The Marine Officer's Guide

SIXTH EDITION

The Marine Officer's Guide

Lieutenant Colonel Kenneth W. Estes
U.S. Marine Corps (Ret.)

Foreword by General C. E. Mundy, Jr.
U.S. Marine Corps (Ret.)
Thirtieth Commandant of the Marine Corps

Naval Institute Press
Annapolis, Maryland

Library of Congress Cataloging in Publication Data

Estes, Kenneth W.
  The Marine officer's guide / Kenneth W. Estes : foreword by C. E. Mundy, Jr.—6th ed.
    p.   cm.
  Includes index.
  ISBN 1-55750-567-5 (alk. paper)
  1. United States. Marine Corps—Officer's handbooks. I. Title.
VE153.E85   1996
359.9'6'0973—dc20   95-3307

First edition by General Gerald C. Thomas, U.S. Marine Corps (Ret.), Colonel Robert D. Heinl, Jr., U.S. Marine Corps (Ret.), Rear Admiral Arthur A. Ageton, U.S. Navy (Ret.)

Second and Third Editions revised by Colonel Robert D. Heinl, Jr., U.S. Marine Corps (Ret.), Rear Admiral Arthur A. Ageton, U.S. Navy (Ret.)

Fourth Edition revised by Colonel Robert D. Heinl, Jr., U.S. Marine Corps (Ret.)

Fifth Edition revised by Lieutenant Colonel Kenneth W. Estes, U.S. Marine Corps

**To All Marine Officers,
into Whose Keeping the Corps
Is Year by Year Entrusted**

Once a Marine, always a Marine

Contents

Figures and Tables

Photographs, unless otherwise indicated, are Department of Defense, U.S. Marine Corps, or U.S. Navy official photographs. Diagrams, where not original, have been reproduced from various official publications.

Foreword

In my thirty-eight years of commissioned service, a constant companion has been my copy of *The Marine Officer's Guide*. First published in 1956, the year before I entered commissioned service, this is the sixth edition of this invaluable book.

It is designed to serve as a bridge between the individual officer and the great body of regulations, directives, customs, courtesies, traditions, and service usages that make up the formal structure of our Corps. Although it has been written with newly commissioned officers in mind, its usefulness extends to officers of all grades and seniority.

We are a Corps that prides itself on an appreciation for the value of tradition, the importance of personal integrity, and the unique responsibilities of officership. The "special trust and confidence" placed in Marine Officers requires that we uphold the very highest standards of personal and professional conduct. Maintenance of these high standards must come from within each officer. This useful and informative book will prove helpful in meeting this responsibility.

Finally, to all new officers, I extend a welcome to the Corps. Your challenges will be many and the road often hard, but the reward of service will be great. Semper Fidelis.

C. E. MUNDY, JR.
General, U.S. Marine Corps (Ret.)
Thirtieth Commandant of the Marine Corps

Preface to the Sixth Edition

On the publication of its sixth edition, and nearing the end of its fourth decade in print, *The Marine Officer's Guide* scarcely requires introduction. Many a well-worn copy sits ready at hand on the bookshelves of the officer corps, and officers of all grades have grown accustomed to its reliability and utility. This sixth edition reflects well the changes in the organization of the Corps fostered by the evolving military establishment of the United States. A modern corps, shaped in so many ways by the Great Pacific War of 1941–1945, now reflects the closing of the era of superpower rivalry and the century of the world wars. What remains remarkably unchanged, however, is the *character* of the Marine Corps and the keen pursuit of excellence in the profession of arms that its officer corps reflects.

The aims of this new edition remain the same as one of the founding editors, Colonel Robert D. Heinl, Jr., wrote: "to assist new officers to learn the ropes as quickly as they can, to digest for all readers the continuing changes which have beset the Defense Establishment, and to help the entire officer corps keep professionally up to date." Given the variety of tasks and challenges that a Marine Corps officer faces today, no single volume can speak to the professional needs of some 18,000 officers likely to be on active duty at any one time. Perhaps as a vital first reference stop, however, it can fulfill many needs of the day.

The Marine Officer's Guide describes in detail the Marine Corps as a military institution of the United States and, in so doing, delineates the characteristics of the men and women who constitute the Corps. The *Guide* supplements, but does not supplant, official regulations and instructions. It can help an officer to acquire quickly a stockpile of information, but it does not relieve the officer of his or her obligation to know the published regulations that govern our Corps. I have endeavored to provide sound advice and up-to-date information on professional matters of note to the Marine officer. I have described customs and usages that are current and not at variance with "the book." I have also deleted some practices that have become anachronistic, and persons in search of nostalgic material can refer to preceding editions for them.

For the most part, I continue to retain the familiar organization of previous editions, while updating much of the material. Many chapters have required considerable revision to reflect changes in defense organization and public laws. I have deleted a previous chapter, "Women Officers," because the conditions of service for women have now become practically indistinguishable from those observed by men. A former appendix, "The Importance of Being Inspected," also fell to my knife because of the ready availability of published instructions and checklists at every echelon of the commands and units. I continue to expand the appendix "Fellow Marines" that lists marine corps and naval infantry organizations of nations around the world, including those not previously considered part of the "free world."

A work of this kind necessarily depends on the help and advice of many people. The staff sections of Headquarters Marine Corps (HQMC) and the information sections of the defense establishment continue to render valuable support. Beyond the hundreds of officers and NCOs who have indirectly influenced my knowledge and opinions during my twenty-four years of service, as well as my collaborators in the fifth edition, I want to particularly thank the following who have contributed to this edition: General Carl E. Mundy, Jr.; Colonels Marshall Buchanan Darling, John R. Kopka, and John Shotwell; Lieutenant Colonels Roger G. Charles, Ray Beaulieu, and Norman Hitchcock; Lieutenant Colonel (USAF) Dennis Shepherd; Majors Bruce Gandy, William G. Leftwich III, and Gary R. Oles; Dr. Helmuts A. Feifs; and S. A. Schallenberg.

Finally, I welcome the comments and corrections of every reader. Is the *Guide* accurate? Is it complete? Does it meet our needs? Does it answer your questions or indicate where you can find the answers? Please send your suggestions to the Editor, *The Marine Officer's Guide*, Naval Institute Press, Annapolis, Maryland 21402. Only with your interest and assistance can this book continue to meet the needs of its readers and thereby best serve our Corps.

KENNETH W. ESTES

Introduction to the First Edition

Preparation of this book was a project which began during my tenure as Commandant of the Marine Corps, and it was one to which I lent sympathetic attention. Now that I see the results, I am well satisfied that I helped to the extent that I did.

It is high time that the Marine Corps had a work of this kind.

Within the memory not of a few senior officers on the verge of retirement, but of the bulk of our most experienced field officers, the Corps has expanded immensely and has pursued its traditional role of national force in readiness on a vastly larger scale.

Thus the Marine Corps is—or could be—in a time of transition. At such times it is all too easy to forget, depart from, or discard the well tested ways which have brought us where we are. Fortunately, those ways are still with us, and such a book as *The Marine Officer's Guide* must be of the greatest value in keeping them with us.

As I write this to readers of *The Marine Officer's Guide*, I am reminded of what must be one of the earliest surviving "fitness reports" on a young Marine officer, submitted by Captain Daniel Carmick, USMC, in April 1799: "Lt Amory is very ignorant of Military duty, as he acknowledges, but he is a smart Gentleman and far preferable to the others." For the young officer of today who (like Lt Amory) is not ashamed to admit the limits of his own experience, and is intelligent enough to profit by the experience of others, *The Marine Officer's Guide* should prove indispensable.

L. C. SHEPHERD, JR.
General, U.S. Marine Corps (Ret.)

The Marine Officer's Guide

1

The U.S. Marine Corps

First to fight.
Retreat, hell! We just got here.
Gone to fight the Indians—will be back when the war is over.
Uncommon valor was a common virtue.
The Marines have landed, and the situation is well in hand.

Phrases like these say more about the U.S. Marine Corps than all the handbooks ever written. As you read this *Guide,* therefore, remember that there is far more to the Marine Corps than can ever be expressed in any manual. If you are fortunate enough to become a Marine, you will soon realize what the Corps is and what it stands for.

101. What Is a Marine Corps?

Beyond the statutes and official definitions, what is a marine corps?

To many observers, it is a military anomaly—a marine is a "soldier and sailor, too." But any cursory reading of military history tells us that navies from their inception had a fundamental need for expert troops to guard ships and stations as well as to extend the force of naval power ashore.

Every world power has an army. Most powers have navies and air forces. Few have had marine corps, but more such corps, based on the examples of their eminent usefulness, have been formed since the Second World War. Some thirty nations now field marine corps or naval infantry units in their orders of battle: Argentina, Brazil, Chile, China, Colombia, Cuba, Ecuador, El Salvador, France, Guatemala, Indonesia, Italy, Republic of Korea, Kuwait, Mexico, Morocco, Netherlands, Paraguay, Philippines, Poland, Portugal, Russia, Saudi Arabia,

Spain, Taiwan, Thailand, Turkey, United Kingdom, Venezuela, and Vietnam. Several other countries have naval commando or coast defense organizations that perform missions similar to those of marines.

Nowhere but in the United States, however, has any marine corps attained the status of our own. This status was not foreseen when the Continental Congress, on 10 November 1775, formed two battalions of Marines. The Corps has gained its unique position through long evolution.

Much of the anomalous quality of the U.S. Marine Corps stems from the fact that the Corps possesses many individual attributes of its brother services. As a result, you can usually discern something suggestive of the other services in the Marine Corps, and this is only natural in a Corps that has spent most of its time spearheading, supporting, or serving beside the Army, Navy, and Air Force. But you can also see much more that belongs only to the Marine Corps.

Certainly, the Marine Corps attitude is peculiar to the Corps.

Fully as important as its attitude, however, is the fundamental mission of the Corps. This primary mission—*readiness*—combined with the Marine state of mind makes the Corps what it is today: a national force in readiness, prepared in fact and required by law to "perform such other duties as the President may direct"—which means "ready for anything."

Most Americans, including some who know little specific about the Corps, recognize Marines as the national force in readiness. Such tried and true phrases as "Call out the Marines!" or "The situation is well in hand," or "Tell it to the Marines" have entered American speech and voice the country's attitude.

The existence of this nationwide feeling makes the Marine Corps a national institution.

As a Marine, you represent a national institution whose standing and reputation are in your hands.

102.   What the U.S. Marine Corps Stands For

The United States Marine Corps exists for one purpose—to fight. Whether the Marine Corps is engaged in shipboard combat, landing operations, or a land campaign, the fundamental reason for its establishment remains unchanged.

The qualities that the Marine Corps stands for might seem old-fashioned. Nevertheless, these attributes have shaped the Corps since 1775, from Princeton to Belleau Wood, from Trenton to Chosin Reservoir to Khe Sanh. Here are some things that the Corps stands for:

Quality and Competence.   A Marine has to be good. In the Marine Corps, your best is just the acceptable minimum. It is expected, as a matter of course, that the technical performance of a single Marine or a whole Marine outfit, whether on parade or in the attack, will be outstanding.

Discipline.   Of all the principles of the Marine Corps, its insistence on discipline is the most unvarying and most uncompromising.

Valor.   After the seizure of Iwo Jima, Fleet Admiral Chester W. Nimitz epitomized the performance of the Marines who took the island. "Uncommon valor," wrote the admiral, "was a common virtue." Three hundred Medals of Honor have been awarded to U.S. Marines. Valor is the Marines' stock in trade. "Retreat, hell! We just got here" was originally uttered in 1918 by a company commander of U.S. Marines.

Esprit de Corps. A Marine is intensely proud of the Corps, loyal to his or her comrades, and jealous for the good name of the Corps. This spirit is nowhere better expressed than in a letter, written in 1800, from William Ward Burrows, 2d Commandant of the Marine Corps, to a junior Marine officer who had been insulted by an officer in the Navy:

> Camp at Washing., Sept 22, 1800
>
> Lt. Henry Caldwell,
>
> Sir—
>
> When I answer'd your letter, I did not Know what Injuries you had received on board the *Trumbull.* . . . Yesterday the Secretary told me, that he understood one of the Lieutenants of the Navy had struck you. I lament that the Capt. of yr ship cannot Keep Order on board of her. . . . As to yourself I can only say, that a Blow ought never to be forgiven, and without you wipe away this Insult offer'd to the Marine Corps, you cannot expect to join our Officers.
>
> I have permitted you to leave the Ship . . . that you may be on an equal Footing with the Captain, or any one who dare insult you, or the Corps. I have wrote to Capt. Carmick, who is at Boston to call on you & be your Friend. He is a Man of Spirit, and will take care of you, but don't let me see you 'till you have wip'd away this Disgrace. It is my Duty to support my Officers and I will do it with my Life, but they must deserve it.
>
> On board the *Ganges,* about 12 mos. ago, Lt. Gale was struck by an Officer of the Navy, the Capt. took no notice of the Business, and Gale got no satisfaction on the Cruise: The moment he arrived he call'd the Lieut. out, and shot him; afterwards Politeness was restor'd. . . .
>
> Yr obdt Svt,
>
> W. W. BURROWS
> LtCol Comdt, MC

Pride. Every Marine is intensely proud of Corps and country and does his or her utmost to build and uphold the Corps.

Loyalty and Faithfulness. Semper Fidelis ("Always Faithful") is the motto of the Corps. In addition, every honorable discharge certificate from the Marine Corps bears the phrase, *Fideli certa merces* ("A sure reward to the faithful"). Marines understand that these are not idle words. Absolute loyalty to the Corps, as well as devotion to duty, is required of every Marine. Percentages of Marines missing in action or taken prisoner by the enemy are minute. A good Marine places the interests of the Marine Corps at the top of his or her list.

The Individual. The Marine Corps cherishes the individuality of its members and, although sternly consecrated to discipline, has cheerfully sheltered a legion of nonconformist, flamboyant individuals and irradiant personalities. It is a perennial prediction that colorful characters are about to vanish from the Corps. They never have and never will. No Marine need fear that the mass will ever absorb the individual.

The Volunteer. Despite occasional acceptance of draftees in times of peak demand, as in the Vietnam War, the Marine Corps is "a volunteer outfit." The Corps relies on those who *want to be Marines.* There is no substitute. In the old phrase, "One volunteer is worth ten pressed men."

The Infantry. The Corps is unique in that no matter what military specialty Marines choose, be it ground or aviation, they are trained as riflemen, and all officers, in addition, must be morally and professionally prepared to function as infantry officers.

Relations between Officers and Enlisted Marines. A commandant of the Marine Corps once wrote:

> The relation between officers and enlisted men should in no sense be that of superior and inferior nor that of master and servant, but rather that of teacher and scholar [i.e., student]. In fact, it should partake of the nature of the relation between father and son, to the extent that officers, especially commanding officers, are responsible for the physical, mental, and moral welfare, as well as the discipline and military training, of the young men under their command. . . .

These words now stand as an enduring testimony to the comradeship among all Marines, whether officer or enlisted.

Traditions. St. Paul's injunction, "Hold the traditions which ye have been taught," could be a Marine motto. Respect for the traditions of the Corps is deeply felt. Every Marine adheres to the traditions that have shaped the Corps.

Professionalism. U.S. Marines are professionals who stand ready to fight any enemy, anytime, anywhere, as designated by the president and Congress, and to do so coolly and capably. They are not trained to hate nor are they whipped up emotionally for battle or for any other duty the Corps is called on to perform. Patriotism and professionalism are their only two "isms."

Readiness. The Corps is perhaps most needed when the nation is demobilized and at peace. Marines are prepared mentally and physically for instant employment, as individuals and in trained units. A former secretary of state once remarked that, as a crisis loomed, his first question to his staff was, "Where are the Marines and the carriers?"

Above all, the public has maintained a consistent view of the Corps; that view is taken for granted, but all Marines could use it as a daily measure of effectiveness. It contains no sophisticated concept of national defense or the exercise of sea power but rather reflects the public appreciation of decades of consistent Marine Corps performance. It goes like this: First, that wherever there is a crisis demanding U.S. military action, there will be Marines ready and able to go there in an instant. Second, once on the scene, those Marines will perform in a highly effective manner and restore the situation in our favor, without exception. Finally, the public believes that the Corps is a good thing to have around and consists of sound, energetic young men and women upon whom the national trust can be bestowed.

103. A Commandant Writes to His Officers

Years ago, Major General John A. Lejeune, thirteenth commandant of the Marine Corps, opened his heart to his officers in a collective letter.

TO THE OFFICERS OF THE MARINE CORPS:

I feel that I would like to talk to each of you personally. This, of course, it is impossible for me to do. Consequently, I am going to do the next best thing, by writing letters from time to time which will go to all the officers. In these letters, I will endeavor to embody briefly some of the thoughts which have come into my mind concerning our beloved Corps.

In the first place, I want each of you to feel that the Commandant of the Corps is your friend and that he earnestly desires that you should realize this. At the same time, it is his duty to the Government and to the Marine Corps to exact a high standard of conduct, a strict performance of duty, and a rigid compliance with orders on the part of all the officers.

You are the permanent part of the Marine Corps, and the efficiency, the good name, and the esprit of the Corps are in your hands. You can make or mar it.

You should never forget the power of example. The young men serving as enlisted men take their cue from you. If you conduct yourselves at all times as officers and gentlemen should conduct themselves, the moral tone of the whole Corps will be raised, its reputation, which is most precious to all of us, will be enhanced, and the esteem and affection in which the Corps is held by the American people will be increased.

Major General John A. Lejeune

Be kindly and just in your dealings with your men. Never play favorites. Make them feel that justice tempered with mercy may always be counted on. This does not mean a slackening of discipline. Obedience to orders and regulations must always be insisted on, and good conduct on the part of the men exacted. Especially should this be done with reference to the civilian inhabitants of foreign countries in which Marines are serving.

The prestige of the Marine Corps depends greatly on the appearance of its officers and men. Officers should adhere closely to the Uniform Regulations, and be exceedingly careful to be neatly and tidily dressed, and to carry themselves in a military manner. They should observe the appearance of men while on liberty, and should endeavor to instill into their minds the importance of neatness, smartness, and soldierly bearing.

A compliance with the minutiae of military courtesy is a mark of well disciplined troops. The exchange of military salutes between officers and men should not be overlooked. Its omission indicates a poor state of discipline. Similarly, officers should be equally careful to salute each other. Courtesy, too, demands more than an exchange of official salutes between officers. On all occasions when officers are gathered together, juniors should show their esteem and respect for their seniors by taking the initiative in speaking to and shaking hands with their seniors. Particularly should this be done in the case of commanding officers. The older officers appreciate greatly attention and friendliness on the part of younger officers.

We are all members of the same great family, and we should invariably show courtesy and consideration, not only to other officers, but to members of their personal families as well. Do not fail to call on your commanding officers within a week after you join a post. On social occasions the formality with which all of us conduct ourselves should be relaxed, and a spirit of friendliness and good will should prevail.

In conclusion, I wish to impress on all of you that the destiny of our Corps depends on each of you. Our forces, brigades, regiments, battalions, companies, and other detachments are what you make them. An inefficient organization is the product of inefficient officers, and all discreditable occurrences are usually due to the failure of officers to perform their duties properly. Harmonious cooperation and teamwork, together with an intelligent and energetic performance of duty, are essential to success, and these attributes can be attained only by cultivating in your character the qualities of loyalty, unselfishness, devotion to duty, and the highest sense of honor.

Let each one of us resolve to show in himself a good example of virtue, honor, patriotism, and subordination, and to do all in his power, not only to maintain, but to increase the prestige, the efficiency, and the esprit of the grand old Corps to which we belong.

With my best wishes for your success and happiness, I am, as always,

Your sincere friend,

JOHN A. LEJEUNE,
Major General Commandant

I have just returned from visiting the Marines at the front, and there is not a finer fighting organization in the world.

—General of the Army Douglas MacArthur
21 September 1950

2

The Organization
for National Security

201. Executive Office of the President

At the highest level in the federal government stands the president of the United States, who is, under our Constitution, commander in chief of the armed forces. The president is assisted and advised not only by the Cabinet but by several agencies that have been organized into the Executive Office of the President. Two organizations, the National Security Council and the Department of Defense, are of particular importance to the armed services, and a third, the Central Intelligence Agency, although directly under the National Security Council, must also be considered on this high level. Figure 2–1 shows the flow of authority and direction through the organization for national security from the president as commander in chief to the secretary of defense and the three military departments.

202. National Security Council (NSC)

Established by the National Security Act, the council has as members the president, the vice president, the secretary of state, and the secretary of defense. The act provides that the secretaries and under secretaries of other executive and military departments may serve as members of the council when appointed by the president and confirmed by the Senate. In addition, other government officials attend meetings as "standing request members" or on an ad hoc basis. The council staff is usually headed by a civilian executive secretary appointed by

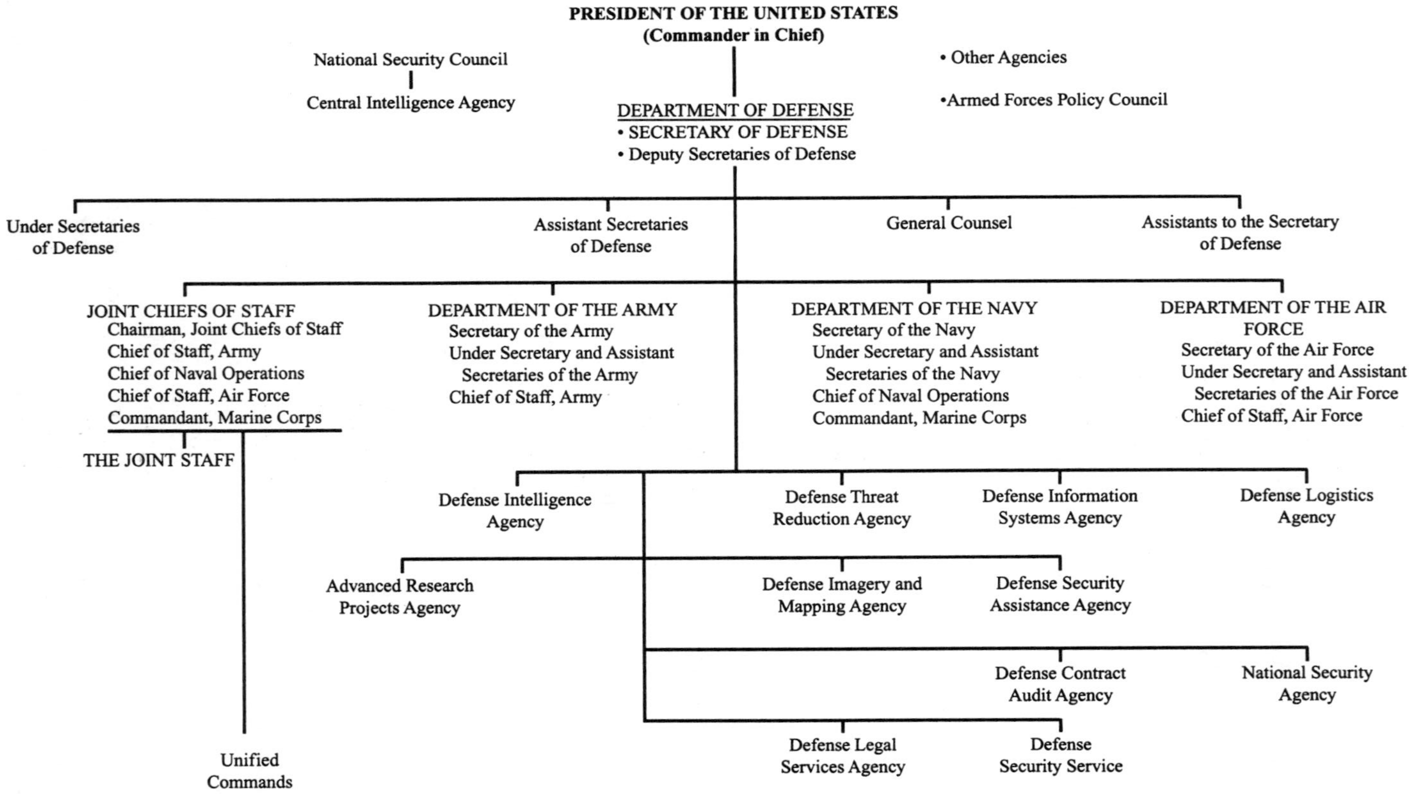

PRESIDENT OF THE UNITED STATES
(Commander in Chief)

National Security Council

Central Intelligence Agency

DEPARTMENT OF DEFENSE
- SECRETARY OF DEFENSE
- Deputy Secretaries of Defense

- Other Agencies
- Armed Forces Policy Council

Under Secretaries of Defense

Assistant Secretaries of Defense

General Counsel

Assistants to the Secretary of Defense

DEPARTMENT OF THE ARMY
Secretary of the Army
Under Secretary and Assistant
Secretaries of the Army
Chief of Staff, Army

DEPARTMENT OF THE NAVY
Secretary of the Navy
Under Secretary and Assistant
Secretaries of the Navy
Chief of Naval Operations
Commandant, Marine Corps

DEPARTMENT OF THE AIR FORCE
Secretary of the Air Force
Under Secretary and Assistant
Secretaries of the Air Force
Chief of Staff, Air Force

JOINT CHIEFS OF STAFF
Chairman, Joint Chiefs of Staff
Chief of Staff, Army
Chief of Naval Operations
Chief of Staff, Air Force
Commandant, Marine Corps

THE JOINT STAFF

Unified Commands

Advanced Research Projects Agency

Defense Intelligence Agency

Defense Threat Reduction Agency

Defense Imagery and Mapping Agency

Defense Information Systems Agency

Defense Security Assistance Agency

Defense Logistics Agency

Defense Legal Services Agency

Defense Contract Audit Agency

Defense Security Service

National Security Agency

Figure 2–1: Organization for National Security (1998)

the president; the staff includes officers and civilian officials from the Departments of State and Defense and the four military services. This secretariat conducts the routine business of the council, prepares agenda for meetings, and correlates and presents for consideration a broad range of information on pertinent topics assembled by the agencies of the membership and by the Central Intelligence Agency.

The council advises the president on domestic, foreign, and military affairs relating to national security. Its duties include the following: to assess the objectives, commitments, and risks of the United States in relation to the actual and potential military power of the nation; to consider policies on matters of common interest to the departments and agencies of the government concerned with national security; and to make recommendations to the president on subjects that may affect that security.

203. Central Intelligence Agency (CIA)

The CIA is administered under the direction of the National Security Council by a director appointed by the president with the advice and consent of the Senate. The director and deputy can be either military officers or civilians; if officers, they retain their service grades and status (being carried as an extra number in grade) but are otherwise exempt from normal military responsibilities.

The agency was established to provide the president and his senior advisers with accurate, comprehensive, and timely foreign intelligence relating to the national security; and to conduct counterintelligence activities, special activities, and other functions relating to foreign intelligence and national security as the president and the National Security Council may direct.

To fulfill its mission, the CIA must collect, process, exploit, analyze, and disseminate foreign intelligence by employing a highly skilled diverse workforce and state-of-the-art technical systems and devices; protect intelligence sources and methods; conduct research on, develop, and procure technical systems and devices; protect the security of its installations, activities, and people; and provide necessary administrative and logistical support, as well as services of common concern to the intelligence community. In carrying out these functions, the CIA prepares "National Intelligence Estimates," that is, analyses of strategic intelligence on which policy decisions are based.

The CIA does not possess police, subpoena, or law-enforcement powers. Nor does it deal with internal security questions. The director is responsible for protecting intelligence sources and methods from unauthorized disclosure.

204. Office of Management and Budget (OMB)

Established in 1921, the OMB has a number of functions: it helps the president prepare the government's budget; it supervises administration of the budget; it improves government administrative management; it helps the president bring about more efficient and economical conduct of government service; it coordinates departmental advice on proposed legislation and makes recommendations as to presidential action on legislative enactments; it assists in consideration, clearance, and preparation of Executive Orders and proclamations; it improves, develops, and coordinates federal and other statistical services; and it informs the president of the progress of government work proposed, initiated, or completed.

Thus, the OMB is in reality far more than its title or even its mechanical functions suggest and is, in fact, a civilian general staff for the president. The power of the office—the ultimate power of the purse—and the continuity of its work give OMB considerable influence over the Department of Defense and the defense policies of the government.

205. Other Organizations

Several other organizations, under direct control of the Executive Office, are connected with national security:

Department of Energy (DOE) administers nuclear research and development, international cooperation, and production of atomic energy and special nuclear materials. The Military Liaison Committee of DOE, made up of representatives of Departments of the Army, Navy, and Air Force, works with the Department of Defense on all military applications of atomic energy.

National Aeronautics and Space Administration (NASA) deals with problems of flight in space and in the earth's atmosphere, develops and operates space vehicles, and is charged with the exploration of space.

Selective Service System provides nationwide standby machinery for the registration and induction—in other words, the draft—of individuals for military service.

Department of Veterans Affairs (VA) administers all laws authorizing benefits for former members of the armed forces and their dependent beneficiaries, together with all government insurance programs open to members of the armed forces. For benefits and services of the VA, see Chapter 20.

DEPARTMENT OF DEFENSE

The Department of Defense is the largest agency in the government. It spends approximately a quarter of the national budget in an ordinary fiscal year. In the five decades since its creation, the Office of the Secretary of Defense has mushroomed from a handful of policymakers (in 1949 the secretary of defense had only three special assistants) to one of the major bureaucracies of the government (see Figure 2–2).

The Department of Defense includes the Office of the Secretary of Defense (OSD); the Joint Chiefs of Staff (JCS) and their supporting establishment; the Departments of the Army, Navy, and Air Force, and the four military services (Army, Marine Corps, Navy, and Air Force) within those departments; the unified and specified commands; and such other agencies as the secretary of defense establishes to meet specific requirements. The central function of the Department of Defense is to provide for the military security of the United States and to support and advance the national policies and interests of the United States.

Office of the Secretary of Defense

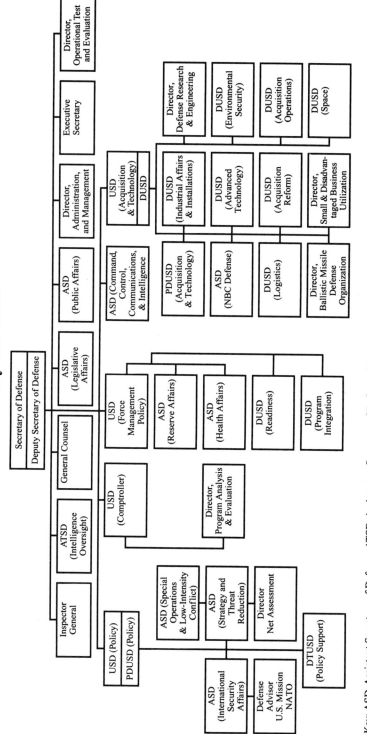

Key: ASD, Assistant Secretary of Defense; ATSD, Assistant to Secretary of Defense; USD, Under Secretary of Defense; PDUSD, Principal Deputy Under Secretary of Defense; DUSD, Deputy Under Secretary of Defense, DTUSD, Deputy to Under Secretary of Defense.

Figure 2–2: Organization of the Department of Defense (1998)

206.   The National Security Act

The National Security Act of 1947, as amended, is the controlling military leg-islation of the United States. The policy section of the act reads: "It is the intent of Congress to provide a comprehensive program for the future security of the United States; to provide for the establishment of integrated policies and proce-dures for the departments, agencies, and functions of the Government relating to the national security." In so doing, the act:

1. Provides three military departments, separately organized, for the operation and administration of the Army, the Navy (including naval aviation) and the U.S. Marine Corps, and the Air Force, with their assigned combatant and service components
2. Provides for coordination and direction of the three military departments and four services under a secretary of defense
3. Provides for strategic direction of the armed forces, for their operation under unified control, for establishment of unified and specified commands, and for the integration of the four services into an efficient team of land, naval, and air forces. The act does not establish a single chief of staff over the armed forces or an armed forces general staff.

Unification has been accomplished by giving the secretary of defense au-thority and virtual military control over the four services, although the secretary does not administer directly the Departments of the Army, Navy, and Air Force. The secretary also has authority in procurement, supply, transportation, storage, health, and research and engineering. The secretary's greatest power lies in administration of the military budgets of the Department of Defense.

The secretaries of Army, Navy, and Air Force no longer enjoy cabinet status, but each secretary has the right to make representations directly to the Office of Management and Budget or to Congress. However, he or she must first inform the secretary of defense of the intention to do so.

207.   Office of the Secretary

The *secretary of defense,* principal assistant to the president in all matters relat-ing to the Department of Defense, is appointed from civil life by the president with the advice and consent of the Senate. Under the president, the secretary exercises direction, authority, and control over the Department (see Figure 2–1). The secretary is a member of the National Security Council, the National Aeronautics and Space Council, and the North Atlantic Council.

The *deputy secretary of defense* is responsible for supervising and coordinat-ing the activities of the department.

The *Armed Forces Policy Council (AFPC)* advises the secretary of defense on matters of broad policy relating to the armed forces and sometimes serves as a final clearinghouse or court of appeal for major administrative decisions. The members are: secretary of defense (chairman); under secretary for acquisition and technology; under secretary for policy; comptroller; secretaries of the Army,

Navy, and Air Force; director of defense research and engineering; chairman of the JCS; chief of staff of the Army; chief of naval operations; chief of staff of the Air Force; and commandant of the Marine Corps.

208. Office of the Secretary of Defense

Various agencies, offices, and positions created by the National Security Act, together with certain other agencies that assist the secretary of defense, constitute the primary staff—civil and military.

The *under secretary of defense for acquisition and technology* is the principal adviser and staff assistant to the secretary of defense in scientific and technical matters. He or she supervises all research and engineering activities in the Defense Department and wields extensive coordinating and directive authority over virtually all materiel programs of the defense establishment.

The *under secretary of defense for policy* is the principal adviser and staff assistant to the secretary of defense in matters of defense and security policy. These include the formulation of national strategy in line with resources and national security requirements, regional security arrangements, nuclear armaments regulation, and special measures for crises short of open warfare. He or she coordinates the formulation of strategic concepts into military force programs and security policies.

The *assistant secretaries of defense*, including the general counsel and certain special assistants, are responsible to the secretary for particular areas. In 1994, there were fifteen of these areas, embracing such fields as health affairs, legislative affairs, program analysis, regional security affairs, manpower reserves and logistics, public affairs, and intelligence oversight.

Responsibilities and functions are periodically rearranged by the secretary according to existing requirements.

209. Joint Chiefs of Staff (JCS)

To promote more personal control of the Army and Navy, to make certain of direct access to the president for principal military advisers, and to improve coordination between the Army and Navy, President Franklin D. Roosevelt directed organization of the Joint Chiefs of Staff in 1942. With the coming of peace and passage of the National Security Act in 1947, the JCS became a permanent part of the defense organization of the United States. When the National Security Act was amended in 1949, a chairman was authorized who would preside at JCS meetings and expedite the conduct of business, but the chairman is now considered the principal military adviser to the secretary of defense and the president. The Joint Chiefs of Staff now have a chairman appointed by the president from one of the four services, with the advice and consent of the Senate.

The Joint Chiefs do not operate on a voting basis. If, after discussing an issue, the Joint Chiefs agree unanimously, all chiefs and the chairman sign (or, as the process is called, "red-band") a paper giving their decision to the secretary of defense and the services. But if, after all views are presented, disagreement remains, the Joint Chiefs come to what is known as a "split." It is the statutory duty of the chairman to inform the secretary of defense and the president of such disagreement.

The chairman, who takes precedence over all officers of the armed services, serves as presiding officer, provides agenda for meetings, and manages the Joint Staff, through its director.

As principal military advisers to the president, the National Security Council, and the secretary of defense, the Joint Chiefs prepare strategic plans and provide strategic direction of the military forces; they prepare joint logistic plans and assign logistic responsibilities in accordance with such plans; they establish unified commands in strategic areas; they formulate policies for joint training of the military forces and coordinate the education of members of the military forces; they review major material and personnel requirements of the military forces in accordance with strategic and logistic plans; and they provide U.S. representation on the Military Staff Committee of the United Nations.

210. Organization of the JCS

The supporting establishment of the Joint Chiefs of Staff is composed of the Joint Staff and a group of other agencies outside the Joint Staff that report directly to the JCS.

The *Joint Staff* provides planning and staff assistance for the JCS. It is limited to four hundred officers (having expanded four times over since it was created in 1947) who are chosen from the Army, Navy, Marine Corps, and Air Force. The director, Joint Staff, an officer of three-star grade, attends meetings of the JCS and serves, in effect, as the expediter and coordinator of the JCS organization. The Joint Staff is divided into directorates: Manpower and Personnel (J-1); [the Defense Intelligence Agency functions as J-2 equivalent]; Operations (J-3); Logistics (J-4); Strategic Plans and Policy (J-5); Command, Control, Communications and Computer Systems (J-6); Operational Plans and Interoperability (J-7); Force Structure, Resources, and Assessment (J-8). There are various special assistants.

Other agencies within the JCS organization, but not part of the Joint Staff, include the Joint Secretariat; the Directorate of Management; and various councils, boards, committees, and representatives.

211. Other Defense Agencies

Other than the unified commands established by the JCS (see below), a number of major agencies and joint service schools come within the aegis of the Defense Department or Joint Chiefs of Staff. Certain of these agencies are of commanding size and stature and perform major functions for the Defense Department that were once considered to be within the operating and administrative purview of the military departments. Agencies included are the following:

- Defense Threat Reduction Agency

- Defense Legal Services Agency (DLSA)
- Defense Contract Audit Agency (DCAA)
- Defense Logistic Agency (DLA)
- Defense Intelligence Agency (DIA)
- Defense Information Systems Agency (DISA)
- Defense Advanced Research Projects Agency (DARPA)
- National Security Agency (NSA)
- Defense Commissary Agency
- Defense Finance and Accounting Service (DFAS)
- National Imagery and Mapping Agency (NIMA)
- Defense Security Service
- Central Imagery Office (CIO)
- Defense Security Assistance Agency (DSAA)

The *Joint Service Schools* are the National Defense University (Industrial College of the Armed Forces, Armed Forces Staff College, and National War College) and a dozen specialty schools, including the DOD Computer Institute, the Defense Intelligence College, and the National Imagery and Mapping School.

212. Unified Commands

Coming directly under the secretary of defense, with orders transmitted by the chairman of the Joint Chiefs of Staff, are the unified commands, predominantly located outside the United States and covering areas of greatest strategic importance. A unified command is a command with a broad continuing mission, under a single commander, composed of components of two or more services. Representation on the commander's staff usually comes from all services, and the command includes "service component commanders" who command all units from their respective services within the unified command. There are nine unified commands:

- Joint Forces Command
- Pacific Command
- European Command
- Central Command
- Southern Command
- Special Operations Command
- Space Command
- Transportation Command
- Strategic Command

For detailed, up-to-date information on the organization and functioning of the Joint Chiefs of Staff, its supporting organization, and the unified and specified command structure, consult *Organization and Functions of the Joint Chiefs of Staff* (JCS Publication 4) and *Unified Action Armed Forces* (UNAAF) (JCS Publication 2).

DEPARTMENT OF THE ARMY

213. Mission of the Army

The National Security Act charges the Department of the Army with providing support for national and international policy and with protecting the security of the United States. The Army is organized, trained, and equipped for prompt and sustained combat operations on land.

This mission is delineated in *Functions of the Department of Defense and Its Major Components,* a defense directive known colloquially as "The Functions Paper" or, from its place of origin in March 1948, as "The Key West Agreement." This document sets out the functions of the armed forces as a supplement to the National Security Act, which is, of course, controlling.

214. Structure of the Army

Command flows from the president, through the secretary of defense and the secretary of the Army, to Army units and installations throughout the world (Figure 2–3).

A field army is composed of a headquarters and two or more corps, each of two or more divisions. The division is the smallest unit that permanently contains a balanced proportion of the combined arms and services and that therefore is constituted to operate independently. Below division level, standing units are mainly composed of the separate arms or services of the Army. The company is the smallest administrative unit in the Army.

The Army is charged with preparing for sustained land combat, including the development of such systems as this M1A1 main battle tank.

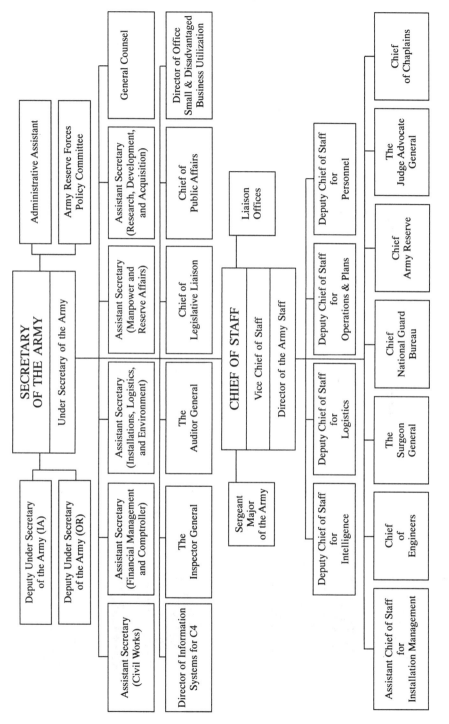

Figure 2–3: Organization of the Department of the Army (1998)

The Army is made up of the following basic and special branches:

Basic Branches	Special Branches
Infantry	Judge Advocate General's Corps
Armor	Chaplains
Artillery	Army Medical Service:
Air Defense Artillery	Medical Corps
Corps of Engineers	Dental Corps
Signal Corps	Veterinary Corps
Adjutant General's Corps	Army Nurse Corps
Quartermaster Corps	Army Medical Specialist Corps
Finance Corps	
Ordnance Corps	
Chemical Corps	
Transportation Corps	
Military Police Corps	
Intelligence Corps	
Aviation	

Officers from all branches are detailed to the General Staff Corps and the Inspector General's Department.

215. The United States Army

The United States Army ensures the security of the United States within its area of responsibility and particularly within the Zone of the Interior. Part of the Army is on full-time duty. Other components are ordinarily inactive in peacetime. All components may be called to active duty during an emergency declared by Congress or in the event of war.

Regular Army.   For nearly two centuries, the regular Army has been the framework upon which we have built our wartime armies. It is the duty of the regular Army to:

1. Perform occupation duties
2. Garrison the United States and overseas possessions
3. Train the National Guard, Organized Reserve, and Reserve Officers' Training Corps (ROTC)
4. Provide an organization for the administration and supply of the peacetime military establishment
5. Provide educated officers and enlisted personnel to become leaders, in event of war, of the expanded Army of the United States
6. Record and expand the body of military knowledge so as to keep the United States up to date and prepared
7. Constitute, with the National Guard and units of the Organized Reserve, a covering force in case of a major war
8. Cooperate with the Marine Corps, Navy, and Air Force in carrying out their missions

National Guard. The National Guard is the militia of the United States. In time of peace, the National Guard of any state can be called to active duty by the governor of that state to perform emergency duties. Units or individual members of the National Guard can be called to active duty by the federal government only during war or national emergency or with their own consent in time of peace. In addition to augmenting the regular Army, the Guard:

1. Trains additional volunteers and assigned selectees
2. Supplies instructors for schools and training centers
3. Furnishes cadres of experienced officers and enlisted personnel for new units
4. Furnishes enlisted personnel who qualify for officer commissions

Ready and Standby Reserve Corps. Like the National Guard, Army Reserve units train in local armories and are subject to orders to active duty under similar conditions. Individual members are assigned to Army Reserve organizations in or near their hometowns. The Organized Reserve, however, is not subject to state control of any kind.

216. Education of Officer Candidates

Three school systems train candidates for commissions in the Army—the Military Academy, Officer Candidate School, and the Reserve Officers' Training Corps.

The *United States Military Academy,* West Point, New York, was established in 1802 to train young gentlemen as commissioned officers. *Duty, Honor, Country*—motto of the Corps of Cadets—has long served to set West Point's high standard. Colonel Archibald Henderson, fifth commandant of the Marine Corps, remarked in 1823:

> It but rarely happens that a graduate from West Point is not a gentleman in his deportment, as well as a soldier in his education.

The Military Academy is commanded by a superintendent, an Army general officer. Marine officers now serve on West Point's academic staff. The four-year curriculum includes cultural subjects as well as military science. The cadet graduates with a B.S. degree and, if physically fit, is commissioned as a second lieutenant in the Army, the Marine Corps, or the Air Force.

Officer Candidate School is conducted at Fort Benning, Georgia. The course is usually six months. Most candidates are chosen from enlisted men and women of the regular Army, the Reserve, and the National Guard.

The *Reserve Officers' Training Corps,* the first unit of which was established in 1862, now has more than 280 civilian universities and colleges that offer the familiar Army ROTC training units. ROTC has long been a major source of officers for our Army (and from time to time for the Marine Corps as well).

DEPARTMENT OF THE AIR FORCE

217. Mission of the Air Force

The Department of the Air Force and the U.S. Air Force were established in 1947 by the National Security Act. The department includes aviation forces, both combat and service (Figure 2–4). It organizes, trains, and equips the Air Force to conduct prompt and sustained combat operations in the air—specifically, forces to defend the United States against air attack, to gain and maintain general aerospace supremacy, to defeat enemy air forces, to control vital air areas, and to establish local air supremacy as required. The Air Force has primary responsibility for: developing doctrines and procedures (in coordination with the other services) for the defense of the United States against air attack; organizing, training, and equipping Air Force forces for strategic air warfare; organizing and equipping Air Force forces for joint amphibious and airborne operations, in coordination with the other services; furnishing close combat and logistical air support to the Army; providing air transport for the armed forces, except as otherwise assigned; developing, in coordination with the other services, doctrines, procedures, and equipment for shore-based air-defense, including the continental United States.

218. Structure of the Air Force

As a result of experience during and after World War II, Korea, and Vietnam, the Air Force has evolved the following basic organizational structure.

Flight. The lowest tactical echelon recognized in the Air Force structure, flights are not formally designated in the structure but are subdivisions of combat squadrons. They provide the basis for combat formations and are used for training.

Air Force–manned bombers, such as this B-1, form part of the U.S. "triad" of strategic weapons.

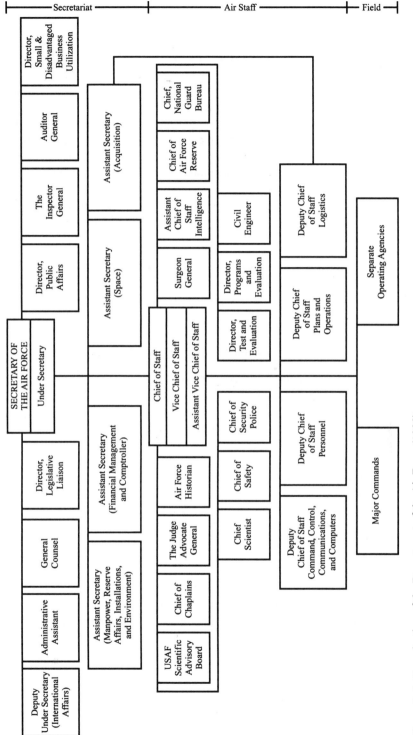

Figure 2-4: Organization of the Department of the Air Force (1998)

Squadron. The basic unit in the organizational structure, a squadron is manned and equipped to best perform a specific military function, such as combat, maintenance, food service, and communications.

Group. A flexible unit, a group is composed of two or more squadrons whose functions may be either tactical or administrative in nature.

Wing. This is the smallest Air Force unit manned and equipped to operate independently in sustained action until replacement and resupply can take place.

Air Division. An air combat organization, a division normally consists of two or more wings. Divisions are operational in nature with minimum administrative or logistics responsibilities.

Numbered Air Force. This intermediate command echelon is designed to control and administer a grouping of combat wings. It is flexible in organization and can vary in size. Usually, a numbered air force has one of three missions—strategic, tactical, or defensive. Its wings may be grouped for operational control under air divisions or be directly under the numbered air force.

Major Command. A functionally titled command echelon directly below Headquarters USAF, it is charged with major responsibility in fulfilling the Air Force mission.

219. Major Air Commands and Field Operating Agencies

Eight major air commands and twelve field operating agencies represent the field organization of the Air Force. The commands are organized on a functional basis in the United States and on an area basis overseas.

Major USAF Commands. The following make up major U.S. Air Force commands:
- Air Force Space Command
- Air Force Special Operations Command
- U.S. Air Forces Europe
- Air Force Materiel Command
- Air Education and Training Command
- Air Mobility Command
- Air Combat Command
- Pacific Air Forces

The Air Mobility Command (AMC) is of special interest, as it provides worldwide air transportation for the Department of Defense.

USAF Field Operating Agencies. The field operating agencies include:
- Air Force Audit Agency
- Air Force Command, Control, Communications, and Computer Agency
- Air Force Logistics Management Agency
- Air Force Inspection Agency
- Air Force Flight Standards Agency
- Air Force Personnel Center

- Air Force Office of Special Investigations
- Air Force Reserve
- Air National Guard
- Air Force Reserve
- Air Force Medical Operations Agency

Components of the USAF. The United States Air Force is composed, in its entirety, of the regular Air Force, Air National Guard, and Air Force Reserve.

220. Education of Air Force Officer Candidates

Candidates for Air Force commissions receive their training in a number of different institutions: Air Force Academy, Officer Training School, Air Force ROTC, and Airman Education and Commissioning Program.

The *Air Force Academy,* Colorado Springs, Colorado, is one of the principal sources for regular Air Force officers. The curriculum includes both academic and military subjects and leads to a B.S. degree and a commission as a second lieutenant in the Air Force (or Army, Marine Corps, or Navy) Reserve.

Officer Training School is located at Lackland Air Force Base, Texas. College graduates may apply for this three-month course. The curriculum includes administration, organization, supply, military law, world affairs, leadership, and human relations. Graduates are either assigned directly to duty or pursue additional training in an aircrew (pilot or navigator) or technical course. Graduates are given the opportunity to apply for regular commissions.

The *Air Force ROTC* is similar in purpose and organization to the Army and Navy ROTC programs.

The *Airman Education and Commissioning Program* provides undergraduate education, followed by officer training and a commission, for selected career-minded airmen on active duty.

DEPARTMENT OF THE NAVY

The Department of the Navy occupies coequal status with the Department of the Army and the Department of the Air Force in the Organization for National Security (see Figure 2–1) and in the Department of Defense. The organization of the Department of the Navy and the place of the United States Marine Corps in the naval establishment are described in detail in Chapters 3, 4, and 5.

COAST GUARD

The Coast Guard is a military service within the armed forces. It operates under the Department of Transportation during peacetime and under the Navy when directed by the president.

Coast Guard personnel receive the same pay and benefits as men and women in the other armed forces, and they are also subject to the Uniform Code of Military Justice. The service's rank and rating system is similar to the Navy's,

High-endurance cutters allow the Coast Guard a wide range of capabilities in answering the needs of mariners near and distant.

with one major difference: there are fewer enlisted ratings. The Coast Guard is headed by a four-star admiral.

The Coast Guard performs a wide range of functions in the United States and around the world. There are three broad mission areas: maritime safety, law enforcement, and military readiness. To carry out these missions, the service operates approximately 2,000 small boats and more than 100 cutters larger than 65 feet; mans hundreds of facilities, mostly small units, throughout the United States and a few abroad; and operates the world's seventh largest naval air force.

Coast Guardsmen are best known for their lifesaving mission, but search and rescue is only one of their duties. They maintain lighthouses, buoys, and other aids to navigation; operate electronic navigation stations, including loran and Omega; track icebergs and operate America's icebreakers; and inspect vessels for safety violations and enforce maritime pollution laws. Their law enforcement responsibility also includes enforcing fisheries laws and stopping drug smuggling. The service is the primary maritime law enforcement agency in the war against drugs.

The Coast Guard has recently assumed an increased military emphasis. It is the lead agency in the Maritime Defense Zone, which is in charge of the defense of America's coast. In past wars, the Coast Guard has engaged in escort duties, antisubmarine warfare, cold-weather operations, riverine warfare, amphibious warfare, port and coastal security, and much more.

Today, the Coast Guard has a total force of about 38,000 men and women, of which approximately 8,000 are officers. The service has an academy at New London, Connecticut. Appointment is by competitive examination, which is open to civilians and enlisted men and women from any armed service between the ages of seventeen and twenty-two. Cadets have a choice of several different majors and graduate with a B.S. degree.

The service was created on 4 August 1790 by the secretary of the treasury, Alexander Hamilton, and was known simply as a system of cutters. In 1915, the name evolved to the United States Coast Guard. Its motto is *Semper Paratus* ("Always Ready").

The principal foundations of all states are good laws and good arms; and there cannot be good laws where there are not good arms.

—Niccolo Machiavelli, *The Prince*

3

The Department
of the Navy

With 6,000 miles of coastline and with 71 percent of the globe covered by water, the United States has long appreciated the need for strong naval forces. The United States is essentially a maritime power, and American strategy must always be fundamentally maritime. In two world conflicts, we have successfully kept war from our shores by superior sea power. Without control of the seas, we could not have transported fighting men, equipment, and supplies to distant battles, nor could we ever project our fighting power from the seas onto the land.

Today, control of the seas is more important than ever. The United States depends on raw materials from overseas to sustain its industry. Our security is bound up with the security of friendly powers in many parts of the world. By maintaining control of the seas, we ensure that our lifelines to these nations and to our far-flung advance bases will not be broken. More important, we ensure the use of the seas for the offensive operations that victory requires. For all these reasons we must maintain the U.S. Fleet. In doing this, the policy of the Department of the Navy is as follows:

> ... to maintain the Navy and Marine Corps as an efficient, mobile, integrated force of multiple capabilities, and sufficiently strong and ready at all times to fulfill their responsibilities ... to support and defend the Constitution of the United States against all enemies, foreign and domestic; to insure, by timely and effective military action, the security of the United States, its possessions, and areas vital to its interest; to uphold and advance the national policies and inter-

ests of the United States; and to safeguard the internal security of the United States.

As you reflect on the import of this policy, remember the words of General Lemuel Shepherd, twentieth commandant: "Both the functions and the future of the Marine Corps are intimately linked with those of the U.S. Navy."

301. Mission of the Department of the Navy

The responsibilities of the Department of the Navy are expressed as follows in the National Security Act, as amended:

> Sec. 206 (a) The term "Department of the Navy" as used in this Act shall be construed to mean the Department of the Navy at the seat of government; the headquarters, United States Marine Corps; the entire operating forces of the United States Navy, including naval aviation, and of the United States Marine Corps, including the reserve components of such forces; all field activities, headquarters, forces, bases, installations, activities, and functions under the control or supervision of the Department of the Navy; and the United States Coast Guard when operating as a part of the Navy pursuant to law.
>
> (b) The Navy, within the Department of the Navy, includes, in general, naval combat and service forces and such aviation as may be organic therein. The Navy shall be organized, trained, and equipped primarily for prompt and sustained combat incident to operations at sea. It is responsible for the preparation of naval forces necessary for the effective prosecution of war except as otherwise assigned and is generally responsible for naval reconnaissance, antisubmarine warfare, and protection of shipping.
>
> All naval aviation shall be integrated with the naval service as part thereof within the Department of the Navy. Naval aviation consists of combat and ser-

The high mobility of naval forces, coupled with their staying power, makes them highly useful in forwarding national policy around the globe. That is the essence of the classical notion of sea power.

vice and training forces, and includes land-based naval aviation, air transport essential for naval operations, all air weapons and air techniques involved in the operations and activities of the Navy, and the entire remainder of the aeronautical organization of the Navy, together with the personnel necessary therefor.

The Navy shall develop aircraft, weapons, tactics, technique, organization, and equipment of naval combat and service elements. Matters of joint concern as to these functions shall be coordinated between the Army, the Air Force, and the Navy.

The Navy is responsible, in accordance with integrated joint mobilization plans, for the expansion of the peacetime components of the Navy to meet the needs of war.

(c) The Marine Corps, within the Department of the Navy, shall be so organized as to include not less than three combat divisions and three air wings, and such other land combat, aviation, and other services as may be organic therein. The Marine Corps shall be organized, trained, and equipped to provide fleet marine forces of combined arms, together with supporting air components, for service with the fleet in the seizure or defense of advanced naval bases and for the conduct of such land operations as may be essential to the prosecution of a naval campaign. In addition, the Marine Corps shall provide detachments and organizations for service on armed vessels of the Navy, shall provide security detachments for the protecting of naval property at naval stations and bases, and shall perform such other duties as the President may direct. However, these additional duties may not detract from or interfere with the operations for which the Marine Corps is primarily organized.

The Marine Corps shall develop, in coordination with the Army and the Air Force, those phases of amphibious operations that pertain to the tactics, technique, and equipment used by landing forces.

The Marine Corps is responsible, in accordance with integrated joint mobilization plans, for the expansion of peacetime components of the Marine Corps to meet the needs of war.

Except in time of war or national emergency declared by Congress after June 28, 1952, the authorized strength of the Regular Marine Corps, excluding retired members, is 400,000. However, this strength may be temporarily exceeded at any time in a fiscal year if the daily average number in that year does not exceed it.

The functions of the Navy and Marine Corps were further defined in the 1948 Key West Agreement (Figure 3–1). Although its primary purpose was to amplify the functions of the Army and Air Force, the agreement did assign collateral functions to the Navy and the Marine Corps and did spell out some basic functions in more detail. Nonetheless, the primary source for Marine Corps functions is the National Security Act, not the agreement.

302. The Executive Branch and the Department of the Navy

The Department of the Navy, as one of the military departments within the Department of Defense, comes under the president and the secretary of defense. Its organization and executive duties are covered later in this chapter.

303. The Legislative Branch and the Department of the Navy

Under our Constitution, Congress is given the authority "to provide and maintain a navy . . . and to make rules for the government of the land and naval forces." In the words of the late Chief Justice Charles Evans Hughes, "Congress provides; the President commands." Congress therefore enacts laws governing the size, scope, functions, and authority of the Navy and the Marine Corps. Congress authorizes and provides funds for construction of ships and shore bases and for all Navy and Marine Corps activities.

Members or committees of Congress, the Department of the Navy, and other offices of the Department of Defense may originate legislation affecting the Navy and the Marine Corps. The Department of Defense then submits comments and recommendations on such military legislation. Officials of the Department of the Navy are frequently summoned to appear at hearings on proposed legislation and at congressional investigations.

304. The Judicial Branch and the Department of the Navy

The Department of the Navy may sue or be sued. It has a right to appear in its own defense or in defense of its officials or members of the services; it may enter briefs and may argue and appear before the courts; and it is bound by decisions of federal courts.

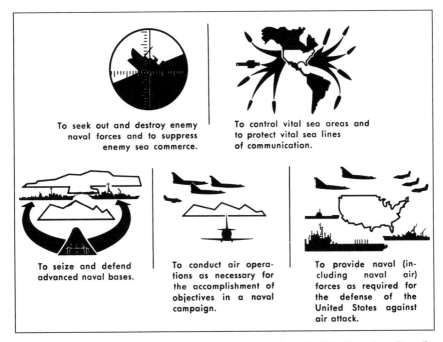

Figure 3–1: The primary functions of the Navy as set forth in "The Functions Paper"

THE DEPARTMENT OF THE NAVY

305. Organization

The Department of the Navy consists of four principal parts: the Operating Forces of the Navy, the U.S. Marine Corps, the Shore Establishment, and the Navy Department (Figure 3–2).

The *Operating Forces of the Navy* include the several fleets, seagoing forces, district forces, Fleet Marine Forces and other assigned Marine Corps forces, the Military Sealift Command, and such other Navy shore (field) activities and commands as are assigned by the secretary of the navy.

The *U.S. Marine Corps,* within the Department of the Navy, includes Headquarters, U.S. Marine Corps; Operating Forces of the Marine Corps; Marine Corps Supporting Establishment; and Marine Corps Reserve (see Chapters 4, 5, and 9).

The *Shore Establishment* consists of all activities of the Navy not assigned to the operating forces and not a part of the Navy Department. These include naval bases, naval air stations, and training establishments not part of the operating fleets.

The *Navy Department* is the central executive authority of the Department of the Navy. It comprises the Office of the Secretary of the Navy; the Office of the Chief of Naval Operations; and the headquarters organizations of the Chief of Naval Personnel, the Bureau of Medicine and Surgery, the Office of the Judge Advocate General, the Office of Naval Research, the offices of the staff assistants to the secretary, and those organizations of the Coast Guard when assigned to duty with the Navy.

306. Secretary of the Navy (SecNav)

The secretary of the Navy is the head of the Department of the Navy and is responsible for the policies and control of the Department of the Navy, including its organization (except as otherwise prescribed in law), administration, operation, and efficiency. As far as practicable, the secretary discharges these responsibilities through civilian executive assistants and other military and civilian assistants. The secretary, however, retains personal direction over activities relating to legislation and to Congress and maintains relationships with the secretary of defense, other principal government officials, and the public.

The secretary of the Navy is the principal morale officer of the Department of the Navy and as such directs a continuing effort to promote the welfare and morale of all hands.

The secretary may communicate directly with any principal official of the Department of the Navy, the Shore Establishment, or the Operating Forces.

The secretary recommends to the secretary of defense and the president appointments, removals, or reassignments of the legally constituted positions of

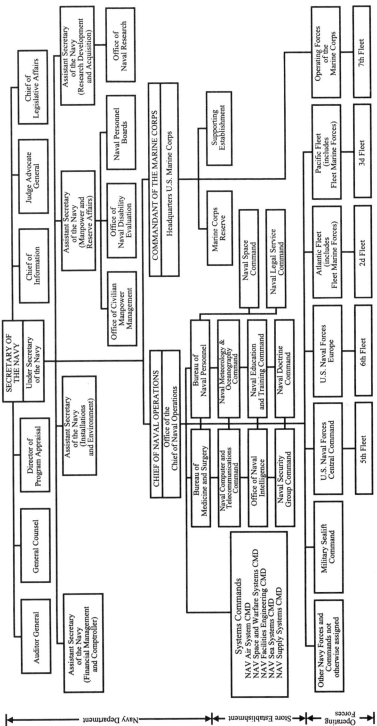

Figure 3–2: Organization of the Department of the Navy (1998)

the Department of the Navy. In his or her own discretion, the secretary controls the selection and assignment of all other principal officials of the department.

Policy Council.   The Department of the Navy Policy Council, chaired by the secretary and composed of the under secretary, chief of naval operations, commandant of the Marine Corps, and the vice chief of naval operations, is one of the secretary's major instruments for military-civilian coordination and for timely consideration of policy.

307.   Civilian Executive Assistants

The under secretary, assistant secretary (financial management and comptroller), assistant secretary (research, development, and acquisition), assistant secretary (installations and environment), and assistant secretary (manpower and reserve) are the principal civilian executive assistants. They exercise top management coordination over the bureau and offices of the Navy Department. Each civilian executive assistant oversees areas of responsibility assigned by the secretary.

308.   Under Secretary of the Navy

The under secretary of the Navy is the principal civilian executive assistant to the secretary of the Navy. The under secretary acts with the authority of the secretary of the Navy during the latter's absence or disability. In addition, the under secretary directly supervises the following bureaus and offices:

Board of Decorations and Medals sets policy regarding, and passes on, all awards and medals for the naval services.

Office of Program Appraisal provides the secretary with an independent capability to appraise progress against approved programs, as well as to analyze proposed programs.

Office of Legislative Affairs advises and assists the secretary and all other principal military and civilian officials of the department in connection with legislative affairs and congressional relations.

Office of Information performs public information and public relations functions for the Navy Department. The chief of information also has collateral public relations responsibility to the chief of naval operations.

Office of the General Counsel. This office furnishes legal services in the field of commercial law. The general counsel is responsible for legal aspects of procurement, contracts, property disposition, and renegotiation.

Office of the Judge Advocate General is described in Section 328.

309.   Assistant Secretary of the Navy (Financial Management and Comptroller)

The assistant secretary of the Navy (financial management and comptroller) is responsible for the financial management of the Department of the Navy, including budgeting, accounting, financing, progress and statistical reporting, and auditing.

310.   Assistant Secretary of the Navy (RD&A)

The assistant secretary of the Navy (research, development, and acquisition) supervises all research, development, engineering, test, evaluation, and procurement efforts within the Department of the Navy. Among other agencies under the assistant secretary is the Office of Naval Research (ONR). In addition, he or she chairs the Research and Development Committee.

311.   Assistant Secretary of the Navy (Installations and Environment)

The assistant secretary of the Navy (installations and environment) supervises all matters relating to real estate and facilities, including utilities, housing, and quarters. Also, the assistant secretary supervises the Navy Petroleum Office, which is charged by law with custody of the federal petroleum reserves, and coordinates Department of the Navy responsibilities in connection with the Mutual Defense Assistance Program.

312.   Assistant Secretary of the Navy (Manpower and Reserve)

The assistant secretary of the Navy (manpower and reserve affairs) supervises all manpower matters, including personnel administration, utilization, and morale and performance. The various naval personnel boards and the Office of Naval Disability Evaluation function under this assistant secretary. The boards include the Board for Correction of Naval Records, Naval Clemency and Parole Board, Navy Discharge Review Board, and Naval Physical Disability Review Board.

313.   Order of Succession

During the absence of the secretary of the Navy, the order of succession as acting secretary is: under secretary; assistant secretaries in the order prescribed by the secretary, or, if no order is prescribed, then the order in which the respective assistant secretaries took office; chief of naval operations; and vice chief of naval operations.

314.   Naval Executive Assistants to SecNav

The *Chief of Naval Operations (CNO),* an admiral, is the senior officer of the Department of the Navy and principal naval adviser to the president and to the secretary of the Navy on the conduct of war. The CNO is naval executive assistant to the secretary of the Navy on the conduct of the activities of the Department of the Navy. As Navy member of the Joint Chiefs of Staff, the CNO is responsible additionally to the president and secretary of defense for certain duties external to the Department of the Navy.

The *Commandant of the Marine Corps (CMC),* a general and the senior officer in the Corps, commands the U.S. Marine Corps and is directly responsible to the secretary of the Navy. The commandant has additional responsibility to the CNO for the forces of the Marine Corps assigned to the Operating Forces of the Navy and to the civilian executive assistants for matters related to them, as well as to the president and secretary of defense for certain duties external to the Department of the Navy.

In addition, the commandant's responsibilities include:

1. Determining the needs of the Corps for equipment, weapons, materiel, supplies, facilities, maintenance, and supporting services, including deciding upon the characteristics of materiel to be procured and the training required to prepare Marines for combat.
2. Developing, in coordination with the Army, Navy, and Air Force, the tactics, techniques, doctrines, and equipment employed by landing forces in amphibious operations.
3. Planning for the future needs, qualitative and quantitative, of regular and reserve personnel of the Marine Corps. This includes ensuring a high degree of competence on the part of all hands through education, training, and equal opportunity and providing leadership to maintain the esprit of Marines and the prestige of a Marine Corps career.
4. Providing for the health of Marines (in coordination with the surgeon general of the navy).
5. Budgeting for the Marine Corps (except as otherwise directed by the secretary of the navy) and supervising the performance of its supporting establishment.
6. Formulating Marine Corps strategic plans and policies and also joint and combined strategic plans and policies.
7. Member of the Joint Chiefs of Staff.

The *Commandant of the Coast Guard* is a naval executive assistant to the secretary of the Navy when the Coast Guard is attached to the Navy in time of war or emergency (see Chapter 2).

315. Naval Professional Assistants

These officials constitute the remaining bureau chiefs, chief of naval research, and the judge advocate general, described later in this chapter.

OFFICE OF CHIEF OF NAVAL OPERATIONS (OPNAV)

316. General Comment

The offices, board, and agencies reporting to and performing duties for the chief of naval operations (CNO) are collectively referred to as the Office of the Chief of Naval Operations (OPNAV).

317. Chief of Naval Operations (CNO)

The eight principal responsibilities of the chief of naval operations are:

1. To command the Operating Forces of the Navy.
2. To organize, train, prepare, and maintain the readiness of Navy forces for assignment to unified commands. This responsibility includes determination of training required by all members of the Navy and Naval Reserve for combat.
3. To plan and determine the materiel support needs of the Operating Forces of the Navy (less Fleet Marine Forces and other assigned Marine Corps forces).
4. To identify present and future needs, qualitative and quantitative, for regular and reserve personnel of the Navy; to make available to all hands education, training, and equal opportunities for promotion; to maintain the morale and motivation of the Navy and the prestige of a naval career.
5. To provide for the health of members of the Navy and their dependents.
6. To budget for the operating costs of the fleets and shore activities of the Operating Forces of the Navy (except as otherwise directed by SecNav) and to supervise the performance of the shore activities assigned to the Operating Forces of the Navy.
7. To formulate Navy strategic plans and policies and to participate in the formulation of joint combined strategic plans and policies.
8. In addition, except with respect to the Marine Corps, the CNO supervises the military administration of the Department of the Navy in such matters as security, intelligence, discipline, communications, and customs and traditions.

318. Vice Chief of Naval Operations (VCNO) (Op-09)

The vice chief of naval operations acts for CNO on all matters not specifically limited to the CNO alone, performs the duties of the CNO during the CNO's absence, and is principal adviser to CNO. Under the vice chief of naval operations are the Plans and Programs Office and the office of the assistant VCNO. In addition, the VCNO supervises the directors of naval intelligence; naval reserve; naval communications; research, development, test, and engineering; and naval education and training and the naval inspector general (who also has certain direct responsibilities to the secretary of the Navy).

The naval inspector general, under the direction of SecNav or VCNO, inquires into all matters affecting the discipline, readiness, effectiveness, efficiency, or economy of the Department of the Navy.

With regard to the Marine Corps Supporting Establishment, these inquiries are limited to management efficiency and to compliance with policies of the civilian executive assistants and technical instructions by the naval professional assistants.

The director, Navy staff (Op-09B), consolidates a number of miscellaneous activities and functions, including, among others, Office of Director of Naval History; Field Support Activity, Career Counselor, and other assistants for various policies.

The following are field activities under the CNO:

1. The Naval Meteorology and Oceanography Command consists of a headquarters, located at the Stennis Space Center, Mississippi, four regional centers, and two production centers. It carries on the work of the former Oceanographic Office, established in 1830 as the Depot of Charts and Instruments, and the former Naval Weather Service.
2. Naval Observatory, Washington, D.C., determines the correct time. These signals establish U.S. standard time, provide navigators with means to determine their astronomical positions, and contribute to other purposes requiring exact time. The observatory takes an active part in designing and constructing its precision optical and electrical instruments. The Naval Observatory's Nautical Almanac Office compiles publications required for fundamental positional astronomy.
3. Naval Weather Service, with headquarters at the Washington Navy Yard, provides worldwide weather forecasts and information for the fleet.

319. Deputy Chiefs of Naval Operations (DCNOs)

Four deputy chiefs of naval operations perform the following functions.

DCNO (Manpower and Personnel) (Op-01) is responsible for coordinating basic training and for instituting personnel policies for the Operating Forces and the Naval Reserve. The same officer serves as chief of naval personnel.

DCNO (Plans, Policy, and Operations) (Op-03/05) has cognizance over the monitoring of daily operations and readiness of the Navy, service planning for present and future military strategy, and working with the Joint Staff on the myriad of military policy matters that occupy the Washington scene.

DCNO (Logistics) (Op-04) plans the logistic requirements of the Operating Forces of the Navy, including ships' materiel readiness, shore facilities programming, and inspection and survey of warships.

DCNO (Resources, Warfare Requirements, and Assessments) (Op-08) plans the organization, readiness, programs, weapons, support, budgeting, and acquisitions actions for the various aviation, surface, and subsurface components of the Navy, to include aircraft and amphibious programs of direct import to the Marine Corps.

THE SHORE ESTABLISHMENT

320. General

The Shore Establishment comprises all field activities of the Department of the Navy, except shore activities assigned to the Operating Forces of the Navy. The Shore Establishment includes those Operating Forces of the Marine Corps that are not assigned to the Operating Forces of the Navy or to a unified or specified command.

The activities of the Shore Establishment are generally distributed along the coasts where they can best serve the Operating Forces. Many activities in which such proximity to the sea is not essential (notably air, ordnance, and supply) are based inland.

321. Status of the Marine Corps in the Shore Establishment

Within the Shore Establishment, the commandant of the Marine Corps exercises military command over the Marine Corps Supporting Establishment, over forces of the Marine Corps not assigned to the Operating Forces of the Navy or to a unified command, and over special activities of the Marine Corps.

322. Naval Operating Bases

A naval operating base centers in one command allied activities that support the fleet. At each major naval base, a single officer is designated as commander naval operating base and is in command over all fleet support activities. A naval operating base includes a shipyard and may include an air station. Commanders of naval shipyards are technically qualified officers who are skilled in industrial management.

Commanding officers of the component activities of a naval base receive instructions on support and technical matters directly from the responsible agencies in the Department of the Navy.

323. Naval Air Bases

A naval air base comprises Shore Establishment activities that furnish aviation logistic support to the Operating Forces of the Navy.

The commander of a naval air base comes under the command and control of the commander, Air Forces, Pacific or Atlantic Fleet. Commanding officers of component activities of naval air bases are subject to the command of their air base commander. Support of such activities stems directly from the Department of the Navy.

Certain air activities are not assigned to the commanders, naval air bases. These include the following:

- Naval Air Training Command
- Marine Corps Air Bases East, Cherry Point, North Carolina, and West, Miramar, California
- Marine Corps Air Facility, Quantico, Virginia
- Naval Air Missile Test Center
- Naval Air Material Center

OPERATING FORCES OF THE NAVY

324. General

The Operating Forces of the Navy comprise the four fleets, seagoing forces, district forces, Fleet Marine Forces (FMFs), Military Sealift Command, and such shore activities of the Navy and other forces as may be assigned by the president or the secretary of the Navy. The chief of naval operations commands the Operating Forces of the Navy.

325. Major Components

The composition of the Operating Forces of the Navy, as assigned by the secretary of the navy, is indicated in Figure 3–2.

Fleet Organization. There are five regularly constituted fleets—the Third and Seventh Fleets in the Pacific (under commander in chief, Pacific Fleet); the Second Fleet (under commander in chief, Atlantic Fleet); the Sixth Fleet (under commander naval forces, Europe); and the Fifth Fleet (under commander, naval forces, Central Command). Normally, commander Third Fleet exercises operational control over all naval forces on the Pacific Coast and in the eastern Pacific, as does commander Second Fleet over similar forces on the Atlantic Coast. The Sixth and Seventh Fleets in the Mediterranean and Far East, respectively, represent the cutting edge of American sea power in those vital regions. Each ordinarily includes one or more embarked "floating battalions," designated Marine Expeditionary Units (MEUs). In addition, the Second Fleet operates floating units of the FMF in the Caribbean.

Type Commands. The major fleets are organized into broad categories under commanders whose titles are self-explanatory and generic, such as commander Surface Force, commander Submarine Force, commander Air Fleet, and commanding general Fleet Marine Force. The purpose of this "type organization" is to prepare and provide forces for operations—not to conduct operations.

The nuclear-powered aircraft carrier remains the principal conventional striking arm of the U.S. Navy. Note the variety of aircraft, hence capability, visible on deck.

The *Military Sealift Command (MSC)* provides ocean transportation for personnel (including sick and wounded), materiel (including petroleum products), mail, and cargoes as directed by the U.S. Transportation Command for the Department of Defense and, as authorized, for other agencies.

A task force directly under the CNO, MSC provides ships and crews for the peacetime needs of the services, keeps available for emergency a nucleus of auxiliary ships that are gainfully employed, and provides an operating and administrative organization capable of rapid expansion.

326.   The Task Force Principle

The task force principle is the name given to the Navy and Marine Corps system of organizing forces for given tasks while preserving a separate administrative organization for training and housekeeping. This is the fundamental organizational principle of the U.S. fleets.

Type Organization.   All forces in the U.S. fleets are grouped into the "type organization" of the fleet. As its name implies, the type organization is based on types of ships or forces. Note that the Fleet Marine Force is a type command, since it comprises all Marine Corps tactical units—air and ground—assigned to the fleet.

Task Organization.   The other facet of fleet organization is the "task organization." The task organization conducts operations, using units prepared and provided by the type organization. Taking the Atlantic Fleet as an example, it includes several permanent task forces. Certain of these, such as the antisubmarine warfare forces, are task-organized from aviation, surface, and submarine forces to maintain control of the sea.

Under this system, a flexible structure is provided, consisting of fleets further subdivided into forces, groups, units, and elements. Each of these descending subdivisions has a numbered designation and appropriate communication call signs. When a task fleet commander receives a task from higher authority, he can then assign necessary forces under his command to do the job by creating an ad hoc organization of ships and units as needed. Such a task organization is adaptable to any magnitude of organization, ranging from the campaigns of entire fleets in general war to a single ship on a temporary mission. For example, an LHD amphibious assault ship might be given a task designation simply to steam across Chesapeake Bay for a Navy Day visit, and, on conclusion of the job, the task designation would cease.

A typical (hypothetical) Task Fleet numbering system would be one in which the commander Seventh Fleet would assign the fleet's major forces to numbered task forces (TF), such as Striking Force, TF 70; Amphibious Task Force, TF 71; Service Force, TF 72; and so forth.

Within each force, the commander would then assign logical subdivisions of that force as task groups (TG), such as TG 70.1, Carrier Group; TG 70.2, Gunfire Support and Covering Group; and so forth.

Within each task group, in turn, would be task units (TU). For example, TG 70.1, Carrier Group, might be divided into TU 70.1.1, Carrier Unit, and TU 70.1.2, Screen Unit.

Note the fashion in which components of a task organization are designated by addition of decimal separators and successive numbers; this enables you to determine at a glance the place of a given unit in an operational command.

Significance. The simultaneous organization of the fleets by types and task is obviously complex. It is, nevertheless, a system precisely adapted to any given job, large or small, temporary or permanent. Moreover, it is flexible and economical.

COMPONENTS OF THE UNITED STATES NAVY

327. Composition

The United States Navy consists of the regular Navy and the Naval Reserve.

328. The Regular Navy

Commissioned officers of the regular Navy (and Naval Reserve) are divided among the line and staff corps. (Figure 3–3.)

Line. Line officers exercise military command and are accountable for the exercise of their authority. Among line officers are several types of "line" specialists: naval constructors, naval engineers, and specialists in such fields as intelligence, oceanography, communications, and public information. Only line officers command at sea, and, in general, only line officers exercise command ashore. Members of certain corps, however, such as Medical, Supply, and Civil Engineer Corps, command shore activities and units (such as Seabees) under the cognizance of their respective bureaus. Although, of course, not eligible to command at sea or to command a Navy base or station, Marine officers are nevertheless line officers of the naval service and have been held, legally, to be naval officers.

Medical Corps. This corps is composed exclusively of graduate doctors of medicine who treat the "sick, lame, and lazy" and administer the hospitals, dispensaries, sick bays, and other medical units of the naval establishment. Medical and dental service for the Marine Corps is provided by Navy doctors, dentists, and hospital corpsmen.

Nurse Corps. Navy nurses are commissioned officers in the Nurse Corps. They serve in hospitals and dispensaries at home and on foreign stations and in hospital ships and transports at sea.

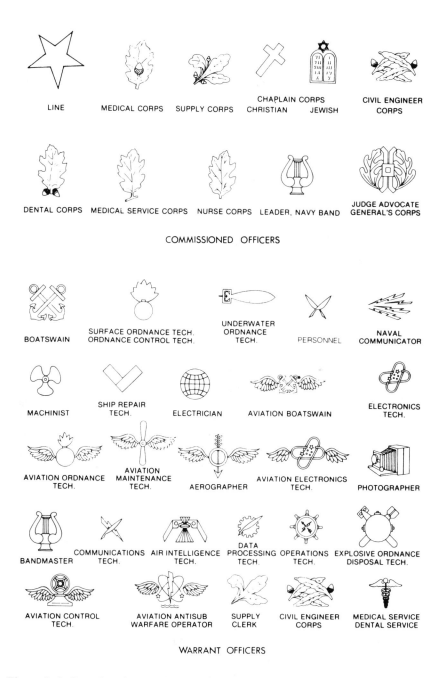

Figure 3–3: Branch and corps devices of commissioned and warrant officers of the Navy (1994)

Dental Corps.   Composed of graduate dental surgeons, this is a separate corps whose members serve at hospitals and dispensaries and on board larger ships. The Dental Corps, like the Medical, Nurse, and Medical Service Corps, comes under the Bureau of Medicine and Surgery.

Medical Service Corps.   This corps is composed of specialists in optometry, pharmacy, and such allied sciences as bacteriology, biochemistry, psychology, sanitation engineering, and medical administration and statistics.

Supply Corps.   This is the business branch of the Navy that administers the Navy supply system and receives and disburses funds for supply and for pay, subsistence, and transportation.

Chaplain Corps.   Ordained ministers of various denominations, officers of the Chaplain Corps conduct religious services and promote the spiritual and moral welfare of the Navy and Marine Corps. The chief of chaplains heads the corps.

Civil Engineer Corps.   This corps is composed of graduate civil engineers, normally restricted to shore duty, who supervise buildings, grounds, and plants at shore stations, as well as construction of buildings and the layout of shore stations. This corps conceived, organized, and commanded the Navy construction battalions (Seabees), which served so illustriously beside Marines during World War II, Korea, and Vietnam.

Judge Advocate General's Corps.   This corps consists of Navy lawyers who have been duly certified to practice and perform staff legal and judicial duties under the judge advocate general and within the system of military jurisprudence.

Warrant Officers.   Navy warrant and commissioned warrant officers possess the most detailed practical knowledge of the complicated mechanisms of our modern Navy and thus provide invaluable technical know-how for the fleet. In spite of recent proposals, based on administrative considerations, that the warrant grades be abolished in favor of limited-duty billets and that no further warrants be issued, it has now been firmly decided that the Navy warrant officer is here to stay. Warrant grade titles include, among others: boatswain, machinist, electrician, aerographer, photographer, supply clerk, ordnance and mine warfare technician, communications and electronics technician, ship repair technician, equipment and building foreman, bandmaster, medical and dental service warrant, aviation maintenance and operations technician, as well as others. (See Figure 3–3.)

Enlisted Men and Women.   Basic legislation allows 500,000 enlistees in the regular Navy. During an emergency, the actual number depends on the size of the fleet and Shore Establishment to be maintained.

Enlisted men and women of the Navy and Coast Guard are divided into rating groups, as illustrated in Figure 3–4. Just as we expect Navy officers to recognize and identify Marine noncommissioned officers, so a Marine officer should be able to identify Navy petty officers in the various ratings.

329.   Education of Officer Candidates

Several systems provide candidates for commissions in the Navy.

United States Naval Academy.   The Naval Academy was established in 1845 at old Fort Severn, at the mouth of the Severn River in Annapolis, Maryland, to train naval officers.

Since the 1880s, the Marine Corps has each year commissioned a number of Naval Academy graduates as second lieutenants. At present one-sixth of the midshipmen per graduating class are permitted Marine Corps commissions, the competition for these vacancies being high.

The strength of the Brigade of Midshipmen is maintained by appointments from senators, congressmen, and territorial delegates; by competitive appointments from regular and reserve enlisted men and women of the Navy and Marine Corps; and by appointments-at-large by the president and vice president. These so-called presidential appointments are made on a competitive basis from among the children of regular and reserve officers and children of any members of the armed forces killed or disabled in the line of duty. In addition, the children of Medal of Honor winners are admitted to the Academy on passing the usual mental and physical examinations.

The Academy is commanded by a superintendent of flag rank. The staff includes officers of all the services, as well as civilian professors. The course is four years and leads to a B.S. degree.

Naval Reserve Officers' Training Corps (NROTC).   The NROTC offers the opportunity for young men and women to qualify for Naval and Marine Corps Reserve commissions while attending college.

Midshipmen are selected competitively in each state. As NROTC students, they lead the same academic life as college contemporaries, but, in addition to normal studies, they receive professional training in naval science.

Tuition and certain related expenses are wholly paid for by the government.

Midshipmen wear uniforms when engaged in naval duties and receive the pay and allowances of a midshipman. After graduation, the NROTC graduate must serve a minimum of four years as a Marine or Navy officer.

Besides the foregoing program for candidates, there is also a nonsubsidized NROTC program for college students.

NROTC units are located at more than sixty institutions throughout the country. To enroll in this program, you should apply either to Commandant of the Marine Corps, Washington, D.C., 20380; or Chief of Naval Personnel, Washington, D.C., 20350.

Officer Candidate School.   Located at the Naval Training Center, Newport, Rhode Island, the Navy's Officer Candidate School trains young college graduates as Naval Reserve officers. Candidates hold the enlisted grade of officer candidate. They are obligated to serve three years on active duty as commissioned officers after passing the four-month course and to continue in the Reserve a total of six years. Meritorious enlisted men and women

Figure 3–4: Specialty marks of Navy enlisted ratings (1994)

selected for integration as regular Navy officers also attend Officer Candidate School.

330. The Naval Reserve

The purpose, classification, and organization of the Naval Reserve are generally similar to the Marine Corps Reserve, discussed in detail in Chapter 9.

The *Ready Reserve* provides trained officer and enlisted reservists, who, added to qualified personnel from other sources, complete the war organization of the Navy. Officers and enlisted personnel of the Ready Reserve must perform annual training and other duties to keep them ready for immediate mobilization in emergency.

The *Standby Reserve* provides a force of qualified and partially qualified officers and enlisted persons who will, except on personal application, be called to active duty only for war or a national emergency declared by Congress.

The *Retired Reserve* is liable for active duty only in time of war or emergency declared by Congress, or when otherwise authorized by law, in the event sufficient qualified personnel are not available in the Ready Reserve and Standby Reserve.

The *Naval Air Reserve* trains at naval air stations about the country, its members functioning in either of the classes of the Naval Reserve described in the preceding paragraphs.

Organization. The basic Ready Reserve unit is the division. A battalion consists of two to five surface or submarine divisions. A brigade is established in cities having more than one battalion. The squadron is the basic unit for the Naval Air Reserve. An air wing consists of a number of squadrons located in the same area. Specialist units exist in communities that have enough reserve specialists to permit such an organization.

In the Standby Reserve, volunteer training divisions and units may be organized in a wide variety of specialties, in order to keep members up to date on their specialties.

NAVAL STAFF ORGANIZATION

331. Organization and Functions of an Operational Naval Staff

This discussion of the naval staff system is important to you because Marine officers serve on every naval staff of any consequence.

The operational naval staff (as in the amphibious group headquarters) is of primary interest to Marine officers. You will find that other naval staffs, ashore or afloat, are organized along much the same lines, with special functions as appropriate. For detailed, authoritative information on naval staff organization and procedure, consult *NWP-12, The Navy Staff.*

Naval staff functions come under two headings: (1) administration and (2) planning and operations. To carry out these functions, the typical large naval staff is organized much like the Office of CNO (see Sections 316–319). This organization comprises the personal staff and the coordinating staff (which is equivalent to the USMC executive staff).

Personal Staff.   The duties of a Navy personal staff are essentially similar to those listed in Section 521 for the Marine personal staff, although titles differ somewhat.

The chief of staff not only carries out the functions the title implies but is also the admiral's personal assistant. He or she is the senior officer on the staff and coordinates all staff activities, thus serving as a member of the coordinating staff as well. In Navy commands headed by officers below flag rank, this billet bears the title of chief staff officer rather than chief of staff.

The flag secretary serves as the admiral's administrative aide and confidential secretary. Like the chief of staff, the flag secretary also has dual status as a member of the coordinating staff, in which he or she heads the administrative section.

The flag lieutenant, in addition to personal services to the admiral, supervises salutes, honors, awards, official calls, uniform, social protocol, and transportation for the admiral and the staff (barge, staff gig, helicopter, and staff cars). The flag lieutenant keeps the staff duty officer (as well as other members of the staff and interested officers of the flagship) apprised of the movements and intentions of the admiral.

Coordinating Staff.   The coordinating staff comprises four or five sections, each headed by an assistant chief of staff.

The Administrative Section (N-1) is headed by the flag secretary. The section combines the shore functions associated with USMC G-1, staff secretary, adjutant, and legal officer.

The Intelligence Section (N-2) performs naval intelligence functions analogous to those performed by the USMC G-2 ashore. In some Navy staffs, the intelligence officer likewise has cognizance over public affairs. Marine officers may serve in Navy intelligence sections—primarily in connection with amphibious intelligence.

The Operations Section (N-3) performs plans (N-5 in larger staffs), training, and operations duties comparable to those of the USMC G-3 on shore. In addition, however, the naval Operations Section has responsibility for matters affecting readiness, and, in amphibious staffs, deals with and conducts the ship-to-shore movement. Marines frequently serve in the Operations Section, not only as *plans officer* but as *military operations officer;* both titles are self-explanatory.

The Logistics Section (N-4) has all the functions of the USMC G-4 section in a Marine staff. In addition, this section plans the availability for overhaul of ships, screens work requests, supervises maintenance, and administers funds for repair and alterations.

The Communications Section (N-6) is sometimes a separate section and sometimes part of the N-1 section. The communications officer not only supervises communications but also controls classified publications for the staff. In amphibious staffs, a Marine communication officer usually forms part of the section.

Specialist Officers. Although the Navy organization does not include a special staff as such, it does, of course, have certain specialists who, in effect, comprise a special staff. While the specialties are not as numerous as on a Marine staff, the duties are quite similar. The following specialist officers would be included in the typical Navy staff: weapons officer, air officer, aerological officer, surgeon, supply officer, chaplain, and legal officer.

332. Staff Duty Officer Afloat

Senior line officers (including Marines) take turns as staff duty officer (see Section 1703).

In port, the staff duty officer takes a day's duty, receives routine reports, acts on routine matters in the absence of officers having staff cognizance, regulates the use of staff boats, and tends the side on occasions of ceremony. In an emergency, the staff duty officer must be prepared to make decisions when the admiral and chief of staff are unavailable.

Under way, the staff duty officer stands watch on the flag bridge and represents the admiral in the same way that the officer of the deck represents the captain. The staff duty officer makes routine reports and signals, supervises navigation and station-keeping of the force, keeps the staff log, and oversees the watch on the flag bridge. To perform efficiently, the staff duty officer must keep

The battleship, repeatedly activated for service in post–World War II crises, might well be the "Marines' best friend."

informed of current operations, expected hazards, conditions of readiness, launching and recovery of aircraft, joining and detaching of units, fueling and provisioning, and so on. The state of relations between the staff and flagship depends in considerable measure on the attitude and consideration of the staff duty officer.

333.   Marine Duties on Naval Staffs

Nowhere more than on a Navy staff is a Marine expected to be "soldier and sailor, too." Thus, when assigned to the Navy, never be surprised, regardless of what duty you find yourself performing.* Your only concern should be to see that that duty is well done, so that as a Marine Corps representative you set an example to your Navy colleagues.

Subject to the foregoing, Marines are usually assigned to one or several of the following staff duties:

Staff Marine Officer.   As division, squadron, force, or fleet Marine officer, you exercise staff supervision over Marine personnel and matters within your command. In practice, this boils down to coordination of landing force activities involving Marines, inspection of ships' Marine detachments, advice and assistance as needed for the several Marine detachment commanders, and supervision of the flag Marine detachment (or "flag allowance"). In addition, the staff Marine officer is usually selected to maintain liaison between his or her staff and any Marine or Army staffs in the vicinity. The senior Marine officer on any Navy staff, regardless of other duties, performs the functions just described.

Military Operations Officer.   The military operations officer has cognizance over all military operations ashore in which the naval staff may be involved. In homely language, the job of the Marine military operations officer is to keep the Navy straight in matters of land warfare and organization.

Combat Cargo Officer (CCO).   The CCO performs the duties of troop loading, billeting, and landing associated with embarkation functions in the Marine staff ashore.

Other Duties.   The foregoing jobs are those to which Marine representatives on Navy staffs are usually assigned. In addition, however (according to your capabilities and the needs of the organization), you could find yourself performing as security officer, logistics officer, intelligence officer, air officer, or plans officer.

Under all circumstances, a decisive naval superiority is to be considered a fundamental principle, and the basis upon which all hope of success must ultimately depend.

—George Washington, 1780

*Note: Never acquiesce in the bad old practice (still occasionally recurrent) of allowing yourself to be assigned duty in a staff section headed by a Navy officer junior to you. Your lineal precedence, based on date of rank, is as binding on a Navy staff as anywhere else.

4

Missions and Status of the Marine Corps

401. Introduction

Every American respects the Marine Corps, but a surprising number of people are quite hazy on what the Corps really is and does. Thus it is up to every Marine officer to have precise knowledge of the roles, missions, and status of the Corps.

402. Marine Corps Roles and Missions

The Law. The statutes of the United States include many provisions, great and small, that affect the Corps. All these provisions have been codified under Title 10 (Armed Forces), U.S. Code.

The "charter" of the Marine Corps, however, has evolved from three laws: (1) the Act of 11 July 1798, "Establishing and Organizing a Marine Corps"; (2) the Act of 30 June 1834, "For the Better Organization of the Marine Corps"; and (3) the National Security Act of 1947 as amended.

The National Security Act, which unified the armed services, is the controlling military legislation of this country. For Marines, though, the Douglas-Mansfield Bill (Public Law 416, 82d Congress, 2d Session) has particular importance. This law amended the National Security Act as regards the Marine Corps. Its debates and hearings (1951–52) contain a mine of information on the Corps.

To summarize briefly, the National Security Act as now amended (see Section 301) makes the following provisions for the Marine Corps:

1. It reaffirms the Corps' status as a service within the Department of the Navy.
2. It provides for Fleet Marine Forces, ground and aviation.
3. It requires that the combatant forces of the Corps be organized on the basis of three Marine divisions and three air wings, and sets a peacetime ceiling of 400,000 personnel for the regular Corps.
4. It assigns the Corps the missions of seizure and defense of advanced naval bases, as well as land operations incident to naval campaigns.
5. It gives the Marine Corps primary responsibility for development of amphibious warfare doctrines, tactics, techniques, and equipment employed by landing forces.
6. It seats the commandant of the Marine Corps on the Joint Chiefs of Staff.
7. It affords the Marine Corps appropriate representation on various joint Defense Department agencies, notably the Joint Staff.
8. It assigns the Marine Corps collateral missions of providing security forces for naval shore stations; providing ships' detachments; and performing such other duties as the president may direct.

In taking stock of Marine Corps missions found in law, it is important not to overlook the short phrase, "... *and shall perform such other duties as the President may direct.*" This phrase, which the Unification Act quotes directly from the 1834 Marine Corps law, stems in turn from similar language in the Act of 1798. It validates in law Marine Corps functions that transcend the Corps' purely naval missions. In mid-1951, the House of Representatives Armed Services Committee highlighted the significance of this clause in a trenchant summary:

> It is, however, the Committee view that one of the most important statutory—and traditional—functions of the Marine Corps has been and still is to perform "such other duties as the President may direct."
>
> The campaign in Korea, in which the 1st Marine Division and the 1st Marine Air Wing are presently participating, can hardly be called a naval mission. Practically every war involving the United States has found the Marine Corps performing duties other than naval. Indeed, the first two battalions of Marines raised in this country were raised specifically for service before Boston with General Washington's army.
>
> Many Marine activities in the War of 1812 involved only land fighting; in the 1840's the Marines saw "the Halls of Montezuma" while fighting with the Army in the War with Mexico; in the early 1900's Marine activities in Central America were repeatedly entirely of a land nature; their participation in the fighting in the Boxer Uprising in China in 1900 likewise was of a land nature; certainly when in May 1917 President Wilson ordered the 4th Marine Brigade to serve as part of the Army's 2d Division in the Battles of Belleau Wood, Aisne-Marne, St. Mihiel, Blanc Mont, and Meuse-Argonne, and later in the occupation forces, these can hardly be described as naval missions; nor can the activities of Marine Maj. Gen. John A. Lejeune, in commanding for a time the Army's 2d Division in France, be called a naval function; nor could the service of Marine aviation in France during 1918 be accurately termed a naval activity.
>
> It is difficult to see how the sending of Marines as the initial force to hold

Iceland prior to the last war, until relieved by Army troops, could accurately be called a naval mission; how the reinforcing of Corregidor by the 4th Marine Regiment sent from China just before war broke out, could be accurately termed a naval action; and if the actions of the 1st Marine Division on Guadalcanal, commencing the first American attack of the war on August 7, 1942, can accurately be called a naval action, then in the same fashion the activities of Army divisions in this area must likewise be so termed. It further is worthy of note that on Mindanao and Luzon in the Philippines, in the last ground action against the enemy in World War II, Marine Air Groups 12, 14, 24 and 32, gave close air support to the 24th, 31st, and 41st Infantry Divisions—an activity that appears to the Committee to be only distantly related (if at all) to exclusively naval activities.

The Committee must also call attention to the fact that, after V-J Day, the V Amphibious Corps, USMC, was part of the forces sent to occupy the Japanese Home Islands; the III Marine Amphibious Corps was sent to North China to accept the surrender of Japanese troops there; that a Marine division, with other forces, was kept in China until the summer of 1947 during the attempt of the United States to settle civil war between the Chinese Government and Chinese Communists. It is a strained construction, indeed, of military activities to characterize such employment of the United States Marines as essentially naval in character.

In line with the foregoing, Marines have on several occasions been temporarily detached by executive order of the president to service under the secretary of war. The last occasion on which Marines were detached to service under the Army was in July 1941, when the 1st Provisional Marine Brigade in Iceland was assigned to the Army by President Roosevelt. Note the distinction between administrative transfer of Marines to Army duty (which can only be effected by order of the president) and operational attachments under unified command, which occur frequently—as was the case throughout the greater part of the Korean and Vietnamese wars, as well as the Persian Gulf Conflict.

So much, then, for the main provisions of law that give the Marine Corps its roles and missions. While those roles are carefully spelled out, the law nevertheless allows employment of Marines anywhere, on any service the president may desire.

Additional Missions of the Marine Corps.   In addition to the missions expressly assigned by Congress, the Corps also performs several tasks either assigned by the Department of Defense or in accordance with long-standing custom.

"The Functions Paper."   Originally known as "The Key West Agreement" (see Sections 213 and 301), the Defense Department directive that states the functions of that department and of its major components is now usually spoken of as "The Functions Paper." This directive is essentially a compilation of interservice agreements dating from 1948, and revised from time to time, as to how the roles-and-missions provisions of the National Security Act are to be implemented. In addition, the directive establishes a number of service rela-

Marine Corps Forces provide units ready to undertake military missions "... in any clime or place. ..."

tionships and common functions within the Defense Department, which affect the Marine Corps equally with the other services. Portions of this paper that specifically provide for Marine Corps functions are as follows:

...To maintain the Marine Corps, having the following specific functions:

(1) To provide Fleet Marine Forces of combined arms, together with supporting air components, for service with the Fleet in the seizure or defense of advanced naval bases and for the conduct of such land operations as may be essential to the prosecution of a naval campaign. These functions do not contemplate the creation of a second land Army.*

(2) To provide detachments and organizations for service on armed vessels of the Navy, and security detachments for the protection of naval property at naval stations and bases.

(3) To develop, in coordination with the other Services, the doctrines, tactics, techniques, and equipment employed by landing forces in amphibious operations. The Marine Corps shall have primary interest in the development of those landing forces doctrines, tactics, techniques, and equipment which are of common interest to the Army and the Marine Corps.

(4) To train and equip, as required, Marine forces for airborne operations, in

---

*The Marine Corps, though repeatedly overruled, has consistently opposed inclusion of the meaningless "second land Army" phrase at this point in "The Functions Paper," since nothing could be further from the objectives or interests of the Corps.

coordination with the other Services and in accordance with doctrines established by the Joint Chiefs of Staff.

(5) To develop, in coordination with the other Services, doctrines, procedures, and equipment of interest to the Marine Corps for airborne operations. . . .

Although many of the foregoing provisions stem directly from and actually include language of the National Security Act, you should never confuse "The Functions Paper," only a departmental directive, with the National Security Act, which is the law and thus governs in any disagreement.

State Department Guards. Under authority of the Foreign Service Act of 1946, the Marine Corps has a collateral mission of providing security guards for American embassies, legations, and consulates. For this duty, which demands the highest discretion and trust, the Marine Corps furnishes over a thousand officers and men who are distributed throughout more than 110 State Department overseas posts.

White House Duties. Dating from 1798, the scarlet-coated Marine Band has been styled "The President's Own" because of its privilege of providing the music for state functions at the White House. Similarly, Marines have established and guarded presidential camps at Rapidan, Virginia; Warm Springs, Georgia; Camp David, Maryland; and elsewhere, while Marine helicopters were the first to carry a president and still routinely do so.

Unwritten Missions. Nowhere do the statute books say that the Marine Corps is *the national force in readiness,* yet our history demonstrates clearly that the fundamental mission of the Corps is just that, and always has been. To quote former Assistant Secretary of the Navy John Nicholas Brown:

> Readiness, the capacity to move anywhere immediately and become effective, is always needed and at the present juncture of events is especially necessary. This is the daily bread of the Marine Corps.

In close corollary to this traditional mission is the Corps' worldwide service, in times of nominal peace, as "State Department Troops" for enforcement of foreign policy and protection of U.S. nationals or their evacuation, under direction of the Department of State.

403. Status of the Marine Corps

"The Marine Corps is *sui generis*" ("something entirely of its own sort"), once ruled a federal judge when construing the legal status of the Corps. This is probably the best one-sentence characterization the Marine Corps ever had.

The Marine Corps is one of the several armed services (Army, Marine Corps, Navy, and Air Force), which, with the Coast Guard (when attached to the naval establishment in time of war), compose the Armed Forces of the United States. It is important that you be aware of this, since you may sometimes encounter the erroneous term "the three services," which is usually a term of exclusion so far as the Marine Corps is concerned.

Side by side with the Navy, the Marine Corps is one of two military services in the naval establishment, under direct control and supervision of the secretary of the navy. Detailed explanation of the relationship of the Marine Corps to the Navy is given in Section 404. For the moment we can let the subject rest with the words of Representative Carl Vinson, distinguished former chairman of the House Armed Services Committee:

> The fact is that the Marine Corps is and always has been, since its inception 175 years ago, a separate military service apart from the United States Army, the United States Navy, and the United States Air Force.

Some account of the evolution of the status of the Marine Corps is useful knowledge for you as a Marine officer.

The Act of 11 July 1798, reconstituting the Corps after its post–Revolutionary War hiatus, provided for a Corps of Marines, "... *in addition to* the present military establishment." In line with this thought, although the Corps' distinct status from the Navy was never questioned, it was nearly forty years before the Corps was firmly dissociated from the Army. During this time, while on shore, Marines (like the British marines) were promoted, paid, rationed, and disciplined under Army Regulations—practices sanctioned not only by custom but by express rulings handed down from time to time by the attorney general of the United States.

To clarify the status of the Marine Corps, Congress in 1834 affirmed the Corps as a separate service but placed it unequivocally under the secretary of the navy and therefore under *Navy Regulations* ". . . except when detached for service with the Army, by order of the President."

For more than a century, the Acts of 1798 and 1834 governed the status of the Marine Corps. In 1947, the National Security Act became law. This law as amended by Public Law 416 not only spells out the missions of our Corps today but defines the Corps in declaratory language as one of the four services given statutory missions under the act. In the first years of unification there was some tendency to assume that the National Security Act had intended to tri-elementalize the armed forces on a three-service basis, with the Marine Corps merely a specialist branch of the Navy. This misconception was set at rest with some emphasis in the debate and hearings on Public Law 416, during which Congress avowed that the Marine Corps was not a mere appendage but a service in its own right.

A final and legally definitive ruling on the foregoing point is to be found in House Report 970, 84th Congress. This is the report by the House of Representatives on the codification of Title 10 (Armed Forces), U.S. Code. This report states:

> ... the legislative history of Public Law 432, the National Security Act of 1947, and Public Law 416 of the 82nd Congress ... clearly indicates that the Marine Corps is legally a separate and distinct military service within the Department of the Navy, with individually assigned statutory responsibilities, and

that the Commandant directs and administers the Marine Corps under delegated command of the Secretary of the Navy.

The status of the Marine Corps can be summed up thus:

1. The Marine Corps is a separate military service possessing distinct statutory roles and missions prescribed by the National Security Act.
2. The Marine Corps is a part of the naval establishment (or Department of the Navy) and comes directly under the secretary of the navy.
3. The commandant of the Marine Corps commands the Corps as a whole, and is directly responsible to the secretary of the navy in a well-defined historical and legal relationship for the total performance, administration, readiness, discipline, and efficiency of the Corps.

404. The Marine Corps and the Department of the Navy

The brotherhood between the Marine Corps and Navy is of such long standing, so close, and so smooth in operation, that the casual observer may be readily pardoned the erroneous conclusion that the Marine Corps forms part of the Navy, or vice versa.

As we have seen, this is not the case. To quote General C. B. Cates, nineteenth commandant of the Marine Corps:

> The partnership between the Navy and Marine Corps had its legal birth more than 150 years ago when Congress placed both Services—which were then some 25 years of age—under a newly created Secretary of the Navy. The partnership was a close one initially, and it grew even closer with the passage of time. Today it is so close that only a handful of people—inside the Naval Services as well as outside—realize that technically the Navy and Marine Corps are separate Services under the command of the Secretary of the Navy. *Practically speaking,* the Navy and Marine Corps have lived, worked, and fought together since their inception.

To understand the place of the Marine Corps in the naval establishment, you must first understand exactly what constitutes the Department of the Navy, or, as it was called for many years in the past, "the naval establishment." As stated in *Navy Regulations,* and in Chapter 3 of this *Guide,* the naval establishment (that is, the Department of the Navy) embraces all activities committed to the care of the secretary of the navy and thus includes the Marine Corps. This does not make the Marine Corps a part of, but rather a partner of, the Navy proper.

The Marine Corps and Public Law 432. The law that defines the position of the chief of naval operations in the Navy is Public Law 432, 80th Congress (original House of Representatives title, "H.R. 3432").

Casual reading of parts of this law by a person not conversant with the intent of Congress in framing it (or of the Navy Department in seeking it) might suggest that this act could be construed as placing the Marine Corps under command of the chief of naval operations. To save confusion on this, it is enough to quote from an official letter by Secretary of the Navy John L. Sullivan, on 17

December 1947, to General A. A. Vandegrift, eighteenth commandant of the Marine Corps:

> The Commandant of the Marine Corps is informed that it is not the intent of the Navy Department, in seeking enactment of H.R. 3432 [Public Law 432], to alter the Commandant's direct responsibility to the Secretary of the Navy for the administration and efficiency of the Marine Corps.
>
> The Navy Department interprets neither Executive Order 9635 [an earlier directive defining the wartime position of the Chief of Naval Operations] nor H.R. 3432 as interposing the Chief of Naval Operations in the administrative chain of responsibility between the Secretary and the Commandant, or as otherwise modifying the historical relationship between the Secretary and the Commandant.
>
> /s/   John L. Sullivan

The Marine Corps as a Naval Service.   Attempts are sometimes made to show that the term "naval service" has a specific organizational meaning that includes both the U.S. Navy and the U.S. Marine Corps, so that together they may be said to constitute one military service—the "naval service." The claim that this term has such a meaning is baseless. Historically, the phrase "naval service" originated as a matter of convenience for the secretary of the navy in issuing orders affecting all military personnel under his jurisdiction. It has occasionally been used for comparable specific purposes in statutes, mainly dating years back, dealing with personnel administration or discipline, and with no general or consistent construction or definition of the term in question. That Marines, within the meaning and purposes of these statutes and regulations, are "members of the naval service" has long been accepted without dispute; but, as the codification of Title 10, U.S. Code, underscores (see Section 403), the Marine Corps is a legally distinct and separate military service. Therefore, the best usage when the term "naval service" arises in connection with Marines or the Marine Corps is to pluralize it as "the naval services," since there are always two naval services—the U.S. Navy and the U.S. Marine Corps—within the Department of the Navy, and, when the Coast Guard is assigned in time of hostilities, there are three.

Working Relations between Marine Corps and Navy.   Although we have emphasized the legally and essentially separate status of the Marine Corps in the naval establishment, such status does not prevent harmonious working relations between the Marine Corps and the Navy.

Not only do individual Marines serve as part of Navy commands, and vice versa, but units are likewise freely interchanged. Every Navy staff of any consequence includes a Marine officer or officers, while all Marine units and stations have Navy doctors, dentists, chaplains, and hospital corpsmen. In addition the Fleet Marine Force includes naval gunfire liaison officers—Navy line officers who, as FMF staff officers, help to obtain gunfire support.

Each major combatant ship of the fleet has a Marine detachment, and most Navy shore stations boast Marine barracks or detachments for security purposes.

On the other hand, Navy units such as Seabees, naval beach groups, and so on, are frequently attached to the Marine Corps.

At higher levels, the Fleet Marine Forces (see Section 505) best exemplify the close relationship between the Marine Corps and Navy. Here we have major Marine operating forces assigned by the secretary of the navy on a continuing basis to duty with the fleets, and, while so assigned, (operationally under the CNO) just as much part of a fleet as its ships or aircraft. Side by side with this operational relationship, however, the commandant of the Marine Corps retains full control over the administration, readiness, and military efficiency of the units concerned. And all hands, Marine Corps and Navy, are governed alike by *Navy Regulations.*

In the words of former Secretary of the Navy Robert B. Anderson, "They are, in every sense of the word, a team."

405. Summary

To summarize, the missions and status of the Marine Corps are prescribed in the National Security Act as amended. Public Laws 432 (80th Congress) and 416 (82d Congress) supplement and affirm the National Security Act, as does "The Functions Paper" (even though without statutory standing). For a detailed discussion and analysis of the tortured struggle of the Corps to achieve its statutory position, read the lively chapters of Lieutenant General Victor H. Krulak in his *First to Fight,* published by the Naval Institute.

The status of the Marine Corps within the Department of the Navy can best be described in the words of Vice Admiral O. W. Colclough, while judge advocate general of the Navy:

> The Marine Corps has been held for years to be a separate Service, although it operates with the Navy, and under the Secretary of the Navy.

Over and above its usual status and duties within the naval framework, the Marine Corps may be, and frequently has been, assigned other duties and status elsewhere in the executive branch, under the plenary powers that the president possesses with regard to the Corps.

In the vast complex of the Department of Defense, the Marine Corps plays a lonely role.

—The Honorable John Nicholas Brown

5

Organization of the Marine Corps

501. Introduction

Major General W. S. ("Bigfoot") Brown, one of the Corps' most loved old-timers, lecturing at a service school, began with these words, "Well, gentlemen, they've given me the job of describing the organization of the Marine Corps. This surprised me somewhat, because I never knew we had any organization. . . ."

Despite that prologue, the Marine Corps does have an organization, and precise knowledge of that organization is one of the first things a Marine officer must acquire (see Figure 5–1).

The Marine Corps is made up of land combat, security, and service forces; Marine Corps aviation; and the Marine Corps Reserve. In many ways, the organization of the Corps resembles that of the Navy. Like the Navy, the Marine Corps is organized into three principal subdivisions:
1. Marine Corps Headquarters
2. Marine Corps Operating Forces
3. Marine Corps Supporting Establishment (including the Reserve Establishment).

Throughout these components, Marine Corps aviation is included as necessary to carry out the missions of the Corps.

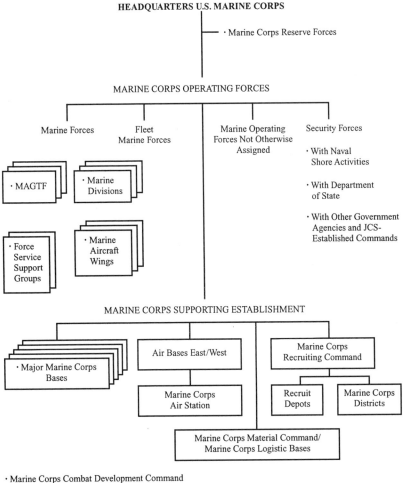

Figure 5–1: Organization of the Marine Corps (1998)

MARINE CORPS HEADQUARTERS

502. Headquarters, U.S. Marine Corps (HQMC)

Marine Corps Headquarters, in Washington, D.C., is the executive part of the Corps. Nominally accommodated in the Pentagon, parts of it operate on board MCB, Quantico; in the Navy Annex, Arlington; and the Clarendon Center, Roslyn.

Although Marine Corps Headquarters exercises some technical functions similar to Navy Department bureaus, one should not conclude that Headquarters is merely another bureau or on the same level as the bureaus. An organization chart of Marine Corps Headquarters appears in Figure 5–2.

Commandant of the Marine Corps.

> I want each of you to feel that the Commandant of the Corps is your friend and that he earnestly desires that you should realize this. At the same time, it is his duty to the Government and to the Marine Corps to exact a high standard of conduct, a strict performance of duty, and a rigid compliance with orders. . . .

In those simple terms, one commandant defined his responsibilities. Phrasing those responsibilities today, we can say that the commandant is directly responsible to the secretary of the navy for the readiness, total performance, and administration of the Marine Corps as a whole, including the Reserve. He commands all Marine forces and activities except those assigned to the naval operating forces, unified commands, or elsewhere. For the readiness and performance of those elements of the Marine Corps operating forces assigned to the operating forces of the Navy (i.e., the Fleet Marine Forces), the commandant is also responsible to the chief of naval operations.

The commandant is appointed by the president, from among the active general officers of the Corps, with the advice and consent of the Senate, for a four-year term. He holds the rank of general. The commandant may be reappointed for more than four years. Archibald Henderson, fifth commandant, who held office more than thirty-nine years, has the record.

The principal duties of the commandant extend, but are not limited, to: procurement, discharge, education, training (individual and unit), and distribution of the officers and enlisted men of the Corps, and all matters of command, discipline, requirements, readiness, organization, administration, equipment, and supply of the Marine Corps. You will find a list of the commandants in Appendix II.

Assistant Commandant.   The assistant commandant is a general who discharges the duties of the commandant during the latter's absence or disability and performs such duties as the commandant may direct.

Director, Marine Corps Staff.   The director, a major general, is the commandant's executive officer. He or she directs, coordinates, and supervises staff activities of Marine Corps Headquarters.

Deputy Chief of Staff.   There are five deputy chiefs of staff. The deputy chief of staff (plans, policies, and operations), a lieutenant general, acts for the director of Marine Corps Staff in his or her absence; has cognizance over unit training and readiness, force structure, amphibious, and other doctrinal matters; and represents the Marine Corps in certain joint service matters. The deputy chief of staff (manpower and reserve affairs), a lieutenant general, has cognizance over manpower planning, budgeting, programs, management and administration, and individual training. The deputy chief of staff (installations and

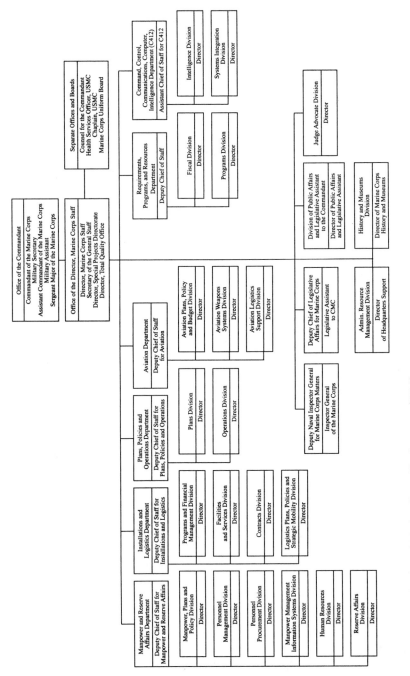

Figure 5–2: Organization of Marine Corps Headquarters (1998)

logistics), a lieutenant general, has cognizance over matters related to logistics policy and management, and facilities and installations. The deputy chief of staff (requirements, programs, and resources), a general officer, has cognizance over Marine Corps programming, requirements, and systems/cost analysis. This officer also represents the Marine Corps in certain external functions related to these areas of cognizance. The deputy chief of staff (aviation), a lieutenant general, has cognizance over matters related to Marine Corps aviation.

The *Military Secretary* manages the immediate office of the commandant.

The *Sergeant Major of the Marine Corps* is the senior noncommissioned officer of the Corps and, by virtue of this billet, is senior to all other enlisted Marines. This officer advises and assists the commandant in all matters within his or her cognizance.

The *Secretary of the General Staff* assists the director of the staff and the staff by coordinating staff action and ensures that staff matters presented to the director of the staff and to the commandant are complete.

The *Legislative Assistant to the Commandant* is the commandant's principal adviser in legal and legislative matters, including liaison with Congress. He or she prepares comments on legislative proposals referred to, or affecting, the Marine Corps (except cases in the province of the fiscal director).

The *Director Special Projects Directorate* assists the commandant in matters related to briefing, symposia, foreign visits, and preparation of speeches and articles.

The *Director of Headquarters Support* has cognizance over administration and management services for HQMC, headquarters security, transportation, internal communications services, and military and civilian personnel for the headquarters.

The *Director of Intelligence* has cognizance over intelligence, counterintelligence, cryptology, and electronic warfare and (as a service intelligence chief) maintains liaison with other government intelligence agencies. He or she also disseminates intelligence information within Marine Corps Headquarters.

The *Director, Judge Advocate Division,* serves as staff judge advocate for the commandant and has cognizance over all legal matters (except certain questions of business or budgetary law, which fall to the legal counsel or to the fiscal director).

The *Director of Systems Integration Division* has cognizance over all Marine Corps automated data processing and programs (ADP), command and control systems, and telecommunications and communications security.

Director of Marine Corps History and Museums. The director of Marine Corps history and museums has cognizance over all Marine Corps historical programs and museums, as well as maintenance of historical reference and library functions, and the Marine Corps archives.

Director of Public Affairs. The director of public affairs heads the Division of Public Affairs. It is his or her delicate, exacting, and sometimes thankless job to represent the Marine Corps to the public. The director of public affairs maintains liaison with Defense Department and government public affairs agencies, and with national public affairs and news media. The director also supervises Marine field activities that disseminate public affairs.

Inspector General.   The inspector general (IG) reports to the Naval IG, the commandant, and the secretary of the Navy as a deputy Naval IG for Marine Corps matters. It is the inspector general's eagle-eyed responsibility to conduct inspections and investigations as directed by the commandant; to coordinate the readiness programs of the Marine Corps; and to maintain liaison with the inspection agencies of the other defense agencies. It is worth comment at this point that, although an "IG inspection" invariably begets trepidation and soul-searching, the mission of the inspector general is to help and to improve by constructive inspection.

Fiscal Director.   The fiscal director heads the fiscal division. It is his or her job to plan and coordinate the Marine Corps budget; to present and justify that budget to other Defense Department agencies and to Congress; to supervise the spending of appropriated funds; to finance military and civilian pay and general expenses; and to analyze, record, and report on expenditures under the Department of Defense budget procedure.

Manpower and Reserve Affairs Department.   Of all agencies in Marine Corps Headquarters, this department has more directly to do with you than any other.

"Manpower" selects and procures you (just as it recruits enlisted Marines). It gives you your commission and administers you from the moment you are sworn in until you rest beneath the trees in Arlington Cemetery. Manpower details you, manages your career, promotes you, and retires you. With one hand, if need be, it disciplines you, while with the other it attends to your welfare. It maintains your records at Marine Corps Headquarters, as it maintains similar records on every officer and enlisted Marine in the Corps. If you become a casualty, Manpower notifies your next of kin, gives you your Purple Heart, and sees that you get the decorations and medals you have earned. Should you have a claim against the government, Manpower adjudicates.

THE MARINE CORPS OPERATING FORCES

503.   Marine Corps Operating Forces

The Marine Corps Operating Forces fall into four categories: Marine Corps Operating Forces assigned to the Operating Forces of the Navy or to unified commands; Marine Corps Operating Forces assigned to shore activities of the naval establishment; Marine Corps Operating Forces assigned to the State Department; and Marine Corps Operating Forces not otherwise assigned.

504. Marine Corps Forces

When Marine Corps units are assigned to the unified commands or to the Operating Forces of the Navy, they report to the senior Marine Corps commander. For the unified command, a *Marine Corps Forces* component commander (COMMARFOR) exercises operational control. That operational control does not include the administration and training responsibilities, which remain under the commandant of the Marine Corps. The Commander, Marine Corps Forces Atlantic, with headquarters in Norfolk, and a similar commander for the Pacific, with headquarters in Hawaii, act as component commanders in the U.S. Atlantic and Pacific unified commands. These same commanders serve as Marine Corps component commanders in the U.S. Joint Forces and Pacific unified commands. COMMARFORs have important strategic and budgetary planning activities, under the unified commanders, that contribute substantially to the determination of the size and composition of the Marine Corps Operating Forces in total.

Marine Corps units assigned to the Atlantic and Pacific Fleets are commanded by the Commanding Generals, Fleet Marine Force, Atlantic and Pacific. These are the same officers serving as COMMARFORs above but exercising command through separate staffs located in the same buildings.

505. Fleet Marine Forces

The Fleet Marine Forces (FMFs) constitute the bulk of the Marines assigned to the Operating Forces of the Navy. Both the Atlantic and Pacific Fleets include

The Fleet Marine Forces constitute the cutting edge of America's amphibious assault potential.

Fleet Marine Forces. The FMFs are integral components in the fleet organization and enjoy status as "type commands" (see Section 326). This Marine expeditionary force integral to the fleet was created by Major General John H. Russell, sixteenth commandant.

A Fleet Marine Force is a balanced force of combined arms, including aviation. It consists of a headquarters, service and support units, one or more Marine divisions or brigades, and one or more Marine aircraft wings. FMFs are organized, trained, and equipped for the following jobs:

1. Service with the fleets in seizure and defense of advanced bases, and for land operations related to naval campaigns
2. Development of amphibious tactics, technique, and equipment
3. Training the maximum number of Marines for war or emergency expansion
4. Immediate expeditionary service where, when, and as directed

The FMF today includes three combat divisions, three aircraft wings, and three service support groups. Based on combat experience, the ratio of one aircraft wing to support one Marine division is the fundamental proportion in the Marine aircraft-ground team.

In addition to the divisions and aircraft wings, Force Service Support Groups include extra engineers, motor transport, air and naval gunfire liaison company, service troops, and numerous specialized units that might be required to form balanced task forces for any kind of operations (see Figure 5–3).

Tables of Organization (T/Os) spell out the organization of every FMF unit, right down to the individual Marine and his or her duties, rank, specialist qualifications, and weapons. *Tables of Equipment* (T/Es) list the equipment required by each unit, and *Tables of Allowance* (T/As) give basic allowances of standard items, such as bunks, helmets, and cleaning gear—to cite examples—which vary in direct proportion to the number of Marines in a unit. *Know your unit's T/O inside out* and acquire more than a nodding acquaintance with your T/E and T/A and with the organization of other FMF units with which you are in immediate contact.

The Marine Division (see Figure 5–4) is the ground fighting organization of the Marine Corps. The division is a balanced force of combined arms, but it does not include organic aviation or logistic support. The division consists of about 16,000 officers and enlisted Marines, more than half of whom serve in the three infantry regiments—the division's cutting edge. To support these infantry regiments, the Marine division includes an artillery regiment, tanks, amphibian vehicles, engineers, motor transport, and medical, signal, and other troops normal for a force of combined arms. During World War II, the Corps reached an all-time high of six divisions.

Fleet Marine Force Aviation. The basic tactical and administrative unit of FMF aviation is the squadron. Two or more tactical squadrons plus a headquarters and maintenance squadron and an air base squadron constitute the *Marine aircraft group.* Two or more groups, with appropriate supporting and service units, make up the *Marine aircraft wing* (Figure 5–5). FMF aviation units, whose

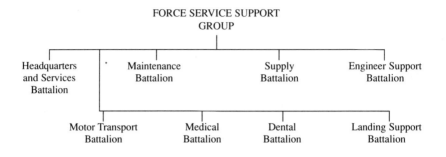

Separate FMF Units:
- Force Communication Battalion
- Surveillance, Reconnaissance, and Intelligence Group

Figure 5–3: Organization of a Force Service Support Group (1994)

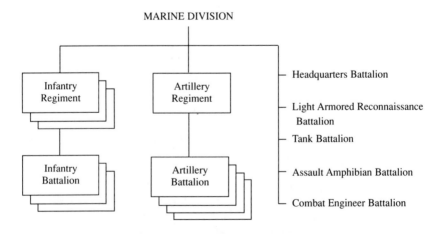

Figure 5–4: Organization of a Marine Division (1994)

aircraft permit carrier operations, are so trained and serve on board aircraft carriers of the fleet. A complete discussion of Marine aviation can be found in Sections 519–520.

506. Marine Air-Ground Task Forces

Marine Corps doctrine normally dictates the employment of Marine forces as integrated Marine Air-Ground Task Forces (MAGTFs). This doctrine emphasizes the employment of all elements of the force under a single commander, thereby obtaining unity of effort. The MAGTF is unique to the Corps (Figure 5–6). It is trained and equipped not only for amphibious warfare but for a variety of combat situations. Its structure and its emphasis on strategic mobility make the MAGTF exceptionally useful in a wide array of crises. Its organization by task enables the commander to tailor the force to a specific contingency. The MAGTF can fight well and harmoniously within a joint or combined task force in a land campaign or provide a one-service force of combined arms for a variety of situations.

When employed in other than amphibious operations, MAGTFs are capable of functioning as self-sustaining forces under the operational command of the unified, subunified, or joint task force commander. Their organization and training for amphibious warfare, which the Marine Corps pioneered and continues to perfect, enhance their capability to deploy rapidly by any means.

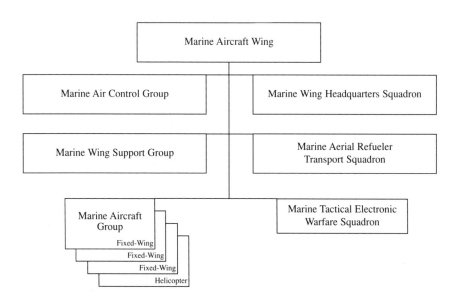

Figure 5-5: Organization of a typical Marine Aircraft Wing (1994)

M1A1 tanks maneuver across the California desert.

The MAGTF is not a permanent organization; it is task-organized for a specific mission and, after completion of that mission, is dissolved in accordance with pre-arranged plans. A MAGTF headquarters is structured to control whatever forces are assigned; thus, the Marine Corps can rapidly converge forces from any or all of its base locations to form a composite MAGTF without regard for parent administrative organization. To shorten the response time and reduce strategic life requirements, the Marine Corps has prepositioned equipment and supplies in or near potential crisis areas. The prepositioning of materiel for use by Marine forces has led to a renewed emphasis on airlifting Marine combat forces to marry-up with that equipment. The Marine Corps endorses airlift as an alternative for rapid deployment of its forces in situations permitting nonhostile entry.

The current and planned uses of Marine forces reflect an understanding by the National Command Authority of the unique role amphibious operations can play in a limited or worldwide war. Marine Expeditionary Units are continuously deployed on amphibious ships in the Mediterranean Sea and Pacific Ocean and visit the Caribbean Sea and Indian Ocean, to provide a peacetime presence and rapid response capability that contributes to deterrence and forward defense strategy.

Deployed MAGTFs provide the means to rapidly project U.S. power in support of vital U.S. interests anywhere in the world. Able to move on and be supported from the sea, MAGTFs, with associated amphibious shipping and carrier battle groups, are free from dependence on basing or overflight rights and provide an effective force presence without political commitment. During peacetime, they provide assurance to our allies and demonstrate commitment to our adversaries.

Regardless of the size of the MAGTF, it will include the following four major components:

The MAGTF integrates the power of Marine Corps ground, aviation, and logistics units.

1. command element
2. ground element
3. aviation combat element
4. combat service support element

    Although a MAGTF is a task organization tailored to accomplish a specific mission, there are three basic types of MAGTFs: the Marine Expeditionary Unit (MEU), the Marine Expeditionary Brigade (MEB), and the Marine Expeditionary Force (MEF). Current doctrine (promulgated in 1994) has supplanted the MEB designation and prefers the designation of MEF (Forward). There is also the designation of Special Purpose MAGTF (SPMAGTF) for any unit smaller than the nominal MEU.

    The Marine Expeditionary Unit is a MAGTF normally built around a reinforced infantry battalion, a composite helicopter squadron, and a MEU Service Support Group (MSSG). The composite squadron normally includes several types of helicopters, although it may include fixed-wing aircraft. The MEU is commanded by a colonel. The MEU is usually considered to be the forward element of a larger MAGTF.

    The Marine Expeditionary Brigade is built around a reinforced regiment, a Marine Aircraft Group (MAG), and a Brigade Service Support Group (BSSG).

Marine Expeditionary Force (MEF) XXX	Marine Expeditionary Brigade (MEB) X	Marine Expeditionary Unit (MEU) III

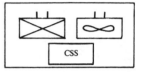

Command Element	Command Element	Command Element
Marine Division	Regimental Landing Team (RLT)	Battalion Landing Team (BLT)
Marine Aircraft Wing	Marine Aircraft Group	Composite Squadron
Force Service Support Group	Brigade Service Support Group	MEU Service Support Group
Commander: Major General	Commander: Brigadier General	Commander: Colonel

Mission Capability

Sustained air-ground combat	Sustained air-ground operations to accomplish limited mission	Mission of limited scope and duration

Figure 5–6: Typical Marine Air-Ground Task Forces (MAGTF)

The Marine Aircraft Group will contain all types of aircraft required by the mission. The MEB is commanded by a brigadier general.

The Marine Expeditionary Force is a MAGTF normally built around a Marine Division, a Force Service Support Group (FSSG), and a Marine Aircraft Wing that will contain all types of aircraft. The MEF is commanded by a major general or lieutenant general.

The command element is the MAGTF headquarters. It is composed of the commander and a separate air-ground headquarters with a staff and communication and service support facilities. The establishment of a single headquarters over the aviation, ground, and combat service support elements provides the command, control, and coordination capability essential for effective planning and execution of operations. In amphibious operations, when Marines constitute the preponderant force, the MAGTF command element serves also as the landing force headquarters.

The ground combat element is a task organization tailored for the conduct of ground maneuver. It is constructed around a ground combat infantry unit and varies in size from a battalion landing team to a reinforced Marine division or divisions. The ground combat element also includes appropriate combat support and combat service support units. Normally, there is only one ground combat element in a MAGTF.

The aviation combat element of a MAGTF is task organized to fulfill the six functions of Marine aviation. These functions—air reconnaissance, anti–air warfare, assault support, offensive air support, electronic warfare, and control of aircraft and missiles—are provided in varying degrees based on the tactical situation and on the size of the MAGTF. Usually, there is only one aviation

Navy landing craft, air cushion (LCACs), impart higher speeds and greater tactical options to the conduct of amphibious operations.

combat element in a MAGTF. It includes those aviation command (including air control agencies), combat, combat support, and combat service support units required by the situation.

The combat service support element provides the primary combat support to all elements of the MAGTF. Depending on the mission, it is task organized to meet any or all of the following functions: supply, maintenance, engineer, medical/dental, automated data processing, materiel-handling equipment, personal services, food services, transportation, military police, disbursing, and financial management. It is capable of providing smaller task organizations for support of MAGTF operations as required.

The MAGTF may be seen as the culmination of some ninety years of U.S. Marine Corps evolution from a ships' police force to a standing ready force. Its genesis lies in the Huntington Battalion of 1898 (Guantánamo), modified by the development of the air weapon, the Pacific War of 1941–45 and joint forces and combined arms experience since the Korean War.

507. Marine Regiments

The Corps has two kinds of regiments: infantry and artillery. They are numbered as follows.
* 1st–9th Marines: Infantry
* 10th–15th Marines: Artillery
* 16th–20th Marines: Unassigned*
* 21st–29th Marines: Infantry

The assignment of regiments to active Marine divisions is as follows.
* *1st Marine Division:*   1st, 5th, 7th, 11th Marines
* *2d Marine Division:*   2d, 6th, 8th, 10th Marines
* *3d Marine Division:*   3d, 4th, 9th, 12th Marines
* *4th Marine Division (USMCR):*   23d, 24th, 25th, 14th Marines.

The above, with one exception, represents the organization for combat of those divisions in World War II. If the numbering at first sight appears illogical, you will find that there are good underlying historical reasons for it in each case.

508. Seagoing Marines

Standing Marine detachments aboard carriers (and formerly aboard flagships, battleships, and cruisers) have been disestablished as of January 1998. FAST platoons and detachments now perform, when required, the security mission once accomplished by these "seagoing Marines." Shipboard marines date from earliest antiquity—from the fleets of Hiram of Tyre, and of Greece and Rome, where, respectively, marines were known as *epibatae* and *milites classiarii*. For more detailed information on seagoing Marines, see Chapter 10 (Service Afloat).

509. Marine Corps Operating Forces with Naval Establishment Shore Activities

Marine forces provide internal security for major shore stations in the naval establishment. At such stations, Marine guards perform the predominantly mili-

* For a period during World War II, these numbers were assigned to Marine engineer regiments that were later disbanded.

tary activities that directly affect the internal security of the base.

Although Marine security forces are part of the naval stations where they serve, they also provide cadres from which the Fleet Marine Force can obtain additional trained regular Marines in a hurry. In fact, until the FMF was established, Marine barracks were the only sources of troops to form expeditionary forces. The Marine security forces therefore conduct training, prescribed by Marine Corps Headquarters, to keep officers and enlisted personnel at each Marine barracks or security force company ready for instant field duty.

510.   Marine Corps Operating Forces on Other Assignment

Because the president can assign Marines to any duty (". . . such other duty as the President may direct"), Marine Corps Operating Forces can be, and frequently have been, detached for service outside the naval establishment, under unified commands, independently, or even under other executive departments (such as the Marine embassy or mail guards). Command of Marine units not otherwise assigned by the president or the secretary of the Navy remains with the commandant of the Marine Corps.

THE MARINE CORPS SUPPORTING ESTABLISHMENT

511.   The Supporting Establishment Concept

The Marine Corps supporting establishment provides, trains, maintains, and supports the operating forces. The supporting establishment includes: Marine Corps Schools; the recruit depots; supply installations; reserve activities; certain Marine Corps bases, barracks, and air stations; Headquarters Battalion, Marine Corps Headquarters; and a number of miscellaneous small activities.

512.   Marine Corps Combat Development Command (MCCDC)

The Marine Corps courses and training activities conducted during World War I took more formal status when General Lejeune established the Marine Corps Schools in 1920. Today's Combat Development Command is the intellectual heart of the Corps. Normally commanded by a lieutenant general, the center serves as the central agency responsible for the training, concepts, and doctrine development necessary for all types of operations by Marine Corps forces.

The command consists of eleven subordinate components: the Marine Corps Base, Quantico; the Marine Corps University; and nine divisions, as follows.

1. Requirements
2. Concepts and Plans
3. Warfighting Integration

4. Doctrine
5. Training and Education
6. Studies and Analysis
7. Coalition and Special Warfare
8. War Gaming and Combat Simulation
9. Marine Corps Presentation Team
10. Science and Innovation

The president of Marine Corps University serves also as the commander of Marine Corps Schools, Quantico, under the Commanding General, MCCDC, who is responsible for Marine Corps Schools as an additional duty. The resident schools at Quantico constitute the principal intellectual activity of the Corps. A brief description of these schools, as of 1994, follows.

The *Marine Corps War College* is a top-level school and convenes annually a class of a dozen colonels, including peers from other services.

The *School of Advanced Warfighting* continues selected graduates of the Command and Staff College course for another year.

The *Command and Staff College,* a nine-month course for majors and lieutenant colonels, is an intermediate-level school. It includes the first phase of joint professional military education in its curriculum.

Amphibious Warfare School is a career-level course of instruction for captains. It prepares them for command at the company level and battalion-level staff work in the Fleet Marine Force.

The *Command and Control Systems Course,* a specialized version of the Amphibious Warfare School, is principally directed at communications and intelligence officers.

The *Basic Communications Officer Course* qualifies officers in the communications specialty, MOS 2502.

Officer Candidate School screens candidates for commissioned rank by providing basic military instruction, leadership instruction, and physical training. Successful candidates are appointed to commissioned rank in the Marine Corps Reserve.

The *Staff Noncommissioned Officers' Academy* provides advanced NCO training for staff sergeants and sergeants selected for promotion to staff sergeant. The academy also conducts an annual Sergeants Major Seminar.

The *Basic School* is the place where newly commissioned lieutenants and warrant officers receive their initial training and are made into officers of Marines.

The *Marine Corps Research Center* provides resources and data to the entire Corps from a new (1993) building located across the street from the Marine Corps University. It contains library, archives, telecommunications media, and conference seminar spaces.

The *Intelligence Activity* provides intelligence services to the command and other activities located at Quantico. These include threat analysis and intelligence awareness.

The *Wargaming Center* is the Marine Corps focal point of all wargaming support and expertise. Its wargaming support assists local activities in validation and refinement of operational concepts and demonstrates them to a wide range of participants.

Supporting activities of the Combat Development Command include Headquarters Battalion, Weapons Training Battalion, and Support Battalion. There are also a Marine Corps Air Facility and a Naval Regional Medical Clinic on board the base.

Tenant activities on board the base, but not reporting directly to the Commanding General, MCCDC, include Marine Corps Systems Command, Marine Security Guard Battalion, Marine Corps Operational Testing and Evaluation Activity, and Manpower Department, HQMC.

513. Marine Corps Recruit Depots

The recruit depots (and Basic School) are the foundation of the Corps. "Boot camp" transforms the average young American into a Marine. Picked officers and veteran enlisted drill instructors (DIs) emphasize the elements of obedience, esprit, and the military fundamentals all Marines must master before taking their places in the fighting elements of the Corps.

The Marine Corps has two recruit depots—at Parris Island, South Carolina, and San Diego, California. Each recruit depot trains and equips the fledgling Marine, or "boot." Recruits from eastern states go to Parris Island, while those from western states go to San Diego. Often in the past, as special conditions have dictated, the Corps has trained recruits at Washington, D.C. (Marine Barracks, Eighth and Eye Streets), as well as at Quantico and Camp Lejeune. After boot camp, the new Marines graduate to advanced individual training at other Marine Corps schools.

514. Marine Corps Supply

The Marine supply services provide logistic support for the Corps. Logistic support refers to supply, service, transportation, and evacuation. The supply establishment procures, stores, distributes, maintains, and repairs all materiel that passes through the Marine Corps supply system, which coordinates and supervises procurement, stock control, and distribution of materiel.

Supply Organization.   The supply organization of the Marine Corps is designed to respond to modern logistic requirements. The Marine Corps supply system heads up what is called an *inventory control point* (ICP) at Marine Corps Logistic Base, Albany, Georgia. The main functions of the ICP are centralized procurement of virtually all materiel for the Corps, centralized processing of all requisitions, and stores accounting. Four additional vital functions are as follows.

1. *Cataloging:* Every item entering the Marine Corps supply system is identified, cataloged, and assigned a national stock number (NSN) in accordance with the federal cataloging program.

Essential field skills form an important part of Basic School training.

2. *Provisioning:* All major equipment or "end-items" entering the Marine Corps supply system, particularly for support of the FMF, require repair parts support. This function of provisioning (which has nothing to do with food) is the selection and procurement of thousands of new repair parts required each year for the support of new equipment.
3. *Technical services:* Users of equipment or maintenance personnel frequently

require engineering or technical assistance, which may vary from the relatively minor determination of the exact characteristics of a repair part to development of a major modification or engineering change.

4. *Publications support:* The publications that are the bibles of the supply system are called *Marine Corps Stock Lists.* You should be as familiar with these (at least in general terms) as with the *Marine Corps Manual* and other basic administrative publications.

The principal Marine Corps logistic establishments (those that physically stock materiel) are called *remote storage activities* (RSA). The two principal RSAs of the Marine Corps are the logistic bases at Albany and at Barstow, California. These RSAs store and issue materiel in accordance with instructions from the ICP, conduct and supervise stores accounting for post supply outlets, and serve as area repair centers.

To facilitate distribution and decentralization within the limits of the system and, at the same time, promote response to supply needs, various smaller supply agencies support certain major posts. These smaller supply agencies, formerly known as "stock accounts," are now also designated RSAs. Communications and actual processing of transactions between the ICP and RSAs are accomplished through a network of computers providing immediate response to supply needs.

Sources of Supply. In recent years, the Defense Logistics Agency (DLA) has emerged as the overall Defense Department manager of materiel. Under DLA, Defense logistic centers exist for the various materiel categories, such as

The Marine Corps logistic system supports equipment distinctive to the Corps, such as these assault amphibious vehicles, as well as common defense user equipment.

petroleum, subsistence, medical supplies, industrial supplies, general supplies, communications/electronics, engineer and construction supplies, automotive and ordnance, and others. In addition, the Defense Clothing and Textile Supply Center makes or procures uniforms and clothing for all the services. The DLA and all logistic centers are staffed by officers from each of the services. Thus, if you enter the supply field, you may reasonably expect to be detailed at some time to one of these joint agencies.

Aviation Supply. To understate, Marine aviation supply is complicated. Marines in aviation units get their clothing, individual equipment, rations, weapons, and pay from the Marine Corps. From the Naval Air Systems Command, however, they receive their vehicles, airplanes, armament, flight gear, and most training aids and manuals. Barracks, quarters, hangars, runways, revetments, and shops for the airplanes come from the Navy's Facilities Engineering Command.

515. Marine Corps Bases and Air Stations

Several Marine Corps bases, camps, barracks, and air stations exist primarily to support other Marine activities. Unlike the barracks for Marine security forces, these stations come under military command of the commandant of the Marine Corps. These posts are:

Marine Barracks, 8th and Eye Streets, S.E., Washington, D.C.

Henderson Hall, Arlington, Virginia

Marines of the Washington Barracks ("8th and Eye") parade weekly during summer months at the Marine Memorial, Arlington, Virginia. The guard unit remains the standard bearer of the pride and bearing of the Corps.

Marine Corps Combat Development Command, Quantico, Virginia
Marine Corps Base, Camp Lejeune, North Carolina
Marine Corps Base, Camp Pendleton, California
Marine Corps Air-Ground Combat Center, Twentynine Palms, California
Camp Allen, Norfolk, Virginia
Camp Garcia, Vieques, Puerto Rico
Camp H. M. Smith, Oahu, Hawaii
Camp S. D. Butler, Okinawa
Marine Corps Air Station, Beaufort, South Carolina
Marine Corps Air Station, Yuma, Arizona
Marine Corps Air Station, Miramar, California
Marine Corps Air Station, Kaneohe Bay, Hawaii
Marine Corps Air Station, Cherry Point, North Carolina
Marine Corps Air Station, Iwakuni, Japan
Marine Corps Air Station (helicopter), New River, North Carolina
Marine Corps Air Station (helicopter), Camp Pendleton, California
Marine Corps Air Station (helicopter), Futenma, Okinawa

In addition to the foregoing major stations, there is also the Marine Corps Mountain Warfare Training Center ("Pickel Meadows") at Bridgeport, California.

516. Marine Corps Districts

The Marine Corps divides the continental United States into regional Marine Corps districts for local representation, recruiting, and officer procurement. Among a wide range of miscellaneous duties, district directors maintain liaison with corresponding agencies and headquarters of the other three services, state adjutants general, other federal field agencies, schools and colleges, and veterans' associations and military societies.

517. The Marine Band

A unique organization in the supporting establishment is the U.S. Marine Band, a part of Marine Barracks, Washington, D.C.

This 120-piece military band is not only the best but the oldest (1798) of the armed forces musical organizations. It has the privilege of providing music for all White House and official state functions in Washington, in addition to its normal duties in military parades and ceremonials. By long custom, the director of the band is ex officio musical director of two of Washington's traditional dining clubs, the Gridiron Club (Washington correspondents) and the Order of the Carabao (military and naval).

518. The Marine Corps Reserve

Although separate from the regular establishment, the Marine Corps Reserve (Chapter 9) forms a vital part of the supporting establishment.

MARINE CORPS AVIATION

519. The Air-Ground Team

The role of Marine Corps aviation in the *air-ground team* is to support Fleet Marine Force operations by close and general tactical air support and air defense. Secondarily, Marine aviation may be called on to replace or augment squadrons for duty with the fleet air arm.

The noteworthy characteristic of Marine aviation is that it forms an inseparable part of the combined arms team operated by the Corps. Thus, the special role of Marines in the air is to support their teammates on the ground. The kind of close air support that Marines are accustomed to demands complete integration of air and ground forces. Pilot and platoon leader wear the same color uniform, share the same traditions and a common fund of experience, and go to school side by side in Quantico. Battlefield and beachhead liaison between air and ground is accomplished by Marine pilots who share frontline foxholes with the riflemen while directing Marine aircraft onto targets just ahead. This makes for maximum reliance by ground on aviation, and for maximum desire by aviation to assist the ground control units.

Probably the outstanding demonstration of this tradition in Marine aviation

Marine aviation exists to support the FMF in any operations that it may conduct. Its method of employment stems from the MAGTF doctrine peculiar to the Corps.

took place during the defense of Wake in 1941. Marine Fighting Squadron 211 provided a heroic air defense of Wake until no more airplanes were left. Then the officers and men of the squadron calmly donned helmets, picked up their '03 rifles, and went down to glory as infantry. Twenty-four years later, in Vietnam, a handful of aviation mechanics made similar history when a suicide demolition section of Vietcong sappers rushed the flight line of MAG-16 at Marble Mountain in an attempt to blow up helicopters with satchel charges. As the Vietcong charged, three mechanics downed tools, seized their rifles, and killed or wounded every attacker in one blast of well-aimed fire.

520. Organization of Marine Corps Aviation

In many respects, aviation is the part of the Corps that most nearly lives up to Kipling's "Soldier and sailor, too," because Marine aviation is very closely related to naval aviation. This relationship stems not only from the long partnership between Marine Corps and Navy, but also because the preponderance of Marine squadrons are organized and equipped for carrier operations and regularly perform tours of duty afloat. In addition, Marine pilots undergo flight training at Pensacola and earn their wings as naval aviators.

The primary function of Marine Corps aviation is to participate as the supporting air component of the Marine Corps Forces in whatever operations they conduct. A collateral function of Marine aviation is to participate as an integral component of naval aviation in the execution of naval functions as directed by the fleet commanders.

The commandant of the Marine Corps controls the administration, individual training, and organization of Marine aviation. The chief of naval operations, however, prescribes (via the commandant) the aeronautical training programs and standards for Marine aviation units. And the aviation materiel used by Marine squadrons comes from the same sources in the Navy as does similar materiel for Navy squadrons.

The organization of Marine Corps aviation falls into subdivisions that correspond to the organization of the Corps as a whole:
• Office of Deputy Chief of Staff for Aviation, Marine Corps Headquarters
• Aircraft, Marine Corps Forces
• Aviation supporting establishment
Office of Deputy Chief of Staff for Aviation. As the headquarters organization for Marine aviation, this office plans and supervises matters relating to the organization, personnel, operational readiness, and logistics of Marine aviation.

Aircraft, Marine Corps Forces. Aviation units in the Marine Corps Forces constitute the combatant part of the organization.

Aircraft, Marine Corps Forces comprises attack squadrons, including all-weather fighter-attack squadrons, reconnaissance squadrons, air-control squadrons, aerial refueller squadrons, transport squadrons (helicopter and fixed-wing), and headquarters and support squadrons for the groups and wings. The wing is the basic tactical unit of Marine aviation, just as the division is the basic ground unit. You should remember, however, that the wing is a flexible, not a fixed, organization, and that different component organizations can be added or deleted.

Aviation is represented in staff and planning billets throughout the ground organization and through the tactical air control parties (TACP) that form part of the battalion, regimental, and division headquarters of Marine Corps Forces.

Aviation Supporting Establishment. The Marine Corps maintains several air stations and base commands in order to support aviation units operating ashore. A commander, Marine Corps Air Bases (COMCAB), supervises all Marine aviation shore establishments supporting aviation units. The Marine Corps Air Bases headquarters occupies Marine Corps Air Station (MCAS), Cherry Point. The air stations and facilities of the aviation supporting establishment are listed in Section 515. The Marine Air Reserve Training Command, described in Chapter 9, has its headquarters at New Orleans.

MARINE CORPS STAFF ORGANIZATION AND PROCEDURE

521. Marine Corps Staff Organization

The general framework of Marine Corps staff organization corresponds to that employed by the U.S. Army. A complete description of that organization and the staff functions it performs can be found in *Field Manual 101-5, Staff Organization and Procedure* (FM 101-5), and the sooner you make the acquaintance of that invaluable manual, the better. Equally important is knowledge of what, in effect, is the Marine Corps' staff manual, *Command and Staff Action, FMFM 3-1.*

To suit differing functional needs of the Marine Corps (particularly in amphibious operations), we modify some of the staff functions described in *FM 101-5*. Moreover, the Marine Corps has evolved several special staff functions peculiar to Fleet Marine Force operations that do not appear at all in *FM 101-5*. These latter, with other staff functions, are listed below.

Staff Organization. The Marine commander's staff consists of three subdivisions: general (or executive) staff; special staff; and personal staff.

As we discuss the staff, one principle should be kept in mind: regardless of how much help the commander receives from the staff, *the commander, and the commander alone, is responsible for all that his or her unit does or leaves undone.* This is the basic principle of command.

General Staff. The general (or executive) staff is a coordinating staff group that plans and supervises all the basic functions of command. In units below divisional or wing level, it is known as the *executive staff;* in divisions or higher headquarters, it is the *general staff.* Except for scale, however, the functions and duties of general and executive staffs are identical.

The basic functions of command are personnel, intelligence, operations and training, logistics, planning, and communications-electronics. These six functions are referred to by number, in the order just given; for example, personnel is "1." If the staff is divisional or higher (a general staff), the numbers are prefixed by the letter "G"; if the staff level is below division or wing (an executive staff), its numbers are prefixed by the letter "S."

The general staff, which is concerned with these command functions, is headed by a chief of staff (or executive officer in units smaller than brigade), who may be assisted by a deputy chief of staff and by a staff secretary, who acts as office manager for the commander, the chief, and the deputy chief of staff. The remaining members of the general, or executive, staff are: the personnel officer (G-1 or S-1); intelligence officer (G-2 or S-2); operations and training officer (G-3 or S-3); logistics officer (G-4 or S-4); plans officer (G-5 level only); and command, control, communications, and computers (C4) officer (G-6 or S-6). In addition to the "G's," as the six assistant chiefs of staff are referred to, the staffs of all major commands, both FMF and non-FMF, include a comptroller, or financial management officer, who is considered to be a member of the general staff.

You will find detailed descriptions of the duties of each of the foregoing officers both in *FM 101-5* and in corresponding Marine Corps publications.

Special Staff.   The special staff includes all the staff who are not members of either the general staff or the personal staff. The special staff is a body of specialist advisers and assistants to the commander who provide technical advice, information, and supervision.

As a special staff officer, you enjoy direct access to your commander regarding any matter that relates to your particular specialty. Your routine activities are coordinated, however, by the appropriate general staff officers described above.

Special staff sections can be organized at will by the commander to fill a particular need, or existing sections can be consolidated or inactivated. Thus, the following list of special staff officers is typical rather than fixed (although, in fact, most of these appear in tables of organization and therefore can be considered "normal" for a major Marine headquarters):

Adjutant
Air base operations officer
Air officer (NA)
Aircraft maintenance officer
Antiaircraft officer
Antimechanized officer
Artillery officer
Assault amphibian vehicle officer
Aviation electronics (avionics) officer
Aviation supply officer

Chaplain (ChC, USN)
Chief air observer
Crash crew officer
Dental surgeon (DC, USN)
Disbursing officer
Embarkation officer
Engineer
Engineering officer
Exchange officer
Explosive ordnance disposal officer
Fiscal officer
Food services officer
Headquarters commandant
Historian
Inspector
Liaison officer
Military government/civil affairs officer
Motor transport officer
Naval gunfire officer
Nuclear, biological, and chemical officer
Ordnance officer
Photographic officer
Postal officer
Provost marshal
Public affairs officer
Shore party officer
Special operations officer
Special services officer
Staff judge advocate
Supply officer
Surgeon (MC, USN)
Tank officer
Utilities officer
Weather officer

Commanding officers of attached units with no special staff representation act as advisers to the commander on matters pertaining to their units.

Personal Staff. The personal staff consists of the staff officers whom the commander wishes to coordinate and administer directly rather than through his chief of staff. The personal staff thus includes such officers as aides-de-camp, and, for certain purposes, selected members of the special staff, such as the public affairs officer or the inspector.

The relationship between the commander and the personal staff is direct,

Effective staff work extends through all phases of operations.

personal, and confidential. The personal staff performs only such duties as the commander personally directs.

522. Staff Procedure and Relationships

Although this chapter deals mainly with Marine Corps organization, it is impossible to discuss staff organization without a few words on staff procedure and relationships. The fundamentals of staff procedure and relationships are staff supervision and completed staffwork.

As a junior officer, you will probably not be assigned to staff duties for a while. Nevertheless, you ultimately face assignment on a staff, and, meanwhile, you will be on the receiving end of staff coordination and supervision. It therefore behooves you to become familiar with the following fundamentals.

Status of the Staff.   No staff officer ever exercises command in his or her own right. The orders voiced by a staff officer are those of the commander—whether or not the commander is aware of them at the time when issued. Regardless of how much authority the commander allows the staff, the commander alone retains the responsibility. The commander holds the sack.

Staff supervision consists of advising other staff officers and subordinate commanders of the policies and desires of the commander; of interpreting those policies when necessary; and of reporting back to the commander the extent and manner in which the policies and desires are being carried out. This supervision does not extend to command.

Completed staffwork is the most important working principle of the staff. Completed staffwork has been variously defined by many commanders and by official or semiofficial publications. The definition that follows is one of the best and most generally quoted.

> Completed staffwork is the study of a problem and presentation of a solution, by a staff officer, in such form that all that remains to be done by the commander is to indicate his approval or disapproval of the completed action. The more difficult the problem is, the greater the tendency to present the problem to the chief in piece-meal fashion. It is your duty, as a staff officer, to work out the details. You should not burden your chief in the determination of those details, no matter how perplexing they may be. You may and should consult other staff officers. The product, whether it enunciates new policy or modifies established policy, should, when presented to the commander for approval, be worked out in finished form.
>
> It is your job to advise the commander what he ought to do, not to ask him what you ought to do. He needs answers, not questions. Your job is to study, write, restudy, and rewrite, until you have evolved a single proposed course of action—the most advantageous course of all that you have considered. The commander then approves or disapproves.
>
> Do not worry your commander with long explanations and memoranda. Writing a memorandum to your chief does not constitute completed staffwork, but writing a memorandum for him to send to someone else does. Your views should be placed before him in finished form, so that he can make them his own views simply by signing his name. In most cases, completed staffwork produces a single document prepared for the commander's signature, without accompanying comment. If the document stands on its own feet, it will speak for itself; if the commander wants further comment or explanation, he will ask for it.
>
> Completed staffwork usually requires greater effort for the staff officer, but it results in greater freedom and protection for the commander. Moreover, it accomplishes two results:
>
> 1. The commander is protected against half-baked ideas, voluminous memoranda, and immature oral presentations.
> 2. The staff officer who has a valid, important proposal can more readily find receptive consideration.
>
> The final test of completed staffwork is this:
>
> If you yourself were the commander, would you be willing to sign the paper you have prepared? Would you stake your professional reputation on its being right?
>
> If your answer would be "No," take the paper back and rework it, because it is not yet completed staffwork.

The foregoing should not suggest, however, that the staff officer operates in a vacuum. Properly prepared, he or she understands the commander's method, character, and desires and takes action in that spirit. Commanders give their appreciations of the situation at hand and should indicate their intentions to their staffs. Staffwork therefore reflects the commander's intent and not the personal whims of the staff officer concerned. When staff officers conceive of

other arrangements, they should present them to the commander as clearly identified alternatives. In higher headquarters, this takes the form of a *decision brief;*
at the regimental or small-unit level, the presentation is less formal.

---

*Fighting spirit is not primarily the result of a neat organization chart nor of a logi-
cal organization set-up. The former should never be sacrificed to the latter.*
—Ferdinand Eberstadt

6

The Story of
the Marine Corps

601. Marines in the Revolution

The Marine Corps dates from 10 November 1775. On that day the Continental Congress authorized formation of two battalions of Marines.

Captain Samuel Nicholas, of Philadelphia, was commissioned captain on 28 November 1775 and charged with raising the Marines authorized by Congress to form part of the naval service. Nicholas remained senior officer in the Continental Marines through the Revolution and is properly considered our first commandant.

The initial Marine recruiting rendezvous opened at Tun Tavern in Philadelphia, and, by early 1776, the organization had progressed to the extent that the Continental Marines were ready for their first expedition. The objective was New Providence Island (Nassau) in the Bahamas, where a British fort and large supplies of munitions were known to be. With Captain Nicholas in command, 234 Marines sailed from Philadelphia in Continental warships. On 3 March 1776, Captain Nicholas led his men ashore, took the fort, and captured the powder and arms for Washington's army.

For the first time in U.S. history, the Marines had landed, and the situation was well in hand.

NOTE: For an operational history of the Marine Corps, see J. Robert Moskin, *The U.S. Marine Corps Story*, rev. ed. (New York: McGraw-Hill, 1991). The definitive institutional and administrative history is Allan R. Millett, *Semper Fidelis*, rev. ed. (New York: The Free Press, 1991).

During the succeeding year, Nicholas, now a major, commanded a battalion of Marines that fought in the Middle Atlantic campaigns of 1776 and 1777, at Trenton, Morristown, Assunpunk, and Fort Mifflin. At sea (notably under John Paul Jones), shipboard Marines played traditional parts as prize crews, sharpshooters, and landing forces (such as in the Penobscot Bay expedition in 1779).

602. Early Years, 1783–1811

After the end of the Revolution in 1783, both Continental Navy and Marines waned into temporary nonentity. Although individual Marines continued to be enlisted for and to serve in the few U.S. armed vessels of the period (such as Revenue cutters), no Corps organization again existed until 11 July 1798, when Congress re-created the Marine Corps as a military service. Major William Ward Burrows, another Philadelphian with Revolutionary War experience, was appointed major commandant of the Corps.

During the decade that followed, the Naval War with France (1798–1800) and the campaign against the Barbary corsairs (1801–05) provided employment for the Corps. Other noteworthy events were the movement of Marine Corps Headquarters to Washington in 1800, the physical retirement of Burrows as commandant in 1804, and organization of the Marine Band in 1798.

The third commandant, Lieutenant Colonel Franklin Wharton, found approximately 65 percent of his small Corps on duty in the Mediterranean. Here, in 1805, First Lieutenant Presley Neville O'Bannon led a mixed force, including Marines, six hundred miles across the Libyan desert to attack the fortress at Derna. O'Bannon's handful of Marines were the first U.S. forces to hoist the Stars and Stripes over territory in the Old World. The "Mameluke" sword, carried by Marine officers to this day, symbolizes O'Bannon's feat.

While events in the Mediterranean held the spotlight, Marines, together with Army and Navy forces, were active in Georgia and East Florida, and in the lower Mississippi, where, in 1804, a 106-man detachment was established at New Orleans.

603. The War of 1812

During the first two years of the War of 1812 the main American achievements were at sea or on the Great Lakes. Marines fought in the great frigate duels of the war, as well as at the Battle of Lake Erie.

The outstanding record among seagoing Marines, however, was set by Captain John M. Gamble, captain of Marines in the USS *Essex,* the raider that virtually destroyed England's Pacific whaling trade. In April 1813, Gamble, with a crew of fourteen Marines and seamen, was placed in command of a prize, the recommissioned USS *Greenwich.* Late in 1813, Gamble and his tiny force joined Captain David Porter in the Marquesas Islands and established a base where they could rest and refit over the winter. In the spring, Porter sailed for the coast of South America and left Gamble with twenty-two volunteers and six prisoners

Sharpshooting Marine riflemen dominate the action between USS *Wasp* and HMS *Reindeer* in 1814.

of war to man the base, should it be needed after a battle with the British. In May, a mutiny broke out aboard the *Seringapatam,* and Gamble was put in a small boat with four others. They made it back to another ship that had been left in the Marquesas. When the natives attacked the small party, Gamble, who had been wounded in the foot during the mutiny, hopped from cannon to cannon to fire them and beat off the attack. Gamble somehow got the ship under way with no charts and a crew of eight scarcely able to sail. He and his men made the Hawaiian Islands, only to be captured in 1814 by a British man-of-war. For all these exploits, he was awarded a richly reserved brevet as lieutenant colonel.

In mid-1813, British forces under Admiral George Cockburn and Major General Robert Ross began a campaign of raids against the Middle Atlantic seaboard. A year later, in August 1814, a column of British soldiers, sailors, and Marines advanced on Washington, D.C. On 24 August, after the government had fled to Frederick, Maryland, an irresolute force of American soldiers and militia under Brigadier General William H. Winder of the Army attempted to halt the much smaller British column at Bladensburg, just east of Washington. Reinforcing Winder's 6,000 soldiers were 114 Marines from Eighth and Eye streets and a contingent of seamen gunners with five guns, the whole force being under Commodore Joshua Barney of the United States Navy.

Winder's soldiers broke and ran at the first volley from the British, who advanced unconcernedly until they hit a piece of high ground occupied by the Marines and seamen, who were standing firm. Marine volleys and Navy gunnery forced the British (seven times stronger) to halt, to deploy, and finally, three times in succession, to charge—at a cost of 249 casualties. After having suffered more than 20 percent casualties and being forced rearward by a double envelopment, the Marines and sailors withdrew in good order, with at least a moral victory to their credit.

The British, having put Washington to the torch, were now determined to seize New Orleans.

Although a peace treaty was even then being signed in Europe, the British expedition forced its way up the Mississippi. On 28 December 1814, the first enemy attack spent itself against an American line generalled by Andrew Jackson, with Marines (under Major Daniel Carmick) holding the center. Less than two weeks later, on 8 January, the British tried again. Despite a courageous assault by the redcoats, Jackson's main battle position stood unbroken. As the British commander, Sir Robert Pakenham, fell mortally wounded, the attack ebbed, New Orleans was saved, and the Marines shared in the glory when Congress recognized "the valor and good conduct of Major Daniel Carmick and Marines under his command."

604. Archibald Henderson Takes Over

The most important event in the history of the Marine Corps following the War of 1812 took place on 17 October 1820, when the adjutant and inspector, Archibald Henderson, succeeded Lieutenant Colonel Anthony Gale and became fifth commandant. Gale's term as commandant had been cut short by a poorly timed row with the secretary of the Navy, followed by a court-martial.

During the thirty-nine years and ten presidential administrations that followed, Henderson dominated the Corps and gave it the high military character it holds to this day. Had it not been for Henderson's firmness, reinforced by a sympathetic Congress, the Corps might well have been abolished as a result of President Jackson's attempt in 1829 (with connivance from certain influential naval officers) to transfer the Marines into the Army. After the smoke of controversy had drifted clear, Congress in 1834 placed the Corps directly under the secretary of the Navy—and increased its strength to boot. This was the first instance of congressional redress and rescue for the Marine Corps—something that has recurred repeatedly since then.

605. Actions against the Creeks and Seminoles, 1836–42

From 1836 through 1842, the Army, Navy, and Marine Corps bent united efforts to transfer the Creek and Seminole Indians of Georgia and Florida to new reservations. Commandant Henderson spent part of this time in the field at the head of a mixed brigade of Army troops and a Marine regiment (the first organization of that size in the history of the Corps). At the Battle of Hatchee-Lustee, Florida, in 1837, Colonel Henderson won one of the few decisively successful victories of the campaign and was thereupon brevetted brigadier gen-

Marines took part in the campaigns against the Creek and Seminole Indians, including service in the Navy's "Mosquito Fleet" of river patrol boats.

eral—the first general officer in the Corps. Despite this success, as well as others against the Creeks, the Seminoles continued an obstinate resistance, and, in 1842, the war ended—with most of the Seminoles still in Florida.

606. To the Halls of the Montezumas

The war with Mexico included three distinct campaigns: Zachary Taylor's against Monterrey, Winfield Scott's against Mexico City; and that against California and the west coast of Mexico. Marines took part in two of these, and were, in fact, the first U.S. forces to set foot on the soil of Mexico proper (at Burrita, 18 May 1846).

A battalion of Marines formed part of General Scott's column that advanced from Veracruz toward Mexico City. The key to the capital was Chapultepec Castle, set on a crag commanding the swamp causeways into the city. In the assault on Chapultepec, the Marines were divided into storming parties to head the attack up the south approach.

Under a hail of fire, the Marines moved out. Major Levi Twiggs, the battalion commander, fell early in the attack, while Captain George H. Terrett, a company commander, pressed home a separate assault toward the city. After a night in the outskirts of Mexico City, the Marines marched into town, in the van of their division—the first U.S. troops to enter—and occupied the palace of the Montezumas. The date was 14 September 1847, and a new phrase had been added to the annals of the Corps.

Commandant Archibald Henderson held tenure for thirty-eight years and shaped the character of the Corps in the nineteenth century.

In the Pacific, Marines joined naval landing parties taking possession of Monterey, Yerba Buena (San Francisco), Los Angeles, and San Diego, while First Lieutenant Archibald Gillespie acted both as confidential agent of President James Polk in the Bear State diplomatic intrigues and subsequently as a bold combat leader.

With California uneasily at rest by 1847, Marines of the Navy's Pacific Squadron secured the Mexican west coast ports of Mazatlán, Guaymas, Mulejé, and San José del Cabo. Mazatlán was garrisoned by Marines until June 1848, when peace was concluded.

607.   Between the Wars

The decade that followed peace with Mexico was hardly one of peace for the Marine Corps, despite postwar reduction of the Corps to approximately twelve hundred.

The opening of Japan in 1853–54 provided a historic setting for the landing of almost one-sixth of the Corps (six officers and two hundred Marines, commanded by Major Jacob Zeilin, Mexican War hero and future commandant). In the best traditions of the Corps, Major Zeilin's Marines were the first Americans to set foot on Japanese soil.

Hardly as peaceful were the landings at Shanghai (1854) and Canton (1856). In each, the conflicts represented trials of strength between Chinese and the

Americans bent on "opening" China. At Canton's "Barrier Forts," 176 Chinese cannon were taken and five thousand Chinese put to flight.

A hemisphere away, in Nicaragua, Panama, Paraguay, and Uruguay, Marines were scarcely less active. With discovery of gold in California, the Panamanian isthmus assumed great importance in 1855, when a rickety U.S. railroad was finally completed across the isthmus. Soon Panama became a hotbed of disorder, which necessitated several landings by Marines, ultimately including a brigade-sized force in 1885. In Uruguay and Paraguay, the story was the same—unsettled times, immature governments—and Marines protected American interests.

And at home, in Washington itself, Marines were called out in 1859 to stand off a gang of Baltimore mobsters who styled themselves the "Plug-Uglies" and who carried a loaded brass cannon for emphasis. While Marines and rioters faced each other across a downtown square, an old man, armed only with a gold-headed cane, stepped forward and placed his body across the muzzle of the mobsters' cannon. It was Brevet Brigadier General Archibald Henderson, fifth commandant of the Marine Corps, now seventy-four years old. While the thugs milled about the steadfast old man, a squad of his Marines rushed the cannon, and that was that.

608. The Civil War

For the Marine Corps, the opening shots of the Civil War sounded almost two years before Fort Sumter. On 17 October 1859, shortly after John Harris had succeeded Henderson as colonel commandant, eighty-eight Marines were despatched by the president to Harper's Ferry, Virginia, to recapture the U.S. Arsenal, which had been seized by the insurrectionist John Brown. The Marine force reported, on arrival, to Colonel Robert E. Lee, the senior U.S. Army officer present. When John Brown refused to surrender, the Marines, led by First Lieutenant Israel Green, smashed their way under fire into Brown's stronghold, wounded the old abolitionist, and quelled the insurrection.

After 1861, the Marine Corps—like the regular Army—was never large enough to fill the demands upon it. A Marine battalion fought in the first Battle of Manassas, and other Marine forces served ashore in the Mississippi Valley and in the defenses of Washington. All along the confederate seaboard, from Hatteras Inlet to Hilton Head and Fort Pickens, shipboard Marines, sometimes in provisional battalions, executed successful landings, which put teeth into the Union blockade. Only at Fort Fisher did Marines share with the Navy a bloody defeat.

By and large, the reputation of the Corps did not gain during the Civil War. Its strength was kept small at only 4,167 officers and men. And, as a Corps, Marines were not called on to perform either the readiness or amphibious tasks peculiar to the organization. As early as 1864 (and again in 1867), attempts were made to disband the Marine Corps and merge it with the Army.

Private Melvin Purvis won one of several Medals of Honor awarded to Marines who stormed the Han River forts of Korea in 1871.

Both times, however, Congress stepped into the breach, and the Corps was saved.

609. Post Civil War

Although the period from 1865 to 1898 has sometimes been spoken of as one of marking time by the Marine Corps, this scarcely holds up. During that time, U.S. Marines landed to protect American lives and property in Egypt, Colombia, Mexico, China, Cuba, the Arctic, Formosa, Uruguay, Argentina, Chile, Haiti, Alaska, Nicaragua, Japan, Samoa, and Panama.

In addition to these and many minor landings, a combined Marine–Navy Asiatic Fleet landing force was sent in to the west coast of Korea in 1871,

Lieutenant Colonel R. W. Huntington (center) led the Floating Battalion of the Navy's Caribbean flotilla to quick success in Cuba in 1898.

where, after storming an elaborate system of Korean forts along the Han River, it captured 481 guns and 50 Korean battle standards. In this fighting, two Marines tore down the Korean flag over the enemy citadel under intense fire and consequently were awarded Medals of Honor, the first of many to be won on the soil of the Hermit Kingdom.

Three able commandants (Jacob Zeilin, Charles G. McCawley, and Charles Heywood) did much to sparkplug the Corps out of the Civil War doldrums, and despite its small strength (still below three thousand), the Marine Corps was in excellent shape when the United States declared war with Spain in 1898.

610.   War with Spain

On the night of 15 February 1898, the USS *Maine* was blown up and sunk in Havana Harbor. Twenty-eight Marines were among the 266 casualties. The gallantry of Private William Anthony, the captain's orderly, in rescuing Captain Charles D. Sigsbee despite great personal danger, made Anthony the first U.S. hero of the impending war.

On 1 May 1898, little more than a week after declaration of war, Commodore George Dewey destroyed the Spanish squadron in Manila Bay. Two days later, Dewey landed his Marine detachments to secure Cavite Navy Yard and settled down for a three-month wait until the Army could get troops to the Philippines.

Just as Marines were first to land in the Philippines, so also were they the first U.S. forces to land and fight in Cuba. On 10 June 1898, an Atlantic Fleet battalion of Marines, commanded by Lieutenant Colonel R. W. Huntington, landed under cover of ships' guns at Guantánamo Bay, Cuba, and seized an advanced base for the fleet. Four days later, at Cuzco Well, Huntington routed the remaining Spanish forces, destroyed their water supply, and completed the victory. The hero of the day was Sergeant John H. Quick, who won the Medal of Honor for semaphoring while under U.S. and Spanish shellfire for an emergency lift of the naval bombardment.

Huntington's battalion was not the conventional ship's landing party of the nineteenth century but rather a self-contained Marine expeditionary force, which included infantry, artillery, and a headquarters complement of specialist and service troops. The battalion formed part of the fleet—a miniature Fleet Marine Force whose primary mission was landing on hostile shores to secure an advanced base.

611. "Our Flag's Unfurl'd to Every Breeze. . . ."

Between 1899 and 1916, the Marine Corps participated in eight major expeditions or campaigns: the Philippine Insurrection, the Boxer Uprising, Panama, the Cuban Pacifications, Veracruz, Haiti, Santo Domingo, and Nicaragua.

At least as important, and possibly more so, Marine Corps developments of this period laid the foundation of American amphibious warfare techniques and ensured the future survival and growth of the Corps.

Long oppressed by Spain, the Philippines in 1899 sought to make a clean break with colonialism and launched the Philippine Insurrection—or rather transferred its insurrection from the Spanish to the Americans. This three-year campaign included the first modern Marine brigade ever organized, as well as three exploits for which the Corps will be remembered: Major Littleton W. T. Waller's march across Samar, the storming of Sojoton Cliffs in Samar (where Captains David Porter and Hiram Bearss won Medals of Honor), and the pacification of the Subic Bay area on Luzon.

As 1900 dawned, China was undergoing one of her periods of antiforeignism— the Boxer Rebellion. In Tientsin and Peking, foreign missions were besieged by the bloodthirsty Chinese mob. In Peking, together with other foreign garrisons, U.S. and British Marines linked arms, as so often in the past, this time to defend the beleaguered Legation Quarter throughout the summer of 1900. In the international relief column despatched to save Tientsin and Peking was a U.S. Marine force commanded by Major Waller and later by Major W. P. Biddle. By midsummer, Tientsin was relieved, and the legations were relieved on 14 August.

Between expeditions, the Marine Corps stood guard over stations and on ships of the U.S. Navy. This detachment guarded the Naval Station, Pensacola, Florida, at the turn of the century.

At almost the same time, conditions in Panama began to threaten free transit of the isthmus. In 1903, on orders from President Theodore Roosevelt, a U.S. Marine brigade—led by Major General G. F. Elliott, the commandant—landed at Colón to protect U.S. rights during Panama's revolt against Colombia. Marines remained in the Canal Zone until the situation became fully routine in 1911, when the Army took over.

First in 1906 and again in 1912, Marine brigades were sent to Cuba to restore order under the so-called Platt Amendment, by which the United States had the right to intervene in that newly liberated country. Twenty-four towns were occupied in 1906 and twenty-six in 1912; considerable fighting took place in eastern Cuba before peace was finally attained.

In 1901, the Marine Corps began special training and organization for the seizure and defense of advanced bases. Succeeding years saw increased use of battalions and regiments based in Navy transports as a means of projecting naval power across the shoreline. In 1910, at New London, Connecticut, General Elliott, the tenth commandant, established the Marine Corps Advanced Base School. For the first time in U.S. history, a school had been created to focus on the thinking of an entire service on the unsolved problems of amphibious warfare, and to develop expeditionary readiness in the Corps.

Hand in hand with establishment of the Advanced Base School was the organization of the Advanced Base Force, a Marine brigade containing all the necessary combined arms, maintained in readiness for immediate expeditionary service with the fleet. The Advanced Base Force was the prototype of the Fleet Marine Force.

When President Woodrow Wilson was obliged to protect American rights, property, and citizens in Mexico in 1914, Marines from the Advanced Base Force were the first to land, at Veracruz. Army forces followed in due course. Veracruz provided the first field test of the Advanced Base Force, a test passed with flying colors.

Early in 1915, Haiti was wracked by revolution. Ships' detachments landed, but Haiti's troubles called for reinforcement by units of the Advanced Base Force. The pacification of Haiti proved to be long and arduous. Bandits were firmly established in the north, where the rugged country gave them every advantage. Under the dynamic leadership of Colonel L. W. T. Waller and Major Smedley Butler, Marines finally brought the bandits to battle in their stronghold at Fort Rivière, in the storming of which Butler won his second Medal of Honor, having won his first at Veracruz. The resulting victory brought peace to northern Haiti. The Marines rebuilt civil government, and, for the time being, Haiti breathed easily.

In 1916, Marine forces were despatched to restore order in the Dominican Republic and again dramatized the ability of the Corps to take effective action on short notice. More than two thousand Marines landed in Santo Domingo, where, until 1924, a protracted campaign was waged to suppress banditry and enable a Dominican civil government to regain control of the country.

By the end of 1916, the Corps had ended a major era of growth. It had become, in fact if not in law, a national force in readiness. In addition, the seeds of

After the War with Spain, U.S. Marines remained in the Philippines on guard duty. The contingent swelled to brigade size to assist in suppressing the Insurrection.

Marine amphibious development had been sown, and the leadership of the Corps had been hardened in continual combat and expeditionary experience, which was destined to pay off for years to come.

612. Marines "Over There"

Although Marines served faithfully around the globe during World War I, and although Marine commitments in Haiti, Santo Domingo, Cuba, and Nicaragua remained little changed, the preeminent Marine story of World War I is that of the 4th Marine Brigade in France.

The 4th Brigade was the largest unit of Marines assembled during World War I, or ever before. Composed of the 5th and 6th Regiments and the 6th Machine Gun Battalion, it totaled some 9,444 officers and men. Of the brigade's succession of notable actions (Belleau Wood, Soissons, Saint Mihiel, Blanc Mont Ridge, the Argonne), Belleau Wood was most significant because it was the greatest battle, up to that time, in the history of the Corps. The casualties of the 4th Marine Brigade in assaulting the well-organized German center of resistance in Belleau Wood were comparable only to those later sustained in the hardest-fought beach assaults of World War II. After Belleau Wood, German intelligence evaluated the Marine brigade as "storm troops"—the highest rating on the enemy scale of fighting men.

By 11 November 1918, the 4th Marine Brigade and Marine aviation units in France had sustained more casualties in eight months of virtually continuous

The 4th Marine Brigade arrived in France, among the "First to Fight," and joined the Army 2d Infantry Division in 1918.

Marines in World War I faced a well-trained and modern opponent for the first time on a major scale.

combat than had the entire Corps during the preceding 143 years. The grim total was 11,366.

613. Marine Aviation

Founded in 1914 as part of the Advanced Base Force, Marine Corps aviation was still in experimental stages when World War I began. During the war, Marine aviation units flew in combat over France and supported the fleet from an advanced base in the Azores. The spark plug of aviation's participation in the war was Major A. A. Cunningham, the Corps' first pilot. Starting from a strength of 7 officer pilots and 43 enlisted men in 1917, Marine aviation, at war's end, mustered 282 officers and 2,180 enlisted men. In the best traditions of the Corps, the 1st Aeronautical Company, destined for the Azores, was the first completely equipped American aviation unit to leave the United States for service overseas.

614. "Beyond the Seas"

While the 4th Brigade was gaining immortal victories, the Advanced Base Force remained hard at work in Haiti, Santo Domingo, and Cuba. One regiment, the 8th Marines (later reinforced by the 9th Marines) was held in east Texas to protect the Mexican oil fields should the Germans try (as intelligence indicated they intended to do) to disrupt that source of the Navy's oil supply.

The 5th Marine Brigade was sent to France but was refused permission by the Army to enter combat. Instead, the Marines were parceled out in noncombatant duties—mainly provost marshal and military police—in the Army communications zone.

615. Expeditions between World Wars

In addition to continuing commitments in the Caribbean, 1919 found the Corps performing occupation duty along the Rhine.

Marines were also occupying eastern Cuba, which was ultimately pacified in 1922. Two years later, in 1924, six hard-fought campaign years in Santo Domingo came to an end, and Marines were finally withdrawn.

Between 1918 and 1920, Haiti was at a boil, with banditry again in full cry. Following suppression of bandit forces in 1922, Brigadier General John H. Russell, an expert in Haitian affairs, was appointed U.S. High Commissioner to Haiti to administer the American protectorate over the troubled republic. It was not until 1934 that the 1st Marine Brigade hauled down its colors in Port-au-Prince and boarded ship for home.

The year 1927 was marked by trouble in both hemispheres—in Nicaragua and China. Naturally, Marines were soon involved.

As early as 1912, Marines had landed in Nicaragua to preserve order but were withdrawn in 1925. No sooner were they out of the country, however, than the worst civil war in the history of Nicaragua erupted, and Marines (spearheaded by the ships' detachments) were again despatched to Nicaragua in 1927, at the mutual request of the leaders of both warring factions. Marine occupation continued after an uneasy peace and consisted of disarming dissidents, conspicuous among whom was Augusto Sandino, a self-styled "patriot" guerrilla supported from Mexico and neighboring Honduras. A native *Guardia Nacional,* much like the *Gendarmerie d'Haiti* (also Marine-trained), was organized under the Marines to facilitate the hard job of policing a population that included thousands of demobilized revolutionary soldiers.

Marine aviation not only played a leading role in supporting ground operations in Nicaragua but also pioneered tactical and logistic air support on a scale hitherto unknown. The technique of dive-bombing (invented by Marine aviators in Haiti in 1919) was greatly refined. Virtually all the isolated patrols and outposts in the heavily jungled northern area of Nicaragua were maintained by air supply. To evacuate Marine wounded, First Lieutenant C. F. Schilt made ten landings and takeoffs from a village street in Quilali in a fabric-covered scout plane under murderous fire. Lieutenant Schilt was awarded the Medal of Honor.

When the Marines left Nicaragua in 1933, they turned over to the Nicaraguan government a well-organized Guardia, a military academy, a system of communications, and a first-rate public health service, plus many less obvious improvements.

As in Nicaragua, Marine embassy guards had been stationed in China for many years before 1927. There, too, civil disturbances of increasing violence reached a peak in 1927, and additional forces—the 4th Marines to Shanghai and a brigade to North China—were hurried in. Mainly because of these precautions, the threatening situation eased, and the brigade was withdrawn. The re-

Major General John A. Lejeune (l) and Brigadier General Wendell C. Neville (r) returned from France in 1919 to lead the Corps into its amphibious era as the thirteenth and fourteenth commandants.

maining units in Shanghai and Peking, and ultimately Tientsin as well, faced crisis after crisis with Chinese warlords and Japanese until World War II closed the ledger.

616.   Guarding the Mails

In 1921, after a series of violent mail robberies in the United States, the president directed the Marine Corps to guard the mails. Within a matter of hours, Marine armed guards were riding mail cars and trucks, with orders to shoot to kill. Not a single successful mail robbery took place against a Marine guard, and in less than a year the Marines were withdrawn. Five years later, when mail robberies again broke out, Marines were called in a second time; this time as well, the robberies ended at once.

617.   Amphibious Pioneering

In the early 1920s, it became clear to Marines that a war with Japan would entail amphibious seizure of a chain of advanced bases across the Pacific, the world's greatest ocean. In 1921, the year after Marine Corps Schools opened at Quantico, the course of a war with Japan was forecast by Lieutenant Colonel Earl Ellis, who subsequently died while on an intelligence mission in the Japanese Palaus in 1923.

These primitive tactical exercises carried out by U.S. Marines between the wars forged the vital doctrine that ensured the defeat of Japan in World War II.

To Major General John A. Lejeune, thirteenth commandant, the prospect of amphibious war was a bleak one. The British failure at Gallipoli had convinced orthodox military thinkers that an amphibious operation could not succeed against strong opposition. Despite the forbidding nature of the problem, General Lejeune set the Marine Corps to solving it.

Quantico was well equipped to undertake the task and became the focal point of American fleet-centered amphibious development. Marine Corps Schools attacked the problem and, by 1934, produced the first comprehensive U.S. manual of amphibious doctrine—*Tentative Landing Operations Manual.* This historic document was adopted intact by the U.S. Navy in 1938, under the title, *FTP-167, Landing Operations Doctrine, U.S. Navy.* In 1941, when the U.S. Army issued its first amphibious publication, Quantico's book was again borrowed verbatim, even down to the illustrations, and appeared this time as *War Department Field Manual 31-5.* The tenets of *Tentative Landing Operations Manual* still constitute much of the basis for publications that compose today's amphibious "bible."

To deal with materiel aspects of amphibious problems, the Marine Corps Equipment Board was established in 1933. Most notable among the board's pre–World War II achievements was the amphibian tractor, or LVT, which joined the FMF in 1940.

Marine aviation came of age in the 1930s. It would prove an essential ingredient to success in the coming war.

During these pioneering years, the Advanced Base Force was redesignated in 1921 as the East Coast Expeditionary Force, and in 1933 as the Fleet Marine Force, after Major General John H. Russell, sixteenth commandant, had persuaded the secretary of the Navy that Marine expeditionary troops should form an integral part of the U.S. Fleet. The Fleet Marine Force not only constituted a force in readiness but also performed an invaluable role in testing the doctrines and materiel evolved by Marine Corps Schools and the Equipment Board, respectively. From 1935 on, annual fleet landing exercises enabled the fledgling FMF to find its footing as well as to keep the thinkers at Quantico progressing along sound lines.

Two architects of amphibious victory: Commandant Thomas Holcomb (left) and future Pacific amphibious corps commander H. M. Smith (right) at Quantico in late 1940.

Because of its pioneering efforts during the 1920s and 1930s, the Marine Corps—ground and aviation—was ready for amphibious war, and ready also to train others to wage it, when the opening salvos of World War II rocked the world. Before World War II had run its course, seven U.S. Army divisions (including the first three Army divisions ever to receive amphibious training) were trained in landing operations by the Marine Corps, and the doctrines of Quantico girdled the globe.

618. Occupation of Iceland

In 1941, under the seventeenth Marine Corps commandant, Major General Thomas Holcomb, the Fleet Marine Force was called on to demonstrate its capabilities.

Iceland, garrisoned by British forces, was critical in the Battle of the Atlantic. President Franklin D. Roosevelt, who well knew Iceland's strategic importance, agreed with Prime Minister Winston Churchill that the island should be more adequately secured, and that U.S. forces should be employed. After the Army found itself unable to provide ready forces for the Iceland mission, the president turned to the Marine Corps. Less than one week later, on 22 June 1941, the 1st Provisional Marine Brigade had been organized and had embarked

Success on Tarawa, as in other battles, rested on the fighting abilities of the individual Marine.

and sailed. On 7 July, more than four thousand Marines debarked at Reykjavik. Once again first on the spot, the Corps had proved itself the national force in readiness.

619. "Uncommon Valor"

When the United States entered World War II in 1941, the Marine Corps totaled some 70,425 men and was organized into two Marine divisions, two aircraft wings, and seven defense battalions (advanced base artillery units). By 1944, the Corps included six divisions, four wings, and corps and force troops to support the two amphibious corps, which were the FMF's highest formations; the Corps' top strength was 471,905.

Despite differences in terrain and character of operations, both the South Pacific and Central Pacific campaigns of World War II highlighted Marine Corps attributes—the South Pacific, *readiness;* the Central Pacific, *amphibious assault virtuosity.*

The Guadalcanal campaign (1942) not only typified the South Pacific, but, more important, Guadalcanal dramatized to the American public the function of the Fleet Marine Force.

In 1942 (on the heels of valiant Marine defensive fighting at Wake, Midway, and Corregidor), it became clear that a U.S. advance base must be established in the southern Solomons. Guadalcanal, where the Japanese were already building an airstrip, was the logical target. Despite high-level prophecies of disaster and recommendations that the assault be delayed until the following year, the earliest that Army troops could be trained to participate, the 1st Marine Division was given the job of retaking Guadalcanal and adjacent Tulagi. On 7 August 1942, the Marines landed.

It was the first U.S. offensive of World War II; the long road back had begun.

Margins were never slimmer during the Pacific War than on Guadalcanal. But by late November 1942, when Army troops began to arrive in strength, battered Henderson Field was firmly secured by U.S. Marine ground and air, and, in the inner councils of Japan, it was already acknowledged that the turning point of the war had been reached.

The lesson of the Guadalcanal campaign was that without a ready Marine Corps, the operation could never have taken place. Undertaken as a purely naval campaign by fleet units and Marines, Guadalcanal demonstrated the dependence of sea power on fleet expeditionary forces, as well as the degree to which the Marine Corps had placed itself in readiness for just such an occasion.

If Guadalcanal and subsequent operations in the South Pacific—New Georgia, Bougainville, Choiseul (all in 1943), and New Britain (in 1944)—proved that the Corps was ready for war, the campaign across the Central Pacific displayed the Marine Corps' virtuosity in amphibious assault.

The succession of Central Pacific battles—Tarawa (1943), the Marshalls, Saipan, Guam, Tinian, Peleliu (all 1944), Iwo Jima and Okinawa (both 1945)—

Marines break from a clearing through the thick brush on Guam in pursuit of the withdrawing Japanese. Medium tanks lead the assault.

was by hard necessity a series of frontal assaults from the sea against positions fortified with every refinement that Japanese ingenuity and pains could produce. To reduce such strongholds, the amphibious assault came of age.

On Iwo Jima, toward the end, as on Tarawa at the beginning, the fighting ability of the individual Marine came into sharp focus. Each battle was one of frontal assault and close combat against fortified positions. Tarawa was the first combat test of the Marine Corps doctrines for amphibious assault, and Tarawa demonstrated that those doctrines worked. Two years later, at Iwo Jima—the largest all-Marine battle in history—Marines reaped the benefit of their Tarawa experience (and experience from many other hard-fought assaults) in the form of a tested, combat-proven assault technique. Without Tarawa, Iwo would not have been possible. Without the U.S. Marine Corps (and without the years of study, experiment, and development at Quantico), neither Tarawa nor Iwo (or the battles between) could have taken place, let alone succeeded.

But the record of the Corps in World War II was not only the great record of its seaborne assaults. Beginning on 7 December 1941 at Wake, Marine aviation was also in the war. At Midway, Guadalcanal, Bougainville, and the northern Solomons, in the Marshalls, at Peleliu, Iwo Jima, and Okinawa, Marine fliers again helped to forge the concept of the air-ground team. And just as World War II brought to fruition the long-studied amphibious assault doctrines of the Corps, so also World War II witnessed the perfection of Marine close air support. In the reconquest of the Philippines, four Marine

In many respects, the Great Pacific War, 1941–45, established the Marine Corps as a fourth armed service of the United States.

aircraft groups working with Marine air liaison parties on the ground reached a high point in Marine tactical air support (even though this support was for Army comrades).

By the end of the war, the Fleet Marine Force, with aviation and ground units, was poised for the invasion of Japan—an invasion rendered unnecessary by U.S. sea and air power. The Corps had grown from 19,354 in 1939 to nearly 500,000 in 1945. The victories in World War II cost the Corps 86,940 casualties. In the eyes of the American public, the Marine Corps was second to none and seemed destined for a long and useful career. Admiral Nimitz's ringing epitome of Marine fighting on Iwo Jima might very well be applied to the entire Marine Corps during World War II: "Uncommon valor was a common virtue."

620. The Postwar Marine Corps

Although the Corps enjoyed high public prestige at the end of World War II and seemed indeed here to stay, the years 1946–49 were devoted to a searching examination into the mission (and in high quarters, behind closed doors, even the need) for the Marine Corps. These doubts were inspired, as two commandants testified before Congress, by the Army General Staff, whose long-term objective (since before World War I) had been abolition of the Marine Corps or, alternatively, its reduction to a minor security and ceremonial unit. The question was firmly—and, Marines hoped, finally—resolved by the National Security Act of 1947, which gave the Corps firm missions and reaffirmed its status as the service charged with primary amphibious responsibility over landing force

Marine Colonel L. B. Puller (right), who distinguished himself during the Inchon landings, studies the terrain before advancing to another enemy objective beyond Inchon.

tactics, technique, and doctrine. Subsequently, the Douglas-Mansfield Bill, enacted in 1952, afforded the commandant coequal status with the Joint Chiefs of Staff in all matters concerning the Marines and legislated today's organization of the Corps.

While the roles, missions, and status of the Marine Corps were being debated in both executive and legislative branches of the government, the Corps maintained occupation forces in Japan and North China and completed an orderly demobilization unmarred by indiscipline or untoward incident.

The Postwar FMF comprised two major forces: Fleet Marine Force Pacific and Fleet Marine Force Atlantic—assigned respectively to the Pacific and the Atlantic fleets. Each force embodied a Marine division and an aircraft wing (both on reduced scales) and supporting logistic units.

621. The Korean War

Like the story of the Corps in World War II, the Marines' part in the Korean War is covered by the official histories. Therefore, this narrative confines itself only to high spots of a grueling three-year war, at the outset of which, to quote Hanson Baldwin, of *The New York Times:*

> The Marines were ready to fight; if they had not been, we might still be fighting in the Pusan perimeter.

On 24 June 1950, when the Russian- and Chinese-supported North Korean troops attacked South Korea, the Corps numbered approximately 75,000. The FMF was deployed in two shrunken divisions at Pendleton and Lejeune. Aviation (which had narrowly missed transfer to the Air Force by Defense Secretary Louis Johnson) was even thinner: eleven squadrons, divided into two wings at Cherry Point and El Toro. The chairman of the Joint Chiefs of Staff, General Omar Bradley, had predicted publicly, hardly eight months before, that the world would never again see a large-scale amphibious landing.

On 2 July, faced with mounting catastrophe, General Douglas MacArthur sent his first request to the Joint Chiefs of Staff for help from the Marines. In the days that followed, General MacArthur sent five more pleas, culminating in a request for a war-strength Marine division and a war-strength aircraft wing.

Less than two weeks later, the 1st Provisional Marine Brigade was crossing the Pacific, as it headed for the Pusan perimeter, into which shaken U.S. Army and Republic of Korea (ROK) units were already streaming rearward. On 3 August, Marine F4Us from the USS *Sicily* scored first blood for the Corps in an air strike over Inchon; on 7 August, eight years after Guadalcanal, ground elements of the brigade were plugging holes in the Pusan perimeter, and, for the first time, helicopters were flown in battle—by Marines.

In Tokyo, U.S. Marine and Navy planners were translating into reality General MacArthur's plan to relieve Pusan and retake Seoul by an amphibious stroke to be delivered at the Korean west coast port of Inchon. Because of extreme tidal fluctuation, 15 September was the only suitable D-day until mid-October.

Despite unprecedented haste in preparation and numerous calculated risks of enemy opposition, geography, and hydrography, the Inchon landing was almost anticlimactic in its success. As favorable reports poured in throughout D-day, General MacArthur signaled:

> The Navy and Marines have never shone more brightly than this morning.

Largely as a result of the amphibious capability and readiness of the Marine Corps, the North Korean Army south of the 38th Parallel had been all but destroyed.

On 25 November 1950, after an eerie lull, Chinese troops hit the right wing of the Eighth U.S. Army, routed and destroyed at least one U.S. Army division, and launched an entire army group, eight divisions, against the 1st Marine Division.

The blow fell when the division's forward elements were west of Chosin Reservoir, at Yudam-Ni. It is enough to record that, in the face of "General Winter" and of every weapon, artifice, and attack in overwhelmingly superior strength, the division concentrated promptly; rescued and evacuated surviving remnants of adjacent, less ready Army formations; and commenced one of the great marches of American history, from Chosin Reservoir to the sea.

Following amphibious withdrawal and a short "breather," the 1st Division spearheaded the IX Corps spring offensive of 1951. At the same time, the 1st Marine Aircraft Wing continued to provide the preponderance of all close-support sorties nominally credited to the Fifth Air Force, under whose control the wing now operated.

In spring 1952, the 1st Division moved to the arena of its final battles in Korea: the line of the Imjin River, astride the Munsan-ni corridor to Seoul. Here, holding a frontage greater than that of any other division in Korea, the division kept Seoul safe, anchored the United Nations' left flank, and over-looked the Panmunjom truce site. From these positions, the Marines fought a series of bloody trench-warfare actions of a type and scale unheard of in the Corps since World War I.

Korea tested "the new Marine Corps" in readiness and fighting quality, and the Corps was found wanting in neither. Korea demonstrated to doubters, in high places and low, that amphibious operations were anything but dead. Korea proved, as had World War II before it, the high caliber and readiness of the Marine Corps Reserve. Most of all, in a time of immense upheaval in military techniques, Korea underscored the fact that the military principles, for which the Marine Corps stood, remained as sound in 1953 as they had been in 1775.

622. At Mid-Twentieth Century

There had been no victory in Korea, so there was no demobilization. The Corps continued within the structure of three divisions and three wings that Congress had established in 1952, with one of each on the East and West coasts of the United States and in the Far East (Okinawa and Japan). From these major forces, floating battalions were maintained on station with the U.S. fleets in the Mediterranean and the Far East and frequently in the West Indies as well. A thorough modernization of the war-tested amphibious doctrines of the Navy and Marine Corps, originally conceived in Quantico in the late 1940s, gave these forces assault helicopters as landing craft and specially designed helicopter carriers as transports. Blending these sophisticated and original methods with the tried and true ones of seaborne assault by landing craft and amtracs, the amphibious assault now had even greater shocking power and flexibility than before.

In the decade following Korea, it became clear that, despite the ever-present threat of nuclear war, the characteristic pattern of the Cold War was one of limited operations, of politico-military guerrilla warfare—in short, the type of small war in which the Marine Corps had become so thoroughly versed during

Improved helicopters brought a new dimension to postwar Marine amphibious doctrine.

the first 150 years of its existence. In the Far East, between 1955 and 1963, Marines landed in the Tachen Islands, Taiwan, Laos, Thailand, and South Vietnam in countermoves against Communist pressure. In the Mediterranean, not only did Marines land at Alexandria to help evacuate U.S. and foreign nationals during the Suez incident of 1956, but, on an appeal from the Lebanese government, Marines secured Beirut against a Communist coup in July 1958. A Marine brigade, subsequently reinforced by Army troops, stood by for ten weeks until peaceful elections had been completed and a constitutional change of government had been duly carried out. In the Caribbean, our October 1962 confrontation with Communism saw Cuba ringed with floating Marine landing forces, while other FMF units ensured that Guantánamo Bay remained safe and secure against Castro aggression.

623.   Explosion in Santo Domingo

On 24 April 1965, what had started as a military coup d'etat escalated into an attempt by leftists to gain control of the Dominican Republic. In a five-day blood bath, the government of Santo Domingo ceased to exist. The American embassy and seven other foreign embassies came under fire or were violated by leftist revolutionaries. In the late afternoon of 28 April, President Lyndon B. Johnson ordered the landing of the 3d Battalion, 6th Marines, at Ciudad Santo Domingo, from the USS *Boxer* lying offshore. It had been thirty-nine years since U.S. Marines last landed in the Caribbean (at Bluefields, Nicaragua, in 1926).

Quickly augmented to brigade size, the landing force, despite appreciable

Among the innovative technical developments pioneered by the Corps in the 1950s, the Ontos demonstrated the potential of mobile, lightweight antitank weapons for the landing force.

resistance in some areas, established a demilitarized international zone protecting the American and other embassies. When, in due course, Army airborne units arrived, the Marines came under command of the Army; when pacification of the city had been effected in June, they were withdrawn.

624. War in Vietnam

Meanwhile, on the other side of the globe, the dragging war in Vietnam heated up. Marine helicopter units (flying half the total sorties and flight hours with 20 percent of the helo-lift in the country) had been in Vietnam since 1962. So had Marine reconnaissance troops and a U.S. Marine advisory mission to train the Vietnamese Marine Corps.

In accordance with long-standing contingency plans, elements of the 3d Marine Division, supported by squadrons of the 1st Aircraft Wing, deployed to a highly strategic enclave, centered around Da Nang and the existing air base complex, in the north of the Republic of Vietnam. This area had not been chosen by chance: it had a port, independent of Saigon and others to the south; it had beaches; it commanded defiles in the coastwise road and rail net. Its main and enduring disadvantage was that it was adjacent to some of the most hard-core Vietcong regions in-country, both south and inland to the west.

On the heels of the 3d Division followed the 1st Marine Division and MAG-36, being split between Vietnam and Okinawa. By the end of the year, almost

Marine helicopter tactics played an important part in the seven-year campaign in Vietnam.

two-thirds of the combat units of the Marine Corps were thus committed to the Vietnamese war.

Adjacent Marine coastal enclaves were established at Da Nang and Chulai, with the objective not only of protecting these important air bases but of pacifying a populous and productive region, using the "oil-stain" tactics originated in this very region by France's master of colonial warfare, Marshal Lyautey. Consolidated under Headquarters, III Marine Amphibious Force, the Marines soon came to grips with the Vietcong. Late 1965 was marked by sustained patrolling, ambushes, and intermittent battles to link up the Da Nang and Chulai enclaves. Not only did 1966 bring more of the same but also more troops. By the end of 1966, approximately 60,000 Marines—more than one-sixth of all U.S. forces in Vietnam—were ashore and in the field. These units included troops from the newly formed 5th Marine Division, not seen on the active list since World War II. In hard fighting throughout I Corps area and especially along the 17th parallel demilitarized zone separating North and South Vietnam, Marines repeatedly turned back crack North Vietnamese Army (NVA) units.

Yet even as successes in combat and pacification mounted for the U.S. Forces and their allies, the war was being lost. The native Vietnamese government proved unsuited to gain and sustain the loyalty and obedience of its population. In the United States, another people grew weary and impatient of the war, amplified on a daily basis on television and the printed media to the extent that Congress began to apply halters to the war effort.

In mid-1969, as the Vietnamese armed forces began to take on more of their own war, American troop withdrawals commenced. By October, the first-in 3d Division and 1st Wing had been phased out. By this time, the Communists had reverted almost completely to the level of terrorism and guerrilla war. At the year's end, 90 percent of the population of the Marines' northern provinces was living in secure areas. Even so, the 1st Division still had ample work holding NVA forays at arm's length from the vital Da Nang area. More and more, however, the ARVN (Army of the Republic of Vietnam) was out front, while the Marines were in support.

One landmark Marine Corps achievement had been to forge the capable, high-spirited Vietnamese Marine Corps, whose splendid fighting during the all-out Communist offensive of 1972 did so much to hold the northern provinces. Yet in the end it was all in vain: abandoned by an America that cut off its weapons and supplies, Vietnam was destined to fall to Communist aggression, which outlasted its foes.

By that time, however (save for Marine landing forces that covered the final evacuation of American embassies in Phnom Penh and Saigon), the Marines' long war was over. In the words of the commandant in April 1972:

> We are pulling our heads out of the jungle and redirecting our attention seaward, reemphasizing our partnership with the Navy and our shared concern in the maritime aspects of our national strategy. . . . With respect to our standards—

Marines train annually in Arctic warfare conditions in support of their global contingency responsibilities.

we will maintain them: in appearance, discipline, personal proficiency, and unit performance. Without them, we would not be Marines.

625. History of the Women Marines

In August 1918, the first women ever to wear the Globe and Anchor enlisted in the U.S. Marine Corps. They totaled 305 in all and were immediately nicknamed "Marinettes," an obvious derivative of the Navy's contemporary "Yeomanettes." Although the duties and scope of action of a Marinette (whose top possible rating was sergeant) were much more limited than today, the spirit was similar.

The "new" women's component was organized in February 1943, when Lieutenant General Thomas Holcomb, seventeenth commandant, authorized creation of the Marine Corps Women's Reserve. The first officer and enlisted women were trained beside Navy WAVES in existing naval schools for women. By May 1943, 75 women had completed officer training, in a special course at Mount Holyoke College and 722 had weathered recruit training. July 1943 saw establishment of the Women Reserve Schools at Camp Lejeune. Here at Lejeune were centralized recruit and officer candidate training, together with a number of specialist schools for the 18,000 enlisted women and 821 officers of the Women's Reserve, or "WR," as it was soon short-titled.

It was an emphatic tradition of the new branch of the Corps that there would be no trick nicknames for the group. As far as Women Marines were—and are—concerned, any cute, coy, or punning sobriquet, official or otherwise, would merely demean the Marine Corps Emblem, which they proudly wore. Today, this tradition is stronger than ever.

Much of the initial tone and standard of the Marine Corps Women's Reserve was set in ordinary course by the parent Corps, but quite as much, if not more, was due to the ability and effort of the first director of the Women's Reserve, Colonel Ruth Cheney Streeter. Colonel Streeter made it her objective to integrate the women reservists into the framework of the Corps. It was her vision that lifted the World War II women from clerical specialization (the World War I role of Marinettes) into more than two hundred separate occupational specialties and billets at every major Marine Corps post in the continental United States and ultimately overseas.

At the end of World War II, save for about 100 women officers and enlisted women retained on duty at Marine Corps Headquarters, under Major Julia E. Hamblet (later to become a director of Women Marines), the Women's Reserve went home. In 1948, however, Congress passed the Women's Armed Services Integration Act, and a new chapter opened. Henceforth, each service would have a career cadre of regulars, in addition to the reservists.

To head the regulars (now called "WM"), General Clifton B. Cates, nineteenth commandant, chose Colonel Katherine A. Towle, former assistant dean of women at the University of California and wartime successor of Colonel Streeter. On 12 June 1948, the Women's Reserve went out of existence, and on the succeeding 4 November, the women Marines came into being. Members of

Violet Van Wagner, Brooklyn (center), and Florence Weidinger, Jersey City, enlisted as the first women to serve in the United States Marine Corps. World War I jackets, a campaign hat, and a helmet were hastily borrowed from male Marines for the official swearing-in ceremony.

the former Women's Reserve were reenlisted into the Marine Corps Reserve, and many became members of the Organized Reserve. Like the remainder of the Organized Reserve, the women found themselves mobilized only days after the onset of war in Korea, with thirteen Organized Reserve women's platoons responding to the call. During the years ahead, regular women Marines continued as an increasingly important part of the Corps, and, during Vietnam (on a strength of some 2,000) filled many key billets, which released other Marines for field service. (A symbolic watershed for the WMs came in 1965 when, during the Dominican Revolt, a staff sergeant on duty at the American Embassy won the first combat campaign medal ever awarded to a woman Marine.)

With the signing of the Paris Peace Accords on 27 January 1973, the war in Vietnam was declared officially ended. Not only a war, but an era, was coming

Within the year, proper uniforms were designed and issued to the Women's Reserve, in which more than three hundred served in 1918–19.

to an end. The draft was replaced by the All-Volunteer Force policy, and societal roles for women were changing rapidly. Both these factors would soon be reflected in the increasing number and widening role of women in the military.

On 1 February 1973—almost thirty years to the day that the first director was sworn into office—Colonel Margaret A. Brewer became the seventh, and final, director of women Marines. The only director without World War II service, she had entered the Marine Corps during the Korean War, immediately following graduation from the University of Michigan at Ann Arbor in 1952.

In many ways, her service career paralleled that of the previous directors. She was commissioned during a war, at a time of acute personnel shortages, and faced the unexpected demands that wartime service entailed. She served as director during a period of sweeping change. In the post-Vietnam years, the Marine Corps took positive steps, within the limits of its combat mission and organization, to integrate women more fully. Many of the actions that were to take place in coming years stemmed from recommendations made by a specially formed ad hoc committee on increased effectiveness and utilization of women in the Marine Corps. In November 1973, the committee's recommendations were approved by the commandant with the written comment, "Let's move out!" Among the most significant recommendations were: (1) the establishment of a pilot program to train women for duty with selected, stateside elements of the Fleet Marine Forces; (2) the assignment of women Marines to all occupational fields except the combat arms; and (3) the elimination of the regulation that prohibited women from commanding units other than women's units.

In 1974, the commandant approved a change in policy permitting the assignment of women to specified rear echelon elements of the Fleet Marine Forces, on the condition that women Marines not be deployed with assault units or units likely to become engaged in combat. The decision came at the conclusion of a successful six-month pilot program and carried the provision "that such assignment not adversely affect combat readiness." Three years later, out of a total of approximately 3,830 women Marines on active duty, 600 were serving in Fleet Marine Force assignments. Another major step was taken in the following year. The Marine Corps approved the assignment of women Marines to all occupational fields except the four designated as the combat arms, that is, infantry, artillery, armor, and pilot and air crew.

Of necessity, some assignment restrictions remained, including the preservation of a rotation base for male Marines; the need for adequate facilities for women; the availability of nondeployable billets for women; and the legal restrictions prohibiting the assignment of women Marines to combat ships and aircraft.

As women became more fully integrated in the Marine Corps, the decision was made to disestablish the Office of the Director of Women Marines following thirty-four years of existence, and its functions were transferred to other Marine Corps staff agencies.

626. The Cutting Edge of Sea Power

In the aftermath of Vietnam, the Corps trained for conventional contingencies involving the reinforcement of NATO and South Korea but also found its operating forces in the Sixth and Seventh Fleets involved in patrolling waters off the Middle East and West Asian hot spots. Middle East tensions brought Marines ashore again in Lebanon during 1983–84. This time, Marines in Beirut drew fire as they interposed themselves between warring factions as part of a four-nation peacekeeping force. One of the rotating Marine battalions fell victim to a terrorist strike in which a fourth of its Navy and Marine personnel died. Emerging undaunted from the rubble, the survivors and a relief battalion continued in their presence mission until withdrawn six months later.

Almost immediately after the Beirut disaster, other Marines played a successful role in a U.S. coup de main on Granada Island in the Caribbean and ousted the Cubans and radicals in control there. Marines exploited light resistance to dash across the island and relieve pressure on bogged down paratroopers and rangers in a model ninety-six-hour intervention exercise.

Expeditionary action proved especially heavy and varied in 1990 as Marine Corps units participated in the U.S. intervention in Panama and evacuated foreign nationals and secured the U.S. embassy in Liberia during a civil war there. Finally, the greatest U.S. deployment since the Vietnam War found the majority of the Fleet Marine Force in and afloat off Saudi Arabia as part of the international expedition sent to protect Saudi Arabia and subdue the Iraqi forces in the 1990–91 Gulf War.

627. The Gulf War and Aftermath, 1990–

In wake of the Iraqi seizure of Kuwait in August 1990, the president of the United States ordered the U.S. Central Command to reinforce and defend Saudi Arabia and the other Persian Gulf states, in concert with a growing coalition determined to resist and ultimately expel the Iraqi forces. Among the first U.S. forces to arrive in Saudi Arabia for this purpose was the 7th Marine Expeditionary Brigade, which deployed to the key port and petroleum center of Al Jubayl, with its aviation based further south on the Gulf of Bahrain. Offloading heavy equipment from its dedicated Maritime Prepositioning Squadron 1, the brigade reported ready for operations on 25 August, a mere ten days after arrival in theater.

The brigade stood alone only for a few days, as the follow-on elements of the I Marine Expeditionary Force (I MEF) began to arrive. Eventually growing to a force of over 90,000 Marines and attached Navy personnel, the Marine Forces, Central Command, included two reinforced divisions, an enlarged aircraft wing containing the majority of the USMC aircraft inventory, and the bulk of two-force service support groups. Over 20,000 Marines and Navy personnel of the 4th and 5th Marine Expeditionary Brigades remained afloat while the I MEF moved into the Kuwaiti-Saudi frontier.

This most rapid and complex strategic deployment in Marine Corps history used all forms of transportation, including military and commercial aircraft, naval and merchant shipping, and the ferrying of hundreds of USMC aircraft, from fighters to the ubiquitous observation planes from bases in California, Arizona, the Carolinas, Hawaii, and Japan. Thousands of reservists and retired Marines were mustered to reinforce or augment the forces, as well as to replace deployed units and personnel in their former garrisons. An infantry regiment, battalions, squadrons, and smaller units of the Marine Corps Reserve took their places in line with regular units in both combat and support echelons.

After long periods of training, marshaling, and waiting, the campaign began with the air offensive against the Iraqi forces on 16 January 1991. Marine aircraft from Saudi bases and the amphibious ships in the Persian Gulf mainly struck targets in Kuwait, with Marine fighter and electronic warfare cover being provided to the coalition forces at large. After air superiority had been established, the ground units began to assemble along the frontier and prepare for their assault. The two reinforced Marine divisions stood south of the Kuwaiti border, free from the observation of the Iraqi defenders, who were being pounded mercilessly by the coalition air forces.

On 24 February, the 1st and 2d Marine Divisions attacked into Kuwait. They forced their way through the Iraqi barriers and brushed aside the frontline resistance. Mounted in a variety of tanks, assault amphibious vehicles, trucks, and light armored vehicles, the attacking regiments destroyed or captured whole battalions of Iraqi troops and swept through the burning oil fields toward the capital, Kuwait City. Artillery barrages and repeated strikes by fighterbombers and attack helicopters supported the advance of the regiments. After one hundred hours of combat, Marines dominated southern Kuwait, and the capital was mopped up by neighboring Arab coalition forces. The cease-fire came too soon for many elements of the Marine force to come into play. The Marines of the landing force, afloat in the Gulf, raided a few islands, landed a tactical reserve in the MEF rear, and provided aviation support to their comrades ashore.

Even faster than their initial deployment to the crisis area, the withdrawal of Marines from the theater proved breathtaking. Except for the service support Marines needed to remove the bulk of the accumulated supplies, the I Marine Expeditionary Force returned to its bases in barely six weeks' time. A total of 24 Marines were killed and 92 wounded in action. The sudden withdrawal of the forces left untouched and unscarred the semifeudal Arab principalities to which the coalition forces had rallied.

Marines in the same year found themselves on humanitarian support missions in Bangladesh, Somalia, and Kurdistan. They would return in strength to Somalia in late 1992, as the leading edge of a great United Nations effort to end starvation and lawlessness there. Increased naval and Marine Corps presence in the Indian Ocean littorals has marked the decade of the 1990s.

These most recent actions illustrate the continuity in the Marine Corps story. In every clime and place Marines have stood vigil ashore and afloat. Readiness and amphibious expertise remain our hallmark. As long as our nation possesses and exercises command of the seas, Marines will form its cutting edge.

No-one can say that the Marines have ever failed to do their work in handsome fashion.

—Major General Johnson Hagood, USA

7

Traditions, Flags, Decorations, and Uniforms

701. "The Thin Line of Tradition"

The traditions of the Marine Corps, its history, its flags, its uniforms, its insignia—*the Marine Corps way of doing things*—make the Corps what it is and set it so distinctly apart from other military organizations and services.

These traditions give the Marine Corps its flavor and are the reason the Corps cherishes its past, its ways of acting and speaking, and its uniforms. These things foster the discipline, valor, loyalty, aggressiveness, and readiness that make the term *Marine* "signify all that is highest in military efficiency and soldierly virtue."

And remember: whenever the Marine Corps is impoverished by the death of a tradition, *you* are generally to blame. Traditions are not preserved by books and museums but by faithful adherence on the part of all hands—*you especially.*

MARINE CORPS TRADITIONS AND CUSTOMS

702. Globe and Anchor

When the late Major General Smedley Butler (winner of two Medals of Honor) was a lieutenant in the Philippines in 1899, he decided to get himself tattooed.

> I selected an enormous Marine Corps Emblem [wrote Butler] to be tattooed across my chest. It required several sittings and hurt me like the devil, but the finished

product was worth the pain. I blazed triumphantly forth, a Marine from throat to waist. The emblem is still with me. Nothing on earth but skinning will remove it.

Butler was somewhat premature in his last sentence. Within less than a year, during the storming of the Tartar Wall in Peking, a Chinese bullet struck him in the chest and gouged off part of his emblem. The rest of it accompanied him to the grave forty years later.

Whether you are a private or general is secondary compared to the privilege you share, of wearing the emblem. The Globe and Anchor is the most important insignia you have.

The Marine Emblem, as we know it today, dates from 1868. It was contributed to the Corps by Brigadier General Jacob Zeilin, seventh commandant. Until 1840, Marines wore various devices, mainly based on the spread eagle or foul anchor. In 1840, two Marine Corps devices were accepted. Both were circled by a laurel wreath, undoubtedly borrowed from the badge of the Royal Marines; one had a foul anchor inscribed inside, and the other bore the letters "USM." In 1859, a standard center was adopted—a U.S. shield surmounted by a hunting-horn bugle, within which was the letter "M." From this time on, the bugle and

Today's emblem, the Globe and Anchor, was adopted by Brigadier General Jacob Zeilin, seventh commandant, in 1868.

The Marine badge before 1868 embodied the hunting-horn symbol traditional to light infantry.

letter "M," without the shield or laurel wreath, were usually worn by Marines on undress uniforms. This type of bugle was the nineteenth century symbol for light infantry or *jäger*—so called because they were recruited from the ranks of foresters, gamekeepers, and poachers, all renowned as skirmishers and riflemen.

In 1868, however, General Zeilin felt that a more distinctive emblem was needed. His choice fell on another device borrowed from the British Marines—the globe.

The globe had been conferred on the Royal Marines in 1827 by King George IV. Because it was impossible to recite all the achievements of Marines on the Corps Color, said the King, "the Great Globe itself" was to be their emblem, for Marines had won honor everywhere.

General Zeilin's U.S. Marine globe displayed the Western Hemisphere (the "Royals" had the Eastern Hemisphere on theirs). The eagle and foul anchor were added, to leave no doubt that the Corps was both American and maritime.

703. The Marine Corps Seal

The official seal of the Corps, designated by General Lemuel C. Shepherd, Jr., twentieth commandant, consists of the Marine Corps emblem in bronze, the eagle holding in his beak a scroll inscribed "*Semper Fidelis*," against a scarlet and blue background, encircled by the words, "*Department of the Navy * United States Marine Corps.*"

The Marine Corps seal, designed by General Shepherd, twentieth commandant, was approved by the president in 1954.

704.   Marine Corps Colors

The colors of the Corps are scarlet and gold. Although associated with U.S. Marines for many years, these colors were not officially recognized until General Lejeune became thirteenth commandant. Today you will see scarlet and gold throughout Marine posts—on signboards; auto tags; bandsmen's drums, pouches, and trumpet slings; MP brassards; officers' hatcords and aiguillettes; and, it sometimes seems, everywhere in sight.

In addition to scarlet and gold, forest green enjoys at least semiofficial standing as a Marine color. During the years since 1912, when forest green was adopted for the winter service uniform, it has become standard for such equipment as vehicles, weapons, and organizational chests and baggage. In addition, forest green is today virtually the distinguishing color of marines throughout the world, being worn as a service uniform by the British, Dutch, Korean, and other corps.

Forest green comes from the same source as the light infantry bugle that was once part of the Corps badge. The costume of eighteenth-century huntsmen was forest green. The riflemen recruited from that calling wore green uniforms—a green that survives not only among marines but also in the uniforms of Britain's Rifle Brigade (the "Greenjackets") and India's Ghurkhas.

705. The Marine Corps Motto

Semper Fidelis ("Always Faithful") is the motto of the Corps. That Marines have lived up to this motto is proved by the fact that there has never been a mutiny, or even the thought of one, among U.S. Marines.

Semper Fidelis was adopted as the motto about 1883. Before that, there had been three Marine Corps mottoes, all traditional rather than official. The first, antedating the War of 1812, was *"Fortitudine"* ("With Fortitude"). The second, *By Sea and by Land,* was obviously a translation of the Royal Marines' *Per Mare, Per Terram.* Until 1848, the third motto was *To the Shores of Tripoli,* in commemoration of O'Bannon's capture of Derna in 1805. In 1848, after the return to Washington of the Marine battalion that took part in the capture of Mexico City, this motto was revised to: "From the Halls of the Montezumas to the Shores of Tripoli"—a line now familiar to all Americans. This revision of the Corps motto in Mexico has encouraged speculation that the first stanza of "The Marines' Hymn" was composed by members of the Marine battalion who stormed Chapultepec Castle.

It may be added that the Marine Corps shared its motto with England's Devonshire Regiment, the 11th Foot, in its day one of the senior infantry regiments of the British Army, whose sobriquet was "the Bloody Eleventh" and whose motto was also *Semper Fidelis.*

706. Marines' Hymn and Marine Corps March

"The Marines' Hymn" is what its name implies, the hymn of the Marine Corps. "Semper Fidelis," one of John Philip Sousa's best-known works, is the Corps march.

"The Marines' Hymn" (Appendix I) is the oldest of the official songs of the armed services. Every Marine knows the words and will sing them at the drop of a field hat. The origin of the hymn is obscure. The words date back into the nineteenth century, and the author remains unknown. The music comes from an air, "Gendarmes of the Queen," in Jacques Offenbach's opera *Geneviève de Brabant,* first performed in November 1859. Regardless of its origin, however, *all Marines get to their feet whenever "The Marines' Hymn" is played or sung.*

"Semper Fidelis" was composed by Sousa in 1888 during his tour as leader of the Marine Band. "Semper Fi," as the troops know it, is habitually rendered for parades, reviews, and march-pasts of Marines.

707. Birthday of the Corps

The Marine Corps was founded by the Continental Congress on 10 November 1775. The resolution that created our Corps reads as follows:

> *Resolved.* That two Battalions of Marines be raised consisting of one Colonel, two lieutenant Colonels, two Majors, & Officers as usual in other regiments, that they consist of an equal number of privates with other battalions; that particular

care be taken that no persons be appointed to office, or inlisted into said Battalions, but such as are good seamen, or so acquainted with maritime affairs as to be able to serve to advantage by sea, when required. That they be inlisted and commissioned for and during the present war with Great Britain and the colonies, unless dismissed by order of Congress. That they be distinguished by the names of the first and second battalions of American Marines, and that they be considered as part of the number, which the continental Army before Boston is ordered to consist of.

Chapter 22 tells how we celebrate the Marine Corps Birthday. Although the Marine Corps joins the other services each May in observing Armed Forces' Day, November 10th remains the Marines' own day—a day of ceremony, comradeship, and celebration.

708.   The Mameluke Sword

The sword that Marine officers carry goes back to the *Uniform Regulations* of 1826 (with a hiatus from 1859 to 1875). Records of the day, however, indicate that swords of this pattern were worn by Marine officers before the War of 1812.

The Mameluke sword gets its name from the cross-hilt and ivory grip, both of which were used for centuries by the Moslems of North Africa and Arabia. The Marine Corps tradition of carrying this type of sword dates from Lieutenant O'Bannon's assault on Derna, Tripoli, in 1805, when he is said to have won the sword of the governor of the town.

Aside from its use on parade, many Marine Corps rituals center about your sword. You wear it when you get married, and you cut your wedding cake with the sword. At many posts, you wear it while officer of the day. Should you ever be unlucky enough to be placed under arrest, you must surrender your sword.*

709.   "First on Foot, and Right of the Line"

Marines form at the place of honor—head of column or on right of line—in any naval formation. This privilege was bestowed on the Corps by the secretary of the Navy on 9 August 1876.

710.   "First to Fight"

The slogan "First to Fight" has appeared on Marine recruiting posters ever since World War I.

Marines have been in the forefront of every American war since the founding of the Corps. Marines entered the Revolution in 1775, even before the Declaration of Independence was signed. Before declaration of the War of 1812, Marines

---

*Never unsheathe your sword inside a mess or wardroom. If you do, custom decrees that you must stand drinks for all present. This tradition goes back to stringent rules against dueling in the early days of the Navy and Marine Corps.

helped to defend the USS *Chesapeake* against the British. At the outset of hostilities against Mexico, Marines helped to raise California's Bear Flag. Before the Civil War, Marines captured John Brown at Harper's Ferry. They were among the few U.S. regulars who fought in the first Battle of Manassas in 1861. In 1898, Huntington's Fleet Marines were the first U.S. troops to occupy Cuban

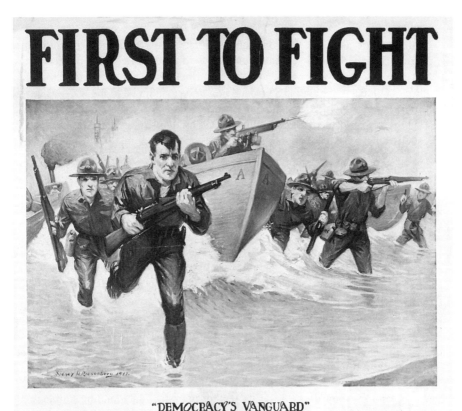

FIRST TO FIGHT

"DEMOCRACY'S VANGUARD"

U·S·MARINE CORPS

JOIN NOW AND TEST YOUR COURAGE
REAL FIGHTING WITH REAL FIGHTERS
APPLY AT
22 TREMONT ROW, SCOLLAY SQ., BOSTON

Marine Corps recruiting poster, used during World War I and later.

soil, and Admiral Dewey's Marines were the first to land in the Philippines. Marines were first to land at Veracruz (1914). In World I, the 5th Marines formed part of the first American Expeditionary Force (AEF) contingent to sail for France. When Iceland had to be occupied in 1941, Marines, the only U.S. troops who were ready, were the first to land. In World War II, at Pearl Harbor, Ewa, Wake, Midway, Johnston Island, and Guam, Marines formed the ready forefront of our Pacific outpost line. At Guadalcanal in August 1942, Marines launched the first American offensive of the war. In the Korean War, the first reinforcements to leave the continental United States were the 1st Provisional Marine Brigade. The first American troops to land in Lebanon in 1958 were Marines. At Santo Domingo, in 1965, Marines were again the first to fight; while, in Vietnam, the first U.S. ground unit to be committed to the war was the 3d Marine Division. In the Persian Gulf War, the Marines opened the ground war.

On this record of readiness, "First to Fight" constitutes the Marine's pride, responsibility, and challenge.

711. "Leathernecks"

The Marines' long-standing nickname, "Leathernecks," goes back to the leather stock, or neckpiece, that was part of the marine uniform from 1775 to 1875. One historian has written:

> Government contracts usually contained a specification that the stock be of such height that the "chin could turn freely over it," a rather indefinite regulation, and, as one Marine put it, one which the "tailors must have interpreted to mean with the nose pointing straight up."

Although many justifications have been adduced for the leather stock, the truth seems to be that it was intended to ensure that Marines kept their heads erect (in battery," the artillery would say), a laudable aim in any military organization, any time.

Descended from the stock is the standing collar, hallmark of Marine blues, whites, and evening dress. Like its leather ancestor, the standing collar regulates stance and posture and thus proclaims the wearer as a modern "Leatherneck."

712. Scarlet Trouser Stripe

Officers and noncommissioned officers have intermittently worn scarlet stripes on dress trousers ever since the early days of the Corps. It is unsubstantiated, even though oft repeated, that the right to wear scarlet stripes was conferred on the Corps as a battle honor after the Mexican War (actually the initial uniform trousers issued after reconstitution of the Corps in 1798 had scarlet piping).

713. Headgear

Two Marine traditions center about headgear. The *quatrefoil* (the cross-shaped braid atop officers' frame-type ["barracks"] caps) has been worn since 1859.

The design, of French origin, is a distinguishing part of the Marine officers' uniform.

The *field hat* was the rugged, picturesque expeditionary headgear of the Corps from 1898 until 1942 and became a universal favorite. As a result, although the hat became outmoded during World War II, General Cates, the nineteenth commandant, authorized its use on the rifle range in 1948 and took steps to issue field hats to all medalist shooters in Marine Corps matches. Subsequently, in 1956, General Randolph McCall Pate, the twenty-first commandant, directed that field hats be worn by all recruit drill instructors, and the hat—later copied and adapted by the Army for the same purpose—has become a symbol of Marine Corps recruit training.

714. Collar Emblems

Although officers have worn collar emblems since the 1870s, enlisted Marines did not rate this privilege until August 1918, when Franklin D. Roosevelt, then assistant secretary of the Navy, visited the 4th Marine Brigade in France, shortly after Belleau Wood. In recognition of the brigade's victory, Roosevelt directed on the spot that enlisted Marines would henceforth wear the emblem on their collars.

715. Marine Talk and Terminology

The 4th Marine Brigade's admired Army commander at Belleau Wood, Lieutenant General James G. Harbord, USA, was quick to note and record the salty Marine way of saying things:

> In the more than a month that the Marine Brigade fought in and around the Bois de Belleau, I got a good opportunity to get the Marine psychology. . . . The habitual Marine address was "Lad". . . . No Marine was ever too old to be a "lad." The Marines never start anywhere: they always "shove off." There were no kitchens: the cooking was done in "galleys." No one ever unfurled a flag—he "broke it out."

This *Guide* contains a glossary of Marine terms (Appendix VII). Never feel self-conscious about using them. Require that subordinates use them. Accept no substitutes.

716. "The President's Own"

Founded in 1798 (more than a century before the bands of the other three services), the Marine Band has performed at White House functions for every president except George Washington and was especially sponsored by Thomas Jefferson. Because of its traditional privilege of performing at the White House, the band is spoken of as "The President's Own." President Kennedy epitomized the band's special position when he remarked in 1962, "I find that the only forces which cannot be transferred from Washington without my express permission are the members of the Marine Band, and I want it announced that we propose to hold the White House against all odds, at least for some time to come."

The Marine Band has been present at many of the most memorable and cherished moments in our nation's history, including the dedication of the National Cemetery at Gettysburg when Lincoln gave his immortal address (and his aide-de-camp was Second Lieutenant H. C. Cochrane, USMC). Among the band's many traditions, including leadership for twelve years by John Philip Sousa, is its scarlet, full-dress blouse, the only red coat worn by American forces since the Revolutionary War. (In 1956, the Marine Corps Drum and Bugle Corps was likewise granted the privilege of wearing red coats.)

The Marine Band tours the country each year, and has done so ever since Sousa commenced the practice in 1891, although one section of the band always remains in Washington to fulfill its traditional primary mission: "To provide music when directed by the President of the United States, the Congress of the United States, or the Commandant of the Marine Corps."

717.   Evening Parade

From May through early September, a ceremonial Evening Parade is held each Friday evening after nightfall at the Marine Barracks, Eighth and Eye. This colorful ceremony, executed under searchlight illumination, features the Marine Band, Marine Corps Drum and Bugle Corps, a special exhibition drill platoon, and a battalion of Marines from the barracks. Evening Parades were first held in 1957 after a Marine Corps ceremonial detachment participated in the Bermuda International Searchlight Tattoo and became a fixed Marine Corps custom following similar participation by a larger Marine detachment in the famed Edinburgh Searchlight Tattoo in Scotland in 1958. Evening Parades are open to the public, and any officer who desires to attend with a reasonable number of guests can obtain reserved seats by telephoning the Marine Barracks adjutant.

718.   "And St. David"

During the Boxer Uprising (1900), at Tientsin and Peking, the Marine battalion in the international relief column was brigaded with the Royal Welsh Fusiliers (23d Foot), one of Britain's most renowned regiments. The resulting fellowship between the two organizations is symbolized each year on St. David's Day (1 March, the Welsh national holiday), when the commandant of the Marine Corps and the colonel of the Fusiliers exchange by dispatch the traditional watchword of Wales: ". . . *And St. David.*"

719.   The Commandant's License Plate

If, in Washington, D.C., you ever bump a car bearing license "1775," climb out of the wreckage at attention. That license plate is set aside for the official sedan of the commandant of the Marine Corps.

720. Rum on New Year's Day

Every New Year's Day since 1804, the Marine Band serenades the commandant at his quarters and receives refreshments in return.

721. Marine Corps Bulldog

Ever since World War I, the bulldog has been associated with the Corps. An English bulldog has been official mascot at Eighth and Eye, and therefore top dog of the Corps, since the 1920s. Prior to World War II, he was always named "Jiggs." Subsequently, however, in an appropriate tribute to one of the Corps' bravest officers, the late Lieutenant General L. B. Puller, the name has been "Chesty."

722. Ship's Bell

All Marine posts (and even some camps in the field) have a ship's bell, usually from a warship no longer in commission. The old tradition of striking the bells, following shipboard routine, has fallen into disuse.

723. Last to Leave the Ship

Marines are always or should be the last—other than the ship's captain—to leave a ship being abandoned or put out of commission. Although the tradition is an old one, it first appears in *Navy Regulations* of 1865:

> When a vessel is to be put out of commission, the Marine officer with the guard shall remain on board until all the officers and crew are detached and the ship regularly turned over to the officers of the Navy Yard or station.

724. Swagger Sticks

The tradition of the swagger stick originated in the British Army and goes as far back as 1790. In the Marine Corps, the stick came into vogue in the latter part of the nineteenth century and was virtually a required article of uniform until World War I. The origin of the swagger stick lay in the whips or batons carried by mounted officers of the eighteenth century. Once carried with relish by many Marine officers, swagger sticks were prohibited in 1960 and adorn only a few mantles in hopes that they might gain favor again.

There was also once in favor a Marine Corps tie with "regimental" colors, scarlet/gold stripes over a forest green background. That tie, and equivalent cummerbund, can be worn at the user's pleasure with civilian attire.

725. "Tell it to the Marines!"

In his book, *Fix Bayonets!*, Captain John W. Thomason, Jr., gives the generally accepted version of the origin of "Tell it to the Marines!":

They relate of Charles II that at Whitehall a certain seacaptain, newly returned from the Western Ocean, told the King of flying fish, a thing never heard in old England. The King and court were vastly amused. But, the naval fellow persisting, the Merry Monarch beckoned to a lean, dry colonel of the sea regiment, with seamed mahogany face, and said, in effect: "Colonel, this tarry-breeks here makes sport with us stay-at-homes. He tells of a miraculous fish that foresakes its element and flies like a bird over water." "Sire," said the colonel of Marines, "he tells a true thing. I myself have often seen those fish in your Majesty's seas around Barbados—" "Well," decided Charles, "such evidence cannot be disputed. And hereafter, when we hear a strange thing, we will tell it to the Marines, for the marines go everywhere and see everything, and if they say it is so, we will believe it."

This yarn (for such it is) was for many years credited to Samuel Pepys, although scholars disclaimed it. On the other hand, the phrase, "Tell it to the Marines," is an old one and can be found in print as early as 1726.

726. At Church Service

Protestant and Catholic services for Marines should always include the Marine Corps Prayer (written at the suggestion of General Shepherd, twentieth commandant, by Bishop Sherrill, former presiding bishop of the Episcopal Church and hero in World War I):

O Eternal Father, we commend to Thy protection and care the members of the Marine Corps. Guide and direct them in the defense of our country and in the maintenance of justice among nations. Protect them in the hour of danger. Grant that wherever they serve they may be loyal to their high traditions and that at all times they may put their trust in Thee; through Jesus Christ our Lord. *Amen.*

It is also customary for Marine Corps religious services to conclude with the traditional naval hymn, "Eternal Father, Strong to Save." When no chaplain is available, the commanding officer (CO), following the traditions of the sea, may conduct divine services, hold funerals, and such. When a chaplain is present, some commanding officers may choose to read the lesson, another traditional prerogative of the CO. This is arranged beforehand with the officiating chaplain. It is a good idea to draw your chaplain's attention to the Marine Corps Prayer, above, as some chaplains are unfamiliar with it.

727. Conduct in Action

Over and above the competence, resolution, and courage expected of every Marine in battle, it is particularly expected that no wounded or dead Marine will ever be left on the field or unattended, regardless of the cost of bringing him in. As for surrender, the Marine Corps code is that expressed by Napoleon:

There is but one honorable mode of becoming prisoner of war. That is, by being taken separately; by which is meant, by being cut off entirely, and when we can no longer make use of our arms.

728. Marine Corps Museums

"The scrapbook of the Marine Corps," as it is sometimes described, is the Marine Corps Museum at the Marine Corps Historical Center, Washington Navy Yard. No summary of the traditions of the Corps would be complete without mention of this central repository of awards, battle honors, historical flags, and other objects of lasting sentimental significance to the Marine Corps. The museum collection documents Marine Corps history from 1775 to the present day. On display is an extensive array of uniforms, weapons, artifacts, equipment, prints, and paintings giving tangible substance to the proud traditions of the Corps. Included among numerous historical flags, for example, are the famous Colors raised by the 28th Marines atop Suribachi Yama on Iwo Jima. The weapons collection is one of the finest in the world, and it is backed up by over 55,000 documents covering design, patent data, and test reports on machine guns and automatic weapons alone. Every Marine officer should be thoroughly familiar with this museum, which ranks among the best military and naval museums in the United States. Larger exhibits and some of the aircraft and vehicles possessed by the Historical Center may be seen at the nearby USMC Air-Ground Museum at Quantico.

In addition, excellent post museums are located at San Diego, Pendleton, and Parris Island. There is the Navy and Marine Museum at Treasure Island, San Francisco. In Philadelphia, at New Hall, a restored building from pre-Revolutionary days, is an outstanding collection of material dealing with the early days of the Corps and its origins in Pennsylvania. The nearby cruiser relic, USS *Olympia*, contains an exhibit depicting Marines of the Spanish-American War.

729. Marine Corps Memorial Chapel, Quantico

The post chapel at Quantico serves, in addition to its regular functions, as the Memorial Chapel of the Marine Corps. Here is kept a "Book of Remembrance" listing the name, rank, and date of death for Marines and members of the Navy serving with the Marine Corps who gave their lives in action in Vietnam.

COLORS, FLAGS, AND STANDARDS

730. Colors, Flags, and Standards in General

A Parris Island recruit once asked his drill instructor, "Sergeant, who carries the flag in battle?"

Came the unhesitating reply, "Son, *every* Marine carries the flag in battle!"

As the soldier's proverb says, "The flag is a jealous mistress," and any Marine will fight and die rather than permit the National Colors or a Marine Corps Color to be dishonored.

Colors or standards must never fall into enemy hands. If capture seems inevitable, they should be burned. Unserviceable colors or standards, or those from disbanded units, are turned in to the supply system. The latter, in turn, forwards flags of historical value to the Marine Corps Museum, which is the Corps repository for historical flags, as well as for flags and war trophies captured by Marines. Soiled, torn, or badly frayed flags, if not historical, are destroyed privately by burning.

731.   Types of Flags

Marine Corps terms that deal with flags are precise and particular. As an officer, you must learn to distinguish the various kinds of flags and to speak of them in the correct terminology.

National Color or Standard.   This is the American flag. When the flag is displayed over Marine or naval posts, stations, or ships, its official title is the *National Ensign.* The national flag carried by Marine organizations is made of silk or nylon and is called the *National Color* (except when borne by a mounted, mechanized, motorized, or aviation unit, when its title becomes the *National Standard*). This technical distinction between a *color* and a *standard* also applies to the battle colors and organization colors described in the following paragraphs.

The National Color is carried on all occasions of ceremony when two or more companies of a unit are present. When not in the hands of troops, the National Color is entrusted to the adjutant. With the Marine Corps Color (discussed below), the National Color is usually displayed in the office or before the tent of the commanding officer. Whenever the National Color is carried in the open, it is escorted by a *color guard* composed of selected Marines, and the Color itself is borne by an outstanding NCO, the *color sergeant.*

The National Ensign, displayed over ships and shore stations, comes in three sizes:

1. *Post flag:* size 10 feet by 19 feet, flown in fair weather except on Sundays and national holidays
2. *Storm flag:* size 5 feet by 9 feet 6 inches, flown during foul weather
3. *Garrison flag:* size 20 feet by 38 feet, flown on Sundays and national holidays as provided in the *Marine Corps Flag Manual* (but never from a flagpole shorter than 65 feet)

For more information on display of the National Color or Ensign, refer to *Navy Regulations* and to the *Marine Corps Flag Manual.*

Marine Corps Colors and Standards.   The commandant issues to every major Marine unit or organization a distinguishing flag, which is carried beside the National Color. These unit flags are called *Marine Corps Colors* (or Standards). A Marine Corps Color bears the emblem and motto of the Corps and the unit title, and follows the color scheme of the Corps, scarlet and gold.

The Marine Corps Color of a Fleet Marine Force unit is called the unit *Battle Color;* the Color authorized for an organization in the Supporting Establishment (such as a Marine barracks) is called the *Organization Color.* No unit smaller than a separate battalion or regiment receives a Battle Color, nor does a temporary or provisional unit unless specially authorized by the commandant.

Certain organized units of the Marine Corps Reserve are likewise authorized to carry organizational flags of the type just described, but bearing a Reserve designation.

Guidons.   These are small rectangular flags, made in the Marine Corps colors, carried by companies, batteries, or detachments, or used as marker flags for ceremonies. *Organizational guidons* carry the Marine Corps emblem and the title of the unit. *Dress guidons* (used as markers) simply bear the initials "USMC."

Personal Flags.   Every active general officer in command displays a *personal flag.* Marine Corps personal flags consist of a scarlet field with white stars, according to the general officer's rank, arranged in the same manner as the stars on Navy personal flags. Regulations governing personal flags are in *Navy Regulations.*

Miscellaneous Flags.   In addition to the ceremonial flags just described, the Corps employs several miscellaneous flags and pennants described in the *Marine Corps Flag Manual.* Examples are:
- Geneva Convention flag
- Church pennant
- Sanitary cordon flag
- United Nations flag

732.   Appurtenances of Flags

The appurtenances of Marine colors, standards, flags, and guidons are: streamers, bands, cords, tassels, and staff ornaments.

Streamers denote participation in combat or award of a collective citation or decoration conferred on the unit as a whole.

A *silver band* is attached to the staff of a Marine Corps Color or Standard for each streamer awarded.

When the unit or organization does not rate streamers or bands, a *cord* and *tassel,* woven in the Corps colors, are substituted.

The heads of staffs bear the following *staff ornaments.*
- Colors and standards: silver lance-head
- Personal flag: silver halberd
- Guidon: plain silver cap

733.   Battle Color of the Marine Corps

The Corps as a whole has one Battle Color entitled *The Battle Color of the Marine Corps.* This Color is entrusted to the senior post of the Corps, Marine Barracks, Eighth and Eye Streets, Washington, D.C. Attached to it are all the battle honors, citations, battle streamers, and silver bands that the Corps has won since 1775. At the time of writing, these honors are the following:

- Presidential Unit Citation (Navy) Streamer with six silver stars and two bronze stars

- Presidential Unit Citation (Army) Streamer with one silver oak leaf cluster
- Navy Unit Commendation Streamer with 23 silver stars and three bronze stars
- Army Valorous Unit Award
- Meritorious Unit Commendation Streamer
- Army Meritorious Unit Commendation Streamer
- Revolutionary War Streamer
- Quasi-War with France Streamer
- Barbary Wars Streamer
- War of 1812 Streamer
- African Slave Trade Streamer
- West Indies Anti-Piracy Campaign Streamer
- Indian Wars Streamer
- Mexican War Streamer
- Civil War Streamer
- Marine Corps Expeditionary Streamer with twelve silver stars and silver "W"
- Spanish-American War Streamer
- Philippine Campaign Streamer
- Cuban Pacification Streamer
- Nicaraguan Campaign Streamer
- Mexican Service Streamer
- Haitian Campaign Streamer with bronze star
- Dominican Campaign Streamer
- World War I Victory Streamer with one silver star, one bronze star, Maltese Cross, and Siberian and West Indies Clasps
- Army of Occupation of Germany Streamer
- Second Nicaraguan Campaign Streamer
- Yangtze Service Streamer
- China Service Streamer with bronze star
- American Defense Service Streamer with bronze star
- American Campaign Streamer
- Asiatic-Pacific Campaign Streamer with eight silver and two bronze stars
- European–African–Middle East Campaign Streamer with one silver and four bronze stars
- World War II Victory Streamer
- Navy Occupation Service Streamer with Asia and Europe Clasps
- National Defense Service Streamer with two bronze stars
- Korean Service Streamer with two silver stars
- Armed Forces Expeditionary Streamer with three silver and two bronze stars
- Vietnam Service Streamer with three silver and two bronze stars
- Southwest Asia Service Streamer with three bronze stars
- Philippine Defense Streamer with one bronze star
- Philippine Liberation Streamer with two bronze stars
- Philippine Independence Streamer

- French Croix de Guerre Streamer (*Fourragère*) with two palms and one gilt star
- Philippine Presidential Unit Citation with two bronze stars
- Republic of Korea Presidential Unit Citation Streamer
- Vietnam Cross of Gallantry with palm
- Vietnam Meritorious Unit Citation

DECORATIONS, MEDALS, AND UNIT CITATIONS

734. Decorations and Medals

"A soldier will fight long and hard for a bit of colored ribbon," said Napoleon, who originated the awarding of personal decorations.

Napoleon's conqueror, the Duke of Wellington, in turn introduced all-hands campaign medals, the first of which went to British troops who fought at Waterloo.

Both Wellington and Napoleon realized that decorations and medals not only express national gratitude to individuals but stimulate emulation and esprit in battles to come.

Today, Marine Corps awards fall into three classes: personal and unit decorations; commemorative, campaign, and service medals; and marksmanship badges and trophies. The *Navy and Marine Corps Awards Manual* gives details on all these, together with guidance for anyone who wishes to originate a recommendation that an award be made.

735. Personal and Unit Decorations

The United States, despite the limitations in Article I, Section 9, of the Constitution, confers numerous military decorations. These range from the Medal of Honor, at the top, to the campaign ribbon in junior position. In order of precedence, these personal or unit decorations are:
- Medal of Honor (Navy)*
- Medal of Honor (Army and Air Force)*
- Navy Cross*
- Distinguished Service Cross (Army and Air Force)*
- Defense Distinguished Service Medal
- Distinguished Service Medal (Navy)
- Distinguished Service Medal (Army and Air Force)
- Silver Star Medal*
- Defense Superior Service Medal
- Legion of Merit[†]
- Distinguished Flying Cross[†]
- Navy and Marine Corps Medal[‡]

*Awarded for heroism only.
[†]Awarded fir either heroic or meritorious acts.
[‡]Awarded for heroism not in combat.

- Soldier's Medal‡
- Airman's Medal‡
- Coast Guard Medal‡
- Bronze Star Medal†
- Purple Heart
- Defense Meritorious Service Medal
- Meritorious Service Medal
- Air Medal†
- Joint Service Commendation Medal
- Navy Commendation Medal†
- Army Commendation Medal†
- Air Force Commendation Medal†
- Joint Service Achievement Medal
- Navy Achievement Medal†
- Coast Guard Achievement Medal†
- Combat Action Ribbon*
- Presidential Unit Citation*
- Joint Meritorious Unit Award
- Distinguished Unit Emblem (Army and Air Force)*
- Navy Unit Commendation†
- Meritorious Unit Commendation
- Navy "E" Ribbon
- Gold Life-Saving Medal (Treasury Department award)‡
- Silver Life-Saving Medal (Treasury Department award)‡
- Prisoner of War Medal
- Marine Corps Good Conduct Medal
- Navy Good Conduct Medal
- Army and Air Force Good Conduct Medal
- Coast Guard Good Conduct Medal
- Selected Marine Corps Reserve Medal
- Marine Corps Expeditionary Medal
- China Service Medal
- Navy Occupation Service Medal
- National Defense Service Medal
- Korean Service Medal
- Antarctica Service Medal
- Armed Forces Expeditionary Medal
- Vietnam Service Medal
- Southwest Asia Service Medal
- Humanitarian Service Medal
- Sea Service Deployment Ribbon

*Awarded for heroism only.
†Awarded fir either heroic or meritorious acts.
‡Awarded for heroism not in combat.

- Navy Arctic Service Ribbon
- Navy and Marine Corps Overseas Service Ribbon
- Armed Forces Reserve Medal
- Marine Corps Reserve Ribbon
- Philippine Presidential Unit Citation
- Korean Presidential Unit Citation
- Vietnam Presidential Unit Citation
- Republic of Vietnam Meritorious Unit Citation Cross of Gallantry
- United Nations Service Medal
- United Nations Medal
- Multinational Force and Observers Medal
- Inter-American Defense Board Medal
- Republic of Vietnam Campaign Medal

Among the foregoing, the *Medal of Honor* rates special mention. The Medal of Honor is the highest decoration conferred by the United States. Ordinarily, you can win it only for gallantry and intrepidity in combat, at the risk of your life, above and beyond the call of duty. Since the Civil War, when the award was created, more than three hundred Medals of Honor have been won by U.S. Marines.

On attaining the age of forty, winners of the Medal of Honor are eligible for a special pension of $400 per month. In addition, if you hold the Medal of Honor, you are entitled to have your son(s) and daughter(s) appointed to Annapolis, to West Point, or to the Air Force Academy. You enjoy lifetime commissary and PX privileges; you may also travel without charge in U.S. armed forces aircraft, and, regardless of military status, you are eligible for medical and hospital care in VA hospitals. It is a tradition (though not officially recognized) that all hands salute a Medal of Honor holder, regardless of rank.

736.   Unit Decorations

All top U.S. unit decorations, or "unit citations," as well as several foreign unit citations, have been won by Marine Corps units. If you are a member of an organization when it wins a collective citation, you are thereafter entitled to wear the citation ribbon or device as a personal decoration.

The *French Fourragère* is the senior unit award (and first collective award) won by Marines. The Fourragère dates from Napoleon's time; it was awarded to the 4th Marine Brigade in 1918 in lieu of awarding all hands the Croix de Guerre. The green and scarlet cord of the Fourragère may still be seen on the left shoulders of members of the 5th and 6th Marines, and of the few remaining Marines who were present when the 4th Brigade won the award.

The *Presidential Unit Citation* is the highest Navy and Marine Corps unit award. It was also the first American collective award, having been personally instituted by President Franklin D. Roosevelt as a citation for the defenders of Wake (1st Defense Battalion and Marine Fighting Squadron 211) in December 1941. The Presidential Unit Citation is considered to represent unit attainments that would warrant award of the Navy Cross if the recipient were an individual.

The *Distinguished Unit Emblem* is the Army and Air Force collective citation roughly equivalent to the Presidential Unit Citation. The Distinguished Unit Emblem has been awarded to several Marine ground and aviation units on detached service with the Army or Air Force.

The *Navy Unit Commendation* ranks next, in the naval service, after the Joint Meritorious Unit Award. Like the latter, the Navy Unit Commendation (NUC) may be won by extremely meritorious service in support of, but not participation in, combat operations. When awarded for combat performance, the NUC is comparable to the Silver Star medal for an individual; for noncombat meritorious service, this commendation is comparable to the Legion of Merit.

Other unit decorations awarded for collective achievements of valor or merit include: Army Valorous Unit Award, Air Force Outstanding Unit Award, and Joint Meritorious Unit Award.

737. Campaign Medals

Campaign or service medals are issued to all hands who take part in particular campaigns or periods of service for which a medal is authorized. In addition to medals for specific campaigns, Marines may be awarded the *Marine Corps Expeditionary Medal* for service ashore on foreign soil, against opposition, for which no other campaign medal is authorized. Or, for similar joint operations in which the Army or Air Force is involved, the *Armed Forces Expeditionary Medal* may be substituted. Campaign medals are often embellished by clasps or bronze stars, which denote participation in specific battles or phases of the campaign.

The *Republic of Vietnam Campaign Medal* is the only foreign service medal authorized for wear without specific individual authorization. It is worn after all other non–U.S. service awards.

In addition to campaign and service medals, certain *commemorative medals* have been struck to commemorate noncombat but notable achievements, such as polar and Antarctic expeditions or pioneer flights.

738. Initiating an Award

One of your responsibilities as a combat leader is to see that your men are promptly recommended for awards you believe they have earned. During active operations, it is usual for every FMF unit, from battalion up, to maintain a *board of awards*. The board evaluates and passes on recommendations for decorations that originate within the organization, but you must see that the board of awards receives recommendations promptly and that the recommendations are accurately stated in whatever form may be required.

Few leadership derelictions are more reprehensible than failure to submit proper recommendations for awards, and then to see an award fail because you were too lazy to recommend it in the right form and with the detailed information required.

Standard Marine Corps procedure for initiating awards is described in the *Navy and Marine Corps Awards Manual.*

739. Wearing Your Decorations and Medals

The Marine Corps has strict rules that govern the wearing of decorations and medals. These rules are in the *Marine Corps Uniform Regulations.* Some of them follow.

Subject to regulations, you may now accept awards from foreign nations.

Most decorations, and all campaign medals, have half-size miniature reproductions known as *miniature medals.* You wear "miniatures" with evening and mess dress, as well as with civilian full dress or dinner jacket, when appropriate. The Medal of Honor, however, is never represented in miniature, and, when miniatures are worn, the Medal of Honor is suspended in the normal fashion, about the collar.

When medals are prescribed instead of ribbons, unit citations and other ribbons for which no medal has been struck will be worn centered on the *right* breast.

Marines with eight or more ribbons of any type may wear them in rows of four rather than three, thus avoiding a top-heavy stack. Large medals may not be worn more than seven (five for women) per single row; and miniatures, not more than ten (eight for women). *Marine Corps Uniform Regulations* now detail the manner of wearing and mounting larger numbers of awards by specific numbers and rows.

With every U.S. decoration (and many foreign ones, too) you receive a lapel device for wear with civilian clothes. This may be worn in the left lapel of your civilian suit when you think fit.

Decorations and medals are part of your uniform and must be worn, *except* that, when ribbons are prescribed for the shirt, you are required to display only personal decorations and unit citations; the wearing of campaign ribbons is optional.

Marksmanship badges may be prescribed for any uniform except evening and mess dress, but it is not customary to wear these badges when medals are prescribed. Nor can you wear *any* ribbon (such as Navy marksmanship ribbons) in lieu of a marksmanship or gunnery badge. Incidentally, you are limited to a ceiling of three badges of your choice, if you rate more than three.

When soiled, faded, frayed, or otherwise unserviceable, the ribbons of decorations and medals should be destroyed by burning, rather than thrown away, not only to prevent reuse by unauthorized persons but because these ribbons symbolize the bravery, devotion, and sacrifice of U.S. Marines.

Even though entitled to wear foreign decorations or medals, you must always display at least one U.S. medal or award at the same time. And remember that U.S. awards take precedence over foreign awards.

UNIFORMS, INSIGNIA, AND PERSONAL GROOMING

740. "... Well-Dressed Soldiers"

"It is proverbial," wrote one commandant, "that well-dressed soldiers are usually well-behaved soldiers." The Marine Corps has always set course by that axiom and has enjoyed success and repute on both counts.

As a Marine officer, it rests squarely with you to maintain the Marine Corps reputation for smart, soldierly, and correctly worn uniforms.

Marine Corps Uniform Regulations is the "bible" on uniforms, insignia, and grooming. You must know *Regulations,* set the example by rigid compliance, and enforce the regulations meticulously.

In *Uniform Regulations* you will find two essential compilations: (1) the listing of required articles of uniform for all officers; and (2) the table showing types and combinations of uniforms authorized for officers. See Tables 7–1 and 7–2 in this *Guide.* They provide a complete checklist of articles (for male officers and female officers, respectively) that should, or should not, be worn as part of each prescribed uniform combination.

741. Wearing the Uniform

Here are important rules that govern the wearing of uniforms:
   a. Uniforms designed to be buttoned *will be worn buttoned.*
   b. Wear headgear whenever under arms or on watch, except when in a space where a meal is being served or divine service is being conducted; or when in quarters (if on watch) or when specifically excused from remaining covered. Remain covered at all times when out-of-doors or on topside spaces on board ship. (But see Section 1014 for shipboard ground rules).
   c. "Mixed uniform" (components of two different uniforms, worn simultaneously—white blouse and utility trousers, for example) is strictly forbidden unless specifically authorized in *Uniform Regulations.*
   d. *Full service uniform* (greens) is worn when:
   Traveling on orders via public conveyance (if desired)
   Reporting for duty ashore
   Paying official visits as defined by *Navy Regulations*
   Serving as a member of court-martial or court of inquiry
   Making boarding calls on merchantmen
   e. *Undress* uniform* (blues or whites with ribbons only) is worn when:
   Reporting for sea duty

---

*"Dress" (large medals in lieu of ribbons) and "undress" (ribbons and badges only) are traditional terms for these uniform categories.

Paying first visit to commanding officer

Visiting foreign officers

f. *Dress* uniform* (blues or whites with sword, when prescribed, and medals) is worn when:

Exchanging calls or ceremonies with foreign officials, or making boarding calls on foreign men-of-war

Exchanging official visits with U.S. civil officials, U.S. armed forces officers, and foreign officials

Attending receptions tendered by or in honor of officials listed in Table of Honors, *Navy Regulations*

Attending informal daytime social functions in an official capacity

Senior officer present considers the occasion appropriate

g. *Evening dress* is worn on formal evening occasions when civilian full dress is prescribed (such as the Marine Corps Birthday Ball) or on semiformal evening occasions. Evening dress will be prescribed for official or military-sponsored events, either formal or semiformal. Any evening function that you attend as an official representative of the Marine Corps is one for evening dress.

h. While the boat cloak is optional, you should feel free to obtain and, more important, wear this handsome, traditional garment. Specifically, the cloak should always be worn (in lieu of overcoat) with evening dress, and, on any social occasion when not in line with troops, over blues. Any officer going on sea duty, other than in tropical waters, should have a boat cloak. By custom, though not prescribed in *Uniform Regulations,* you may also wear your boat cloak over civilian evening dress (dinner jacket or white tie).

i. If invited to the White House, check with the aide-de-camp to the commandant, Marine Corps Headquarters, as to the correct uniform and other questions of protocol.

j. You must buy and maintain in good condition all articles of uniform that the commandant prescribes for officers, as listed in *Uniform Regulations.* You must keep your full assignment of uniforms with you at all times except when in the field.

k. The law prohibits anyone not in the armed forces from wearing the uniform or any distinctive part thereof (10 USC 771, 772, 18 USC 702). This does not apply to honorably discharged Marines, who may continue to bear the title, and, on occasions of military ceremony, wear the uniform of highest rank held during war service.

l. Wearing the uniform is prohibited in connection with nonmilitary commercial or business activities or in any circumstances that might compromise the dignity of the uniform or the Corps.

---

*"Dress" (large medals in lieu of ribbons) and "undress" (ribbons and badges only) are traditional terms for these uniform categories.

Table 7–1.   Types and components of authorized uniforms for male officers

Designation	Cap	Coat/Belt or Jacket	Shirt	Necktie	Trousers/Belt
Evening dress "A"	Dress	Evening w/strip collar and white waistcoat	White w/pique placket	None	Evening (suspenders optional)
Evening dress "B"	Dress	Evening w/strip collar and waistcoat or cummerbund (c)	White w/pique placket	None	Evening (suspenders optional)
Blue dress "A"	Dress	Blue w/strip collar	White plain front	None	Sky blue (g) w/web belt or suspenders
Blue dress "B"	Dress	Blue w/strip collar	White plain front	None	Sky blue (g) w/web belt or suspenders
Blue dress "C" (i)	Dress	None	Khaki long sleeve	Khaki w/clasp	Sky blue (g) w/web belt
Blue dress "D"	Dress	None	Khaki short sleeve	None	Sky blue (g) w/web belt
White dress "A" (d)	Dress	White	None	None	White w/web belt or suspenders
Blue-white dress "A" (d)	Dress	Blue w/strip collar	White plain front	None	White w/web belt or suspenders
Service "A"	Garrison/ optional frame cap	Green	Khaki long sleeve	Khaki w/clasp	Green w/web belt
Service uniform with sweater	Garrison/ optional frame cap	Green sweater	Khaki long or short sleeve	None	Green w/web belt
Service "B"	Garrison/ optional frame cap	None	Khaki long sleeve	Khaki w/clasp	Green w/web belt
Service "C"	Garrison/ optional frame cap	None	Khaki short sleeve	None	Green w/web belt
Utility uniform	Utility	Utility	Not worn	None	Utility w/web belt

a. If required or prescribed.
b. Black gloves always worn or carried with all-weather coat during winter uniform period.
c. Scarlet waistcoat for general officers only. Scarlet cummerbund for all other officers.
d. Dress "B"—ribbons, no medals, badges optional but may be prescribed.
e. Green cushion socks previously authorized may still be worn.
f. Black gloves optional during winter uniform period unless all-weather coat is worn.
g. Dark blue trousers for general officers.
h. Green scarf optional for wear with all-weather coat during winter uniform period and may be prescribed for formations.
i. Can be varied to include blue sweater.
j. Tanker jacket optional.

Gloves	Footwear	Outer coat (a)	Insignia	Medals/Ribbons	Badges	Sword
White (b)	Black shoes and socks	All-weather coat (AWC)/ optional boat cloak	Dress (collar/ cap)	Miniature medals	Not worn	Not worn
White (b)	Black shoes and socks	AWC/optional boat cloak	Dress (collar/ cap)	Miniature medals	Not worn	Not worn
White (b)	Black shoes and socks	AWC/optional boat cloak	Dress (collar/ cap)	Large Medals	Not worn	May be prescribed
White (b)	Black shoes and socks	AWC/optional boat cloak	Dress (collar/ cap)	Ribbons	Optional/ may be prescribed	May be prescribed
(b)	Black shoes and socks	AWC (j)	Dress (cap)	Ribbons optional/ may be prescribed	Optional/ may be prescribed	Not worn
(b)	Black shoes and socks	AWC (j)	Dress (cap)	Ribbons optional/ may be prescribed	Optional/ may be prescribed	May be prescribed
White	White shoes and socks	AWC	Dress (collar/ cap)	Large Medals	Not worn	May be prescribed
White	Black shoes and socks	AWC	Dress (collar/ cap)	Large Medals	Not worn	May be prescribed
(b, f)	Black shoes and socks	AWC (h)(j)	Service (collar/ cap)	Ribbons	Optional/ may be prescribed	May be prescribed
(b, f)	Black shoes and socks	AWC (h)(j)	Service (cap)	Not worn	Not worn	Not worn
(b)	Black shoes and socks	AWC (h)(j)	Service (cap)	Ribbons optional/ may be prescribed	Optional/ may be prescribed	May be prescribed
(b)	Black shoes and socks	AWC (j)	Service (cap)	Ribbons optional/ may be prescribed	Optional/ may be prescribed	May be prescribed
(b, f)	Combat boots/ black socks (e)	AWC or field coat	Decal/ tape	Not worn	Not worn	Not worn

Table 7–2.   Types and components of authorized uniforms for female officers

Designation	Cap	Coat or Jacket	Shirt	Necktab	Skirt/Slacks
Evening dress "A"	Dress	Evening w/cummerbund	White ruffled front w/black tab	(See "Shirt" column)	Long black skirt
Evening dress "B"	Dress	Evening w/cummerbund	White ruffled front w/black tab	(See "Shirt" column)	Long/short black skirt
Blue dress "A" (e)	Dress	Blue	White plain front	Red w/skirt or black w/slacks	Blue skirt/slacks
Blue dress "C" (h)	Dress	None	Khaki long sleeve	Black	Blue skirt/slacks
Blue dress "D"	Dress	None	Khaki short sleeve	None	Blue skirt/slacks
White dress "A"	Dress	White	White plain front	Scarlet	White skirt
White dress "B"	Dress	White	White plain front	Scarlet	White skirt
Service "A"	Green service/ garrison	Green	Khaki long or short sleeve	Green	Green skirt/slacks
Service uniform with sweater	Green service/ garrison	Green sweater	Khaki long or short sleeve	None	Green skirt/slacks
Service "B"	Green service/ garrison	None	Khaki long sleeve	Green	Green skirt/slacks
Service "C"	Green service/ garrison	None	Khaki short sleeve	None	Green skirt/slacks
Maternity uniform	Green service/ garrison	Green tunic	Khaki long or short sleeve	Green (if required)	Green skirt/slacks
Utility uniform	Utility	Utility	Not worn	Not worn	Utility trousers w/web belt

a. If required or prescribed.
b. See regulations on wear of hose/socks.
c. Black gloves always worn or carried with all-weather coat during winter uniform period.
d. Oxfords may be worn. Oxfords always worn with slacks.
e. Dress "B"—ribbons, no medals, badges optional but may be prescribed.
f. Black gloves optional during winter uniform period unless all-weather coat is worn.
g. Green scarf optional for wear with all-weather coat during winter uniform period but may be prescribed for formations.
h. Can be varied to include blue sweater.
i. Green cushion socks previously authorized may still be worn.
j. Tanker jacket optional.

Handbag/ Purse	Gloves	Footwear	Outer Coat (a)	Insignia	Medals/ Ribbons	Badges	Sword
Black clutch	White (c)	Black pumps (cloth/ suede)	All-weather coat (AWC) optional cape	Dress (collar/ cap)	Miniature medals	Not worn	Not worn
Black clutch	White (c)	Black pumps (cloth/ suede)	AWC/optional cape	Dress (collar/ cap)	Miniature medals	Not worn	Not worn
Black handbag/ clutch purse (optional)	White (c)	Black pumps (d)	AWC/optional cape	Dress (collar/ cap)	Large Medals	Not worn	May be prescribed
Black handbag (optional)	(c)	Black pumps (d)	AWC (j)	Dress (cap)	Ribbons optional/may be prescribed	Optional/ may be prescribed	Not worn
Black handbag (optional)	(c)	Black pumps (d)	AWC (j)	Dress (cap)	Ribbons optional/may be prescribed	Optional/ may be prescribed	May be prescribed
White clutch	White	White pumps	AWC	Dress (collar/ cap)	Large Medals	Not worn	Not worn
White clutch	White	White pumps	AWC	Dress (collar/ cap)	Ribbons	Optional/ may be prescribed	Not worn
Black handbag (optional)	(c, f)	Black pumps (d)	AWC (g)(j)	Service (cap/ collar)	Ribbons	Optional/ may be prescribed	May be prescribed
Black handbag (optional)	(c, f)	Black pumps (d)	AWC (g)(j)	Service (cap)	Not worn	Not worn	Not worn
Black handbag (optional)	(c)	Black pumps (d)	AWC (g)(j)	Service (cap)	Ribbons optional/may be prescribed	Optional/ may be prescribed	May be prescribed
Black handbag (optional)	(c)	Black pumps (d)	AWC (g)(j)	Service (cap)	Ribbons optional/may be prescribed	Optional/ may be prescribed	May be prescribed
Black handbag (optional)	(c, f)	Black pumps/ oxfords	AWC (g)	Service (cap)	Ribbons optional/may be prescribed	Optional/ may be prescribed	Not worn
Not worn	(c, f)	Combat boots/ black socks (i)	AWC or field coat	Decal/ tape	Not worn	Not worn	Not worn

m. No Marine (including retired or reserve personnel) may wear the uniform while attending (unless on duty) or participating in any demonstration, assembly, or activity, the purpose of which is furtherance of personal or partisan political, social, economic, or religious issues. In other words, *demonstrations and the Marine Corps uniform or emblem don't mix.*

742. Uniform Accessories

The following rules concern the wearing of uniform accessories:
 a. Belts are worn with buckle centered. Belt buckles (except on 782 equipment) must be brightly polished.
 b. Leather gloves may be worn or carried with the winter service uniform, without topcoat, overcoat, or raincoat, at the option of the individual. Gloves are required with winter service when wearing topcoat, overcoat, or raincoat. Local commanders designate whether gloves will be worn by troops in formation.
 c. Shoes (and all leather) worn with service uniforms must be plain, without fancy stitching, and of regulation shade. Socks must match shoes in color.
 d. Swords may be prescribed only with dress, undress, or service uniforms and must be carried in line with troops in dress uniforms. Male officers must possess swords, but no longer must have their names engraved on the blade. Sons of Marine officers may carry their fathers' swords.
 e. Marines may not wear jewelry, fobs, pens, or pencils exposed on the uniform, except:
 Wrist watch
 Regulation tie-clasp
 Rings
 Sunglasses (conservative design—but may not be worn in line with troops unless by medical requirement)
 Women may carry umbrellas and, in dress uniform, wear small earrings.
 f. You wear the regulation black mourning band on your left arm between the shoulder and elbow:
 When a pallbearer or attending a military funeral in an official capacity
 During prescribed official mourning
 For family mourning (optional)
 g. The Sam Browne belt is authorized and worn as organizational equipment in organizations when the sword is required for wear or an individual is considered "under arms." Presently, no optional wearing is permitted on any other occasion by the regulations.

743. Civilian Clothes

As an officer you are expected to maintain a high standard of civilian dress. Your clothes should be conservative in cut and color, of the best quality, and well maintained. Never forget, incidentally, that your general neatness and grooming at all times are marked on your fitness report. This includes not only uniform but civilian clothes as well.

When off duty, wear civilian clothes. If on duty abroad, however, be sure to check local directives on wearing of plain clothes. Unless you have permission from the commandant, you may not wear uniform when on leave outside the United States or its territories.

Here are rules on civilian clothes:

- No distinctive articles of uniform (except items not exclusively military such as sweater, gloves, purse, shoes, socks, underwear, and so forth) may be worn with civilian clothing.
- On board government transports and aircraft, you must wear your uniform unless your orders permit plainclothes. When traveling singly by other means, you may and usually should wear mufti.

744. Grooming

a. Although most military grooming has simply reflected society's standards through history, Marines since the 1950s have stressed neat and close trimming of hair. Although three inches is the maximum permissible length on top, hairstyles approaching the maximums are regarded as somewhat foppish by many Marine officers and insubordinate by more than a few. Therefore, this *Guide* must, in good faith, encourage more junior officers to remain wary and well-trimmed.

b. Keep clean-shaven, except for a mustache, if desired (traditionally, Marines have always rated mustaches, and naval officers, beards, but not the reverse). Eccentricities of mustache will not be tolerated.

c. All leather must be maintained in very high polish.

d. To keep shirt collars trim and scarves in place, wear a collar stay.

e. To make utility trousers look smartest with field boots, turn up the trousers so as to form interior cuffs, and place a strong rubber band, sleeve garter, or section of inner tube inside this interior cuff. This produces a neat overhang. Most post exchanges stock garters for this purpose.

f. Keep the overlap of your khaki web belt within the prescribed 2–4 inches, $2^3/_4$–$3^3/_4$ inches for coat belts.

g. Although your uniforms contain many pockets, the safest rule is to carry nothing in them. Specifically, you should never place anything in exterior pockets of a dress or service uniform (exceptions: pencil out of sight in a shirt pocket; notebook in hip pocket; wallet, cigarette case, and handkerchief kept flat in trousers pockets). Do not, under any circumstances, follow the sailor practice of carrying cigarettes in the cuff of a sock.

h. At least a fortnight before the seasonal change from summer to winter uniform variants and vice versa, break out the forthcoming uniform, have it cleaned and pressed, and check it for completeness and repair.

Marine Corps uniforms are distinguished in their elegant simplicity, smart cut, and the evident pride and bearing of their wearing.

i. With standing-collar uniforms (as well as evening dress), it is convenient—and military—to carry your handkerchief unobtrusively tucked inside your left sleeve; this obviates convulsive dives into the interior of the uniform when a handkerchief is needed.

j. Read and follow the advice on care and marking of uniforms to be found in *Uniform Regulations.*

Old breed? New breed? There's not a damn bit of differences so long as it's the Marine breed.

—Lieutenant General Lewis B. Puller

This modern tendency to scorn and ignore tradition and to sacrifice it to administrative convenience is one that wise men will resist in all branches of life, but more especially in our military life.

—Field Marshal Wavell

8

Posts and Stations

Only the globe itself—trademark of Marines—limits the number of places where you, as a Marine, may ultimately serve.

In this chapter, we take a look at the permanent posts and stations of the Corps. These are the places where, between expeditions, you will spend much of your career. In addition, the chapter describes the organization and general conditions at a typical post, as well as the facilities and services that a post or base offers to you and your family members.

801. Posts of the Corps

A number of major bases, posts, and air stations form part of the Marine Corps Supporting Establishment and are maintained exclusively for Marine Corps forces. Marines in the security forces man more than twenty Marine barracks and shore-based Marine detachments at home and abroad. (Figure 8–1 lists major Marine Corps installations.)

Except for posts with missions directly reflected in their titles (such as the Recruit Depots), the Corps has the following kinds of stations.

Marine Corps Bases (MCB) and *Marine Barracks* (MB) are the basic permanent posts for support of ground units of the Corps. Both are administratively autonomous and self-supporting. Marine Corps bases and camps are devoted to field training and support of major tactical units, whereas Marine barracks perform security missions.

ARIZONA
MCAS Yuma, Yuma 722.4, 1959

CALIFORNIA
MCLB Barstow, Barstow, 8.9, 1942
MCAGCC Twentynine Palms,
Twentynine Palms, 930.3, 1952
MCB & MCAS Camp Pendleton,
Oceanside, 196.8, 19426
MCRD San Diego, San Diego,
0.675, 1942

DISTRICT OF COLUMBIA
Marine Barracks, Washington, D.C.,
0.008, 1801

HAWAII
MCAS Kaneohe Bay, Kaneohe, 4.7, 1952
Camp H. M. Smith, Honolulu, 0.658, 1955

JAPAN
MCAS Iwakuni, SOFA 1958
MCB Camp Butler, SOFA 1957

NORTH CAROLINA
MCAS Cherry Point, Havelock, 43.8, 1941
MCB Camp Lejeune, Jacksonville, 192.1, 1941
MCAS New River, Jacksonville, 4.3, 1941

SOUTH CAROLINA
MCAS Beaufort, Beaufort, 11.6, 1955
MCRD Parris Island, Beaufort, 12.6, 1912

VIRGINIA
HQMC, Henderson Hall, Arlington, 0.039, 1943
MCB Quantico, Quantico, 86.9, 1917

MARINE CORPS MUSEUMS

U.S. Marine Corps Museum	Washington, D.C.
U.S. Marine Corps Air-Ground Museum	Quantico, Virginia
Ranch House Museum	Camp Pendleton, California
U.S. Marine Corps Amphibian Vehicle Museum	Camp Pendleton, California
U.S. Marine Corps Recruit Depot Museum	San Diego, California
U.S. Marine Corps Air Station Museum	El Toro, Santa Ana, California
U.S. Marine Corps Museum and Memorial, New Hall	Philadelphia, Pennsylvania
U.S. Marine Corps Recruit Depot Museum	Parris Island, South Carolina

Figure 8–1: Major Marine Corps installations (with listings of nearest city, square miles, and date opened)

Marine Corps Air Station (MCAS) is the aviation counterpart of a Marine Corps base. Like MCBs, air stations are also permanent, autonomous, and self-supporting. All MCASs have a common mission: support of Marine aviation units.

Marine detachments are the smallest organizations of the Corps. A Marine detachment depends administratively and logistically on some larger organization, sometimes Navy, and often enjoys less permanent status than other Marine activities.

A TYPICAL POST

802.   How a Post Is Organized

With allowances for different missions and locations, most posts follow the same organization. Figure 8–2 shows the organization of a hypothetical post.

Command.   The *commanding officer* (CO) (if a general, called commanding general) commands the post. The CO is responsible for all that the command does or leaves undone.

The *executive officer* is the line officer next junior in rank to the CO. As the commanding officer's alter ego, the executive officer relieves the commander of administrative detail and succeeds to command in the latter's absence. The extent and character of the duties vary somewhat according to the policies and peculiarities of the CO. On a post commanded by a general, the executive officer is entitled *chief of staff,* and the latter, in turn, may be assisted by a deputy.

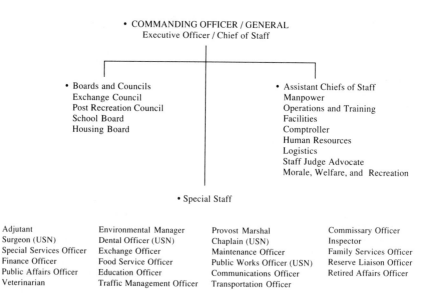

Figure 8–2: Organization of a typical post or base

Staff.   Just as in tactical units, a post commander is assisted by an executive and special staff much like those described in section 521. The executive staff includes assistants for manpower, operations, facilities, fiscal matters and the full range of services that posts and stations must provide.

In addition, most posts have a few special staff functions that differ materially in scale or scope from similar FMF staff jobs, where housekeeping is not quite so important as on a post.

Provost Marshal.   This is the post "chief of police," or "sheriff," responsible for public safety, traffic control, criminal investigation, internal and external security, regulation of pets, and law and order in general. Frequently, the provost marshal acts as *fire marshal* and thus also becomes responsible for fire protection. Law-abiding members of the post usually encounter the provost marshal in connection with licensing of vehicles or pets and obtaining passes for guests and family members.

Maintenance Officer.   This officer bears responsibility for minor construction, repair, and upkeep of the physical plant of the post. He or she is also responsible for its cleanliness and shipshape appearance.

Public Works Officer (CEC, USN).   On large stations, this is a Navy (CEC) officer who supervises new construction, improvements, and plans for post development.

Boards and Councils.   To supplement the staff, most stations include one or more standing boards or councils. Some are required by regulations, while others exist to meet local needs. Typical examples are:

Exchange council
Recreation council
School board
Athletic and sports council
Housing board

803.   Facilities and Services

In many ways a post resembles a small community. Most if not all the facilities and services you could expect in such a town have counterparts on a Marine post. Like small towns, however, stations of various age, locality, and mission exhibit considerable local disparities. Thus, what you find on one post might not exist, or hardly exists, at another.

One key to gaining the most benefits from the military community resides in the USMC family programs and family service centers maintained by all bases and activities. Family service centers provide a single point of reference for Marines as they change location. Relocation specialists provide the latest information on new duty stations and civilian communities: housing, child care, schools, employment, vehicle and firearms registration; and non–Marine Corps activities.

The centers offer seminars and orientation courses on the many aspects of family and personal development. Trained counselors and social workers provide guidance and referrals to outside agencies. Courses, home visits, and specialized assistance are available for new and expectant parents. For those families experiencing crises, family advocacy counselors supplement the wide variety of counseling services. Also offered are employment counseling for family members and retirement preparation for Marines, services often not available in communities except at considerable expense. A Marine assigned to another service's installation and his or her family may also use the host command's center.

If you and your family have never visited a family service center, the time to do so is now. If you are already en route, call one of the toll-free numbers, (800) 336-4663 or (800) 253-1624 for East Coast or West Coast services, respectively.

804. Medical and Dental Care

Every Marine post includes medical installations for the health and sanitation of the command. These may range from a *dispensary* (sick bay) to a *clinic* (dispensary with limited facilities for inpatient care) or, on the largest posts, a *naval hospital* that can handle any medical or surgical emergency. Routine treatment and consultation are afforded daily at "sick call"—a fixed time of day when the sick bay is fully staffed. Emergencies, of course, are dealt with at any time, day or night.

The Medical Department not only cares for ailments but wages a ceaseless preventive campaign. All Marines must undergo certain immunizations and every officer must have a thorough physical examination. These examinations are ordered every other year until the officer reaches thirty-five years of age and annually thereafter.

805. Medical Care for Family Members

Medical care for service families and for retired officers and their families is provided by the government on a space-available basis. CHAMPUS (Civilian Health and Medical Program, Uniformed Services) permits civilian medical care and hospitalization. A small percentage of the total annual cost of a civilian's medical care and hospitalization is borne by the individual.

Eligibility.   Virtually all family members (spouse and unmarried children under age twenty-one—subject to a few exceptions) of Marines on active duty are eligible for civilian medical care and care in service medical facilities. In order to receive such care, however, armed forces personnel must enroll their families in the DEERS (Defense Enrollment Reporting System) Program. Check your Personnel Office or, on larger posts, the DEERS Office for appropriate forms and actions. Do not put this off, as your family cannot be treated without DEERS certification. Retired officers and their dependents likewise have such eligibilities, but under differing provisions (see Chapter 21). If you die, whether on active duty or after retirement, your surviving dependents remain eligible for care at armed forces or U.S. Public Health Service medical facilities (subject to availability of space and staff), as well as for certain civilian medical care and hospitalization.

Civilian Medical Care.   Under CHAMPUS, civilian semiprivate hospitalization, outpatient care by civilian facilities, routine doctor visits, prescribed medicines, laboratory and X-ray tests, rental sick-room equipment, artificial limbs and eyes, and so forth are available to family members of active-duty Marines on a cost-sharing basis. In general, you pay a minimum annual fee per person or family and 20 percent of the cost of the medical care; the government pays the remaining 80 percent.

A program of financial assistance is also provided for active-duty personnel whose spouses or children are mentally retarded or physically handicapped. This program authorizes diagnostic services, treatment, and use of private nonprofit and nonmilitary institutions for such handicapped family members, with you (the sponsor) paying a varying amount according to rank and the government paying the remaining portion of the cost up to a given maximum.

Medical Care at Service Facilities.   When medical staff, space, and facilities are available, the Navy Medical Department will provide the following care for your family:
- Diagnosis
- Treatment of:
    acute medical conditions
    surgical conditions
    contagious diseases
    acute emergencies of any kind
- Immunization
- Maternity and infant care

All care receiving during and for a pregnancy that results in hospitalization is considered, for payment purposes, as part of that hospitalization, and oral contraceptives are considered to be prescription drugs.

Outpatient service, essentially of free-clinic character, is given family members (including parents, if in fact dependent upon you). Virtually all post medical installations in the continental United States and outlying stations have dependent outpatient service.

The extent and quality of medical services for family members vary widely with the limitations of local dispensaries, or hospitals, and with the medical workload as a whole. Isolated outlying stations usually have more self-sufficient medical and dental services.

In some regions, available health services are coordinated among various government health providers. In effect, you and your family may be assigned to a specific primary clinic for all outpatient and referral services. Consult your unit or base medical department or retired affairs office, as appropriate, to obtain information on local procedures.

On outlying stations, in addition to the service medical care noted above, dental care frequently can be provided to family members, subject to limitations of workload and facilities, provided adequate civilian dental services are not available. The government will also, in appropriate cases, provide transportation for family members from outlying stations where medical care is inadequate to centers where proper care can be provided (with round-trip expenses for attendants when they are found to be required).

A few cautionary words are in order on the subject of family medical care.

First and foremost, the medical needs of military personnel are the primary concern of the Medical Department. This means that care for family members takes second place and always gives way, when conflict arises, to military medicine functions.

Second, although members of the Marine Corps and Navy receive free dental care, dependents do not (except on remote, overseas stations or as otherwise required in connection with medical or surgical treatment). As compensation, you are offered the Delta Dental Plan, a government cost-sharing program equivalent to CHAMPUS.

Third, to receive medical assistance from any Navy (or armed forces) establishment, your family member must possess and present a family member identification card (see Section 806 below). Obtain these cards and have each family member carry a card.

Fourth, make sure, before seeking CHAMPUS treatment in a civilian hospital, that military medical treatment and hospitalization are not available (and that you have a nonavailability certification, currently Form DD 1251). If in doubt, check with your medical officer or nearest sick bay.

Finally, if you wish, and can afford the more personal attentions of a private practitioner and civilian hospital, you are free, at your own expense, or under CHAMPUS when applicable, as just noted, to obtain such services.*

806.   Identification and Privilege Cards for Family Members

The Department of Defense issues (on application) a standard *Identification and Privilege Card* (Form DD 1173) for family members (except children under age ten) of all active-duty personnel. This card is essential to enable your family to use the medical facilities, commissary, exchange, and post theaters. It is honored not only on Marine and Navy posts and stations but on those of the other services as well. As soon as you have family members, you are required to apply to your commanding officer for their identification and privilege cards and DEERS enrollment.

---

*The Defense Department authorizes military medical facilities to fill prescriptions written by licensed civilian physicians and dentists for military personnel, retirees, and family members, in reasonable quantities of nonnarcotic items stocked routinely.

807. Commissary

The military equivalent of the supermarket is the commissary, where prices are slightly lower than those charged by grocers ashore. The privilege of making purchases is limited to regular and retired personnel; to reservists on active or training duty; and to certain government civilians. Family members of anyone entitled to commissary privileges may also use the commissary. Use of the commissary is a privilege, not a right, and all purchases must be for your own use and that of your household.

Everyone entitled to commissary privileges must be prepared to present identification. Active personnel, as well as retired personnel, are identified by the ID card, dependents by the identification and privilege card.

Stock and services available in commissaries vary somewhat according to the size of the post and the availability of adequate civilian facilities off post.

808. Marine Corps Exchanges

Marine Corps exchanges (post exchanges, or PX, as they are known) are maintained by all posts of any size. Any regular Marine Corps organization may, with the approval of the commandant, establish its own exchange.

Post exchanges go far back into U.S. military history. During the nineteenth century, when the Army pushed our frontier westward, each isolated post had its "post trader" or sutler, authorized to keep store at the post. One of the trader's perquisites was the right of trading with Indians, trappers, and hunters, and from this arose the title, "post exchange." After the frontier vanished, the name remained, carrying over from the Old Army into the Old Marine Corps. In early times, the perquisite of keeping the post trader's stores at the various Marine barracks was awarded to the widow of some officer or senior NCO. The modern post exchange system was established by General Heywood, the ninth commandant.

Today's exchange is the post general store. On large stations, it approximates a small department store, but the size of an exchange depends on the size of the post and the accessibility of civilian shopping centers.

The missions of Marine Corps exchanges are: (1) to afford service personnel (including family members), at reasonable prices, articles necessary for health, comfort, and convenience; and (2) through reasonable profits, to finance recreation and amusement. The latter mission is realized through donation of exchange profits to unit recreation projects and to the Marine Corps Morale, Welfare, and Recreation Fund, a nonappropriated fund maintained by Marine Corps Headquarters for the entire exchange system and for welfare and recreation.

Eligibility to use the exchange, like the commissary, is a privilege that extends only to active or retired service personnel; to their eligible family members and surviving spouses; and to reservists on active or training duty. The *Marine Corps Exchange Manual* gives the various classes of eligible individuals. If in civilian clothes when making a purchase, be prepared to show your ID card. Take note, as well, of the dress codes pertaining to the exchange and commissary and ensure that your family members comply at all times.

809. Welfare Activities

In addition to welfare services provided by the chaplain, special services officer, and legal assistance officer, most large posts have representatives of the American Red Cross, Navy Relief Society, and Navy Mutual Aid Association. The assistance furnished by these groups is described in Chapter 21.

810. Educational Facilities

Many posts have their own public schools for the children on the post. Because of wide variations between post school systems, however, you should investigate carefully before you assume that you will find schools that meet your needs at the post. If overseas where U.S.–owned school facilities are not available, you may claim a modest schooling allowance for each child you place in a local private school of approved standards.

Every post has a free library, open to Marines and their family members. Marine Corps Headquarters provides the books. A few large posts have museums.

Even the smallest station and detachment features an Education Office, charged with providing information on educational opportunities available on and off post, including correspondence courses. Many of these programs lead toward various types of college degrees. The same office will advise you of tuition aid, veteran's assistance, and loan and scholarship programs.

811. Recreation

Most posts feature excellent on-station recreation opportunities. Facilities for athletic activities and hobbies are open to all. Frequently, instruction in various sports and hobbies will be available at little or no cost, and you would do well to avail yourself and your family of the opportunity to learn new skills for present and future enjoyment. Depending upon space and demand, posts may have golf courses, tennis courts, marinas, gymnasiums, skeet and small bore ranges, swimming pools, stables, flying fields, and various workshops. Take advantage!

MAJOR POSTS AND STATIONS

812. Marine Barracks, Eighth and Eye Streets, S.E., Washington, D.C. 20390

"Eighth and Eye" is the senior post of the Corps, both because of its age and because it houses the commandant. The post has been a Marine Barracks since 1801, and quartered Marine Corps Headquarters throughout its first century. It is the "spit-and-polish" post of the Corps, famous for its weekly Evening Parades, and constructed about a historic barracks square in the heart of Southeast Washington.

The Barracks provides ceremonial troops for official occasions in the nation's capital; it supports the U.S. Marine Band and the Marine Corps Drum and Bugle Corps, and the Marine Corps Institute (see Section 1510); and its officers and men are assigned to certain special security duties in and about Washington and in the Navy Yard.

Transportation.

Rail. Amtrak.

Bus. Greyhound.

Airports. Washington National Airport; Andrews Air Force Base; Dulles International Airport, Chantilly, Virginia (35 miles distant).

Quarters. Center House BOQ for officers permanently attached; nearest transient officer accommodations are at Naval Facility, Andrews AFB. Family quarters are not available.

Schools. In addition to a metropolitan school system, Washington has numerous private and parochial schools. Suburban public schools are adequate, with those in Montgomery Country, Maryland, generally considered best.

Recreation. Other than the Barracks gymnasium, the only on-post facility at Eighth and Eye is Center House, but facilities are abundant in the metropolitan area.

Commissary and Exchange. Commissary privileges are available at various commissaries in the Washington area. Excellent Marine Corps and Army exchanges are at Henderson Hall and Forts Myer and McNair, in addition to the small exchanges located at Eighth and Eye and Washington Navy Yard.

Neighboring Marine Activities. The Washington area includes Marine Corps Headquarters in Navy Annex, Navy Department, and Henderson Hall, Arlington, Virginia, which supports Headquarters Battalion, HQMC.

813. Marine Corps Combat Development Command, Quantico, Virginia 22134

MCCDC is, in many ways, the showplace of the Marine Corps. It is located on the Potomac River, approximately thirty-five miles south of Washington, D.C. It is the only base in the Marine Corps to be the site of a national cemetery. The base also includes the Marine Corps Air Facility (MCAF), Quantico, and the Naval Medical Clinic. Because of its educational and developmental roles, MCCDC is called the "Crossroads of the Marine Corps."

Transportation.

Rail. North to and from Washington, D.C., and south to and from Richmond and Fredericksburg, Virginia.

Bus. Greyhouse serves adjacent town of Triangle, Virginia.

Airports. Commercial air service is available at Washington National Airport (more than thirty miles distant) and at Dulles International Airport (more than fifty miles distant). MCAF Quantico serves military aircraft.

Highways. U.S. 1 and Interstate 95 serve MCCDC north and south. No major highway west.

Quarters. Government quarters are available and sufficient to accommodate all eligible personnel. Off-base housing is available in the surrounding area and north to Woodbridge, Virginia, and south to Fredericksburg, with rapid seasonal turnovers in rentals. Because of the proximity to Washington, D.C., housing costs are slightly higher than at other Marine Corps bases. Transient and permanent bachelor quarters are available.

Schools. Two elementary schools, one middle school, and one high school are located aboard MCCDC.

Recreation. Quantico abounds in recreational opportunities. There are the Commissioned Officers' Mess, an eighteen-hole golf course, boat docks, stables, a rod and gun club, a sky-diving club, a flying club, an auto hobby shop, swimming pools, a gymnasium and Nautilus center, a theater, bowling alley, the Marine Corps Air-Ground Museum, a base library, and the Marine Corps Research Center. Special Services offers a variety of discounted tickets, tours, and recreational classes.

Commissary and Marine Corps Exchange. The commissary and exchange, located together to make parking more convenient, are outstanding. The exchange is designed like a shopping mall, and the commissary offers shoppers the variety of a major supermarket.

814. Marine Activities in the Norfolk, Virginia, Area, 23551

Although the Norfolk–Hampton Roads area includes no major Marine Corps posts, it is the location of Headquarters, U.S. Marine Corps Forces, Joint Forces Command, and its supporting Camp Allen; Landing Force Training Command, Atlantic Fleet; and the Marine Corps Security Force Battalion. In addition, because Norfolk is the home of the United States Joint Forces Command (USJFCOM) and the primary East Coast base of the Atlantic Fleet, many Marines serve in the area as part of the USJFCOM and Fleet staffs. Thus, Norfolk and the surrounding area can be considered a Marine Corps station of importance.

Transportation.
Rail. Amtrak.
Bus. Greyhound.
Airport. Norfolk International Airport.
Highways. U.S. 13, 17, 58, and 60, and Interstate 64.

Quarters. Although relatively few government quarters are available, there is a wide range of excellent private housing reasonably priced. Temporary lodging and unaccompanied officer quarters are abundant throughout the area.

Schools. Norfolk has good public, private, and parochial schools—kindergarten through postgraduate.

Recreation. Plentiful in the region. Naval Air Station, Norfolk (Breezy Point), has an outstanding Commissioned Officers' Mess, and there are other excellent clubs and messes in the area with recreational facilities of all types. Virginia Beach, adjoining Norfolk, is one of the most attractive shore resorts on the East Coast.

Commissary and Exchanges. Excellent and plentiful throughout the area.

815. MCAS, Cherry Point, North Carolina 28533

Commissioned in May 1942, Cherry Point is the largest Marine Corps air station in the world and is one of the best all-weather jet bases. It is home to the 2d Marine Aircraft Wing, the only Marine Corps–operated Naval Aviation Depot, and a naval hospital.

Transportation.

Rail. Amtrak (nearest main-line stop, Rocky Mount, North Carolina, which is one hundred miles away).

Bus. Carolina Trailways.

Highway. U.S. 70.

Airport. Craven County Regional Airport, New Bern, North Carolina, twenty-five miles from Cherry Point, serviced by USAir/Henson Regional Airlines and American Airlines/American Eagle.

Quarters. There are 326 sets of family quarters for married officers aboard the air station, as well as one bachelor officers quarters and one temporary officers quarters. Private housing is available in adjacent Havelock and nearby Newport, New Bern, Beaufort, and Morehead City.

Waiting periods of several months for government quarters are not uncommon. Officers reporting in should consider leaving their families in comfortable and familiar surroundings elsewhere before checking into the air station or 2d MAW.

Schools. There are five public elementary schools, one middle school, and one high school, as well as a Roman Catholic parochial grade school, in Havelock. The Joint Education Center provides a wide range of education-related services. Programs ranging from adult high school completion to master's degree programs are offered by Craven Community College and university extension programs.

Recreation. Commissioned Officers' Mess; bowling alley; movies; swimming pool; tennis courts; golf (eighteen holes); hunting and fishing; boating and sailing; gym.

Commissary and Exchange. Excellent.

816. MCB, Camp Lejeune, North Carolina 28542

Camp Lejeune is the East Coast base for the ground units of the Fleet Marine Force. It accommodates the Command Element, II MEF, 2d Marine Division; 2d Force Service Support Group; 6th Marine Amphibious Brigade; Naval Hospital, Camp Lejeune; and adjoins Marine Corps Air Station (Helicopter), New River. Its neighboring community is Jacksonville, North Carolina.

Transportation.

Rail. Amtrak connections at Rocky Mount, North Carolina.

Bus. Greyhound and Carolina Trailways provide scheduled service to and from Camp Lejeune bus terminal.

Sheltered amid the pines of North Carolina, MCAS Cherry Point supports most elements of the 2d Marine Aircraft Wing.

Airports. Albert Ellis Airport, Jacksonville, twenty miles from Camp Lejeune, and airports at Wilmington and Kinston, each about forty-five miles distant, are served by scheduled airlines. Connections with major airlines can be made at Raleigh or Charlotte, both in North Carolina.

Highways. U.S. 17 and N.C. 24. U.S. 258 originates at Jacksonville and runs north into Virginia.

Quarters. A DD Form 1746 (application for quarters assignment) should be sent to Director, Family Housing Division, Camp Lejeune, prior to detachment from previous duty station; on reporting, check in with the Base Housing Office. Because mandatory quarters assignment is sometimes necessary, do not arrange for off-base housing until Base Housing gives a green light. Married company officers can anticipate a six- to twelve-month wait, depending on type of requested quarters. There is a minimal waiting period for bachelors. Limited guest or temporary accommodations, if desired, may be provided for officers with their families, but advance reservations with the Director, Unaccompanied Personnel Housing, are mandatory.

Schools. Base schools from kindergarten through high school are open to children of service families residing on federal property. Families not on federal property must rely on county or other local schools. East Carolina University operates a branch and an extension division at Camp Lejeune, and major extension universities offer degree programs at the base. Coastal Carolina Community College at Jacksonville offers courses leading to an associate degree.

Recreation. Commissioned Officers' Mess; four base theaters; hunting; fresh and saltwater fishing; swimming pool; surf bathing; golf (two eighteen-hole courses); boating and sailing.

Commissary and Exchange. Excellent.

817.   Marine Corps Recruit Depot, Parris Island, South Carolina 29905

In the mid-1500s, colonial empires clashed on the shores of Parris Island as Spanish and French explorers sought strategic footholds in the New World. Although more than four hundred years have passed, the military tradition continues to be as vital today as it was then. More than one million recruits have been trained on Parris Island since "boot camp" was established there in 1915. Currently, male recruits from the eastern United States and females from throughout the nation are trained at the place "Where the Difference Begins." The commanding general of Marine Corps Recruit Depot, Parris Island, is also commanding general for the Eastern Recruiting Region.

Transportation.

Rail. The nearest Amtrak station is Yemassee, South Carolina, twenty-eight miles northwest of Parris Island. Amtrak has service to many East Coast destinations.

Bus. Greyhound.

Airports. Savannah (forty-five miles) and Charleston International (sixty-one miles) airports are the nearest.

Highways. From south: Interstate 95 to Exit 8, Route S-88; follow signs to Beaufort via Routes 170 and 278. From north: Interstate 95 to Exit 33; follow signs to Beaufort via U.S. 17N and Route 21. From both directions, follow signs to the Parris Island main gate on Route 802.

Quarters. Bachelor officers quarters, senior officer guest house, and a temporary lodging facility that accommodates individuals and families. Married field grade officer quarters are available on the depot, on a priority basis, and Capehart housing is available at Laurel Bay, a military housing facility about ten miles from Parris Island. Civilian housing is available throughout Beaufort County.

Schools. First- through sixth-grade children attend one of two DoD schools (K–2 and 3–6) at the Laurel Bay housing complex. Seventh through twelfth graders attend Beaufort County Public Schools. Bus transportation is provided for all grades. Private schools are also available. There is a child development center resident on the depot.

Recreation. Commissioned Officers' Mess (Open); senior officer guest house; swimming pool; racquetball; tennis; sailing and boating; golf course; bowling; theater; Rod and Gun Club; skeet; fishing; shrimping; ball fields, gym-

Recruit training at Marine Corps Recruit Depot, Parris Island, continues to bring the best out of marines-to-be.

nasiums; auto, wood, and ceramic hobby shops; fitness center; picnic areas; War Memorial Museum. Variety of activities and resort areas in Beaufort County, including historic Beaufort and Hilton Head Island.

Commissary and Exchange. Excellent with convenient hours.

Neighboring Activities. Marine Corps Air Station, Beaufort, seven miles north and Naval Hospital, Beaufort, three miles from the gate.

818. MCAS, Beaufort, South Carolina 29904

MCAS, Beaufort (pronounced "Bewfort") is a major jet air base capable of supporting two Marine aircraft groups and associated service units. It is close to Parris Island and provides it with military air services.

Transportation.

Rail. Amtrak via Seaboard Coast Line to Yemassee, South Carolina, twenty-six miles northwest, is the most convenient mode to or from northern or southern points.

Bus.   Greyhound.

Airports.   Savannah, Georgia (forty-five miles), and Charleston, South Carolina (sixty-five miles) are the nearest commercial airports.

Highways.   U.S. 17 or Interstate 95, thence by U.S. 21 to Beaufort.

Quarters.   In addition to bachelor officers' quarters, the station has one community of quarters at Laurel Bay, five miles west, with 228 sets of officers' quarters. All quarters are modern two-, three-, or four-bedroom units, air-conditioned. Off-station housing conditions are the same as those described for Parris Island.

Schools.   There are two federal government grade schools (grades K–6) at Laurel Bay, open only to children of families occupying government quarters. The state provides bus transportation for children attending school in Beaufort. A nursery/kindergarten is operated by Special Services for children in government quarters.

Recreation.   Commissioned Officers' Mess; tennis; swimming pool; hobby shop; fishing; hunting; boating; golf (Parris Island); outstanding ocean beaches near at hand.

Commissary and Exchange.   Air station personnel use the Parris Island commissary, but there are two excellent seven-day stores at MCAS, one on the station and the other at Laurel Bay. The small post exchange is excellent.

819.   Marine Corps Logistic Base, Albany, Georgia 31704

The Albany Base is one of the newer posts of the Corps. Its missions, all logistic, include: acquisition, storage, and disposal of materiel; technical direction of Corps stores distribution; procurement, repair/rebuild, storage, and distribution of supplies and equipment. The base has more than 3.8 million square feet of closed storage in nineteen warehouses, and more than 7.7 million square feet of open storage lots.

Transportation.

Rail.   Amtrak has no passenger service for Albany, although the base is served by one of the largest freight rail complexes in the Southeast.

Bus.   Trailways; Greyhound.

Highways.   U.S. 82 and 19.

Quarters.   Modern bachelor officers quarters and married quarters are available in adequate numbers to meet the requirements; most of the MOQ are three-bedroom, while a few have four. There are also on-post guest accommodations.

Schools.   Civilian county system.

Recreation.   Commissioned Officers' Mess; golf (nine holes); swimming pools; tennis; bowling; skeet and pistol ranges; movies; fishing.

Commissary and Exchange.   Excellent, medium-sized.

820.   MCAS, Yuma, Arizona 85369

One of the newest of the Marine Corps air stations, MCAS Yuma has a 13,300-foot main runway, an instrumented range, and some of the finest flying weather to be found.

Marine Corps Logistic Base, Albany, rightly boasts one of the finest drum and bugle corps on the East Coast.

Transportation.
Rail.   Amtrak via Santa Fe at Yuma (seven miles east).
Bus.   Greyhound.
Airport.   Yuma International Airport.
Highways.   Interstate 8; U.S. 95 and 80.
Quarters.   More than 84 sets of officer family quarters and 300 bachelor officers rooms are available, together with thirteen transient accommodations in the Hostess House. Civilian housing is readily available in Yuma. Since 1993, however, the waiting list for government quarters has been as long as six to eight months.

Schools.   The station has a child care center, including preschool. Public and parochial elementary schools, a high school, a junior college, and a college are in Yuma.

Recreation.   Commissioned Officers' Mess; stables (boarding only); swimming pools; auto hobby shop; bowling; tennis; fishing, camping, and boating at Lake Martinez; station-operated recreational area.

Commissary and Exchange.   Modern and adequate.

821.   Marine Corps Air-Ground Combat Center, Twentynine Palms, California 92278

With its 932 square miles of area, twice the size of Los Angeles and big enough to encompass Pendleton, Lejeune, and Quantico with room to spare, MCAGCC is not only the largest post in the Marine Corps but also a primary training and experimental center for Marine artillery and guided missiles. It is also the loca-

This view of the main entrance to MCAS Yuma demonstrates its renowned flying weather.

tion of the Communication-Electronics School and has facilities for the major part of the 7th MEB. The base also includes the Tactical Exercise Evaluation and Control Group, which exercises the combined-arms capabilities and readiness of FMF units in a live-fire environment.

Transportation.

Rail. Amtrak via Southern Pacific (Indio).

Bus. Local bus to Palm Springs, California, for connections with Greyhound.

Airport. Twentynine Palms Airport.

Highway. U.S. 66 to Amboy, thence by county highway to Twentynine Palms.

Quarters. Government married quarters and bachelor officers quarters are available. Temporary lodging is available, depending on exercises.

Schools. The base has a nursery school for children, ages three to six, as well as a child care center. The town of Twentynine Palms has elementary, junior high, and senior high schools, as well as a parochial grade school (through eighth grade). Undergraduate and graduate educational opportunities are available through on-base extension universities.

Recreation. Commissioned Officers' Mess (both Open and Closed); swimming; bowling; skeet; hunting and fishing; tennis; golf (nine holes); hobby shop. The base is almost at the center of the southern California recreation area, and practically any kind of outdoor or indoor recreation is available.

Commissary and Exchange. Excellent.

822. Marine Corps Logistic Base, Barstow, California 92311

The Marine Corps Logistics Base at Barstow is located to take advantage of a confluence of transportation routes and the Mojave Desert's hot, dry climate, which inhibits deterioration of stored material. Barstow supports all Marine organizations west of the Mississippi and in the Far East, operates a central repair shop for all FMF equipment except aircraft, and stores designated items. The ten-acre repair shop at Yermo is the largest building in the Marine Corps and is surrounded by a forty-acre concrete platform.

Transportation.

Rail. Amtrak via Santa Fe.

Bus. Greyhound and Trailways.

Airports. The nearest airport with scheduled service is Ontario, California,

Only a portion of the industrial sprawl of MCLB, Barstow, can be captured in a single photograph.

(eighty miles distant); but McCarran Field, Las Vegas, Nevada, and Los Angeles International Airport are normally used.

Highways. Interstates 15 and 40; California 58.

Quarters. The base has fifty married and eight bachelor officer quarters. Officers on accompanied tours are required to occupy government quarters, but suitable housing is available nearby for cases where off-base housing may have been approved as an exception.

Schools. Public schools are located in the towns of Barstow, Yermo, Daggett, and Hinkley; the high school as well as five parochial schools are in Barstow. Public school buses are provided.

Recreation. Consolidated Officer–Staff Noncommissioned Officer Club; swimming pools; tennis; racquetball; golf (nine holes); equitation; bowling; skeet and fishing. Like Twentynine Palms, Barstow is in the southern California playground area, which offers extensive recreational opportunities.

Commissary and Exchange. Good.

823. Marine Corps Recruit Depot, San Diego, California 92140

The primary mission of MCRD, San Diego, is twofold. First is the recruiting of new Marines from the Western Recruiting Region, which is composed of the 8th, 9th, and 12th Marine Corps Districts. Second is the training of Marine recruits using facilities at San Diego and Camp Pendleton, California. Also located at MCRD is the Recruiters' School and the West Coast Drill Instructors' School. The depot is located in central San Diego on the Pacific Highway.

Depot Headquarters, San Diego, typifies the base's Spanish colonial architecture and atmosphere.

Transportation.

Rail. Amtrak via Santa Fe: Coaster.

Bus. Greyhound; Trailways.

Airport. San Diego International Airport.

Highways. Interstates 5 and 8.

Quarters. Except for five sets for key senior officers, there are no government quarters on the depot and no guest house. Married officers with families are eligible for Navy housing—mainly Capehart—operated by the 11th Naval District under agreement with the depot. Officers with families must report to CO, Navy Public Works Center, San Diego, for an endorsement as to quarters availability prior to accepting private quarters.

Schools. No depot schools, but San Diego has excellent public, private, and parochial primary and secondary schools. Also, there are three major colleges in the city, plus numerous junior colleges.

Recreation. Southern California supplies virtually every type of recreation from swimming to skiing. The Mess is one of the finest and oldest in the Corps.

Commissary and Exchange. There are several Navy commissaries in the San Diego area. MCRD has an outstanding Marine Exchange.

824a. MCB, Camp Pendleton, California 92055

"Pendleton" is the prime amphibious training base in the Corps. It serves as the major West Coast base for ground units of the Fleet Marine Force and provides facilities and support for the 1st Marine Division and the I MEF. Other tenant units include the 1st Force Service Support Group (FSSG), elements of Marine Aircraft Group 39, and the Marine Corps Tactical Systems Support Activity (MCTSSA). Recruits from Marine Corps Recruit Depot, San Diego, spend two weeks at Camp Pendleton's Edson Range and Weapons Field Training Battalion for weapons training; those who go into infantry attend the School of Infantry at Camp San Onofre after graduation from San Diego. Several other formal schools are also conducted at Camp Pendleton.

The Marine Corps' role in Camp Pendleton history dates from 25 September 1942, when the 125,000-acre tract of land was dedicated by President Franklin D. Roosevelt and named in honor of Major General Joseph H. Pendleton. The area where Camp Pendleton is located emerged through Spanish land grants as Rancho Santa Margarity y Las Flores y San Onofre. Custody of these lands was originally held by Mission San Luis Rey de Francia. It passed through the hands of Don Pio and Don Andres Pico in the mid-1800s, and on through several other owners until the federal government purchased a major portion of the rancho for use as a Marine Corps training base during World War II. The ranch house, in which the rancho owners once lived, is now the residence of the base commanding general. Nearby are the historic chapel and bunkhouse (now a museum).

During World War II and the Korean and Vietnam conflicts, Pendleton was the training "funnel" through which the majority of Marine battle replacements passed on their way to combat. Today, the base's 196 square miles of varied terrain provide training areas for thousands of Marines each year, as well as for Reserve and other service personnel.

Transportation.

Rail. Amtrak via Santa Fe, at Oceanside, California, the adjacent civilian community.

Bus. Westwind Express; Greyhound; North County Transit; intrabase.

Airport. Lindbergh Field, San Diego. The Marine Corps Air Facility at Pendleton handles most military traffic.

Highways. U.S. 395; Interstate 5.

Quarters. In addition to limited unaccompanied officers housing, Pendleton has approximately 700 sets of three- and four-bedroom quarters for married officers and more than 160 rooms for bachelors. There are ample transient bachelor accommodations; transient officers with families may stay at the Hostess House, by advance reservation, up to two weeks. Private housing ashore is available in Oceanside, Carlsbad, Vista, Fallbrook, San Clemente, and other, more distant, communities. Before bringing families to Camp Pendleton, it is nevertheless advisable to write to the Base Housing Office for information. This office can update you on the quarters situation and can, if necessary, help in finding civilian housing.

Schools. Educational facilities for Camp Pendleton Marines and their families are excellent. Public, parochial, and some private schools, together with MiraCosta and Palomar community colleges in the immediate area, offer courses for qualified Marines and their families, as do other colleges in the San Diego area. Five elementary schools (one K–8) are located on board the base, and a number of college and high school completion courses are taught on board.

Child Care Centers and Preschools. Six separate facilities provide child care and preschool programs for children of military and civilian workers at Camp Pendleton. Located in five different areas of the base, the centers are open Monday through Friday and offer care on a regular (monthly) and walk-in (hourly) basis. The centers provide cribs and beds, toys, and well-equipped, fenced playgrounds. Enrichment programs are available for all ages. School-aged children may be cared for before and after their school sessions.

Naval Hospital. The Camp Pendleton Naval Hospital, located near Lake O'Neill, is a 600-bed facility that provides outpatient and inpatient care to active duty members and, subject to availability of staff and funds, to authorized family members from all the armed services. Retired persons, their authorized family members, as well as the authorized family members of deceased retirees, are also eligible for care in this facility. Outpatient medical care is also provided to active-duty personnel in twelve branch clinics located throughout the base. An average of 31,000 outpatient visits are recorded monthly, and more than 175 babies are delivered each month at the hospital.

Recreation. The Commissioned Officers' Mess has three convenient locations, one with swimming pool. Surfing beaches, freshwater and deep-sea fishing, skeet and trap, tennis, riding stables, golf (eighteen holes), hunting, additional swimming pools, bowling, track and field, gymnasiums and weight rooms, theaters, sailing, playgrounds, miniature golf, archery, picnic areas, libraries, hobby shops, and recreation instruction and rental equipment are all available. Youth activity programs are numerous.

Commissary and Exchange. A modern commissary is available near the main gate, with an annex in the northern section. Exchanges are modern and complete and are located within each of the major camps.

Family Service Center. The Family Service Center provides counseling and assistance with a range of family problems. Referral to off-base social service agencies is done in many cases. The center also conducts orientation for newly arrived families, and provides hospitality kits for those whose household effects have yet to arrive.

824b. MCAS, Miramar, California 92145

Miramar has become the Marine Corps' largest aviation facility, following its reversion to USMC control in the late 1990s. A former cattle and citrus ranch, it first served Army infantry training in 1914 as Camp Kearny. After World War I, Miramar became an auxiliary field for the Navy and an air base for the Marine Corps. When World War II broke out, Miramar quickly expanded. At the end of the war the Marines moved to El Toro, and Miramar was developed as a master jet station. In 1973 E-2C Hawkeye Squadrons joined the Miramar fighters. "Fightertown" was the center of tactical training for the Tomcat Fighters and Hawkeye Wizards. Highly technical aviation maintenance schools trained men and women to repair and maintain the aircraft. On 1 October 1997, Naval Air Station Miramar reverted to a Marine Corps air station, bringing fighter and helicopter squadrons from El Toro.

Transportation.

Rail. Amtrak Coaster service to coastal neighborhoods.

Airport. Lindbergh Field, San Diego.

Bus. Greyhound; North County Transit local Route 20 express stops at various locations on base; Route 30 express takes you to the north gate.

Highways. Interstate 15; also nearby Interstate 5 and 805.

Quarters. 7284 one-to-five bedroom units are reserved for enlisted personnel. 561 one-to-five bedroom units are reserved for commissioned and warrant officers. Most of the housing areas are located in civilian communities, but there is on-base housing at MCAS Miramar and NAS North Island, reserved for personnel assigned to those installations.

Military housing is under the control of COMNAVBASE San Diego and is scattered throughout the county in thirty-six locations. More units are constantly being added through lease and acquisition of existing structures, as well as expanding through construction. Members must choose a specific property to be placed on the waiting list, and waiting time will be dependent on that property. Average waiting time is six to thirty-six months. A housing referral package is available upon request.

Medical. Active duty persons are seen at sick call on base. Family members are seen by appointment only at the Family Practice Clinic. All specialty care is referred by consult to Balboa Medical Center.

Commissary and Exchange. Large commissary and exchange. There are several Navy commissaries in the San Diego area, and MCRD has a large Marine Corps Exchange.

825. Marine Activities in the Hawaiian Area
     Camp H. M. Smith, Hawaii 96861
     MCAF Kaneohe Bay, Hawaii 96863
     Marine Barracks, Pearl Harbor, Hawaii 96860

The island of Oahu includes several permanent Marine Corps installations with diverse missions. The headquarters (and nerve center) of all Marine Forces Pacific activities is at Camp H. M. Smith, overlooking Pearl Harbor from the site of the World War II Aiea Naval Hospital. In addition to Camp H. M. Smith, there is MCAF, Kaneohe, on the "windward" side of the island, home station of the 3d Marine Regiment and 1st Radio Battalion, and one of three Marine Corps air facilities outside the continental United States; here, both ground and air units of the FMF train and operate as an integrated air-ground team. The Pearl Harbor Marine Barracks performs security missions. Because of its superb site and outstanding facilities, Camp H. M. Smith was chosen by the commander in chief, Pacific, for his headquarters, which is a tenant activity. Camp Smith is thus the only Marine Corps station that also serves as the headquarters of a unified command. Other Marines serve at the Makalapa headquarters of commander in chief, Pacific Fleet.

Quarters. The quarters situation on Oahu has improved somewhat in recent years. Bachelor and transient officers' quarters are available. Married quarters are located six miles from Camp Smith and at Kaneohe. Quarters are also available for officers assigned to the security forces at Pearl Harbor. Up-to-date information concerning waiting time for quarters can be obtained from individual commands.

Schools. In most areas, public and parochial schools of acceptable quality are located on government property or in or near housing areas. Public high schools are also conveniently located but require bus transportation in some cases. Numerous private and parochial schools are to be found on Oahu and are accessible by bus.

Recreation. Oahu and its naval and military installations afford some of the best all-around recreation and liberty in the Marine Corps. In addition to several

MCAF Kaneohe Bay, home of the 3d Marines, lies on the windward side of Oahu.

excellent clubs and messes, the Hawaiian area provides opportunity for virtually every sport or taste.*

Commissary and Exchange.   All services maintain commissaries and exchanges on Oahu, although prices are higher than on the Mainland.

826.   MCB, Camp Smedley D. Butler, Okinawa (FPO AP 96373)

Located at Camp Foster, Headquarters, MCB Camp Butler, is responsible for operation of all Marine facilities on the island (Camps Schwab, Kinser, McTureous, Hansen, Courtney, and Foster, and MCAS, Futenma). Headquarters, III/MEF; 3d Marine Division; 1st Marine Aircraft Wing; and 3d Force Service Support Group are garrisoned at Camp Butler.

Transportation.   Chartered commercial airlift planes use Kadena AFB, while commercial airlines use Naha International Airport. MCAS, Futenma, handles propeller-driven and helicopter military traffic for Marine units on Okinawa; Marine jets deployed to Okinawa operate from Naval Air Facility (NAF), Kadena.

Quarters.   Government quarters are available for dependents of officers assigned to accompanied tours only. Waiting times can vary from eight to twelve months, but comfortable Western-style housing may be obtained in the civilian community. Though off-base rentals are available, some units are old, expensive, and small, and some are lacking in storage space and modern conveniences.

---

*If you are interested in a Hawaii vacation on Waikiki Beach at affordable rates, investigate the Hotel Hale Koa (House of Warriors), a government-built, fifteen-story hotel located at Fort DeRussey and open to armed forces personnel and their families. Reservations are first-come, first-served, with active-duty people having priority.

Recreation. Commissioned Officers' Mess; fishing; aquatic sports; hobby shops; movies; various major sports; AFRTS radio-television; local cultural and recreational activities.

Commissary and Exchange. Excellent exchanges, operated by the Army and Air Force, and a large, well-stocked commissary are available at Camps Kinser and Courtney.

827. MCAS, Iwakuni, Japan (PSC 561, FPO AP 96310)

Iwakuni is the home station of all tactical jet aircraft units of the 1st Marine Aircraft Wing (whose headquarters is at Camp Butler, Okinawa) and of Japanese naval aviation units as well.

Transportation.

Rail. Japan National Railways has outstanding local and high-speed service to all points in Japan except Okinawa.

Air. Semiweekly Military Aircraft Command (MAC) flights handle military traffic directly in and out of Iwakuni. Commercial flights go from Hiroshima Airport (twenty-seven miles distant), with connections for international flights at Tokyo.

Quarters. Besides bachelor officers' quarters, Iwakuni has government quarters for officers on accompanied tours.

Schools. Matthew C. Perry School (K–12) is the only Western-style school available. The station provides school busing for children whose families live off-station. Special Services operates a children's day care and preschool center (ages three through five).

Recreation. Commissioned Officers' Mess; tennis; swimming; flying club; hobby shop; fishing; hunting; golf; local cultural events.

Commissary and Exchange. Excellent.

SMALLER POSTS

828. "From the Dawn to Setting Sun. . . ."

In addition to the large posts just described, the Corps maintains a dozen units of the Marine Corps Security Forces (MCSF) ashore. Formerly made up of Marine Barracks and Detachments, these reformed in 1986 into MCSF companies, monitored by a battalion headquarters. Two of the old barracks have retained their original status. If you should be ordered to any of these posts, write the commanding officer for local information.

829. Posts in the Continental United States

Here, as of 1998, are the most important smaller Marine Corps stateside posts.

California: Expeditionary Warfare Training Group (EWTG), NAB, Coronado; Mountain Warfare Training Center, Bridgeport

Georgia: MCSF Co, Submarine Base, Kings Bay
Maryland: MCSF Co, NAS, Patuxent River
Missouri: Defense Finance and Accounting Service, Kansas City Center
Virginia: MCSF Bn/1st Fleet Antiterrorist Support Team (FAST) Co, Norfolk;
    2d FAST Co, Yorktown; EWTG, NAB, Little Creek
Washington: MCSF Co, Submarine Base, Bangor

830. Overseas Posts

Marines serve in the overseas states and possessions of the United States, as well as in foreign countries (not including the embassy guards), as follows.
Bahrain: MCSF Co, Naval Activities, Bahrain
Cuba: MB, Naval Operating Base (NOB), Guantánamo Bay
Iceland: MCSF Co, Naval Air Station (NAS), Keflavík
Italy: MCSF Co, Naval Activities, Naples
Spain: MCSF Co, Naval Activities, Rota
United Kingdom: MCSF Co, Naval Activities, London

831. Embassy Guards: The Marine Security Guard Battalion

In addition to the foreign posts listed above, the Marine Corps maintains more than 120 State Department security detachments, commanded by NCOs, in most of the capital cities of the world. These detachments are under the immediate supervision of regional company headquarters located at Frankfurt, Casablanca, Manila, Panama City, and Nairobi.

The Marine Corps has no responsibility in which individual quality and outstanding performance are of higher importance than the Marine Security Guard program, which the Corps administers and operates for the Department of State.

Under this program, more than one thousand carefully selected Marines maintain the internal security of the American embassies, legations, missions, and consulates throughout the world. All of these vitally important security posts are under the independent command of staff noncommissioned officers. With the possible exception of recruiting duty and drill instruction at the recruit depots, the Corps has no other program that depends so directly and singly on the loyalty, devotion to duty, military character, self-discipline, and good sense of its noncommissioned officers.

Our flag's unfurl'd to every breeze, from the dawn to setting sun . . .

—"The Marines' Hymn"

9

The Marine Corps Reserve

The Marine Corps Reserve has proved itself repeatedly to be the true backbone of the Marine Corps. The highly motivated, well-trained, and characteristically spirited Marine Corps Reserve assists the active component in maintaining its position as the national force in readiness. The reserve has one fundamental mission: to provide trained units and qualified individuals to be available for active duty in the Marine Corps in time of war or national emergency and at any other time as national security may require.

For decades, the reservist maintained this capability with the stance of the "weekend warrior," drilling monthly on weekends and for two weeks in the summer with his or her unit to maintain the required individual skills and unit capabilities. That routine was judged adequate to provide Reserve forces with the capability to mobilize and prepare for eventual operations at the side of active duty forces. Doctrine generally held that a "grace period" of sixty days would ensue while the reservists could prepare for such operations.

Operations at the end of the twentieth century, however, ushered in an era of increasing dependence on the day-to-day readiness of the reservist and quick reinforcement by the Reserve unit. The expenses of maintaining active-duty forces, their typical worldwide commitments, and the difficulty of providing certain skills all have demanded an unconditional readiness of the Reserve and an increasing willingness to put it into action in situations short of declared war. Thus, today's reservists train with the knowledge that their commitments to operations might be required in mere days versus months.

Two concepts dominate the doctrine for preparing and deploying the Reserve. *Augmentation* brings units and selected individuals to join the active forces as required for operations, national emergency, or war. *Reinforcement* provides depth, replacement, and capabilities not resident in the active forces for operations, national emergency, or war.

901.   History of the Reserve

The Marine Corps Reserve came into being in 1916 with an initial strength of 3 officers and 33 enlisted men, while Major General George Barnett was twelfth commandant. Like many other forward steps during the period, the Reserve was, in fact, the product of the foresight and imagination of Barnett's assistant, Colonel Lejeune, later to become thirteenth commandant. Despite its eventual importance, the Reserve played no significant role in World War I. Indeed, it nearly died on its feet in the early 1920s as a result of fiscal starvation. But for the loyalty and single-mindedness of pioneer reservists of that decade, there might not be a Marine Corps Reserve.

Following enactment by Congress of the Naval Reserve Act of 1925, the Marine Corps Reserve began to come into its own. This legislation for the first time permitted individual training duty with pay, as well as the organization of drilling units in pay status. Training programs were instituted, and units sprang up in 1927. This prosperity was short-lived, however, for the depression years of 1929–33 found the Reserve again without funds. During those lean years, most units continued to drill and train without pay—even buying their own uniforms—and thus again saved the Reserve from oblivion.

It was 1935 before the Reserve was finally able to stand on its own feet. In that golden year, these developments occurred:
1. Appropriations for training an organized and volunteer Marine Corps Reserve (ground and aviation) totaling almost 10,000 officers and enlisted Marines
2. Inauguration of the Platoon Leaders Classes in order to obtain a steady input of well-trained, carefully selected junior Reserve officers from colleges not participating in Army or Navy ROTC
3. Dawn of the Reserve pilot program for Marine Corps aviation—an extra dividend of the Naval Aviation Cadet Act of 1935

In 1938, the 1925 Naval Reserve Act was brought up to date by Congress in many aspects—perhaps the most important being the provision, for the first time, of a charter of rights and benefits for the Reserve. Among these milestones were: hospitalization; death and disability benefits; equitable promotion; retirement with pay for active service; and the right to participate in formation of Reserve policy. Under the National Reserve Act of 1938, the Marine Corps Reserve has twice accomplished its job of providing a trained force in readiness.

The solid success of the peacetime Reserve was amply attested in 1939, when individual reservists were brought to active duty after President Roosevelt's proclamation of limited national emergency in September of that year, and a year later, in 1940, when mobilization of the remainder of the Reserve brought 15,138 additional Marines to the Colors. The extent to which the Reserve had hewn its place in the Corps was proved, in 1945, by the fact that, of 471,000 Marines, the largest number in the Corps' 170-year history, approximately 70 percent were reservists.

Much of the Reserve's effectiveness throughout World War II stemmed from the philosophy behind its mobilization, a philosophy that today is stronger than ever. Although the 1940 Reserve was built around thirty-six hometown battalions and squadrons, each with its distinctive temper, local associations, and comradeship, Major General Holcomb, then commandant, took the position that no Marine, regular or reservist, should, while on active duty, claim any home but the Corps. Thus, as Reserve units reached mobilization points, they disbanded and their members simply became individual Marines headed for service in the expanding regular formations of the Fleet Marine Force. To drive home the import of this decision and to emphasize that every man privileged to wear the Globe and Anchor was a Marine, no more and no less, General Holcomb decreed that, except where required by law for administrative purposes, the word, "Reserve" and its corresponding abbreviation, "R," following the "USMC," would not be used. All hands, reserve and regular, were Marines.

Following World War II, the postwar buildup of its Reserves was one of the great achievements of the Corps. Through good leadership (regular and reserve), through willingness to invest capable personnel in the Reserve program, and because of the unflagging loyalty of Marine alumni—*"Who ever saw a sorehead ex-Marine?"* asked a prominent journalist—the Reserve was in unmatched readiness to back up the attenuated regular Corps when the Korean War flamed up.

In the field in Korea, as in Pacific battles before then, it was literally impossible to distinguish reservist from regular. Once again, as always, all hands were Marines. Among those who had originally started as reservists, however, it is worth noting that, in World War II and Korea, fifty-seven won Medals of Honor.

Soon after the end of the Korean War, Congress passed legislation (the Reserve Forces Act of 1955) that continues to exercise a profound effect on the reserve components of all the armed forces, including the Marine Corps. This law provided for the so-called Special Enlistment Program whereby young men, after receiving not less than twelve weeks of hard training with and by regular forces, enter the Ready Reserve for a prescribed period of years of obligated service. The Reserve was reorganized on 1 July 1962, to provide a distinct unit mobilization structure, embodied in the 4th Marine Division, 4th Marine Aircraft Wing, and 4th Force Service Support Group. These were to be mobilized and employed as units; however, the Ready Reserve still maintains additional units whose function is to provide trained individual Marines for fleshing out regular and Reserve units.

When U.S. forces deployed to the Arabian Peninsula and its seas during 1990–91 for the liberation of Kuwait from Iraqi occupation, Marine Corps forces moved in the vanguard. As the conflict deepened and the eventual campaign took shape, some 30,000 Marine reservists deployed to augment and reinforce the FMF and to operate the bases nearly vacated in the United States.

Today, the Department of Defense "Total Force Policy" integrates active, Reserve, and National Guard forces into all military planning, especially major campaigns requiring more than the forward-deployed segment of the active forces. The Marine Corps Reserve Establishment reflected this sea-change by creating the Commanding General, Marine Reserve Forces, to command its various components under the direction of the CMC.

ORGANIZATION AND COMPOSITION

902. Organization of the Marine Corps Reserve

The Marine Corps Reserve today is organized and maintained under the Armed Forces Reserve Act of 1952, which superseded the 1938 Naval Reserve Act. This law incorporated the basic principles of its predecessor but modernized the Reserve. (This and other laws bearing on the Reserve have been codified under Title 10, U.S. Code.)

Because the Reserve is a component of the Marine Corps as a whole, command and administration of the Reserve stem directly from the commandant. Thus the department and offices of Marine Corps Headquarters bear the same relationships and responsibilities toward the Reserve as they do toward the remainder of the Corps.

903. Reserve Branch, HQMC

The Reserve Branch, Manpower Department, Headquarters Marine Corps, serves to monitor the current operations and budget actions of the Reserve Establishment for the commandant. The headquarters staff no longer enters directly into the chain of command of the Reserve forces.

904. Marine Corps Reserve Forces

Commanding General, Marine Corps Reserve Forces, exercises command under the commandant of the components of the Reserve Establishment under the "total force concept." With headquarters and staff located at New Orleans, Louisiana, the commanding general exercises command over the 4th Marine Division, 4th Marine Aircraft Wing, 4th Service Support Group, 2d and 3d MEB, and the individual Ready Reserve (see Figure 9–1).

905. Marine Corps Reserve Units

To a greater extent than many Marines realize, the Corps entrusts its readiness to the units of the Selected Reserve. They are the backbone of the Reserve and constitute the mobilization backbone of the Corps.

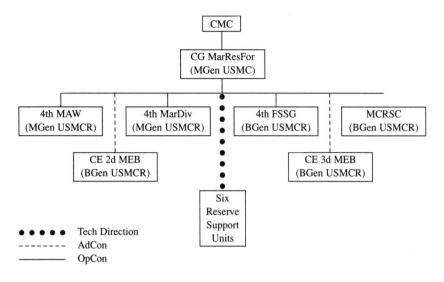

Figure 9–1: Organization of the Marine Corps Reserve (1994)

Leaving out the mobilization training units (discussed below), organized units of the Marine Corps Reserve are formed almost entirely from Class II reservists (see Section 906). Both ground and aviation units are mainly organized at or below the battalion/squadron level. Units parallel prototype units in the FMF. Thus, in the ground portion of the Selected Reserve, you will find infantry, artillery, tank, amphibian tractor, engineer, air and naval gunfire liaison (ANGLICO), and signal units—the preponderance, of course, being infantry. Reserve aviation likewise follows the FMF pattern and includes, in various cities, most of the principal operating units of a Marine aircraft wing—fighter-attack squadrons, transport squadrons, helicopter squadrons, and wing headquarters and service units as well.

Because Selected Reserve units follow the Fleet Marine Force pattern, the administration and functions of these units are carried on in the same way as in similar units in the regular establishment.

Selected ground units are commanded by Reserve officers who have been selected for their professional experience and background. Like all commanding officers, they must administer, train, and maintain the readiness of their commands. In addition, however, they must stimulate and promote whatever recruiting is needed to keep their units up to strength. Reserve commanding officers usually serve for a two-year tour, which may be extended to three or more years under certain circumstances. This gives them adequate experience in command and, at the same time, ensures the advantages of healthy rotation.

Aviation units, like ground units, are commanded by Reserve officers whose responsibilities are much like those of ground unit COs in the Ready Reserve.

Because of the large amount of technical training, the paramount requirement for safe flight operations, and the quantities of expensive materiel (including airplanes) required by an aviation reserve unit, the inspection-instruction organization for Reserve aviation outfits differs somewhat from that used with ground units.

At the home station of each Reserve aviation unit, a parent Marine Air Reserve Training Detachment is located. This detachment is commanded by a regular Marine Corps aviator and includes assistant instructors and maintenance crews to support the Reserve squadron. The Reserve unit's commanding officer comes under command of the CO of the Reserve training detachment, or MARTD.

Staff groups permit drill pay and Organized Reserve status for more senior Reserve officers for whom mobilization requirements exist but who cannot train with other Organized Reserve units. Staff Groups attend paid drills and annual field training.

Mobilization training units (MTUs) are not part of the Selected Reserve but afford training in staff and command functions, ground and air, for Reserve officers and enlisted men and women ordinarily not associated with a unit, who want to stay with the Corps, keep up professional training, and amass credits for Reserve retirement.

A mobilization training unit may be made up of six or more members (officer or enlisted) of any military specialty or combination of specialties. Most MTUs train under a specified syllabus provided by Marine Corps Combat Development Command (MCCDC), but some specialize in given fields when all members hold the same or related military occupational specialties. Each MTU is assigned an adviser, usually the nearest inspector-instructor (see Section 907) or commanding officer, MARTD.

If you are a member of the Reserve but not affiliated with a unit, or if you live in a locality without a local unit, the district director's office can help you maintain contact with the Corps. If you wish to join the Reserve but have no hometown unit, your district director can help you in this, too.

Marine Reserve affairs outside the United States are administered by the Reserve Branch, Manpower Department, HQMC.

906. Composition of the Reserve

The Marine Corps Reserve includes individual classes for mobilization planning and assignment that vary according to the preferences and background of the reservist. Thus the Reserve affords various opportunities for activity, which can usually be adjusted to the desires of anyone qualified to be a Marine.

Fleet Marine Corps Reserve (Class I). Usually short-titled "the Fleet Reserve," Class I is composed entirely of former regular enlisted Marines who enter this status under various laws which, in general, allow transfer to the Fleet Reserve after twenty years' service as a regular. Thus the Fleet Reserve provides a backlog of experienced enlisted Marines who may be employed without further training if the bell rings for full mobilization. Fleet reservists remain in Class I (which in peacetime amounts practically, if not legally, to semiretirement on retainer pay) until they complete thirty years' combined regular and Reserve service. Then they are eligible for retirement.

Selected Marine Corps Reserve (Class II). The Selected Reserve comprises over thirty thousand officer and enlisted members of organized units that can be immediately assimilated into the FMF. For this reason, Selected Reservists must measure up to physical and professional standards comparable to those required of regulars. Today, the majority of the men and women in the Reserve are young, intelligent, highly motivated six-month trainees with a six-year military obligation; the balance are prior-service noncommissioned officers who provide the necessary hard-skill experience and seasoned leadership. Members of the Selected Reserve attend semimonthly or monthly drills, go to camp for annual training with their unit, and get paid for the drills and training they perform. If you wish to become a Class II reservist (over and above required individual standards), you must be able to attend the regular drills of your unit or its home station. This does not ordinarily present too serious a problem, however, since more than two hundred U.S. cities and towns boast organized units of the Marine Corps Reserve.

Individual Ready Reserve (Class III). Class III, effectively speaking, includes all physically qualified Marine reservists not assigned to Classes I and II. The mission of the IRR is to provide the Marine Corps with personnel for complete mobilization in time of war or emergency.

This means that the Individual Ready Reserve largely falls into two categories: reservists who cannot take part in a unit and people with specialist qualifications who do not need or desire the unit training and group participation that Class II entails.

The Individual Ready Reserve gives an opportunity for Marine Corps membership to many men and women whose personal commitments might otherwise preclude this, and the Reserve program includes voluntary training opportunities designed to suit almost any combination of individual convenience or specialization that may apply to you.

Limited Assignment (Overage) Category. Some Reserve officers have special qualifications that are of value to the Marine Corps regardless of their age in grade. When such officers become over age for their rank, they may be transferred to the limited assignment category and thus be retained for special mobilization assignments.

NOTE: Current law authorizes the president, without a prior declaration of war or a national emergency, to order not more than 200,000 members of the Selected Reserve (of all of the branches of our armed forces) to active duty for not more than ninety days for purposes other than training.

RESERVE TRAINING

907. The Inspector-Instructor

To ensure that the Reserve has the benefit of coordinated and professional up-to-date training, advisory personnel from the regular Marine Corps are detailed to duty with the Reserve.

Each Selected Marine Corps Reserve (SMCR) ground unit has a regular Marine officer (with a small staff) whose title is *Inspector-Instructor* (I&I). This title describes the job exactly. The I&I must, as instructor, provide training assistance and general guidance to the unit. As inspector, however, he or she must make certain that the unit is up to the standards set by Marine Corps Headquarters. Inspector-instructors are under the direct command of the respective commanding generals of the 4th Division (ground I&Is) and 4th Wing (aviation). As seen in Section 905, functions comparable to those of the I&I are performed for aviation reserve units by the CO, air reserve training detachment.

The I&I's job (and for that matter, *any* duty in connection with the Reserve) calls for grade-A–certified leadership, imagination, and tact. Responsibilities are heavy (much heavier than they look on paper). Authority is slight. Nevertheless, the job presents great challenges and can give you corresponding rewards. In most cases, the I&I alone represents the active Marine Corps in the community. By your conduct, example, and loyalty to the ideals of the Corps, your fellow townsmen form their impression of the whole Marine Corps.

908. Training Opportunities in the Reserve

Every Selected Reserve unit has to complete a carefully worked out annual training cycle. In addition to this unit training program, you, as an individual reservist, may avail yourself of a wide selection of courses, volunteer periods of training duty, and gratis home study courses (both Marine Corps Schools Extension Courses and Marine Corps Institute—see Section 1510). Reserve training affords something for every individual's interests and opportunities.

Selected Reserve Training.   Training of the average SMCR unit consists of twelve paid weekend drill or flying periods, and two weeks' annual active-duty training.

Reserve training is as meaningful as human effort can make it. It involves realistic field training, including overnight problems. The amount of air-ground and combined arms training is considerable, with two or more neighboring units joining in weekend exercises. Selected Reserve artillery units (generally located near Army or Marine Corps bases with range facilities) conduct live firing throughout the year.

The hometown Selected Reserve training cycle culminates annually in two weeks' training by the unit at a Marine Corps station. It follows a cycle to include desert, mountain, jungle, amphibious, air-ground, combined arms, and specialist training. When possible, the Marine Corps arranges the movement of

The Marine reservist receives equipment and essential training identical to that operated by active Marine Corps Forces.

Selected Reserve outfits to and from annual training by military airlift or in amphibious shipping. This increases the adaptability, professional know-how, and experience of the unit concerned.

As a member of the Selected Reserve, you receive drill pay for each drill you attend, as well as for summer camp, and this pay can provide a welcome augmentation for your income.

Individual Ready Reserve Training. If you are in the Individual Ready Reserve, you do not have to attend drills but may be required to perform training duty not exceeding fifteen days a year. (Enlisted personnel in certain categories must perform thirty days' active duty annually.) Many opportunities are open to you to train with Ready Reserve units or mobilization training units on your own initiative, with or without pay. If you aim to maintain your professional proficiency and to accrue credits for reserve retirement with pay (see Section 911), you can keep up to date by periodic spells of training duty and through MCCDC Extension School correspondence courses. A typical training cycle for an Individual Ready Reservist might include: completion of an Extension School course; a two-week Reserve summer staff course at Quantico; and perhaps a few days' training duty without pay at a Fleet Marine Force post to brush up in a specialty. If you keep professionally up to date, you may have the opportunity of performing training duty as an umpire during a large maneuver, where qualified Reserve officers often serve in this capacity.

MISCELLANEOUS

909. Transfer into the Marine Corps Reserve

The Armed Forces Reserve Act permits certain members of reserve components of the armed forces to transfer from one service to another. Thus, if you are a member of another reserve component and desire to complete your obligated military service in the Marine Corps Reserve, it may be possible for you to do so.

Generally speaking, if you are not on active duty but do have a period of obligated service in your Reserve component, you may be discharged (or resign, if a Reserve officer) to accept an appointment in the Marine Corps Reserve. The Marine Corps Reserve Division can advise you on your eligibility for transfer and can assist you in the administrative paperwork.

910. Privileges and Perquisites of the Marine Reservist

A Marine recruiting poster alleged to date from Revolutionary War days tells the privileges and perquisites of the Marine of 1776:

> You will receive SEVENTEEN DOLLARS BOUNTY, And on your arrival at Head Quarters, be comfortably and genteelly clothed—And spirited young boys of a promising Appearance, who are Five Feet Six Inches high, WILL RECEIVE TEN DOLLARS, and equal advantages of PROVISIONS and CLOTHING with the Men. In fact, the Advantages which the MARINE possesses, are too numerous to mention here, but among the many, it may not be too amiss to state—That if he has a WIFE or aged PARENT, he can make them an Allotment of half his PAY; which will be regularly paid without any trouble to them, or to whomsoever he may direct; that being well Clothed and Fed on Board Ship, the Remainder of his PAY and PRIZE MONEY will be clear in Reserve, for the Relief of his Family or his own private Purposes. The Single Young Man, on his Return to Port, finds himself enabled to cut a Dash on Shore with his GIRL and his GLASS, that might be envied by a Nobleman. . . .

Times have changed somewhat.

Today, the preeminent privilege that you gain as a member of the Marine Corps Reserve is the right to wear the Globe and Anchor and call yourself a Marine. But you do have other substantial privileges and perquisites, which are summarized below.

Pay, a short but important word, is certainly a perquisite of the reservist. For each regular drill or equivalent, you draw one day's pay, according to rank. This also applies to all active or training duty, unless you elect to perform these in nonpay status.

Uniforms worn by reservists are, of course, regular Marine Corps uniforms. They are worn, or may be prescribed, during and when going to and from drills and instruction, and on other appropriate occasions, such as military ceremonies, military dinners or dances, and the like.

As a Reserve officer, you purchase your own uniforms but receive an initial allowance when you first report for active duty.

Every Reserve officer must possess a required kit but may, in addition, buy other uniforms, such as blues, whites, and evening dress, if one desires them and can find proper occasions to wear them. Marine Corps Headquarters publishes, from time to time, lists of uniforms that Reserve officers must have.

It goes without saying that the right to wear Marine Corps uniforms is a privilege, which members of the Reserve have always treasured. While you wear that uniform, you are accountable to every high standard of the Corps and its discipline.

Clubs and messes extend a hearty welcome to the Marine Corps Reserve officer, whether active or inactive. Thus you will always find a friendly greeting (and, likely as not, old comrades) in the open mess at the Marine Corps or Navy station nearest your home.

Exchange and commissary privileges: On drill days, reservists enjoy unlimited exchange privileges. Commissary privileges are available on a limited basis for those on duty less than seventy-two hours. If your period of duty exceeds seventy-two hours, you rate the same exchange and commissary privileges as an active-duty Marine.

Promotion opportunities afford reservists the chance to enhance prestige and responsibility and, of course, to be eligible for increased retirement pay. (For information on Reserve retirement, see Section 911 below.)

Decorations and medals are awarded to Marine reservists as to all other Marines—strictly as earned. They are worn on the uniform, or, on certain occasions, with civilian clothes, in the same way as by regulars (see *Marine Corps Uniform Regulations*).

The Marine Corps Association, which publishes the professional magazine of the Corps, the *Marine Corps Gazette,* is open to membership by officers and enlisted men of the Reserve. So also is the U.S. Naval Institute, which publishes the *United States Naval Institute Proceedings,* professional journal of the naval services.

Government insurance benefits: Marine reservists may qualify for Serviceman's Group Life Insurance (SGLI), Veteran's Group Life Insurance (VGLI), and, for those completing twenty years of satisfactory federal service for entitlement to retired pay, the Reserve Component Survivor Benefit Plan (RCSBP).

Employment protection: The Universal Military Training and Service Act (P.L. 632, 86th Congress), as amended, protects reservists against loss of seniority, status, pay, and vacation while they are away from their jobs on Reserve training duty. Also, if you should unfortunately become disabled while training and can no longer perform the duties of your civilian job, you are entitled to reemployment on other jobs whose duties you may be able to perform. If you are hospitalized incident to training duty, you may delay reemployment application for a period up to one year. On the other hand, the law requires that you request leave of absence from your employer before going on training duty and that you must report back to work immediately on completion of training.

In addition to the foregoing, federal employees, if in the Reserve, rate up to fifteen days' extra leave with pay per year to cover periods spent on training duty and are protected by law against "loss of time, pay or efficiency rating" while availing themselves of this additional leave for training. Government-employee reservists ordered to active duty must, by law, be restored to the job they held before being called up.

911. Reserve Retirement

Retirement, both honorary (without pay, that is) and with pay, can be earned by members of the Marine Corps Reserve. In general, leaving out the Fleet Reserve, the fundamental prerequisite for Reserve retirement with pay is twenty or more years' active service (not necessarily consecutive), or twenty years' "satisfactory federal service," not all of which need be active.

Although Reserve retirement may be effected under various provisions of law, the principal one affecting most reservists is a section of Public Law 810, 80th Congress, which makes retirement pay available to all Marine reservists who accumulate sufficient "retirement points" (credit points earned by service and training). The number of retirement points you chalk up also determines the amount of retired pay you earn.

Here is a brief description of this retirement system.

To qualify for Reserve retirement, you must earn at least fifty points a year for a minimum of twenty years, but these years need not be consecutive.

You must earn at least fifty points a year in order to have that year count toward Reserve retirement. The amount of retired pay you get is determined by the total number of points you accumulate. The number of points you earn depends largely on the amount of effort put into training, home study courses, and other kinds of equivalent instruction: the more you give as a reservist, the more you get.

After you have met all the requirements, you become eligible for Reserve retirement pay the first month after your sixtieth birthday.

Your retirement pay is computed as follows: Divide by 360 the sum of *all* points earned. Then multiply the result by 2½ percent. Then multiply this result by the combined annual base pay and longevity pay you would get if on active duty in the highest grade, permanent or temporary, satisfactorily held by you during your twenty years' service. The answer is the annual Reserve retired pay you will be eligible to receive on attaining the age of sixty.

In addition to all the foregoing, physical disability retirement rules that govern regular Marines extend with equal force to reservists who incur service-connected disabilities.*

---

*Reservists retired *with pay* are eligible to use armed forces medical facilities on a space-available basis and to participate in civilian outpatient care provided for retired personnel.

912. Additional Information on Reserve Matters

The Marine Corps Reserve can supply more detailed information on the Reserve, not only to Marines, but to potential reservists and friends. The Division is always glad to answer individual queries and to assist reservists in solving professional problems. However, before you write Marine Corps Headquarters, look under "United States Government" in your telephone directory, and see if there is a local Marine Corps activity, either regular or reserve. Your local Marine officer—whether inspector-instructor, recruiter, NROTC instructor, or district director—will always be ready to help you find out what you want to know.

In its outstanding service to our Corps, the Marine Corps Reserve has earned the right to be called our "Secret Weapon."

—General L. C. Shepherd, Jr.

10

Service Afloat

Sea duty, dating from the Athenian fleets of the fifth century B.C. and carrying on through Roman times when separate legions of *milites classiarii* ("soldiers of the fleet") were assigned to duty afloat, is the oldest and original duty of marines. In the seventeenth century, when the British and Dutch organized the first modern corps of marines, it was for duty as ships' detachments, and it was for this same purpose that U.S. Marines were first employed. The anchor in our Marine Corps emblem today symbolizes that the Marine is first and foremost a maritime soldier whose natural medium is the sea.

Since World War II and the Korean War, and even more today, the great permanent expansion of the Marine Corps has unfortunately been accompanied by a corresponding reduction in the number of Navy ships carrying Marine detachments, with the result that sea duty is a much rarer tour for the young Marine officer than in the past. Thus when you receive orders to report on board the USS *Tuscarora* for duty, you are not only embarking upon a tour that previous experience has little prepared you for, but you may not even be able to turn for advice to a contemporary in your outfit. Nonetheless, sea duty is one of the most rewarding tours that can come your way. It is an opportunity and a professional privilege.

1001. Fleet Security Force Training and Indoctrination

Because the Navy forms its opinions to a large extent from the direct observation of the Marine Corps, and because Fleet Security detachments represent the Corps "in every clime and place," officers and enlisted personnel assigned to the Marine Corps Security Force Battalion must be carefully selected and prepared. Marines are first trained by the Marine Corps Fleet Security Force Training Company, Chesapeake, Virginia. They are then assigned either to a permanent station or one of the Fleet Antiterrorist Security Team companies (1st FAST Company, Norfolk, Virginia, and 2d FAST Company, Yorktown, Virginia) for direct support assignments afloat and ashore worldwide.

Sea duty remains the oldest and original duty of U.S. Marines. Seagoing Marines have played traditional roles as prize crews, landing parties, and gunners throughout U.S. history.

By way of background and reference reading, you should be familiar with Marine Corps Orders on assignment criteria for security forces and on the personnel reliability program. The nominal cost of a current *Bluejacket's Manual* (U.S. Naval Institute, Annapolis) and *Watch Officer's Guide* (U..S. Naval Institute) will be repaid many times. In addition, obtain a copy of the Marine Corps Educational Center's pamphlet ECP 1-17, *Service Afloat*, as well as of Admiral Mack's invaluable *Naval Ceremonies, Customs, and Traditions* (U.S. Naval Institute). If you have a file of *Marine Corps Gazette* handy, turn to the September 1961 issue for an excellent article on sea duty by Major W. M. Cryan and, much earlier, to June 1927 for a similar article—essentially still valid and containing much excellent advice—by Captain L. C. Shepherd, Jr.

THE SHIP AND SHIPBOARD LIFE

The words Marine and Mariner differ by one small letter only;
but no two races of men, I had well nigh said no two animals,
differ from one another more completely.

—Captain Basil Hall, RN, 1832

1002.   Reporting Aboard

Your orders, in case of sea duty, will direct you to report to a ship for duty and, in peacetime, will ordinarily state the port in which you are to report. When this is impossible for security reasons, you will be directed to report to some shore command, such as a naval base, a naval shipyard, or a naval district. This headquarters will further direct you where and when to join your ship. Arrive in the specified port at least as early as the night before you are expected to report.

Ships in port periodically send boats to the regular fleet landings. Plan to have your baggage and yourself at the landing by 0730. Better still, if you know your ship is in port, go to the landing and take the next boat; that way you will run no risk of missing ship.

As you reach the top of the gangway or accommodation ladder, come to a halt, fact aft, and salute the Colors. Then face and salute the officer of the deck (OOD), saying, "I request permission to come aboard, sir. I am Lieutenant Holcomb reporting aboard for duty."

The OOD will return your salute, probably shake hands and welcome you aboard, and then ask for a copy of your orders for the log. The OOD's messenger or a side boy will escort you below to the ship's executive officer. You will find the other activities to which you must report much more conveniently located than ashore.

Within forty-eight hours, make a reporting call on the captain in his cabin; the executive officer will arrange the time, if you ask. Ascertain that the captain is in. Give the captain's orderly your card and ask the orderly to report to the captain, "Lieutenant Holcomb would like to pay his respects to the captain." The uniform will be prescribed by the executive officer. Remove your cap before entering the cabin. Be alert for the captain's dismissal; the call will usually last not longer than ten minutes. (If your ship is in home waters, the captain may desire that you call on him ashore at home rather than in his cabin.)

After reporting to the executive officer, next report to the department head, who knows the ropes and will advise you as to subsequent moves. They will ordinarily follow in this sequence:

- Report to the first lieutenant, the "housekeeper" of the ship, who assigns the rooms. You will mess in the wardroom.
- Report next to the mess treasurer and pay your mess entrance fee (known as "the mess share," see Section 2210).

1003. Ship's Organization

One of your first tasks should be to study the ship's organization. Each ship prepares its own organization book, but all ships have certain essentials in common (see Figure 10–1).

The captain of a naval vessel, the senior line officer assigned to the ship's company, has full command and responsibility for the ship, and exercises authority and precedence over all persons serving in the ship. Also, the captain is charged with the supervision of all persons temporarily embarked in the ship. The captain's authority, responsibility, and duties are described in *Navy Regulations,* which every officer going to sea should study.

The executive officer is the executive arm of the commanding officer. As such, he or she is the captain's direct representative and is responsible for the prompt and efficient execution of orders. The executive officer works through the heads of departments, who assist the executive officer in organization, administration, operation, and fighting the ship. In addition to these general responsibilities, the "exec" directly oversees such administrative functions as morale, welfare, berthing, training, personnel administration, religious, and legal matters.

Under the executive officer, the tasks of the ship are divided among the departments and activities and then further subdivided into divisions.

1004. Ship's Regulations

Usually in one binder with the Ship's Organization, Ship's Regulations (which are the captain's standing orders to all hands) contain indispensable information

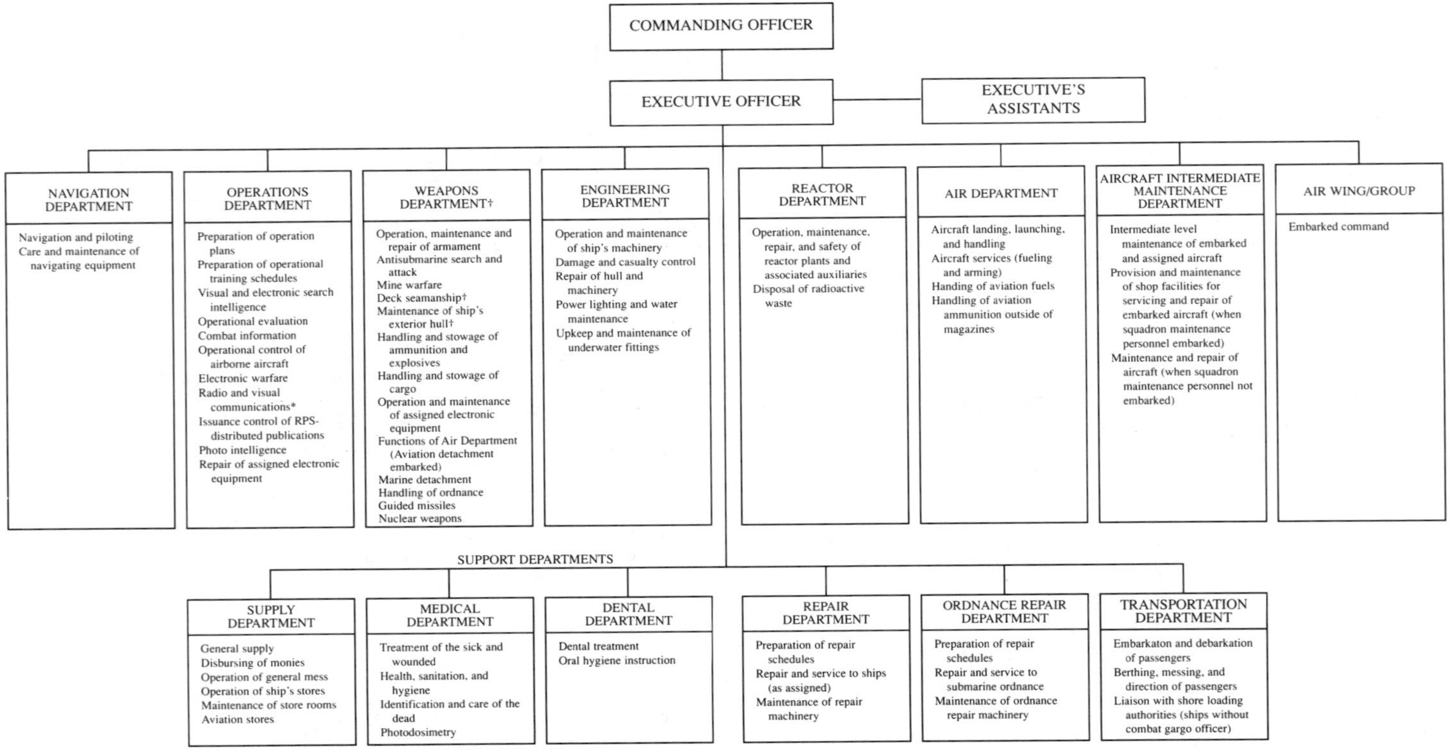

COMMANDING OFFICER

EXECUTIVE OFFICER

EXECUTIVE'S ASSISTANTS

NAVIGATION DEPARTMENT
Navigation and piloting
Care and maintenance of navigating equipment

OPERATIONS DEPARTMENT
Preparation of operation plans
Preparation of operational training schedules
Visual and electronic search intelligence
Operational evaluation
Combat information
Operational control of airborne aircraft
Electronic warfare
Radio and visual communications*
Issuance control of RPS-distributed publications
Photo intelligence
Repair of assigned electronic equipment

WEAPONS DEPARTMENT†
Operation, maintenance and repair of armament
Antisubmarine search and attack
Mine warfare
Deck seamanship†
Maintenance of ship's exterior hull†
Handling and stowage of ammunition and explosives
Handling and stowage of cargo
Operation and maintenance of assigned electronic equipment
Functions of Air Department (Aviation detachment embarked)
Marine detachment
Handling of ordnance
Guided missiles
Nuclear weapons

ENGINEERING DEPARTMENT
Operation and maintenance of ship's machinery
Damage and casualty control
Repair of hull and machinery
Power lighting and water maintenance
Upkeep and maintenance of underwater fittings

REACTOR DEPARTMENT
Operation, maintenance, repair, and safety of reactor plants and associated auxiliaries
Disposal of radioactive waste

AIR DEPARTMENT
Aircraft landing, launching, and handling
Aircraft services (fueling and arming)
Handling of aviation fuels
Handling of aviation ammunition outside of magazines

AIRCRAFT INTERMEDIATE MAINTENANCE DEPARTMENT
Intermediate level maintenance of embarked and assigned aircraft
Provision and maintenance of shop facilities for servicing and repair of embarked aircraft (when squadron maintenance personnel embarked)
Maintenance and repair of aircraft (when squadron maintenance personnel not embarked)

AIR WING/GROUP
Embarked command

SUPPORT DEPARTMENTS

SUPPLY DEPARTMENT
General supply
Disbursing of monies
Operation of general mess
Operation of ship's stores
Maintenance of store rooms
Aviation stores

MEDICAL DEPARTMENT
Treatment of the sick and wounded
Health, sanitation, and hygiene
Identification and care of the dead
Photodosimetry

DENTAL DEPARTMENT
Dental treatment
Oral hygiene instruction

REPAIR DEPARTMENT
Preparation of repair schedules
Repair and service to ships (as assigned)
Maintenance of repair machinery

ORDNANCE REPAIR DEPARTMENT
Preparation of repair schedules
Repair and service to submarine ordnance
Maintenance of ordnance repair machinery

TRANSPORTATION DEPARTMENT
Embarkation and debarkation of passengers
Berthing, messing, and direction of passengers
Liaison with shore loading authorities (ships without combat cargo officer)

*In some ships, there is a separate communication department.
†In carriers, battleships, and cruisers, there are both weapons and deck departments.

Figure 10–1: Typical organization of a large ship

as to the administration of the ship and of the department and division to which you are assigned. The ship's secretary or the aide to the executive officer will issue them. Study them carefully; these regulations will answer many questions and save much embarrassment.

Study the ship's plans, a copy of which can be borrowed from the first lieutenant. Supplement them by a tour of the ship. If no guide is provided for such a tour by new officers, ask your roommate or some friendly officer to show you around. Visit the bridge, forecastle, combat information center, crew's quarters, galley, central station, plotting rooms, all directors, one mount or turret in each battery, handling rooms, ship control stations, one engine room, and one fireroom.

The Plan of the Day is an important document, issued daily by the executive officer, giving the next day's schedule of routine work or operations and any variations or unusual additions. The Plan of the Day promulgates the orders of the day, drills and training, duty and liberty sections, working parties, and movies or recreational events.

The Boat Schedule is promulgated when in port and not lying alongside a dock or pier. Obtain a copy and keep it with you, especially when going ashore.

1005. The Quarterdeck

The quarterdeck is a portion of the ship's main deck (or occasionally a prescribed area on another deck) set aside by the captain for official and ceremonial functions. Certain parts of the quarterdeck (usually the starboard side) are reserved for the captain or for an admiral if embarked. The remainder is reserved for the ship's officers. The detachment parade of the Marines is either on or immediately adjoining the quarterdeck. The rules, traditions, and etiquette of the quarterdeck are among the most venerable in the service, and their strict observance by all hands is the mark of good sea manners.

Never appear on the quarterdeck unless in the uniform of the day, except when crossing to enter or leave a boat, or when otherwise required by duty.

Do not be seen on the quarterdeck with hands in pockets or uncovered, and do not remain on the quarterdeck for any length of time if in civilian clothes.

Salute the quarterdeck every time you come on board.

Do not smoke on the quarterdeck until after Evening Colors.

Do not skylark or engage in recreational sports on the quarterdeck unless specifically so authorized by the captain, and then, of course, only after working hours.

Remain clear of those portions of the quarterdeck reserved for captain or admiral.

1006. The Wardroom

The wardroom is your home—and your club. Here you meet and get to know your fellow officers; it's up to you to make them shipmates.

In Navy messes, tradition is important and seniority is well recognized. The executive officer sits at the head of the senior table; other officers are seated down the table in strict order of seniority, and on down the other junior tables to the last, which is called "the Fourth Ward." On aircraft carriers, the hundreds of embarked officers are messed in shifts in cafeteria fashion.

Unless you are on duty under arms, remove your cap when entering the mess. Never unsheathe your sword in a mess (see Section 2210). Save your quarrels for elsewhere.

This does not mean that the silence of a library need be maintained. A noisy mess is often the sign of a happy mess. Between meals, you gather in the wardroom for a moment of relaxation, discussion of problems, a game of acey-deucey or cribbage, or a quiet cup of coffee. It is also often a place for fun, on a Mess Night, when spouses and dates are entertained, or on the occasion of a ship's party. It can be all these things, or it can be just a place to eat. It depends upon you and upon the other members of the mess.

Officers' messes (see Sections 2208–2211) are organized as business concerns, with a mess fund to which you contribute your share on joining. Monthly assessments are made, from which costs of food, periodicals, decorations, and other essentials and conveniences are paid. This fund is administered by a mess treasurer. In addition, on board some ships a junior officer—it could be you—is designated as "mess caterer" and put in charge of menu planning, detailed supervision of meal service, and so on. A good way to get this job is to complain about any of these matters. Avoid doing so unless you have better ideas.

Enlisted mess specialists man the wardroom, "steerage," pantries, and officers' galleys, and take care of senior officers' rooms.

The senior Navy line officer (usually the executive officer) is mess president. Be in the mess before mealtime so that you can take your seat when the "exec" sits down. Etiquette once required that an officer remain seated (unless excused) until the mess president rose. Although this custom is not observed in all ships today, this does not excuse you from showing ordinary politeness and deference.

Wardroom country is "out of bounds" to enlisted persons except when on duty or in special circumstances. Do not use your stateroom as an office. See that enlisted persons have little need to enter wardroom country. When they do, require that they uncover (unless under arms), keep quiet, and refrain from profane language.

1007.   Wardroom Etiquette

Be punctual for meals. If unavoidably delayed, express your regrets to the senior member.

If necessary to leave before the senior member has risen, ask to be excused.

Do not lounge about the wardroom out of uniform. Some latitude may be allowed during "all hands" evolutions, which require working uniform, but be certain that the captain approves such departure from the basic rule.

Introduce guests to as many wardroom officers as possible, and *always* to the senior member and those at your own table. Entertain only such guests as your messmates and their families will be happy to meet.

Each guest is considered a guest of the wardroom. Be friendly and sociable with all guests.

Except on mess or party nights, officers' guests should leave the ship by four bells of the first watch (2200).

Only officers on the sick list may have meals in their rooms. This does not preclude your having a cup of tea or coffee in your cabin when you are working there.

Do not loaf about the wardroom during working hours. If you have nothing else to do, catch up on your professional reading and study the ship's organization and regulations.

Do not be boisterous in the wardroom; be considerate of your messmates.

When a visiting officer enters, introduce yourself, extend the courtesies of the ship, and try to help the visitor in any way you can.

Observe mess rules—not to talk shop at meals, not to talk religion or politics, not to play the radio or phonograph during meals—or whatever they may be.

Be just and pleasant in your dealing with mess specialists; make complaints to the mess treasurer.

Do not abuse the privilege of the watch mess specialist by sending him or her on long errands. The watch mess specialist is there to serve *all* officers.

Gambling, drinking, and possession of liquor on board ship, except for medical purposes, are serious offenses.

Pay your bills promptly. Within twenty-four hours of reporting, pay the mess treasurer your mess bill and mess share in advance.

When necessary, admit ignorance. Experienced officers respect a frank admission and detest bluff. But endeavor to find out what you did not know.

1008. Shaking Down

Your stateroom will be small, or, if large, crowded. Junior officers are usually doubled or quadrupled up. But the CO of a Marine detachment is assigned his or her own stateroom.

Space will be cramped. You will probably have an upper bunk, comfortable but not luxurious, a share in a desk with drawers for stowing clothing, a chest of drawers or part of one, and some hanging space. Some rooms have air ports, but most are force-ventilated or air-conditioned.

Your mess specialist will supply you with bed linen, blankets, and towels and pick up laundry. Deal with the mess specialist tactfully but firmly.

As the junior Marine, you can expect considerable good-natured running. Get to know your roommates, and, if possible, to like them. In cramped quarters in a ship, it requires a nice adjustment to live in harmony with a number of other positive personalities.

As just suggested, Marines at sea traditionally get a certain amount of teasing harassment from Navy shipmates. Remember it is in fun, don't let it get under your skin, and don't hesitate to slip in your own digs as targets present themselves.

Make a definite effort to get along. It's a matter of give-and-take; be sure you give more than you take.

MARINE SECURITY FORCE ORGANIZATION

1009. Types of Units

Since their inception, MCSF Battalion units have conducted the following missions: reinforcement of U.S. embassies, naval station installation security, protection of special weapons, nuclear refueling and defueling security missions, security during Strategic Arms Reduction Treaty inspections, and training in a wide array of antiterrorism and force protection scenarios.

Under the reorganized concept of fleet security, the 1st and 2d FAST Companies deploy three FAST platoons in support of selected fleet CINCs or commanders, generally one platoon each for COMUSNAVCENT, CINCUSNAVEUR, and CINCPLACFLT on a six month rotational basis.

Standing Marine detachments onboard ships disappeared in 1998 and the mission will be performed by FAST platoons and detachments when required.

When assigned onboard a man-of-war, such security units no longer form part of ship's company, but are embarked as a direct support unit. As such, they report to the commanding officer of the ship to perform assigned missions:
1. Security for special weapons
2. Internal security for the ship
3. Other force protection tasks

1010. The Afloat Detachment Commander

The FAST platoon or detachment commands "task organized security forces to augment Navy security to protect against terrorist acts at designated installations, units, ships, and critical assets, and perform other emergency security operations." Since their first deployment in February 1998, the platoons have conducted installation and airfield security, reinforcement of bombed U.S. embassies, and protected ships and flagships.

The assignment of shipboard security detachment commander will give you one of the finest opportunities for responsibility and independence that is open to a company grade officer. At sea, you are truly on your own; in general, as long as you discharge your mission responsbilities and tasks detailed in your orders, you will be left alone to get results in your own fashion by both Marine Corps and naval authorities. Occupying the traditional roles of the Marine shipboard detachments commanders of yore, you could not ask for more. Moreover, the intimate

Shipboard detachments of Marines still pay traditional attention to the guns. Here, a heavy machine gun is prepared for action on board an aircraft carrier.

experience that you gain as to Navy ways, operating procedures, capabilities, and limitations will prove invaluable to you throughout the rest of your career. In later years, as a senior officer, you will find relative ease in transacting Marine Corps business with your Navy counterparts as an old acquaintance. Such rare sea duty should be coveted whenever available.

The commander of the security force unit will report to the captain of the ship for the efficiency and performance of the detachment. He or she remains responsible to the Marine Corps chain of command for the detachment's personnel administration, training, and the Marine Corps property in his or her charge. The detachment commander may report to a designated ship's department head for specific assignments, augmentation by Navy personnel and equipment, and for the operation of any assigned shipboard systems.

The former duties of shipboard officer or shore patrol officer will normally not be performed by a security detachment commander, except as authorized in orders. However, the detachment commander will still assign detachment personnel to shipboard duties and stations under the ship's Watch, Quarter, and Station Bill. This is a chart that lists every person in the ship by name, rank, bunk and locker assignjment, cleaning station, watch and liberty section, and battle station. The bill is arranged in standard tabular form and gives a graphic picture of what everyone in the detachment does and when, according to the readiness condition of the ship.

1011. Embarked Marines

With the extinction of seagoing Marine Corps detachments on board Navy ships, the common type of service afloat for Marine officers comes with the embarkation of your unit for duty with the fleet or for exercises. Such duty reflects the essence of the modern Marine Corps, which has provided landing forces for the fleet throughout our history.

There remains a typical set of misconceptions that can cloud the experience of embarkation for all. This is the notion of some uninitiated Marines that the U.S. Navy exists primarily as a taxi service for Marines and should conduct itself in an appropriately service-oriented manner. Then, on the other extreme, are the occasional Navy personnel who think that Marines exist solely to interrupt a ship's routine, clutter spaces, and make a mess of the paintwork on vehicle and cargo areas. Neither concept could fall farther from the truth. The amphibious force doctrine of the Navy and Marine Corps provides one of the most striking military capabilities of the history of warfare, *primarily* through the unique concepts of teamwork, cooperation, and integration that have evolved over decades of training and operations. Your first charge as an office embarking with your troops must be to readdress ruthlessly all instances of real and pretended friction that can rise from untrained and inexperienced personnel reacting to the obvious conditions of shipboard life.

1012. Commanding Officer of Troops

Under *Navy Regulations*, the authority of the commanding officer of a ship governs embarked personnel and units as well. In order to ensure the maximum cooperation and understanding for mutually satisfying results, the commanding officer requires embarked units to organize themselves under a single troop commander, responsible to that commanding officer for all matters pertaining to them.

The CO of troops therefore functions with respect to the ship's organization as another department head, reporting for the embarked detachments to the commanding officer and executive officer of the ship. Musters, duty assignments, working parties, and the all-important needs of the troops for training and maintenance support on board ship require much attention from the CO of troops.

Shipboard duties for Marine officers embarked with their units may include the following: team embarkation officer, ship's platoon commander, troop officer of the day/guard officer, billeting officer, troop mess officer, officer's mess treasurer, and troop communications officer. These and other requirements are made clear by the ship CO before embarkation occurs, mainly through liaison with the advance party that your unit will send to the ship. Your unit will provide a standing working party (ship's platoon), cooks, and messmen on a fairshare basis to assist in the functioning of the ship, which will be your collective home for the period of embarkation.

Your unit also will be responsible for the care and cleaning (but not repair) of the berthing and working spaces assigned. The daily cleanliness of a ship is of paramount concern to all, especially considering the obvious closeness of shipboard life. Don't let your personnel be found lacking. Above all, cultivate the respect of the ship's executive officer by following the standards to the letter and never quibbling over them. Be a good guest, as well as an effective professional.

Shipboard routine soon becomes second nature to embarked personnel. Training periods and maintenance of troop weapons, equipment, and cargo will take up most of each day, but these will be supplemented as required by ship drills and exercises that, of necessity, must involve you and your Marines. Be familiar with the various watch bills and emergency bills, particularly for general quarters, man overboard, abandon ship, and fires. Learn the rules for movement through the ship during general quarters. Learn your way around, and memorize the compartment numbering system in order to locate yourself and ship spaces. Many areas will be designated as "restricted spaces," both to afford requisite security for sensitive equipment and documents and to keep the limited space from becoming overcrowded. These restrictions largely apply to enlisted personnel. Embarked officers should feel free to include these spaces in their familiarization tours, being sure to ask the assigned Navy personnel kindly to explain to you their duties and the capabilities of their equipment.

1013. Guard Duty in Embarked Marine Corps Units

When a Marine Corps unit *not* part of the ship's company goes to sea, the guard duty required is a combination of that maintained ashore and that described above for a Marine detachment.

Bear in mind two principles of command relations: first, the captain of a ship has paramount authority and responsibility for safety, good order, and discipline over everyone embarked in the ship, whether or not under the captain's military command; second, the commanding officer of troops embarked in a ship retains his or her military command authority and responsibility for his or her officers and enlisted persons, subject only to the overriding authority and responsibility of the captain.

Consistent with the foregoing principles, the captain of the ship can call upon the embarked troop units to establish a guard to assist in maintaining the security and safety of the ship by manning such posts as life-buoy, control of circulation of passengers, and communications and by performing any other necessary guard duties. For internal order, security, and control of embarked units, the troop commander, with the concurrence of the captain, may establish any posts he or she considers necessary. In general, the troop commander organizes the guard like an interior guard ashore and provides an officer of the day as his or her direct representative for supervising the troop guard and carrying out troop orders, ship's regulations, and special instructions of the ship's captain.

All orders to troops embarked in a ship, including instructions for the troop guard, are transmitted through the commanding officer of troops.

COURTESTY, ETIQUETTE, AND HONORS

1014.   Shipboard Courtesy and Etiquette

On many occasions during your career, you will find yourself serving or embarked in naval vessels, on a Navy staff, as part of the ship's Marine detachment, or as a passenger. Because of this and because, as a Marine officer, you are a member of the naval services, you must comply meticulously with the courtesies and customs practiced on board men-of-war.

Ladders and Gangways.   The starboard accommodation ladder is reserved for officers; if there are two starboard ladders, one ladder may be designated for flag and general officers. The port ladder is for enlisted persons. When a ship is alongside a dock, the officers' gangway usually leads to the quarterdeck; the enlisted's gangway is forward or aft, as the case may be.

Coming on Board and Leaving a Man-of-War.   As a Marine officer, whether on duty or as a visitor, you always will be welcome on board a Navy ship. In fact, you should seize every opportunity to visit each type and class of ship so that you may increase your seagoing knowledge. The Navy is rightly flattered by such visits and will do everything possible to make your stay instructive, as well as socially pleasant. Always pay your respects to the Marine officer when visiting a warship that has a Marine detachment.

If the ship is docked, there will be little complication. If the ship is anchored in the stream, obtain permission from the ship's senior officer present at the landing (or from the boat coxswain, if no officer is on hand) to go out in one of the ship's boats. If no boats are at the landing, ask the shore patrol representative when the next boat is due. If you come off in a motor launch loaded with enlisted passengers, you will probably be taken to the port ladder.

Observe boat etiquette. Defer to seniors in the boat, and introduce yourself.

On reaching the quarterdeck, either from the gangway or an accommodation ladder, halt, face aft (or toward the national ensign), and salute the Colors. Immediately afterward, render a second, distinct salute to the officer of the deck or junior officer of the deck, and say, "Sir, I request permission to come on board." When it is time to leave the ship, render the same courtesies in reverse order, saying, "Sir, I request permission to leave the ship."*

Boat Etiquette. When boarding a small boat, juniors embark first and sit forward, leaving the sternsheets for seniors, who embark last (Figure 10–2). The most senior officer in the boat sits farthest aft, at the centerline, or elsewhere as he or she wishes. When debarking, officers do so in order of rank (Figure 10–3). Officers or enlisted persons in the boat rise and salute when a senior officer boards or debarks.

When another boat passes close aboard with a senior officer embarked and in view, or when a senior officer passes close aboard on shore, the senior officer and the coxswain in each boat render hand salutes (Figure 10–4). Seated officers do not rise to salute; coxswains rise unless to do so would be dangerous or impracticable. When a boat is crowded, juniors rise and yield seats to seniors. If there are not enough seats, take the next boat.

Marine officers (although line officers) and officers of the Navy staff corps, when senior in a boat, receive and return salutes and are otherwise accorded the deference due individuals of their seniority, but the senior Navy line officer or petty officer in the boat, regardless of how junior he or she may be, is in charge of the boat and is responsible for its navigation and for the safety of personnel and materiel embarked. This is provided by *Navy Regulations* and should be remembered by you as a Marine officer, in case you are inadvertently directed to act as a boat officer.

During Colors, boats under way within sight or hearing lie to or, if necessary, proceed at slowest safe speed. The coxswain (or boat officer, if embarked) stands and salutes unless dangerous to do so. Other persons embarked remain in place and do not salute.

Shipboard Amenities and Saluting. In general the amenities and rules for saluting set forth in Chapter 18 apply on board ship, but the following special points should be observed.

Men at work, at games, or at meals, are not required to rise when an officer other than the captain, or a flag or general officer, or an officer senior to the captain

---

*If you are a member of the ship's company, or embarked in any capacity, you report to the OOD as follows: On coming aboard, "I report my return on board, sir." On Leaving the ship, "I have permission to leave the ship, sir."

Figure 10–2: When embarking, junior officers board first

passes, unless attention is called, or when a passageway must be cleared. It is customary for all officers to uncover when entering a sick bay or space in which food is being prepared or served; when a senior officer does so, this indicates that he or she does not desire the people present to be brought to attention.

Juniors give way to seniors in ship's passageways and particularly when going up and down ladders.

"Gangway!" is a command given by anyone who sees an officer or civilian dignitary approaching a gangway, ladder, or passage that is blocked. Never use "Gangway!" except for an officer or senior civilian. For others, "Coming through!" is appropriate. The senior officer, NCO, or petty officer present must clear passage afer "Gangway!" has been given.

The ship's captain, any officer senior to the captain, all flag and general officers, the executive officer, and inspecting officers are saluted at every meeting except in officers' country, heads, and messing compartments.

On the first meeting of the day, salute each officer senior to you; thereafter, salutes are dispensed with except when an officer is directly addressed by a subordinate or in the cases of senior officers listed above.

Sentries at gangways salute all officers coming on board or leaving the ship. Sentries posted on the topside also salute officers passing close aboard in boats.

When passing honors are being exchanged between men-of-war or when ruffles and flourishes are sounded on the quarterdeck, all personnel on weather decks, not in formation, come to attention and salute.

Figure 10–3: When disembarking, senior officers are first to leave the boat

Navy (*but not Marine*) formations on board ship are dismissed with the command, "Leave your quarters," whereupon all members of the formation salute, the officer in charge returns the salute, and all hands fall out.

Ship's sentries posted on the dock, when a ship is moored alongside, carry out normal saluting procedures for sentinels ashore.

When Colors go in port and the ship is in port, all hands on weather decks or on the pier (if the ship is berthed alongside) face aft and salute.

1015. Display of Personal Flags and Pennants Afloat

On Board Ship.   A flag officer or unit commander afloat displays his or her personal flag or command pennant from the flagship but not from more than one ship at a time. If two flag officers are embarked in the same ship, only the senior's flag flies. When a civil official who rates a personal flag is embarked for passage in a naval vessel, his or her flag is flown, but if an officer rating a personal flag or command pennant is also on board, both the officer's flag and that of the civilian are displayed.

In Boats.   An officer in command or chief of staff acting for that officer, when embarked officially in a naval boat, flies his or her personal flag or command pennant from the bow. Officers who rate neither display a commission pennant. Officers who rate personal flag or command pennant may display a miniature of such flag or pennant from the vicinity of the coxswain's station when

Figure 10–4: The coxswain and the senior officer in the boat render hand salutes

embarked on other than official occasions. Civilian officials display their flags, if any, from the bow, if embarked in a naval boat.

1016.   Official Visits and Calls on Board Ship

Official Visits.   Insofar as practicable, the same honors and ceremonies are rendered for an official visit afloat as for one ashore. In addition, however, on board ship the compliments mentioned in Section 1820 are added, such as manning the rail and piping and tending the side.

If *Navy Regulations* call for a gun salute on departure of the visitor, the salute is fired when the visitor is clear of the side (to avoid blast), and the flag or pennant (if that person rates one) is hauled down with the last gun of the salute.

Official Calls on Board Naval Vessels.   The procedure for receiving official callers on board U.S. Navy ships is more formal than ashore. According to the rank of the visitor, and the occasion, the side may be piped; side boys, guard, and band are paraded; and certain officers attend the side. If you or your ship is on the receiving end of the call, you can find the details (and should check these carefully in advance) in such publications as *The Watch Officer's Guide* or *The Naval Officer's Guide*, both of which will be readily available on board, as well as in *Navy Regulations*. For a table of honors to be rendered for the various military and civil officials of the United States and foreign countries, see Chapter 18.

1017.   Housekeeping Afloat

Much advice and information presented in Chapter 20 applies to Marine detachments on board ships. A man-of-war's Marine detachment is also a weapons division, and the commanding officer of Marines thus has additional duty as "division officer," a status roughly analogous to that of a company commander ashore. The Marines man and maintain certain equipment and have their own part of the ship (where the detachment lives, works, and maintains its headquarters—styled, sailor-fashion, as "the Marine office").

The term "housekeeping," however, has no exact equivalent afloat. "Ship's work," or "keeping the ship," includes some housekeeping functions but does not encompass all shoreside connotations of the phrase. In examining housekeeping for Marines at sea, some of the similarities and differences are noted.

Police. "Police," in the Navy sense, means the ship's police force. Under the chief police petty officer (or "chief master-at-arms," to use the old Navy title), each division, other than the Marines, details a police petty officer ("master-at-arms" or "jimmy-legs") whose job is to act as a kind of military policeman in enforcing good order and ship's regulations. It is a popular misconception that Marines perform this function and act as "the Navy's police force" on board ship. Nothing could be farther from the truth.

Within the Marine detachment, however, the term "police" has its normal meaning, as in Section 2001, and the detachment police sergeant performs the duties usually associated with that title anywhere in the Corps.

Subsistence and Mess Management. Like "police" (in the Navy sense), subsistence and food service are functions of the ship's executive officer. The supply officer and assistants perform the duties that ashore would fall to the post food service officer, as described in Section 2003. In most ships, a central enlisted mess is operated on a cafeteria basis. Among enlisted persons, only chief petty officers have a separate mess; the Marine first sergeant and gunnery sergeant are, for messing purposes, considered to rate as chief petty officers.

Messmen are detailed from privates and privates first class of the Marine detachment on the basis provided by *Navy Regulations.* Never detail an NCO as a messman. If the detachment includes a rated cook, he or she should be assigned to duty in the ship's galley. *But never lose sight of the cook as a Marine.* *

Clothing and Small Stores. Marine Corps clothing for the detachment is obtained via Sea Duty Supply Officers at San Diego and Norfolk.

Marines may likewise avail themselves—for cash purchases—of the ship's "Clothing and Small Stores," where many items of regulation (Navy) clothing, such as handkerchiefs, socks, and underwear, may be bought at considerable saving over shoreside prices. Obviously, the Marine officers and NCOs must prevent Marines from improper wearing of Navy articles of uniform in lieu of prescribed Marine items of similar type.

Ship's Store. The ship's store is the seagoing equivalent of the post exchange ashore. The ship's store is operated by the supply officer. It stocks stationery, candy, toilet articles, insignia, and the usual selection of post exchange supplies, including, in most ships, "pogey bait" and soda-fountain ("gedunk") delicacies such as are found ashore.

---

*In recognition of Marines' continuing and important security functions, many ships do not call on the Marine guard for messmen. If you have any latitude in this, bend every effort to prevent detail of a Marine for mess duty.

Ship's Welfare and Recreation.   On board ship, Welfare and Recreation embraces the gamut of activities associated with Special Services on the beach. Both as individuals and as a division, Marines take part in the ship's athletic and recreation programs. A ship's *special services officer* administers the funds for these purposes. Be sure the Marine detachment gets its share.

1018.   Shipboard Cleanliness and Upkeep

As its "part of the ship," the Marine detachment usually has a berthing compartment, a storeroom, an office, several guns, a gunnery control station, and adjacent topside deck space. The cleanliness and upkeep of these spaces and structures are the responsibility of the Marine detachment's CO in his or her capacity as a division officer. Each division performs its own minor repairs; more extensive repair, when needed, is the job of the shipfitters and "repair gangs," based on "work requests" submitted by the division officer (detachment commander).

As ashore, your detachment will have a police sergeant. Instead of a police shed, though, he or she will have a *gear locker.* In lieu of a police gang—career men in their field—the police sergeant will levy on every Marine in the detachment to keep the ship's "Marine country" a model space, spic and span, an example to the bluejackets.

In your responsibility for structural upkeep and cleanliness of the ship, you should assign certain "cleaning stations" to your NCOs, and, if you are in command, to your junior officer(s). On board some ships, the immediate approaches to the captain's cabin (or flag quarters if an admiral is embarked) are assigned as a Marine cleaning station and should be a source of special pride and solicitude by the detachment. Marines get this duty because the captain *knows* the job will be well done.

1019.   Navy Property Accounting

Much of the equipment and supplies in the hands of the Marine detachment will be Navy, rather than Marine Corps property, and thus must be handled and accounted for under the Navy property system. In this system, all items are divided into functional accounting categories, or "titles." You will be concerned with Titles B and C.

Equipage (Title B).   Title B covers nonexpendable equipment on board ship. Anything classed as "Title B" must be carefully safeguarded, inventoried, and covered by receipts and records. The ship's supply officer keeps records on Title B items on *Equipage Stock Card and Custody Records*, which serve the same purpose as consolidated memorandum receipts ashore. The Marine detachment CO signs for Title B gear on this form and keeps a duplicate in his or her own files. In turn, responsibility for Title B items is subdivided within the detachment by means of similar forms. As equipage is received or expended, the respective custody cards must be kept up to date.

Title B gear is inventoried at least annually and also whenever the ship's supply officer or other responsible custodian changes. By Navy custom, routine inventory usually takes place during the third quarter of the fiscal year. An incoming custodian must complete the Title B inventory within twenty days of assuming actual custody; shortages or unserviceable items must then be reported and recommended for survey.

Shipboard control of equipage is a prime responsibility, which the Navy takes very seriously. Just as on the beach, ability to control valuable property, both in fact and on the record, is rightly considered a significant index of your military efficiency.

Operating Expenses of Ships in Commission (Title C).   Although a multitude of maintenance and running expenses (even crew's pay and rations) is chargeable to Title C, the Title C items that concern the Marine detachment consist mainly of expendable supplies issued for cleaning, repair, and administration. Anything classed under Title C is expended when issued. Examples are: stationery, toilet paper, chipping hammers, swabs, and paint. Ordinarily, the ship's first lieutenant and gunnery officer establish allowance lists for each division, covering Title C material, which is then drawn once a week, usually on Monday morning. Then it is up to the division concerned (the Marine detachment, in our case) to see that the supplies are not carelessly expended or wasted. If for some unforeseen reason, the routine apportionment of consumables runs out, the division officer can ordinarily get more through a special written request to the head of department. Needless to say, this situation should be avoided.

HINTS FOR SEAGOING MARINE OFFICERS

In addition to Marine duties, seagoing Marine officers perform the usual duties of a division officer. Don't be too proud to learn from the Navy. Make it your goal to be as salty (in a military way) as any of your messmates. Never lean on the lifelines; always know which is the lee side; learn what the different boatswains' calls mean. Make yourself into a true seagoing man-of-warsman.

Know which NCO is responsible for each cleaning station.

Keep a sharp eye on the corners, out-of-way areas, and tops of angle irons and beams, under lockers, and behind and under gear. The center of the deck takes care of itself.

Give special attention to gaskets, knife-edges, and dogs on hatches, scuttles, ports, and doorways. The condition of these items is a direct measure of the watertight integrity of the ship.

Timely, energetic scrubbing prevents wasting paint to cover up dirt. Paint not only costs money but greatly increases danger from fire.

Know your whole ship; know every fitting, rivet, and detail in your own spaces.

Take a turn around your battery daily with the gunnery sergeant and with the battery gunner's mate. Visit all security spaces daily with the gunnery sergeant and sergeant of the guard.

Ship's detachments are just noted for the splendid appearance of rifles. By applying several coats of a preparation of olive oil and orange shellac to previously scraped rifle stocks and bayonet grips, the grain of the wood can be brought out in a beautiful glosslike finish. This work preferably should be done by a single individual, such as the detachment armorer, who can master the technique and mix, and thus get very best results. M-16 rifles simply receive careful cleaning.

Avoid oversupervising your NCOs. This is more difficult on board ship, not only because of the proximity in which officers and men work and live but also because the Navy expects junior officers to concern themselves with many details that, in the Marine Corps, are entrusted to noncommissioned officers. Do not spoil NCOs—and also pick up bad supervisory habits—by breathing down their necks at every turn. Tell your people the "what"; leave the "how" to them.

In most ships, custom requires division officers to be in their parts of the ship by 0800 each working day. Your presence shows interest in the work in progress. When anything important is going on in your part of the ship, be there.

If on board a carrier, be exceedingly careful on the flight deck and be sure your Marines are well schooled as to safety precautions. Sad but true, while pilots are the most likely to sustain injury about the flight deck, the second most likely are the Marines.

Be scrupulously neat and clean. A self-respecting male officer never appears unshaven before his shipmates and his men. If you find one of your men unshaven, make him shave immediately.

Salute admiral, captain, executive officer, and any other officer of the rank of commander or above whenever you meet them about the ship, except when standing watch on the bridge. Salute whenever making reports. Salute all officers senior to you when you meet them for the first time during the day and give them a cheerful, "Good morning, sir."

Observe the local rule for permission to leave the ship. In some ships, you must obtain permission not only from the Marine officer but from the head of department also; in other ships permission is assumed to be granted after working hours, if your work is done. A few ships require one Marine officer on board at all times.

Learn about RHIP ("Rank has its privileges"). Tread safely until experience, higher rank, and increased responsibility bring you greater privileges. Reserve jokes and wisecracks for your contemporaries. Toward seniors, maintain an attitude of respectful friendliness.

Try to get as much accomplished during normal working hours as you can, so that your Marines get the benefit of their free time. But work as long as a job remains to be done, working hours or not.

Most Navy personnel at all levels have a high regard for Marines, which usually lasts as long as the Marines continue to function at the level of professional competence that the Navy has a right to expect of them. Relationships between Navy and Marines on board ship are therefore generally healthy and rewarding. If you cannot adjust yourself to cooperating and working with those whose methods admittedly differ from your own, you have no business on sea duty.

Ensure that you (and if possible new Marines coming on board) have a full seabag before reporting. Items of uniform are hard to come by in the middle of the Indian Ocean. (In particular, you should have not less than three dress white cap-covers, which soil easily on board ship but must be kept white and spotless.)

If your sword drill is weak or rusty, you should brush up intensively prior to coming to sea.

Take every opportunity to get your detachment ashore for training, even if no more than close-order drill on a Navy Yard pier. If at bases where the terrain permits, such as Guantánamo Bay, Guam, Panama, or Roosevelt Roads, get permission to land the Marines for a day of hiking and field training. Be alert for opportunities for competitive rifle and pistol shooting with units ashore, with military units in friendly foreign countries, or with other ships. Remember that the inspector general will visit your detachment once a year and will inspect training, physical fitness, weapons qualifications, close-order drill, and so on. All the above requirements, and more, must be concurrent with shipboard duties. You cannot afford to coast.

Finally, when on sea duty never neglect to call upon the local Marine commanding officer ashore or overlook the help you can receive from brothers in arms who wear the Globe and Anchor.

GLOSSARY FOR SEAGOING MARINES

See *Naval Terms Dictionary* for commonly used shipboard terms and phrases that every Marine should know. By using and understanding these, you will prove to Navy shipmates that Marines can be, and are, just as salty as any sailor.

NAVY RATING ABBREVIATIONS

The Navy's system of ratings (that is, petty officer ranks and specialties) with its many different abbreviations may at first appear confusing but is something seagoing Marines must understand. The *Naval Terms Dictionary*, Appendix B, gives the basic abbreviations and their titles.

. . . that no persons be appointed to offices, or inlisted into said battalions, but such as are good seamen, or so acquainted with maritime affairs as to be able to serve to advantage by sea.

—Resolution of the Continental Congress
to raise Marines, 10 November 1775

A ship without Marines is like a coat without buttons.

—David G. Farragut

11

You Become a Marine Officer

The *Marine Corps Gazette* recounts that a young man from the hinterland, when shipping into the Corps, was asked if he intended to try for a commission.

"I don't think so," the recruit answered, "I'm not a very good shot. I'd better work on a straight salary."

Whether it is the commission that attracts you or just the salary, here are the ways in which you can become a U.S. Marine officer and what happens to you in the process.

There are many ways in which you can obtain a commission. The variety of approaches to officer status in the Corps ensures that the base of experience, background, and education among Marine officers remains broad. It also means that, no matter what your origin, once you qualify for a Marine commission, you stand on equal footing with every other officer candidate, regardless of source or education.

1101. General Requirements to Become an Officer

To be eligible for a commission in the Marine Corps, you must be a U.S. citizen, morally, mentally, and physically qualified, and your application must be approved by Marine Corps Headquarters. If you are already a veteran, you must of course have an honorable discharge, and if you are a member of the reserve component of any other service, you must obtain a conditional release from that organization. Under certain limited conditions, officer transfers are authorized from the other services into the Marine Corps; for such transactions special regulations and procedures apply which are beyond the scope of this chapter.

1102. Roads to Your Commission

To obtain a commission in the Marine Corps, you may follow any one of the several roads summarized in Table 11–1 and subsequently described.

U.S. Naval Academy.   Each graduating class from the Naval Academy at Annapolis includes midshipmen who have been selected for Marine Corps commissions. Entrance into the Naval Academy, first step toward a commission via this route, is open to civilian preparatory school and high school graduates and to qualified enlisted personnel from the Marine Corps and Marine Corps Reserve. Information regarding appointment to the Naval Academy may be obtained by writing to the Superintendent, U.S. Naval Academy, Annapolis, Maryland 21402. If you are already in the regular Marine Corps or Reserve, consult your commanding officer. At present, up to 16⅔ percent of each graduating class of midshipmen may be commissioned in the Marine Corps. All USNA graduates have a five-year service obligation.

U.S. Military and Air Force Academies.   Limited numbers of graduates of West Point and of the Air Force Academy are also eligible for regular commissions in the Marine Corps, with preference going to former Marines or children of Marines. Information regarding appointment to these academies may be obtained from the Departments of the Army and the Air Force, respectively.

From Civil Life.   If you are attending an accredited college or are a college graduate, you may enter the Marine Corps as an officer under the following programs.

Naval ROTC.   Any college student enrolled either as a scholarship midshipman in the Naval Reserve Officers' Training Corps (NROTC) or as a "College Program Student, NROTC," can, if selected for the Marine Corps, obtain a commission. NROTC is today the largest single source of regular officers in the Corps. The NROTC scholarship midshipman goes to college, when selected and approved, with tuition, fees, and books paid for by the Navy. He or she also receives a retainer of $100 a month. The midshipman spends summer "cruises" afloat with the fleet and ashore at OCS, Quantico (after selection for the Marine Corps). On graduation from college, with a B.A. or B.S. degree, he or she is commissioned and enters Basic School. A limited number of entry-level scholarships are earmarked for the Marine Corps. Civilian high school graduates may apply for these through their local USMC recruiter.

The NROTC "College Program Student" receives no government financial support, other than $100 a month retainer pay during the last two years in college, but takes the same naval science instruction in college as the scholarship midshipman. If selected for a Marine commission while in college, the contract student spends one summer on a "cruise" at OCS, Quantico. After graduation, he or she is ordinarily commissioned in the Marine Corps Reserve. If you are in

NROTC and want to become a Marine officer, see the Marine officer attached to your NROTC unit.

Platoon Leaders Class (PLC).   The Platoon Leaders Class is a summer officer-candidate program designed to train college men and women either as ground officers or as prospective pilots or naval flight officers (NFO) in Marine aviation. PLC training is limited to two summer periods of six weeks each at Quantico. In the case of college juniors, all training is completed in a single ten-week summer period. At the completion of that training, and upon graduation, you are eligible for commission as a second lieutenant in the Marine Corps Reserve. No uniforms, training, or other work is required of you during the academic year.

To enter PLC, you must be enrolled in an accredited college as a freshman, sophomore, or junior. You must be at least seventeen years old on enrollment, and less than twenty-eight on 1 July of the year in which you expect to receive your degree.

Training consists of two six-week tours (Junior and Senior Course, respectively). During each period, you receive the pay—but not the allowances—of a sergeant.

Training for both ground and aviation candidates is intensive, with initial emphasis on the basic instruction and careful screening required for all Marine officers. Aviation candidates, however, take flight examinations as part of their program, and, if found qualified on graduation, are ultimately sent to flight training on graduation from Basic School.

In addition to pay and transportation to and from Quantico, you get living quarters, uniforms, and medical and dental care. And, during off-hours, you have full privileges at the library, post exchange, theater, swimming pool, and athletic field, and of course weekend liberty.*

Officer Candidate Course (OCC).   The Officer Candidate Course is conducted for college graduates who are over twenty years of age and less than twenty-eight on 1 July of the year in which commissioned.

The course provides the practical military training needed to qualify for the specialized training to be received as a second lieutenant and, in the case of aviation officer candidates, for flight training. It consists of ten weeks intensive training at Quantico, Virginia. Upon successful completion of this course, you are commissioned a second lieutenant in the Marine Corps Reserve.

In addition to preofficer training, OCC and PLC candidates, after being commissioned, attend Basic School in Quantico before being assigned to a unit, while aviation officer candidates, if found qualified, go on from Basic School to

---

*If you are headed for law school, you should investigate the special PLC (Law) program, under which individuals who have successfully completed PLC are allowed to remain in law school in inactive status as second lieutenants in the Reserve until they obtain their law degrees and are then brought to complete their required active duty as Marine lawyers. PLCs may also be deferred from active duty to obtain a master's degree in most recognized major fields.

Table 11–1. Avenues to a career as a Marine officer

Program or Source of Input	Age Limit	Education Requirements	Open to	Leads to
U.S. Naval Academy		Graduation from USNA	Midshipmen USNA	2d Lt. USMCR[1]
U.S. Military or Air Force Academies[2]		Graduation from USMA or USAFA	Cadets USMA or USAFA	2d Lt. USMCR[1]
NROTC (Marine Option NROTC Scholarship Program)	Be 17 but not 21 years of age by 30 June of the year entering college	B.A. or B.S. degree[3]	NROTC midshipmen	2d Lt. USMCR[1]
NROTC (College Program)	Be 17 but not 21 years of age by 30 June of the year entering college	B.A. or B.S. degree[3]	NROTC midshipmen	2d Lt. USMCR[1]
Platoon Leaders Class (Ground or Aviation)	Be at least 17 years old and less than 28 (27½ for aviation) at time of appointment to commissioned grade	B.A. or B.S. degree[3]	College freshmen, sophomores, juniors[2]	2d Lt. USMCR[1]
Officer Candidate Course	Be at least 20 but less than 28 (27½ for aviation) at time of commissioning	B.A. or B.S. degree	Regularly enrolled senior in good standing, or a graduate, of an accredited institution granting a 4-year baccalaureate degree in a field other than medicine, dentistry, veterinary, pharmacy, chiropody, hospital administration, optometry, osteopathy, or theology[4]	2d Lt. USMCR[1]
Marine Corps Enlisted Commissioning Education Program (MECEP)	Be at least 20 but less than 26 years old by 1 July of the year entering college	B.S. degree[3]	USMC enlisted, with GCT 120 or higher and 6 years' obligated service	2d Lt. USMCR[1]

Program	Age/Service Requirement	Education/Test	Eligibility	Rank
Enlisted Commissioning Program	Be at least 19½ and less than 27½ on date of application	High school graduate (or GED certificate issued by State Department of Education) and have satisfactorily completed not less than 1 year of unduplicated college work at an accredited institution.	Private and above, USMC and WACR with GCT of 120 or higher and at least 12 months remaining on current enlistment and who have completed recruit training	2d Lt. USMCR[1]
Limited Duty Officer	WO applicants who have a minimum of 10 and a maximum of 20 years' active service and who have not reached their 46th birthday by 1 January of the fiscal year in which the appointment is to be made	EL 110 (ASVAB)	Permanent warrant officers in grades W-2 through W-4	1st Lt. USMC
Warrant Officer	Must be of an age to allow 30 years' total active service by age 62	GCT 110 or higher	Sergeant or above with 5-12 years' active service. COs may recommend waivers for preeminently qualified NCOs with up to 14 years of service	Warrant Officer (W-1) USMC

[1] Initial commission in USMCR with opportunity to augment (integrate) if qualified and selected.

[2] Military Academy and Air Force Academy graduates may by law be commissioned in the Marine Corps, but the Departments of Army and Air Force will only grant approval in exceptional cases.

[3] Successful college graduation and completion of program are prerequisites for commissioning.

[4] Aviation candidates must meet flight physical standards and will be sent to flight training on completion of required ground training. Current regulations require all to attend Basic School prior to reporting for flight training.
(To be eligible for any program, you must be able to meet the general requirements stated in Section 1101.)

Marine officers are commissioned from a variety of sources, with the universal goal of providing leadership to U.S. Marines.

fifteen to eighteen months' preflight and flight training in commissioned officer status.

Qualified enlisted Marines may also enter either the Officer Candidate or Aviation Officer Candidate courses.

From the Ranks. The Marine Corps pioneered the award of officer commissions to meritorious enlistees long before the practice was accepted among the other three services. In the Marine Corps, the door remains open through several programs.

Marine Enlisted Commissioning Education Program (MECEP). Under this program, qualified enlisted Marines are assigned to a special preparatory course and then to college, during which they remain on active duty. On successful completion of college, preceded by summer officer candidate training, they receive commissions as second lieutenants in the Marine Corps Reserve.

Limited Duty Officer (LDO). Warrant officers of the Marine Corps may apply for LDO commission in specialized fields, such as administration, intelligence, infantry, logistics, artillery, engineers, tanks, amphibian tractors, ordnance, communications, supply, food, motor transport, and aviation. (See Section 1207.)

Warrant Officer. Long-service NCOs may obtain appointment as warrant officers (WOs) in specialized fields. Because qualifications for LDO and WO vary appreciably from time to time, the requirements for such appointments are not summarized here.

Temporary Officer. In addition to the established programs shown in Table 11–1 and described so far, authority exists in law to issue temporary commissions as second lieutenant and above to selected warrant officers and enlisted men in order to meet pressing or particular needs. Individuals so commissioned as temporary officers retain their permanent grades and status and revert thereto when the requirement for their services in the advanced rank ceases. Temporary officers have been commissioned during all twentieth-century wars, including Vietnam. As in the case of LDOs and WOs, programs and requirements are variable.

Former Regular Officers. Former regular officers of the Marine Corps who have not attained their thirtieth birthday at time of appointment and who resigned from the Corps in good standing may be reappointed with the approval of the secretary of the Navy. Former officers of the other armed services may, within certain limits, be appointed by transfer in the Marine Corps Reserve, but under no circumstances in a grade higher than that held in the former service.

1103. Becoming an Officer

No matter how you earn your appointment as a Marine officer, the day finally arrives when you are to be sworn in as a second lieutenant.

Your commission and orders will be forwarded to your commanding officer (if you are already in the service in some capacity) or to a Marine activity near your home for presentation. The swearing-in ceremony and required administrative steps will ordinarily be taken care of by the presenting officer. Bear in mind, however, that pay and allowances do not begin for officers until they are sworn in and commence active duty, nor can you assume title and status as an officer until you have taken your oath and formally accepted your appointment. *You should therefore be sworn in at the earliest opportunity.*

Of that oath, one of the Navy's greatest and best-loved fighting admirals, Arleigh A. Burke, once wrote:

> It is a responsibility that should not be taken easily. And its phraseology is disarmingly simple. When an officer swears "to support and defend the Constitution of the United States against all enemies, foreign and domestic"—he is assuming the most formidable obligation he will ever encounter in his life. Thousands upon thousands of men have died to preserve for him the opportunity to take such an oath. What he is actually doing is pledging his means, his talent, his very life, to his country. This is an obligation that falls to very few men.

The U.S. Supreme Court has more succinctly ruled:

> The taking of the oath of allegiance is the pivotal fact which changes the status from that of civilian to that of soldier.

As you raise your right hand and stand at attention to take your oath, you are at a turning point in your life. In a matter of seconds, you will become an officer in a Corps whose valor, renown, and honor are second to none. From the moment you complete your oath *"to support and defend the Constitution of the United States of America against all enemies, foreign and domestic . . ."* you are a lieutenant of Marines responsible to the president and your superior officers, and fully amenable to military justice. It is a great moment.

1104. Your Commission

After you are sworn in, you receive your commission.

A *commission* is the formal written authority, issued in the name of the president of the United States, which confers on you your rank and authority as a Marine officer. It is signed for the president and by the secretary of the Navy and is issued under the seal of the Department of the Navy and countersigned by an officer in the Manpower Department, Marine Corps Headquarters. Your commission states your rank and the date from which it is effective (your date of rank, so-called) and enjoins all officers, seamen, and Marines to obey any lawful order you may give. You receive a new commission for each rank to which you are promoted.

1105. "Special Trust and Confidence . . ."

Before you file away, or even frame (as many do) your first commission, reread its opening phrase:

Know ye, that reposing special trust and confidence in . . .

With these words, the president of the United States certifies, via the secretary of the Navy, that you, as a commissioned officer, have been set apart from your fellow citizens as one in whom "special trust and confidence" are placed. On the basis of this special trust, you as an officer are granted special privileges; on the same basis you are subject to special responsibilities and obligations. In the words of the old French motto, *noblesse oblige.*

In specific implementation of the foregoing, the *Marine Corps Manual* states: "The special trust and confidence which is expressly reposed in each officer by his commission is the distinguishing privilege of the officer corps." As a commissioned officer, you should be vigilant to discharge and, where necessary, enforce performance of all responsibilities, and thereby guard the privileges.

1106. Basic School

The orders that accompany your appointment and initial commission will direct you to proceed to Quantico, Virginia, and report as a student at Basic School. The mission of Basic School is:

> . . . to educate newly commissioned officers in the high standards of pro–fessional knowledge, esprit de corps, and leadership traditional in the Marine Corps in order to prepare them for the duties of a company-grade officer in the Fleet Marine Force.

Ordinarily, your orders specify a date by which you must report. *It is vital that you comply carefully with your orders, and, above all, that you report on time.* There is no poorer way to start a Marine career than by being late for Basic School.

In reporting, be guided by Sections 1401–1402 of this *Guide.* These give the procedure for joining a new station. You may wear civilian clothes when first reporting to Basic School.

Hints on Reporting at Basic School.   You are specifically *not* required to possess any articles of uniform upon reporting. You should, however, take care that your hair is closely trimmed and that you present a neat appearance.

You should have enough money available for living and other expenses until your first payday, which will be about three weeks after you join. Joining instructions that accompany your orders will suggest minimum amounts of cash single or married new lieutenants should have.

Travel light and bring little baggage, as stowage space is limited. Bring two combination locks to secure lockers assigned.

Outside working hours, like any other officer, you may wear civilian clothing. This, however, must conform to accepted standards within the officer corps: clothes of eccentric design or color are not tolerated. As a minimum, you should have one suit, of conservative cut and color, as well as sports attire.

Except for commissioning uniforms, utilities, and working uniforms, do not purchase or contract for uniforms before you report to Basic School.

Year after year, students report with uniforms and accessories bought in good faith, only to find them ill-fitted, nonregulation, and far too costly. Beware of high-pressure uniform salesmen and so-called package deals for uniforms. One of the first items of business after you join will be a uniform orientation session conducted by the school. Only after that should you begin acquiring your uniforms.

Basic School, the oldest Marine Corps school, is an institution whose importance to the Corps is equaled only by that of the two recruit depots. Basic School traces its history to 1 May 1891 when, as the "School of Application," it was founded at Marine Barracks, Eighth and Eye Streets, Washington, D.C., by Colonel Charles Heywood, ninth commandant of the Corps. At various times the school has been located at Annapolis; at Port Royal, South Carolina (later to become famous as Parris Island); at Norfolk; at Philadelphia Navy Yard; and, finally, at Quantico.

Today, Basic School is located approximately twelve miles from the main post of Quantico. The headquarters of Basic School is located at Camp Barrett, one of the outlying camps of the Guadalcanal Area, which constitutes the greater part of the 57,000 acres of the training reservation.

No matter how you earned your commission, your first assignment as a second lieutenant will be as a student in the Officer Basic Course, a course of approximately twenty-one weeks' duration. In addition to the *Officer Basic Course* for newly commissioned second lieutenants, Basic School conducts a *Marine Warrant Officer Basic Course* for newly appointed warrant officers.

Quarters for the officer students at the Basic School are found in O'Bannon and Graves halls. This BOQ houses the Basic School dining hall and bar, a snack bar, television lounge, library and reading room, and reception room.

Heywood Hall is the main administration building of Basic School. Adjoining Heywood Hall are four modern, air-conditioned classrooms with a total seating capacity of 1,150 students. Conveniently located between these classrooms is the barber shop.

Additional facilities at Camp Barrett include a small post exchange and snack bar, post office, gymnasium, outdoor theater, chapel, armory, additional classroom facilities, gas chamber, combat conditioning facilities, clinic, PX gas station, and a lighted playing field for baseball, softball, or football.

When you report to Basic School, you will turn in your orders to the personnel officer, who will then assign you to a student company. The average class is made up of a company of about 200 students, including young officers from various allied countries around the world. The company is commanded by a major with a captain as executive officer and captains and lieutenants as platoon leaders. Upon reporting to your company commander, you will receive an orientation on the course: what will be expected of you and what you can expect from the school. You will be assigned to a platoon and given a room in the BOQ. You will then be issued your field equipment, individual weapons, and textbooks for your forthcoming courses. You will do theoretical work in the classroom and then go to the field and work it out practically. About one-half of your training is in the field and about one-fifth of this takes place at night.

Immediately after Basic School, every officer goes to "follow-on training" in some school or course, for example, flight training, to qualify the officer in his or her new military specialty. Officers with an infantry (03) MOS (military occupational specialty) remain at Quantico for additional advanced infantry training. Thus, in all, your professional apprenticeship, including Basic School, lasts a minimum of six months.

Quarters at Basic School are not luxurious, although you will find them clean and quite comfortable. If married, you may live on or off the station. You will be given a locker in which you can secure your field equipment, rifle, and extra clothing.

The Basic School curriculum, including intense and rugged fieldwork, provides graduates with a foundation of leadership and professional knowledge upon which they may build their careers. All of the subjects included in the Basic Course are grouped under the following major categories: tactics, weapons, general military subjects, and physical conditioning.

Within the foregoing academic framework, the objects of Basic School are twofold: first, to instill the Marine Corps attitude; and, second, to teach new lieutenants the basic professional techniques that a Marine officer must know. In other words, it is up to Basic School to make a Marine officer of you. The extent to which the school succeeds, however, is largely up to you. Officer students who do not measure up to the standards set for Marine officers are dropped from Basic School, their commissions are revoked, and they are returned to civilian life. Remember that, at Basic School, you are under continual experienced observation.

1107.   Officer Candidate School

In obtaining your commission via the Platoon Leaders Class, NROTC, MECEP, or through any of the inputs that lead you to Officer Candidate Class, you will receive pre–Basic School instruction while assigned to Officer Candidate School. Conducted at Camp Upshur and old Brown Field, Quantico's original air station and later the immediate post–World War II site of Basic School, prebasic training is primarily concerned with imparting to officer candidates the knowledge required of the basic enlisted Marine, while at the same time rigorously screening all candidates to be sure they are officer material. In effect, Officer Candidates School is an officer candidates' boot camp, and a very exacting one.

HINTS FOR NEW OFFICERS

1108.   Do's, Don't's, and Pointers

As a Marine officer, you now represent the Corps. Conduct yourself with dignity, courtesy, and self-restraint.

Avoid any show of self-importance. Do not bluster, especially toward civilians or enlisted personnel.

Be wary of situations beyond your depth. A new lieutenant is not expected to be all-wise. You are expected to keep your head and to possess enough common sense and knowledge of your own limitations to prevent you from overextending yourself.

Something else will be expected of you: *not to make the same mistake twice,* particularly after having been told about it by a senior. Learn to accept criticism positively and with grace.

On joining a new organization, you will be closely looked over by all hands, officer and enlisted. The first impressions can make (or break) you. Be natural and courteous, prompt and punctilious, "squared-away" in uniform and deportment. At all costs avoid the impression of a brash young know-it-all.

From the moment you become a Marine, you should cultivate the habit of punctuality. Along with discipline, dedication, obedience, and loyalty, it should be a matter of pride never to be late. *Always be five minutes early* for any formation or official commitment.

Avoid the habit of complaining or whining, and avoid those who do. Refrain from criticizing unless you are ready and able to provide a better solution. By the same token, cultivate the habit of optimism. An optimist is like a breath of fresh air and cheers all with whom he or she comes into contact. One of the great sayings of the greatest of all naval officers, Lord Nelson, was, "I am not come forth to find difficulties, but to remove them."

Be industrious and persevering, attentive to duty, and attentive to essential detail. Whether ashore or afloat, in garrison or in the field, the best officers are those who possess powers of observation, and, having those powers, know how to use them. Akin to observation is the power and habit of forethought.

Learn to control and to hide your feelings. In addition to being alert, always try to look alert.

Whatever you do, do thoroughly, and do it with enthusiasm and imagination. Do not confine yourself to doing only what you are told to do. Do more than you are told to do. And bear in mind that it is the smart, quick, and, if possible *cheery* voice that gets the job done and makes people hop.

If you are asked a question and are unfamiliar with the answer, don't bluff. The proper answer from a young officer in such circumstances is, "I'll find out."

Do not procrastinate. When you have a job to do, do it at once. If you have several items to be accomplished, do the important thing first. If you find yourself stymied, don't shove the matter aside or report back that you can't do it— try some other way, and keep on trying. Remember that in the service it is results that count, and that if you can acquire the reputation of a capable officer, you are on your way to success.

Always give thought to the service reputation that you build and acquire day by day. An officer's reputation for character and efficiency is his or her vested capital. Take this away and the officer's usefulness is gone. And remember, you cannot fool your contemporaries. Working closely together, officers soon learn the ins and outs of each other's lives and character.

Personal appearance is most important in the service, and although most young officers must and should economize wherever possible, purchasing inferior uniforms is a false economy of the worst kind. The only way to economize on uniforms and equipment is to get the best and then take care of them. Economize on your bar bill rather than your tailor's. Nobody in the world looks more shabby than a shabby officer.

Keep fit. Avoid fat. The Marine Corps will help you with this by periodic physical fitness tests and by vigorous training all year, but fitness is a continuous matter and must be a continuous concern to every officer. No Marine can afford to become fat.

Stand straight. Keep your hands out of your pockets. Never chew gum or smoke in public. Do not carry packages when in uniform. Male officers should never appear unshaven after 0800.

As you acquire clothing, mark each article as laid down in *Marine Corps Uniform Regulations.* Stencil baggage and personal kit with your name, rank, and service number. Inside each piece of baggage, stencil or affix the same information in a permanent manner. You can buy clothing-marking sets at the post exchange. Once deployed off foreign shores and using field or ships' laundry services, it's too late to mark your clothing properly.

In your relations with your fellow officers, avoid joining factions or, if there is any bad feeling between others, avoid taking sides. Don't gossip; gossip always finds its way back. Only say of a fellow officer who is absent what you would say to his or her face.

Never, under any circumstances, speak ill of the Corps, or of your own organization, in the presence of civilians or members of the other services. Before you voice any criticism, however merited or carefully thought out, be sure it cannot be construed by outsiders so as to derogate the Corps. By the same token, avoid criticizing other units or services, at least in public.

Conduct all your business through proper channels. "Channels" is a highly important word in the service. The phrase, "Go through channels," which you will hear repeatedly, simply means, "Don't go over people's heads." In giving instructions or in doing or getting things, be careful not to go over someone's head or infringe on his or her areas of responsibility. This is a sure way to trouble in the service.

Now that you are a Marine yourself, keep your eyes open for likely recruits and for potential officers among your friends. Such individual recruiting of new Marines by convinced and loyal old Marines is one of the principal ways in which the Corps maintains its quality.

Obtain suitable visiting cards, as described in Section 2207.

When the telephone rings, answer up smartly, in Marine Corps fashion, with your name and rank: "Lieutenant Burrows"—not "Hello." When you make a call, identify yourself immediately: "This is Lieutenant Wharton, Marine Corps." Be sure to add that "Marine Corps." It prevents mix-ups with the other services.

Since you are now a member of the most professional of the services, you should join the Marine Corps Association and subscribe to the professional journals listed in Appendix III. If you are a regular, you should by all means immediately join the Army and Navy Club in Washington, while you can still do so (as a newly commissioned officer) without payment of initiation fees. See Section 2214 for details.

Know where to find information. Set out to go through all the basic professional publications, page by page—read *Navy Regulations, The Marine Corps Manual, Uniform Regulations, Drill and Ceremonies Manual,* and of course all the basic field manuals relating to Marine weapons and basic tactical principles. Basic School will direct your attention to the most important provisions in all the foregoing, but, by going through these publications on your own, you will learn where to find information that lazy or inattentive young officers will say is not included in the manuals.

Get into the habit of being systematic and methodical. In Lord Chesterfield's words, "Dispatch is the soul of business, and nothing contributes more to dispatch than method. Fix one certain day and hour in the week for your accounts, keep them together in their proper order, and you can never be much cheated." By so doing, you will be able to accomplish two or three times as much as an equally capable but unsystematic officer.

As an officer embarking on your new career, you should do everything possible to make your living arrangements becoming to your new station. Your pay

Rigorous training and critical evaluation remain the hallmark of Marine Corps officer schools.

is given you for this purpose, and you owe it to the service to dress and live, however simply, like an officer.

If you don't have one already, open a checking account with a substantial bank, preferably one accustomed to handling officers' accounts on a worldwide basis. Begin systematic savings with your first paycheck. Take out life insurance immediately (see Chapter 21).

Be extremely circumspect in any kind of financial transactions with fellow officers. "Neither a borrower nor a lender be" is golden advice; be not a cosigner either—many an officer has discovered that his or her signature on a "friend's" note has resulted in the loss of both the friendship and the amount of the loan. Other than in line of duty, you are prohibited by Navy Regulations from any pecuniary dealings with enlisted persons, and this prohibition should be strictly observed.

Do not intrude among enlisted persons. They are entitled to privacy among themselves as you are. Do not enter noncommissioned officers' messes except by specific invitation of the senior NCO present. If you have been commissioned from the ranks, remember that now you are an officer. You cannot turn back the clock.

An officer is much more respected than any other man who has as little money.
—Samuel Johnson

It's not hard to be an officer, but it's damn hard to be a good officer.
—Gunnery Sergeant Daniel Daly

12

Officers' Individual Administration

Although a few administrators may convey the reverse impression, there is nothing inherently complicated or darkly mysterious about individual administration. This term merely comprises a number of administrative matters that concern you personally: your record, rank, promotions, retirement, official correspondence, leave, and liberty. Pay and allowances, and official travel, closely related, are covered in Chapter 13.

To give you working familiarity and ready reference in "quill driving," and to prevent its seeming a black art known only to a chosen few, read and study *Navy Regulations, The Marine Corps Manual,* and pertinent Marine Corps orders—and let individual administration serve and help but never get the better of you.

OFFICERS' RECORDS

1201. Your Official Record

Throughout your career, correspondence that concerns you accumulates at Marine Corps Headquarters. Adverse matter cannot be placed on record without your knowledge and must always be referred to you for statement. If you wish to give your side of the matter, you may do so; if you have nothing to say, you so state in writing. In either case, the adverse matter goes back to the commandant of the Marine Corps, via the reporting officer and thence through normal channels. Whether favorable or unfavorable, correspondence once rightfully included in your record cannot be removed without authorization by the secretary of the Navy.

The vital importance to you and your career of your official record cannot be overstressed. The entries in your record form the basis of your service reputation. Without vicious intent, many young officers, by carelessness or misdirected high spirits, have written into their records an accumulation of minor lapses that prove as detrimental to their service reputations as serious missteps.

Your record in Washington comprises a correspondence file and certain additional files, some of which may be kept by the judge advocate general of the Navy.

The *Correspondence File* has two sections:

1. *Orders:* Copies of orders issued by Marine Corps Headquarters, and all modifications thereto, regardless of origin; orders to or from active duty, retirement, and so forth.

2. *Miscellaneous correspondence and forms:* Matter pertinent to your military history, such as correspondence relative to original commissioning; medical data; pay and insurance; detailing correspondence; final security clearance; and Record of Emergency Data.

The *Officer's Military Performance File* (on microfiche) contains only matter that bears directly on your fitness as an officer; it has three sections:

1. *Administrative data* (fiche "S"): Diplomas and other evidence of completion of instruction while in the Marine Corps; requests for changes of orders; official photograph; court-martial order (when acquitted); and any other matter neither clearly favorable nor unfavorable but of interest to a selection board in appraising you.

2. *Commendatory and derogatory materials* (fiche "C"): (a) Anything that reflects favorably on you, such as citations and awards; recommendations for awards; letters of commendation; favorable remarks in forwarding endorsements; letters of appreciation from civilians, and so forth. (b) Anything that reflects unfavorably on your moral, mental, or professional qualifications, such as court-martial orders (when convicted); letters of censure and related correspondence; correspondence concerning marital difficulties reflecting unfavorably on your moral attitude or conduct; indifference to indebtedness; and statements by you concerning any of the above unfavorable matters.

3. *Fitness reports* (fiche "P"): Fitness reports; statements by you, your reporting senior, or the reviewing officer regarding a particular report; letters of commendation or censure attached to fitness reports when such letters have not previously been filed in your record.

The *Confidential File* contains any correspondence to or about an officer that must be kept in a confidential status. Most officers have no material on confidential file.

Proceedings of Courts or Boards that affect your record are filed by the judge advocate general (JAG) of the Navy. You may examine these records in the JAG files. If unfavorable, such matter is referred to you before being filed.

Access to Record. The only persons who enjoy access to your record are you (on personal application to the Officer Files Unit); your personal representative, armed with proper proof; designated headquarters personnel; and, when authorized by the secretary of the Navy, the courts. No person (including you or your agents) without proper authority can withdraw official records and correspondence from the files or destroy them.

Make it a habit to review your record every time you find yourself in Quantico. Every two years, request a copy of the microfiche from HQMC (Code MMSB-10), Quantico, VA 22134-5002.

1202. Your Personal Records

The only administrative records that accompany you now, as distinct from records filed in Washington, are your *Health Record* and *Dental Record.*

Your *Health and Dental Records* are opened by the Navy's Bureau of Medicine and Surgery and contain your life history, the results of your physical examinations, and the medical history of every ailment that befalls you.

1203. Your Personal File

The day you are commissioned, start a personal file. This should contain, in one folder, all original travel orders and, in another, all official correspondence from, to, and concerning you. In addition, remember that some unofficial letters you write or receive are just as important to your career as the official ones.*

1204. Fitness Reports

Fitness reports provide the periodic documentation for the Marine Corps Performance Evaluation System. The system provides for the reporting, recording, and analysis of the performance, potential, and professional character of all Marines in the grade of sergeant and above. The fitness report form, when properly completed, constitutes the principal record of your performance of duties and conduct for a designated period of time. Linked together, these reports assist selection boards of all varieties in determining which officers are best suited for the services desired. They also provide the commandant and staff with information as to your desired duty assignments and locations for the future.

The form consists of several principal parts. Section A contains data on you, the period covered in the report, your duty assignments, physical and small personal weapons qualifications, and preferences for future assignments. It re-

---

*The History and Museums Division, Marine Corps Headquarters, encourages retired officers to donate personal files and papers to the Marine Corps archives.

mains *your* responsibility to provide the report to your reporting senior with the information in this section correctly stated. Section B is then filled out by the reporting senior, normally that officer next above you in your chain of command (unless he or she is of the same grade). This section rates your personal attributes. Generals are evaluated by letter reports, annually for brigadier generals.

Your fitness reports obviously will constitute a running record of your performance of duty throughout your career, as seen through the eyes of your various commanders. It is the most vital single source of your personal and professional record. It will merit your attention and review through your last day of service.

Occasions for Reports. There are nine occasions when a fitness report must be prepared on Marines in the grades of sergeant through colonel:

1. Change of reporting senior
2. Transfer
3. Assignment or return from temporary duty
4. End of Service
5. Grade change
6. Direction of the commandant
7. Annual (active duty)
8. Annual (reserve duty)
9. Reserve training

The annual periods for Marines vary by grade, in order to correspond to the needs of the promotion boards (reservists not on active duty fall under a different schedule):

Grade	Regular	Reserve
Colonel	May	June
Lieutenant Colonel	May	November
Major	July	December
Captain	July	January
1st Lieutenant	November/May	February
2d Lieutenant	January/July (semiannual)	April
Warrant Officers	March	February

Reporting Senior. Normally, the reporting senior is the next senior officer (or civilian in grade GS-9 or above) in your chain of command. Such a senior may be in the same grade as the Marine reported on, if that officer is the commanding officer or officer-in-charge, or has the specific authorization of the reviewing officer. The system values the reporting officer's viewpoint as the best position from which to observe a Marine's performance and the officer as the person most responsible for setting the Marine's daily tasks and the standards to which they are performed.

Reviewing Officer. The reviewing officer next receiving your fitness report is normally that officer (or civilian in grade GS-12 and above) next senior to the reporting officer in the chain of command. The reviewing officer occupies a critical link in the performance evaluation system by ensuring adherence to the stated regulations and exerting the leadership, supervision, and detached point of view to obtain unbiased and accurate reports. Errors by either the Marine reported on or the reporting officer are returned to them for correction. The reviewing officer fills out printed portions of the reviewing officer certification to indicate agreement or disagreement with the report. Written remarks, based upon the reviewing officer's personal knowledge of the Marine, are encouraged, especially to determine the Marine's potential to serve at a higher grade and also the Marine's general value to the service, in comparison with the other officers of the same grade serving with the reviewing officer. Remarks must be provided to clarify disagreement with the reporting senior or, in the case of adverse reports, to adjudicate the respective positions of the Marine and the reporting officer.

Initial reports on Marines joining the organization within ninety days of the end of the fitness report period are normally omitted (annual) or completed as "not observed" (all other occasions). This rule is excluded when, in the view of the reporting officer, sufficient observation occurred and the report provides important information to the commandant and remains fair to the Marine thus observed. A typical case would be during high-intensity or combat operations where close, daily, and detailed personal observation occurs.

Adverse reports contain any one of several possible ratings or phrases reflecting unsatisfactory performance and require special handling in addition to the normal processes. Generally, any of the following cases would constitute an adverse report:

• A report of failure of physical fitness testing or weight control program
• Any rating of "adverse"
• Any comments in Section I of a derogatory nature, comments on failures, unsatisfactory performance of duty or on a required program of training or education, or comments of a failure to measure up to norms and expectations.
• Similar adverse material contributed by the reviewing officer.

The revised performance reporting system introduced in 1999 greatly altered the scope and nature of fitness reports, their completion, and handling. After the first major overhaul in several decades, the revised system reduces the amount of writing and limits the scope of evaluation to assigned duties and tasks. It virtually eliminates gratuitous or freewheeling commentary, which in the past contributed to an acknowledged "inflation" and distortion of the system's goals. The new system will permit the use of automated technology which greatly enhances the quality of procedures, processes, and accountability.

Under the revised system, the reporting seniors are themselves "rated" with a profile revealing their tendencies in marking fitness reports. Marines will always receive a copy of the report as written by the reporting senior, and adverse reports will be referred back to the subject officer now by Headquarters Marine Corps for final comment, vice attaching it to the initial report at the unit level. Reviewing officers must make an evaluation of all officers of the same grade as the subject officer, if known, within that officer's command.

Records. A few months after you have seen your fitness report, you will receive a computer-generated receipt from HQMC that contains a recapitulation of the tabulated markings. Keep this in your personal file and verify later transfer to your Master Brief Sheet. The latter is mailed annually to all officers and can be requested at will from the HQMC Career Counseling Section (Code MMOA-4). Whenever you are in the Washington area, visit the records branch at Quantico to draw a copy of your microfiche record for study (also available by mail). Look at your trends, as displayed in the reports, and objectively strive to improve the weaknesses reported by your seniors, many of which you share with most other officers. If you desire professional help in interpreting or planning your career, seek the guidance of the HQMC Career Counseling Section, via appointment. That section's counselors have the advantage of knowing how the other officers of your grade and year group are performing and can advise you in clear and dispassionate terms.

In the event that after all interviews and reviews of your record have been accomplished, you believe a report reflects errors or injustice on the part of the reporting senior or reviewing officer, you have the final recourse of an appeal to the Board for Correction of Naval Records (BCNR) of the Department of the Navy. Any officer seeking such redress should obtain first the advice and recommendations of the HQMC Career Counseling Section before presenting the petition. The procedure goes as follows: The petitioner fills out the appropriate application form for correction of error or injustice, attaching copies of fitness reports, amplifying statements, and supporting evidence as applicable. Before reaching the actual board, however, the petition for redress must receive a review by the Performance Evaluation Review Board (PERB) of the relevant service, in this case the Marine Corps. If the PERB agrees with the petition, the records will be amended or removed without further authority to meet the applicant's requirements. If the PERB recommends the retention of the records, then the BCNR takes the matter for consideration. This three-member board will recommend, based upon a majority vote, the final actions to be taken by the secretary of the Navy. A final report of the BCNR to the petitioner will report the decision of the secretary and the actions, if any, taken with respect to the petitioner's records.

1205. Marking Fitness Reports

Because fitness reports are decisive in the career of an officer, the preparation of a fitness report is one of the most weighty tasks you will ever perform and an opportunity for you to contribute materially to the overall improvement of the Marine Corps. Instructions governing fitness reports are found in pertinent Marine Corps Orders, which you should review before you make out a report or a recommended report.

The suitability of an officer for future assignments, selection, or retention is based in large degree on the evaluations made by reporting seniors. For most officers in today's large services, there is little else on which decisions can be based.

Officer appraisal should be a continuous process rather than an intermittent one performed only at fitness report time. Shortcomings should be pointed out as they arise—not saved up. Counseling policy, now distinct from performance evaluation, requires you periodically to sit down with the officer and candidly discuss his or her general performance and personal qualities. This is not always an agreeable session for either party, but it is a responsibility of command.

You must therefore make out fitness reports carefully, impartially, and with a full appreciation of the task at hand and the responsibility that goes with it. A report that is unduly negative or fails to accent the positive might cost the Marine Corps a fine officer. On the other hand, your failure to point out weaknesses can cause the selection and promotion of an officer unsuited for higher rank at the expense of one who is. Reporting seniors can virtually ensure selection or force the separation of a given officer. Thus, as a reporting senior, you can add luster to a career or destroy it.

Put aside prejudice or partiality as you evaluate. Compare the officer being reported on with other officers of the same rank and experience. Guard particularly against the attitude of the moment; you are grading an officer's total performance during *the whole period covered*. Make initial drafts of the report, then review it for consistency and fairness. Ink in the final marks on the form, and type the comments.

Bear in mind that any group contains a few individuals at the top and bottom, respectively, who stand out favorably or unfavorably. The majority represents a fairly level standard of performance in between. If you find that your ratings tend to put most officers at the top or at the bottom, be quite sure you can justify this departure from the normal distribution (as you are specifically required to do in the case of certain outstanding or unsatisfactory marks). Remember that most officers are average officers. It is the easy way out to give high ratings to all officers, rationalizing that "everyone does." But overrating an average officer leaves no scope for the brilliant one.

Do not hesitate to use the "not observed" rating for any characteristic for which your observation has been too limited to warrant sound evaluation. An overall report of "not observed" may be provided if you have had less than ninety days' observation of the officer reported on, except in the cases of lieutenants or persons returning from temporary duty or changing status, in which cases the observation period must be less than thirty-one days. An "observed" fitness report can also be written on an officer or NCO of the Marine Corps Reserve on active duty for training for twelve to thirty days. If you feel that you can make a normal observed report in less than ninety days, other than in the preceding occasions, you will be required to justify that action. In contrast to earlier systems, a "not observed" report may still reflect certain mandatory comments, such as failure to complete a course, failure to pass the physical fitness test, or placement on the weight control program.

The final written section of the new fitness report, Section I—Directed and Additional Comments, carries much less weight than the former single space furnished for written comments. Because the new type report contains sections on the billet description, billet accomplishments, and an evaluation of some thirteen attributes among four categories, comments in this section must be clear, objective, and to the point—not an attempt to provide superlative descriptions and superfluous statistics to enhance one's image. The section may be left blank, given the depth covered previously in the report. Otherwise you will begin the section with the phrase "directed comments" or "additional comments" and supply objective, clear, and concise statements either required by the evaluation system or considered necessary by you to complete an accurate picture of the officer or NCO you are evaluating.

PROMOTION AND PRECEDENCE

1206.   The Marine Corps Promotion System

The Marine Corps and Navy share a system of officer promotion that has been under continuous evolution since 1915 and, in recent years, has served as a model for the other services. Under this system, officers who are best fitted are selected for advancement, while those least fitted are passed over and must ultimately retire. Determination of who is best fitted for promotion is accomplished by boards of senior officers, known as selection boards.

Promotion never comes automatically. To qualify for promotion, you must not only perform effectively and loyally in your present rank, but you must develop and prove your capacity to handle the increased responsiblities of higher rank.

1207.   Officer Distribution

The Defense Officer Personnel Management Act of 1981 provides officer promotion machinery for the Army, Marine Corps, Navy, and Air Force. The Navy and Marine Corps provisions are generally similiar. One of the most important things that this law does is to establish certain categories of officers for promotion purposes. It also regulates the number of officers who may be assigned to each grade. This is known as "officer distribution" and determines how many vacancies for promotion each rank contains.

Officer Categories.   All Marine officers are line officers. Some commissioned officers, however are designated "restricted in the performance of duty," in contrast to all other Marine officers, who are described as "unrestricted officers."

Existing law provides for two categories of *restricted officers:* permanent regular limited duty officers (LDO) and permanent warrant officers. All other officers in the Corps are considered for promotion and assignment purposes as not being restricted in the performance of duty.

Limited duty officers are former warrant or noncommissioned officers who have been commissioned for duty in the particular fields in which they have specialized, such as ordnance, motor transport, and so on. If the officer so applies, and is qualified, an LDO may be designated as an unrestricted officer, and the limited duty designation ceases.

Like limited duty officers, warrant officers are also appointed for duty in particular fields and are thus restricted to performance of duty in the appropriate field. Warrant officers selected from certain "line duty" MOS carry the title of "Marine Gunner" and wear the gunner's bursting bomb insignia. The MOS from which Marine gunners are usually appointed are 0302 (infantry), 0802 (artillery), 1802 (tank), 1803 (amphibian tractor), 2502 (communications), and 4915 (range officer).

Reserve officers, unless on active duty with the regular establishment, are selected separately. If on active duty with the regular establishment, Reserve officers are selected and promoted along with regular contemporaries. The Marine Corps has a continuing requirement for Reserve officers on active duty beyond their obligated service and now offers them a career program comparable to that of regular officers.

Distribution of Officers in Grades.   The number of officers who may be promoted above first lieutenant depends on the authorized numbers for each grade. These ceilings are computed by Marine Corps Headquarters and approved by the secretary of the Navy. The maximum in each grade (FY 1994) is:

General officers (not more than half may be major general or above; includes excess authorization for joint assignments)	66
Colonel	639
Lieutenant colonel	1,569
Major	3,056
Captain	5,844
Lieutenant (1st or 2d)	5,774
Warrant officer	1,947

If the secretary of the Navy decides that fewer officers than those computed are required in any grade, the secretary can establish that lesser figure as the authorized number for that grade.

Limited duty officers are not "additional numbers," but the actual number of LDOs may not exceed 3.64 percent of the total number of unrestricted officers at each grade.

General Officers.   Without summarizing all provisions of the Officer Personnel Act dealing with general officers, the following are noteworthy.

The commandant and vice commandant of the Marine Corps are four-star generals. A Marine as chairman of the Joint Chiefs of Staff or commander of a unified command also would be a four-star general.

The president may appoint up to eight of the authorized number of unrestricted general officers as lieutenant generals to head certain high commands or for duty of great responsibility. At present, the three-star billets of the Corps are:

Deputy Chief of Staff (Plans, Policy, and Operations), HQMC
Deputy Chief of Staff (Manpower), HQMC
Deputy Chief of Staff (Aviation), HQMC
Deputy Chief of Staff (Installations and Logistics), HQMC
Commanding Generals of the two Fleet Marine Forces
Commanding General, MCCDC
Commanding General, IMEF

1208. Promotion Procedure

Promotion to first lieutenant is by seniority on completion of twenty-four months' service in grade. From captain to major general, inclusive, promotion is by selection. The standard of selection is "best fitted"; eligibility requirements, selection procedures, and so forth are the same for all.

Eligibility for Selection.   You become eligible for selection when, approximately, you have completed service as follows:

	Years in Service
Colonel	22 (±1)
Lieutenant colonel	16 (±1)
Major	10 (±1)
Captain	4
First lieutenant	2

Eligibility for selection does not necessarily mean you enter a promotion zone, as described below. Once you become eligible, though, your eligibility for promotion continues, regardless of failure of selection, as long as you remain on active duty.

The Mechanics of Selection.   Each selection board receives the names and files (see Section 1201) of officers who are eligible for consideration. In addition, each board is informed of the names of the eligible officers who constitute the *promotion zone* for that grade. Whenever a selection board convenes, the secretary of the Navy determines how far down the eligible list the board must go in making selections, if a satisfactory flow of promotion is to be ensured.

Beginning with the most senior officer of the grade under consideration who has not previously failed to be selected, the promotion zone goes down to the last unrestricted officer needed to maintain the flow of promotion "up or out," as determined by the secretary of the Navy.

A separate promotion zone is established for limited duty officers, and the selection board is allocated separate quotas of limited duty vacancies to be filled by selection. These officers are considered only upon their specialist qualifications. They do not compete for selection with unrestricted officers.

Any officer eligible for selection may forward to the president of the board a letter inviting attention to any matter of record that the officer deems important in his or her case. This, however, is a privilege that should be exercised with the utmost prudence. Don't rock your boat.

All officers senior to or in a promotion zone fail of selection (that is, are "passed over") if not recommended for promotion. The effects of failing of selection, in terms of mandatory retirement, are covered in Section 1211.

Except for LDOs, a selection board must go below the promotion zone, among the eligibles, and select outstanding officers for accelerated promotion. But no officer below the promotion zone is considered passed over, even if an officer junior to him is selected for accelerated promotion, and not more than ten percent of the total number of officers whom the board is authorized to select may come from below the zone, except in the case of colonels and brigadier generals being considered for the next higher grade.

Once selected, your name is submitted by the board to the commandant, secretary of the Navy, and finally the president. If, as is usual, all names are approved, you are then promoted, subject to Senate confirmation, according to vacancies.

Selection Boards.   Marine selection boards usually consist of nine active or Reserve officers and are convened by the secretary of the Navy annually. The typical composition, by rank, of selection boards for the various grades is as follows:

	Number of Members by Grade		
Promotion to:	*Maj. Gen.*	*Brig. Gen.*	*Col./Lt. Col.*
Major general	9*		
Brigadier general	3*	6	
Colonel	3*	6	
Lieutenant colonel		2	7
Major		2	7
Captain		1	8
Chief warrant officer			5

*Senior selection boards virtually always include at least one lieutenant general.

The board is usually balanced in numbers of ground and aviation officers with representation of service support MOSs, and, if LDOs and reservists are to be considered by the board, it includes one of each as members.

No officer may be a member of two successive boards for the same grade. This ensures that eighteen different officers must pass on your case before you twice fail of selection.

Members of selection boards are sworn to act without prejudice or partiality and, like members of a court-martial, may not disclose their deliberations. Specifically, their sworn duties and obligations are as follows:

- To recommend the best-fitted officers for promotion
- To give equal weight with line duty to equally well-performed administrative staff duty, aviation duty, supply duty, or duty in any technical specialty
- Not to consider as prejudicial the fact that an officer under consideration may have been previously passed over
- Not to select more officers than the number set by the secretary of the Navy

(but the board need not select the full number if there are insufficient qualified names under consideration)

Effecting Promotions. When selected for promotion, your name goes on a promotion list in normal order of seniority. As vacancies occur, you are then promoted. All officer promotions, regular and reserve, however, are subject to such physical, mental, moral, and professional qualifications as the secretary of the Navy may prescribe. On promotion, you rate the pay and allowances of the higher grade from the date of the appointment.

1209. Precedence

Precedence is your right of seniority over other officers, based on rank and on the date of your appointment within a grade. The rank and precedence of officers on active duty is shown in numerical order in *The Combined List of Officers on Active Duty in the Marine Corps,* otherwise known as "The Blue Book." Your date of rank is also stated on your commission. Although complex methods previously determined the order of precedence of officers appointed to the same date of rank, today class standing at Basic School remains the sole criterion for that order, which will change thereafter only as officers are selected, "deep selected," or passed over for promotion.

Your Social Security number serves, in effect, as your service number instead of the "file number" every officer used to have. In addition to the Social Security number, every Marine officer has a number in grade, which is his or her number, in order of precedence within grade, in "The Blue Book." Your number in grade gives an exact indication of your precedence.

Precedence of officers of different services is in accordance with their relative grades and, within grade, in accordance with respective dates of rank, the senior in date of rank taking precedence. Among officers of different services of the same relative grade and the same date of rank, precedence is determined according to the time each has served on active duty as a commissioned officer.

RETIREMENT AND SEPARATION

1210. Introduction and Basic Definitions

Retirement is removal from active duty following completion of certain service and longevity requirements, after which the retired officer receives retired pay. Although no longer on duty, a retired officer remains a member of the Marine Corps, retains his or her rank and status as an officer (being entitled to all military courtesies of that rank), and may under certain conditions be recalled to active duty.

Separation or discharge is an absolute termination of officer status. Depending on the character of discharge, the officer being separated may or may not receive lump-sum separation pay. *Resignation,* as distinct from retirement, is total, voluntary separation from the service.

Revocation of commission may separate any officer who has been on continuing active duty for less than three years as a commissioned officer in the Marine Corps or Navy. An officer whose commission is revoked does not receive any advance pay or allowances or separation pay.

1211. Involuntary Retirement and Separation

Except for physical reasons, you retire upon reaching a certain age, on completing certain periods of service, or after failure of selection for promotion.

Retirement for Age. Officers still on the active list must retire at age sixty (sixty-two in the case of flag officers), unless the president in a particular case defers retirement. Such retirement may not be deferred beyond age sixty-four.

Limited duty officers, if not otherwise subject to retirement, must retire after completing thirty years' active Marine Corps or Navy service.

Retirement Requirements.

Major Generals. Major generals (as well as lieutenant generals) normally retire within a month of the date that they complete five years' service in grade and thirty-five years' commissioned service. They may stay on active duty from year to year if so recommended by a board convened for the purpose and approved by the secretary of the Navy.

Brigadier Generals. Brigadier generals retire within a month of the date that they complete thirty years' service or five years in grade.

Colonels. Colonels retire within a month of the date that they complete thirty years' total commissioned service, if they have twice failed for brigadier general, or the date that they complete five years' service in grade.

Lieutenant Colonels. Lieutenant colonels retire within a month of the date that they complete twenty-eight years' total commissioned service, if they have been passed over for colonel.

Majors. Majors retire within a month of the date that they complete twenty years total commissioned service, if they have twice been passed over for lieutenant colonel. They have to retire six months after their second failure, though present policy continues them to twenty years' service, provided no more than six years' continuation is thus required.

Captains and Lieutenants. Captains and first lieutenants who are twice passed over for major and captain, respectively, are honorably discharged (*not* retired) six months following the second failure, with separation pay based on length of service. An LDO, however, has the option of reversion to prior enlisted status.

Warrant Officers. Warrant officers who are twice passed over for promotion to the next higher permanent warrant grade, and decline reversion to enlisted status, are discharged with separation pay if they have less than eighteen years' active service since initial appointment as a warrant officer; if warrant officers so passed over have eighteen but less than twenty years' service since the original appointment, they will be retired (unless picked up in the interim) two months after completing twenty years. Any regular male warrant officer who has at least twenty years' active service in the armed forces will be retired at age sixty-two, or, short of that age, on completing thirty years' active service in the armed forces.

Selective Early Retirement. Defense Department policies authorize the services to convene boards to select officers for retirement in advance of the statutory limits of service. Such measures seek to retain the desired annual vacancies in grade and allow promotion opportunities for juniors at the desired rates (see Section 1207). The boards convene when directed by the service secretary and have the same composition normally as the board convened to promote to the next higher grade. Officers so selected will be retired on the date seven months after the board's results are approved. Such officers who choose to retire before the seven months elapse are considered "voluntary" retirements. Normally, such boards perform their duties only in time of forced personnel reductions by the services.

Officers Reported as Unsatisfactory. If at any time before completion of twenty years' service, your name comes before a selection board in normal course and you are specifically reported by that board to be unsatisfactory in performance of your duties, you are honorably discharged with separation pay (*not* retired) on 30 June following approval of the report by the president. An LDO so reported has the normal option of reverting to his former status. Do not confuse this procedure with being passed over (which is bad enough).

Revocation of Commission. The secretary of the Navy may revoke the commission of any officer who has less than three years' continuous service. Discharge of this type does not include separation pay. The most usual causes for revocation of commission are academic failure at Basic School, general low-caliber or unsatisfactory performance of duty, or temperamental unsuitability.

1212. Voluntary Retirement

When a regular or Reserve officer completes twenty years' active duty in the Marine Corps, Army, Navy, Air Force, or Coast Guard (including Reserve), ten years of which must have been active commissioned service, he or she may, in the discretion of the president, retire with the highest grade satisfactorily held, as determined by the secretary of the Navy.

When an officer has thirty year's active service, he or she may, in the discretion of the president, retire with 75 percent of active-duty base pay.

Retirements take effect on the first day of the month after the secretary of the Navy approves the request, *except* in cases of voluntary retirement in which a later date has been approved.

If you are considering voluntary retirement or are subject to involuntary or statutory retirement and you have any doubt as to your physical qualification for release from active duty, obtain a preliminary physical examination *three months ahead of estimated retirement date.* If a disability is discovered at this time, you might be eligible for physical retirement. Information as to your physical condition must be received by Headquarters Marine Corps in time to modify action on your retirement papers.

After the president or secretary of the Navy approves a request for retirement, or approves involuntary retirement proceedings, and the retirement has become effective, there is no process of law whereby the retired status can be changed except through disciplinary action or because of physical disability incurred subsequently while serving as a retired officer on active duty.

1213. Disability Retirement

Disability retirement is governed by Title 10, U.S. Code. Its important provisions are summarized below.

A *temporary-disability retired list* exists in each service, to which are transferred individuals whose physical condition prevents proper performance of duty but who may yet recover. Persons whose disability is less than 30 percent may be discharged with separation pay. Pay on the temporary-disability retired list may be either 2½ percent of active-duty pay per year for the number of years of service, *or* the percentage of disability fixed; but retired pay may not be less than 50 percent or more than 75 percent of active-duty pay. Disability retirement pay is tax-exempt.

If you are on the temporary-disability retired list, you must have a physical examination at least every eighteen months, for not more than five years. During that time, if your disability becomes permanent and is 30 percent or more, you are permanently retired for physical disability. If, upon examination, you are again found physically fit while on the temporary-disability retired list, you may, at your own consent, be reappointed to the active list in a rank not below that held when you went on the temporary-disability retired list. If you do not wish to return to active duty or are not qualified for duty but are still rated less than 30 percent disabled, you may be separated from the service, with separation pay.

If you are hospitalized for more than three months, a clinical board (or board of medical survey) at the hospital considers your case and usually recommends that you be (1) returned to duty, (2) given further treatment, (3) ordered to limited duty and reexamination after a stated period, (4) given sick leave and reexamination thereafter, or (5) ordered before a Marine Corps physical evaluation board.

You may waive the right to appear in person, but *should be very chary of this* unless the medical evidence in your case is uncomplicated and the result certain. You should also have counsel.

Appearance before the board requires less than a day; final action is taken by the secretary of the Navy. If you are incapacitated but do not require hospitalization, you may take leave or be assigned to temporary duty. If found qualified for continued active duty, you are ordered back to duty. If retired, you must complete travel home within one year from the date of retirement, in accordance with *Joint Travel Regulations.* You may choose any residence desired, even overseas, without regard to your current address of record in headquarters.

The report of a physical evaluation board is extensively reviewed in the Navy Department. The final reviewing authority is ordinarily the judge advocate general of the Navy. Retirement takes effect on the first day of the month after the secretary approves.

If you have less than eight years' active service and if disability is less than 30 percent, the physical evaluation board must determine whether your disability is the proximate result of active service. If the board so finds, you may be discharged with separation pay. Eight years or more of active service is considered proximate result.

CORRESPONDENCE AND MESSAGES

1214.   Official Correspondence

Both Marine Corps and Navy employ the same forms and procedures for official correspondence. These are prescribed in *Navy Regulations,* in the *Navy Correspondence Manual,* and in the *Marine Corps Manual.* "Correspondence" embraces letters, endorsements, speedletters (shortcut, urgent communications that do not require telegraphic or radio transmission), and memoranda. Correspondence is filed in accordance with *Navy Filing Manual.*

As an individual, you may originate official correspondence that pertains to you personally (including any recommendations for improvement or innovation that may benefit the Marine Corps). Correspondence affecting a command as a whole can be originated only by, or in the name of, the commanding officer.

Except for speedletters, official correspondence must be conducted through channels and must be promptly forwarded. Failure to do so (if in proper form and language) is a very serious dereliction.

Avoid unnecessary, verbose, imprecise correspondence. Joseph Pulitzer's rule for the staff of the old *New York World* applies with considerable force to military correspondence: "Accuracy, brevity, accuracy!"

During the past few years, government correspondence has grown less precise and less effective. Vague expressions, superlatives, and affectations have become commonplace, replacing, in many cases, clear and understandable terms. Complex language is used, not because it contributes to clarity, but because it makes the user feel self-important. It is not consistent with the character of the Marine Corps or with efficiency to dilute correspondence with unmilitary expressions or unnecessary language.

Admirable advice regarding official correspondence, and military writing in general, was offered recently in the thoroughly revised *Navy Correspondence Manual*. Read and heed.

1215. Official Letters

According to the nature of the correspondence, official letters may follow either the *naval form* (which is used throughout the naval establishment) or the *business form*. Examples and detailed instructions covering both forms can be found in the *Navy Correspondence Manual*. Speedletters, however, may follow the abbreviated form and language employed in dispatches and naval messages.

Hints for Official Letter Writers.   Until you are quite familiar with the prescribed forms for official correspondence, do your writing within arm's reach of the *Navy Correspondence Manual*. See that your unit clerks do likewise. Keep an up-to-date dictionary at hand.

Avoid pointless letters. Correspondence with higher authority should be confined to specific requests, reports, and concrete recommendations.

One letter should deal with one subject only. Cover separate subjects to the same addressee by separate letters. Answer official letters by letter, not by endorsement on the letter received, unless specifically directed to do so.

Write in terse, unadorned, direct, and clear language. Generally, use short sentences and paragraphs. Avoid the passive voice ("Please arrange the following," *not* "It is requested that the following arrangements be effectuated"). Don't be afraid to use the first person.

Be as temperate and courteous in correspondence as you would be in discussing the subject face to face with your correspondent.

Organize your facts and ideas before you write. The standard sequence for a staff study is a good one for almost any kind of official correspondence:
1. Statement of the problem
2. Facts bearing on the problem
3. Discussion
4. Conclusions
5. Recommendations

Do not send official letters to other officers in the same command. Intraunit and intraheadquarters correspondence should be by memorandum.

Block out important official letters in double-spaced rough draft. This permits you to make legible corrections and interlineations.

Shun like leprosy the demeaning practice, sometimes encountered in official correspondence or directives, of using the word "member" where "Marine," "officer," or "enlisted person" is meant; or "personnel" in lieu of "Marines" or "all hands." In expressing time, use the Navy twenty-four-hour system and never add the superfluous word "hours"—write "1230," not "1230 hours." Always choose a short, simple word over a long one. Write "pay," "help," "mistake" instead of "compensation," "assistance," "inadvertency."

Here is an example of gobbledygook, canned language, and jargon excerpted from a sampling of official correspondence. We would all be better off if most of these were never written again:

pursuant to
in conformance with
the full impact
pertinent facts
unprecedented—as a substitute for "unusual"
thorough and complete investigation
infeasible of accomplishment
at the earliest practicable moment
top management
rendered mandatory
salient data
materially impaired effectiveness
interface incompatibility (except in information management)
in light of the foregoing
above-named personnel
management—as a substitute for "command" or "leadership"
considered opinion
VIP
deobligate
firm up
formalize
outload, offload, onload
frame of reference
effectuate
definitive—where "definite" is meant
maximize
as appropriate
finalize
logisticswise
personnelwise
appraise—where "apprise" is intended
forward—as a garble for "foreword"
marshall—as a misspelling of "marshal"
throughput

1216. Official Mail

Official correspondence may be mailed with official postage stamps in envelopes bearing an official return address and the notation *"Official Business"* in the upper left-hand corner. As an officer you are entitled to use such envelopes for correspondence that clearly involves government business and for government parcels within prescribed weight limits. Be scrupulous in exercising this privilege. Remember you also are a taxpayer.

1217.   Personal Correspondence

Because you change stations every few years, keeping correspondents advised of your correct mailing address can be quite a problem.* Get change-of-address cards from your mail clerk or station post office and send them to all your regular correspondents every time you are detached. Should you wish to write an officer but not know his present address, simply address the letter as follows:

c/o Worldwide Locator
Headquarters Marine Corps (Code MMSB-17)
Quantico, VA 22134-5002

Fleet Post Office (FPO) and Army Post Office (APO).   Mail may be sent to units and persons afloat or overseas at domestic postage rates via East Coast and West Coast military postal centers. This privilege merits your use, as it saves you and your correspondents considerable money in postage charges, especially for publications and parcels. Units that deploy or are at sea receive their mail via the tracking and routing efforts of military postmasters in the shortest time possible. Generally speaking, if a ship or FMF unit is on the East Coast, the Atlantic, Europe, or Africa and adjacent waters, its mail goes via FPO AE or APO AE [zip code], with domestic postage charges to New York. Ships and units in the Pacific, Far East, or Indian Ocean receive mail via FPO AP or APO AP [zip code] with domestic charges paid to San Francisco or Seattle. A ship or station based in one geographic area, but deploying temporarily to another, will retain its original address, even though the postmasters will route the mail through different theaters. Finally, be aware that current postal privileges allow free mailing of letters and small parcels *within* a given postal theater, by writing "MPS" in the corner normally reserved for stamps. Be sure to obtain specific instructions, however, before attempting to use this procedure.

1218.   Personal Radio Traffic

If you are serving at sea or at a station outside the continental limits of the United States where there are no commercial cable services, you may file personal traffic for stateside addresses via what is known as "Class E Messages." In this system, your message is transmitted by naval communications to the nearest Naval Communication Station in the United States, which relays your message to its ultimate addressee via commercial telegraph. You pay for the cost of commercial relay only. If you want to send a Class E message, see your communications officer. Many bases also feature a Military Affiliate Radio Station (MARS), linking with amateur radio operators, for radiotelephone communications around the world.

---

*For guidance of your family or parents at your permanent home address, Postal Laws and Regulations permit postage-free forwarding of any class of mail addressed to a member of the Armed Services, if marked, *"Change of Address Due to Official Orders, Postal Reg. 157.4."*

SECURITY OF INFORMATION

1219. Personal Security

After taking your oath and becoming a new Marine officer, in your new life and status you receive access to information not generally available to civilians. One of your most important responsibilities then becomes the safeguarding and discreet use of this information in such a way that it can never fall into the hands of enemies of the United States. Remember that, war or peace, the battle for information goes on continually. Our success in this battle will determine whether the odds of physical combat are on our side or our enemies' sides.

Indiscreet conversation and personal letters constitute great menaces to security. Guard against unthinking discussion of classified "shop talk," even with your family and friends. Avoid loose talk in public places. When you are on the telephone, you can never tell who may be listening. Automatic self-censorship is a responsibility of all Marines.

1220. Security of Classified Matter

Classified matter is anything—either information or materiel—that, in the public interest, must be safeguarded against unauthorized or improper disclosure. *Navy Regulations,* as well as the *Navy Security Manual for Classified Matter* and the *Registered Publications Manual,* contain detailed instructions that must be followed to the letter when you handle classified matter. The security of classified matter is the security of the United States.

Classifications.   The categories of security classification are *Top Secret, Secret,* and *Confidential.* In addition, certain information regarding nuclear weapons and related subjects is classed as *Special Information.* It is up to the originator of matter—if so authorized—to assign it the appropriate classification, and he or she, as well as higher authorities, may reclassify it when appropriate. Reclassification can involve either "upgrading" or "downgrading."

Handling of Classified Matter.   The precautions regarding preparation, marking, custody, handling, transmitting, stowage, disclosure, control, accounting for, and disposal of classified matter may be found in the references at the beginning of this section, and of course you must follow them to your utmost. If, however, you find yourself in a situation where you cannot physically comply with certain of these rules, you are bound simply to do your utmost, in common sense and zeal, to safeguard whatever may be entrusted to you. Should you have reason to believe classified information has been compromised, through your fault or anyone else's, you must inform your commanding officer at once.

No one, regardless of rank or position, is automatically entitled to knowledge or possession of classified matter. Such information goes only to those who *need to know.*

LEAVE AND LIBERTY

1221. Leave of Absence

Subject to the needs of the service, leave of absence provides time off for mental and physical relaxation from duty and gives you opportunity to settle your affairs when the time comes for change of station. Every officer on active duty accrues leave at the rate of thirty days a year (that is, $2^1/2$ days per month).

Without jeopardizing the readiness of your command, your commanding officer sometimes cannot grant every officer all the leave he or she rates. Whatever leave is not taken "goes on the books" until you have a maximum of sixty days' unused, or accrued, leave. Earned leave that accrues above sixty days must be automatically dropped on 30 September each year, and when you retire. As you approach retirement, it is a good idea to let leave accrue to a minimum of thirty days, since you receive a lump-sum payment for such accrued leave when you retire. Short of final years, however, take leave as you can; the days that are dropped each first of October can never come back.

Leave of absence describes authorized vacation or absence from duty, as distinguished from *liberty,* which is merely authority to be away from your place of duty for short periods and is not charged to leave.

Accrued leave is the unused leave to your credit "on the books" each 1 October. You cannot bank up more than 60 days' accrued leave.

Annual leave is leave taken as routine vacation from duty. Annual leave is limited to your total accrued leave plus forty-five days' advance leave but may not exceed periods of sixty days.

Sick leave is given to convalescents on recommendation of the medical authorities or to repatriated prisoners of war. Sick leave does not count against accrued leave.

Emergency leave may be granted to help alleviate some personal emergency, such as death or serious illness in the immediate family. Emergency leave is charged against accrued leave and may not exceed 105 days.

Excess leave is leave in excess of all your accrued leave plus forty-five days' advance leave. Avoid taking excess leave when you can possibly do so because your pay and allowances are checked while you are on excess leave.

Earned leave is the term used to describe the leave potential of an individual at any given date during the fiscal year. Earned leave is calculated as follows: From the amount of accrued leave, subtract whatever leave has been taken since the outset of the fiscal year to the date in question. To that remainder add the amount of leave earned since the beginning of the fiscal year. Earned leave may exceed sixty days during the fiscal year but will always be cut back to sixty days at the beginning of the new fiscal year.

Advance leave is an accounting term to describe leave granted in advance of accrual.

Delay in reporting is leave authorized to be taken after detachment from one permanent station and before reporting to another. Only the commandant can grant delay to an officer.

Graduation leave is granted to officers newly commissioned from one of the service academies (*not* to officers from any other source). It is thirty days, not chargeable to the officer's leave account, and you must take it prior to reporting to the first permanent duty station (ordinarily Basic School) or CONUS port of embarkation if ordered to permanent duty beyond the seas.

1222. Computing Leave and Delay in Reporting

No small amount of low-order bookkeeping and finger counting centers about the average officer's computations of leave and delay. Here is how to make these computations:

Amount of Leave or Delay	Date of Departure	Must Return and Report Not Later Than
10 days' annual leave	10 April (day of duty, not leave)	21 April (before forenoon quarters [0900] or beginnng of working hours
20 days' delay, with 5 days' travel time, and 4 days' "proceed" time (permanent change of station)	1 August (date of detachment, day of duty)	30 August (without delay, you would be due 10 August; add 20 days' delay, making it 30 August)

Your day of departure on leave, if after 1600, counts as a day on duty (and hence is not charged as leave).

If you return after the beginning of working hours on shore station, or after the hour of 0900 on board ship, the calendar day of return counts as a day of leave. If, however, you return before working hours or before 0900 on board ship, the calendar day of return is a day of duty.

1223. Leave Requests and Records

Requesting Leave. When you want leave, give your commanding officer advance notice. Some organizations have an annual leave plan that permits all officers to book leave well in advance. After you have informal approval for your projected leave, submit a written request using the standard leave-authorization form when available (via channels, if necessary) to the officer who is authorized to grant leave—usually your battalion, squadron, or post CO. Your leave request should include the number of days and type of leave desired, the number of days' leave you have already taken during the fiscal year, your address while on leave, whether you are a member of any court or board, and any other pertinent information or special justification for the request.

If approved, your leave request is returned by endorsement. Keep it with you throughout your leave.

Address during Leave. It is your responsibility to keep your commanding officer apprised of your address at all times while on leave. If your plans change, inform him or her by telephone or telegram. If you are touring, set up a number of check-in points, such as hotels where you expect to stay, American Automobile Association offices, or homes of friends. You have no leg to stand on if, while on leave, your commanding officer tries to communicate with you and cannot reach you.

Your Leave Record. Every officer has a leave record (Leave and Earnings Statement, or "LES"), on which all leave taken is debited and all leave earned is credited each month. This record is compiled by the headquarters that administers you, but it is your responsibility to see that your leave record is correct.

1224.   Foreign Leave

Officers going on foreign leave may travel, on a space-available basis, in government aircraft, in uniform. Unless you are authorized by the commandant to wear uniform while on foreign leave, you must wear civilian clothes.

Permission to visit certain foreign countries while on leave must be granted by the commandant, except for visits to certain foreign areas specified from time to time in current directives, for which blanket authorization is granted.

1225.   Liberty

Liberty is local free time, within limits, that does not count as leave. It may be granted at any time for up to forty-eight hours. If the period includes a legal holiday, any commanding officer can extend a "forty-eight" to a "seventy-two." Commanding officers so authorized by the commandant may grant ninety-six hour liberty. But liberty cannot be used as a device to extend leave.

Unless you have specific permission to the contrary, while on liberty you must remain within the general vicinity of your post. Almost all posts and units have standing orders that designate "liberty limits," beyond which ordinary liberty does not extend. The purpose of this is to prevent Marines from going so far afield that they cannot count on returning within the prescribed time.

IDENTITY DEVICES

1226.   "ID Card"

The "ID card," or Armed Forces Identification Card, is the most important identifying document you have. It identifies you as a Marine officer and must be safeguarded with great care. Regular and active-duty Reserve officers carry a green card, whereas inactive Reserve personnel carry a red card. Retired officers and enlisted persons are issued a grey card. Loss of an ID card is serious and must be reported immediately. Carry the card at all times, and never surrender it. The ID card, however, is not a pass, but an identifying device.

1227. Identification Tags

Every Marine on active duty is issued two "dog tags" for identification should he or she be killed or wounded in action. These tags are items of equipment. When not required to be worn, they must remain in your possession. Note that *both* tags must be worn, when tags are required.

1228. Official Photograph

As soon as you are commissioned, and prior to any consideration by a regular promotion board, you must submit an official photograph. This photo cannot be more than six months old when the board convenes. This is then filed in your official record. Considering its purpose, you should take care to look your best. See your adjutant to determine the uniform, pose, and data desired under current directives. If your board is about to convene, mail the photo directly to the Promotion Branch (HQMC Code MMPR-1).

1229. Dependents' ID Cards

Your spouse and each family member over age ten are entitled to an Armed Forces Dependent's Card. This card, like your ID Card, is an identity device and does not in itself entitle the bearer to anything. It ordinarily serves, however, to establish identification for medical care, post exchange, and similar privileges extended to dependents. (See Section 806.)

1230. Standard Vehicle Stickers

The Department of Defense has standard bumper decals for personal vehicles of active and retired officers and enlisted people of the Navy and Marine Corps. Officer stickers are blue; enlisted, red. To obtain stickers and register your car, consult your provost marshal. Properly displayed, they permit routine entry into military bases and facilities.

My Lord—If I attempted to answer the mass of futile correspondence that surrounds me, I should be debarred from all serious business of campaigning.

I must remind your Lordship—for the last time—that so long as I retain an independent position, I shall see that no officer under my command is debarred, by attending to the futile drivelling of mere quill driving in your Lordship's office, from attending to his first duty—which is, and always has been, so to train the private men under his command that they may, without question, beat any force opposed to them in the field.

—Letter attributed to the Duke of Wellington

13

Pay, Allowances, and Official Travel

It is related that, during the early days of World War II, a lofty-minded civilian visited Guadalcanal. During his tour, war aims were mentioned. Addressing Lieutenant Colonel L. B. Puller, one of the most hard-bitten professionals on the island—or, for that matter, in the Marine Corps—the visitor inquired, "And what, colonel, are *you* fighting for?"

Colonel Puller reflected for a moment, then answered, "$649 a month."

Whether you incline to this view or to the sentiments of George Washington, quoted at the end of this chapter, the importance of knowing about pay and allowances is self-evident.

Every member of the service is paid monthly, or twice monthly, based on rank and length of service. Regardless of whether your rank is temporary or permanent, you are paid at the rates prescribed for that grade.

The military term for your pay is *military compensation*. The military equivalent of a civilian salary includes basic pay, quarters allowance, subsistence, and, often overlooked, the federal income tax advantage deriving from tax-exempt allowances. Your pay normally increases each January, in line with pay levels in the private economy.

Besides regular pay, just described, officers whose duties or status so qualify them are entitled to incentive and special pay, including flight pay (see Section 1306).

1301. Pay System

Marines, both active and Reserve, are paid through a centralized automated Marine Corps Total Force System (MCTFS), which constitutes part of an integrated armed forces pay and personnel system.

Under MCTFS, a master pay account is maintained for each Marine at the Defense Finance and Accounting Service, Kansas City Center, Missouri. Monthly "leave and earnings statements" (LES) are produced from information in your master pay account; are distributed to you, your commanding officer, and your finance officer; and are filed at the MCFC on microfiche for permanent record. Your LES reflects what you are due, tax withholding, leave balance, and any deductions, and forecasts the amount payable for the next two paydays.

1302. Service Creditable for Pay Purposes

In determining your length of service for pay purposes, you receive credit for all service, active or inactive, in the Marine Corps, Navy, Army, Air Force, Coast Guard, and Reserve components thereof. In addition, full time is allowed to Marines for service in the Army Nurse Corps, the Navy Nurse Corps, the nurse corps of the Public Health Service, and Reserve components thereof. Full time is also allowed for service as deck officer or junior engineer in the Coast and Geodetic Survey. Active service in the appointive grade as aviation cadet and officer candidate (PLC) may be counted as service for pay purposes. Further, captains and lieutenants with more than four years' active duty (including active duty for training) as enlisted persons receive a separate, slightly higher rate of pay.

Service not creditable for longevity increases is service as cadet or midshipman; service in inactive National Guard, or in State, Home, or Territorial Guard; service in ROTC; and time spent in voided fraudulent enlistment.

You count, in the computation of basic pay, the total of all periods authorized to be counted in any of the services.

1303. Family Members

Some allowances vary according to your family size. The law defines family as:
- Your spouse (whose dependency is presumed)
- Unmarried children under age twenty-one (twenty-three if enrolled in higher education), or over age twenty-one if handicapped and incapable of self-support
- A parent (or one who has stood *in loco parentis*), if chiefly dependent on you for over half support
- Stepchildren and adopted children, if dependent
   Except for your spouse or unmarried minor children, you must be able to prove dependency for any persons for whom you claim allowances.

1304. Subsistence

Every officer on active duty receives a basic monthly subsistence allowance, regardless of his or her family status.

1305. Quarters Allowance

If you have a family, you receive quarters allowance except when assigned government quarters for yourself and family. If you are assigned quarters adequate for yourself but not adequate for your family members, or if they are prevented by official orders from joining you, you continue to receive quarters allowance. While on authorized delay or in transit between permanent stations, you rate quarters allowance, as well as for the interval between the date when sworn in and reporting for first duty.

Without family, you receive quarters allowance, except:

- When on sea duty (unless on temporary duty not exceeding three months)
- While in the field (unless on temporary additional duty of less than three months or required to procure quarters at own expense)
- While occupying or assigned adequate public quarters

Officers without family members who do not qualify for a full quarters allowance because they are on sea or field duty or living in government quarters are entitled to a partial quarters allowance.

In general, the status of an officer without family members at the permanent station (as long as that duty station remains unchanged) determines his or her right to quarters allowance. This is true even though quarters may be occupied at some other place than the permanent duty station, including time while on temporary additional duty (TAD), on leave, or hospitalized.

For quarters purposes, an officer without family is, in general, considered to be on sea duty when on temporary additional duty on board ship even though one's primary duty is ashore. An officer is considered on field duty when on service with troops operating against an enemy, either actual or potential.

1306. Incentive Pay

Incentive pay is additional pay for undertaking an aviation career, submarine duty, or performance of hazardous duty in obedience to competent orders.

The following hazardous duties currently rate incentive pay:

- Frequent and regular participation in aerial flights in a nonrated status or as a noncrew member
- High- or low-pressure chamber inside observer; diving or submarine duty
- Parachute jumping
- Demolition of explosives as a primary duty, including training for such duty
- Duty as a human test subject in stress experiments

The president may suspend hazardous duty pay in wartime. Finally, you may not receive it for more than two purposes at the same time.

In addition to hazardous duty pay, Marine officers frequently qualify for two other types of incentive pay:

- Career sea pay compensates persons assigned for thirty-six *continuous* months to a ship performing missions while primarily under way. Over $100 per month is paid for each additional month assigned to such duty.
- Foreign language proficiency pay (FLPP) provides up to $100 per month for persons demonstrating proficiency in one or more foreign tongues, validated by examination on an annual basis. Only those assigned to billets requiring a language proficiency or holding MOS, which include language skills, will receive FLPP.

1307. Advance Pay

An advance of pay ("dead horse" in slang) incident to a permanent change of station (PCS) provides funds to meet the extraordinary expenses of a government-ordered relocation. It assists with out-of-pocket expenses that exceed or precede reimbursements incurred during a PCS move, which are not typical of day-to-day military living.

You may draw advance pay any time after receipt of orders involving detachment from permanent duty station until sixty days after reporting to a new permanent station, provided the orders are not incident to separation from the service or trial by court-martial. Temporary duty en route is no bar to drawing advance pay. The amount advanced normally does not exceed one month's pay, but as much as twelve months' basic pay (less income tax, deduction for Social Security, and indebtedness to the government) may be drawn.

1308. Midshipmen and Cadets

Midshipmen and cadets from the other academies receive $543.90 (1994) per month as base pay. They receive rations in kind or commuted rations at rates periodically fixed by regulations.

1309. Uniform Allowances for Officers

All Marine officers, regardless of source of commission or previous enlisted status, receive an initial uniform allowance.

Reserve officers who have not received a uniform allowance during the preceding two years may draw it if, during that time, they have completed at least ninety days of active duty.

Civilian clothing allowances for officers depend on an assignment to a high-risk area outside the United States, certified as such by the Department of State or Defense. In such a case, where officers wear civilian clothing for all or a substantial part of their duties, a one-time allowance is paid for the two- or three-year tour length.

The subject of uniform allowances remains complex. For the final word, consult *Part A, Volume 7, DOD Financial Management Regulation Military Pay, Policy and Procedures.*

1310.   Flight Pay

To qualify for flight pay (or, as it is now technically termed, "Aviation Career Incentive Pay," or ACIP) you must be designated as a student naval aviator or student naval flight officer, or rated as naval aviator or naval flight officer, and be assigned to an aviation unit having aircraft. During your first twelve years' service, besides having a minimum number of operational flying assignments, you must also meet annual and semiannual prescribed minimum required flight hours. After your initial twelve years in flight status, your continued qualification to fly for pay depends on satisfactory passage of "gates" set by law and listed in Table 13–1.

1311.   Pay of Enlisted Personnel

The monthly basic pay of enlisted personnel of the Marine Corps, Navy, Coast Guard, Army, and Air Force may be found in current pay tables and is the same, grade for grade, in all services.

Enlisted Marines may be authorized *commuted rations* in lieu of rations in kind at a current per diem rate determined by law and regulation. If rations in kind be unavailable, they are entitled to basic *allowance for subsistence* at a per diem generally larger than for *commuted rations.*

In general, enlisted Marines are entitled to a quarters allowance, with or without family, under the same conditions as officers.

Leave rations are granted to enlisted Marines on leave (if they are not furnished rations in kind) at a per diem rate.

1312.   Enlisted Clothing Allowances

An initial in-kind clothing allowance is granted to each enlisted person. Six months after assignment to active duty, a monthly basic clothing maintenance allowance accrues to each enlisted person for the first three years of service; thereafter, an increased standard clothing maintenance allowance continues while the individual remains on active duty.

1313.   Family Separation Allowance

Family separation allowance equal to "without-quarters" basic allowance for quarters is payable to a Marine, with family members, who is on permanent duty in Alaska or outside the United States under certain conditions when dependents are not permitted to join him or her.

An additional allowance of $75 per month may be paid to a Marine, with family members, who is away from home under certain conditions.

Both of these allowances may be paid at the same time and in addition to any other allowances or per diem to which you are entitled.

Table 13–1.   Gates and flight pay entitlement

Number of Years Aviation Service	Years in Operational Assignment*	Entitlement to ACIP
12	9 or more	First 18 years of aviation service
18	10 or 11	First 22 years of officer service
18	12 or more	First 25 years of officer service

*Operation duty assignments are listed and defined in MCO 3710.1D.

1314. Reenlistment Bonus

The purpose of this bonus is to encourage Marines with costly or specialist skills to reenlist. Enlisted Marines, who have critical skills and have completed less than fourteen years' active service, may be paid "shipping-over money" of as much as $45,000.

1315. Retired Pay

Retired pay consists of the retainer received by an officer on the retired list. No allowances are paid retired officers. Separation pay is a lump-sum payment made to an officer involuntarily discharged from the service, based on 10 percent of active-duty pay for each year of commissioned service.

Computation.   Originally, retired pay was based on the active-duty pay of the grade in which an officer was serving at the time of retirement, plus periodic increases. Except for physical disability retirement, retired pay was computed by multiplying $2^1/_2$ percent of the officer's active-duty base pay at time of retirement by the number of years' service creditable for pay purposes, the total not to exceed 75 percent of such basic pay.

Marines entering the Corps after 7 September 1980 may retire after 20 years of service and receive a monthly retainer based on 50 percent of their averaged high three years of pay. Those entering after 1 August 1986 can retire after twenty years of service and receive payment based upon 40 percent of their high three years of pay. The percentage increases above 40 percent by $3^1/_2$ percent for each year of additional service beyond the twenty years.

Retired Pay Accounts.   Defense Finance and Accounting Service, Cleveland Center, Box 99191, Cleveland OH 44199-1126, telephone (800) 321-1080, maintains all retired pay accounts for all services. Marine Corps accounts were transferred there in 1994.

Income tax continues to be withheld on retired pay except for physically disabled officers wholly exempt from payment of income taxes. Unless otherwise requested, all allotments are automatically continued when you retire.

1316. Settlement for Unused Leave

Each member of the Marine Corps or Marine Corps Reserve having unused leave to his or her credit on discharge or separation from active duty is compensated for such unused leave on the basis of basic pay. Payment is made for a career total up to sixty days' unused leave. Thus, as retirement approaches, it is advantageous to keep the maximum accrued leave on the books.

TRAVEL OF MILITARY PERSONNEL

1317. Travel Expense and Mileage

The law provides travel expenses for military personnel on a mileage or per diem basis, by rail, private conveyance, steamer, or aircraft, the allowances for travel being computed on the basis of mileage rates and/or per diem expenses. The actual rates of reimbursement and the regulations governing issuance of transportation are contained in the *Joint Travel Regulations* and *Marine Corps Travel Instructions*. Check with your finance officer for guidance. Basically, your options are:

a. Transportation in kind, reimbursement therefor, or a monetary allowance in lieu of cost of transportation based on distance in official mileage tables

b. The allowance in (a) plus a per diem in lieu of subsistence

c. For travel within continental United States, a mileage allowance according to current mileage tables

1318. Travel Orders

Travel status is travel away from your duty station, under orders on official business.

When you apply for reimbursement for travel performed, or for transportation for travel to be performed, you must have travel orders.

Authority to issue travel orders rests with the commandant, who delegates this authority to certain commands.

All travel orders must contain the following nine items:

1. The Marine's name
2. Reference to authority other than the commandant
3. The place or places to which the Marine is ordered to travel
4. The date on which the Marine will proceed
5. The delay authorized in reporting, if any
6. The modes of transportation authorized
7. The duty (official/public) to be performed
8. The person to whom the Marine shall report (if so required)
9. The accounting data for cost of travel

Omission of any of these items can delay reimbursement and might cause rejection of a travel claim as invalid. Be sure you understand your orders before departure, and carry them out exactly.

"Proceed" Time.   The dates when you must comply with travel orders, and when you must report, depend on certain phraseology that always appears in orders. Check to see which of the following expressions appears, then govern yourself accordingly.

"Proceed."   If your orders have no limiting date and no haste is required in execution, you are directed simply to "proceed." You are allowed four days' proceed time before commencement of travel (unless you have also been granted delay in reporting.

"Proceed Without Delay."   When haste in execution is demanded, you are directed to "proceed without delay." You are allowed only forty-eight hours' proceed time before commencement of travel.

"Proceed Immediately."   When maximum haste is required, orders are worded "proceed immediately." In this case you rate only twelve hours' proceed time before commencement of travel.

A number of additional ground rules apply to computation and availability of proceed time when travel orders require temporary or temporary additional duty (TAD) or are received while on such duty. For these rules, consult Chapter 4, *Assignment, Classification, and Travel Manual.*

Types of Orders.   Four types of travel orders are generally encountered.

Permanent Change of Station.   This includes transfer from one permanent station to another; travel to first duty station after appointment; call to active duty; change in home port or home yard of a ship (for family members); travel home from last duty station upon retirement, separation, or relief from active duty.

Temporary Duty (TD).   This is duty at a place other than permanent station, under orders that direct further assignment to a new permanent station. While on temporary duty—as distinguished from temporary *additional duty*—you have no permanent station.

Temporary Additional Duty (TAD).   This includes travel away from permanent station, performance of duty elsewhere, and return to permanent station.

Blanket or Repeat Travel Orders.   These are temporary additional duty orders issued to individuals for regular and frequent trips away from permanent duty stations in connection with duty.

1319. What to Do about Your Orders

Here is what you do when you receive a set of orders. (This is written to apply specifically to temporary additional duty orders as they are the most frequently encountered.)

1. On receiving orders, read them through and check the following points:
   - Correct rank, name, Social Security number, and MOS
   - Departure date
   - Place or places to be visited
   - Whether you are to report to a given headquarters or command
   - Mission you are to accomplish

- Security clearance
- Modes or options of transportation
- Whether the orders are signed
- First (receiving) endorsement completed
- Statement on requirement to use government quarters and meals
  If your orders appear incorrect, or if it appears that you cannot carry them out as directed, return them immediately to the issuing officer with an explanation of the difficulty.
2. Check out before departing and check in on return with your adjutant during working hours, or with the officer of the day or staff duty officer at all other times.
3. If your orders so direct, you will have to report to some other headquarters or command (these are known as "reporting orders"—those not requiring you to report to anyone are known as "nonreporting orders"). When your TAD is completed at the distant place or station and before reporting, be sure your orders are endorsed and signed, stating the time and date you reported, the date your TAD was completed, and the availability or nonavailability of quarters and messing facilities.
4. If your orders do not direct you to report (that is, are "nonreporting") and if you intend to claim full per diem, and if your TAD at a place is twenty-four hours or longer, you must obtain a certificate of endorsement from the CO at that place, to the effect that government quarters and mess were not available for your occupancy while there on TAD. This entitles you to higher per diem.
5. If, while away from your parent command, you find you cannot carry out your orders as written without incurring additional expense, or if some unforeseen contingency arises that is not provided for in the orders, request instructions by message or telephone (which can be reimbursed at government expense) before proceeding further. Reimbursement for unauthorized additional expenses or unauthorized travel might not be paid.
6. If orders specify travel by government aircraft where available, you must use government air unless a transportation officer certifies that government air transportation is not available. Under current regulations, government air is considered "available" if there is a *scheduled* government plane departing for your destination within forty-eight hours of the time you plan to leave. If no special mode of transportation—or some other option—is specified in your orders, take your choice.
7. Keep an accurate itinerary and a record of authorized travel expenses for which you can claim reimbursement (see Section 1321).
8. Turn in your orders, complete with itinerary, to your finance office the third working day after your return to home station.

1320. Travel Time

Travel time allowed in connection with permanent change of station is either the actual time required or "constructive travel time," whichever is less.

Actual travel time is computed in whole days regardless of the length of time actually spent traveling in any given day. This requires completion of an itinerary showing all stops of one calendar day or more.

Constructive travel time for commercial transportation is one hour for each forty miles of travel by rail or bus, with a proportionate part of one hour allowed for any fraction of forty miles; and one hour for each five hundred miles of air travel, with similar proportionate allowances for fractions of five hundred miles. One day of travel time is allowed for each eighteen hours of commercial constructive travel time.

Constructive travel time for travel by privately owned vehicle (POV) is based on one day for each three hundred miles and for any fraction above one hundred fifty miles.

Regardless of the actual sequence of travel, constructive travel time is computed in order of POV, commercial surface, and commercial air. It is computed on the basis of the official distance between the points of duty contained in the *Official Table of Distances.*

Regardless of the mode or modes of transportation, only one day of travel time is allowed if the ordered travel is four hundred fifty miles or less.

Government and commercial vessel travel time is the actual time required to complete the trip.

Proceed, delay, and travel time are covered in detail in Chapter 4, *Assignment, Classification, and Travel Manual.* There are few parts of the *Manual* more important for a young officer to know thoroughly.

1321. Reimbursement

On permanent change of station, except when traveling in a group or with troops, you may choose one of the following optional allowances for travel within the United States:
* Mileage at prescribed rate
* Reimbursement for common carrier travel plus per diem
* Government transportation, if available, plus per diem
* Common carrier transportation on government travel request (T/R) plus per diem

When you make your own travel arrangements, you may choose between mileage or reimbursement of common carrier costs (which is limited to cost for travel over the direct route between the points of travel).

Mileage is computed via official common carrier distance or official highway distance, depending upon the mode of transportation used. These distances are given in the *Official Table of Distances.*

For temporary duty (TD), reimbursement for travel is the same as for permanent change of station as shown above.

On temporary additional duty orders (TAD), which permit per diem reimbursement, transportation is furnished in kind or by transportation request, and reimbursement is at specified per diem. If you choose to pay your own travel expenses rather than use a T/R, you will be reimbursed at a given prescribed rate per mile for the official distance. If travel by private automobile is authorized and used—as more advantageous to the government—you get a different rate plus a per diem allowance. On this mode of travel, you are authorized travel time and per diem for the actual time necessary to make the trip. If the orders authorize you to travel by private conveyance, you are authorized travel time at three hundred miles per day but your per diem will be based on common carrier schedules, not to exceed time actually used. When orders direct a specific mode of transportation but you perform travel via another mode, including privately owned conveyance, for your own convenience, you will not be entitled to reimbursement for cost of transportation, or to the monetary allowance in lieu of transportation, unless the authority responsible for furnishing the transportation requests certifies that T/Rs were not available or the mode of transportation directed was not available at the time and place required in time to comply with the orders. Travel time in excess of that authorized by the directed mode is chargeable as annual leave.

1322.   Per Diem Allowances

These are designed to cover hotel, meals, tips, taxi fares (other than to and from carrier terminal), laundry, and other incidental expenses. You get per diem for temporary additional duty or temporary duty, including periods of necessary delay while awaiting transportation and at ports during permanent change of station.

In the United States.   Per diem rates within the United States are given in *Joint Travel Regulations.* Where government quarters and/or mess is available, the allowance is reduced proportionately. If you claim maximum per diem, you must secure a certificate from the local commander that government quarters and/or mess were not available.

Outside the United States.   Per diem allowances vary widely from country to country and are subject to frequent change. They are discussed in *Joint Travel Regulations,* Chapter 4.

1323.   Reimbursable Expenses

Certain travel expenses (in addition to per diem) are separately reimbursable. These include:
1. Taxi fares or other local transportation between places of abode and terminals, and between terminals when free transfer is not included; also taxi fares between terminal and place of duty
2. Tips to porters; fees for checking baggage; excess baggage, when approved
3. Fares and tolls, when traveling by government transportation
4. In government aircraft: cost of fuel, repairs, nonpersonal services, guards, and storage at other government fields

5. In government auto: storage charges, repairs, fuel, when government facilities are not available
6. Telephone and telegraph charges incident to duty and arrangement of transportation but not hotel reservations
7. Registration fees at technical, professional, or scientific meetings and so forth, when attendance is authorized
8. Passport and visa fees, including cost of photographs and birth certificates required in connection therewith, and cost of traveler's checks
9. Entry fees, port and airport taxes, and embarkation or debarkation fees upon arrival or departure from foreign countries
10. Any incidental expense that can be justified as necessary

On all the foregoing items, except tips, you may be required to produce receipts in order to support claims in excess of $25. If in doubt on any point, consult *Joint Travel Regulations* as well as your finance officer. If you and the finance officer disagree as to whether a given item is reimbursable (or if you differ on any computation of pay and allowances), you have the right to submit a claim for adjudication by the comptroller general. The finance officer will explain how to go about this.

1324. Travel Advance

Before departure under orders on permanent change of station, you may, if you request, draw an advance on mileage allowance, known as a *travel advance*. An advance of per diem on temporary duty or TAD orders is also considered a travel advance. Do not confuse these advance payments with a "dead horse," described in Section 1307.

1325. Travel Reimbursement

After reporting at your new station and getting your orders endorsed, present your original orders with two complete copies, to the designated administrative officer, who will help you prepare your claim for mileage and per diem on your orders. Your completed claim should then be presented to your finance officer within three working days. A claim must be filed even if you have drawn an advance.

1326. Travel in Government Conveyance

Travel by government aircraft or any other government conveyance is travel in kind. You rate per diem at the prescribed rate. On extended navigational flights for proficiency purposes, if authorized at your request, no per diem is payable.

TRANSPORTATION OF FAMILY MEMBERS AND HOUSEHOLD GOODS

1327. Transportation of Family Members on Permanent Change of Station

Costs of transporting family members on permanent change of station are paid by the government.

If you are not traveling by private vehicle, it is simplest to obtain tickets for family members by Government Transportation Request. You may, however, transport family members at your own expense and claim reimbursement afterward at prescribed mileage rates within certain maximum ceilings.

In the event you plan to marry while en route to a new duty station (for example, en route to your first station after graduating from Basic School), your proceed time, leave, and excess travel time are added to your date of detachment to determine the effective date of your orders for the purpose of entitlement to dependent's travel. *It will be to your advantage to discuss this with your finance officer and ask for his or her advice.*

Claims for reimbursement must be signed by you unless you are in a casualty status. When family travel is incident to your having been reported as a casualty, the claim will be signed by the senior family member.

1328. Shipment of Household Goods

Household goods include baggage, clothing, personal effects, and professional books, papers, and equipment. Not included, however, are vehicles and boats, wines and liquors, pets, and articles not belonging to your family.

Shipment can be made (including crating and drayage) at government expense on permanent change of station, within weight allowances, under the following circumstances*:

- Entrance into the service, or orders to more than twenty weeks of active duty
- Orders to sea or duty overseas, where family may not follow
- Permanent change of station orders while on active duty
- Orders to duty under instruction of twenty or more weeks' duration
- Orders to or from *prolonged* hospitalization
- Honorable separation or retirement
- Death on active duty, or reported dead, missing, or interned
- Transfer between ships having different home ports
- Orders changing home port of ship to which attached
- Transfer between ship and shore station, where shore station is not ship's home port
  Shipment cannot be made in the following circumstances:
- Before receipt of orders, unless specially authorized by competent authority
- If separation is other than honorable, or if transfer is incident to trial
- For change of station by reservists on duty for less than six months.

1329. Weight Allowances

Current tables of weight allowances show the maximum weight of household goods that may be shipped by you on either permanent or temporary change of

---

*There is also a "do-it-yourself" household-goods shipment program under which you move your own effects by commercial or rental vehicle and are paid up to 75 percent of what it would have cost the government to ship the goods. Before doing this (which requires specific authorization), you should get the advice of your traffic management officer.

station. Remember that professional books, papers, and equipment (the adjective "professional" being construed generously) are moved without charge to your allowance.

On permanent change of station, you may ship "by expedited mode" (in most instances, simply a phrase for express shipment) up to 1,000 pounds net weight of personal property classified as *unaccompanied baggage*. This shipment should include only high-priority items necessary to permit you to carry out your duties or to prevent undue hardship to you or your family, and the net weight is charged against your total weight allowance. This type of shipment is invaluable for uniforms and effects required immediately after reporting.

Household goods in excess of weight allowance may be shipped, but excess costs will be charged to you. Remember, however, that weight allowances shown are net, that is, they do not include packing materials.

1330. Storage of Household Goods

Nontemporary Storage. There are many situations under which an officer may be entitled to "nontemporary" storage of household effects, not exceeding prescribed weight limitations. Because the length of storage at government expense varies and you are subject to excess costs for storage beyond the authorized time limit, you should check with the traffic management officer. Among the most common situations under which you are entitled to nontemporary storage are the following:

• Temporary duty pending detail overseas
• Change of station from within the United States to outside the United States
• Permanent change of station with temporary duty en route
• Retirement, discharge with severance pay, or reversion to inactive duty with readjustment pay (up to one year's storage allowed)
• Assignment to government quarters

Temporary Storage. You are entitled to temporary storage at government expense for up to ninety days in connection with any authorized shipment of household goods. Under certain conditions arising from circumstances beyond your control—such as unavailability of quarters at the new station, arrival of your effects before you do, early surrender of quarters, and so forth—competent authority may authorize an additional ninety days' storage. This added time in storage is not automatic; to arrange it, you should consult your traffic management officer.

Prohibited Articles. You may not store automobiles, inflammables, ammunition, or liquor.

1331. Dislocation Allowance

When an officer with family has completed a permanent change of station, he or she gets a dislocation allowance to help pay the numerous extra expenses of moving. This allowance is equal to two months' quarters allowance for grade; it is payable only once in any fiscal year, except by special authorization or when the officer is ordered to or from a course of instruction. It is not payable on orders to or from active duty. An officer without family is authorized dislocation allowance on permanent change of station if not assigned government quarters at the new post.

1332.   Trailer Allowance

An officer on a permanent change of station is entitled to a trailer allowance for transportation of a "house trailer," if owned, within the United States for use as living space. Trailer allowance therefore means the moving or transporting of a trailer at government expense or subject to reimbursement. If you elect to claim trailer allowance, you cannot claim dislocation allowance or transportation of household goods. Always consult your transportation or supply officer and your finance officer before taking any action in transporting your trailer. It will be to your advantage.

1333.   Transit Insurance

The liability that the government will accept for a lost or damaged shipment of household goods will not exceed $40,000. In addition, the carrier's liability for loss or damage varies on the actual weight of the shipment, but collection of claims against a carrier is a complicated, frustrating, and often fruitless process. Thus, where the value you set on your household goods exceeds the government's liability you may be wise to purchase additional protection in the form of a commercial *transit insurance policy.*

Should you take out such a policy, be careful to find out exactly what type of coverage you are getting. It is well to note, for example, that most such policies expire when your effects are delivered. Thus, when effects are delivered by van to a warehouse for temporary authorized storage, your policy will very likely expire as soon as the goods are accepted by the warehouse unless you have made special arrangements to extend your coverage. Further, reimbursement on such policies is computed on the ratio of the declared value of your shipment to the amount of insurance purchased. For example, if you state that your effects to be covered are worth $4,000 but only insure for $2,000, the insurance company will pay only $50 for an item worth $100. A personal property insurance policy, for a few additional dollars, may prove more comprehensive.

1334.   Check-Off List for Shipping Household Goods

Here is a summary of things you should do and think about when you ship household goods.

Have enough certified copies of your orders (usually ten copies for each shipment). Then see your traffic management officer three months before you plan to move.

Tell the traffic management officer if you have professional books and papers to be shipped so that they may be weighed separately and packed without being a charge against your weight allowance.

If you plan to reach your new station before your household goods are shipped, leave or send your spouse enough certified copies of orders to initiate shipment; also leave him or her a power of attorney or written authority to make the shipment.

If you have valuables to be shipped, inform your traffic management officer in order that special arrangements can be made.

Get all possible information about your housing situation at the new station before you request shipment of your goods.

Request storage at point of origin (your old station) whenever you are in doubt as to where to ship your goods.

If goods go by van, be sure to get a copy of the inventory sheet from the driver. *Never* sign a blank "certificate of packing," which the driver might present you.

If your orders are modified or canceled, or a change of destination of the shipment is desired, notify your traffic management officer immediately.

Get from your traffic management office (TMO) the ETA (estimated time of arrival) of your goods at destination, as well as the destination TMO telephone number.

Be at home on the day of the expected move.

Make arrangements for receipt of your household goods at destination. If you can't be there yourself, check with your TMO to find out whether storage is authorized. In cases of direct delivery by van, you or your representative must be at the new home to receive it.*

If possible, turn over all your household goods for the same destination at the same time, except items to be shipped by express.

Let the movers know about fragile items, such as chinaware and delicate glassware.

Keep groceries and food supplies together for proper packing.

Arrange to have your telephone and utilities disconnected.

Here is a summary of things *not* to do:

Do not request shipment to some place other than your new station without finding out first how much it will cost you.

Do not contract for shipment with commercial concerns unless you have been authorized in writing to do so by your traffic management officer.

Do not be upset if the movers don't show up at your quarters exactly at the appointed hour. It is hard to schedule a move by the minute.

Do not try to get special services from the carrier until after you have checked with your traffic management officer.

---

*If returning from foreign shore-duty overseas, your legitimate household effects are allowed to enter the United States duty-free.

Do not pack dishes or bric-a-brac yourself. Leave this to professional packers. Usually commercial firms won't pay claims on items they didn't pack.

Finally, although service people have scant option as to when they move, the best time of year to schedule movement of household effects is from October through May (a period when only about 30 percent of all moves take place). In any given month—according to the Defense Department's Military Traffic Management Command—the best time to move is between the 3d and 25th. In other words, if you want better, quicker, more careful handling of household effects, do not move in the summer or at the end of a month—if you have a choice.

ALLOTMENTS AND TAXES

1335. Allotments

As a matter of convenience and to facilitate regular monthly payments, you may make allotments of your pay for certain purposes. When you make an allotment, your pay is checked that amount, and the Marine Corps transfers it monthly to the designated recipient. To start or stop an allotment, notify your finance officer or commanding officer.

You may grant allotments to a bank, and you may make allotments for purchase of U.S. Saving Bonds. You cannot grant allotments to repay indebtedness, *except* for life insurance premiums, for repayment of emergency loans from Navy Relief or the Red Cross, or for repayment of indebtedness to the government.

Allotments are credited on the last day of the month of checkage.

You should register an allotment for support of your family as soon as you are ordered overseas so that your family can rely on uninterrupted support—especially if you are headed for combat.

1336. Income Tax

Your pay is taxable income and is subject to federal and state withholding tax at its source. Not taxable, however, are quarters and subsistence allowances, disability retired pay, and family separation allowance. Tax exemptions for personnel serving in combat zones during hostilities are covered in Section 1338.

Marine Corps withholding tax procedure provides that the finance officer establishes your withholding rate, based on your rate of pay; this rate changes when your pay changes. Tax deductions are checked on your pay record in the same fashion as allotments. At the end of the year, the finance officer furnishes you a withholding statement to be filed with your income tax return. You in turn must inform the finance officer of your tax-exemption status by filing a W-4 form, so that the correct rate is applied.

When hospitalized in a naval hospital as a result of wounds, disease, or injury incurred while in a combat zone, you may, if certain conditions are met, exclude from taxable income a certain portion of your pay, which is known as "sick pay." Check with your legal assistance officer (or that of the naval hospital) to determine eligibility. This can be a substantial tax benefit and should not be overlooked.

1337. Social Security Tax

Social Security coverage extends to Marine officers on active duty and requires the withholding of Social Security deductions from your pay. These taxes are computed on your base pay for grade and length of service and are deducted at rates prescribed by law.

The amount subject to withholding and the amount of tax withheld are reflected on the IRS Form W-2 furnished you by your finance officer at the end of each year, as well as your monthly leave and earning statement.

1338. Combat Pay and Tax Exemptions

Combat pay (technically termed "Hostile Fire Pay") is provided for all military personnel serving within geographic limits established by the secretary of defense during hostilities and meeting certain criteria of exposure to hostile fire or enemy action. This pay is the same for all grades and is taxable to the same extent as other pay. The rate is currently $150 per month. Your finance officer can advise you as to eligibility.

Income tax exemption for officers and enlisted persons serving in combat areas may be placed in effect by executive order of the president. This exemption extends to all military pay of enlisted men and warrant officers and to the first $500 per month of taxable income received by commissioned officers. Here again, your finance officer can advise you as to eligibility and the precise provisions of the effective executive order. Note that the geographic areas of this tax exemption bear no relation to, and do not necessarily coincide with, the combat pay geographic limits mentioned above.

As to pay, I beg leave to assure the Congress that, as no pecuniary consideration could have tempted me to accept this arduous employment at the expense of my domestic ease and happiness, I do not wish to make any profit from it.
—George Washington (to Congress, on his appointment as commander in chief, 16 June 1775)

14

New Station

No statistician has ever totaled the endless adages about the importance of good beginnings, but one thing is certain: as far as your Marine Corps career is concerned, all of them are true.

The instant you show your face on a new station, you come under close observation and appraisal. And when you report for duty on your first station—whether in garrison, in the field, at sea, at school, or beyond the seas—you begin to lay the foundation of the service reputation that will make or break your future.

How you conduct and carry yourself; how you wear your uniforms; how you behave; how much you know, pretend to know, or don't know—by all these details you are judged.

1401. Preliminaries

After completing Basic School and military occupational specialty (MOS) training, you will have received your primary MOS (see Chapter 15) and orders to your first station. In the majority of cases, this will be a Fleet Marine Force unit. You also will have been authorized some delay in reporting, which will give you an opportunity to catch your breath after training and to square yourself away for further adventures. If you are ordered to one of the Marine divisions or aircraft wings, your first assignment will be predetermined by your MOS, that is, by your military specialty. If, however, you are ordered to a non-FMF unit or command, it is good practice to write ahead in order to introduce yourself and to assist your new CO in deciding where and how you can best be fitted in. A good example of such a letter (which should be formal but unofficial) follows:

Chief of Staff
Marine Corps Recruit Depot
San Diego, California 92140

Dear Sir:

I have just received orders to report to the Recruit Depot not later than 20 June 1985. My present intention is to arrive in San Diego on the 18th and report for duty at 0800 on the 19th.

I am married but have no children, and my wife will remain on the East Coast for the time being until I have an opportunity to find suitable housing and get settled in whatever duties may be assigned me.

Although commissioned under the NROTC program, I have had three years' enlisted service in the Marine Corps, including one year with the rifle range detachment at Camp Lejeune, and believe I could do well on the range or with any of the recruit battalions.

Having had no previous duty at San Diego, I would appreciate it if I could be sent any orientation or general information literature as to the Base, together with any particular instructions you may have for me.

I am looking forward to this tour of duty with pleasure and hope I may render useful service.

Very respectfully,

Wharton Burrows,
2dLt USMC

Remember you will be reporting in to your new station or unit in uniform of the day. This requires prior planning on your part to ensure that you have a complete uniform while traveling between duty stations. You should also have enough uniforms (for example, utilities) so you can go to work immediately if the need arises. In no case should you ship all your uniforms and assume they will be ready and waiting at your new post.

REPORTING IN GARRISON

1402. Reporting on Board in Garrison

There are as many ways to report in to a new post as there are individuals. During your career, you will see them all: the procrastinator, tearing out in a taxicab five minutes before midnight on the last day his orders allow; the travel-worn parents with house trailer, children, and wilted clothes; the careful officer who arrives two days early and scouts the lay of the land before reporting.

Without considering the trouble in store if you miscalculate your reporting date, or if you arrive late for *any* cause, legitimate or not, you may be sure that last-minute arrival is a risky business, and one that can start you out off balance. So allow ample time, whatever else your personal logistics call for.

Let's assume, then, that you have budgeted "proceed, travel, and delay" (if any), that you've arrived at a city adjoining your first station, and that you're there in plenty of time—at least a day to spare.

So here you are, at the threshold of your first station.

Put on your best civilian clothes (or, if you prefer, service A). Get a haircut. Drive out to the base, show your identification card (or orders, if you have not yet been issued an ID card) to the sentry at the main gate, and ask the sentry to direct you to the adjutant's office. The adjutant is the staff officer who traditionally receives newcomers to the command. Large posts (such as Camp Lejeune), which include several commands, now have a "Joint Reception Center" where all company officers report initially. After leaving the JRC, you proceed as described herein, reporting to the adjutant of the command to which you have been assigned.

Before you enter the adjutant's office, knock (or hesitate in the doorway until invited in), and have your orders handy. Introduce yourself informally: "Sir, I'm Second Lieutenant Nicholas. I have orders to report in tomorrow, and would like to find out where and when I report, the uniform, and any information you may have on my assignment. Also, perhaps you can tell me if there's any mail for me at this station?"

The adjutant probably will have advance information of you and will know a good deal about your immediate future. In any case, the adjutant will look over your orders and, unless extremely busy, chat a few minutes, if only to size you up and get you off to a proper start.

Find out the exact time and place for reporting, the name and title of the officer to whom you report, and the required uniform. This last information allows you to visit the post exchange to purchase any uniform items you may have overlooked.

Usually an officer reports for duty at the commencement of office hours, or at such other time during the forenoon as the commanding officer desires. This information can be ascertained in advance of reporting. If, in order to comply with the letter of orders, you must report at night or after working hours, the officer of the day or staff duty officer will receive you, log you in, and, if necessary, provide overnight accommodations. Next day, you then report formally to your new commanding officer.

From the moment you step on board, you must be on tiptoes, fit and ready to do whatever may be required—and do it instantly.

Your service dress "A" should be freshly cleaned and pressed. Your shoes should shine, your brightwork gleam. Your hair should be cut and your face newly shaven. Check to make sure that pockets are buttoned and that all insignia are in place and correct. Look yourself over in the mirror for a last-minute check.

With you should be: your original orders, two dozen copies, personal records, and miscellaneous papers that have to do with the day's business (baggage checks, check-in sheet, information booklet, and so on).

If you are staying off post and have no transportation, or if you arrive by train or air, telephone the post and ask for the motor transport dispatcher. Identify yourself, explain that you are reporting under orders, and ask that transportation pick you up and drive you to post headquarters. Be sure to tell where you are and who you are (so that the driver will know whom he is to look for) and emphasize that you are traveling under orders. Have the dispatcher tell you when you may expect to be picked up. If, for any reason, the dispatcher cannot provide for you, you are authorized to take a taxi and claim reimbursement on your travel orders.

Once on board, enter post headquarters and present yourself at the time and place previously ascertained, if you've conducted a preliminary reconnaissance; if you are in any doubt, report to the adjutant. He or she will take your orders and have them endorsed. The adjutant will show you to the office of the commanding officer or executive officer (on large posts, possibly the chief of staff, the deputy chief of staff, or the G-1).

On cue from the adjutant, step smartly into the office, uncovered, halt at attention two paces before your senior's desk, and say, "Sir, Second Lieutenant Zeilin reports on board for duty." *Do not salute;* Marines do not salute uncovered or indoors (except when under arms).

The officer to whom you are reporting will then have you sit down, will put you at ease, and will chat with you a few minutes, both as a matter of courtesy and to fix you in mind. Do not get flustered; answer questions briefly and directly, and sit erect without slouching or fidgeting. The end of the interview usually will be indicated by instructions that you report to some lower headquarters or commence the prescribed check-in procedure. Unless you are urgently needed, your commanding officer will almost always ask whether you have had time to "get squared away" and will allow you reasonable opportunity to attend to such personal matters as housing, administration, and the like.

After you leave, retrieve your orders with their reporting endorsement. You'll need them all day.

Your next stop probably will be the supply office, for *quarters information.* At large posts, there is usually a housing office, which not only assigns government quarters but can give you leads on off-post housing. Because government quarters are assigned (with few exceptions) on a first-come, first-served basis, present yourself immediately to the person who runs the quarters list, and see that your name is placed on that fateful roster, which determines when you move in. (At some posts, your control date on the quarters list is determined by the date of detachment from your previous station; it is of course in your interest to verify that this is correct.) Before making any arrangements, let alone leases, for off-post housing, be sure to get your change-of-station orders endorsed to the effect that public quarters are not available. If you lease ashore before getting an endorsement, you may find yourself being moved into quarters anyway and, in any case, losing your quarters allowance.

Once you've gotten yourself housed, the *finance office* will be your destination. Ask for the NCO or officer who handles officers' pay accounts. Here you'll provide certain personal statistics and here, also, you can draw pay. In addition, the finance office will pay you whatever *travel allowances* are due—a much-needed bonus that helps bring your pocketbook back to level after the expenses of travel. During their long careers, paymasters become familiar with the fact that most officers who report in are low on cash, so don't hesitate to reveal your needs and ask to be paid as soon as practicable.

With orders endorsed, quarters arranged, and pay in your pocket, you'll be ready to claim whatever baggage and effects you may have shipped from your home or former station. The Traffic Management Office (TMO) takes care of this by holding your gear until you report in and claim it. Again, your orders are necessary. You are entitled to temporary storage of your effects. If your baggage and effects have not arrived, leave word with TMO where you wish to be notified when your gear gets in. TMO will deliver it to government quarters or to any point off post within a reasonable radius. After that, it's your problem.

You should now leave your health record at the sick bay (if it hasn't been mailed separately from your old station). Find out where this is before you leave post headquarters. If your new station has a standard check-in procedure for officers newly reporting, the check-sheet will tell you where to find the sick bay. With health record in hand, enter and ask for the record office. Here a Navy hospital corpsman will accept your health record, enter you on the records, and, perhaps, verify that you are up to date on your immunizations. If you need dental work or any routine medical assistance, now is the time to make your needs known.

By the time you've covered the rounds just described, you will more than likely be ready for a bite to eat. This can usually be obtained at the Commissioned Officers' Mess. If you're pressed for time, most post exchanges have a short-order cafeteria; here you can eat on the run—less elegant, perhaps, but enough. Lunch at the mess, however, will enable you to take care of another reporting obligation, that of joining the mess. Here you receive your membership card, pay dues, and ascertain the privileges and obligations of the mess.

Last, but by no means least, if driving your own car, present yourself to the provost marshal and have your car registered. Marine Corps stations require that cars pass safety examinations and that you possess liability insurance. Nothing can be more troublesome than not being able to meet post requirements for registration of a car; without post registration you park outside and walk from there. Advance precautions to have your car in good shape and fully insured can save you days of walking, plus much vexation. Never park in a space reserved for someone else. Such spaces are usually marked by signs or numbers painted on the curb or surface. Few events annoy a senior more than to find his or her space preempted by a junior.

1403. Shaking Down

As you settle down in your outfit and assignment, your success will depend largely on your common sense, application, willingness to learn, and skill in human relations. Here, however, are a few tips.

Learn quickly to associate as many names, faces, and jobs of the officers and enlisted Marines about you as you can. Study your Marines' records (which include background information).

Read bulletin boards—not only the current, but all the past accumulation that most bulletin boards display; it may be old hat to the plankowners, but it's background to you.

Don't forget your official calls (see Chapter 22).

Study the Tables of Organization and Equipment for your organization. The S-1 and S-4 can provide these.

Read Post Regulations; they can keep you out of much trouble.

Study your organization's general orders and standing operating procedures ("SOPs"). You can get copies from your first sergeant.

Find out the mission of your organization.

Learn the geography of your post and training areas by map and personal reconnaissance. "I'm a stranger here myself" is a poor reply for an officer to give.

Above all, strive to know your Marines. As you begin this ceaseless, vital Marine Corps task, take down your *Marine Corps Manual* and read the article entitled "Relations Between Officers and Men."

1404. Orienting Yourself

As you shake down, the sergeants in your unit can be a new lieutenant's best professional friends. Both parties observe proper military courtesy and maintain mutual respect.

An officer—especially a new one—should never be too stiff-necked or proud to learn from anybody who knows more about a particular subject.

Some commanding officers work out an informal orientation dealing primarily with internal administrative matters—mess, supply, paperwork—for new junior officers. If nothing of the kind is directed, you may find it desirable, after touching base with your captain, to do the following:

1. Ask the first sergeant to assemble copies of standing orders and manuals you ought to read—and read them carefully. Make friends with, and respect, the first sergeant.
2. Go to the supply room and find out the basics of obtaining, caring for, and accounting for supplies, equipment, and other property. There is a lot to learn about these subjects. Find out how weapons are safeguarded and about ammunition stowage. (Incidentally, familiarize yourself with safety regulations.)
3. Visit the battalion or other mess that feeds your unit. Catch the mess sergeant at a slack time and ask how the mess and galley are operated, how rations are drawn, and how the mess force is handled.

Besides all the foregoing, read up on your job. Use the fine professional manuals, both Marine and Army, that bear on your duty and unit. You will be surprised how soon you become recognized as professionally qualified.

REPORTING IN THE FIELD

1405. Actions upon Arrival

The circumstances under which you join your first command in the field are as various as the world's geography and climate. A force on occupation duty leads a different life from a Marine division or aircraft wing at the peak of a campaign. Nevertheless, in preparing for field duty, here are some useful rules.

Get all the briefing you can, especially from those who have recently returned. Accept only guardedly advice or information from anyone who has not been on the spot recently. Find out, if you can:

• The local climate.
• The uniforms worn; also whether these uniforms may be procured after you arrive or whether they should be brought with you.
• The correct mailing address. This will enable correspondence to meet you rather than lag weeks behind.
• Local shortages or hard-to-get items. These are the things you'll want to have with you.

Don't tarry in moving forward. The "pipeline" affords many delays. Overcome them, and press forward to your destination.

Travel lightly. For a junior officer this usually means Valpack, hanging bag, briefcase, and little more. Keep your baggage tagged with your name and destination.

Keep your travel orders and service records on you. Get a notebook and pencil, and keep them handy.

Try to reach your destination with two or more hours of daylight to spare. Night is no time for strangers to be stumbling about a new unit. When you report in, follow the procedure described in Section 1402 as closely as circumstances permit. As soon as administrative formalities are complete, you should immediately:

• Obtain needed uniforms and field equipment ("782 equipment") from the unit supply officer.
• Find out where and when you wash, sleep, and eat.
• Ascertain the likelihood of enemy attack and the degree of readiness being maintained. This includes blackout rules and where and when you wear sidearms and helmets. Learn the password and countersign and the location of mine fields and entanglements. Find out immediately what to do if an enemy attack takes place.

1406. Taking Command in the Field

If you are taking over a command, especially one in contact with the enemy, you must:

- Understand your mission and know the degree of readiness required of your unit.
- Meet your subordinate leaders, so that you can identify them and they can identify you. Meet your leading NCO and keep him or her with you.
- Walk your front lines or perimeter. Locate your unit's boundaries on the ground. Identify adjacent units. Inspect individual positions. Locate the enemy. *Show yourself to your Marines.*
- Inspect your unit's weapons and equipment. If the situation permits, hold emergency alerts and battle drill.
- Check your interior and exterior guard and security.
- Verify your communications. Be sure you are familiar with all emergency signals.
- Ascertain plans for and amount of supporting arms available. Know how to obtain them.
- Check your supply situation. This includes, at minimum, ammunition, water, and rations—"beans and bullets,"the old phrase puts it.
- Make a thorough sanitary inspection, covering heads, urinals, garbage and trash disposal, and water supply. Don't overlook general policing of your area.
- Know how to get medical assistance and how to evacuate casualties.
- And, finally, remember that you can count on the Marines around you, just as they are depending on you.

OVERSEAS TRAVEL AND FOREIGN STATIONS

1407. General

About a fifth of your career (other than expeditionary or war service) is spent on foreign stations.

Probably you will be visiting a country that is new to you. You may miss some conveniences and facilities to which you are accustomed at home. Language, customs, national characteristics, and living habits may well differ markedly from your own.

Learn to view foreign usages and characteristics with understanding and without insularity or provincialism. If only for the success of our missions overseas, Marines must earn the friendship of the people in whose countries we serve. Self-discipline, courtesy, tolerance, good humor, and generosity are the best ambassadors.

And one word more: remember Laurence Sterne's dictum on foreign travel— "An Englishman does not travel to meet English men." When abroad, meet the people and live the life of the country where you are stationed. Otherwise you might just as well never leave home.

1408. Personal Effects

One thing you must bear in mind: even though ordered to sea or foreign service in one part of the world, you may suddenly find yourself on the way to some place quite different. Thus you must select wardrobe and personal effects that, with minimum weight and bulk, keep you prepared for duty anywhere—from the Arctic to the Caribbean, or from Asia to Alaska.

Your maximum travel baggage should comprise: seabag, Val-pack, and brief-case. To be absolutely sure none of your essential gear goes adrift, there is but one safe rule, as voiced by a well-seasoned old-timer in the Corps: "Sit on your baggage and keep your orders in your pocket."

Common sense and the advice of officers who know your destination are the surest guides on what to take overseas. Regardless of destination, however, never be without a complete service uniform (with garrison cap, to save space) and accessories, at least one suit of utility clothing, field boots, field jacket, and regulation raincoat.

Do not take valuable papers, such as insurance policies, deeds, stocks, bonds; irreplaceable jewelry; or anything else you cannot afford to lose. Leave such items in a safe-deposit box. And be sure your spouse's or next-of-kin's power of attorney contains authority to get into the safe-deposit box. Consult Section 2114 with regard to this.

1409. Moving Family Overseas

Overseas travel of your family on an accompanied tour via government transportation is usually contingent on your having adequate housing (or good assurance thereof) for them at the destination.

When possible, the Marine Corps tries to arrange for you and your family to travel together to an overseas station. If there must be delay and separation before the overseas area commander allows your family members to join you, the Corps will do its level best to get them moving quickly.

Get the latest information on living conditions in the overseas area, including climate, housing, food, educational facilities, shopping, recreation, servants, and medical care. Such data will help you decide what to take. For information, check with the Transportation Section, Marine Corps Headquarters.

1410. Preparations for Travel Overseas

Passports. You and each member of your family will require passports, unless you are ordered to one of a few areas where this rule is waived. Your change of station orders will normally include instructions that you obtain a passport, and Marine Corps Headquarters will usually obtain it with minimum delay. If you are anywhere near Washington, get your passport in person. If you cannot work through Washington, apply to the State Department Passport Office in New York, Chicago, New Orleans, Boston, or San Francisco—or, if no other source is at hand, apply to the clerk of the nearest United States Court or Post Office. In any case, notify Marine Corps Headquarters by telegraph when you apply. Regardless of what agency you deal with, have the following items with you when you apply:

- Birth certificates for yourself and family members
- Evidence of naturalization if you or your family members are not native U.S. citizens
- The number(s) of past U.S. passports held
- Your ID card and other supporting identification
- Two passport-size photos, full-face and uncovered, of each person

Visas.   Be sure you have all visas required by countries en route and at your destination. Again, your most reliable source is the Manpower Department, Marine Corps Headquarters. The nearest consulates of the countries on your itinerary can of course answer your questions and issue visas when needed. Remember that you cannot get a visa until you have your passport.

Physical Examinations and Immunizations.   You and your family members must have physical examinations and complete certain immunizations before going overseas. The requirements for both vary from time to time. Have your immunizations recorded and certified on your Navy Medical Department *International Certificate of Inoculation and Vaccination of the World Health Organization* (PHS Form 731), and be sure that every shot is recorded in your health record. Otherwise, you may find yourself getting a double dose of inoculations every time you step ashore.

You can get the necessary physical examinations and immunizations from your medical officer. If your family members are moving alone from an area without a Navy surgeon nearby, have them consult the nearest armed forces medical activity, or, under outpatient provisions for family medical care, they may receive examinations and immunizations from civilian sources.

Medical service for families is usually variable overseas. So is dental service. Both you and your family should make every effort to be in tip-top repair before going overseas.

Baggage.   Before you pack, ascertain what restrictions are in force as to weight allowances, what items may accompany you, and the precise address to which baggage must be shipped. All this information may be obtained from Marine Corps Headquarters. Mark and tag your gear clearly and indelibly. Put one copy of your basic orders *inside* each piece of baggage.

Forwarding Mail.   If you can be absolutely sure, find out your new mailing address in advance and send out official change-of-address cards to all your correspondents and to all business firms and publications with which you deal. If you are not sure, wait until you arrive, then send the cards *at once.* Your unit mail clerk can give you as many of these cards as you need. When stationed in a foreign country, have your magazines, parcels, and any dutiable articles sent to you via the nearest Fleet Post Office (FPO) or Army Post Office (APO). This not only gets you domestic rather than appreciably higher overseas subscription rates but enables you to receive stateside parcels without the red tape of foreign customs. *Leave a forwarding address everywhere you stop.*

1411. On Foreign Station

Arrival.   Because you are traveling under orders (and with an official or perhaps a diplomatic passport), you will have few, if any, problems with foreign customs or immigration authorities. You probably will be met by some representative of the military community that you are entering. The area or port commander will try to move you expeditiously to your destination. If delay is unavoidable, the commander will provide accommodations. But keep in touch with the officer you are relieving (if you know him or her)—that is the person directly interested in your safe and speedy arrival.

Language.   Where your duties make it desirable, the Marine Corps makes every effort to give you language training before sending you to a foreign billet. Your spouse should also enroll in some type of language instruction. Your young children will pick up the language of the country soon enough from servants and other children. To enable them to learn the country and its ways, as well as the language, give serious consideration to enrolling the children in local schools, if this is feasible. In certain overseas areas, the Department of Defense will pay all or part of the cost of private schooling in eligible local schools for your children. This is an opportunity you should not overlook.

Regardless of whether you are in a U.S. service community or on detached service alone, you will be working with the citizens of the country where you are serving and you must perfect your command of the local language. Some commands maintain language tutors and conduct regular classes. If you cannot avail yourself of them, you can almost always hire your own tutor for a nominal fee. Educate the entire family.

Ability to speak the language vastly extends your opportunities, protects you against imposition, and earns the respect of all with whom you deal.

Sanitary Precautions.   Sanitation and public health abroad may not attain the levels to which you have been accustomed at home, depending on the country. Find out the local sanitary situation as soon as you arrive. Take nothing for granted. Be especially careful against insect-borne and enteric diseases. Keep up your immunizations. Drink only pasteurized or boiled milk and water that has been boiled. Avoid raw fruit and vegetables unless you are quite sure "night soil" is not used as the local fertilizer. Make your own ice at home, using pure water. Your medical officer can advise you on what you can get away with and what you must watch.*

Shopping.   The "bargains" you and your spouse may find on foreign station will sometimes seem unbelievable. If you do not know quality, values, and the local market, take along some friend who does.

---

*Most experienced officers traveling overseas carry a bottle of bismuth and paregoric, the tried and true Navy diarrhea mixture, which you can get from your sick bay. A word to the wise . . .

Look into the foreign exchange, currency, and tax situations. Find out where you can get the best legal rate of exchange (although your hotel will almost always change money, hotels usually charge a commission or give you a poor rate). In some countries, dollar purchasers are accorded purchase-tax exemptions; in others, some types of currency are more readily negotiable and thus get better rates of exchange. Know these fine points and take advantage of them. On the other hand, never demean your country or your Corps by black marketeering. This sort of thing is emphatically not done by Marines and is sternly dealt with in the few cases that arise. If you know quality, style, and value, a relatively small outlay may obtain furniture, linens, rugs, bric-a-brac, silver, chinaware, and other fine goods you might never be able to afford at home.

Take it easy at first, however. Look for a while, then buy. Don't bypass your post exchange. Purchase through an exchange gives you some assurance of quality and equity in price. Often, in fact, exchanges can do better than you as an individual because of mass purchasing and bargaining experience.

Well begun is half done.

—Horace, Epistles, I

15

The Profession of Arms

Military professionals exist to provide effective armed forces to the nation for use as an instrument of policy. In peacetime, this mission demands that an officer exert every effort to ready and prepare the military organization to fight a war that he or she hopes will never be fought. That feature leads to the salient way in which the profession of arms stands apart from all others. Although the armed forces use many terms in common with the learned professions—rights, duties, rewards, and privileges—only the profession of arms carries the obligation to surrender life itself if duty so demands. That liability is not often called upon in time of peace, but Marines of every epoch have faced considerable violence and borne many casualties in operations short of war.

Order distinguishes the profession of arms. Because the military operates by applying force, even violence, toward the resolution of a political question, properly vested authority exists at all levels of the military structure. On the other hand, one cannot say that initiative and latitude are not offered to the officer. The increasingly complex and sophisticated skills that a Marine must acquire through the period of active service exert a fascinating challenge for those intent upon mastering the nuances of military science. Many officers remain Marines simply because of the satisfaction gained in attaining a high degree of expertise in association with a like-minded cohort.

The professional officer continually seeks education and increased levels of qualification. Unlike other professions where a lengthy period of initial education qualifies a practitioner for life, the military professional's initiation merely suffices for the apprentice years. Thereafter, the officer returns to school frequently for specialist, technical, command, and staff courses. Perhaps up to one-fifth of an officer's career will be spent studying, expanding one's experiences, and preparing for greater responsibilities. This amount far exceeds the preparation for law and significantly exceeds that for medicine. In addition to

Teamwork, dedication, esprit . . . the way of the Marine.

formal courses, the officer reads relevant periodicals and books and seeks out ideas and innovative methods in an ongoing process to acquire knowledge and extend abilities.

In fact, the skills required for military purposes know no real bounds. The Marine Corps encourages intellectual endeavors of all sorts and frequently provides time and funds in their support. Officers may work toward a doctorate in physics or master a foreign language. The Corps can and will make direct use of such qualifications. There also seems no doubt that learning to paint, ski, sail, ride, play a musical instrument, or climb mountains will prove of benefit to the Corps, indirectly if not directly. As long as you strive to improve your military skills, your fellow officers will respect and support your most eccentric hobbies and activities. This freedom of individual expression, in the midst of an ordered world, features in no other line of work but the military. The Corps remains necessarily a closely knit group with high values, fairness, and consistency. People are at the heart of the profession of arms.

1501.   A Balanced Career

If you aim for the top, you must have a balanced career. A rounded career guarantees decision, judgment, steadiness, and practicality at the top. Raw material for these attributes is found in most officers. But the extent to which you develop those qualities results largely from the kind of career you pursue.

For a balanced Marine career, you should seek the following:
• Experience in command
• Professional education
• Combat experience
• Joint staff experience
• Fleet Marine Force duty

Remember, as you go from duty to duty, that while it is the commandant who assigns you, it is still *your* career. Watch that career as anxiously as a chemist compounding a critical formula. Your career is your critical formula.

1502.   Assignment and Detail

The right balance in your career results largely from assignment or "detail," as it is sometimes still known in the Marine Corps. Your assignments send you to school, to sea, and to the FMF and determine which of the thousand-and-one Marine jobs you fill. Thus, a balanced career can be attained only through a sound pattern of assignment. It is one of the important functions of Marine Corps Headquarters to see that, during the first twenty years of service, every officer gets assignments designed to develop his or her potentialities, to afford equal opportunity for advancement, and to qualify the officer for command responsibility appropriate to rank.

Figure 15–1 represents the "typical career pattern" often spoken of by career counselors. Too many variations exist to speak realistically these days of such patterns. Typically, a ground officer will serve in some sequence such as FMF, non-FMF, career-level school, and staff duty as a captain, followed by more FMF, non-FMF, and staff tours intermingled with intermediate and perhaps top-level schools and high-level staff duty as a field grade officer. Aviation officers tend to spend much more time in flying tours and comparatively less time on staff duty than do ground officers.

To manage your career, and at the same time meet the needs of the Corps, is the job of the Officer Assignment Branch (Code MMOA), Marine Corps Headquarters. The "monitors" distribute officers to all Marine commands immediately subordinate to Headquarters. These commands in turn assign you according to your experience and military specialty.

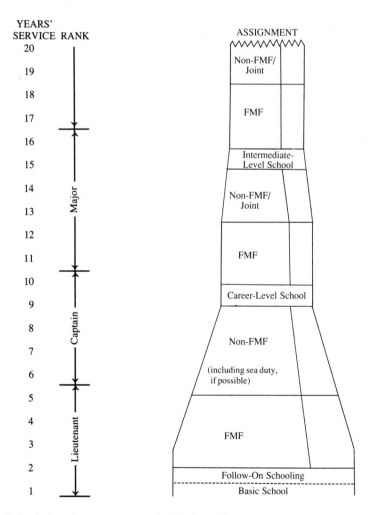

Figure 15–1: Typical assignment patterns for Marine officers

Assignments are classed as follows.

Command: duty as commanding officer or executive officer of any Marine organization.

Staff: duty on the general, special, or executive staff of any organization above company or squadron level.

Instructor: duty on the staff or as instructor at any U.S. or foreign military school.

Student: duty under instruction at any school.

Joint service assignment: duty on the staff of a joint command or component of the Department of Defense.

Special duty: A range of varied and miscellaneous duties, such as sea duty, supply duty, duty as an aide-de-camp, and duty involving flying.

The normal tour of duty for Marine officers on duty ashore is three years, although the demands of the service sometimes require departure from this or any other standard duration of tour.

Overseas (and certain other) tours are classed as either "unaccompanied" (without family) and "accompanied" (with family). You may receive one accompanied foreign tour during your career and about three unaccompanied.

Although it is up to Marine Corps Headquarters, and every commanding officer, to balance your assignments, the fact remains, as has been emphasized, that it is *your* career. This is well recognized, and you have ample opportunity to put your wishes for assignment on record.

On each fitness report, you state your preference for next duty, and your reporting senior must in turn give his or her own recommendation as to what assignment should be made. In addition, any officer may write an official letter (usually an Administrative Action form) to the commandant to request a future assignment.

Factors involved in determining who moves where are: date of last unaccompanied overseas tour, school requirements, moves precipitated by school and/or unaccompanied tour completions, career development, time on station, and, of course, special requirements—the exceptional cases—as well as economy. Timing and individual availability for assignment also bear heavily on final decisions.

You can generally expect to be assigned to overseas unaccompanied tours on the basis of your date of return from previous unaccompanied duty, with respect to all other officers of your grade and military occupational specialty (see Section 1505).

The normal process of detailing officers to the various billets of the Corps revolves around annual preparation of "slates," or lists showing the assignments in each rank that are planned for the forthcoming year. Based on a normal three-year turnover, about one-third of the officer corps should be transferred each year. But because some billets have shorter tours than three years, a larger percentage usually moves.

Slating is essentially a cross-matching of Marine Corps officer requirements (based on tables of organization, approved manning levels, school quotas, and so on) with officers available for transfer in a given calendar year. The decisions on individual assignments in each case are based on: optimum career pattern (including need for schooling); individual qualifications (such as MOS, college degree, language skill); present station (to avoid costly, time-consuming cross-country or Atlantic to Pacific moves); and, of course, the individual's requests.

Over and above all the foregoing, the factor of overriding importance in slating (and thus in shaping careers) is *performance*. No matter what duty you have had in the past, the singular consideration that will shape your future assignments is an established record of and reputation for consistently high performance across the range of your career.

You often hear it loosely said that "nobody pays any attention" to individual officers' requests. This is not true; contrary to all rumor, the Officer Assignment Branch does have a heart.

The literal heart of the process lies with carefully selected officers at Marine Corps Headquarters called *monitors* (or, in Navy parlance, "detailers"). The responsibility of a monitor is to assign officers under his or her cognizance in the most efficient manner to meet the needs of the Marine Corps. At the same time, your monitor tries to harmonize your best interests and expressed desires with the requirements of the Corps.

To accomplish the above, the Marine Corps maintains an open door policy, in which informal, frequent contact between individual officers and their respective monitors is encouraged. You can always write, call, or, when in Washington, visit your monitor. In addition, the Manpower Department tries to have selected monitors visit major commands on the East and West coasts each year, together with a special trip to the Western Pacific (WESTPAC).

So never hesitate to make your desires known, especially when you feel your career might be broadened by some assignment that may seem professionally necessary to you, such as Fleet Marine Force or schooling. If you pass through Washington, stop by Headquarters Marine Corps and consult your monitor. Fortunately, the Corps is small enough to accommodate its own needs and the desires of its officers pretty consistently. But you must do your part.

1503. Initial Detail

Undoubtedly, one of your major concerns is where you will be detailed upon graduating from Basic School, and here are the procedures used to determine that.*

Early in the course, you will have a chance to submit a form showing your preference for duty. Here you indicate, in order, choices of occupational field

---

*In virtually all cases, lieutenants graduating from Basic School are immediately ordered to follow-on training to qualify them in their MOSs. They are then ordered to their new permanent stations or organizations.

(see Section 1505), preferences of geographic area, and any reasons to support these choices. Your company officers recommend, assign, and endorse this form with your leadership and academic grades and appraisal of your attitude, motivation, and general value to the service. The form then goes to the Officer Assignment Branch, HQMC.

The ground officer assignment section controls the detail of officers into the occupational fields. Just before receipt of the Basic School "Preference Statements," the monitors review their respective quotas based on future requirements. On arrival of the preference forms, the monitors consult and tentatively select candidates for their respective occupational fields.

How do the Basic School staff and monitors make up their minds?

As to occupational field, the monitors' choice depends on the following factors:

- Current requirements of the Marine Corps
- Previous military education and experience
- Civilian education and experience
- Your desires
- Basic School staff recommendations

As regards geographic area, you will be ordered where the Marine Corps needs you, with your preference taken reasonably into account if possible. In any case, however, you can usually expect orders to the Fleet Marine Force.

1504.   Initial and Permanent Precedence

Every new second lieutenant is assigned a date of rank. Those with the same date of rank are assigned temporary initial precedence (see Section 1209), which governs their seniority until publication of the first lineal list, or "Blue Book," after they have finished Basic School. At this time, their names are rearranged in permanent precedence within groups having the same date of rank, according to Basic School standing.

1505.   Your Military Occupational Specialty (MOS)

As you look down a roster of officers, you may at first be puzzled to see some such entry as this:

1STLT JOHN HEYWOOD, 579-52-8180/0802/0840/0805

Those mysterious numbers, you will soon realize, are individual identifying badges worn by today's Marines. Those numbers indicate the military occupational specialties, or MOSs, of the individual concerned.

Your *primary MOS* describes the type of unit you are considered qualified to command; your *secondary MOS* may indicate either other command qualifications or staff qualifications.

The MOS system thus provides the Marine Corps with a running inventory of talent and indicates at a glance the professional qualifications of each officer and enlisted Marine. For example, returning to Lieutenant Heywood, just mentioned, a translation of the numbers after his name would run:

1STLT JOHN HEYWOOD, 579-52-8180: (Name and Social Security number)

0802: (Qualified field artillery officer)

0840: (Qualified naval gunfire spotter)

0805: (Qualified artillery air observer)

Obviously, those MOSs and the skills they represent are extremely important to you. When you report to a new station, those numbers generally determine your assignment because every duty, or "billet," in the Marine Corps carries the MOS appropriate to that billet.

When you report to Basic School, you are classified as a basic officer. You retain this classification only until basic training is completed and the Marine Corps has had opportunity to size you up. Before you leave Basic School, you are assigned a primary MOS by the commandant of the Marine Corps in one of the following major fields of command specialization.

Personnel administration: Occupational field 01

Intelligence: Occupational field 02

Infantry: Occupational field 03

Logistics: Occupational field 04

Field artillery: Occupational field 08

Engineer: Occupational field 13

Tank/assault amphibian: Occupational field 18

An officer will spend almost a third of his or her career working within a primary occupational specialty, such as field artillery, the 08 field.

Communications: Occupational field 25
Signal intelligence: Occupational field 26
Supply: Occupational field 30
Auditing, finance, and accounting: Occupational field 34
Motor transport: Occupational field 35
Data systems: Occupational field 40
Public affairs: Occupational field 43
Legal services: Occupational field 44
Military police: Occupational field 58
Aviation ground: Occupational field 60–73
Pilot/naval flight officer: Occupational field 75

If you later qualify for command in other fields, you receive a secondary MOS to denote this fact. As you acquire staff specializations (for example, as an embarkation officer, naval gunfire officer, or operations officer), these are reflected by secondary MOSs.

Every Marine officer below colonel (regular and Reserve), as well as every enlisted Marine, is classified under this system. Once you have your primary MOS, it can be changed only by the commandant. Should you feel that you have not been correctly classified in accordance with your skills or experience, or wish to qualify in a new field, you may so request in an official letter to the commandant, who then approves or disapproves the change you desire, taking into consideration the needs of the Corps, your skills, and your wishes.

One word of caution:

Although our MOS labels you for certain duties and patterns of assignment, never let that MOS be a pair of blinders. Avoid overspecialization in fact or attitude. Remember that *every Marine, regardless of MOS, must always be prepared for all duties* appropriate to his or her rank. The genius of the Corps lies

Throughout your career, you must hold tactical and technical proficiency as the greatest of your personal goals.

in the fact that Marine officers have never let themselves be "jurisdictionalized" into competing branches or watertight professional cliques.

You are, first and foremost, a line officer of Marines; secondary to that, you pursue a major professional specialty. Command and leadership are the only universal military occupational specialties of *all* Marine officers and NCOs.

1506.   Assignment of Women Officers

Successive revisions of Title 10, U.S. Code, have provided an integrated career for men and women officers through the grade of general. In 1981, the lineal lists of men and women officers merged and all were selected for promotion under direct competition among contemporaries. In 1994, policy changes removed the former restrictions on women serving in combat units, in combat aircrews, and on board combatant ships. Today, women serve in all units except those primarily concerned with ". . . engaging the enemy on the ground with individual or crew served weapons, while being exposed to hostile fire and to a high probability of direct physical contact with the hostile force's personnel."

Translated into current assignment policies, this means that women will not be assigned to infantry units; artillery, tank, assault amphibian, combat engineer, and reconnaissance battalions; force reconnaissance companies; and low-altitude antiaircraft defense (LAAD) batteries. Thus, women officers will find assignment to most of the units of the FMF, with 95 percent of the primary MOSs available to them.

Pregnancy may not bar assignment or retention of women in the Marine Corps. Those who become pregnant have the option to remain on active duty or be discharged. If they elect to remain on active duty, they are treated the same as their male counterpart parents in terms of assignments. There are no special considerations based solely on the fact of family responsibilities.

A request for separation by reason of pregnancy may be denied if a woman has incurred an additional active-duty obligation following receipt of special compensation, funded education, or advanced technical training, or when she serves in an MOS requiring her retention based upon the needs of the service. A request for separation will be considered under any of the above conditions if the woman can show overriding or compelling factors of personal need.

1507.   Professional Schools

You cannot overemphasize the importance of professional education.

In school, you learn from the hard-won experience of others and you develop your own professional bent. The schooling you pursue and your application to professional studies probably exercise more immediate leverage on your career than any other factors.

Types and Levels of Schools.   Professional schools are classified by instructional level as being resident or nonresident; as being of general curriculum, or specialized; as being Marine schools or schools of other services.

The levels of Marine officer schooling are: Basic (followed immediately by follow-on training in MOS), Career-Level, Intermediate, and Top. You will find examples in Section 1508.

So far as numbers permit, it is Marine Corps policy that every permanent unrestricted officer goes to school at each level through intermediate. You may not attend two schools on the same level. For the top-level schools (such as the National Defense University), only specially qualified officers are selected. If you aspire to attend such a school, you must buck stiff competition from your equally ambitious fellow officers.

In addition to resident schooling, the Marine Corps encourages all officers to enroll in nonresident (correspondence or extension) courses. You can pursue these on your own time, thus adding to your professional knowledge and better preparing yourself for resident instruction when the time comes. It is the advice of many successful officers that, during your first fifteen years' service, you should *always* be enrolled in some course (see Section 1510).

Schooling Outside the Corps. Many Marine officers attend schools conducted by other U.S. services and foreign nations. This ensures a wide base of professional thinking throughout the Corps and fosters insight by Marines into every aspect of the profession of arms—land, naval, and air.

It is a Marine tradition, which you should never forget, that when you attend the school of another service or country, you should return at or near the head of the class, or—as is said half-jokingly—not return at all.

Marine Corps Schools. Although many Marines attend school outside the Corps, the Marine Corps University at Quantico provides the bulk of the professional education for Marines. At Quantico are schools from basic through intermediate levels, together with several specialist schools. Quantico's students come from all officer ranks of the Corps, from other U.S. services, and from numerous foreign countries. Quantico is the goal of every Marine officer who wants to make the most of his or her career. For more information about "the Schools," read Sections 512 and 1106.

1508. Resident Schools

A "resident school" is one that you attend in person, as distinguished from a "nonresident school," whose instruction is conducted by correspondence. Marine officers attend resident schools at Quantico, the majority of the schools conducted by the other services, a number of civilian schools, and a few schools conducted by foreign countries. The list varies from time to time, and Marine Corps Headquarters periodically lists each course or school open to officer or enlisted Marines.

Here are certain courses and schools that you might attend. You may find names of still more in the current directive on this subject.

Basic Level:
The Basic School, Quantico, Virginia

Career Level:
> Amphibious Warfare School, Quantico, Virginia
> Command and Control Systems Course, Quantico, Virginia
> The Infantry School (USA), Fort Benning, Georgia
> The Field Artillery School (USA), Fort Sill, Oklahoma
> The Engineer School (USA), Fort Belvoir, Virginia
> The Armor School (USA), Fort Knox, Kentucky
> The Signal School (USA), Fort Monmouth, New Jersey

Intermediate Level:
> Marine Corps Command and Staff College, Quantico, Virginia
> Command and General Staff College (USA), Fort Leavenworth, Kansas
> The Naval War College, Newport, Rhode Island
> Air Command and Staff College, Maxwell AFB, Alabama
> Armed Forces Staff College, Norfolk, Virginia
> British Joint Services Staff College, Latimer, England
> NATO Defense College, Rome, Italy

Top Level:
> Marine Corps War College, Quantico, Virginia
> Naval War College, Newport, Rhode Island
> National War College, Washington, D.C.
> Army War College, Carlisle Barracks, Pennsylvania
> Air War College, Maxwell AFB, Alabama
> Industrial College of the Armed Forces, Washington, D.C.
> British Imperial Defense College, London, England
> NATO Defense College, Rome, Italy

(Occasional assignments are made to other foreign schools at intermediate and top levels in Spain, France, Norway, Germany, Australia, and Japan.)

Generally speaking, the duration of resident courses increases with the level of the school. In quiet times, instruction is more leisurely, whereas, during war or emergency, courses are compressed to the maximum extent. The average length of a peacetime resident course is from seven to nine months.

The resident schools of the Marine Corps at Quantico are open without distinction to officers from the line and from aviation.

1509. Flight Training

If you have a yen to fly; if you can pass the searching battery of physical and psychological tests; if you are a lieutenant with less than three years of service, under age twenty-seven when you apply, and a Basic School graduate or student, you may apply to Marine Corps Headquarters and be duly assigned as a student naval aviator or naval flight officer. Initial flight training is conducted at the Naval Air Training Center, Pensacola, Florida. It does not count as schooling on any of the levels described above, and whether or not you succeed does not debar you from normal schooling to which your rank and length of service

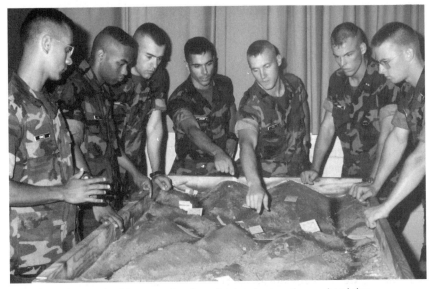

The Basic School provides entry-level professional education and training.

otherwise entitle you. Once you complete flight training and are given your wings, you will be assigned to duty in an aviation unit, probably in the Fleet Marine Force.

1510. Correspondence Courses

All Marine Corps correspondence schooling is free of charge to Marines and Navy personnel serving with the Corps. In addition, Marine officers are eligible to take correspondence courses conducted by the U.S. Naval War College, Newport, Rhode Island, and, if no equivalent Marine correspondence course exists, correspondence instruction offered by the Army and Air Force war colleges, and the National Defense University.

The Marine Corps Institute (MCI).   Located at Marine Barracks, 8th and Eye Streets, Washington, D.C., MCI is the oldest correspondence school in the U.S. Armed Forces, having been founded in 1920 to permit World War I Marine veterans to complete interrupted education. Over the years, MCI has changed from a general, semiacademic correspondence school to one that focuses on the professional development of enlisted Marines.

The following personnel are eligible for enrollment in the Marine Corps Institute:

- Marines of any rank on active duty
- Marines of any rank in the Organized and Volunteer Reserve (provided that the courses requested are commensurate with the rank of, and are appropriate for, the individual reservist)
- Retired Marines, members of the Fleet Marine Corps Reserve, and disabled former Marines

- Eligible members of other armed services (as determined by the service concerned)
- Civilian employees of the Marine Corps who, in the opinion of their military supervisors, would improve their efficiency and service to the Marine Corps by completing a Marine Corps Institute course related to their specific duties.

You may apply for an MCI course through your commanding officer or, if retired, directly to: Director, Marine Corps Institute, Marine Barracks, Box 1775, Washington, D.C. 20013.

In all, the Marine Corps Institute has some 150 courses, in which there are approximately 100,000 enrollments yearly. Also available are Extension School courses equivalent to the resident instruction at the Basic School, Amphibious Warfare School, Command and Staff College, and MAGTF Joint Warfighting Course.

Naval War College. The Naval War College extends its correspondence courses to Marine officers. Typical but not inclusive are courses in intelligence, international law, and strategy and tactics. In addition, the College Library makes loans of certain professional books and promulgates annual lists of recommended professional reading for Navy and Marine officers. If you wish to enroll, or if you seek further information, address the President, Naval War College, Newport, R.I., via your commanding officer.

Other Service Courses. If you want to take a correspondence course offered by the Army, Navy, Air Force, or Department of Defense (DOD), for which the Marine Corps does not have an equivalent, apply directly to the school of interest.

For younger officers of marked ability, the White House Fellows Program is worth looking into. In this program, officer college graduates (age 23–36), as well as civil servants, educators, and journalists, are given a year of first-hand, high-level experience in the workings of the U.S. government at the White House and Cabinet level.

1511. College Degree Program

One of the basic educational goals of the Corps is that any officer who does not have a baccalaureate degree will be offered the opportunity to earn one.

Officers who have completed two or more years' undergraduate work are eligible for the *college degree program* (sometimes referred to as "Operation Bootstrap") for not more than twenty-one months' residential instruction at an approved institution. In this program, you are ordered in a duty status to the institution in question. You receive normal pay and allowances but in turn meet the various academic fees and expenses out of pocket. (Most tuition and other academic expenses normally can be funded through the individual officer's Veterans Affairs entitlements.) To be selected, you may be in any grade, as a permanent regular officer, from warrant rank to that of lieutenant colonel. Applications must reach Marine Corps Headquarters at least six months before the start of the college term specified by you. Special consideration is given officers who have demonstrated interest and accomplishment in off-duty educational programs.

1512.   Special Education and Advanced-Degree Programs

The Corps has three programs in which officers can be encouraged and assisted to obtain advanced degrees above baccalaureate level.

The *tuition aid program* is a strictly do-it-yourself arrangement on your own time, but the Marine Corps pays 75 percent of tuition costs.

The *special education program* (SEP) officers study in a variety of disciplines for periods up to twenty-four months. Chosen curricula are tailored to billet needs of the Corps and may or may not lead to an advanced degree. (Officers, however, are at liberty to take on extra course loads, which, taken with the prescribed curriculum, would earn a degree.) All tuition and related expenses are paid by the Marine Corps while you continue in pay status.

The *advanced-degree program* (ADP) is essentially an advanced-level version of "Bootstrap." An officer, paying his own way, gets eighteen months in which to gain a degree. Again, in most cases, GI Bill entitlements cover academic expenses.

Typical, though by no means inclusive, of fields open to officers in the SEP and ADP are: applied mathematics (statistics); aeronautical engineering; communications engineering; computer engineering; computer science (technical); defense systems analysis; education, curriculum, and instruction; electronics engineering; financial management; management operations analysis; and public relations/journalism.

Selection for SEP and ADP is made on application to the commandant, by a Headquarters Marine Corps selection board.*

1513.   Professional Reading

Read and re-read the campaigns of Alexander, Hannibal, Caesar, Gustavus Adolphus, Turenne, Eugene, and Frederick. Make them your models. This is the only way to become a great general and to master the secrets of the art of war.

—Napoleon Bonaparte

A few officers attain high rank without having mastered the history of war, but they are few indeed. The habit of systematic, planned reading of history, biography, and literature enables you to live up to your profession and to apply the

---

*In addition to all the formal, organized schooling just described, there still remains a place for the traditional battalion or squadron officers' school, conducted by the CO and best-qualified officers of the unit. A well-tested arrangement is to hold it each Friday afternoon, followed immediately by a happy hour.

lessons of the past to the future. Remember Metternich's remark: "The past is chiefly useful to me as the eve of tomorrow—my soul wrestles with the future." Professional reading means more than studious application to field manuals and the regulations by which we steer our course. That type of reading should be taken for granted. So should the reading of service journals. Professional reading even transcends military matters (remember Clemenceau's barbed dictum: "War is too important a matter to be left to the generals"). Your professional reading ought to embrace military and naval history and biography; U.S. history; literature; international affairs; economics; and psychology.

That sounds like a large order. It will not seem so large once you begin. The most important part of a professional reading program can be summed up in one verb: *Read!*

Right now, subscribe to your professional journals: The *Marine Corps Gazette;* the *U.S. Naval Institute Proceedings;* and—for service news—the authoritative, widely read, and well-informed *Navy Times*. If you have a bent for military history, take *The Journal of Military History*.

In Appendix III, look over the list of Marine books that every officer should know, and start reading them. Better still, start acquiring them. Both the Naval Institute and the *Marines Corps Gazette,* incidentally, sell current books to subscribers at discounts of 10 percent or more. If you want a more extensive compilation of outstanding professional books, the Naval War College, Newport, Rhode Island, will be glad to send you its recommended reading list for Marine and Navy officers.

A relatively new program, the Commandant's Reading List, has fostered unit libraries and reading seminars to assist Marines in reading two to four of the listed titles each year.

A final must are the high-quality Marine Corps operational histories prepared by the History and Museums Division, Marine Corps Headquarters. Every officer should know them.

So now it's time to build your professional library and get the habit of reading professional journals. The Marine Corps packs and ships your professional library from station to station at no charge against your weight allowance and at no cost to you.

1514. The Service Author

Every officer with professional ideas worth expressing should support his or her service journals by contributing. There are three good reasons why you should do this:

1. You support the publications that spread military knowledge and raise professional standards.
2. You give readers the benefit of your ideas and experience.
3. You acquire a service reputation for professional keenness.

  It is widely believed that elaborate and drastic regulations hamper an officer who chooses to write for publication. This is by no means the case if you confine yourself to semiofficial service journals, such as the *Gazette* or *Proceedings*. Material prepared by active officers for outside publication, however, may require clearance by the secretary of the Navy and usually by the Department of Defense, as well.

In any case, you cannot reveal classified information in an article for publication any more than you can disclose the same information in a letter or in careless conversation. Nor can you represent that you are an official spokesman of the Marine Corps or the Department of the Navy, or give such an impression. Finally, whatever you write for publication should constitute a constructive contribution to the primary missions of the Department of Defense.

If, however, you are in any doubt as to the classification or general propriety of an article or manuscript, you may always submit it to the director of public affairs, Marine Corps Headquarters, who will advise you as to its suitability for publication.

1515. Public Speaking

The Importance of Speaking Ability.   Distinct, forceful speech is an essential quality for a successful officer. Public speaking ability is a primary tool of leadership. Because a large part of your career will be devoted to explaining, announcing, and teaching, you should learn at least the fundamentals of speaking technique—and the sooner, the better.

Some believe that public speaking ability is a magic gift, bestowed on some but denied to others. This is far from true. Public speaking, like the technique of shooting a rifle, can readily be, and has to be, learned. Good speakers are made, not born.

The Qualities of an Effective Speaker.   What are the qualities of effective military speakers?

Be purposeful. You must have a clear view of your objective—of what you are trying to put across. You must be able to balance the time spent against achievement of your objective. Avoid digression into irrelevancy.

Know your stuff. You must have a thorough grasp of your subject, backed up, if possible, by practical experience. Conversely, avoid, if you can, having to talk about matters in which you lack experience.

Take pains. Even if you have all the knowledge, skill, and experience needed to put your subject across, there is no shortcut in preparation. Choose the right approach and method of presentation; arrange your material in logical phases, each one followed by a summary; if you are instructing, use visual aids to help your audience *see* your points. Psychological studies show that 75 percent of all we learn is taken in through the eye, whereas only 13 percent comes through hearing.

Be enthusiastic. Enthusiasm is as catching as boredom. It is the driving force of a good speech or lecture. Your enthusiasm must be balanced and seasoned. If

The officer, above all else, must be a skilled teacher and be able to communicate concepts at many levels of knowledge.

you make your hearers feel that you are a fanatic with a wild gleam in the eye, they will discount what you say, and soon become bored. And enthusiasm unseasoned by intelligence and humor soon exhausts the hearer.

Cultivate a dramatic sense. Don't be content with dull, stodgy presentations; cultivate what show business people call "sense of staging." Get in touch with the mood of your hearers. Use variety of pace, surprise, and emotional and dramatic appeal to drive home your points. If you can tell a funny story well, don't be afraid to use it. But don't indulge in a gag just for the gag's sake. Remember also that there are other (and usually more effective) ways to introduce a subject than by telling an irrelevant "funny" story.

Have a confident, easy manner. Give your hearers confidence in what you say by having that confidence yourself. Speak clearly and distinctly. Remember that distinctness of speech stems from distinctness of ideas. Don't be flowery.

Have the right approach. Your particular approach should be determined by the nature of the audience. Regardless of the kind of audience you face, however, avoid the following.

- Flippancy: A flippant speaker displays disrespect for his subject and usually for the audience also.
- Cheap humor and vulgarity: Don't play the clown to get a cheap laugh. Vulgarity offends most hearers and, if repeated, bores all. By cheapening your remarks, you cheapen yourself and the Marine Corps.

- Slangy diction: Judiciously used, slang can be quite effective. But if you use slang indiscriminately, you lose your effect and grate on the audience's nerves.
- "Big words" and pedantry: Overuse of technical terms or of involved, long-winded constructions wraps your subject in a fog. Five-dollar words used merely for effect do not impress your listeners with anything but your stuffiness.

Make the most of your voice and body. Voice is your basic weapon. To exploit your voice, develop power, distinctness, and variety of delivery. Your body supports your voice through erect, confident posture, natural movement, meaningful gesture, and eye contact with every listener. Make it a rule to look every hearer in the eye while you speak to a group.

1516. Public Affairs

Intelligent and candid relations with the public form an important part of every Marine's career, from private to general, regardless of specialty.

The Marine Corps has long benefited from an aggressive and positive public affairs program, in which attention is drawn to the mission, capabilities, and security that the nation derives from the Corps' existence. Public affairs specialists assist commanders to handle community and media relations in presenting and explaining Marine Corps activities in order to broaden the public view of the Corps. In many cases, this means that prompt attention is paid to good and bad news in order that the unsparing eye of the citizen will see that the Corps measures up to the high standards of discipline, devotion to duty, individual smartness, and valor—hallmarks of the Corps.

In spite of your not being a public affairs specialist, know that your every action in public view will enhance or degrade the carefully won reputation the Corps enjoys today. The best advertisement the Corps has is the individual Marine. Deal truthfully, pleasantly, and respectfully with the public and its media representation. Be aware of what the public affairs program has outlined for appropriate remarks to the press and public. The Corps belongs to the nation, and your individual contribution, however isolated, will only enhance public knowledge and appreciation.

The future success of the Marine Corps depends on two factors: first, an efficient performance of all the duties to which its officers and men may be assigned; second, promptly bringing this efficiency to the attention of the proper officials of the Government, and the American people.

—John A. Lejeune

16

Leadership

Service in peacetime and even more in wartime makes great demands on the mental, moral, and physical strength of the individual Marine. In battle, character traits weigh more heavily than intellectual acuity. Even in this age of highly developed technology, it is still humans who must stand the test. Hence leadership assumes extraordinary importance, for it convinces the Marine of the necessity of service and encourages faithful performance of duty. The Marine's readiness to serve and, in wartime, to risk his or her life closely relates to the integrity of the nation and the survival of its free and democratic order.

The foundations of an individual's performance as a Marine are discipline, a sense of duty, courage, self-assurance, and cooperative thinking. These qualities support the Marine as he or she endures hardships and strives to accomplish the mission. Establishing such foundations remains the salient objective of leadership. Of them, discipline plays the indispensable role in maintaining the combat power of a unit. Undisciplined behavior must be countered immediately and appropriately. In well-disciplined units, a sense of comradeship emerges and soldierly values—such as confidence and unselfishness—predominate. It is the duty of commanders at all levels to gain the trust of subordinates and establish solidarity in their units. This is accomplished primarily through the demonstration of knowledge and wisdom, example, fairness, patience, and thoughtfulness and through the administration of appropriate strictness. Most destructive to comradeship are misguided ambition, selfishness, and insincerity. A unit that has grown together into a "band of brothers" will be able to withstand severe stress.

All leaders, regardless of their fields or styles of leadership, share one characteristic—confidence, in themselves and in their cause. A person gains self-confidence by surmounting difficulties through intelligence and judgment. That confidence transmits itself to others and is a source of inspiration to Marines serving under that individual. The leader also understands the obligation to look after those in the command. The more arduous their situation, the more intensely subordinates must feel that their commanders, their leaders, are vigilant on their behalf. Again, this relates to the feeling of comradeship that should pervade a unit, holding true up, down, and across the ranks. This is one reason it is nearly always a mistake to break up a unit, particularly in combat.

In wartime, troops face enormous psychological pressures brought on by the force of the weapons being used against them, by disruption of communications and isolation from other friendly forces, and by rumors planted by the enemy. The natural fear resulting from any of these causes can escalate into unrestrained, unreasoning, and self-destructive fear—panic. All signs of panic must be nipped in the bud by the commanding officer before losing influence over the troops. But before the situation reaches a point where a commanding officer must use drastic measures to quell the first signs of panic, he or she can follow a course of action that can help prevent panic. By providing the unit with up-to-date, factual, and objective information and by reiterating that their fight is meaningful and their political and military leadership sound, the commander can psychologically equip the troops to withstand the pressures of war.

This chapter describes characteristics, techniques, and procedures that contribute to effective leadership. As you peruse these paragraphs (or any so-called text on leadership), remember that the royal road to leadership is not merely to read, but rather to *lead*.

THE MARINE LEADER

1601. Attributes of a Marine Leader

> The young American responds quickly and readily to the exhibition of qualities of leadership on the part of his officers. Some of these qualities are industry, energy, initiative, determination, enthusiasm, firmness, kindness, justness, self-control, unselfishness, honor, and courage.

So Major General John A. Lejeune summarized the attributes of a Marine leader. Although Lejeune's list can scarcely be improved, it can be enlarged on.

The contagion of example is the central thought in General Lejeune's passage. It is not enough that you merely know a leader's qualities and not enough that you proclaim them; you must *exhibit* them. To exact discipline, you must first possess self-discipline, and to demand unsparing attention to duty, you must not spare yourself.

Much of the power of example, in turn, stems from "command presence," or the kind of military appearance you make.

Command presence is the product of dignity, military carriage, firm and un-hurried speech, and self-confidence. Command presence is one useful adjunct of leadership that can be systematically cultivated. "Spit and polish" should not be confused with command presence.

Resolution and tenacity—an unfaltering determination to achieve the mission assigned to you—is the fuel of leadership.

Ability to teach and speak usually denotes an effective leader and enhances whatever latent leadership talents you possess. Cultivate this gift at every opportunity. It is a lever that can decisively influence your career.

Protection and fostering of subordinates distinguishes Marine Corps leadership. Leaders assume responsibility for their subordinates' actions (their mistakes, too) and see to it that credit is received where it is due. Leadership means looking out for your people.

Encouragement of subordinates is a tradition of Marine leadership. Give subordinates all the initiative and latitude they can handle. Encourage them in professional studies and reading. Make them seek professional schooling.

Professional competence may not make your Marines like you but will surely elicit their respect. "You can't snow the troops" is an old Marine saying. If you are professionally able, your enlisted Marines will be the first to get the word. Conversely, they will be mercilessly quick to spot a fraud. Demonstrate competence and keenness as an officer, and your Marines will be content to be led by you. Never be ashamed to be known as a "hard charger," as long as your aim is the best interest of the Corps.

Here is a classic remark by one of the Corp's hardest-charging generals, the late Graves B. Erskine:

> The first thing, a man should know his business. He should know his weapons, he should know the tactics for those weapons, and he should not only be qualified for the grade he is assigned to, but at least for the next higher grade.

Education contributes to professional competence. Education and study give you technical proficiency, help you think clearly, enable you to express yourself, and command respect from all.

Physical readiness, though not an end in itself, is essential for every Marine and thus doubly so for every leader. Unless you can confidently face your physical fitness test, you are not fit for active command.

The spirit of "can-do" and "make-do" is as old as the Corps itself. To do the best you can with what you have, to do it promptly, cheerfully, and confidently, marks you as a leader in the best traditions of the Marine Corps. The world is divided into "can-do" and "can't-do" types. Be sure you are in the former class.

Adaptability marks a seasoned Marine. As a leader, keep loose; roll with the punches. Cultivate that most admirable trait, "grace under pressure."

Devotion to the Marine Corps and its standards begets equal earnestness and devotion from subordinates. Take the Marine Corps and its time-honored ways with full seriousness, and so will your command. That is the Marine Corps attitude.

As both summary and comment on the foregoing, here is a thought-provoking list of attributes. How do you measure up?

Serious	Competent	Inventive
Disciplined	Aggressive	Austere
Loyal	Knowledgeable	Purposeful
Authoritative	Tenacious	Compassionate
Courageous	Proud	Sensitive
Tough	Resolute	

Marine officers must offer their skills and knowledge in a tactful, understanding, and cooperative fashion to allies and officers of other services.

YOU AND YOUR SUBORDINATES

1602. Dealing with Subordinates

Whether your subordinates are officers or enlisted Marines, support and back them to the hilt. They will turn to you for encouragement, guidance, and material support. Never let them down. Nothing should ever be "too much trouble" if it is needed for your outfit. Protect, shelter, and feed them before you think of your own needs.

Demand the highest standards and never let those standards be compromised. Field Marshall Erwin Rommel stated this in slightly different words:

> A commander must accustom his staff to a high tempo from the outset, and continually keep them up to it. If he once allows himself to be satisfied with norms, or anything less than an all-out effort, he gives up the race from the starting post, and will sooner or later be taught a bitter lesson. . . .

Live, lead, and exercise command "by the book." Let this be understood by your Marines.

Keep *responsibility* centralized—in *you*. Decentralize *authority*. Give subordinates wide authority and discretion. Tell them what results you want, and leave the "how" to them. Never oversupervise.

Avoid overfamiliarity of manner or address. If you have feet of clay—and most humans do—overfamiliarity with subordinates is the surest way to advertise it.

Develop genuine interest in your Marines as individuals. Study each personality. Seek out background information from service records. Learn names, and address your Marines by proper names. Never let any Marine picture himself or herself as "a mere cog" in the machine. No Marine is a cog.

In your daily exercise of command, avoid the "hurry-up-and-wait" tendency that characterizes ill-run commands. That is to say, think twice before you apply pressure to speed up something if the result is simply that your people will have to stand around waiting at some further stage. Don't get them out unduly ahead of time for formations and parades, especially if every other echelon has added its few minutes of anticipation, too. And always be on time and on schedule as far as you yourself are concerned. One of the most basic rules of military courtesy is to never keep the troops waiting.

Respect the skill and experience of your NCOs. Learn from the wisdom of NCOs, but never let them snow you. Do everything in your power to enhance the skill, prestige, and authority of NCOs, except at the expense of your own prestige and authority. In public, address NCOs by name and rank. In private, you may call them by their last names only. *Never address an enlisted person by his or her first name or nickname.*

Be accessible to any subordinate who wishes to see you. It is a tradition of the Corps that any enlisted Marine who desires an interview with the commanding officer must obtain the first sergeant's permission. It is equally a tradition of the Corps that permission is unhesitatingly given unless the Marine is drunk or flagrantly out of uniform. In connection with such requests, you should give your first sergeant direct and positive instructions that he or she must report to you, the commanding officer, every complaint received from an enlisted Marine. Most of these need never come to your attention otherwise or in any official form, but this rule helps to avert trouble before it becomes serious.

1603. Issuing and Enforcing Orders

> Promulgation of an order represents not over 10 per cent of your responsibility. The remaining 90 per cent consists in assuring through personal supervision on the ground, by yourself and your staff, proper and vigorous execution.

So wrote General George S. Patton on the subject of orders. Issuing and enforcing orders constitute one of the main functions of an officer.

Before you issue an order, ask yourself if it can be reasonably carried out. If, in the circumstances, an order cannot be executed as given, it should not be given.

Never give an unlawful order; that is, an order that contravenes law or regulations or demands that your subordinates break the rules. A good test of a lawful order is, "Could a subordinate be court-martialed for failing to comply?"

Issue as few orders as necessary. Keep them concise, clear, and unmistakable in purpose. Anything that can be misunderstood, will be.

Never contravene the orders of another officer or NCO without clear and pressing reason. If possible, make this reason evident when you countermand the order in question. If orders to you conflict, obey the last one.

When you have once given an order, be sure it is executed as you give it. Your responsibility doesn't end until you have assured yourself that the order has been carried out. Never shrug off half-hearted, perfunctory compliance. "If anyone in a key position appears to be expending less than the energy that could properly be demanded of him," wrote Rommel, "that man must be ruthlessly removed."

An order received from above should be passed on as your order and should be enforced as such. Never evade the onus of an unpopular directive by throwing the blame on the next higher echelon.

It cannot be too often repeated that when you issue an order, make it clear what you want done and who is to do it—but avoid telling subordinates how it is to be done. Remember the old promotion-examination question for lieutenants, in which the student is told that he or she has a ten-person working party, headed by a sergeant, and must erect a seventy-five-foot flagpole on the post parade ground. Problem—How to do it?

Every student who works out the precise calculations of stresses, tackle, and gear, no matter how accurately, is graded wrong. The desired answer is simple: The lieutenant turns to the sergeant, and says, "Sergeant, put up that flagpole."

1604. "R.H.I.P."

As an officer, you are entitled to take precedence ahead of your juniors and all enlisted persons. This privilege is admitted in the service proverb "R.H.I.P."—

The peculiarities of aircrew and flight leadership place special demands on officers in aviation fields.

"Rank has its privileges." Just when and where you "pull rank," though, is a matter of some delicacy.

Generally speaking, you should assert your privilege when your time is circumscribed by duty or when failure to do so would demean your status as a commissioned officer. For example, an officer should not waste his or her own time and the government's by falling in line behind privates in a clothing storeroom or hesitate to claim the attention of an administrative functionary hemmed in by enlisted persons. Conversely, in situations where all persons are equal, take your place with the others regardless of rank. In the mess, at the barber shop (unless there is an officer's chair), at the post exchange, or at games, avoid taking advantage of rank.

Finally, every Marine officer pulls rank in reverse when it comes to looking out for the troops. In the field, before you yourself eat, every enlisted Marine must have had a full ration. Before you take shelter, your Marines must have shelter. "There is no fatigue the soldiers go through," said Baron Friedrich von Steuben in 1779, "that the officers should not share."

MILITARY DISCIPLINE

1605.   The Object and Nature of Discipline

Effective performance by Marines in combat is the direct result and primary object of military discipline. Discipline may be defined as prompt and willing

Marine leaders command from the front of their units, share hardships, and demand the utmost efforts of their subordinates.

responsiveness to orders and unhesitating compliance with regulations. Since the ultimate objective of discipline is effective performance in battle, discipline may in a very real sense spell the difference between life and death (or, more important to the Marine, between victory and defeat). It is that standard of deportment, attention to duty, example, and decent behavior that, once indoctrinated, enables Marines, alone or in groups, to accomplish their missions.

To many persons, discipline simply means punishment. In fact, discipline is a matter of people working well together and getting along well together—and, even if there be a lack of harmony among them, discipline is a means of cementing them as a fighting organization. In the Marine Corps, as in any military organization, it is necessary for people to do certain things in prescribed ways and at given times. If they do so, we say they are well disciplined.

Discipline exists in everyday life: people obey traffic lights, pay greens fees, go in through entrances and out through exits. Nevertheless, military discipline differs fundamentally from the disciplines of civilian life, because a Marine, having taken an oath to serve an allotted time, is committed to his or her duty while a civilian worker is free to quit a job at any time. For this reason, "management," a popular word in the civilian sector, is an impoverished one in military circles compared with "leadership."

1606. The Basis of Discipline

The best discipline is self-discipline. To be really well-disciplined, a unit must be made up of individuals who are self-disciplined. In the ultimate test of combat, the leader must be able to depend on the Marines to do their duty correctly and voluntarily whether anyone is checking on them or not. If time and the situation permit, you should make known to your subordinates the reasons for a given order because this knowledge will increase the desire of your people to do the job and will enable them to do it intelligently. You must know what you want of your people, let them know, and then demand it of them.

1607. Characteristics of Effective Discipline

Until severely tried, there is no conclusive test of discipline. Troops remain relatively undisciplined until physically and mentally exerted (a fact that shapes much of the programs of recruit and officer training). No body of troops could possibly enjoy the dust, the heat, the blistered foot, and the aching back of a road march. Nevertheless, hard road marching is a necessary and sound foundation for the discipline of combat foot troops. The rise in spirit within any unit, which is always marked when Marines rebound from a hard march or after a record day, does not come from a feeling of physical relief but from a sense of accomplishment.

Another key factor in sound discipline is consistency and firmness. You cannot wink at an infraction one day and put a person on the report for the same offense tomorrow. You must establish and make known your standards of good discipline, and be consistent, firmly consistent, every day.

Discipline imposed by fear of punishment will inevitably break down in combat or any other severe test. If you threaten your troops, discipline will also break. Discipline will not break under stress, however, if troops understand why they are enduring hardship and danger.

PRAISE AND REPRIMAND

1608. Occasions for Praise

A basic rule is to *praise in public and reprimand in private.*

Never let a praiseworthy occasion pass unmentioned. This means more than occasional back-pats. Here are ways in which you can make the most of opportunities to praise subordinates.

Promotion. When an officer is promoted (although regulations no longer so require), he or she should be sworn in at Office Hours by the senior Marine officer present. Administration of the oath adds greatly to the solemnity of the occasion and enables the officer to reaffirm the original oath taken on receiving his or her first commission. If practical, the spouse and children should be invited. All fellow officers who can be spared should attend. The officer administering the oath should always give a set of insignia to the individual being promoted—if possible, a set of his or her own insignia from an earlier rank, a gift that is always appreciated.

Enlisted promotions are effected by presentation of the individual's warrant for the next higher rank. This should be accomplished at a formation. If a parade or other formation cannot be arranged, the person should receive the warrant from the commanding officer at Office Hours, in the presence of his or her immediate commanding officer and first sergeant. If enlisted offenders are to appear at the same Office Hours, parade them in the rear, in order to give them occasion to reflect on "the other side of the coin."

Under no circumstances should a Marine be called into the company office and receive the warrant from the first sergeant or clerk. This is the wrong way and reflects directly on you if you permit such procedures.

Presentation of Decorations. The *Drill and Ceremonies Manual* describes the ceremony for presenting decorations. Even at some inconvenience to the unit, decorations—particularly those earned in combat or awarded for heroic action—should be presented with utmost formality at a parade or review, as laid down in the book. Avoid the easy solution of calling in the Marine to Office Hours and presenting the medal with a handshake. The fundamental purpose of awards is to inspire emulation. To do this, you must present medals or commendations where the maximum number of other Marines know about it.*

In combat, when an award can be made immediately, it is sometimes effective for a senior commander to visit the recipient at the unit, call together com-

---

*A modified version of the awards ceremony can serve equally well for such occasions as presentation of Good Conduct Medals, civilian commendations, commissioning of meritorious NCOs as warrant officers or second lieutenants, and so on.

rades, and give the medal on the spot. With decorations, even more than other rewards, "he gives thrice who gives quickly." As a combat leader, be alert for every deserving act, especially by an enlisted Marine. Know the criteria and Marine Corps standards for every award, and how to initiate proper recommendations. (See Section 738.)

Retirement.   The honorable retirement or transfer to the Fleet Reserve of any officer or enlisted Marine should be habitually effected at a parade or review. In the case of an officer, it is also appropriate for the officers of the unit to "dine out" at a mess night, as described in Section 2203.

Completion of Correspondence Course.   Any Marine who completes a Marine Corps Institute (MCI) correspondence course should receive the diploma from the commanding officer at Office Hours or formation.

Reenlistment.   When a number of Marines ship over on the same day, arrange a formation in their honor. Otherwise, individuals should be shipped over at Office Hours. If practical, make this the occasion for a day off—and, if warranted and possible, there is no better moment to effect a promotion. Nothing starts a new cruise so handsomely as another chevron.

1609.   Reprimand

One basic rule of reprimand has already been stated—*do it in private.*

A second rule is found in the Marine proverb "Never give a Marine a dollar's worth of blame without a dime's worth of praise."

And avoid collective reprimands, let alone collective punishments. Nothing so rightly infuriates an innocent person as to be unfairly included in an all-hands blast or all-hands punishment.

Before you issue reprimand or censure, be sure that an offense or dereliction of some kind has been committed. This is basic. You cannot call down a Marine just because you don't like the color of his or her eyes. Before telling off any individual, ask yourself if what that person has done, pushed to the limit, would sustain charges under any article in the *Uniform Code of Military Justice.* This can save you much embarrassment and injured innocence at the hands of sea-lawyers, while it sometimes cuts the other way to protect a subordinate against hasty rebuke when not warranted.

Know what you intend to say before you launch into reprimand. A sputtering, inconclusive rebuke only makes an officer look silly.

Avoid uncontrolled anger, profanity, or abuse. Many experienced Marines, officer and NCO, know how to valve off anger into indignation. Make this your object but at all costs avoid "acting tough."

Never make a promise or threat that you are not capable of fulfilling, or that you do not intend to fulfill. Never bluff, or you will be called in short order.

Like reward, the effectiveness of reproof is in direct proportion to its immediacy. When you spot something amiss, take corrective action at once. Never let a wrongdoing Marine slide by with the thought, "Well, he's not one of *my* troops. Let his own outfit handle it." *Every* U.S. Marine is one of *your* troops.

If you have occasion to call down a Marine not under your command, find out who the Marine is, and see that his or her commanding officer knows about it. This will be appreciated by the CO, who is just as anxious as you are to have his or her Marines up to snuff. Moreover, the derelictions of an individual are the responsibility of the immediate senior. A Marine with a dirty rifle is a black eye for the squad and fire-team leader; a man in your platoon who fails to salute is a discredit to your leadership. Napoleon's dictum, "There are no bad regiments—only bad colonels," applies with equal force to fire teams, squads, platoons, companies, and battalions as well.

1610.   Office Hours

Office Hours, the Marine Corps equivalent of Captain's Mast, is the occasion when the commanding officer awards formal praise or blame, hears special requests, and awards nonjudicial punishment. Detailed treatment of Office Hours procedure and nonjudicial punishment is contained in Chapter 19.

Remember that Office Hours is a ceremony, and that much of the desired effect depends upon the manner in which it is conducted. And when you hold Office Hours, do so with the greatest respect for each person's individuality. Not only must the punishment fit the *crime,* it must fit the *person.* Never let anyone leave Office Hours with a sense of injustice or frustrated misunderstanding.

A special and important variation of Office Hours is Request Mast, an occasion set aside for individuals who may have special requests or grievances that they wish to present to the commanding officer. It is one of the responsibilities of command to keep this opportunity open to any Marine who, *in good faith,* wishes to utilize it. In holding Request Mast, one important point to remember is that the individual is entitled to complete privacy. Unless requested otherwise, you should see Marines alone, and should take all necessary steps to avoid any prejudice to their interests that might arise out of a bona fide complaint or special request.

INSPECTIONS

1611.   Inspections

Inspection is one of the most important tools of command. Throughout your Marine Corps career, you will be continually inspected or inspecting. Inspections serve two purposes: first, to enable commanding or superior officers to find out conditions within an organization; and second, to impart to an organization the standards required of it.

There are several types of inspection, varying from inspection of personnel in ranks to inspections of materiel, supplies, equipment, records, and buildings. Each inspection has a particular purpose, which the inspecting officer will keep foremost in mind. Thus it is up to you to ascertain or forecast the object of the inspection and to prepare yourself and your command accordingly. For example, if the inspection is to deal with the crew-served weapons and transportation in your unit, it does no great good to emphasize clean uniforms and haircuts at the expense of materiel upkeep. On the other hand, good-looking vehicles do not excuse greasy, worn clothing at a personnel inspection.

1612. Preparation for Inspection

Once you know the purpose of an inspection, you must prepare your outfit. The best way to do this is by putting yourself in the inspector's shoes. Be sure your leading NCOs also understand the "why" of the inspection so that they can cooperate intelligently in getting tuned to concert pitch. Many an inspection crisis has been averted by a quick-witted, loyal NCO with a ready answer.

While your unit prepares for inspection, move about with a leading NCO, usually your police sergeant, and/or first sergeant. This enables you to see that preparations are what you want, and it reminds your people that you have direct interest in the hard work they are engaged in. It also lets you discover weak spots in good time.

Time preparation for inspection so that everything is ready about thirty minutes before the appointed hour. This gives your Marines a final opportunity to get themselves ready. It also gives you a margin to handle last-minute emergencies.

Ten minutes beforehand, have your responsible subordinates standing by their respective posts, or, if the inspection is to be in formation, have your troops paraded, steady and correct. You yourself should be either at the head of them or at the entrance to your area, poised to meet the inspecting party. As a platoon leader, you should have your platoon sergeant and guide assist you in the inspection. If you are the company commander, you should have your first sergeant and gunnery sergeant in your inspection party. The "top" should have a notebook and pencil ready to take notes. The police sergeant should have a flashlight. All rooms, compartments, sheds, and so forth should be unlocked and open. Tents should be rolled, unless the weather is foul.

When the inspecting party arrives, salute and report your unit ready for inspection. Post yourself at the left rear of the inspecting officer. Answer questions calmly and with good humor. Avoid alibis. Remember, there is only one inspector and you should take no actions or make comments yourself, except to attend the inspector. Do not reprimand your troops during inspection for shortcomings the inspection brings out. It is your outfit; the shortcomings are *yours*. Be alert for the inspecting officer's comments. These forearm you for the next inspection.

Afterward, if results have been notably good or notably poor, assemble your people and tell them about it. Give every Marine a personal stake in the success of each inspection.

1613. Conduct of the Inspection

Nothing else can raise the standards of a command like an intelligent program of inspection, carefully followed up. Some officers unwisely discount the value of formal inspections, saying that these result in unbalanced, artificial impressions, and that COs ought to observe informally in order to find out "real" conditions. While it is certainly true that every CO must keep on the move and keep his or her eyes open, the periodic formal inspection is vital because it requires all hands to overhaul their areas of responsibility. Moreover, formal inspection is the only way to determine accurately the degree of progress being made by a unit.

Before you inspect, you, like the unit being inspected, must also make careful preparations. As an inspector, you should:

1. Know what you intend to concentrate on—in other words, the purpose of the inspection.
2. Have a planned route and sequence of inspection designed to cover the entire unit and area.
3. Organize your inspecting party. This should include one Marine to take notes, one with flashlight, plus the requisite specialist talent (such as hospital corpsman, technicians, and so forth) needed to advise and assist.
4. See that you and your party are perfectly turned out and neatly uniformed. Inspections also operate in reverse.
5. Be up to date on details of maintenance and function of any materiel you are to inspect. If materiel is on the program, leaf through the appropriate technical manual, which will contain a checklist for inspection. Become familiar with the nomenclature, functioning and maintenance indicators associated with the equipment. When you inspect, do so impartially and pleasantly. Avoid a fault-finding spirit; the object of inspections is to help and inform, not to antagonize. Praise individuals when you properly can. As you uncover defects, be sure that the responsible individuals understand what you have discovered and why it constitutes a defect. Avoid a dead level of criticism or complaint.
6. Inspect yourself. Never walk in front of another Marine to inspect at less than your best. The Marines you look at are inspected once, by you. All of them, on the other hand, inspect you as you pass down the ranks. Don't be found lacking.
7. Inspect in cadence and at attention. Having a leading NCO—sergeant major or first sergeant—precede you.

Finally, regardless of the purpose of the inspection, never overlook the individual Marine. See that he or she is smart and military. Look the Marine in the eye. Make the Marine feel that he or she is the ultimate object, and that you are deeply interested in him or her as a person and a Marine.

1614. Inspection Follow-up

An inspection loses value if you fail to follow it up. This is the main reason for keeping careful notes on the comments of the inspecting officer.

Inspection notes should be disseminated to everyone concerned, broken down into items for corrective action, so that they can serve as a checklist. When you reinspect, review previous inspection notes as a guide for follow-up. On the receiving end, you can use past notes to prepare for future occasions. It is a grave reflection on you as a leader if the same defects continue to show up on consecutive inspections.

1615. IG Inspections

Via the long-standing previous title, "The Adjutant and Inspector," the Inspector General of the Corps ("the IG") can trace roots back to 1798. Today, the IG's job is to assist and examine by periodic inspections the effectiveness of Marine Corps commands in terms of ability to carry out their missions; unit leadership, economy, policies, and doctrine; work and health conditions; and discipline.

After a visit to a command by an IG team, one of three grades is awarded: satisfactory, noteworthy, and unsatisfactory. Although it may seem difficult for a unit under such searching inspection to believe, the IG is there to help: inspections are always a search for causes, not an inventory of symptoms.

OTHER ASPECTS OF LEADERSHIP

1616. Weapons Proficiency

A Marine leader has few better ways of setting the right example to his troops than by maintaining high proficiency with infantry weapons—notably, the rifle and pistol. Marines respect a good shot and an officer who is handy with small arms. Do your best each year when you go to the range. Every enlisted Marine will be watching to see how you do. Make yourself a model of marksmanship technique. Demand no special favors: behind a rifle, on the firing line, all Marines are equals. Clean and maintain your own weapon, pick up your own brass, keep your own scorebook, and keep your mouth shut.

Never violate a safety precaution. Remember the shooter's proverb: "There is no such thing as an accidental discharge."

Although you will never match your best enlisted Marines, seek knowledge and skill in firing and employing crew-served weapons, such as machine guns, assault, and antitank weapons.

1617. Looking Out for Your Marines

In the final analysis, the essence of Marine leadership is looking out for your people.

For the sake of your unit, you must be tireless, you must be imaginative, you must be willing to shoulder responsibility. Their good must be your first preoccupation. Their interest and advancement must be always on your mind.

- Are they comfortably clothed, housed, and sheltered?
- Are they well fed?
- Are they getting their mail?

- If sick and wounded, can they rely on help?
- Are they justly treated?
- Are they trained to accomplish their mission?
- Are you available to everyone who needs counsel?
- Are you alert to help each one in his or her career?

As an officer, you demand a great deal of your Marines. But they, in fact, demand much more of you. If you let down one of your Marines, you are letting down the entire Corps.

The general must know how to get his men their rations and every other kind of stores needed in war. He must have imagination to originate plans, practical sense and energy to carry them through. He must be observant, untiring, shrewd, kindly and cruel, simple and crafty, a watchman and a robber, lavish and miserly, generous and stingy, rash and conservative. All these and many other qualities, natural and acquired, must he have. He should also, as a matter of course, know his tactics; for a disorderly mob is no more an army than a heap of building materials is a house.

—Socrates

If the trumpet give an uncertain sound, who shall prepare himself to the battle?

—I Corinthians 14:8

17

On Watch

One of the most stirring guard orders ever received by U.S. Marines was issued on 11 November 1921 by Navy Secretary Edwin Denby, himself a former Marine. The nation was in the grip of a crime wave, which had been highlighted by armed robberies of the U.S. Mails. Four days before Secretary Denby penned his letter of instruction, the president had directed that the Marine Corps take over the job of safeguarding the mails, and fifty-three officers and twenty-two hundred enlisted Marines were already on watch in post offices, railway mail cars, and postal trucks throughout the country. "To the Men of the Mail Guard," wrote Edwin Denby:

> I am proud that my old Corps has been chosen for a duty so honorable as that of protecting the United States mail. I am very anxious that you shall successfully accomplish your mission. It is not going to be easy work. It will always be dangerous and generally tiresome. You know how to do it. Be sure you do it well. I know you will neither fear nor shirk any duty, however hazardous or exacting.
>
> This particular work will lack the excitement and glamor of war duty, but it will be no less important. It has the same element of service to the country.
>
> I look with proud confidence to you to show now the qualities that have made the Corps so well-beloved by our fellow citizens.
>
> You must be brave, as you always are. You must be constantly alert. You must, when on guard duty, keep your weapons in hand and, if attacked, shoot and shoot to kill. There is no compromise in this battle with the bandits.
>
> If two Marines, guarding a mail car, are suddenly covered by a robber, neither

must hold up his hands, but both must begin shooting at once. One may be killed, but the other will get the robber and save the mail. When our men go in as guards over mail, that mail must be delivered or there must be a Marine dead at the post of duty.

To be sure of success, every Marine on this duty must be watchful as a cat, hour after hour, night after night, week after week. No Marine must drink a drop of intoxicating liquor. Every Marine must be most careful with whom he associates and what his occupations are off duty. There may be many tricks tried to get you, and you must not be tricked. Look out for women. Never discuss the details of your duty with outsiders. Never give up to another the trust you are charged with.

Never forget that the honor of the Corps is in your keeping. You have been given a great trust. I am confident you will prove that it has not been misplaced.

I am proud of you and believe in you with all my heart.

/s/ Edwin Denby

Mail robberies ceased within a matter of days after Secretary Denby penned his order, and not a single piece of mail was lost to a robber while Marines stood watch.

1701.   Watchstanding

The Importance of Guard Duty.   In the Marine Corps and Navy, the safety and good order of the entire command depend on those who stand guard. Thus, watchstanding is your strictest routine duty.

The importance of guard duty is underscored by the fact that sleeping on watch can be punished by death in time of war and in peace by heavy penalties.

In addition to combat missions, the Marine Corps is the combat security force for the naval establishment and is thus not only responsible for the good order and protection of its own posts but also of all stations and ships where Marines are assigned. As a Marine officer, you are therefore expected to be an authority on watchstanding and guard duty, as well as a model watch officer, ashore or afloat.

Semper Fidelis never demands more than when you are on guard. Marines maintain four kinds of guard: an exterior guard ashore; an interior guard ashore; a ship's guard afloat, and special guards.

In addition, Marines frequently perform military police and shore patrol duties for the regulation and assistance of Marines and seamen on liberty.

An *exterior guard* is maintained only in combat or when danger of attack exists. An exterior guard protects the command against outside attack and is organized and armed according to the tactical situation.

Interior guards have the threefold mission of protecting life, preserving order and enforcing regulations, and safeguarding public property.

Ships' guards carry out the same general missions afloat as interior guards do ashore but differ in details of organization and duty because of shipboard conditions.

Special guards include all guards organized for special purposes (for example, train or boat guards and so on). In addition, most posts having custody of special weapons have a separate main guard for that purpose alone, leaving other normal security functions at the post to the station main guard.

Status of Marines on Watch. Any Marine on guard, whether officer or enlisted, represents the commanding officer. In the execution of orders or the enforcement of regulations, the Marine guard's authority is complete. When you receive a lawful order from a member of the guard, comply without hesitation and ask your questions afterward. Remember that an armed sentry has full authority to *enforce* instructions.

THE INTERIOR GUARD

1702. The Interior Guard

The interior guard—established to preserve order, protect property, and enforce regulations—derives its authority directly from the commanding officer. Figure 17–1 shows the organization of a typical interior guard. The guard is composed of a main guard, and, when needed, special guards.

1703. Duties of the Guard

The duties of the guard (and the CO's responsibilities in connection with the guard) are as follows.

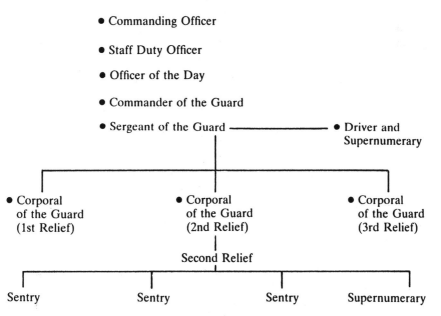

- Commanding Officer

- Staff Duty Officer

- Officer of the Day

- Commander of the Guard

- Sergeant of the Guard ——————— • Driver and Supernumerary

- Corporal of the Guard (1st Relief)

- Corporal of the Guard (2nd Relief)

- Corporal of the Guard (3rd Relief)

Second Relief

Sentry   Sentry   Sentry   Supernumerary

Figure 17–1: Organization of a typical interior guard. There are as many sentries in each relief as there are posts. On a small station, the staff duty officer is omitted.

The *Commanding Officer* establishes the guard and sees that it functions properly. Either the CO or representative (usually the executive officer or adjutant) receives the daily reports from, and relieves, the officers of the day, examines the guard book, and issues whatever special instructions may be needed.

The *Staff Duty Officer* may be required on a large post where subordinate commands maintain separate guards. The staff duty officer coordinates subordinate guards, and acts for the post commander in an emergency.

The *Officer of the Day (OD)* supervises the main guard, executes all orders that pertain to the guard, and is responsible that the guard performs effectively. While officer of the day, you are the direct representative of the commanding officer.

The *Commander of the Guard,* a staff NCO, is responsible for the proper instruction, discipline, and performance of the guard. A commander of the guard is usually required only for a large guard.

The *Sergeant of the Guard,* whatever his or her actual rank, is the senior NCO of the guard. The sergeant of the guard assists the commander of the guard, or, if the guard does not include one, performs the latter's duties. The sergeant of the guard supervises the enlisted members of the guard and is responsible for government property charged to the guard.

Nonrated members of the guard are organized into three reliefs, each of which includes a sentinel for each post and one supernumerary and is commanded by a *Corporal of the Guard.* The corporal of the guard instructs and supervises the relief, which takes its successive turn on guard throughout the tour of duty.

1704.   Duties and General Orders for Sentinels

The sentry is the workhorse of the guard. The universal respect accorded a U.S. Marine sentinel is based on that person's high military efficiency and the fact that he or she is habitually armed and prepared to defend his or her post and person in the execution of orders. A sentinel's duties are to carry out the general orders for a sentinel on post, as well as special orders applicable to the particular post. Every Marine, officer or enlisted, must know the general orders by heart:

1. To take charge of this post and all government property in view.
2. To walk my post in a military manner, keeping always on the alert, and observing everything that takes place within sight or hearing.
3. To report all violations of orders I am instructed to enforce.
4. To repeat all calls from posts more distant from the guardhouse than my own.
5. To quit my post only when properly relieved.
6. To receive, obey, and pass on to the sentinel who relieves me, all orders from the commanding officer (field officer of the day), officer of the day, and officers and noncommissioned officers of the guard only.
7. To talk to no one except in line of duty.
8. To give the alarm in case of fire or disorder.

9. To call the corporal of the guard in any case not covered by instructions.
10. To salute all officers, and all colors and standards not cased.
11. To be especially watchful at night, and, during the time for challenging, to challenge all persons on or near my post, and to allow no one to pass without proper authority.

In addition to routine sentry duties, nonrated members of the guard are assigned to certain special duties, such as the following.*

Guardhouse Sentinel (Post No. 1):   If one is assigned, the sentinel assists the corporal of the guard in carrying on guardhouse routine. Your guardhouse sentinel should be picked for intelligence, reliability, and smartness.

Main Gate Sentinel: This sentinel ensures that only authorized persons enter or leave the post through the main gate; he or she also directs traffic and assists visitors. Your main gate sentry stands watch in the show window of the station; therefore select the sentry for soldierly appearance, judgment, and thorough knowledge of the post. *The main gate is a spot for outstanding Marines.*

Supernumerary: One additional sentry stands by as a supernumerary to replace anyone who must be relieved. The supernumerary can be kept busy as a messenger and general factotum in the guardhouse.

Driver: A motor transport operator is assigned to the guard to drive the guard truck. Always keep the driver up to standard in uniform and appearance; it is a notorious failing among guard drivers to lag behind the rest of the guard in this respect.

1705. Daily Guard Routine

The daily routine of an interior guard varies somewhat according to the wishes of the commanding officer and the size and missions of the post. But, in the main, guard duty runs as follows.

The normal tour is twenty-four hours. Anyone detailed for guard duty must be on board and fit for duty at least four hours before commencement of the tour.

Details for guard duty should be published well in advance, by written order, and should specify uniform and equipment, together with any other information not covered in standing orders. *Officers detailed for guard duty must be notified in person or by written order, preferably both.* This is the adjutant's responsibility. The adjutant also keeps the officer-of-the-day roster, which determines the order in which officers stand watch.

A tour on guard begins in formal situations with *guard mounting,* when the old (outgoing) and new (incoming) guards are paraded and inspected. After guard mount, old and new officers of the day and sergeants of the guard relieve

---

*The policy of the Marine Corps is that all sentinels will be armed. Detailed safety instructions, as well as restrictions on the use of the weapon, should be known to all members of the guard, from OD to sentry. Improper or careless use of firearms is an extremely serious matter.

each other. Thereupon the officers of the day report to the commanding officer, and the new officer of the day assumes duty.

The guard's routine includes execution of Colors, posting and relief of sentinels, supervision of meal formations, and rendition of honors to the commanding officer, visiting officers, and civilian dignitaries.

Each relief stands watch for four hours before turning over to the next relief. Thus, in a twenty-four-hour tour, each relief stands a total of eight hours on watch—four by day and four by night.

1706. Challenging and Countersign

"Halt! Who goes there?" the traditional challenge, has been employed by Marines since 1775. As an officer, you should know exactly how to challenge and reply because a faulty challenge or reply may not only embarrass you but in combat can cost one's life.

The *challenge* is used at night or in low visibility to identify anyone approaching a sentinel.

On hearing any suspicious noise, the sentinel brings his or her weapon to a ready position and commands, "Halt! Who goes there?" The person challenged halts and then identifies himself or herself either by a password or by some such answer as "Friend" or "Officer of the Day." The sentinel replies, "Advance, friend, and be recognized." The person is allowed to approach near enough to the sentinel to be recognized and is halted again, at which time the sentinel examines the person. When satisfied, the sentinel commands, "Pass, friend"; or, if being visited by the officer of the day, reports, "Post Number . . . secure, ma'am."

It is extremely important, not only as military etiquette, but for your own safety, to reply audibly and promptly when challenged and to comply exactly with the sentry's orders. The sentry is the person behind the gun. You are in front of it.

Challenge and countersign (sometimes called the "password") are used to distinguish between friend and enemy. In the use of this procedure, which takes place only when prescribed by the commanding officer, the person or party approaching a sentry is challenged in the usual way, as described above. Then, after advancing the person for recognition, the sentry repeats the secret challenge, an agreed code word to which the person being challenged must respond with the countersign, a second code word that validates the reply. Challenge and countersign change daily and must be kept from the enemy at all costs.

OD AND COMMANDER OF THE GUARD

1707. Officer of the Day

Because officer of the day (OD) duties will take up much of your energies as a company officer, this section discusses the responsibilities of that job. In addition to what you read here, however, you must be thoroughly familiar with the *Interior Guard Manual,* as well as post and unit standing orders that deal with guard duty.

1708.   Duties of the Officer of the Day

As officer of the day, you must attend to the following routine duties. More important, however, as the CO's representative, you must be ready to act promptly and sensibly in any contingency not covered by the letter of your orders.

Inspect each relief of the guard by visiting sentinels at least once while that relief is on post. One inspection must take place between midnight and reveille. When visiting sentinels, cover the following points:

• Verify that the sentinel is on post, alert, in correct uniform, and correctly armed and equipped.

• Question the sentinel on special orders, checking particularly that the sentinel knows the limits and designation of the post; the location of fire-fighting gear on the post, and how to sound a fire alarm; any recent changes in special orders for his post; the reason the post is required; and restrictions, if any, on use of a weapon.

• Verify that the sentinel knows verbatim, and understands, the general orders for sentinels. Have the sentinel repeat several and explain them in his or her own words.

Supervise and coordinate the inspections to be made by your commander of the guard and sergeant of the guard. See that these do not conflict with or duplicate yours.

Take immediate steps, in an emergency, to protect life and public property and to preserve order. As soon as the situation permits, report what has happened and what you are doing about it to the commanding officer (or to the executive officer, or staff duty officer if your post has one).

Always inform the guard where you can be reached when not in the guardhouse. If possible, leave a telephone extension.

Abstain from alcohol throughout your tour.

Unless otherwise authorized, remain fully clothed at all times. This enables you to turn out immediately in case of fire or other emergency. Nothing can get an OD into more trouble than arriving late and drowsy at the scene of trouble.

Inspect galleys and messes, in accordance with local orders, at each meal during your watch.

Review the OD logbook before guard mount and correct any mistakes. In it, log the times when you visited sentries, together with any other information you think proper to place on record. Then attest the correctness of the entire report by signing the logbook, which constitutes your official report.

1709.   Relieving as Officer of the Day

After guard mount, old and new officers of the day both report to the executive officer (XO) for relief and posting.

March in, at attention, covered and wearing side arms (sword or pistol as prescribed by the executive officer), and halt in front of the executive officer (old OD on the right). You both salute together. Thereupon the old officer of the day says, "Sir, Lieutenant . . . reports as old officer of the day," and hands the guard book to the XO. The latter reads the guard report, asks any questions that come to mind, and comments as necessary. Then the XO informs the old officer of the day, "You are relieved." Thereupon the old OD salutes and withdraws. Then the new officer of the day again salutes, and says, "Sir, Lieutenant . . . reports as new officer of the day." The executive officer gives the new officer of the day instructions, whereupon the latter salutes and withdraws. All movements during relief and posting as officer of the day are carried out at attention and in cadence. If an emergency strikes between guard mount and the time when you report to the XO, the senior of the two ODs takes charge of both guards, old and new.

1710. Duties of the Commander of the Guard

As you have seen, the duties of commander of the guard are carried out by the sergeant of the guard if no commander of the guard is detailed. Regardless of whether performed by SNCO or NCO, they constitute a useful checklist by which, as officer of the day, you can ensure that your guard is running smoothly.

Inform your officer of the day of any orders that have come to you from anyone other than the OD. Pass on to your own relief all instructions and current information.

See that your guard is properly instructed and that it performs properly.

Make certain that all inspections (yours and the sergeant of the guard's) are carried out on time and as directed by the OD.

See that sentinels are relieved, Colors executed, the proper bugle calls sounded, bells struck, and guard routine followed.

Ensure that legible copies of general and special orders for each post are mounted both in the guardhouse and under shelter on each post.

Inspect guardhouse and brig thoroughly at least once during your tour.

Inspect each relief of the guard while it is on post. Like the officer of the day, you must make one inspection of sentinels between midnight and reveille.

Parade the guard for inspections as required. In emergency, turn out the guard, sound the appropriate call or alarm, and promptly notify your officer of the day.

If any sentry calls, *"The Guard!"* send help immediately. This is the SOS for a sentinel on post. If in serious danger, the sentry may fire his or her weapon three times.

Like the officer of the day, you must keep the guard informed of your whereabouts whenever you leave the guardhouse—if possible, by a telephone number.

Report to the officer of the day if any member of the guard takes sick, quits his or her post, or has to be relieved for any reason.

It is up to you to keep the guard in prescribed uniforms and equipment.

Make up the details to execute Morning and Evening Colors, and attend Colors to be certain that this ceremony is correctly performed. Ensure that the Colors are properly stowed and are handled only in performance of duty. Finally, report to the OD if a set of Colors is unserviceable (see Section 1817).

Detain any suspicious persons, and report the circumstances to the OD.

Write your report in the guard book, and, at the end of your tour, present the logbook to the OD.

1711.   Hints for the Officer of the Day

Of all officers, you are the one who can least tolerate any discrepancy or violation of orders. *Never overlook a dereliction or infraction, however minor.* Be especially alert for:

- Unmilitary behavior
- Marines out of uniform
- Traffic offenders
- Safety hazards
- Unsanitary, unusual, or unsightly conditions
- Security of restricted areas

Keep closely posted on the movements and whereabouts of the commanding officer and the executive officer. Try to see the post as it would appear through their eyes and act accordingly.

Be meticulous in bearing, and conspicuous by your neatness, when on watch. A neat OD has a well turned-out guard. Keep your leather shining. Polish your brightwork and sword. Wear your best uniforms. Set an example for the whole command.

No matter how many times you have stood watch before, review the guard orders as soon as you take over. Changes have a way of sneaking in without warning. "That isn't the way it used to be" is no excuse for a bobble.

Prevent your guard from idling. See that it is instructed in guard orders and routine, and especially in safety precautions. More so-called accidental discharges of firearms take place during guard duty than anywhere else. Sad but true, the overheads of many guardrooms are pockmarked by 9-mm bullet holes.

See that reliefs and sentinels are posted in military fashion, by the book.

Keep an eye on the Colors. Such avoidable fumbles as Colors unwittingly hoisted upside down have, on occasion, provided the hapless OD with several days' enforced leisure. Never allow Colors to become fouled or snarled about the pole or halyards.

Visualize every emergency that could happen during your watch. Decide now what you will do. What if fire breaks out? A serious automobile accident occurs? Electric power or utilities fail? Disaster occurs in a nearby community? Is there a bomb threat or terrorist threat? Know your answer in advance.

Visit the main gate during rush hours. Let yourself be seen, and let the main gate guards know you are on hand to back them up.

Be unfailingly courteous, especially to civilians and visitors. The good name of the post is in your hands when you are on watch.

Avoid gumshoeing. It is one of your main functions to be seen.

Enforce orders to the hilt. If an order is unwise, impractical, or out of date, the best way to get it modified is to enforce it and to report that you are doing so. Never slough over an order because *you* think it is a "dead letter."

The guard must never be relaxed. Shown here is the aftermath of a terrorist strike.

Avoid personal dealings with drunks. Let enlisted members of the guard deal with them while you keep in the background. This will not only save you potential embarrassment but may also save the drunken man from some offense much more serious if done toward an officer. Never allow a drunk to be roughly treated, and, above all, *never detain a supposed drunk without medical examination.* It is easy to confuse seeming intoxication with the symptoms of serious head injury.

Be immediately accessible at all hours. Don't let members of the guard, however well meaning, interpose themselves between you and any sober caller, whether in person or by telephone. You never know who may be calling.

Finally, run your guard the way you know it should be run. You have the responsibility, backed up by almost unlimited authority. If the guard is below standard, you have only yourself to blame.

MILITARY POLICE AND SHORE PATROL

1712.   Concept of Patrols

Whenever enlisted men go ashore on liberty, it is customary to provide military police (MPs), whose job is:
- To assist the civil authorities in dealing with members of the armed forces
- To maintain discipline and good behavior among Marines and bluejackets ashore, and get them back in good order
- To aid and safeguard liberty personnel in every possible way

This duty is described as "military police" when performed by a Marine organization; when a ship or Navy shore station provides such a guard, it is known as "shore patrol" (SP). Shore patrol routine and duties are covered in the *Navy Shore Patrol Manual.* In a few places where large military populations are present from all services, a joint patrol is sometimes organized. This has the title of "Armed Forces Police Detachment."

Never resist, obstruct, or fail to cooperate with a shore patrolman or an MP, even if he or she comes from the Army or Air Force. Under joint regulations, MPs and SPs have all-service authority, with power to enforce any lawful acts or instructions. If you have any complaints, make them through military channels to the proper superior authorities.

1713.   Hints on MP and SP Duty

Remember that you are a *military* police officer. Do not assert police authority over civilians. That is a job for the civilian police. By the same token, keep your charges reminded that they are Marines, first and foremost, and police only in a secondary and qualified sense. Do not tolerate any symptoms of "lawman" or highway-patrol swagger on the part of any of your Marines.

Never imbibe alcohol while on MP or SP duty. It is a long-standing naval custom that the least evidence that an MP or SP has partaken of alcohol while on duty demands a court-martial.

Make yourself and your MPs or SPs conspicuous. This helps to hold down violations and gives assurance to all that the situation is well in hand.

If possible, have medical assistance ready at hand. Should your patrol not include a doctor or corpsman, know where you can get medical aid without delay.

Get on easy working terms with the local police. Cooperate sincerely with them, and they will do the same with you. Be unfailingly courteous toward civilians.

If in a foreign port, obtain a trustworthy interpreter who knows the local customs. Try to select enlisted Marines who know the language.

Let your enlisted people deal with drunks. Be sure to give a medical examination to any seemingly intoxicated prisoner.

Handle prisoners "by the book." Allow no undue force, "third degree," or abusive behavior toward a prisoner, no matter how he or she provokes you. Unauthorized treatment of a prisoner is unworthy of a Marine officer.

Avoid disorderly public scenes, prolonged disputes, or heated brawls. Get troublemakers back to headquarters, and deal with them in private.

Know your orders, *Navy Regulations,* and *Uniform Code of Military Justice,* down to the last comma.

Above all, exercise common sense and tact. It is your job to prevent trouble as well as to quell it. When you see a Marine or bluejacket in difficulty, ask yourself, "How can I help this person?"

A Marine on duty has no friends.

—Marine Corps proverb

Duty is the great business of a sea officer; all private considerations must give way to it, however painful it may be.

—Horatio Nelson

18

Military Courtesy, Honors, and Ceremonies

MILITARY COURTESY

Military courtesy is the traditional form of politeness in the profession of arms. Though sharing many elements with courtesy in civilian life, military courtesy stems firmly from a traditional code of rules and customs. Just as courtesy in general is said to be "the lubricant of life," so military courtesy helps to ease us along well-worn, tried, and customary paths. Because, by its very nature, the life and discipline of the service is formal, so too is its form of courtesy.

Military courtesy embraces much more than the salute or any other rituals, important as these are. Courtesy is a disciplined attitude of mind. It must be accorded to all ranks and on all occasions. Courtesy to a senior indicates respect for authority, responsibility, and experience. Courtesy toward a junior expresses appreciation and respect for his or her support and for that person as a fellow Marine. Courtesy paid to the Colors and to the National Anthem expresses loyalty to the United States and to the Constitution, which we are sworn to uphold and defend.

Military courtesy is a prerequisite to discipline. It promotes the willing obedience and unhesitating cooperation that make a good outfit "click." When ordinary acts of military courtesy are performed grudgingly or omitted, discipline suffers. Discipline and courtesy alike stem from and contribute to esprit de corps. The Marine Corps has always stood at the top of the services by full and willing observance of the twin virtues of soldierly courtesy and discipline.

1801.   Conduct toward Members of Other Services

The minutiae of military courtesy vary little from service to service, and from nation to nation. As a Marine (and therefore, as a professional), you must learn the meaning and traditions behind the badges, insignia, and titles of the officers and enlisted personnel of other military services, both American and foreign.

When you go to duty with another service or in another country, make it a particular point to know and defer to the customs and traditions of that service or country. On the other hand, never forget that you are a Marine, never feel self-conscious about holding fast to Marine Corps standards of uniform or to the Marine way of doing and saying things.

1802.   Military Titles, Phraseology, and Address

In Section 715, you will find emphasis on the traditional Marine way of saying things, and, in Appendix VII, a glossary of Marine Corps terms. Know, employ, and enforce the use of those terms. Insignia of rank appear in Figures 18–1 and 18–2.

Addressing Seniors.   Never forget that "sir" or "ma'am" is an important word in conversation with anyone senior. While you may not be reprimanded on the spot for omission of "sir" or "ma'am," that omission is quickly noted and usually remembered.

Speaking to Juniors.   To help promote subordination and respect among your juniors, address them by their proper titles *and* their names. Follow the principles laid down in Section 1602; and be wary of overly casual use of first names or nicknames. Formality in speaking to a subordinate is never wrong, whereas informality can be risky and is liable to compromise your position. In particular, never allow casual or even unintentionally disrespectful reference to an absent third person, particularly one senior to one, on the part of one of your juniors.

Shortcuts.   It is proper to use shortened titles in conversation or unofficial correspondence. Table 18–1 shows the correct military forms of address on official and unofficial occasions and when dealing with civilians.

Here are some informalities that usage sanctions.

Medical and dental officers below the rank of commander may be addressed as "Doctor."

Any chaplain may be addressed by another officer as "Padre" and Roman Catholic chaplains of whatever rank (and Episcopal chaplains who so prefer) as "Father."

Although no longer prescribed in regulations, custom sanctions a second lieutenant's being addressed or spoken of as "Mr." or Ms. In the presence of enlisted people, however, it is preferable to use "Lieutenant."

Lieutenant colonels should be addressed as "Colonel."

Generals and admirals, of whatever grade, are spoken to as "General" or "Admiral."

Where the male officer is addressed as "sir," a woman officer may be addressed as "ma'am," or by rank, as "Yes, Major," or "Good morning, Lieutenant." Women warrant officers may be addressed informally as "Ms.," as may female nurses below the grade of commander.

The first sergeant of a company, battery, or detachment may be addressed by officers of the unit as "Top." The title "top sergeant," however, is not used in the Marine Corps.

Avoid the unfortunate practice, which has occurred in instances, of referring colloquially to enlisted Marines as "troopers." This is an Army—not a Marine or Navy—term, going back to horse cavalry, and more recently used to refer to paratroopers; it is inappropriate for Marines (and sounds like the highway patrol). Marines should be referred to collectively as "Marines" or less formally in the traditional Marine usage as "people" (as in the injunction, "You people, square yourselves away").

Address enlisted personnel by rank and last name.

Navy chief petty officers are habitually spoken to as "Chief."

1803. Pointers on Military Etiquette

This subsection compiles a miscellany of Marine Corps and Navy customs, courtesies, and points of etiquette, some written, others unwritten—but all important for you to know and observe.

The CO's "Wishes." When your commanding officer says, "I wish," "I desire," "I would like," or similar expressions, these have the force of a direct order and should be complied with on that basis.

Accompanying a Senior. The position of honor for one's senior is on the right. Therefore, in company with a senior, you walk, ride, and sit on the left. When entering a vehicle or a boat, juniors embark first and take the less desirable places in the middle or on "jump" or front seats (or forward in a boat); when debarking, the senior leaves first, while juniors follow in order of rank.

When a senior is inspecting, he or she is followed by the immediate commander of the unit being inspected, who remains on the senior's left, one pace to the rear—*except* that, during inspection of troops in formation, the immediate commander remains on the *right* of the inspecting officer and *precedes* him or her while inspecting in ranks. For other pointers on inspections, turn to Sections 1611–1615.

Acknowledging Orders. When a Marine officer or enlisted Marine receives orders or instructions, he or she replies, "Aye, aye, sir," or "Aye, aye, ma'am." This phrase, which descends from the earliest days of the Marine Corps and Navy, is used in both services. It means: "I understand the orders I have received, and will carry them out." Never permit a subordinate to acknowledge an order by "Very well," "All right," "Yes," or "OK."

Mounted Juniors. Mounted juniors dismount before addressing or report-

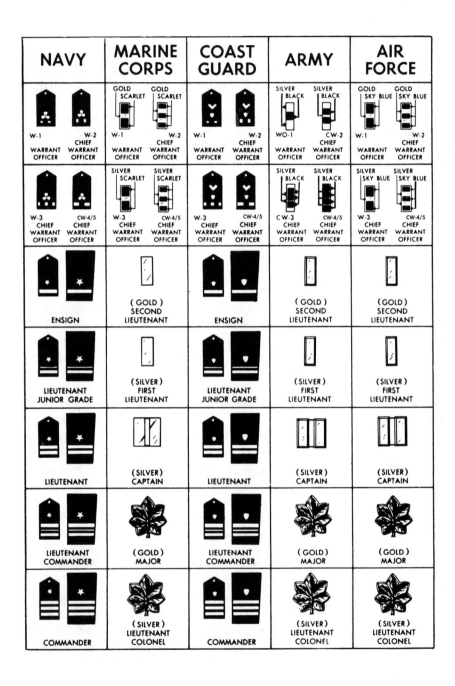

Figure 18–1: Commissioned insignia of rank

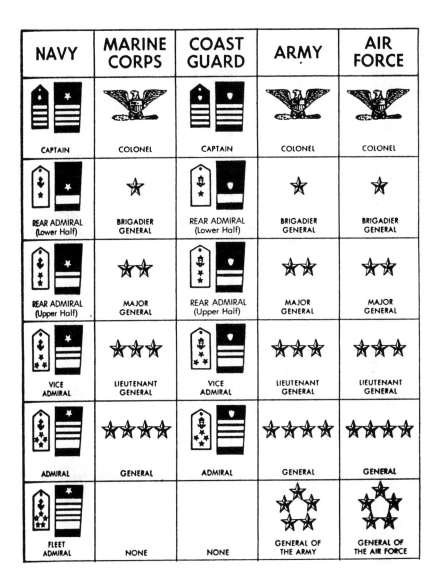

NAVY	MARINE CORPS	COAST GUARD	ARMY	AIR FORCE
CAPTAIN	COLONEL	CAPTAIN	COLONEL	COLONEL
REAR ADMIRAL (Lower Half)	BRIGADIER GENERAL	REAR ADMIRAL (Lower Half)	BRIGADIER GENERAL	BRIGADIER GENERAL
REAR ADMIRAL (Upper Half)	MAJOR GENERAL	REAR ADMIRAL (Upper Half)	MAJOR GENERAL	MAJOR GENERAL
VICE ADMIRAL	LIEUTENANT GENERAL	VICE ADMIRAL	LIEUTENANT GENERAL	LIEUTENANT GENERAL
ADMIRAL	GENERAL	ADMIRAL	GENERAL	GENERAL
FLEET ADMIRAL	NONE	NONE	GENERAL OF THE ARMY	GENERAL OF THE AIR FORCE

Figure 18–1 (*cont.*): Commissioned insignia of rank

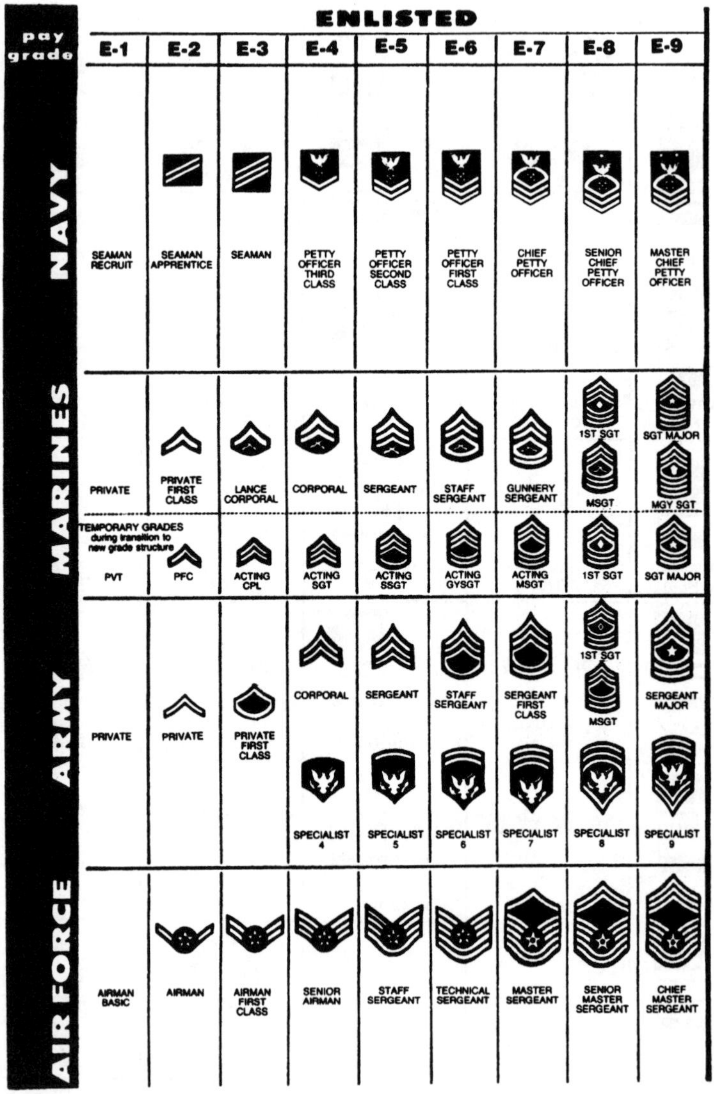

Figure 18–2: Enlisted insignia of rank

ing to seniors, except when in the field. Even then, however, dismount if practical.

Meeting a Senior Indoors. When you meet a senior indoors, either in a passageway or on a stairway, give way smartly and promptly.

Senior Entering a Room. When a senior enters a room or passes close aboard unorganized groups either indoors or outside, the senior officer or NCO of the group or groups commands "Attention!" All hands come to attention and remain so until the senior has passed. If out of doors and covered, all hands salute.

Uncovering under Arms. The only exception to the rule that Marines under arms never uncover is at a religious service, such as a wedding, when officers may wear swords and still uncover. You do not unsheathe your sword inside a church, however, unless express authority is granted by an appropriate religious functionary.

Permission to Speak to Senior Officers. When one of your enlisted people wishes to speak to the company or detachment commander, the enlisted person first obtains the first sergeant's permission (see Section 1602). If he or she desires to speak to an officer of still higher rank or position, the enlisted person must in turn have the company or detachment commander's permission.

Similarly, as a junior officer, you obtain your immediate CO's permission before you seek an official interview with any higher officer. The reason for this is that the first sergeant or CO can probably solve the problem satisfactorily without the matter having to go higher.

Entering an Office. Enlisted Marines entering any office should be required to observe the following procedure, regardless of whether or not an officer is in the office: (1) knock; (2) enter and stand at attention immediately inside doorway, uncovered (unless under arms); (3) identify oneself by name and rank, and state business.

Although the foregoing sequence is not mandatory for officers, it is a prudent procedure for junior officers to bear in mind, especially when entering the office of one who is appreciably senior. In general, an officer should not "freeze" on entering, however. Having once made an entrance, the junior officer should distinctly come to the position of the soldier (to signify respect for the senior) and then as quickly assume a less formal stance of alert composure.

Never enter the office of a senior while you are smoking, and do not smoke in the senior's office or presence until invited to do so.

On the Telephone. Use moderate and respectful tones, and identify yourself and your organization. Be brief. For example, in answering a call: "Company B, 5th Marines, Captain Griffith." Never "Hello."

On a Ladder or Stairway. When you encounter a senior on a stairway or in a passageway or doorway, you should always give way. In such an instance, greetings are normally exchanged.

Table 18–1. Correct forms of address for naval and military personnel

Person Addressed or Introduced	To Military Personnel		To Civilians	
	Introduce as:	Address as:	Introduce as:	Address as:
Marine, Army, or Air Force Officer	Major (or other rank) Smith[a]	Same	Major Smith[a]	Same
Naval Officer	Captain Smith	Same	Captain Smith[a]	Same
Navy Staff Corps Officer	Commander Smith[b] Chaplain Smith	Same Same	Commander Smith[b] Chaplain Smith	Same Same
Coast Guard and Coast and Geodetic Survey Officers	Same as for same rank in Navy[c]	Same	Same	Same
U.S. Public Health Service Officer (M.D. or D.D.S.)	Dr. Smith[c]	Same	Dr. Smith of the Public Health Service	Dr. Smith
U.S. Public Health Service Officer (Sanitary Engineer)	Mr. or Ms. Smith[c]	Same	Mr. or Ms. Smith of the Public Health Service	Mr. or Ms. Smith
Commissioned Warrant Officer[d]	Chief Warrant Officer[d] Smith	Same[d]	Chief Warrant Officer Smith[d]	Same

Midshipman or Cadet	Midshipman (or Cadet) Smith	Mr. or Miss Smith	Midshipman (or Cadet) Smith	Mr. or Miss Smith
Warrant Officer[d]	Warrant Officer Smith[d]	Same[d]	Warrant Officer Smith[d]	Same[d]
Staff NCO or Chief Petty Officer[e]	Sergeant Major Smith,[e] Master Chief Gunner's Mate Smith	Sergeant Major or Chief	Sergeant Major Smith, Master Chief Gunner's Mate Smith	Sergeant Major or Chief
Noncommissioned Officer or Petty Officer	Corporal Smith or Gunner's Mate Smith	Corporal Smith or Gunner's Mate Smith	Corporal Smith or Petty Officer Smith	Same
Private or Seaman	Private (or Seaman) Smith	Smith	Private (or Seaman) Smith	Smith

a When not in uniform, an officer should be introduced as "of the Navy" or "of the Marine Corps" to distinguish the rank from similar-sounding ranks in the other armed services. Suggested phraseology: "This is Lieutenant Smith of the Marine Corps." Such a form of introduction indicates the officer's rank, service, and the proper form of address.

b Add "of the Medical Corps," "of the Civil Engineer Corps," or other corps, when helpful to indicate status of officer. If a senior officer of the Medical or Dental Corps prefers to be addressed as "Doctor," such preference should be honored. Some senior members of the Chaplain's Corps prefer to be addressed by their rank, but it is always correct to address a chaplain of any rank as Chaplain.

c In any case where there is reason to believe that the officer's insignia might not be recognized, it is correct to add, "of the Public Health Service," "of the Coast Guard," or "of the Coast and Geodetic Survey."

d Male Marine Corps warrant officers appointed in certain occupational fields bear the title of (Chief) Marine Gunner, addressed as "Gunner."

e All staff NCOs (that is, those with rank of staff sergeant and higher) are addressed by their particular titles, such as, "Gunnery Sergeant Hayes," "Master Sergeant Wodarczyk," "Staff Sergeant Basilone."

SALUTES AND SALUTING

1804.   The Military Salute

Saluting is a military custom observed by men and women who follow the profession of arms. It is a matter of pride among Marines, from general to private, to salute willingly, promptly, smartly, and proudly. The good Marine stands out from the other services by a smart, correct, and cheerful salute, which is as much a hallmark of the Corps as the Globe and Anchor. When you salute or receive a salute, you mark yourself as a Marine who has pride in self and Corps.

As a junior officer, you must recognize and teach that the salute is a privilege enjoyed only by military people and is a mutual acknowledgment of comradeship in the profession of arms.

Origins of Saluting.   Over the centuries, men-at-arms have rendered fraternal and respectful greetings to indicate friendliness. In early times, armed men raised their weapons or shifted them to the left hand (while raising the empty right hand) to give proof of amicable intentions. During the Middle Ages, knights in armor, on encountering friendly knights, raised their helmet visors in recognition. If they were in the presence of feudal superiors, the helmet was usually doffed. In every case, the fighting man made a gesture of friendliness—the raising of the empty right hand. This gesture survives as today's hand salute, which is the traditional greeting among soldiers of all nations.

Like the original hand salute and doffing of the cap, the discharge of weapons, presentation of arms, and lowering of the point of the sword were all intended to signify good will. In every case, the one so saluting, in good faith, momentarily rendered himself incapable of using his weapon offensively. The descendants of these earlier gestures are the modern sword salute, present arms, and gun salutes.

Whom to Salute.   Those entitled to salutes are:

1. All commissioned and warrant officers of the Army, Marine Corps, Navy, Air Force, and Coast Guard; of the Reserve components of those services; and of the National Guard
2. Officers of friendly foreign powers
3. In addition, by service custom though not by regulation, any high civilian official who is entitled to honors by *Navy Regulations*

Officers of the same rank exchange salutes on meeting. The first one to recognize the other initiates the salute.

Enlisted Marines salute other enlisted Marines only in formation when rendering reports. Prisoners may not salute or wear the Marine Corps emblem.

Definitions.   The following definitions apply to Marine Corps saluting procedure.

Out of doors means "in the open air; or the interior of such buildings as drill halls and gymnasiums when used for drill or exercises of troops; or on the weather decks of a man-of-war; or under roofed structures such as lanais, covered walks, and shelters open at one or both sides to the weather." It is synonymous with "on the topside" when used afloat.

Indoors means "the interior of any building ashore, other than a drill hall, gymnasium, or armory."

Between decks means "any shipboard space below a weather deck, other than officers' country."

Covered and *uncovered* means "when and when not wearing headgear."

Under arms is a term indicating that a Marine is carrying a weapon in his hand; is equipped with side arms; or is wearing equipment pertaining to an arm, such as a sword sling, pistol belt, or cartridge belt. Any Marine wearing an "MP" or "SP" brassard is considered under arms.

Saluting distance means "the maximum distance within which salutes are rendered and exchanged," prescribed as thirty paces. This figure is considered to be one within which recognition of insignia is possible, and approximately that within which friends or acquaintances can recognize and greet each other. The salute should be rendered when six paces from the person (or Color) to be saluted. If the person or Color to be saluted obviously will not approach within this distance, the salute is rendered at the point of nearest approach.

1805. Hand Salutes

Significance. In some services, the hand salute (Figure 18–3) has been deemphasized almost to the vanishing point, based on an erroneous perception that rendition of a salute, rather than being an act of courtesy and soldierly recognition, signifies inferiority and subservience. Nothing could be further from the truth. As in civil life "on the outside," where you render courtesy to older or

Figure 18–3: Hand salute

more important persons, so, as a junior Marine, you salute first. In returning your salute, the senior in turn salutes you as a fellow in arms. Thus, the exchange of salutes is a two-way street.

The manner and enthusiasm with which you render or receive a salute indicate the state of your training, your individual esprit, the discipline of your outfit, and your quality as a Marine. Correct saluting habits characterize a good Marine.

How to Execute the Hand Salute.   Salute at quick time only. If you are at the double and must salute or receive a salute, slow to quick time. Stand or walk at attention: head up, chin in, and stomach pulled in. When halted, come to attention distinctly as a preliminary motion to the salute. Look directly at the person or Color you are saluting. If walking or riding, turn your head smartly toward the person being saluted, and catch that person's eye. Execute the first movement, holding position until the salute is acknowledged or you see that it is not going to be, then complete the salute by bringing your hand down smartly. When doing this, keep your fingers extended and joined, your thumb streamlined alongside. In returning a salute, execute the two counts at marching cadence.

In the Marine Corps and Navy, it is customary to exchange a greeting with a salute. The junior should always say, "Good morning (or evening), sir (or ma'am)," and the senior should unfailingly reply in the same vein—with a smile.

In the Marine Corps and Navy, one does not salute when uncovered—that is, when not wearing headgear. The only exception to this rule is that the salute *may* be rendered uncovered when, in a special circumstance, not to salute might cause misunderstanding. For example, when serving with the Army or Air Force (who *do* salute uncovered), you may, if you wish, depart from the naval procedure but beware of contracting the habit.

How Not to Salute.   A sloppy, grudging salute, or a childish pretence not to notice anyone to whom a salute is due, indicates unmilitary attitude, lack of pride in self and Corps, and plain ignorance.

Never salute with pipe or cigarette in your right hand or your mouth. If you are chewing tobacco or gum, bring your jaws to rest during the exchange of salutes. As under any other circumstances, it is highly unmilitary to be caught saluting with one hand in your pocket, your blouse unbuttoned, or your cap not squared.

Avoid—and, as an officer, never tolerate—trick salutes. The most common aberrations are:

• Right wrist bent
• Left elbow stuck out at exaggerated, unnatural angle
• Palm turned inward, knuckles kept forward
• Fingers on right hand bent and flexed inward
• Right thumb extended away from fingers
• Hips thrust forward, shoulders swayed back

When you find a Marine doing any of these things, no matter how hard he or she seems to be trying, correct the Marine on the spot, and see that he or she knows and practices the right way to salute.

1806. Rifle Salutes

The rifle salute may be executed from the following positions:
- Right or left shoulder arms
- Order arms
- Trail arms
- Present arms

Any individual under arms with rifle salutes by one of the foregoing rifle salutes. The only occasion where a hand salute is executed by a Marine with a rifle is at "sling arms."

In its four forms, the rifle salute is rendered as follows under the conditions given:

Right or left shoulder arms—when out of doors, at a halt or at a walk.

Order arms—when at a halt, either indoors or out of doors.

Trail arms—when at a walk, indoors or out of doors.

Presenting arms is a special compliment, as a Marine at present arms represents
the authority of the nation. The privilege of saluting by presenting arms is
reserved for troops in formation and for sentinels on post.

Marines armed with weapons normally carried slung use the hand salute only, and, when so saluting, carry the piece at sling arms, with the left hand grasping the sling to steady the weapon.

1807. Sword Salutes and Manual

You will find the manual of the sword described in *Marine Corps Drill and Ceremonies Manual,* and further information on the sword is given in Sections 1815–1816. Every Marine officer takes pride in being precise, dexterous, and at ease with the sword (see Figure 18–4).

When armed with the sword, you render or return salutes in the following ways.

Rendering the Salute.

1. *If your sword is sheathed,* and you are not in formation: execute the normal
   hand salute.
2. *If your sword is drawn and you are halted,* either in or out of formation,
   execute present sword as prescribed in the manual of the sword. If commanding a formation, which will usually be the case if your sword is drawn, bring
   your troops to attention before you do so.
3. *If your sword is drawn and you are under way in formation,* execute the
   sword salute, having first brought your command to attention, if necessary.

When You Are Returning a Salute.

1. *If your sword is sheathed,* acknowledge by the hand salute.
2. *If your sword is drawn,* acknowledge by the sword salute.

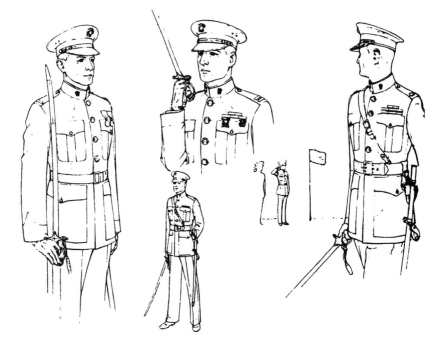

Figure 18–4: Sword salutes and manual

1808.   Individual Saluting Etiquette

Whether to Salute Once or Twice.   After an officer has been saluted initially, if that officer remains nearby and no conversation takes place, no further salutes are required.

When a junior is spoken to by, or addresses, a senior officer, he or she salutes initially, and again when the conversation ends or the senior leaves. Throughout the conversation, the junior stands at attention unless otherwise directed by the senior. It should be an instinctive military courtesy on your part, as an officer, to give your subordinates "at ease" or "carry on" during any extended conversation.

Reporting, Indoors.   When you report indoors to an officer senior to you, unless under arms, you uncover, place your cap under your left arm, visor forward, knock, and enter when told to do so. Two paces in front of the senior, halt and report, "Sir, Lieutenant Neville reporting." Remain at attention unless told to carry on or be seated. On being dismissed, take one backstep, halt, and then face about and march out. If under arms, remain covered, and salute on reporting, and again on being dismissed. The latter salute is rendered after completion of your backstep.

After entering, do not report until recognized by the officer and until he or she has completed the business at hand.

The foregoing procedure also applies to enlisted Marines who report to you.

Enlisted Marines Not in Formation.   When an officer approaches enlisted Marines who are not in formation, the first to recognize the officer calls the group to attention as soon as the officer comes within ten paces. Out of doors, if covered (as they should be), all hands salute when the officer is within six paces. The salute is held until returned. The group remains at attention until the officer has passed or until commanded, "Carry on," which an officer should be quick to do under informal circumstances.

Profit in this by the example of Major General Lejeune, later the thirteenth commandant, during the Meuse-Argonne Battle in 1918. General Lejeune approached a group of Marines, whom an NCO called to attention. As the men sprang to their feet, General Lejeune checked them, saying "Sit down, men. It is more important for tired men to rest than for the division commander to be saluted."

Overtaking.   When you overtake an officer senior in rank proceeding in the same direction, draw abreast on the senior's left, coming to the salute as you do so, and say, "By your leave, sir." The senior officer acknowledges the salute and replies, "Granted."

When you overtake a Marine junior to you, pass on the right. As you come into view, abreast, salutes are exchanged.

Indoors.   Marines not under arms do not salute indoors. *In an office,* however, work need not cease when an officer enters unless called to attention. When addressed by an officer, the person so addressed should rise.

In the Mess Hall.   At meals, do not rise when called to attention but stop eating and keep silent. If spoken to by an officer, an enlisted person gets to his or her feet and stands at attention. If not under arms, be sure to uncover when you enter a galley, mess hall, or ship's messing compartment.

In Sick Bay.   Formal military courtesies are neither rendered nor required in a sick bay. Always uncover when you enter a sick bay or ward.

In Vehicles.   Except when on board public conveyances, such as street cars, buses, and trains, officers in vehicles are saluted as if afoot. Other passengers salute or return salutes as necessary.

When Mounted.   Mounted persons salute in the same manner as if on foot, but salutes are not rendered by anyone standing to or leading a horse. A mounted junior always dismounts before addressing a senior who is not mounted; this rule applies to vehicles as well as horses.

During Games.   Games are not interrupted at the approach of an officer. Spectators do not rise or salute unless individually addressed by an officer.

On Guard.

1. *When armed with the rifle,* sentries salute by presenting arms. A sentry walking post halts, faces the officer being saluted, and comes to the present. If then spoken to by the officer (or by any other person), the sentry executes port arms and holds this position throughout the conversation. If speaking with an officer, the sentry does not interrupt the conversation to salute another officer, unless the officer with whom one is speaking likewise salutes;

if so, the sentinel presents arms. At the end of the conversation, the sentry presents arms again. During hours of challenging, the first salute or present arms is rendered when the officer has been duly advanced and recognized, as described in Section 1706.

2. *When not armed with the rifle,* a sentry renders hand salutes in the usual way. A sentry armed with a submachine gun, pistol, or carbine does not salute during hours for challenging. While challenging, a sentry armed with the pistol remains at raise pistol; one armed with a submachine gun or carbine remains at port arms.

If circumstances are such that payment of compliments interferes with a sentry's performance of duty, the sentry does not salute.

Prisoner guards ("chasers") do not salute except when addressed by an officer.* If marching prisoners, the chaser halts them and takes necessary precautions for their security before rendering the salute. If armed with the rifle, a chaser executes a rifle salute but does not present arms. Prisoners may not salute at any time.

When in Doubt. If you are uncertain as to whether a salute is required, always salute. For a properly trained Marine, there should never be any doubt. Should a doubtful situation arise, however, do not go out of your way to avoid saluting. Having made up your mind to salute, do so properly and smartly. Never give a hesitant, half-hearted salute, which suggests only too plainly that you really don't know the score. Remember, it is better to render five unnecessary salutes than to omit one that you should give.

1809. Group Saluting Etiquette

Troops in Formation. Troops in formation salute on command only. Officers and NCOs in command of formations render salutes for their respective units. Before rendering a salute, the person in command brings the unit to attention. Individuals armed other than with a rifle (and officers and NCOs whose swords are not drawn) execute the hand salute.

If an officer speaks to an individual in ranks when the unit is not at attention, the person spoken to comes to attention. At the end of the conversation, the person resumes the position of the remainder of the unit.

Troops at Drill and on the March. Troops drilling do not render compliments. The person in command renders salutes for the unit. An officer in a formation is saluted only if in command of the entire formation, and that officer alone returns all salutes. NCOs in charge of detachments or units do not exchange compliments with other units so commanded, except at guard mounting, when the old and new guards do exchange compliments.

Troops marching at ease or route step are called to attention on the approach of a senior entitled to a salute.

---

*Never pass between a guard and prisoners, and be sure to correct any guard who permits you or any other person to do so.

Marine units always begin and end a march at attention.   March your unit at attention while within barracks and central areas and on main roads of your post. No matter how tired you are after a day or a night in the field, bring your outfit home with a short, snappy step, pieces aligned, ranks dressed, at regulation cadence, at attention. That is the Marine way.

Groups of Officers.   When officers are walking or standing together, or are embarked in a vehicle, *all* render and return salutes as if each were alone (see Figure 18–5).

Formations in Vehicles.   Members of formations embarked, as units, in military vehicles do not salute individually. The senior person in each vehicle renders and acknowledges salutes. Only the hand salute is employed.

Working Parties.   The NCO in charge renders salutes for the entire detail. Individuals come to attention and salute if addressed by an officer but do not interrupt work at the approach of an officer unless the detail is called to attention.

While Honors Are Being Rendered.

1. During ruffles and flourishes by the band or field music, while honors are being rendered, the guard presents arms to the recipient of honors. All persons in the vicinity come to attention and salute, following the motions of the guard (for example, hand salute on present arms; terminate salute on order arms).
2. If ruffles and flourishes are followed by a gun salute, persons in the vicinity but not in formation stand fast at attention until the last gun has fired.
3. On board ship, all hands on the quarterdeck salute while an officer is being piped over the side. If the guard is paraded, follow the motions of the guard in your hand salute.

At Military Funerals

1. The basic rule for saluting at military funerals (Sections 1813–1814) is to salute each time the body bearers move the coffin and during volleys and "Taps." If you are wearing civilian clothes, uncover and hold your headgear over your left breast.
2. During prayers, stand at parade rest without arms, head bowed. During the firing of volleys, come to attention and salute.
3. Body bearers remain covered, both indoors and outdoors, when carrying the coffin. When the remains are lowered into the grave, body bearers stand at attention, holding the flag waist-high over the grave. The officer in charge of the escort presents this flag to the next of kin after the ceremony.
4. When a military funeral cortege passes, all hands come to attention and salute the remains, using the hand salute if in uniform, and uncovering in the civilian salute, if wearing civilian clothes.

1810.   Saluting the National Anthem

When the National Anthem is played, or "To the Color" is sounded, all military personnel come to attention, face toward the music, and salute. You hold your

Figure 18–5: Group saluting

salute until the last note of the music but remain at attention until "Carry On" is sounded. If the anthem or call is being played incident to a ceremony involving the Colors, face toward the Colors rather than the music.

Troops in Formation. Troops in formation are halted (if on the march) and brought to attention, and the commander salutes, facing in the direction of the unit's original front. If participating in a ceremony that includes rendition of the National Anthem or "To the Color," troops present arms.

Personnel Mounted in Vehicles. During the playing of the National Anthem, all vehicles within sight or hearing of the ceremony stop. Passengers do not debark, but remain seated at attention and do not salute. If the passengers comprise a military detail in an official vehicle, the person in charge debarks, faces toward the flag or music and salutes.

Personnel on Horseback. Those on horseback halt and salute without dismounting.

Sentries. Sentries halt, face in the direction of the flag or music, and render the hand salute or present arms as appropriate (see Section 1808).

In Civilian Clothes. If wearing plain clothes, come to attention, remove your headgear, and hold it over your left breast with your right hand.

Indoors. When the National Anthem is played indoors, you come to attention and face the music. Only those under arms salute.

Foreign National Anthems. Accord the national anthems of friendly foreign powers the same courtesies as your own.

1811.   Courtesy to the Flag

This section confines itself to the courtesies that apply to the National Color (or National Ensign). You will find additional information dealing with flags, colors, and standards in Chapter 7, and Section 1818 covers execution of Morning and Evening Colors, the daily ceremonies that take place when the flag is raised and lowered.

Saluting the Flag.   Except at Morning and Evening Colors and on board a man-of-war at anchor or pierside, the flag is not saluted when displayed from a mast or flagstaff, nor is any flag saluted unless it is a National Color or Standard as defined in Section 731. When Colors are encased in a protective cover (and said to be "cased"), they are not saluted.

Colors and Standards not cased are saluted when either you or they approach or pass within six paces. Hold your salute until the Colors have passed or been passed by that distance.

In the field or camp, it is customary to display the National Color and unit Battle Color in front of the commanding officer's tent. According to one's wishes, this may be done every day or only on Sundays and national holidays. All hands who approach within saluting distance (six paces) execute a hand or rifle salute as appropriate, holding the salute until six paces beyond. If a Color sentinel is posted, he or she acknowledges salutes rendered by enlisted Marines; when officers salute the Colors, the sentinel holds his or her salute or present arms until the officer has completed the salute.

Motor Vehicles Passing Colors.   When passed by an uncased National Color, all persons embarked in a vehicle remain seated at attention. Vehicles approaching and passing Colors reduce speed; mounted personnel remain seated at attention but do not salute.

Individuals Not in Formation.   At the approach of Colors, persons not in formation come to attention, face the Colors, and salute when within saluting distance; if you are passing Colors, continue at attention and salute within saluting distance. Construe this distance literally. Hold your salute and keep your head and eyes turned smartly toward the Colors until they have passed or have been passed by six paces. In civilian clothes, render the civilian salute with headgear held over your left breast. If mounted, bring your horse to a walk, and salute without dismounting.

Dipping the Battle or Organizational Color. In military ceremonies Battle and Organizational Colors (see Section 731) are dipped in salute during the playing of the National Anthem, "To the Color," or "Retreat" (in place of the National Anthem), or "Hail to the Chief"; when rendering honors to the organizational commander or individual or higher rank; and, during military funerals only, on each occasion when the funeral escort presents arms.

On these occasions, when passing in review, the Battle Color or Organizational Color (but never the National Color) is dipped when six paces from the individual receiving the salute and remains dipped until six paces beyond.

Dipping the National Ensign. The National Color or Ensign is never in any circumstances permitted to touch the ground or deck. At sea, however, it is customary for merchantmen to dip their Colors when passing close aboard a man-of-war, and, in reply, the warship runs her Ensign halfway down and then back up again. This is the only time when a National Color or Ensign may be dipped.

1812. Pointers on Saluting

All salutes received by you must be returned unless you are uncovered or unless both hands are fully loaded or occupied. If you are physically unable to return a salute, you should acknowledge it verbally, and should, if possible, excuse yourself to the individual who rendered the salute. If you are uncovered, or in any circumstance when you cannot render a correct salute, you should, if standing still, come to attention.

When wearing civilian clothes, you should use the civilian salute (headgear held over left breast, in lieu of hand salutes) for:

• Salutes to the Colors
• Salutes to the National Anthem
• Salutes during military funerals

If salutes are to be properly exchanged, both junior and senior must be alert. The junior must spot the approaching senior, and the senior must respond with alacrity. The attitude of seniors toward salutes has a profound effect on the spirit with which any salute is rendered. Enlisted persons are discouraged from saluting (and rightly so) if you overlook their courtesy or seem not to observe them. Such an attitude on your part as a Marine officer is discourteous and at times downright insulting.

You can do much to foster correct rendering of salutes by inviting them. A pleasant, direct look at an approaching junior encourages that person to salute with goodwill and generally puts the junior on his or her mettle. It is an old trick, when a junior officer seems to need a reminder in saluting manners, for the senior to salute the junior first, with a solicitous greeting, thus extending a courteous reprimand.

In saluting, *do:*
• Begin your salute in ample time (at least six paces away)
• Hold your salute until it is returned or acknowledged
• Look squarely at the person or Colors being saluted
• Assume the position of attention
• Have thumb and fingers extended and joined
• Keep hand and wrist in same place, not bent
• Incline forearm at 45 degrees
• Hold upper arm horizontal while hand is at salute
Do not:
• Salute with blouse or coat unbuttoned
• Salute with cigarette, pipe, or cigar in mouth

- Have anything in your right hand
- Have your left hand in a pocket
- Salute when in ranks, at games, or part of a working detail
- Salute at crowded gatherings, in public conveyances, or in congested areas, unless addressing or being directly addressed by a senior
- Salute when to do so would physically interfere with performance of an assigned duty

One of the most unmilitary habits encountered among some Marines, both while saluting and even in ranks, is the ludicrous habit of leaning over backwards (literally) in an effort to stand straight. This swaybacked stance, with stomach and pelvis thrust forward, jaw jutting out, and shoulders too far back, is a caricature of the position of attention. A Marine at attention should stand straight as an arrow, not like a bow.

MILITARY FUNERALS

1813.   General Information on Funerals

Navy and Marine Corps funerals are conducted in accordance with *Navy Regulations* and the *Drill and Ceremonies Manual,* both of which you should check carefully if, in any role other than that of principal, you are to take part in a military funeral. Chapter 21 of this *Guide* contains administrative information on funerals and burials.

Classification.   Military funerals are classified as follows:

1. By size of escort (depending on rank of deceased) and type of ceremony, for example, full, simple, or modified honors. Some next of kin may wish only gravesite honors or a reduced escort; some may not wish the firing of volleys. Such wishes are of course governing.
2. By location of military ceremony, that is, church or chapel service (remains received at church and escorted to graveside); transfer (remains received at station, airport, or cemetery gate and escorted to gravesite); gravesite (remains conveyed to graveside by civilian undertaker, military participation and ceremony at gravesite only)

Uniforms and Equipment.   If the organization providing the funeral escort is authorized blues, then the uniforms should be dress blue A or dress blue/white A, according to season. Otherwise the uniform should be service dress with large medals instead of ribbons, if blouse is worn.

Body bearers should not wear bayonets or scabbards.

For difficult terrain, mud, or foul weather, units and individuals—such as body bearers, music, and firing party—who must leave paved areas may wear shined boots instead of dress shoes.

Officers of funeral escorts wear mourning band and mourning sword knot, as do pallbearers; noncommissioned officers armed with the sword wear mourning sword knot only (except if acting as pallbearer, when mourning band will also be worn).

When sanctioned by the denomination concerned (as in the case of the Episcopal Church), the officiating clergyman, if so entitled, should wear military ribbons on vestments.

Dependents' Funerals. Military honors (firing of volleys and sounding of "Taps") are reserved for deceased military or former military persons. For the funerals of Marine dependents, body bearers may be assigned and, if desired, the funeral service will be conducted by a Navy chaplain.

Musical Honors. If prescribed by *Navy Regulations,* musical honors are rendered during each transfer of remains into, or from, hearse or caisson to church (or vice versa) and from hearse or caisson to gravesite. Next of kin should have an opportunity to select hymns or funeral music to be played by the band, but the Navy Hymn, "Eternal Father, Strong to Save," always should be included.

Rehearsals and Reconnaissance. Unit rehearsals obviously cannot be conducted at the church or gravesite, although the various evolutions can be adequately rehearsed on the parade ground. Careful but unobtrusive reconnaissance, however, should be conducted by the adjutant (who acts as officer-in-charge unless otherwise prescribed) and by the escort commander. All Marines assigned to funeral details—especially firing party and body bearers—must have attained the necessary high standards of individual proficiency in their duties for these occasions.

1814. Funeral Escorts

Officers' Funerals. The basic escort for a deceased officer consists of:
- Escort commander (same rank as deceased, if possible)
- Staff (colonels and flag officers only)
- Band
- Color guard
- Body bearers
- Firing party (eight riflemen with NCO-in-charge)
- Field music
- Personal flag bearer (flag officers only)

Troop escort is as follows for the respective officers.

Major General or Senior: Three ceremonial companies (two platoons of three eight-person squads each)

Colonel or Senior: Two ceremonial companies composed as above

Major or Senior: One ceremonial company composed as above (escort commander commands company and has no staff)

Company and Warrant Officers: One ceremonial platoon (three eight-person squads; escort commander serves as platoon leader and has no staff)

Enlisted Marines' Funerals. The funeral escort for a deceased enlisted Marine consists of a noncommissioned escort commander (same rank as deceased, or senior), body bearers, firing party (eight riflemen), field music, and, in the case of gunnery sergeants or above, troop escort consisting of a rifle squad.

Simple Honors Funerals.   When next of kin does not desire full honors, the simple honors funeral escort, for all ranks, consists of an escort commander (not above rank of captain), body bearers, firing party, and field music.

YOUR SWORD

1815.   Rigging Your Sword

Correct wearing of your sword is a point of professional punctilio. Derived from "Rig It Right," an excellent article in the *Gazette* (June 1961), by Majors T. N. Galbraith and R. N. Good, here is an account of how you should rig and wear your badge as a commissioned officer.

The first step is to get your sword knot squared away. The way to begin assembly of the knot is to reeve its small end through the eye of the "pommel," slip it back through the two keepers, and hook it to the small metal eye adjacent to the large end. Draw one keeper tight against the pommel, the other over the hook and eye, and you are ready to tie the knot.

Now loop the large end of the knot under the cross guard of the hilt and tie a hitch as shown in Figure 18–6. If you check this diagram closely, you will see that the knot shown is a clove hitch, not the double half hitch specified in regulations. The fact is, a double half hitch won't hold the knot tight to the cross guard, whereas a clove hitch will.

When the hitch is bent on, draw it taut and, at the same time, work the knot so that the large end doesn't hang below the upper ring mounting on the scabbard. Depending on the length of your particular knot, the portion from the eye of your pommel to the cross guard will possess some degree of looseness. This is all right: the determining factor is the length of the bight hanging free below the cross guard. If the knot hangs down farther than it should, you may find yourself slapped in the face when you present sword.

Mourning Knot.   Secure the mourning knot to the leather sword knot between pommel and cross guard by (1) doubling the mourning knot in two; (2) passing its two free ends together around the sword knot and through the middle bend, drawing it taut. Figure 18–6 shows how it should look.

Nomenclature of the Sword and Accessories.   Attaching the knot may be the most troublesome part of rigging the sword, but the nomenclature of the sword also may be a source of confusion (see Figure 18–7). Sword and scabbard are suspended from the *sword sling.* If you are wearing a blouse, the sword sling is attached to your Sam Browne belt by the frog, or, if with cloth belt, to the *shoulder sling;* if you are not wearing a blouse, the sword sling is attached to the *frog* on your belt. In either case, the frog and shoulder sling serve the single purpose of providing a D-ring to which you attach the sword sling.

Attaching Scabbard to Sword Sling.   One easy way to attach your scabbard to your sword sling is shown in Figure 18–7. With the sword sling on and its

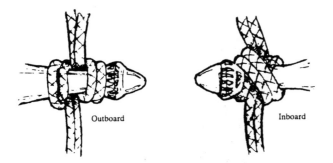

Outboard   Inboard

Figure 18–6: Rigging your sword

straps hanging free, attach the sling strap snaps to the scabbard rings. Holding the scabbard by its upper ring, give it a half twist toward the body (clockwise) and hang the upper ring over the sword sling hook.

1816. Manual of the Sword

This is shown in the *Drills and Ceremonies Manual*. In addition to the manual just mentioned, however, two additional positions are sometimes used.

Standing at Ease. When it is desired to stand at ease or at rest but with sword drawn (as distinct from "Parade Rest"), thus facilitating quick return to the carry for the purpose of giving commands, the old (naval) position formerly used at rest is both military and convenient. Simply stand with the feet apart, as in "Parade Rest," but with the sword blade carried horizontally without constraint across the front of the body, hilt in the right hand and lower blade in the left.

Carrying Sword When Not in Formation. As your sword is not a fishing pole, a hoe, or a golf club, it should be carried and handled in a military way even when you are not in formation and the sword is unrigged. The proper way to do this is to crook your left arm at right angles across the front of your body and to place the sword (sheathed in its scabbard) in the crook, *curve of the blade downward* and hilt rearward. The sword will ride easily here as long as you hold your forearm steady, and the appearance will be formal and soldierly.

Marching. When under way, with sword drawn, the scabbard will hang and move naturally. Despite jokes to the contrary, it is next to impossible to trip over a scabbard. Few things make you appear more unsure of yourself than clutching at your scabbard while carrying or saluting with your sword.

DISPLAYING THE FLAG

1817. General Concept

Routine Guidelines. Throughout the Navy and Marine Corps, the National Ensign is displayed from 0800 to sunset (except in ships under way, which fly

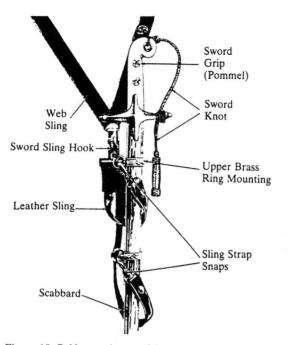

Figure 18–7: Nomenclature of the sword, scabbard, and sling

the ensign continuously). On shore, the flag is flown near post headquarters, or at the headquarters of the senior when two or more commands are located so close together that separate flags would be inappropriate. Outlying commands or activities display the National Colors in order to make clear their governmental character.

Except when intentionally lowered to half-mast, the flag must be "two-blocked" at all times—that is, it must be hoisted and secured at the very top of the staff, or gaff, since any flag not so secured is technically considered to be at half-mast (see Figure 18–8). Display of the flag at half-mast indicates official mourning. On Memorial Day, the flag is half-masted until the completion of the required gun salute, or until noon, if no salute is fired.

The position of half-mast is midway between the peak (or truck) and the base of the flagstaff, except when the latter has yardarms or is supported by guys, stays, or shrouds, in which case half-mast is halfway between the peak and the yardarm or the point at which guys, stays, or shrouds join the staff.

The church pennant is the only flag ever flown above the ensign. It is hoisted at the sounding of "Church Call" for divine services on shipboard, and the National Colors are lowered to a position just under the church pennant. When divine services have concluded, the church pennant is hauled down and the National Colors are "two-blocked."

Colors must never be allowed to become fouled. It is an important responsibility of the guard to prevent this. To avoid fouling, they should be raised or lowered from the leeward side of the pole. Should it become necessary to exchange a set of Colors already hoisted, a new set is first run up on a second halyard (this is why flagpoles have two sets of halyards), and the original set is lowered as soon as the new one has been two-blocked.

It is a recognized international *distress signal,* afloat or ashore, sanctioned by law, to fly the National Ensign upside down.

In Battle.   It is a very old tradition, although no longer prescribed by *Navy Regulations,* that, on joining action, ships break out the National Ensign at the truck of each mast. The spirit of this tradition should be observed on shore. Any position under attack, at which Colors are normally flown, should keep those Colors flying throughout action, night and day, just as the original Star Spangled Banner flew through the night over Fort McHenry at Baltimore (where Marines formed one of the defending units).

Half-Masting the Flag.   First, two-block the flag at the truck (top) of the staff, and keep it there until the last note of the National Anthem or "To the Colors"; then lower it to the half-mast position. In lowering the flag from half-mast, hoist it smartly to the truck at the first note of the music, then lower it in the regular manner, as described in Section 1818.

Displayed with Other Flags.   The National Colors are always on the right (to your left as you face the displayed flags). If other flags are flown from adjacent poles, the American flag will be the first one raised and the last one lowered.

When displayed from crossed staffs, the National Colors are on the right, and the staff is in front of the staff of the other flag with which it is crossed.

When displayed over a street, the blue field (or "union") of the flag should point north on a street running east-west, and point east on a street running north-south.

When used to drape a coffin, the flag should be placed so that the union would cover the head and left shoulder of the body within.

Foreign Flags.   Except in cases of official ceremonies, the carrying of foreign flags by members of the U.S. Armed Forces is not authorized. An example of an official ceremony would be the arrival or departure of a foreign head of state. Rulings as to whether given events may be considered official ceremonies should be obtained from Marine Corps Headquarters.

1818.   Morning and Evening Colors

Colors are the most important ceremonies of the working day and must be conducted with precision and ceremony. Executing Colors is the responsibility of the guard of the day and should be personally supervised by the commander of the guard (see Chapter 17). Honors to be rendered by individuals and formations are described in Section 1810.

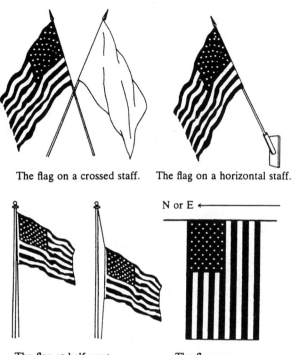

The flag on a crossed staff.   The flag on a horizontal staff.

The flag at half-mast.   The flag over a street.

Figure 18–8: Correct ways to display the flag

Raising the Flag (Morning Colors). The color guard, a noncommissioned officer and two privates, forms at the guardhouse, with the NCO (carrying the folded Colors) in the center. The color guard marches to the flagstaff, halts, and bends on the flag to the halyards. The halyards are manned by the two privates, and the NCO holds the flag until it is hauled free of his grasp. The NCO must see that the Colors never touch the ground. At precisely 0800, the signal to execute Colors is given from the guardhouse by the corporal of the relief on watch. The field music then makes eight bells, and, after the last stroke, the music begins, and the flag is hoisted smartly. When the flag is clear, the NCO comes to hand salute. As soon as the flag is two-blocked, the privates manning halyards likewise come to hand salute and hold this position throughout the National Anthem or "To the Colors," after which the halyards are triced. In saluting during Colors, members of the Color detail should avoid looking up at the Colors, and should salute in the normal manner and stance.

The guard of the day and band, or field music, parade facing the flagpole. At Morning Colors, following the last stroke of eight bells, attention is sounded by bugle, followed in turn by the National Anthem (if a band is present) or "To the

Colors" (by field music). The guard is brought to present arms on the call to attention. If foreign forces are present, the band renders prescribed honors to foreign ensigns after playing the U.S. National Anthem. Hand salutes and present arms end on the last musical note, after which "Carry On" is sounded.

In the absence of a band, "To the Colors" is sounded by field music. If no music is present, the signals for attention, hand salute, and carry on must be given by whistle, which is most undesirable. Even if your outfit does not rate or include music, you should make every effort to obtain a bugle and train a non-rated Marine to sound the calls required for Colors. This is where initiative, enterprise, and spirit of "make-do" can show.

Lowering the Flag (Evening Colors). Evening Colors is executed by the same guard details as Morning Colors, and the ceremony is virtually a reverse performance of the latter. The flag is lowered precisely at sunset, the exact daily time of which should be kept in a table in the guardhouse. Beginning with the first note of the music, the flag is slowly lowered, in time with the music, so that it will be in the hands of the NCO of the color guard as the last note sounds. In the absence of a band, "Retreat" is sounded by field music.

After being lowered, the flag is folded in the shape of a cocked hat. The correct procedure for folding a set of Colors may be found in Figure 18–9 and should be followed.

Standing lights (such as streetlights and aircraft obstruction lights) throughout the post should not be turned on until after the last note of Evening Colors.

1819. Display of Personal Flags or Pennants

At Commands Ashore. The personal flag or pennant of a general or flag officer is displayed, day and night, in the headquarters area (usually from a staff on the headquarters building). When an officer entitled to a personal flag makes an official visit or inspection at some other activity of the command, the personal flag is hauled down and shifted to the activity that the officer is visiting. If this latter activity is in turn commanded by a flag or general officer, the senior officer's personal flag displaces that of the local commander.

When a foreign ensign or personal flag is displayed ashore during an official visit by, or gun salute to, a foreign officer or civil official, it is broken at the normal point of display of the local commander's flag or pennant, and the latter is in turn shifted to some other point within the command.

If the points of display of two or more personal flags are so close together that it would be inappropriate to fly them in competition, so to speak, the senior officer's personal flag is displayed alone. Similarly, if two or more civil officials who rate personal flags are present officially at the same time, only the flag of the senior is broken.

It is a Marine Corps custom that, on conclusion of a tour in command, a general officer may retain a personal flag.

On Vehicles. Any officer entitled to a personal flag or pennant may display this forward on a vehicle in which the officer is riding officially. Alternatively,

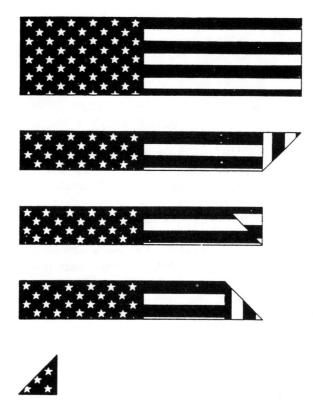

Figure 18–9: Folding the flag

one may mount plates, forward and aft, bearing the number of stars appropriate to rank. Marine Corps and Army generals have scarlet plates (but the arrangement of stars on Marine general officers' flags and plates corresponds to that of flag officers of the Navy rather than to that of Army generals). Navy and Air Force flag or general officers have blue plates. A personal flag and a set of such plates are never displayed at the same time from the same car. When the officer who rates the flag or plates is not in the car, the flag should be furled and cased, and the plates cased. This is a point on which drivers should be carefully schooled.

On Board Ship or in Boats. The rules for display of personal flags and pennants afloat are complex and precise, and they must be carefully followed. They are given in *Navy Regulations*.

HONORS, OFFICIAL VISITS, AND CALLS

1820. Honors, Official Visits, and Calls

As a junior officer, your first contacts with honors, official visits, and official calls will probably occur on board ship or when you find yourself detailed to command a guard of honor. Like all military etiquette, the subject demands precise attention and compliance with every rule. Because the Marine Corps prides itself on being the most military of the services, make a point to know and observe all the ins and outs of honors and official visits.

The following definitions may be helpful.

Official visit: A formal visit of courtesy that requires special honors and ceremonies.

Official call: An official but informal visit of courtesy that does not require honors or ceremony. Note the distinction between official calls, discussed in this chapter, and personal calls, which are covered in Chapter 22.

Guard of the day: For rendering honors, *Navy Regulations* provides that the "guard of the day" (normally not part of the interior guard, except on board ship) shall be not less than one rifle squad.

Full guard: Not less than one rifle platoon.

Guard of honor: Any guard, not part of the interior guard, that is paraded ashore for rendition of honors. When the interior guard turns out in compliment to an individual, it is spoken of as "the guard," not as a guard of honor.

Compliment of the guard: This honor consists of an interior guard turning out and presenting arms, as a compliment to visiting officers or civilian dignitaries.

Shipboard compliments: In addition to honors by a guard, shipboard compliments may include any or all of the following elements, which are dispensed with ashore:

- Manning the rail on weather decks by the ship's company
- Piping alongside and over the side
- Sideboys.

Because Marines in a ship's company are fully occupied with other elements of rendering honors to visitors, these shipboard compliments are performed only by Navy officers and enlisted personnel.

Honors.   Arrangements for rendering honors ashore are usually coordinated by the commanding general's aide. On a post or unit not commanded by a general officer, arrangements are made by the adjutant.

Ashore and afloat, we render the same salutes, honors, and ceremonies, as practicable, at Marine Corps posts and stations and in naval ships and stations. Wherever Marines are present, they provide the honor guard. Detailed pointers and procedures on honors are in Section 1822.

It goes without saying that troops paraded as honor guards must be the best. See to it that your guard is correct, snappy, and immaculate—a reflection of the Marine Corps at its smartest.

Official Visits and Calls.   Official visits and official calls, as we discuss them here, are paid only by officers in command and are distinct from the personal calls described in Chapter 22.

Generally speaking, official visits are more often paid by commanders afloat, whereas on shore official calls are substituted.

On taking over a command, you must make an official call on the senior to whom you have reported for duty. This call is at the senior's headquarters and is not the domestic "visit of courtesy," mentioned in Chapter 22, that is customary.

In addition, unless the senior indicates otherwise, the following other official calls are required:

1. A call by the commander of an arriving unit on his or her immediate superior, if present, and on the senior Marine or Navy officer present.
2. A call by commanding officers on an immediate superior in the chain of command upon arrival of the latter.
3. A call by an officer, who has been senior officer present, upon that officer's successor.
4. A call by the commander of a unit or ship arriving at a Marine Corps post or naval station, upon the commander of such activity; except that when the arriving commander is senior, the local commander makes the call.
5. Calls on high civil officials (state and territorial governors and U.S. diplomatic and consular officials) as prescribed in *Navy Regulations*.
6. When in the vicinity of a command ashore belonging to another U.S. armed service or to a friendly foreign power, the senior Marine officer present in command arranges with the other commander concerned for an exchange of official visits or calls as appropriate. Check *Navy Regulations* for calling procedure on foreign officials.

When you leave your command for an official visit, or return therefrom, you receive the honors prescribed for such a visit, except that your own organization remains in uniform of the day and omits gun salutes.

Official calls or visits must be paid expeditiously as they become due, or on the first working day thereafter. They must be returned within twenty-four hours or on the first subsequent working day.

Circumstances permitting, generals and flag officers return in person official visits or calls by officers of the grade of colonel or higher. The chief of staff or deputy commander returns official calls or visits by officers below colonel.

Officers below general or flag rank return all calls and visits in person.

High foreign officials (other than chiefs of state) return in person visits or calls by a general or an admiral. Otherwise they return such visits by a suitable representative.

Before making or returning an official visit or call, check both *Navy Regulations* and *Marine Corps Uniform Regulations* for the proper uniform. If unable to get access to these publications, or if you cannot find your answer, you will never be far wrong wearing undress blue or white, according to season and climate.

1821. Official Visits and Calls Ashore

Before you make or receive an official call or visit ashore, be sure to have all arrangements taken care of well in advance. This requires liaison between the maker and the recipient of the call, which is up to the aide or the adjutant, as the case may be. Coordinate the following details especially:

- Time and exact place call is to be paid
- Uniform
- Entrance to post, station, and headquarters that caller will use
- Transportation
- Honor guard, if required (see Section 1822)
- Use of calling cards
- Refreshments to be served, if any
- Specific units, places, or installations to be visited
- Arrangements to break or haul down personal flags or to fire gun salutes

1822. Procedure and Pointers on Rendering Honors

Preparations. The general's aide (or the adjutant) virtually always has ample advance notice to prepare for an official visit that requires honors and to notify those concerned. Ashore, the casual or surprise official visit is rare.

When detailed to command an honor guard, you should immediately visit the aide (or report to the adjutant) and obtain all possible information. Check with the bandmaster on the timing of ruffles and flourishes and with the NCO in charge of the saluting battery. If the saluting guns are remote from the honor guard's parade, see that absolutely foolproof communications are established between the parade and the saluting battery. It is elementary, but vital, that the saluting battery knows how many guns are to be fired; also ensure that a standby piece (if available) and spare rounds are in instant readiness to fire in the event of hangfire or malfunctions of a saluting gun.*

Make a personal reconnaissance of the honor guard's parade, and know exactly where the guard and band and the recipients of honors are to be posted. Determine what markers and guidons are required, and who will supply and locate them. If possible, give your platoon leaders and leading NCOs an opportunity to look over the ground. If you are going to provide an escort of honor, verify the route of march.

As to the guard itself, spare no effort to make it the finest in the Marine Corps. See that every person is immaculately turned out, that the guard is perfectly sized, and that the entire formation, if possible, is adequately rehearsed. If troops for the guard come from units other than your own, have no hesitation in returning substandard individuals to their units, reporting that you have done this (and why) to the adjutant.

Procedure for Honors on an Official Visit Ashore. The following general procedure can serve as a guide for rendering honors ashore. (Remember, how-

---

*If for any reason your saluting battery doesn't have a stopwatch for timing the rounds (or if the watch stops permanently), the NCO in charge can obtain the correct interval between sounds by repeating, "If I wasn't a gunner, I wouldn't be here—Fire One (two, three, etc.)." This is a trick that dates back to early days in the sailing Navy.

ever, that almost every post has its ground rules and standing operating procedures, and be sure to consult these when preparing to render honors.)

1. Well before the time of arrival of the visiting official, complete the preparations discussed above, parade your guard and band, have the Color detail standing by to break or haul down personal flags involved, and have the saluting battery manned and ready. If possible, especially on a large post, have communications that can apprise you, up to the last moment, of the visitor's movements and approach.

2. When the recipient of honors arrives and debarks from boat, train, car, plane, or helicopter, "Attention" is sounded by bugle. The local commander (or whoever is receiving the dignitary) greets that individual and conducts him or her to the post front and center of the guard.

3. When the official takes post, the commander of the honor guard brings the guard to present arms. All hands in the vicinity, but not those in formation, come to hand salute, following the motions of the guard.

4. When the guard has been presented, and the commander has executed the salute, the band sounds off with ruffles, flourishes, and other musical honors. The personal flag or National Color, as specified for the dignitary, is broken on the first note of the music.

5. The guard is brought to the order after the last note of the music, or when the commander of the guard has exchanged salutes with the official, if there is no music. If a gun salute is rendered, the first gun is fired immediately after the last note of the music, and the guard remains at the present throughout the salute, as do all hands in the official party who hold salutes throughout the gun salute. Persons not in the official party, but in the immediate vicinity, remain at attention during the gun salute. If the National Color, or a foreign flag or ensign, is to be displayed during the gun salute only, it is broken on the first gun and hauled down on the last.

6. On completion of the musical honors or the gun salute, if fired, the honor guard commander brings the guard to order arms, executes present sword to the person being honored, and reports, "Sir, the honor guard is formed." If the personage desires neither to inspect the guard nor that it pass in review, the honor guard remains at attention. For procedure to be followed for marching the guard in review or for its inspection by the personage, see *Drill and Ceremonies Manual.*

Honors on Departure from an Official Visit Ashore.   In general, departure honors reverse those given on arrival.

1. Departure honors commence when the visiting official has completed personal leave-taking from the senior officer present. Either the latter officer or the aide will signal this to the commander of the guard.

2. Gun salutes, if rendered on departure, must begin before the individual actually leaves (that is, while within earshot). The personal flag, or any national ensign displayed, is hauled down on the last gun.

3. An honor guard is not normally inspected on departure. Hold the guard on parade until the official is out of sight.

Pointers on Honors, Ashore and Afloat. Your "bible" for honors incident to official visits and calls is *Navy Regulations.* The table of honors and ceremonies given here (Table 18–2) is a compilation of the information in those articles, assembled for quick reference. You must also be meticulously familiar with the *Drills and Ceremonies Manual,* which gives detailed instructions for rendering all types of honors.

In addition to guards paraded in receiving the president, or any foreign sovereign or chief of state, or member of a reigning royal family, all officers not required elsewhere form on the left of the honor guard, in dress uniform with swords. Troops not otherwise occupied should form on parades adjacent to the guest's route of inspection and also line the route. On board ship, persons not manning the rail fall in at quarters.

Afloat, all ships present, other than the one receiving the president or foreign guest, man the rails and fire the required national salute on the arrival and departure of the distinguished guest.

The officer of the day or officer of the deck attends the arrival and departure of any distinguished visitor, whether or not the visit is official.

Afloat, side honors only (that is, side boys only, no guard or band) are rendered when a general officer, flag officer, or another commanding officer comes on board without flag or pennant flying. If so requested, full honors may be rendered on departure, otherwise side honors only are again the rule. While side honors are being rendered, all hands on deck and in view of the gangway stand at attention, facing the gangway; they salute as the officer reaches the top of the accommodation ladder or brow, and remain at the hand salute until the end of the boatswain's pipe, following the motions of the side boys.

Honors are dispensed with under the following circumstances:

• When the visiting officer is in plainclothes or visits the post unofficially
• Between sunset and 0800 (except that foreign officers may be rendered honors at any time during daylight)
• During meal hours for the troops (except in the case of foreign officers)
• When a ship is engaged in maneuvers, general drills, or undergoing overhaul in a navy yard, or is in action
• When a unit or post ashore is carrying on tactical exercises or emergency drills
• On Sundays or national holidays (except in the case of foreign officers)

Honors in the Field. Despite the rigors of field service, Marine units make every effort to render appropriate honors when so serving. The spirit, if not the letter, of the preceding paragraphs must be faithfully observed. It is the distinguishing mark of really professional troops that in face of handicaps and obvious obstacles to smartness, they nevertheless remain smart and military and do the best they can with what they have. Marines in the field may well remember what was said of England's Brigade of Guards: "They die with their boots clean."

For rendition of honors in the field, the most important points are that:
* Marines be in clean, homogeneous uniforms
* Equipment (especially weapons) be first-class and serviceable
* Individuals be smart, keen, and clean
* The place for rendering honors be not subject to enemy observation
* Military readiness or combat operations be not interrupted

POINTERS FOR AIDES-DE-CAMP

1823. Duties and Relationships

Duty as an aide-de-camp (usually short-titled "aide") is one of the most exacting details that a young officer can receive. If you are so assigned, you may take it as a compliment to your military and personal character—a compliment that you must do your best to live up to.

As an aide, you are always on duty, and this duty is always personal and confidential and always official. Your duties are only such as your general personally directs. On the other hand, if you are to succeed, you must quickly learn to anticipate your general's desires and needs and take care of them without having to be told. No matter what the circumstances, your first thoughts should be for your chief's safety, reputation, convenience, and pleasure. Any duty asked of you should therefore be promptly performed.

Intelligence, tact, loyalty, absolute discretion, and military smartness are the most important characteristics of a good aide, with sensible frankness not far behind. Although, by direction, an aide must often serve as an extra pair of eyes and ears for the chief, the aide must avoid becoming a tale-bearer and should, whenever consistent with loyalty and fairness toward the chief, do the utmost to protect other officers' chance indiscretions from reaching the attention of higher authorities.

Aside from your chief, the two most important persons with whom you routinely deal are the chief of staff and spouse. Establishment of a cooperative, deferential, helpful relationship with the chief of staff—while being careful never to betray any confidence of the general—is essential.

To sum up, virtually all arrangements that concern the general end up as your responsibilities. Functionally, your job breaks down into (1) scheduling, (2) paperwork, (3) protocol, and (4) personal needs.

Keeping your general on schedule is of overriding importance; it is also one of your most difficult tasks. Remembering that "punctuality is the politeness of kings," you must stay on top of the itinerary or other program for each hour and minute.

At briefings, ensure that the general has good background familiarity with the subject. On visits, see that your chief is prepared for and familiar with the people one can be expected to meet, and, where appropriate, with the missions and general situation of units concerned.

Your main job in the realm of paperwork is to keep track of all papers going

Table 18–2. Table of honors for official visits

Rank	Uniform	Gun salute — Arrival	Gun salute — Departure	Ruffles and flourishes	Music	Guard	Side boys	Crew	Within what limits	Flag — What	Flag — Which truck	Flag — During
President	Full dress	21	21	4	National anthem*	Full	8	Man rail[1,2]	....	President's	Main	Visit
President or sovereign of a foreign country	do.	21	21	4	Foreign national anthem	do.	8	do.	....	Foreign ensign	do.	do.
Member of reigning royal family	do.	21	21	4	do.	do.	8	do.	....	do.	do.	Salute
Ex-president or president-elect	do.	21	21	4	Admiral's march	do.	8	Quarters	....	National	do.	do.
Secretary of state when acting as special foreign representative of the president	Full dress	19	19	4	National anthem	Full	8	Quarters[3]	....	Secretary's	Main	Visit
Vice president	do.	...	19	4	Admiral's march	do.	8	do.	....	Vice president's	do.	do.
Speaker of the House of Representatives	do.	...	19	4	do.	do.	8	....	....	National	Fore	Salute
Governor of a state of the United States	do.	...	19	4	do.	do.	8	....	Area under governor's jurisdiction	do.	do.	do.
Chief Justice of the United States	do.	...	19	4	do.	do.	8	....	....	do.	do.	do.
Ambassador, high commissioner, or special diplomatic representative whose credentials give him or her authority equal to or greater than an ambassador	do.	...	19	4	National anthem	do.	8	....	Nation or nations to which accredited	do.	do.	do.
Secretary of defense	do.	19	19	4	Honors march†	do.	8	Quarters	....	Secretary's	Main	Visit
Deputy secretary of defense	do.	19	19	4	do.	do.	8	do.	....	Dep. secy.'s	do.	do.
Prime minister or other cabinet officer of a foreign country	Dress	19	19	4	Admiral's march	do.	8	....	....	Foreign ensign	Fore	Salute
Cabinet officer other than secretary of defense	do.	...	19	4	do.	do.	8	....	....	National	do.	do.
Secretary of the Navy	Full dress	19	19	4	Honors march†	do.	8	Quarters	....	Secretary's	Main	Visit
Secretary of the Army or Air Force	Dress	...	19	4	do.	do.	8	....	....	National	Fore	Salute
President pro tempore of the Senate	do.	...	19	4	do.	do.	8	....	....	do.	do.	do.
Assistant secretary of defense	Dress	17	17	4	Honors march†	Full	8	Quarters	....	Asst. Secy.'s	Main	Visit
Under secretary and assistant secretaries of the Navy ..	do.	17	17	4	do.	do.	8	do.	....	Under or asst. secy.'s	Main	Visit

Official	Uniform	Gun salute	Gun salute	Ruffles and flourishes	Music	Dress of ship	Side boys	Guard	Display area	Flag	Position	Salute
Under or assistant secretary of the Army or Air Force	do.	17	17	4	do.	do.	8		Area under official's jurisdiction	National	Fore	Salute
Governor general or governor of territory, commonwealth, or possession of the U.S. or area under the administration of the U.S.	do.	17		4	Admiral's march	do.	8			do.	do.	do.
Committee of Congress	do.	17		4	do.	do.	8			do.	do.	do.
Envoy extraordinary and minister plenipotentiary	Dress		15	3	Admiral's march	Full	8		Nation to which accredited	National	Fore	Salute
Minister resident	do.		13	2	do.	do.	6		do.	do.	do.	do.
Charge d'affaires	do.		11	1	do.	do.	6		do.	do.	do.	do.
Career minister or counselor of embassy or legation	do.			1	do.	do.	6		do.			
Consul general or consul or vice consul when in charge of consulate general	do.		11	1	do.	do.	6		District to which assigned	National	Fore	Salute
First secretary of embassy or legation	Of the day with sword					Of the day	4		Nation to which accredited			
Consul or vice consul when in charge of consulate	do.		7			do.	4		District to which assigned	National	Fore	Salute
Mayor of an incorporated city	do.					do.	4		Within limits of mayoralty			
Second or third secretary of embassy or legation	do.						2		Nation to which accredited			
Vice consul when only representative of the U.S. and not in charge of consulate or consulate general	do.		5			Of the day	2		District to which assigned	National	Fore	Salute
Consular agent when only representative of the U.S.	do.					do.	2		do.			
Military and Naval Officers, United States and Foreign[4-7]												
Chairman of the JCS	Dress	19[8,9]	19[8,9]	4	Admiral's march[10]	Full	8	Quarters				
Chief of Staff, U.S. Army	do.	19	19	4	General's march	do.	8	do.				
Chief of Naval Operations	do.	19	19	4	Admiral's march	do.	8	do.				
Chief of Staff, U.S. Air Force	do.	19	19	4	General's march	do.	8	do.				
Commandant of the Marine Corps	do.	19	19	4	Admiral's march	do.	8	do.				
Fleet Admiral or General of the Army or the Air Force	Dress	19	19	4	Admiral's march[10]	Full	8	Quarters				
Admiral or general	do.		17	4	do.	do.	8					
Naval or other military governor, commissioned as such by the president, within area under jurisdiction	do.		17	4	do.	do.	8		For United States officers, personal flag at the main during the salute			
Vice admiral or lieutenant general	do.		15	3	do.	do.	8[11]					

Table 18–2. (Continued)

Rank	Uniform	Gun salute Arrival	Gun salute Departure	Ruffles and flourishes	Music	Guard	Side boys	Crew	Within what limits	Flag What	Flag Which truck	Flag During
Rear admiral or major general	do.	...	13	2	do.	do.	6	...	...	For officers of foreign nations, the foreign ensign at the fore during the salute		
Rear admiral (lower half) or brigadier general	do.	...	11	1	do.	do.	6	...	...			
Captain, commander, colonel or lieutenant colonel	Undress	...	...			Of the day	4	...	...			
Other commissioned officers	Of the day with sword					do.	2					
Official not herein provided for	Honors as prescribed by the senior officer present; such honors normally shall be those accorded the foreign official, when visiting officially a ship of own nation, but a gun salute, if prescribed, shall not exceed 19 guns.											
Foreign officer of the armed forces, diplomatic or consular representative in country to which accredited, or other distinguished foreign official ..	Honors for an official or officer of the United States of the same grade, except, that equivalent honors shall be rendered to foreign officers who occupy a position comparable to Chairman JCS, CNO, CMC, Chief of Staff Army, Chief of Staff Air Force, or CMC.											

NOTES

1. All other ships present man rail and fire national salute at official reception or departure of president.

2. For president of United States, president of a foreign republic, foreign sovereign or member of reigning royal family, officers assembled on quarterdeck in full dress, crew man rail, and other officers unemployed formed forward of guard, personnel not occupied fall in at quarters.

3. For others for whom full dress uniform is prescribed designated officers assembled on quarterdeck and formed forward of guard.

4. When side honors only are rendered to a flag or commanding officer, officers and personnel on deck and in view from the gangway shall stand at attention facing the gangway, and salute as the officer appears over the side and shall remain at the salute until the end of the pipe.

5. All honors except attendance at gangway by the officer of the deck, except as social courtesy may demand, shall be dispensed with:
 a. When officers are in plainclothes.
 b. From sunset to 0800 (except that for foreign officers, side shall be piped during daylight).
 c. During meal hours of the crew for officers of U.S. Navy or Marine Corps.
 d. When exercising at general drills or when undergoing Navy Yard overhaul, for officers of USN and USMC.
 e. For ships with less than 180 personnel in the seaman branch, for officers of USN, USMC, USCG, USA, and USAF, except when advance notice of an offical visit has been received.

6. The guard and band shall not be paraded on Sunday for USN, USMC, USCG, USA or USAF officers.

7. All sentries on the upper deck or in view from outside shall salute all commissioned officers passing them close aboard, in boats or otherwise.

8. If a flag or commanding officer comes on board without flag or pennant flying, only side honors shall be given unless officer should request full honors on departure. All persons on the quarterdeck shall stand at attention by command without bugle.

9. No officer in civilian clothes shall be saluted with guns or have a guard paraded in his or her honor.

10. Admirals and Marine Corps Generals receive the "Admiral's March"; Generals (Army/Air Force) receive the "General's March."

11. The officer of the deck shall attend at the gangway on the arrival or departure of any commissioned officer or distinguished visitor.

* "Hail to the Chief" may be used in lieu of National anthem on either arrival or departure. When specified by the president, "Hail to the Chief" may be used while the president and immediate party move to or from their places while all others stand fast.

† Honors march is a 32-bar medley in the trio of "The Stars and Stripes Forever."

in or out and set them into proper priority, depending on deadlines, actions required, and importance.

The responsibilities of protocol and personal needs are covered in subsequent paragraphs.

1824. Travel Arrangements

Before Leaving. Prepare an itinerary, giving hours and modes of arrival and departure at destination and all intermediate stops, and furnish a copy to the chief of staff and any other interested parties.

Obtain a program for each official stop, to include schedule of events, uniforms required, times, and other necessary information. This program, of course, must have been coordinated with the host activity.

Inform your chief of the uniforms required throughout the trip.

Obtain your chief's orders and transportation requests (if required), and see that transportation is arranged.

Issue instructions for forwarding mail or messages.

See that all baggage for the official party is suitably tagged and identified.

Determine what, if any, papers or files the general will require on the trip and arrange for their handling and stowage, especially that of any classified matter.

Check communications arrangements to be sure the general can be reached rapidly during any part of the trip.

During Travel. If traveling commercially, keep air and railroad timetables handy, and, no matter how you travel, know hours scheduled for arrival and departure. Know places and times for connections.

Prescribe uniforms for aircrew and stewards and ensure that other members of the party are informed as to correct uniform during travel, on arrival, and for scheduled events.

When on board government aircraft, be sure the pilot sends a message ahead, stating the composition of the party, ETA, and transportation required on arrival. If traveling commercially, send such a message yourself. Be sure that the host activity is informed if any guests are in the party or of changes in schedule.

Take care of all tickets, baggage checks, baggage handling, and transportation. In this capacity, your first responsibility is to take care of the general's gear and keep track of it at all times. This particularly includes official and classified papers.

Obtain copies of daily papers published at the principal places en route, and see that they reach your chief.

Keep track of time zone changes and the dateline. Remind the general to set his or her watch.

Take with you: station lists or rosters of officers at activities to be visited; a copy of the "Blue Book"; official and personal stationery and postage stamps as required; notebook, pen, and sharp pencils; a supply of the general's visiting cards; ample cash and a supply of personal checks on the general's bank; cleaning gear; liquor and refreshments as may be required; spare insignia and ribbons; and the general's personal flag and vehicle plates (if visiting an activity where such are possibly not available).

Keep a running record by name, rank or title, and address, of all persons to whom "bread and butter" notes or letters should be sent; if you have time, rough out such notes before memory fades.

After Return. Write or prepare, for the general, official and personal letters of appreciation to all who extended special courtesies.

Prepare for the general's signature the itinerary and travel claim, being careful not to omit miscellaneous expenses that can be properly claimed.

Obtain and deliver all personal mail held for your chief.

1825. Duties of an Aide in Garrison

Because you are expected to be the social arbiter and expert on the staff, you should know and possess both *Service Etiquette* (Oretha D. Swartz, published by the U.S. Naval Institute) and *Naval Ceremonies, Customs, and Traditions,* (Mack and Connell, also a Naval Institute publication). These sheet anchor books can be relied on for tested and correct advice in virtually any situation involving service social usage or protocol. In addition, you should keep an up-to-date *Combined Lineal List,* being careful to annotate all promotions, retirements, changes of status, and yearly promotion zones.

Courtesy and thoughtfulness are indispensable in an aide. You should never be too busy to be courteous to all comers. Especially avoid a nose-in-the-air attitude toward fellow officers.

Stay as much as possible within call of your chief.

Make a daily appointment schedule for your chief (and, if the general desires, save it for record). Keep track of engagements and commitments, and calls to be returned and remind as necessary.

Whenever anyone calls on the general officially or semiofficially, meet the visitors on arrival and accompany them to departure.

It is not only proper but in order for you to invite your chief's attention to anything that may be amiss as to uniform or dress, and also to remind the general of any social amenities or courtesies that may have been overlooked. It is up to you to know your chief's shortcomings, and to protect him or her against them.

Supervise the performance of drivers, enlisted aides and all others who serve the general. Keep them on their toes personally and professionally and weld them into a team. See that the general's office and the outer office are attractive and efficient.

Assist your general and spouse in preparations for all social functions to be given by them. Supervise the issuance of all invitations, making sure that dates and times are correct and that the desired uniform or costume is correctly specified, and keep track of RSVPs. (It is a helpful practice to put the guest list on the back of each invitation.)

On social occasions, keep close by and see that your chief and the persons with whom he or she may be talking are supplied with refreshments. Take post in the receiving line next to your chief, on the approach side. You need not shake hands except with guests you know. The most important thing is to get each name correctly and announce it clearly and distinctly to your chief, even in the cases of people your chief knows well.

Make the acquaintance of aides assigned to other flag or general officers in the immediate area. By close coordination and mutual support, you may be able to prevent many slipups.

1826.   Duties of an Aide in the Field

Your duties as an aide to a general officer in the field are quite different from those in garrison, although the spirit in which they are performed and the basic relationships remain unchanged.

Subject to the general's wishes, you must accompany your chief everywhere. In any case you must always keep a personal situation map and other maps or status boards absolutely up to the minute. Pay particular attention to locations of front lines, of installations to visit, and above all, of unit command posts. The last information is important not only to the general and driver, but also to you, as the general may often use you to convey personal messages to other commanders.

Be alert as to the military situation and be ready to obtain any information the general wishes, either from staff sections and subordinate headquarters or, if necessary, by personal reconnaissance.

See that your chief's personal wants are cared for. Have arrangements been made for laundry? For keeping weapons and gear in shape? For the foxhole?

Introduce visiting officers, official visitors, correspondents, and other persons having business with the general.

Arrange and control all transportation for the general.

Supervise the general's drivers, orderlies, cooks, and stewards as you would in garrison, but be sure these people are reminded that, in the field, they are combat Marines, too, and must be prepared to defend the general and the area in the event of surprise attack or enemy penetration of the command post area.

Supervise and act as caterer for the general's mess. Be sure that any fatigued, wet, or cold officer or enlisted Marine who sees the general (especially people from frontline units) always gets a cup of hot coffee or, if appropriate, a drink. Have plenty of coffee for drivers and runners, day or night.

Supervise the security arrangements for the general's area.

Work closely with the headquarters commandant in such arrangements as digging a suitable head, erection of tentage, digging in tents, camouflage of the area, water supply, electricity, and facilities.

Above all, do everything in your power to protect and defend your general, and to shelter the general from unnecessary strain and fatigue.

CEREMONIES

Ceremonial duties are written deep into our history as a Corps. Marines have always striven to excel in this field, and we have good reason to be proud of our record. We should continue so to strive and succeed. Every officer taking part in a ceremony—especially when, as is often the case, little time is available for practice—should realize how broadly revealing of wider professionalism our parade ground performance can be. Precision drill, immaculately turned-out troops, disciplined marching, and fine bearing—all these furnish, for the public to see, evidence of Marine Corps alertness, determination to put out only our best, and pride in Corps and selves. It is no coincidence that among the units and corps famous for ceremonial prowess and split-and-polish are also to be found some of the world's most redoubtable fighting formations.

1827.   Types of Ceremonies

The Marine Corps and Navy have eight military ceremonies that may be performed on shore. These ceremonies are in the form prescribed by the *Drill and Ceremonies Manual* and may be modified only when the nature of the ground or exceptional circumstances require that change be made.

The title and a brief description or discussion of each ceremony follow.

A *review* is a ceremony at which a command or several commands parade for inspection by, and in honor of, a senior officer, or in honor of a visitor or a civilian dignitary. In a review, the individual being honored passes on foot or in a vehicle throughout the formation, which is then marched past the honoree.

Presentation of decorations is the ceremony at which decorations are presented. This ceremony follows, in part, that prescribed for a review; it is noteworthy in that, regardless of rank, the individuals who have been decorated receive the review side by side with the reviewing officer. In modified form, this ceremony can be adapted for such occasions as presentation of commissions or enlisted warrants, commendations, and so forth.

A *parade* is the ceremony at which the commanding officer of a battalion or larger unit forms and drills the entire command and then marches them in review. The battalion parade is the most common form of periodic ceremony, and, under normal garrison conditions, is usually performed each Saturday morning. Together with guard mounting, described below, the parade is probably the most important ceremony for you to know by heart. "Memorize every comma in it!" Captain Lewis" ("Chesty") Puller used to enjoin his Basic School lieutenants.

Escort of the National Color is known less formally as "Marching on (or off) the Colors." That is, when the Colors are to take part in a ceremony, be presented to a unit, or turned over to some institution or person for safekeeping, they are ceremonially received and escorted from their place of safekeeping (usually the CO's headquarters), and are similarly returned, by a picked escort. The ceremony for this occasion corresponds somewhat to portions of the famous British ceremony *Trooping the Color* and is derived from that.

Escort of honor is the ceremonial escorting of a senior officer or other dignitary during an official visit or on arrival or departure.

Military funerals are covered in the *Drill and Ceremonies Manual,* as well as in Sections 1809, 1813, 1814, and 2117 of this *Guide.* The ceremonial forms followed in military funerals are among the oldest in the profession of arms; some parts, such as the firing of volleys (originally to frighten evil spirits) can be traced to pagan times.

Inspections, as you have seen from Section 1611, run to all types. The ceremonial inspection of troops in ranks has as its object the general military appearance and condition of individual uniforms and equipment within a command. Officers headed for sea duty should note that personnel inspection on board ship follows considerably different lines and frequently varies from ship to ship. Be sure you know your own ship's ground rules and inspection procedure.

Guard mounting is the ceremony whereby a guard is organized from guard details, is inspected before assuming the guard, and then relieves an outgoing or "old" guard. This is a very old ceremony, portions of which antedate the Revolutionary War and go back to the British Army. Guard mounts may be *formal* or *informal,* according to weather, size of guard, availability of music, or local conditions.

Morning and Evening Colors, although sometimes regarded as parts of the daily routine, should be conducted with the same gravity as ceremonies, if only out of respect to the significance of the daily raising and lowering of the National Ensign.

In addition to the foregoing eight ceremonies of general character, we employ specific ceremonial forms on the occasion of *change of command, relief of the sergeant major,* and for celebration of the *Marine Corps birthday.*

Another form of ceremony not covered in any official regulations is the *tattoo* (sometimes called "searchlight tattoo"). A tattoo is an evening parade conducted under floodlights or searchlights; embellished with traditional, historic, or display drills and special musical features; and usually climaxed by lowering of the Colors, playing of "Taps," and sometimes a traditional evening hymn. Evening parades at 8th and Eye, though not so entitled, are in fact a form of tattoo.

1828. Precedence of Forces in Parades or Ceremonies

To avoid conflicts at parades or ceremonies, the places of honor are allocated in order of service seniority. Because you may readily find yourself at the head of a Marine detachment in a parade or ceremony, you should know your own place and those of other components relative to your own. As prescribed in law (*Federal Register,* volume 14, 19 August 1949, page 2503), the precedence of U.S.

forces in parades or ceremonies is as follows (reading from the head to rear of column, or from right to left in line):

1. U.S. Corps of Cadets (U.S. Military Academy)
2. Midshipmen, U.S. Naval Academy
3. Cadets, U.S. Air Force Academy
4. Cadets, U.S. Coast Guard Academy
5. United States Army
6. United States Marines
7. United States Navy
8. United States Air Force
9. United States Coast Guard
10. Army National Guard of the United States
11. Organized Reserve Corps, U.S. Army
12. Marine Corps Reserve
13. Naval Reserve
14. Air National Guard of the United States
15. Air Force Reserve
16. Coast Guard Reserve
17. Other training organizations of the Army, Marine Corps, Navy, Air Force, and Coast Guard, in that order.

When the Coast Guard is serving as part of the Navy, in time of war or emergency, the precedence of Coast Guard units and personnel shifts to position immediately after Navy units and personnel.

Bear in mind, as a Marine, that although the Air Force is one of the three larger services, it is nevertheless junior in ceremonial precedence to the Marine Corps. Never accede to erroneous assignment of fourth, or junior, place to Marines, following Air Force units, as is sometimes carelessly done on the basis of size.

The place of honor is the head of column or right of the line, and foreign units should be assigned that post of honor in any American ceremony or procession. Where several foreign units of mixed nationality are present, they should be placed in alphabetical order, ahead of any U.S. forces, if the ceremony is conducted by U.S. forces or on American soil.

The official who organizes and coordinates a street parade or procession is entitled the *grand marshal* or, sometimes, the *marshal*. If your unit is misplaced, this official should rectify the mistake.

1829. General Appearance of Troops and Units

The Marine Corps has long enjoyed a worldwide reputation for smart appearance and soldierly performance of every task. This reputation has been enhanced by continually demonstrating to the American public that our execution of peacetime functions is excelled only by our performance in battle.

During peacetime, the reputation of the Corps is maintained to a considerable degree by creating favorable, highly military impressions in parades, ceremonies, and other functions. It is therefore a responsibility of all officers, and especially commanding officers, that marching units in the public eye fully meet the standards by which the Marine Corps is measured. Those in key positions must have perfect posture; troop leaders must excel in command presence; uniforms and equipment must be outstanding in condition and appearance. All such public appearances should be preceded by ample drill and specific rehearsal as needed.

1830.   Pointers on Ceremonies

Know Your Parade Ground.   If possible, not only make a personal reconnaissance of the parade ground or area where a ceremony is to be held but conduct a rehearsal on the ground. At a minimum, be sure your leading NCOs and unit guides know the layout of the ground, and how the field is to be marked.

Markers.   Dress guidons (see Section 731) mark the boundaries and the reviewing point for a parade ground. In addition, it is sometimes customary to place small metal discs on the ground to mark the posts of unit guides and other key personnel. The adjutant places markers and guidons, but every officer and NCO must know the system and layout of markers. In addition, guides and leaders should know the lineup of "landmarks" adjacent to and visible from the parade ground, so as to be able to march in exactly straight lines and column without wavering or falling off to right or left. Guides and leaders should keep their heads up and their lines of sight directly to the front and well out, so as to be able to "navigate" on guidons, markers, and landmarks.

Officers Center is an evolution that should be gone over until all concerned are perfect. Every individual participant is on display, and this evolution comes at the high point of the parade. Properly executed, "Officers Center" should seem to be the movement of a single Marine. Manuals of sword and guidon count here as at no other time.

Photographers.   Photographers, both official and otherwise, can do more to detract from the formality and solemnity of a military ceremony than anyone else. Keep them under strict control, preferably in a suitably located, enclosed vantage point, from which they can get good pictures but will not mar the occasion by capering about.

Cadence.   The regulation cadence is 120 steps per minute, and this is the "tempo" at which a military band plays marches. That is, the bass drummer hits the drum 120 times per minute, with a heavier downbeat or thump on the first and succeeding alternate beats. For parades or ceremonies, it makes for smarter appearance to have a short, snappy step and, if possible, a slightly accelerated cadence. Thus cadence should never fall below 120. When the band is not playing, individual foot movements during a ceremony, notably those by the adjutant when taking post, are traditionally executed at markedly accelerated cadence, with short steps.

Use of PA Systems and Amplifiers.   In general, except for the largest ceremonies and under special conditions, it is most unmilitary to employ a public address system for commands or other purposes incident to military ceremonies. Regimental and battalion commanders and adjutants should pride themselves on their voice of command and should, if necessary, practice to strengthen and increase its carrying power.

Stepping Off in Time with the Music.   Units must step off on the left foot, as is well known, and must accomplish this on command of the leader, and on the first beat of the music—a combination that often defeats inexperienced junior leaders, and one that you, as a Marine, must be prepared to perfect.

One method of achieving this result—which requires briefing your unit and some rehearsing but well worth it—is to give your preliminary command just in advance of the music, and have all hands drilled to step off automatically on the first note of the music, without any command of execution from you; in other words, to *let the first note of the music be the command of execution.* This is particularly effective on parade, after the commands have been given to pass in review.

For guard mounting, and for many other ceremonies where units march onto their parades to music, troops must be brought to right shoulder arms at the first note of "Adjutant's Call" and marched off at the first note of march music. This, too, requires coordination by leader and unit. A recommended sequence for these evolutions—"by the numbers"—is summarized as follows:

1. Bear in mind that Adjutant's Call is a sixteen-beat call, and the first note of march music therefore will be count seventeen.
2. The signal for the first note of Adjutant's Call is given by the drum major, who brings down the baton and can thus be seen by all hands.
3. Give your commands in time with Adjutant's Call, on successive beats as shown in this diagram, in which numbers correspond to beats in the call:

1	2	3	4
Right	Shoul-	der	Arms
5	6	7	8
	(troops execute the movement)		
9	10	11	12
	(pause)		
13	14	15	16
For-	ward	(pause)	March

4. Rehearse this a few times with music, and, in the old Marine phrase, "You've got it made."

Command of Mixed Detachments of Seamen and Marines.   When a mixed (or composite) detachment of seamen and Marines is formed for a parade, the Marines occupy their post of seniority and honor at the head of column or on right of line, *but* the senior line officer present, of the Marine Corps or the Navy, according to date of rank, commands the entire detachment. This rule does not apply when Navy and Marines form separate detachments. It usually occurs when a ship parades as a unit (of which the Marines form part).

Close Order Drill. The object of drill is to teach troops by exercise to obey orders, and to do so in the correct way. For this reason, slovenly drill is harmful. Close order drill is one foundation of discipline and esprit de corps. Well-executed, confident, precise ceremonial close order drill is therefore the foundation of success in ceremonies.

Uniform for Inspections, Parades, and Ceremonies. Where possible, undress or dress uniforms should be prescribed for inspections, parades, and ceremonies. Additionally, swords should be worn on such occasions in preference to pistols and belts. If blues are not authorized for the command, large medals may be prescribed on ceremonial occasions for wear with the service blouse.

Music Played during "Sound Off." At a review or parade, when a foreign visitor or officer of another service is being honored, the march played during "Sound Off" should if possible be one traditional to the officer's country or branch of service. At ceremonies conducted by Marine artillery units, "The Caisson Song" is normally played during "Sound Off." For a parade on the occasion of a Marine's retirement, it is a pleasant and appropriate courtesy to ascertain whether there is any particular march the officer would like to have played on "Sound Off." When several individuals are being so honored, the senior, of course, gets the choice. At the very end of a retirement ceremony, the band should play "Auld Lang Syne."

Law, order, duty and restraint, obedience, discipline . . .
— Rudyard Kipling, *M'Andrew's Hymn*

19

Notes on Military Justice

This chapter contains a general description of the system of military justice in force in the U.S. Marine Corps and, with minor differences, throughout all the U.S. armed forces. This chapter is not intended as an exhaustive review or as a source of legal authority; it merely covers some major points in military law. Because the military justice system is complex, technical, and, at times, inflexible, there can be no substitute for consultation with a knowledgeable individual. Should a substantive or procedural question arise, refer to your staff judge advocate or legal officer.

Military law governs individual conduct and performance of duty in the naval services. It also provides a means for enforcing the rules—nonjudicial punishment and trial by court-martial. As a Marine officer, you must be familiar with military law and its sources. It is part of the tradition of Marine Corps discipline that legal proceedings are conducted expeditiously, firmly, and expertly. Marine officers are frequently called upon to perform various legal functions, and they must set an example with their competence and knowledge.

1901. Sources of Military Law

The sources of military law include the Constitution of the United States, the Uniform Code of Military Justice (UCMJ), and other acts of Congress. The implementation and administration of these laws in the military is accomplished by the president, who has promulgated the *Manual for Courts-Martial (MCM)*

1984, and the secretary of the Navy, who has promulgated the *Manual of the Judge Advocate General of the Navy (JAG Manual).* These two manuals constitute the primary sources of military law that applies to the Navy and Marine Corps. You must be familiar with these publications and pertinent general orders.

Other sources of military law include: decisions of the Court of Military Appeals and Navy–Marine Corps Court of Military Review; directives from the president, secretary of defense, secretary of the Navy, and commandant of the Marine Corps; and customs and usage of the service.

1902. Civil and Military Law

In addition to being subject to the federal and state laws that bind all citizens of the United States, members of the armed forces are subject to a second body of law and a separate jurisprudence. This body of law includes the statutes and regulations setting forth the rights, liabilities, powers, and duties of officers and enlisted persons in the military services. Thus, members of the armed forces may be brought before civil or military tribunals and are generally answerable to both bodies of law. Breaches of the peace and other minor offenses by service personnel that violate both civilian and military law will often be tried by court-martial, although this does not exclude exercise of civil jurisdiction as well. When an offense violates state, federal, and military law at the same time—for example, a serious crime, such as murder—the authority that first obtains control over the offender may try him. For, just as civil courts may not interfere with military courts (other than by writ of *habeas corpus*), neither do military authorities have the power to interfere with civil courts.

A member of the Marine Corps accused of an offense against civil authority may, upon proper request, be delivered to the civil authority for trial. Regulations promulgated by the secretary of the Navy covering this are found in the *JAG Manual.*

In foreign countries, Marines are subject to the laws of those countries and may be tried and punished by foreign authorities. In certain countries, the United States has "status of forces agreements," which among other things prescribe conditions under which U.S. military personnel may be delivered to local authorities for trial in local courts (or, alternatively, tried by U.S. military courts). These agreements vary from country to country.

1903. Uniform Code of Military Justice (the Code)

On 5 May 1950, the Uniform Code of Military Justice (hereafter cited as the Code) was approved by President Harry S Truman. The authorities that, under the present revised Code, administer military justice are shown in Figure 19–1.

Instructions and Publication.   Certain articles of the Code must be carefully explained to every enlisted person entering active duty, then again after six months, and also when reenlisting. A complete text of the Code

Nonjudicial — Commanding Officer's Office Hours

Judicial — Court-Martial

	Nonjudicial: By commanding officer (Art. 15)	Nonjudicial: By officer in charge (Art. 15)	General (Art. 16)	Special (Art. 16)	Summary (Art. 16)
Members			Five or more members plus a military judge	Three or more members plus a military judge	One commissioned officer
Convening Authority			(Art. 22) (1) President of the United States (2) Secretary of a department (3) Commander in chief of a fleet, CO of a naval station or larger shore activity beyond limits of United States (4) CG of a Marine Corps division, separate brigade, separate wing, etc. (5) COs designated by the secretary of a department or the president.	(Art. 23) (1) Persons who may convene a general court-martial. (2) CO of any naval or Coast Guard vessel. (3) CO of any independent Marine Corps unit where members of that corps are on duty (4) COs and OsINC designated by the secretary of a department	(Art. 24) (1) Persons who may convene a general or special (2) CO or OINC when empowered by the secretary of a department.
Jurisdiction	(Art. 15) Officers and any other personnel in his or her command	(Art. 15) Enlisted personnel under his or her charge	(Art. 18) All persons subject to the code for all offenses made punishable by the code.	(Art. 19) All persons subject to the code for any non-capital offenses made punishable by the code; further for capital offenses under such regulations as the president may prescribe.	(Art. 20) All enlisted personnel subject to the code for any non-capital offense made punishable by the code unless the accused objects to trial thereby, in which case trial may be ordered by special or GCM.
Punishments and Limitations	(Art. 15) See list below		(Art. 18) Any punishment not forbidden by code including death when specified. President may prescribe limitations.	(Art. 19) Any punishment not forbidden by code except death, dishonorable discharge, dismissal, confinement in excess of 6 months, hard labor without confinement in excess of 3 month's confinement in excess of 3 month's pay per month or forfeiture of pay for a period exceeding 6 months. A BCD may be adjudged only if complete record of proceedings and testimony before the court has been made.	(Art. 20) Subject to presidential limitations any punishment not forbidden by code except death, dishonorable or bad conduct discharge, dismissal, confinement in excess of one month, hard labor without confinement in excess of 45 days, restriction in excess of two months, or forfeiture of pay in excess of ⅔ pay for one month.
Qualifications of Members			(Art. 25) Any officers on active duty shall be eligible to serve on all courts-martial. Any warrant officer on active duty shall be eligible to serve on general and special courts-martial for the trial of any person except an officer. Any enlisted person on active duty who is not a member of the same unit shall be eligible to serve on general and special courts-martial for the trial of any enlisted person if prior to the convening of the court the accused personally has requested in writing that enlisted persons serve on it. Upon such request the membership must include at least one-third enlisted personnel.		

PUNISHMENTS INCLUDING ADMONITIONS OR REPRIMANDS AS FOLLOWS

Officers and Warrant Officers

1 Restrictions to limits, with or without suspension from duty, for 30 days (60 days if by flag/general officer)
2 Arrest in quarters for 30 days (if imposed by flag/general officer in comd)
3 Forfeiture of ½ pay for 2 months (if imposed by flag/general officer in comd)
4 Detention of ½ pay for 3 months (if imposed by flag/general officer in comd)*

Enlisted

1 Three days' confinement on bread and water or diminished rations (if imposed on a man attached to or embarked in a vessel
2 Thirty days' correctional custody (limited to 7 days if imposed by officer below maj/ltcdr)
3 Forfeiture ½ pay for 2 months (limited to 7 days' pay if imposed by officer below maj/ltcdr).
4 Reduction: to next inferior rating (if imposed by officer below maj/ltcdr) or reduction to lowest or intermediate pay grade (by ltcdr/maj or above). Reduction may only be accomplished from grade within promotion authority of officer imposing punishment, and no person above E-4 may be reduced more than one grade.**
5 Forty-five days' extra duties (14 days if imposed by officer below maj/ltcdr).
6 Sixty days' restriction to limits with or without suspension from duty (4 days if imposed by officer below maj/ltcdr)
7 Detention of ½ pay for 3 months (14 days if imposed by officer below maj/ltcdr).*

*The president has excluded use of this punishment.
**The secretary of the Navy has limited reduction to one pay grade.

Figure 19–1: Administration of military justice under the Uniform Code of Military Justice (revised 1984)

must be available to every person on active duty in the armed forces of the United States.

At frequent intervals, the "punitive articles" (those dealing mainly with offenses and punishments) must be published to troops and posted so that the crew of a naval vessel and the personnel of shore stations may read them. This is known—in the old Navy phrase—as "reading the Rocks and Shoals."

Jurisdiction. All persons in the armed forces are subject to the Code. Reciprocal jurisdiction between services is provided, but the exercise of jurisdiction over a member of another service is limited to those circumstances prescribed by the president in the *Manual for Courts Martial,* that is, when a joint service command is specifically authorized to refer such cases or when manifest injury to the armed forces will result from the delivery of the accused to the accused member's service.

Rights of the Accused. In addition to the Constitutional rights enjoyed by all American citizens, an accused person under the Code has the right to be warned before interrogation of any suspected offense; the right to a preliminary investigation before trial for an offense; the right to challenge members of the court, both for cause and peremptorily; the right, if convicted, to testify under oath or to make an unsworn statement to the court regarding extenuating or mitigating matters; the right to forward a brief of matters that should be considered in review of the case; and the right to counsel at specified stages of the foregoing proceedings.

Review and Appeals. The Code establishes elaborate machinery and channels for review and appeal of courts-martial. In all cases the convening authority must take action to approve, remit, or suspend an adjudged sentence. The accused may waive appellate review by higher authority. If not waived, the case may be reviewed by various officers in the chain of command; by *Courts of Military Review* (composed of three or more officers or civilian lawyers qualified to practice before federal courts or before the highest court of a state); by the *judge advocate general of the Navy;* by the *Court of Military Appeals* (a court composed of five civilian judges); and by the U.S. Supreme Court.

Approval. Sentences of death must be approved by the president. Sentences dismissing an officer, cadet, or midshipman must be approved by the secretary of the Navy. Sentences to a dishonorable or bad-conduct discharge are not executed until appellate review is completed and the trial case affirmed by the Court of Military Review (unless appellate review has been waived).

Legal Duties. Officers who perform legal duties include the following.

The *staff judge advocate* is the senior Marine officer lawyer, certified in accordance with the Code, and performs the staff legal duties of a command.

A *judge advocate* is a Marine officer lawyer certified in accordance with the Code, to perform duties as trial and/or defense counsel. In addition, the judge advocate is authorized to review trial records of summary, special courts-martial, and general courts-martial.

A *military judge* is a judge, appointed by the judge advocate general of the

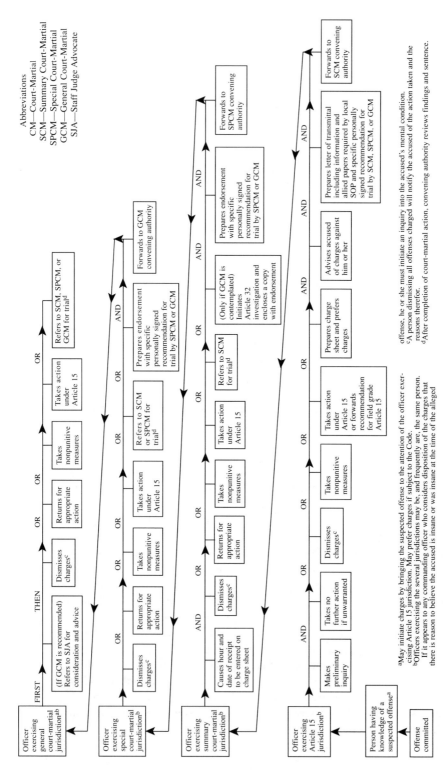

Figure 19–2: Disposition of a case under the Uniform Code of Military Justice

Navy, who serves on general and special courts-martial in a capacity similar to that of a civilian judge. If the accused requests and the military judge consents, a military judge may sit as a one-officer court-martial to determine the issue of guilt or innocence and adjudge sentence if found guilty.

An *initial review officer* is a disinterested and detached officer who reviews command decisions to confine individuals prior to trial by court-martial. Not later than seven days after imposition of pretrial confinement, the initial review officer must determine whether confinement will continue or the Marine will be released.

A *legal assistance officer* is a Marine officer lawyer designated by the commander to give legal advice to members of the command on personal legal problems involving civilian law generally.

A *legal officer* is an officer (nonlawyer) designated by a commanding officer to perform legal duties, of purely military nature, within the command. This officer does not render legal assistance (see above), but can answer questions regarding the Code.

1904.   Common Offenses and the Small Unit

The Punitive Articles.   Articles 77–134 of the Code ("the Rocks and Shoals") divide punishable offenses into three general groups: (1) crimes common to both civil and military law, such as murder, rape, arson, burglary, larceny, sodomy, and frauds against the United States; (2) purely military offenses arising out of military duties and having no counterpart in civilian life, such as desertion, willful disobedience of lawful orders of superior officers and noncommissioned officers, misbehavior before the enemy, and sleeping on watch; and (3) a general group of offenses based on two articles that do not specify any particular acts of misconduct but cover a variety of transgressions harmful to the service in general terms. Article 133 applies only to officers and midshipmen. It makes punishable "conduct unbecoming an officer."

Article 134 applies to all persons who are subject to military law. Offenses punishable under this article include disorders and neglects prejudicial to good order and discipline, conduct tending to bring discredit upon the armed forces, and crimes and offenses covered by federal laws other than the Uniform Code of Military Justice. This general article ensures that there will be no failure of justice simply because an offense is not specifically mentioned in an article of the Code.

Among the foregoing punitive articles, those frequently violated include:

85:    Desertion
86:    Unauthorized absence
87:    Missing ship or unit movement
92:    Disobedience of orders, dereliction of duty
107:    False official statement
108:    Unlawful disposition of government property

111: Drunken or reckless driving
112a: Wrongful use, possession of controlled substances
113: Drunk or asleep on watch, or quitting post without proper relief
121: Larceny, wrongful appropriation
128: Assault
132: Fraud against the United States
134: General article (conduct to prejudice of good order and discipline; scandalous conduct).

Offenses in the Small Unit. As a company officer, you should familiarize yourself with the most commonly encountered offenses, mainly order violations, which arise within the platoon or company/battery. These are:

86: Unauthorized absence
89: Disrespect toward superior commissioned officer
90: Assaulting or disobeying a superior commissioned officer
91: Insubordinate conduct toward warrant officer, noncommissioned or petty officer
92: Failure to obey orders or regulations
112a: Drug offenses
113: Drunk or asleep on watch
121: Larceny and wrongful appropriation
128: Assaults.

In order to deal effectively with the above offenses, you should familiarize yourself with the elements that form each, together with the possible defenses against such charges. Otherwise, you cannot effectively use the Code as a tool for maintaining effective discipline.

1905. Investigations, Warnings, and Evidence

Criminal investigations of felonies and other serious offenses are performed by the Naval Investigative Service (NIS) and the Criminal Investigation Division (CID) of the provost marshal. There are two types of investigations relating to offenses that are frequently performed within the chain of command: preliminary inquiries (preliminary to an Article 15 hearing, see below) and Article 32 investigations, which are preliminary to a general court-martial. Since the latter is normally performed by a field grade officer, it lies beyond the purview of this *Guide*.

Preliminary inquiries are a common occurrence within units and should thus be understood by all officers. Typically, within the Marine division, a company commander who receives a report of misconduct directs that a preliminary inquiry be conducted by an officer or staff NCO of the command. The purpose is to provide the CO with sufficient information so that he or she can intelligently dispose of the case. Depending on the CO's wishes, the inquiry may be oral or written.

What you are looking for in a preliminary inquiry boils down to three elements: (1) Has any offense chargeable under the Code been committed? (2) Who committed it? (3) What is the gravity of the offense in light of the circumstances?

Your job is not to perfect a case or "hang" an accused but to collect all evidence, favorable or unfavorable, to enable your commander to dispose of the matter.

A preliminary inquiry is inherently informal. It is up to you to go out and get the information. Likely places to start include the logbook of the OD, military police "blotter," civilian police, hospitals and dispensaries, judges advocate, and witnesses otherwise identified. What you learn should be distilled into findings of fact, together (if requested by the CO) with any opinions or recommendations arising out of the inquiry.

Warnings. Because both the Constitution and Article 31 of the Code protect a Marine from being forced to incriminate oneself, every accused or suspect must be fully warned of certain rights or evidence that has been obtained cannot be used against the individual. Such a warning should inform the individual of the following:

- The nature of the offense of which the individual is suspected
- That the individual has an absolute right to remain silent
- That any statement made may be used against the individual in any subsequent trial or proceeding
- That the individual has the right to consult a lawyer and have counsel present during all questioning and that he or she may seek counsel's advice before answering any question
- That the individual may obtain a civilian lawyer at his or her own expense
- That if the individual cannot afford or does not desire civilian counsel, he or she may have a military lawyer at no cost
- That the individual may discontinue an interrogation at any time at his or her own option.

Evidence. Without attempting to summarize the laws of evidence, which are precise and complex, it is enough to say that even junior officers should be familiar with them for two reasons: (1) evidence that is obtained in any manner contrary to law generally cannot be used against an offender; and (2) much evidence is originally uncovered, either at first instance (for example, by an OD) or during preliminary inquiry, by junior nonlawyer line officers—that is, you. Thus the admissibility (which is to say, the usability) of evidence often depends on correct decisions at the outset, based on your knowledge of the rules.

Two kinds of searches that frequently turn up evidence are: (1) the limited search of an individual and the immediate area, incident to a lawful apprehension based upon probable cause; and (2) searches authorized by a commanding officer on probable cause within the command (that is, a barracks). The laws of search, which are part of those of evidence, are also precise and complex, but you should be acquainted with them. Many an otherwise well-founded case has failed because an officer has conducted an overbroad or otherwise improper search, which in turn denies admissibility of evidence so obtained.

NONJUDICIAL PUNISHMENT

1906. Convening Nonjudicial Punishment (CO's Office Hours)

Commanding officers and officers-in-charge are authorized by Article 15 to impose nonjudicial punishment (at "Office Hours" in the Corps, "Captain's Mast" in the Navy) upon members of their command. Under Article 15, a commanding officer is defined as a commissioned or warrant officer who, by virtue of rank and assignment, exercises primary command authority over a military organization or prescribed territorial area, which under pertinent military directives is recognized as a command. Under the law, distinctions are made between officers in command, with progressively increased limitations on their powers, as follows. Flag and general officers in command and officers having general court-martial jurisdiction have the greatest scope of nonjudicial punishment. Among commanding officers not in the foregoing class, those of or above the rank of major/lieutenant commander have considerably increased authority over that possessed by COs of company grade and officers-in-charge (see Figure 19–1).

Nonjudicial punishment is a disciplinary measure more serious than administrative corrective measures but less serious than trial by court-martial. Nonjudicial punishment provides an essential and prompt means of maintaining good order and discipline and also promotes positive behavior in Marines without incurring the stigma of a court-martial.

Preliminary Report and Investigation. The customary procedure for putting a Marine on report is as follows.

An officer may submit a report against a Marine directly to the executive officer or adjutant of the command concerned. Otherwise a written report is sent up the accused's chain of command to the executive officer or the adjutant, giving the name of the offender, the offense charged, the name of the NCO making the charge, and any witnesses.

The executive officer or adjutant makes, or causes to be made by the offender's company commander, the provost-marshal, or other responsible person, a thorough investigation of the charges. (See Section 1905 for details on the conduct of the preliminary inquiry, or investigation into an offense.) For company-level proceedings, see Figure 19–3.

At company level each morning, the first sergeant informs the commanding officer of Marines placed on report during the preceding day. At battalion level, this is done by the executive officer or adjutant.

Officer offenses, when they occur, are by custom the province of battalion commanders or higher. They are dealt with by special reports and handled separately and privately.

Unit Punishment Book (UPB).   Every unit whose commander has Article 15 powers must keep a Unit Punishment Book, which is simply a record of each case considered at Office Hours. The UPB also records each individual's acknowledgement that he or she has been apprised of the individual's rights under Articles 15 and 31 and his or her waiver of right to trial by court-martial. The first sergeant or sergeant major takes care of this prior to Office Hours and obtains the individual's initials in the appropriate spaces in the UPB. At this time, the accused is also told that, although he or she has no right to legal representation at Office Hours, the individual may obtain a personal representative to speak in his or her behalf and also call witnesses and cross-examine witnesses against the accused.

The UPB is an important administrative record, which is liable to inspection at any time, incident to a case, or by higher authority or the IG. A sloppy or improperly kept UPB can get you into trouble.

1907.   Office Hours Procedure

Office Hours, as we have seen, is the Marine Corps equivalent of Mast. Like Mast, Office Hours can be, and frequently is, devoted to nondisciplinary matters such as praise, special requests, and the like. Here, however, we are concerned only with the legal and disciplinary aspects of Office Hours. Bear in mind that Office Hours is not merely an administrative procedure but also a ceremony intended to dramatize praise and admonition. Like any ceremony, it should be dignified, disciplined, especially set apart in the daily routine, and carefully planned (see Section 1610).

Office Hours should be:
- Held at a set time and in a set place, usually the office of the commanding officer
- Attended by immediate commanding officers and first sergeants (or platoon sergeants if within a company) of those required to appear, whether for praise, reproof, or request
- Supervised by the adjutant and sergeant major if at battalion level, otherwise by the company first sergeant
- Held in full, immaculate uniform of the day.

Every officer attending Office Hours should review the cases of personal concern. If one of your Marines is up, take a careful look at the Marine's service record and talk with the squad leader and platoon sergeant. Assure yourself that your Marine is in tip-top condition as to uniform, cleanliness, and military demeanor. If you yourself hold Office Hours, be sure to review the service records and individual cases before you call in the individuals concerned. This does not mean that you should prejudge the case in any sense of the word. However, it does ensure that you focus your thoughts on the Marine and on the case.

Under the provisions of Paragraph 4, Part V, *Manual for Courts Martial,* 1984, a Marine receiving Office Hours has the right to personally appear at the

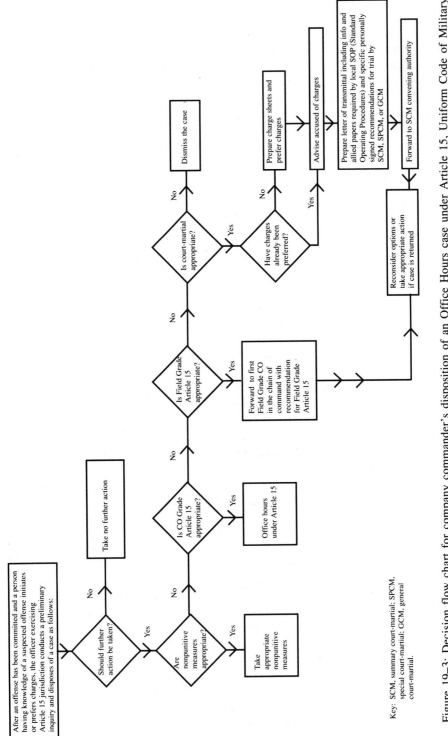

Figure 19–3: Decision flow chart for company commander's disposition of an Office Hours case under Article 15, Uniform Code of Military Justice

hearing or waive appearance and submit written matters for the CO's consideration. To make an impression on the Marine, the CO may desire that the Marine be present for the hearing or at least for announcing punishment, even when appearance has been waived. In such cases, the Marine will be ordered to be present but cannot be forced to participate in the proceedings.

Here is a typical Office Hours procedure:

1. Ten minutes before the scheduled time, the sergeant major (first sergeant) assembles all who are to appear, together with any enlisted witnesses and the respective first (or platoon) sergeants, who bring the service records (if these are not already in the hands of the sergeant major). At the same time, immediately commanding officers and any officer witnesses report to the adjutant, who conducts the officers into the commanding officer's office, where they are then seated.

2. At the appointed time, the adjutant (or company executive officer) stands on the left of the commanding officer with relevant documents; these should be opened, tabbed appropriately for ready reference. First (platoon) sergeants stand in a group to one side. The sergeant major (first sergeant) conducts in the first accused and reads aloud the charge or report against the accused, while the adjutant (executive officer) places the documents before the CO. The accused stands uncovered and at attention throughout, one pace in front of the commanding officer's desk.

3. After the charges have been read, the CO must be satisfied that the accused understands his or her rights under Articles 15 and 31, UCMJ, and, as a matter of prudence, should again warn the Marine as follows: "Private _____, you do not have to make any statement regarding the offense of which you are accused or suspected. I must warn you that under Article 31 of the Code any statement made by you may be used as evidence against you in a trial by court-martial. Also that, if you so desire, you have the right to a trial by court-martial rather than accept nonjudicial punishment here at Office Hours. Do you understand? What have you to say?" This gives the accused a chance to tell that individual's side of the case if desired. Witnesses may be called—usually the reporting officer and witnesses to the offense. The accused must not be compelled to make a statement, nor does the accused have to admit guilt or produce evidence.

4. After all explanations have been heard and the commanding officer has considered the report of preliminary investigation, the CO has four courses of action (see Figures 19–2 and 19–3):
   - Dismiss the accused, either accepting the explanation or giving a warning.
   - Award nonjudicial punishment.
   - Order the accused to be tried by special or summary court-martial (or recommend such trial, if the CO is not authorized to convene these courts).
   - For a very serious offense, order or recommend that an investigation be conducted under Article 32 to determine whether the accused should be tried by general court-martial. An Article 32 or pretrial investigation must

be conducted before a case can be referred to a general court-martial.
5. At the conclusion of the hearing, the sergeant major (first sergeant) commands, "About FACE, Forward MARCH." On the command "MARCH," the person marches out of the office, and the process is repeated in the next case.

When meritorious cases (such as presentation of Good Conduct Medals, promotions, or special commendations) are involved, disciplinary cases should be paraded in the rear of the CO's office, to watch the proceedings. They are then marched out and individually brought in again as described above.

1908. Appeal from Nonjudicial Punishment

When nonjudicial punishment is imposed at Office Hours, the Marine must be informed of the right to appeal the punishment to the immediate superior in command if he or she feels (1) the punishment is unjust; or (2) it is disproportionate to the offense. This appeal must be in writing and must be presented within five days. A Marine who has appealed may be required to undergo any punishment imposed while the appeal is pending, except that if action is not taken on the appeal within five days after the appeal was submitted, and if the Marine so requests, any unexecuted punishment involving restraint or extra duty will be stayed until action on the appeal is taken. The immediate superior in command (or the officer who imposed punishment) may, at any point, suspend probationally any part of the unexecuted punishment or remit, mitigate, or set it aside.

1909. Limits of Nonjudicial Punishment

At Office Hours, under Article 15, the commanding officer, in addition to, or in lieu of, admonition or reprimand, may impose one, or certain combinations, of the sentences which are given below:
Upon officers and warrant officers:
1. by any commanding officer—restriction to specified limits, with or without suspension from duty, for not more than thirty consecutive days
2. if imposed by an officer exercising general court-martial jurisdiction or an officer of general or flag rank in command
   * arrest in quarters for not more than thirty consecutive days
   * forfeiture of not more than one-half of one month's pay per month for two months
   * restriction to specified limits, with or without suspension from duty, for not more than sixty consecutive days.
Upon other military personnel of the command:
3. by any commander:
   * if imposed upon a person attached to or embarked in a vessel, confinement on bread and water or diminished rations for not more than three consecutive days
   * correctional custody for not more than seven consecutive days

- forfeiture of not more than seven days' pay
- reduction to the next inferior grade, if the grade from which demoted is within the promotion authority of the officer imposing the reduction or any officer subordinate to the one who imposes the reduction
- extra duties, including fatigue or other duties, for not more than fourteen consecutive days
- restriction to specified limits, with or without suspension from duty, for not more than fourteen consecutive days

4. if imposed by a commanding officer of the grade of major or lieutenant commander or above:

- if imposed upon a person attached to or embarked in a vessel, confinement on bread and water or diminished rations for not more than three consecutive days
- correctional custody for not more than thirty consecutive days
- forfeiture of not more than one-half of one month's pay per month for two months
- reduction to the lowest or any intermediate pay grade, if the grade from which demoted is within the promotion authority of the officer imposing the reduction or any officer subordinate to the one who imposes the reduction, but enlisted members in pay grades above E-4 may not be reduced more than one pay grade, except that during time of war or national emergency this category of persons may be reduced two grades if the secretary concerned determines that circumstances require the removal of this limitation
- extra duties, including fatigue or other duties, for not more than forty-five consecutive days
- restriction to specified limits, with or without suspension from duty, for not more than sixty consecutive days

Although the law permits reduction of more than one pay grade, Navy Department regulations provide that no person can be reduced more than one grade at a nonjudicial punishment. Even more important as far as Marines are concerned, *no staff NCO may be reduced nonjudicially at Office Hours under Article 15 of the Code, except by the commandant, as the commandant is the only one who has the authority to promote a staff NCO.*

On the point as to who may impose commanding officer's punishment aboard ship, only the captain has such power *over members of the ship's company* (the Marine detachment included), even though the title of the CO, Marine detachment, is also that of commanding officer. On the other hand, the disciplinary authority of the commanding officer of an embarked, separate organization of Marines (a floating battalion, for example) remains unaffected whether afloat or not, insofar as members of the CO's command are concerned (see Section 1013).

Office Hours punishment is not considered as a conviction insofar as the offender's record is concerned. Remember, also, that under no circumstances may an offender awarded extra duty be placed on guard to work it off. And do not forget to keep the unit record of nonjudicial punishment as required by the Code and departmental regulations.

NAVAL COURTS-MARTIAL

1910. Summary Courts-Martial

Summary courts-martial may be convened by any person who may convene a general or special court-martial, the CO of all battalions and squadrons, and the commanding officers or officers-in-charge of any other commands, when empowered by the secretary of the Navy.

A summary court-martial (SCM) consists of one commissioned officer, whenever practicable not below the rank of captain, USMC, or equivalent. This officer will be of the same armed force as the accused, although the Navy and the Marine Corps are considered the same service for this purpose. When only one officer is attached to a command, the commanding officer will be the summary court-martial, in which case no convening order is required. The summary court-martial officer is not sworn but performs his or her duty under the overall sanction of the oath of office.

Commissioned officers, warrant officers, cadets, midshipmen, and those accused of capital offenses cannot be tried by summary court-martial. Witnesses testify under oath. Examination is conducted by the summary court-martial officer. Rules of evidence are binding.

Right to Counsel.   The accused at a summary court-martial does not have the right to counsel. If the accused hires civilian counsel, that counsel will be permitted to represent the accused if it will not delay the proceeding unreasonably and if military exigencies do not preclude it.

Limits of Punishment.   Summary courts-martial may adjudge any sentence not in excess of confinement at hard labor for one month, forfeiture of two-thirds pay per month for one month, and reduction to pay grade E-1. Within specified guidelines, restriction for up to sixty days, hard labor without confinement for forty-five days, or three days on bread and water may be substituted for or combined with hard labor with confinement at hard labor or each other. Enlisted Marines above pay grade E-4 will not be reduced more than one pay grade and cannot be adjudged confinement or hard labor without confinement. An admonishment or reprimand may be adjudged in all cases.

Objection to Trial by the Accused.   No person may be tried by summary court-martial over his or her objection. Each person must consent to the trial or the case is returned to the convening authority for further action.

Record.   The record of a summary court-martial is written on a standard record of summary court-martial form (DD Form 2329). Detailed instructions and examples of the record of trial are found in the *MCM*. The accused has seven days after the sentence is announced to submit matters to the convening authority. The convening authority can then act to approve or disapprove the findings and sentence. An entry reflecting trial by SCM is also made in the Marine's service record book.

1911. Special Courts-Martial

Special courts-martial may be convened by any of the officers shown in Figure 19–1 and, specifically insofar as the Marine Corps is concerned, by any officer with general court-martial authority; any general officer in command; commanding officer of any battalion or squadron; directors of Marine Corps Districts, commanding officer of any Marine brigade, regiment, detached battalion, or corresponding unit; commanding officer of any aircraft group, separate squadron, station, base, or Marine barracks; commanding officer of any independent Marine Corps unit or organization where members of the Corps are on duty; any inspector-instructor; and by any other CO or officer-in-charge when so designated by the secretary of the Navy. A special court-martial may try officers or enlisted persons for any offenses (except capital) that the convening authority deems appropriate.

A special court-martial is composed of a military judge, optionally with not less than three members, who may be commissioned officers, warrant officers, or (if the accused is an enlisted person and so requests) enlisted persons of any of the services, including members of the National Oceanic and Atmospheric Administration and the Public Health Service, when assigned to and serving with the armed forces.*

When a full special court-martial sits, the function of the members (sometimes called "the panel") is to determine guilt or innocence and adjudge sentence. The senior member of the court, usually a major or higher—even though no longer presiding (which is the judge's duty)—is called the president.

The trial counsel conducts the prosecution's case; the defense counsel acts as defense attorney for the accused. In the naval services, a reporter transcribes the testimony and keeps the record under guidance of the trial counsel. The bailiff acts as guard and messenger and, if need be, escorts the accused.

If an accused enlisted person requests in writing that enlisted members be included in the special court-martial trying the case, at least one-third of the members must be enlisted, unless that many cannot be obtained. Enlisted members cannot be from the same unit as the accused. When enlisted members cannot be obtained, the trial may still be held, but convening authority must give the reasons in writing. No member of a court-martial should be junior to the accused, and warrant officers or enlisted persons may not, under any circumstances, sit as members for the trial of an officer.†

---

*An accused has the option in both general and special courts-martial to request trial by military judge alone, in which case the judge alone hears arguments, adjudges guilt, and hands down sentence. In this case, there are no other members of the court.

†While the law provides for a variant form of special court without military judge and with diminished powers, it is the policy of the Marine Corps that all Marine special courts shall have military judges and full powers. For that reason, this *Guide* omits other reference to the lesser type of court.

1912.   General Courts-Martial

General.   The highest naval court, the general court-martial, may be convened by the president; the secretary of the Navy; the commandant of the Marine Corps; the commanding generals of the Fleet Marine Forces; the commanding general of any corps, division, aircraft wing, or brigade; the commander in chief of a fleet; the commanding officer of a naval station or large shore activity beyond the continental limits of the United States; any general officer or immediate successor in command of a unit or activity of the Marine Corps, and such commanding officers as may be authorized by the president and the secretary of the Navy. General courts may try anyone who is subject to the Code and award any punishment authorized by law (see Table 19–1).

Composition.   A general court-martial is composed of not less than five officers (one-third enlisted members, if an enlisted accused so requests). A military judge serves with each general court-martial. The president should be a senior officer. Unless unavoidable, all members should be senior to the accused.

Investigation of Charges.   Charges may not be referred to a general court-martial unless they have been formally investigated or such investigation has been waived by the accused. This investigation may be ordered by court-martial convening authority. The officer conducting the investigation should be of field grade and should possess legal training and experience. The investigating officer's job is neither to build up nor to whitewash a case, but simply to ascertain the facts thoroughly and impartially under Article 32 of the Code.

Proceedings.   A general court-martial is conducted with special military formality. The military judge presides, while trial counsel prosecutes and defense counsel defends.

Although special courts have jurisdiction to try officers, by custom of the Marine Corps, officer cases are reserved for general court-martial. All cases involving a sentence to death must be approved by the president before that portion of the sentence is executed. Dismissal of a commissioned officer, cadet, or midshipman may be approved and ordered executed only by the secretary of the service concerned or designated under secretary.

1913.   Duty as a Court Member

Second lieutenants rarely serve as court members, but first lieutenants and captains often do. Despite the importance of this duty, no special preparation is required. Your one big responsibility as a member is to be there, smartly turned out in the prescribed uniform, prepared to look and be alert. From the time court convenes until it finally adjourns, no matter how pressing may be your regular duties, your duty as a member is primary and comes first.

As trial progresses, the military judge will explain all applicable points of law. Your job is to listen to the evidence adduced by both sides, determine the facts fairly and impartially, and then apply the law, on which the judge will

Table 19–1.   Court-martial punishments

Type of Punishment	General Court-Martial	Special Court-Martial	Summary Court-Martial
Bad conduct discharge (enlisted only)	Yes	Yes	No
Confinement	Yes	Yes (enlisted only; not in excess of 6 months)	Yes (only enlisted below 5th pay grade; not in excess of 1 month)
Bread and water*	Yes	Yes	Yes
Death	Yes	No	No
Dishonorable discharge (warrant officers and enlisted only)	Yes	No	No
Dismissal (officers only)	Yes	No	No
Fines	Yes	Yes	Yes
Forfeiture	Yes	Yes (not in excess of ⅔ pay per month for 6 months)	Yes (not in excess of ⅔ of 1 month's pay)
Hard labor (without confinement— enlisted only)	Yes (not in excess of 3 months)	Yes (not in excess of 3 months)	Yes (not in excess of 45 days; only enlisted below 5th pay grade)
Life imprisonment	Yes	No	No
Loss of numbers, lineal position, seniority	Yes (seniority only)	No	No
Reduction of officer	No	No	No
Reduction to lowest enlisted grade	Yes	Yes	Yes (only enlisted below 5th pay grade)
Reprimand	Yes	Yes	Yes
Restriction to limits	Yes (not in excess of 2 months)	Yes (not in excess of 2 months)	Yes (not in excess of 2 months)

* Subject to various administrative limits; enlisted personnel only.

have instructed you, to the facts as you see them. Every member has an equal vote regardless of grade. You may not divulge your deliberations.

1914. Role of Counsel

Counsel on both sides before Marine Corps courts-martial must be qualified judge advocates.

Trial counsel prosecutes cases for the government, but he or she is more than a prosecutor; the trial counsel has a responsibility to help the court develop the truth and safeguard the rights of the accused. You will often have dealings with trial counsel in preparation for cases in which you may have conducted an inquiry or investigation or may be called as a witness.

Defense counsel conducts the defense, to which every accused is entitled. It is the duty of defense counsel:

- To undertake the defense regardless of personal opinion as to the guilt of the accused
- To disclose to the accused any interest the defense counsel may have in connection with the case, or any ground of possible disqualification, and any other matter that might influence the accused in the selection of counsel
- To represent the accused with undivided fidelity
- Not to divulge the secrets or confidence of the accused

1915. Arrest, Restriction, and Conditions on Liberty

When charged with an offense, anyone subject to the Code may be subjected to pretrial restraint (moral or physical restraint) as follows: conditions on liberty, restriction in lieu of arrest, arrest, or confinement. These are administrative acts, not punishment.

Conditions on liberty are imposed by orders directing a person to do or refrain from doing certain acts.

Restriction in lieu of arrest is the restraint of a person by oral or written orders directing the person to remain within specified limits; a restricted person shall perform full military duties unless otherwise directed.

Arrest is the restraint of a person by oral or written orders directing the person to remain within specified limits; a person in the status of arrest may not be required to perform full military duties.

Confinement is physical restraint depriving a person of freedom.

Pretrial restraint should be no more rigorous than the circumstances require. Pretrial restraint is not punishment and should not be used as such. Personnel should not be placed in confinement pending trial by court-martial unless it is foreseeable that (1) the individual will not appear at trial or will engage in serious criminal conduct and (2) less severe forms of restraint are inadequate. Personnel in pretrial confinement may not be subjected to punishment (including hard labor). They must be visited periodically to ascertain their condition and to care for their needs.

An officer under arrest must remain within the limits assigned; an arrested officer arrested cannot officially visit commanding officer or other superior officer unless sent for, or on approval of a written request for a meeting.

An officer under arrest should not ordinarily be deprived of the use of any part of the ship or post to which the officer had access before arrest. But, on board ship, if suspended from duty, an arrested officer may not visit the ship's bridge or quarterdeck, except in case of danger to the ship.

You should distinguish between pretrial restraints, which are discussed, and the officer punishment, awarded by a commanding officer, of restriction to limits, suspension from duty, or arrest in quarters—all generically known in the Naval Services as "hack." An officer in such status is spoken of as being "under hack." (See Section 1909.)

Physical Restraints.   As an officer of the day, you will frequently have the decision of arresting, apprehending, or confining enlisted people, and, on certain occasions, of applying such physical restraints as irons or straitjackets, whose use is carefully restricted by Navy Regulations and other instructions.

On probable cause to believe that an offense has been committed, any of the following may apprehend (arrest) any enlisted person: (1) officers; (2) warrant officers; (3) NCOs; (4) enlisted personnel on duty as military police. As OD, you may apprehend and also confine. Orders for confinement (which you may receive from a commanding officer) may be oral or written, direct or conveyed through a staff officer.

You (as an OD) are required by the Code to accept any prisoner brought in to you by a commissioned officer with a signed, written report of an offense. Not later than your relief as officer of the day, you must report to the commanding officer the full details of any such confinements.

Instruments of restraint (handcuffs, for example) can never be used for punishment. They are authorized only for safe custody and no longer than is strictly required: (1) to prevent escape during transfer; (2) on medical grounds certified by the medical officer; or (3) by order of the CO or officer-in-charge to prevent a Marine from injuring himself or herself.

OTHER CONVENING BODIES

1916. Courts of Inquiry and Investigation

General. Courts of inquiry and investigation (sometimes called "*JAG Manual* investigations") are administrative fact-finding bodies convened by commanders under the regulations of the *Manual of the Judge Advocate General.*

They perform no real judicial function and are in no sense the trial of an issue or of an accused person. They are convened to inform the convening authority of the facts involved. The court of inquiry is the most formal fact-finding body and is used for the most serious matters, for example: loss of life under peculiar circumstances; a serious fire; loss, stranding, or serious casualty to a ship of the Navy; or major loss or damage to government property.

In case of loss of life, a medical officer should be a member of the court of inquiry or investigation. The investigating body must determine, if possible, whether death was caused through the intent, fault, negligence, or inefficiency of any person in the naval services. No opinion will be expressed, however, regarding the misconduct and line-of-duty status of an individual in the report of investigation of his or her death or any endorsement thereon.

Type of Fact-Finding Bodies. There are three types of *JAG Manual* investigations: court of inquiry, board of investigation, and single individual investigations.

Court of Inquiry. The court of inquiry is the formal fact-finding body of the naval services. It may be convened by anyone authorized to convene a general court-martial or by anyone else designated by the secretary of the Navy. A court of inquiry consists of three or more commissioned officers and a commissioned officer as counsel for the court. Any person whose conduct is subject to inquiry shall be designated as a party to the inquiry. Any person who has a direct interest in the subject of inquiry may request to be designated as a party. Any person so designated must be advised and accorded the right (among other rights) to be present, to be represented by counsel, to testify or remain silent, to cross-examine witnesses, and to introduce evidence. Witnesses may be summoned to be examined upon oath before courts of inquiry just as for courts-martial. Courts of inquiry return findings of fact and do not express opinions or make recommendations unless required to do so by the convening authority.

Board of Investigation.   A board of investigation consists of two or more officers, one of whom should be of field grade. Such boards are usually convened by battalion or more senior commanders. Proceedings may be either formal or informal; the board has authority to examine witnesses, to receive depositions and other documents, and to make such findings, together with such opinions and recommendations, as may be directed by the convening authority. Do not confuse reports of such proceedings (or of individual investigations) with certain reports required by *Navy Regulations* or with reports of investigations conducted by the inspector general.

Investigations.   An investigation, consisting of an informal proceeding conducted by one or more officers, may be ordered by any commander with Article 15 powers. Save that it is nonpunitive and thus outside the disciplinary process, it is not unlike the preliminary inquiry into an offense, as described earlier in this chapter. The conduct of an investigation may well be one of your earliest legal assignments on your own, so it behooves you to handle it in competent fashion.*

Lost, Damaged, or Destroyed Government Property.   A common form of investigation often falling to junior officers is an investigation into the loss, damage, or destruction of government property. When such an investigation falls to your lot, it is imperative that you first consult *Marine Corps Supply Manual, Vol. I,* which supplements the *JAG Manual* with much special information.

1917. Administrative Discharge Boards

These boards, convened by officers with general court-martial jurisdiction, hear cases of individuals whose separation from the Corps by administrative dis-

---

*An important part of any investigation dealing with death, injury, or individual performance of a Marine (for example, a serious traffic accident involving a government vehicle) is to determine whether it took place in line of duty or involved individual misconduct. Such findings have wide repercussions in subsequent handling of claims against the government, determinations by the Department of Veterans Affairs, and so on. For this reason, the responsibility of an investigation or board of investigation is heavier than may at first seem to be the case.

charge (as distinct from a punitive discharge) has been recommended. The *Marine Corps Separation Manual* requires that the board consist of at least three officers, one of which must be field grade. Junior officers may serve as board members and frequently have to appear before such boards as witnesses.

In general terms, the board, like an investigation, seeks to determine facts and, based on these, recommends either that a Marine be retained in the Corps or that he or she be given an administrative discharge of a character and type recommended by the board.

Law is a regulation in accord with reason,
issued by a lawful superior, for the common good.
　　　　　　　　　—Thomas Aquinas, *Summa Theologica*

20

Housekeeping

In military parlance, the term "housekeeping" connotes the humdrum but necessary stewardship of administration, services, and maintenance that a unit requires for day-to-day existence. Housekeeping thus embraces such matters as police and maintenance, food service management, supply and property, clothing, equipment, transportation, pay, post exchange, and special services. Afloat, housekeeping focuses especially on cleanliness and upkeep.

The organization where housekeeping is below par finds itself perpetually beset with irksome disorders and nagging minor problems. A prerequisite to tactical efficiency is housekeeping so streamlined that the unit can pursue its military missions unhampered by distracting administrative demands.

Good housekeeping characterizes a smart, professional command and is expected of every Marine.

2001. Police and Maintenance

Police and maintenance are the janitorial side of administration. Except on large posts, both functions come under a single officer. "Police" has to do with tidiness and good order; "maintenance" means upkeep.

Every unit, afloat or ashore, designates a *police sergeant,* a noncommissioned officer who supervises cleaning details, trash collection, minor repair, and upkeep. Despite the title, the police sergeant may be any rank from corporal up. This NCO should be selected by virtue of cost-consciousness, powers of observation, forceful character, ability to work independently, ingenuity, and tinkering bent. The police sergeant is the key person in your unit's housekeeping setup.

The police sergeant's workshop is known as "the police shed." This is anything from a storeroom to a separate building that houses tools, scrap materials, cleaning gear, paint, and salvaged items, which an energetic police sergeant will habitually recover wherever found adrift. As can be realized, the police shed, properly administered, may resemble a miser's lair.

The labor force for police details comes from varying sources. Except in small organizations, the police sergeant has one or more assistants, ordinarily jackleg artificers known collectively as "the police gang." The police gang is supplemented by working details of prisoners from the brig and by those awarded extra duties. Much of the effectiveness of extra duties as a disciplinary measure depends on the personality and executive abilities of the police sergeant. If the supply of malefactors is inadequate, the first sergeant supplies working parties from those available. Needless to say, close liaison should be maintained between the first sergeant, the police sergeant, and the gunnery sergeant.

When police and maintenance efforts bulk sufficiently, a unit or station *maintenance officer* (see Section 802) is detailed. The duties, on enlarged scale, are much the same as those of the police sergeant. Whenever the commanding officer conducts an inspection, he or she is accompanied, among others, by the maintenance officer (if there is one) and the police sergeant.

2002.   Subsistence and Mess Management

"An army travels on its belly," wrote Napoleon, and so does the Marine Corps. There is no more direct way to the heart of a Marine than through the stomach. This being the case, every officer must know the rules and arts of food service management, which are set forth in the *Marine Corps Manual* and presented in greater detail in the *Marine Corps Supply Manual* and in the *Marine Corps Subsistence Manual.*

A word is in order to describe how messes are organized. The term "mess" refers to the enlisted dining facility, where enlisted members of the command are fed, rather than any of the various types of officers' mess. Marine Corps messes today mainly operate on a cafeteria system.

The dining facility and its management represent one of the most important responsibilities of command. The commanding officer must ensure without fail that the troops are served meals which, in the traditional officer of the day logbook phrase, are "well served and well prepared, of good quality, and sufficient in quantity."

On large posts with several separate messes, and in Marine divisions and aircraft wings, a *consolidated food service system* is employed. This simply means that all messes are centralized for operations, under a single *food service officer*; that a central butcher shop is maintained; and that central storage is provided for dry stores and other mess supplies. In addition, the food services officer supervises training of mess personnel, advises the CO and supply and commissary officers on mess matters, and systematically inspects all messes. On small posts, there is no food services officer. For that matter, on many small posts, Marines eat in the Navy mess.

The food service officer is a specialist, but *unit mess officers* are not—and that is where you come in. Every unit with its own mess has a mess officer, usually a lieutenant. This officer in turn has a noncommissioned assistant, the *mess sergeant*. The quality and standing of any given mess usually reflect the energy, imagination, and capability of the mess officer and mess sergeant, working as a team.

You may be a unit mess officer at some time in your career, and the experience will be invaluable in preparing you for command. Thus you should know how a typical mess is organized and how it operates.

The mess sergeant is the leading NCO of the mess. This billet demands a capable executive, a good cook, and an efficient culinary planner.

The chief cook is senior cook in the galley force and supervises the cooks in preparation of food.

The chief messman, usually an NCO, is in charge of messmen. He or she is responsible for the cleanliness of the galley and mess hall. The chief messman is a key billet assignment. Although most tables of organization do not contain a chief messman billet, you should nevertheless try to find the right person and detail that individual permanently. A slipshod mess hall manned by idle, unclean messmen usually can be traced back to an inefficient chief messman.

The storeroom keeper assists the mess sergeant by keeping the galley stores and provisions.

Cooks are divided into watches, regulated by the chief cook. Each watch should be headed by a rated cook, known as the "cook on watch." Depending on the size of the galley and galley force, the cook on watch may be assisted by other cooks or by "strikers," as apprentice cooks are known. Messmen who show a bent for cooking are assigned as strikers.

Messmen are the "hewers of wood and drawers of water" for the mess. Messmen serve food, wash dishes, wallop pots, police the mess hall and galley, and function as the mess sergeant's labor force. On posts where civilian messmen are not authorized, messmen are detailed monthly from the nonrated Marines of the command, in accordance with the *Marine Corps Manual*. The normal assignment of messmen is one for every twenty-five to thirty members of the command. An NCO should never serve as a messman (except as chief messman).

2003. The Unit Mess Officer

The duties of the unit mess officer are as prescribed by the commanding officer. If you are detailed as unit mess officer, immediately look up appropriate references in the *Marine Corps Manual, Marine Corps Supply Manual,* and the *Ma-*

rine Corps Subsistence Manual. Despite some variations from unit to unit, all unit mess officers should make frequent spot checks and inspections of the galley and mess hall, paying particular attention to:

- Personal cleanliness of cooks and messmen (clean, regulation clothing; clean hands and fingernails; obvious general health)
- Cleanliness and good order of cooks' and messmen's quarters, including condition of weapons and individual equipment
- Contents of garbage cans (to eliminate waste and to spot badly prepared food)
- Good order and sanitary condition of storerooms and reefers (look especially for signs of spoilage or evidence of rodents or insects)
- Cleanliness of mess halls (properly washed dishes and utensils; immaculate decks and tabletops; condiments covered)
- Sanitary garbage stowage and disposal

Attend at least one meal daily. Attend breakfast at least once a week. See that food is served hot and appetizingly and that there is enough for all. Enforce wearing of prescribed uniform by troops being fed.

Subject to unit policies, provide separate messing spaces in the General Mess for officers (when subsisting in the mess); for staff NCOs; for sergeants and corporals; and for nonrated enlisted. Special tables for staff NCOs and sergeants and corporals—screened off, if possible—are most important and should be provided whenever physically possible.

Stand by the mess and galley area for all inspections by the commanding officer. Have your mess sergeant and chief messman with you.

Be prepared at all times (especially if in an FMF mess) to take the field and serve rations under field conditions.

See that no Marine ever goes hungry or misses a meal because of a conflict of duties. This means that special servings, both group and individual, may be frequently required for those on watch and for drivers, travelers, and the like. Indoctrinate your mess force that any Marine who has unavoidably missed a meal must receive hot chow and hot coffee, day or night. A proper galley has hot coffee available to all comers, all the time.

2004. Clothing Your Marines

Instructions for wearing the uniform and specifications of all articles of uniform are found in *Marine Corps Uniform Regulations.* Procurement, issue, and inspection of clothing are covered by *Individual Clothing Regulations.*

It is your responsibility, as a Marine officer, to see that every Marine under your command is always properly uniformed and always possesses the required regulation clothing correctly marked.

Every unit has periodic *clothing inspections* for all hands. When inspecting, ensure that:

- Each person has the required quantities of clothing
- Clothing is marked as required by *Uniform Regulations*; that it bears correct

rank insignia; and that it is in the hands of the person whose name appears thereon

- Clothing is serviceable or that serviceable items are being replaced

Whenever a Marine is transferred or joins, the platoon leader should hold an individual clothing inspection.

Special clothing, such as cooks' and messmen's uniforms, cold-weather gear, flight gear, and chemical warfare clothing, is organizational property and issued to individuals on receipt, like equipment. If someone loses clothing, the Marine must then replace it by cash purchase. At stated intervals, each Marine receives a *clothing replacement allowance,* a pay-record credit to permit replacement of worn-out items. If a Marine needs clothing but hasn't enough money, the issue is made and checkage entered against future pay. This system makes it impossible for a Marine to have an excuse for not having required and serviceable uniforms. It is your responsibility to make this system work.

2005. Supervision of Uniforms

Here are ways to keep your Marines properly uniformed.

Carry out frequent, systematic clothing inspections with careful follow-up of deficiencies. This means keeping written individual records.

Place full-length mirrors in passageways and exits of barracks and in headquarters entrances to encourage the habit of self-inspection.

Rotate the command through various uniform combinations on successive days or at troop inspections.

Obtain cleaning, washing, and pressing equipment (irons and ironing boards) for squad rooms and barracks.

Inculcate officers and NCOs with their responsibility to enforce proper wearing of the uniform by Marines at all times. You have no excuse for disregarding a breach of uniform regulations with the famous last words: "He isn't one of *my* men. Let his own outfit catch up with him." When you encounter an individual out of uniform, require immediate correction. If the violation is conspicuous, report the incident to the Marine's organization commander.

2006. Individual Equipment

In addition to uniforms, every Marine is issued a weapon and individual equipment (known as "782 equipment"). It is one of your first responsibilities to see that the arms and equipment of your Marines are on hand, ready, and serviceable.

Upon joining the unit, a Marine is issued pistol or a rifle. It is up to that Marine to keep that rifle (or its successors) in top condition, since all will have to depend upon it in combat. Even when temporarily armed with other organizational weapons, the Marine is responsible for that rifle's safekeeping and maintenance. A Marine's rifle is a mirror of its owner; the rifles of a platoon or a detachment are the mirror of the platoon leader or detachment commander.

Officers must ensure that equipment and weapons are properly maintained and accounted for. The battlefield is unforgiving of neglect.

In addition to the weapon, a Marine's individual equipment comprises other items that one needs to fight and survive in the field. These articles are issued on memorandum receipt by the organization and are recovered or exchanged as necessary. The major items of individual equipment are pack, bayonet, magazine pouches, mess gear, cartridge belt, canteen and cup, poncho, first-aid packet, shelter half, helmet, cover, and entrenching tool.

Your responsibility for your troops' equipment is similar to your responsibility for their clothing. It is a matter of constant supervision and inspection. Remember that each item of equipment is government property, bought and paid for by the taxpayers—including you and the Marine who carries it. Field service and combat consume equipment, and this is to be expected. What is not to be expected, and will not be tolerated in the Marine Corps, are carelessness and negligence toward the weapons and equipment on which Marines' lives depend.

2007. Pay

Detailed information on pay is contained in Chapter 13. From a housekeeping point of view, interest lies in the command responsibilities involved in paying the troops. These responsibilities are simple.

The most important responsibility of a commanding officer, insofar as pay is concerned, is to see that Marines are paid correctly. When a Marine finance officer is present, this will present fewer problems. For outlying detachments, or for units dependent on other services or on visiting finance officers, the problem sometimes requires close supervision.

Officers have the duty of advising their people in money matters and of encouraging them to save and to take advantage of the opportunities that the government provides.

2008. Property

Handling and accounting for public property consume much of the energy of the Marine Corps. The golden rules on property are found in *Marine Corps Supply Manual*. You, and every officer in the Corps, should know these rules and definitions, the most important of which are summarized in the following paragraphs.

Anyone who possesses government property or who commands those who possess it, whether it is in use or in storage, has *responsibility* for that property, whether or not that individual has signed a receipt for it. Responsibility—in the supply sense—means the obligation of anyone who is required to have personal possession of, or supervision over, public property, to ensure that it is procured, used, and disposed of only as authorized. When you have public property in your custody, you assume, as a public trust, responsibility that this property will be utilized only as authorized by law or regulations.

The CO of any post or unit, however, has *command responsibility* over all the public property of the command. It is the CO's job to ensure that all such property is safeguarded, maintained, and accounted for. An officer has *accountability* (and is known as "an *accountable officer*") when specifically detailed to duty involving pecuniary responsibility for government funds and property. An accountable officer—as distinguished from a responsible officer—must keep formal records and stock accounts subject to audit by higher authority.

As you can see, virtually every Marine officer has some type of responsibility for government property, whereas relatively few officers are accountable. It is unlikely that you will become an accountable officer unless you specialize in supply; you may well be a responsible officer tomorrow.

2009. A Responsible Officer's Duties

As a responsible officer you have certain basic obligations with regard to public property.

You are personally (and pecuniarily) responsible for all nonexpendable property issued to you. You are also responsible that all nonconsumable but expendable property issued to you be used only for the purposes authorized. Most such items, like 782 gear (see Section 2006), which, owing to their nature, may often be in short supply and are always pilferable, require control by individual memorandum receipt.

You must inspect your property frequently to ensure serviceability, safekeeping, and proper use. At least quarterly, you must take physical inventory and adjust discrepancies with the accountable officer.

You must possess in serviceable condition all equipment shown on your unit's *allowance list*. The allowance list for a unit is prepared by the supply officer and contains all items allowed for the organization by tables of equipment (T/E) and tables of allowance (T/A) and any supporting allowance items except repair parts.

You must keep records reflecting the status of equipment and property for which you are responsible.

It is desirable that you designate in writing one or more representatives, officer or enlisted, who are authorized to receipt for property in your name. An officer representative is known as the "property officer," and an NCO as the "property sergeant."

Turn in to the appropriate supply agency any property grossly in excess of authorized allowances or not needed for fulfillment of your missions.

When relieved by another officer, you must conduct a joint inventory and adjust any discrepancies with the accountable officer. Your relief must then sign for all nonexpendable property carried on the equipment custody records. If you are relieving, and circumstances prevent joint inventory and immediate signature, you are nevertheless responsible for all property on hand. Before you sign any equipment custody records, however, be sure to make an immediate inventory of all property.

Ensure that your officers and enlisted persons are instructed in care, use, and maintenance of government property and that all hands are totally cost-conscious. The persons you select for safekeeping property—your property sergeant, in particular—must be chosen with great care. Do not entrust keys of storerooms or chests to enlisted persons or civilians without constant officer supervision.

2010. Expenditures of Property

Even with the most careful stewardship, property wears out and supplies are expended. The Marine Corps recognizes this; the supply system permits expenditure of material, and there are procedures for fixing responsibility for unusual or improper loss or damage to government property.

Nonconsumable expendables and consumables are expended on issue by the supply officer. Thus, no formal accountability exists for these items. Nevertheless, you must ensure that there is sufficient control over such materiel to guarantee proper use as well as ordinary economy.

If nonexpendable property is unavoidably lost or destroyed, this fact should be brought immediately to the attention of the supply officer, who may drop the property, with the approval of the commanding officer, through a special adjustment to the account.

If culpability or negligence is the suspected cause of loss of a nonexpendable item, an investigation should be held to determine the exact circumstances surrounding the loss.

Checkage of individual pay is a means of recovering the value of lost, damaged, or destroyed property from anyone who acknowledges responsibility therefor. An individual cannot be compelled to checkage of pay but can be subjected to disciplinary action, which most Marines are anxious to avoid (see *Marine Corps Supply Manual*).

2011.   Hints on Property

In addition to the advice in *Marine Corps Supply Manual,* a few hints on the management of your property are in order.

Make friends with your accountable officer. Keep that officer candidly informed on the state of your property account. Though you may have shortages, the accountable officer in turn may have overages. Share your problems.

Keep in touch with salvage and reclamation activities. It is often possible to adjust an awkward debit balance through assists from reclamation.

Look and plan ahead. Nothing is worse than getting caught short because of lack of ordinary foresight.

Be cost-conscious. The money available to your unit is not limitless, and supplies cost your unit money.

Follow through. Your responsibility doesn't end with the placing of requirements for material with the supply officer. It ends only when the items in question are physically either in the hands of the user or in your storeroom. As the Duke of Wellington wrote in 1810:

> It is very necessary to attend to all this detail and to trace a biscuit from Lisbon into a man's mouth on the frontier and to provide for its removal from place to place by land or by water, or no military operations can be carried out.

Take pains to determine and enforce responsibility for government property among your subordinates. When one of your Marines loses or damages property, institute checkage against that person. This not only reimburses the government for the loss and thus clears your books, but it also reminds all hands that property is to be respected and cared for.

Keep a neat, uncluttered storeroom. Allow no "grab-bag" accumulations in dark corners. Inspect your storeroom frequently—and unannounced.

Finally, remember the old saw that supposedly covers every known category of government property: "If it's small enough to pick up, turn it in; if you can't move it, paint it."

2012.   Special Services and Recreation

"Special services" embrace a number of nonmilitary morale, welfare, and recreation (MWR) activities within the Marine Corps, chief among which is unit recreation. *Marine Corps Special Services Manual* compiles all information on special services. Remember, however, that no matter what machinery may be set up for MWR purposes, nothing can supersede or diminish the commanding officer's paramount responsibility to lead, care for, counsel, and educate those under command.

Special services include recreation, athletics, education (nonmilitary programs intended to raise the general educational level of the Corps), information, and "personal affairs." To implement these programs, every command has a *special services officer,* and (often as additional duty), education, family services, athletic, and personal affairs officers.

The mainstay of post or unit recreation is the *recreation fund,* which provides for the recreation, amusement, and welfare of all hands. The recreation fund gets its money from exchange profits and from the Central Marine Corps MWR Fund. Because recreation funds are "nonappropriated funds" (that is, not provided from government appropriations), some latitude exists in spending them for items not covered by official grants but nevertheless desirable for the welfare or morale of the command. Some expenditures that may be made from a recreation fund are athletic equipment; athletic and marksmanship prizes; dances, picnics, and beer parties for the unit as a whole; musical instruments; washing machines and electric irons for barracks; and television and radio sets. The foregoing items, remember, are only examples. Before making a purchase from recreation funds, consult the *Manual,* not only to ensure that your project is authorized but also to make certain it does not fall among the prohibited transactions also covered.

The MWR fund is administered by the *MWR council,* which consists of not fewer than three officers, one of whom is the special services officer. On small posts, the exchange officer may also serve as custodian of the MWR fund. The council audits the fund, inventories and controls all property, and ensures compliance with established MWR policy.

The *custodian of the MWR fund* takes charge of funds and property and supervises MWR activities. This person is usually the special services officer.

2013. Transportation

Every unit or station that has vehicles includes a *motor transport officer,* who, under the S-4, is responsible for the upkeep and operation of the unit's transportation. The motor transport force is made up of drivers and mechanics. Motor transport operations are supervised by a noncommissioned *dispatcher,* who assigns vehicles to particular runs and keeps the unit's transportation operating in accordance with policy and regulations. When you need transportation, you call the dispatcher, the "front man," so to speak, of the motor transportation organization.

When dealing with drivers and transportation, keep the following pointers in mind.

Cars and drivers are for official business; use them accordingly. However, commanding officers, senior staff officers, and aides-de-camp frequently have cars and drivers assigned for use as required. Misuse of government transportation is a serious matter.

If you are the senior officer in an official vehicle, you are responsible for its safe operation and proper employment. If the driver breaks rules, you are responsible. Never, except in an emergency, order a driver to transgress a regulation or safety precaution. If you do, be ready to explain.

You cannot drive a Marine or Navy vehicle without a government motor vehicle operator's license. In addition, some commands require a unit driver's license. Other commands prohibit any officer from driving official vehicles except in emergency.

When duty requires a driver to make a run during meal hours, it is your responsibility to see that arrangements are made to feed that Marine (not just a cup of coffee and a sandwich, but a proper hot meal). Always ask your driver if he or she has been fed, and see the matter through. If you are not satisfied, call the dispatcher or, if necessary, the motor transport officer. In extreme cases, you may have to arrange directly with the mess sergeant. Regardless of how you do it, see that your driver is fed.

Avoid keeping vehicles waiting. Send them back to the motor pool, with instructions to return at a specified time (or call when you need a return trip). When using an official car in connection with an official social function, avoid having your driver wait outside at your pleasure. Be meticulously punctual; keep to schedule.

Play fair with the dispatcher, and the dispatcher will play fair with you.

Require drivers to be military and correct in manner and uniform. When not otherwise employed, see that the drivers perform routine checks, upkeep and maintenance on their vehicles, regardless of whether they are normally assigned to you or not.

If you are concerned with motor transport operations, "safety" and "preventive maintenance" are key words.

Let all things be done decently and in order.

—I Corinthians, 14:40

21

Personal Affairs

Your first responsibilities as a Marine officer are to Corps and country. Hardly second, however, are your responsibility to your family and your responsibility to organize your affairs so that they can continue undisturbed through all the ups and downs and sudden turnings in a service career.

Sudden death is only one contingency you must anticipate. What if you are captured? Prematurely retired? Ordered overseas where your family cannot follow?

Reflect on these possibilities. Put your house in order. *Keep* it in order.

YOUR ESTATE

2101. A Balanced Estate

Under the selection system of promotion, most officers retire between ages forty-five and sixty, and all must retire by age sixty-two. Thus a service career is shorter than that in any other profession. Today's laws have considerably lessened assurance of adequate retirement income, even for the physically retired. If you are over age fifty or physically disabled after retirement, your prospects for employment are poor. For all these reasons you must lose no time in laying the foundations of a balanced estate—an estate that reflects well-planned objectives; that is built on a prudent insurance program, wise investments, and property ownership; and that affords protection against the unexpected.

2102. Survivor Benefits

Current laws, which took effect in 1957 and have since been amended and extended, provide a greatly improved structure of benefits for eligible survivors of all officers and enlisted who die on active service or after separation from active service if, in the latter case, death results from a condition incurred or aggravated on active service. These benefits are described in this chapter as follows: federal government insurance; Social Security; Survivor Benefit Plan (SBP); death benefits (including back pay, death gratuity, dependency and indemnity compensation, pension for non–service-connected death, compensation for unused leave); and, finally, other benefits.

2103. Life Insurance

From the moment you take out life insurance, you create a cash estate of the amount of that policy, an estate whose proceeds are not taxable under the inheritance laws of most states. Life insurance provides an estate while you are in a low-income bracket and protects the future of your spouse and family during your younger years against the occupational hazards of your profession. Finally, certain types of life insurance give a modest return on your investment and can help maintain your standard of living after retirement.

On a straight life policy, you pay premiums over a lifetime. It is the most widely used type of insurance because it provides lifetime protection at less cost than any other permanent insurance.

Term insurance, which has no cash value and only gives temporary protection over a certain period, is the cheapest of all. With this type, you pay premiums for a set term—usually from one to fifteen years—and its protection stops at the end of that period. Term insurance also goes up (in most cases) at the end of each five years and becomes virtually prohibitive at age seventy.

Limited payment policies provide lifetime protection and contain cash values just as straight life policies do. This type is more expensive than straight life, however, because it is designed to give you a paid-up policy at the end of a certain number of years or at a certain age. After that, you are still fully protected, but you no longer have premiums to pay.

Endowment policies are essentially a form of insured savings. This type of policy provides for the payment of its face value to you at a future date elected by you. If you die before that date, the face value goes to your beneficiary. Premiums on endowment policies are higher than on any other insurance, because the emphasis is on savings rather than protection.

Your Life Insurance Program.   A sound life insurance program varies with income, age and number of your children, your own age, and your probable number of years remaining upon the active list. Periodically, you must overhaul your program, and consider carefully the number of years your children will remain dependent, their educational requirements, your outside income, your spouse's employment capabilities, your income after retirement, and any experience qualifying you for civil employment.

Consider the needs of your family five, ten, and twenty years from now and your probable income. Think about retirement income, education, and cash for the down payment on a house. Contrary to some opinion, not all endowment policies are bad; neither are short-term policies. Short-term policies cost more in the long run, but you buy them while receiving full pay; when you retire, they are paid up.

But, first, by all means join the *Navy Mutual Aid Association.* The association gives more than helpful assistance to beneficiaries of its members. Details on Navy Mutual Aid are given below and in Section 2105.

Only second to Navy Mutual Aid, you should immediately enroll in the *Group Insurance Plan of the Marine Corps Association* (MCA), which pays an active-duty death benefit up to $350,000. Details on the MCA Group Benefits Plan are given below.

At least every five years, review your program. You may well find that changes in income or employment and a different family situation indicate modifications. Look through a sound guide on insurance.

Government Life Insurance. *Servicemens Group Life Insurance (SGLI)* provides up to $200,000 term life insurance, in addition to any other government insurance carried, for all persons on active duty. Your pay is checked up to $16 per month for this coverage, and you are covered for the full amount until and unless you cancel all or part of your coverage, or until (as the law permits) you convert SGLI into VGLI (see below) upon separation or retirement, with the ultimate option of further conversion into permanent protection, *without medical examination,* provided by a commercial insurance company. Death claims are handled by Marine Corps Headquarters and by the commercial company that is the prime insurer.

Veterans Group Life Insurance (VGLI), which took effect on 1 August 1974, is a five-year nonrenewable term policy that has no cash, loan, paid-up, or extended values. VGLI automatically covers Marines who, after the above date, are separated or retired (or reservists released from active duty over thirty days). VGLI takes effect at the end of the 120-day free coverage under SGLI following separation or retirement as above, only if payment for at least the first month of the required premium has been made before the end of the 120-day SGLI free period. Depending on age, monthly VGLI premiums vary and must be paid directly to: Office of Servicemen's Group Life Insurance (OSGLI), 213 Washington Street, Newark, NJ 07102, which will answer any questions on SGLI/VGLI.

At the end of its five-year term, VGLI may be converted to an individual insurance policy with an eligible company *without medical examination,* as noted above.

On government insurance matters, refer to the *Handbook for Retired Marines,* published by Headquarters, U.S. Marine Corps, and frequently updated.

NMA and MCA Insurance. *The Navy Mutual Aid (NMA) Association,* Arlington Annex, Room G-070, Washington, DC 20370, is a semiofficial, nonprofit life insurance group for all personnel of the Navy, Marine Corps, Coast Guard, National Oceanic and Atmospheric Administration, and Public Health Service. Rates are minimum for three coverage plans. On receipt of notice of your death from the Navy Department, the association instantly wires $1,000 to your beneficiary, and the rest of the benefit will be paid in accordance with the desires of the beneficiary. NMA will also render help to your surviving dependents in settlement of all other claims. Perhaps the most important service of this kind performed by NMA is the assistance provided in securing service-connected compensation for spouses, children, and dependent parents of deceased members of the association (see Section 2124). In the event compensation is disallowed initially (as sometimes happens), the association provides, without charge, competent legal representation before the Veterans Administration Board of Appeals, in order to obtain the best possible settlement. Every Marine officer should be a member of Navy Mutual Aid. *Attend to this now.*

Marine Corps Association Group Benefit Program (MCAGBP) incorporates term insurance plans designed and operated by Marines. It is open to any member of the Marine Corps Association on active duty, if under age seventy. Depending on the plan chosen and on the age of the insured, benefits may go as high as $250,000. Rates are minimum. One of the attractive features of this plan is that, unlike most group insurance schemes, you may, after separation or retirement, continue your low-cost protection until age seventy so long as you retain MCA membership (another good reason to take the *Gazette*).

To inquire, or better, join, address the Administrator, MCAGBP, P.O. Box 335, Quantico VA 22134-9906.

Notes on Life Insurance. If you hold it, don't let government insurance lapse. In service or out, it is the *best* insurance you can get.

Don't take out insurance haphazardly. Follow a program.

Keep your beneficiaries up to date. Name contingent beneficiaries. Remember to include the phrase ". . . or to the survivor or survivors thereof," which is all-inclusive. If a beneficiary dies, make a prompt change in beneficiary. Consider the effect if both beneficiary and you should die in the same accident.

Review settlement arrangements with your insurance agent or broker periodically to ensure that they are adapted to your present circumstances.

Will your spouse have funds immediately after your death? Navy Mutual Aid is splendid for this purpose.

Pay premiums by allotment. Regulations permit indefinite allotments for insurance premiums that continue after retirement. Payment by allotment prevents lapse of policies.

Don't overload yourself with insurance against remote dangers, but be sure your policies protect against all expected military hazards. Many insurance companies have restrictions as to war, flying hazards as pilot or crew of a military aircraft, and so on.

Do not place all your insurance with any one company. Protection is enhanced by diversification among several good companies.

If you have your policy made payable to your estate, payment of proceeds will be delayed until completion of administration. This could be costly and reduce your estate, while delaying benefits to your dependents.

Although insurance is something you should attend to promptly, be wary before you start signing. Avoid fly-by-night companies and insurance agents who hover about newly commissioned lieutenants. Deal with sound, well-known companies, and select your agent with discrimination.

2104. Social Security

Contributory Social Security coverage is extended to all hands in uniform. Your contribution is made through an automatic checkage of a percentage of your basic pay. In addition to your military retirement pay and any disability compensation paid by the Veterans Affairs, Social Security provides monthly income for:

- You, on reaching age sixty-five (or age sixty-two, if you apply to receive the smaller payments due at that time)
- Your spouse, if you die and your minor children remain in your spouse's care
- You, your spouse, and children, if you should be totally disabled
- Your spouse, if not entitled earlier, on attaining age sixty
- Your children under age eighteen, or older if incapable of self-support, after your death or while you are disabled
- Your dependent parents

The payments for a family group may go as high as the legal maximum even though you have only paid into the Social Security program through taxation of your basic pay for a few years. The amount of your Social Security benefits is determined by your "average monthly wage" during the years you were contributing. The exact amount differs in almost every case and must be worked out. If you are eligible for any of the Social Security benefits just mentioned, you must apply for them; benefits are not paid automatically. You must file an application and it must be in the hands of the Social Security Administration (or with a U.S. Foreign Service officer, if outside the United States) before it can pay you. File immediately when you become eligible because back payments are limited by law. The local post office can furnish you with the address of the nearest Social Security district office. You should get in touch with the district office on attaining age sixty-five, or when your spouse reaches age sixty, or at any time if disabled before reaching age sixty-five. When you die, your next of kin should check with the Social Security office to see if there is an entitlement to survivor's insurance.

You need not have wage credits for military service added to your record currently. These credits are recorded when a claim is made for retirement or survivor's insurance payments.

Your Social Security number is important for both you and your family to know, and it must, of course, accompany claims or inquiries. Moreover, it is your basic number for military administrative purposes and is used by the Internal Revenue Service in connection with all your tax returns and related records. Record it in your safe deposit box and with any emergency papers you keep, such as insurance policies and so forth.

To assist in computing where you stand under Social Security, the Social Security Administration encourages every insured individual—you—to request a Statement of Wages every three years from the Social Security Administration. In this way you can determine whether the records are complete and you are getting credit for all earnings on which Social Security tax has been paid.

You can get full information on these and other matters of interest by applying to the nearest Social Security Administration office and usually from your unit personal affairs officer. Before retirement, investigate your Social Security rights and credits, and be sure your spouse is acquainted with his or her rights under this law.

2105. Insurance Death Claims

Government Insurance Death Claims. If you were on active duty, your beneficiary will be mailed forms by the Department of Veterans Affairs (VA) The VA is notified by Marine Corps Headquarters; no further proof of death is required. Your beneficiary must fill out the form and return it.

If you were retired or separated from the service, your beneficiary should apply to the nearest VA regional office for necessary forms or see the legal assistance or personal affairs officer at the nearest Navy or Marine Corps station; and if these are inaccessible, the beneficiary should seek assistance from his or her nearest state or other service organization. Proof of death must be furnished; the beneficiary should get certified copies of the public death record, coroner's report, death certificate of attending physician, or death certificate of naval hospital. If one of these is not available, the beneficiary should obtain an affidavit from persons who viewed the body and knew the deceased when living.

Because of a backlog of VA claims in central and regional offices, there may be appreciable delay before payment. Navy Mutual Aid, if you are a member, can keep claims moving.

The beneficiary should hold your government policy until claim is paid; it should *not* be sent with the claim.

Commercial Policy Death Claims. The beneficiary should consult local representatives of each company or write directly to the head office. The following steps are required:

- Give insured's name.
- Give insurance policy numbers.

- Request necessary forms to make a death claim.
- Return *by certified mail* the accomplished forms, with return receipt requested.
- Send a certified copy of death certificate, and affidavit of death as described above, or, if death occurred at sea or abroad, a certified copy of the official notification of death.

You yourself should list the commercial insurance companies that insure your life in the Record of Emergency Data in your computer file; Marine Corps Headquarters will notify the companies in case of death. Most companies accept such notification as proof of death.

Some companies require submission of the policy before paying the claim. Your insurance agent will assist your beneficiary with this paperwork.

Navy Mutual Aid.   Deaths occurring on active duty or at a naval hospital are reported to Navy Mutual Aid via official channels. In case of death occurring elsewhere or under circumstances wherein an official death message may not have been sent to the Navy Department, the next of kin should notify Navy Mutual Aid via the most rapid means. As previously noted, $1,000 will be immediately transmitted to the beneficiary, and the rest of the benefit will be paid in accordance with the desires of the beneficiary. A letter containing details of what must be done, enclosing all forms to be signed, is sent to your beneficiary at once. Navy Mutual Aid also notifies civilian insurance companies, with which you may be insured, of your death and the address of your next of kin. The finance officer holding your accounts is notified of your death and the name and address of next of kin for the purpose of expediting payment of arrears of pay, unused leave compensation, and death gratuity, if eligible.

In general, it is unwise for your family to put claims for government benefits in the hands of private attorneys, as this may simply cause unnecessary delay and will certainly entail added expense.

2106. Survivor Benefit Plan (SBP)

This plan provides survivor income of up to 55 percent of your retired pay to your surviving spouse and dependent children.

In the past, surviving members of a retired Marine's family often found themselves with little or no income after the retiree's death. The SBP fills that gap; until its enactment, retired pay ended with the retiree's death, unless he or she had elected to take part in the old Retired Servicemen's Family Protection Plan (RSFPP), known in turn originally as the Contingency Option Act (COA).

You will be automatically enrolled in the SBP with maximum coverage when you retire, if you have a spouse or dependent child at retirement time, unless you specifically elect a lesser coverage or decline participation, with concurrence of your spouse, before the day you become entitled to retired pay.

If you have no spouse or dependent child when you retire, you may either join the plan then by naming someone else as beneficiary or begin participation later if you acquire a spouse or child after retirement, but within one year of acquiring said family members.

The cost of SBP will be checked from your retired pay (6.5 percent of insured portion).

Because the government pays a substantial part of the SBP costs, your loss of retired pay for participation might be considerably lower than if you had purchased the same commercial coverage at retirement time.

SBP survivor benefits are based on your retired pay at time of death, or escalated base amount, not that initially received or elected when you began.

The decision to elect or not to elect the SBP is a big one. It is not a substitute for life insurance (it is taxable as an annuity, you have no equity in the plan, and you cannot cash it in or borrow against it). Whether it is best for you depends on your personal situation. Basically, if you have a long life expectancy on retirement, are well-fixed, with adequate life insurance and a solid estate, the plan has the disadvantages that you will probably receive reduced retired pay for many years, your surviving spouse may remarry (at which time payments cease unless remarriage is after age fifty-five) or die soon (at which time payments cease), and he or she would receive little benefit. On the other hand, if you are in such poor health that you cannot obtain additional insurance, it could be an excellent means of augmenting insurance and other survivor benefits, at a relatively small cost, and should be carefully pondered.

2107.   Other Kinds of Insurance

Automobile Insurance.   Your car can cause you much grief if not properly insured.

Auto insurance is available to cover liability for bodily injury; property damage; medical payments; collision or upset; fire and lightning; and transportation, theft, windstorm, earthquake, explosion, hail, or water damage. Liability awards for bodily injury and property damage are very high and are rising. Your insurance agent can recommend how much coverage you should carry in each category. Collision or upset coverage is also very expensive; you should therefore take out a "deductible" policy—$200 deductible for each accident, as nearly every accident now costs that much or more. This protects you against heavy damage to, or total loss of, your car.

Many states and all Marine posts require public liability and property damage insurance before you can be issued a license for your car.

Personal Property Insurance.   Personal property (clothes, jewelry, silverware, furniture, and so on) should be covered against fire, theft, and breakage or other damage at home or during transportation. Inexpensive "floater" policies for officers are written by many companies. One of the best and least expensive underwriters is United Services Automobile Association, San Antonio, Texas, an association of officers of all services who mutually insure each other against automobile liabilities and loss incurred to personal effects. Reflect upon this fact: *Government liability for effects destroyed or damaged while in government custody is limited to $40,000, regardless of how much more you may lose.*

Fire Insurance and Personal Liability Insurance. Take out fire insurance on any house or other real property of your own. Another valuable coverage is personal liability insurance, which protects you against claims for injuries by persons visiting your home or by servants or workmen; damage done by pets, children, spouse, or self (usually including damage arising out of sports); and damage done to the property of others by such accidents as falling trees or fire originating on your property. This insurance is inexpensive but invaluable when trouble comes.

2108.   An Insurance Checklist

Over and above Social Security coverage, do you have Navy Mutual Aid insurance? Do you have enough commercial life insurance, in addition, to provide an adequate cash estate? Is there an educational provision for each child?

Is your car insured for bodily injury, property damage, and the contingencies listed in Section 2107? Do you carry a personal property "floater" policy? Is your home insured against fire or other disaster?

Do you have the name and address of your insurance agent(s)? Does your beneficiary?

2109.   Real Estate

While you are young, with small income and few obligations, it is probably better to rent quarters for your family. As you get older and have children, you may agree with many officers that it is advantageous to own your own home. Marines have some advantage in this, as there are a few localities where they may be ordered to duty over and over again. For example, a ground officer would serve most stateside duty in the vicinity of Camp Lejeune, Washington-Quantico, and San Diego or Pendleton; an aviator would have maximum service in the vicinity of Yuma, Washington-Quantico, and Cherry Point or Beaufort.

Some officers find it financially advantageous to buy a house where they have duty and are not assigned quarters, then sell or rent when ordered to other shore duty, or else leave the family in its own home while on sea or expeditionary service. Although absentee landlord is certainly a difficult role, it is worthwhile to have a home available when you return, and you can approach retirement with something besides canceled checks and rent receipts. When retirement comes, you have an asset that will permit you to buy a house wherever you decide to settle, if the city where you already own a house does not suit you. And if you die on active duty, your family will have a home or an income from the real estate you leave. Moreover, the Federal Housing Authority (FHA), in most cases, will grant a long-term mortgage, which will facilitate purchase or construction of the home you want, or purchase of a second home provided that your first FHA-sponsored home had to be sold because of military orders.

Consider carefully the terms of ownership of any real property before the deed is prepared. Joint ownership or transfer of property to your spouse by deed may offer material advantage to your estate. Leave with your valuable papers a list of your real estate holdings that gives description and location of all holdings; location of deeds, mortgages, or other papers; and original cost, depreciated cost, estimated present value, and present ownership status.

If you do rent housing, you should insist on a "military clause" in the lease. This clause generally states that the tenant may terminate the lease subject to payment of a certain sum and allows the tenant to end the lease on thirty days' written notice to the landlord, for any one of several reasons, such as permanent change of station or release from active duty. Your legal assistance office can give you desired wording and other details.

2110. Control of Property

An individual may use or control an estate himself or herself or through an agent acting under power of attorney. Remote control of one kind or another is often necessary during a service career.

Joint Ownership. To facilitate use of property and to provide for its disposition on death, an individual may arrange for most property to be held in joint tenancy (with spouse or other beneficiary) with right of survivorship, thus enabling the joint tenant to use and control the property jointly during the individual's lifetime and, after his or her death to obtain full title as survivor. Property held jointly cannot be disposed of by will if your joint tenant survives you, but it is wise to include provision for its disposal should your joint tenant die before you do.

The advantages of joint tenancy are less expense, less inconvenience, and less time required to dispose of property after a death. But there are also disadvantages. Be aware, too, that the provisions of the Soldiers' and Sailors' Civil Relief Act exempting military personnel from state or municipal taxation do not apply to your spouse's interest in property.

Real estate is not the only property that can be held in joint tenancy. Joint bank accounts and joint ownership of securities, with right of survivorship, have some advantages.

Note that joint ownership of government savings bonds, if held in safekeeping with the Treasury Department, does not necessarily ensure flexibility. Such a bond cannot be withdrawn by a joint owner unless the purchaser has registered with the safekeeping agency a sample of the co-owner's signature, along with written authority to withdraw the bond.

Automobiles. Joint ownership of the family car also has advantages. Serious loss may result if your spouse or another family member drives your individually owned car after your death. The best plan is to hold the title to the car in joint tenancy. The certificate of title and the insurance policy should bear the names of the *joint* owners.

Although joint ownership of automobiles is desirable, your spouse's interest in this personal property is taxable. Payment of taxes in a state where you live temporarily can be avoided under the Soldiers' and Sailors' Civil Relief Act of 1940, if the car is registered in your name, in your own state of legal residence. A power of attorney to your spouse, however, will enable him or her to transfer title, secure registration, sell, or buy a car during your lifetime.

Joint Bank Accounts. If suddenly ordered to expeditionary service or upon sudden death, an officer who carries a bank account in his or her own name only may deprive the family temporarily of access to funds at a time when they are most needed. Investigate the advantages of joint accounts—at least during times when you are separated from your family.

2111. Investments

The complexity of the financial environment, particularly in light of the many new investment instruments that have become available, may prove, at first, overwhelming to you. In investments, as in your military career, you must remain informed and consistent in your approach. A good place to begin your familiarity with the world of investment is the library or bookstore, where generally accepted references can help you to navigate the reef-strewn waters of high finance.

Investments should be viewed as a part of a well-conceived and comprehensive personal financial plan (see Figure 21–1). Your aim should be twofold: the preservation and the increase of your capital base. Take note of these priorities: preserve your capital, so that you can increase it. The old adage that it's tough to make something out of nothing is never more applicable than in the area of investments.

2112. Borrowing Money and Loans

Because the first few years of a junior officer's career may well be spent paying off debts, it may be wise to underscore Shakespeare's advice, "Neither a borrower nor a lender be . . ." if you can help it. Avoid loan sharks, and *equally avoid private loans to fellow officers,* however deserving the case may appear; particularly avoid acting as cosigner to any note—this makes you just as liable as the borrower.

Interest Rates. The amount of interest you pay on a loan is a matter of vital concern and often a source of confusion. This is because most lenders charge different rates from those they quote. There are four ways of quoting interest: (1) monthly (1 percent per month); (2) add-on rate (6 percent per year); (3) discount rate (6 percent per year); (4) simple annual rate (6 percent per year). Only the last—simple annual interest—is quoted in *true* terms.

To convert quoted rates to simple annual interest, and thus to true interest:
- Multiply a monthly rate by 12
- Multiply add-on or discount rate by 2.

Whenever you borrow, ask what kind of interest is being charged—add-on, discount, monthly, or simple. Convert the quoted rate to true annual interest.

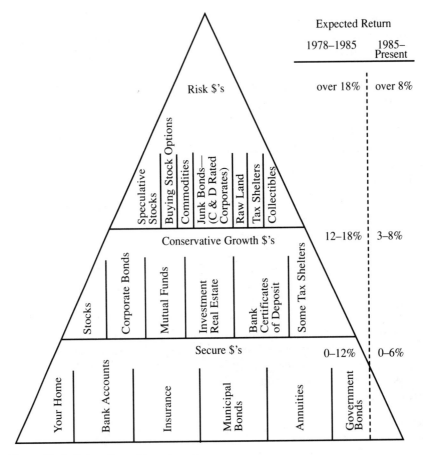

Figure 21–1: Categories of investments

Then compare interest costs and other charges to determine which lender offers you the best terms.

If you need credit, investigate the *Navy Federal Credit Union.* Both for borrowing and saving, whether by mail or in person, this nonprofit organization is tailored to the needs of the young officer—its charges are very low, and interest is generous. Navy Federal Credit also covers loans with life insurance at no extra cost, which is of great benefit to a young officer.

2113.   Soldiers' and Sailors' Civil Relief Act

This legislation, as amended, is designed to relieve officers and enlisted from worry over certain civil problems and obligations.

The Civil Relief Act—as it is sometimes short-titled—temporarily suspends enforcement of some civil liabilities of military personnel on active duty if your inability to meet your obligations results from your military status. The act also provides that, in most cases, if you are a legal resident of one state but are stationed in another, you may not be subjected to certain taxes imposed by the latter state. Included are personal property taxes and state income taxes. It applies to auto licenses only if you purchase home state tags. No state tax exemption is applicable to your family members.

Legal advice is necessary in any application of the Civil Relief Act because of the many technicalities. The act is designed to provide a shield against hardship; it is not a device to evade civil liabilities. Information and advice may be obtained from your legal assistance officer.

POWERS OF ATTORNEY AND WILLS

2114. Powers of Attorney

A power of attorney authorizes someone else to act in your name in the same manner and extent as you yourself could act. The power permits your representative to do only acts expressly stated therein.

When you are on expeditionary duty "beyond the seas," a power of attorney enables your family to carry on your affairs without interruption. Thus, when ordered overseas, you should consider whether to execute a power of attorney covering your affairs generally and particularly with reference to reimbursements from the United States. If you wish to include authority to transact business in general, consult the legal assistance officer to ensure that the power is legally sufficient but not needlessly broad.

Whether general or limited, your power of attorney should include phraseology as follows:

> To execute vouchers in my behalf for any and all allowances and reimbursements payable to me by the United States, including, but not restricted to, allowances and reimbursement for transportation of family members or shipment of household effects as authorized by law or Navy or other regulations; to receive, endorse, and collect the proceeds of checks payable to the order of the undersigned drawn on the Treasurer of the United States for whatever account, and to execute in the name and on behalf of the undersigned, all bonds, indemnities, applications, or other documents, which may be required by law or regulation to secure the issuance of duplicates of such checks, and to give full discharge of same.

Such a power of attorney for governmental transactions should be executed in the presence of three witnesses and acknowledged before a notary public, or, if outside the United States, by any officer of the United States authorized to administer oaths. For purposes other than those given, each specific power must be mentioned to be effective.

Bear in mind that not everyone needs to execute a power of attorney, as it can be a dangerous tool in the hands of the uninitiated.

2115.   Your Will

Considering occupational hazards of our profession, it is important that you have a will. A will simplifies settlement of your estate, reduces expenses, conserves assets, and enables your last wishes to be carried out.

Definitions.   A *will* is the legal document by which an individual leaves instructions for disposition of property after death. *A holographic will* is in the handwriting of the testator.

A *testator* is a person who leaves a will. An *intestate* is a person who dies without a will.

Settling an estate is a general term used to denote the entire process of collecting assets, filing inventories and accounts, paying claims, distributing assets in accordance with the will or laws of descent and distribution, and filing final accounting with the court.

An *executor* is appointed by your will to execute its provisions after your death. If you die intestate, the court appoints an *administrator,* who discharges the duties of an executor in settling the estate.

A *codicil* adds to, or qualifies, a will; it revokes the will only to the extent that it is inconsistent therewith. Will and codicil are construed together. A codicil is drawn in the same way as a will. When possible, the best procedure is to make a new will rather than to add a codicil to an old will.

Probating a will is the process of presenting the will for record to the proper authority in the county where the deceased had legal residence.

Before Making a Will.   Analyze your estate; estimate state and federal taxes, and plan to minimize them. Then, if not sooner, confer with a competent legal adviser. See your legal assistance officer or a member of the local bar for this advice. It is well at this time to discuss, and preferably put in writing, the lawyer's expected charges for settling the estate.

Confer with the trust officer of your bank for help with administering expenses and taxes.

Provide liquid assets in your estate to meet taxes.

List the property that you cannot dispose of freely—property limited by joint tenancy, community property, your share of trust funds, life insurance already assigned to individuals, and so on—and put down opposite each the amount that is yours to distribute:

• Cash
• Real estate
• Securities
• Life insurance payable to the estate
• Business interests
• Automobiles in your name
• Household furniture and furnishings that are not community property
• Personal effects
• Other property

Estimate expenses and debts to be paid from your estate, such as:
- Expense of last illness
- Funeral expenses
- Unpaid household bills
- Personal debts
- Mortgage or notes payable (just your share, if joint)
- Expense of administering estate
- Taxes, such as real estate, estate, and inheritance

Be careful in making cash bequests; if your estate decreases, you may cut off residual legatees with little or nothing.

For a small estate, it is probably best for husbands and wives to make the other the executor of each's estate. For a large estate or a complicated will, give consideration to your bank as executor or coexecutor. The trust department of a bank has officials trained to handle large or complicated estates; a bank is a continuing institution; a bank is financially responsible; a bank receives no more for its services than an individual. Seek advice from your lawyer and banker.

When your executor has accepted the assignment, discuss your plans, go over your affairs—and take him or her into your confidence.

If your estate is within the amount exempt from a tax, a simple holographic will may be adequate. Your lawyer can express your thoughts and wishes in legal language; he or she can give you advice that will help ensure a well-planned estate.

File the original of your will in your safe deposit box (or with the Navy Mutual Aid Association, if you belong), and be sure that your spouse and your executor know the location and the date of your latest will.

During your lifetime, you will probably make a new will several times. Certain milestones indicate when to reconsider your will and bring it up to date:
- Change of legal residence
- Removal of executor to another state or his or her death
- Radical change in your estate
- Sale of property mentioned in your will
- Major changes in tax laws
- Marriage, divorce, or remarriage
- Birth or death of child
- Death of spouse.

Check your will on changing legal residence (*not* change of station) to another state, as the provisions of your will may not be legal in that state and your executor may not be able to function there.

2116. Drawing a Will

A will must be in writing, but no particular form is required if its wording intelligently expresses your intent.

If you dispose of real property, your will must be made in accordance with the law of the state where the real property is located. If you dispose of personal property, your will must be made in accordance with the law of the state in which you are a resident. If both realty and personality are disposed, your will must conform to the laws of all states among which the property is distributed.

The number of witnesses required for a will varies from none (for a holographic will) to three; *have three witnesses* to your will, and be safe. Sign in their presence, so that they see you sign and understand that it is your will you are signing. Witnesses, then, in your presence and in the presence of each other, sign the attestation. Be sure that none of the witnesses is mentioned in the will; attestation by an interested witness may invalidate the will, or the witness may lose a legacy. Witnesses should write opposite their signatures their places of residence. Because the authenticity of signatures must be proved in court at the time of probating, take care to select witnesses who will be available.

A Simple Will.   The following short form of a simple, holographic will has been used by many officers:

> All my estate I devise and bequeath to my wife, for her own use and benefit forever, and I hereby appoint her my executrix, without bond, with full power to sell, mortgage, lease, or in any other manner dispose of the whole or any part of my estate.
>
> JOHN WHARTON (Seal)
>
> (Date)
>
> Subscribed, sealed, published, and declared by John Wharton, testator above named, as and for his last will in the presence of each of us, who at his request and in his presence, in the presence of each other, at the same time, have hereto subscribed our names as witnesses this (date) at the City of Washington, in the District of Columbia.
>
> (Signatures and addresses of witnesses, preferably three in number. Be sure that the word "Seal" is written in parentheses after each signature, as shown above.)

A Simple Codicil.   If possible, write a codicil on the same sheet of paper as the will; if written on a separate sheet, fasten the two together securely. Here is a simple form of codicil:

> I, John Wharton, of Washington, District of Columbia, make this codicil to my last will dated . . . , hereby ratifying said will in all respects save as changed by this codicil. Whereas, by said will I gave Robert Anderson Wharton, my son, a legacy of $5,000, I now give him a second legacy of $10,000, making $15,000 in all.

(Then follow the testator's signature and seal, the attestative clause, and the witnesses' signature and seals.)

If you decide to modify your will, once it is executed, do not make alterations or interlineations. Consult your legal assistance officer on what to do.

Probate. If executed according to law of your legal domicile, a will made anywhere in the world will be admitted to probate in the jurisdiction of your domicile without question.

Probate establishes the validity of the will and evidences the right of beneficiaries to succeed to title to property in the estate. The place of probate is usually the country and state in which you are domiciled at the time of death; the will must also be probated in any other county and state where you own real property.

DEATH AND BURIAL

2117. Burial Arrangements

When Death Occurs near a Navy or Marine Activity. When a Marine officer on active duty dies at or near his or her station, the commanding officer takes charge and arranges for local burial or for shipment of the body at government expense. (For burial in Arlington National Cemetery, see Section 2119 and the *Marine Corps Casualty Procedures Manual.*)

In case of death in a naval hospital, the hospital authorities handle the arrangements.

Death at a Remote Place. When an officer on active duty dies at some distance from a Marine Corps or naval station or hospital, the next of kin should contact the nearest Marine Corps or Navy activity for aid; if unable to contact a local activity, he or she should telegraph or telephone the deceased's commanding officer or the commandant of the Marine Corps, Washington, DC, giving the deceased's full name, rank, and service number; the date, place, and cause of death; and the place where burial is desired. Request instructions as to burial arrangements and give the address to which a reply may be sent.

Death in a Naval, Military, or Veterans Hospital (while in Inactive Status). Where death of a veteran or a retired or inactive officer occurs in a naval or military hospital or in a facility, the hospital authorities will make necessary arrangements upon request of the next of kin.

The Navy Mutual Aid Association has an outstanding pamphlet, *What To Do Immediately in Case of Death,* which is available on request. Obtain a copy of this and keep it with your important papers, as it is a complete checklist of essential information and actions required.

2118. Burial Expenses

The expenses of burial or shipment of the remains of Marine officers who die on active duty borne by the surviving spouse or another individual may be reimbursable. When the place of death is remote from a Marine Corps or naval station or hospital and it is impossible to obtain instructions from Marine or Navy authorities, the surviving spouse may employ a local undertaker, or, if necessary, arrange shipment of the body to the place of burial, but in such cases he or she should obtain itemized bills and receipts. Reimbursement in the case of a regular or Reserve officer who dies on active duty in an area where an armed forces contract is available and not used is not to exceed what services and supplies would have cost the Navy. Where an armed forces contract is not available, the amount is not to exceed $1,750.

In the case of an honorably discharged, inactive, or retired veteran, the limit of disbursement is $300 (payable by the VA), or $1,500 in the event of a service-related cause of death. In addition, Social Security will pay a death payment up to $255 if the deceased was covered. This claim must be filed with the nearest Social Security office. A $150 burial plot allowance will be paid by the VA if burial is in a private cemetery.

Generally, no expenditure is authorized for shipping the remains of an officer who dies on inactive duty. There is no interment expense for burial in a federal cemetery.

If the remains of an officer who dies on active duty are forwarded to the next of kin for private burial, the expenses of preparation, encasement, and transportation will be borne by the Department of the Navy; and after the body has arrived, the Navy will allow $3,100 for burial in a private cemetery or $2,000 for remains consigned to an undertaker prior to burial in a national or naval cemetery. If the remains are consigned directly to a national or naval cemetery, $110 is available.

If funeral expenses have been paid, claim for reimbursement should be submitted by letter to the Commandant of the Marine Corps (Code MHP-10) stating name and rank of deceased, date and place of burial, and enclosing itemized bills in triplicate, receipted to show by whom payment was made, and the dates when rendered.

If funeral expenses have not been paid, unpaid bills in triplicate are forwarded to the commandant as above. (All claims for burial expenses must be submitted within two years after permanent burial or cremation.)

If remains are claimed at the place of death for private burial, and the service of the government is refused, the next of kin thereby relieves the government of any obligation for funeral or transportation expenses.

2119. Place of Burial

You may be buried at the place of death, in a private cemetery near your home, or in an open national cemetery. Leave written instructions as to your choice. If burial is to be in a national cemetery, the undertaker should telegraph the superintendent of the national cemetery selected; if your family lives near the selected national cemetery, the next of kin may request burial directly from the cemetery superintendent.

Remains are cremated only on written request from the next of kin.

Arrangements for burial at sea may be initiated via either Marine Corps Headquarters or local naval authorities. Burial at sea is not a right but a privilege, which might not be feasible to accord. Expenses incurred for delivery of remains to point of embarkation aboard a naval vessel must be paid by your survivors.

Military Funerals, Arlington National Cemetery.   Funeral arrangements for burial in Arlington National Cemetery are made with the superintendent by the shipping activity, undertaker, or next of kin. Headquarters Marine Corps can make hotel reservations for family and friends, meet trains or planes, explain the different types of military funeral, and assist in selection of honorary pall-bearers and furnish their transportation. Headquarters Marine Corps will also put the surviving spouse in touch with the Navy Mutual Aid Association (if deceased was a member) or another organization that can assist in preparing applications for pensions, compensation, or other claims on the government.

After the next of kin has received confirmation from Arlington of the request for burial, he or she should contact the office of the Superintendent of Arlington (and also pass the information on to Headquarters Marine Corps), stating the number in the funeral party; the means of transportation; the date and hour of arrival; and whether local transportation and hotel reservations are required.

When you think of burial, remember that Quantico now has a national cemetery, which ought to be considered as a special place for our own in the Corps.

2120.   Other Information

Funeral Flag.   A U.S. flag accompanies the remains and may be retained by the family. When death is remote from a naval or Marine activity, the postmaster of the county seat may furnish a flag.

Honors.   When practicable, and if requested, full military honors will be provided at the funeral of an officer (see *Marine Corps Manual*). But at cemeteries remote from Marine Corps or naval stations, military honors are not practicable, and relatives must make their own arrangements for funeral services. Veterans organizations usually can assist.

Gravestones.   The government will provide a standard white headstone inscribed with the name, grade, and branch of service of the deceased. If burial is in a national cemetery, do not order a private monument until the design, material, and inscription have been approved by Office of Memorial Programs, National Cemetery System, Department of Veterans Affairs, Washington, DC 20420. The superintendent of the national cemetery concerned should be informed of plans for the headstone when you apply for the burial lot; many national cemeteries allow private markers only in certain areas. The VA will furnish a government headstone prepaid to the railroad station nearest to the place of private burial.

Government headstones are provided for officers' dependents buried in national cemeteries.

Transportation for Family.   One person may escort the body of an officer who dies on active duty to the place of burial. The escort may be a relative or friend (not in the service), with the government providing transportation in kind. If private burial is desired, a military escort usually accompanies the remains.

Household Effects.   The household and personal effects of an officer who dies on active duty may be shipped from the last duty station or place of storage to the place the next of kin selects as home. Arrangements are made in the usual manner with the local supply officer, but shipment must take place within a year of death.

Death Certificates.   For a death on inactive duty, the undertaker will obtain as many certificates as may be requested, at a nominal cost ($1 to $2 each, depending on the locality). They are needed for each insurance company, for the will, for each claim, for Commandant of the Marine Corps, for the pay office carrying your accounts, and for the transfer of each security held in joint ownership. For deaths on active duty, Marine Corps Headquarters furnishes five copies of the official Report of Death, which will serve as a legal death certificate. Additional copies may be obtained on request.

The next of kin should also ask two officers or other friends, who knew the deceased, to identify the remains. These witnesses will then be prepared, if required, to furnish the affidavit of death sometimes demanded by commercial insurance companies.

Burial Privileges for Family Members.   If a family member of any Marine on active duty dies at or while traveling to or from place of active duty, certain government allowances are payable for transportation of remains.

SURVIVOR BENEFITS AND ASSISTANCE

2121.   Death Benefits

Back Pay.   Pay and allowances to the credit of a deceased are payable to the persons as designated on the Record of Emergency Data to receive them. If the deceased did not make such a designation or if the person designated dies first, this payment is made to the surviving spouse or, if predeceased, to the children, then the parents. Headquarters Marine Corps will send the necessary form to the person(s) eligible to receive this payment.

Death Gratuity to Active Personnel.   When death occurs on active duty, six months' pay (including flight and hazardous duty pay), in an amount not less than $800 or more than $6,000, is payable to the spouse of the deceased, or, if predeceased, to children; if he or she is not survived by children then to any parents or brothers and sisters so designated. Payment to the spouse or children is mandatory and is not affected by designations. *This gratuity cannot be checked to liquidate overpayment or any debt to the United States, and it is nontaxable.* In most cases, payment by the cognizant commander is proper and authorized and, in fact, should be paid within twenty-four hours after receipt of notification of death. In all other cases, Headquarters Marine Corps will institute claim for death gratuity to the eligible beneficiary upon notification of death of a Marine; therefore, it is not necessary for your next of kin to request this benefit. In case of financial distress, your spouse may apply to the nearest Marine command for help. The Navy Relief Society will also help with either a grant or loan (see Section 2124). The death gratuity just described is also paid if death occurs within 120 days after retirement or separation from the service, provided death is due to disease or injury incurred or aggravated while on active duty.

Compensation for Unused Leave. Your spouse or estate is eligible to claim and receive compensation for any unused leave to your credit, should you die on active duty.

Death Compensations and Pensions. For veterans who die on active duty as a result of disease or injury received in service, the award granted survivors is referred to as "compensation." If an award is based only on the fact of service in a war, it is called a "pension." Pensions may be payable by the VA to surviving spouses and to children of certain retired Marines who die from causes not connected with their active military service. If, for example, you served in World Wars I or II, the Korean War, or Vietnam, your unremarried spouse and unmarried children under age eighteen (twenty-one, if attending an approved school) are eligible for pension. So would be any children over age eighteen if incapable of self-support. If your spouse has other income of given categories, it may reduce or terminate his or her pension during periods when the spouse receives income in disqualifying amounts.

Payment of pension commences as of the day following death of the veteran, if a claim is filed within a year following death; otherwise, it commences from the date of receipt of the application. Claims should be filed with Dependents' Claims Service, Department of Veterans Affairs, Washington, DC 20420. Considerable investigation is required before a pension claim can be approved, and the following evidence must accompany a claim:

- Proof of death (death of a veteran in active service, on the retired list, or in a government hospital does not need to be proved)
- Proof of marriage of the claimant to the veteran (if either had been married previously, proof of death of or divorce from the former spouse is required)
- Proof of date of birth of children
- Proof of birth of veteran (showing filial relationship, if a parent makes the claim)

If claimant qualifies under more than one rate, the maximum rate is awarded.*

2122. Other Benefits

Hospital and Medical Care. Dependent parents, spouses, and children under age twenty-one of deceased Marines are eligible for certain civilian medicare on a cost-sharing basis and, in general, for admission to armed forces hospitals. They may receive outpatient medical service where such service is available (see Section 805).

Educational Assistance for Children of Marine Corps Personnel. From time

---

*If the veteran in question has ever previously filed a VA claim, he or she has been assigned what is called a "C Number," a file number of permanent record that relates to all future VA correspondence or dealings involving the person in question. It is important that a living veteran or next of kin know and record the C Number and use it in all VA claims or contacts.

to time, the Department of the Navy publishes a list of schools, colleges, universities, and other organizations that grant concessions and scholarships to service children. For this information, write to Commandant of the Marine Corps (Code MHEP).

Navy Relief Educational Loans. The Navy Relief Society (see Section 2124) will lend up to $1,000 per year, interest-free, for college or vocational education above high school, or for preparatory work to enter a state or service academy, to eligible children (not over age twenty-three) of active or retired regular Navy or Marine Corps officers or enlisted, and to children of reservists on extended active duty. Information may be obtained from the Navy Relief Society, Washington, DC 22203.

Family Educational Assistance. Administered by the VA, this program provides up to thirty-six months' schooling for spouses of deceased veterans, spouses of living veterans, and children of either (ages eighteen–twenty-six) when death or total, permanent disability arose from service. Spouses and children of Marines missing in action (MIA), prisoner of war (POW), or forcibly detained or interned by a foreign power for more than ninety days are also eligible.

In certain cases, children with disabilities may begin special courses as early as age fourteen. In most cases, a child's eligibility ends with the twenty-sixth birthday.

Generally, eligibility for a spouse extends to 30 November 1978, or ten years from the veteran's date of death or total, permanent disability, whichever is later. For spouses of MIAs or POWs, eligibility extends to 24 December 1980, or ten years from the date the serviceman or servicewoman was listed, whichever is later.

Naval Academy Preparatory Scholarships. The Society of Sponsors of the U.S. Navy awards preparatory school scholarships to enable high school seniors who are the children of active, retired, or deceased Marine Corps, Navy, or Coast Guard personnel to prepare for entrance to the Naval Academy. For information, write Commandant of the Marine Corps (Code MHEP).

Exchange and Commissary Privileges. Armed forces exchange and commissary privileges are available to the families of Marine Corps personnel upon presentation of a valid Identification and Privilege Card. Before going overseas, be sure that these ID cards are current for each family member and that those over ten years of age have their own cards.

Employment. Important civil service preference benefits are granted to service surviving spouses, not remarried, in connection with examinations, ratings, appointments, and reinstatements under civil service and in connection with government reductions in force. Those interested should also apply to the nearest U.S. Employment Service office for job information.

2123. Marine Corps Casualty Procedures

The next of kin recorded on your Record of Emergency Data is notified in case you are seriously injured, wounded, killed, or missing. Your next of kin is kept advised of your condition while you are on the critical list.

When an officer dies or is missing in action, a casualty assistance officer is appointed from a nearby Marine Corps organization to provide advice and assistance to the survivors. The casualty assistance officer outlines rights and benefits of survivors, helps prepare claims, and so forth.

Chaplain. The survivors of a deceased Marine (active or retired) should not fail to seek assistance from the chaplain of the nearest Marine Corps or naval activity. Not only can chaplains minister spiritually at this difficult time, but they are also ready to help with burial arrangements, transportation, and all the problems that arise after the death of the head of the family. Chaplains will likewise arrange for burial in government or civilian cemeteries and will conduct the funeral service.

Marine Officials. The nearest Marine commanding officer, recruiting officer, or inspector-instructor is competent and glad to assist families of deceased Marines with their problems.

2124. Aid from Organizations

Several organizations offer advice and assistance to families of deceased officers.

American Red Cross. This organization assists families with all types of government claims, as well as other problems. Proof of dependency is necessary; family members should consult the Red Cross field director at the post or station or the Red Cross chapter in their town.

Navy Mutual Aid Association. In case of death of a member, the secretary of the association should be the very first resort. This association can be depended upon to handle all matters pertaining to pensions and other government claims.

Navy Relief Society. This organization provides aid to members of the naval services and their dependents. Aid includes financial assistance (loan or gratuity); services of a Navy Relief nurse; help with transportation and housing; information about dependency allowances, pensions, and government insurance; location of and communication with naval personnel; and advice about community services. Apply to the Navy Relief Society, Navy Department, Washington, DC 22203.

Veterans' Groups. The Retired Officers Association, American Legion, Veterans of Foreign Wars, Disabled American Veterans, Military Order of the World Wars, and other veterans' groups may also render aid to survivors of Marine veterans.

RETIRED OFFICER BENEFITS

When you retire, you rate various Marine Corps benefits and perquisites. In addition, you may be entitled to various veterans' benefits if you apply for them. Some of these have already been mentioned, and this section sums up the most important ones remaining. In connection with most veterans' benefits, it is important to know that, although your retired pay is taxable, it is not classed as "other income," and thus does not bar you from receipt or limit the extent of benefits for which you are otherwise eligible, except that, if you receive disability compensation from the VA, your retired pay is reduced by the amount of the VA disability payment.

2125.   Medical Care and Hospitalization

Retired Marines entitled to retired or retainer pay are also entitled to medical and dental care in uniformed services medical facilities on the basis of availability. Their family members are also eligible on this basis, except as to dental care.

Retired personnel of the Marine Corps, their spouses and children, and the spouses and children of deceased active or retired Marines, are eligible for CHAMPUS civilian hospitalization and outpatient services (routine doctor visits, drugs, and so forth) on a cost-sharing basis, whereby the government pays the major part of fees involved. For outpatient services, a single family pays a deductible fee per person treated per year and 25 percent of the remaining cost; the government pays the remaining 75 percent. For hospitalization, the government pays 75 percent of the cost (including doctors' bills), and the retired Marine or family member pays the remaining 25 percent. On reaching age sixty-five, when you become eligible for Social Security Medicare, you no longer rate the civilian-type military medicare just described, and your access to armed forces medical facilities expires.

At the time of retirement, when your active-duty health record is closed out, ask your sick bay to make a copy for personal retention in case of future VA claims or whenever you need attention from any medical facility.

2126.   Eligibility for U.S. Naval Home

Aged and infirm retired regular officers are eligible for admission to the U.S. Naval Home, Gulfport, Mississippi, on approval by the secretary of the Navy (see *Marine Corps Civil Readjustment Manual*). Residence at the home does not entail forfeiture of retired pay. Retired Navy and Marine officers and their spouses or surviving spouses are also eligible for Vinson Hall, the Navy-Marine-Coast Guard Residence Foundation home at Fairfax, Virginia.

2127.   Veterans' Benefits

As a veteran of military service, whether in time of war or peace, you have certain privileges and benefits. Although some of these are subject to expiration, Congress adds others from time to time. The following are the most important current benefits.

Department of Veterans Affairs.   The VA offers a multitude of benefits to persons honorably discharged from the armed forces: special care and pensions for the physically and mentally impaired; hospital and domiciliary care; vocational rehabilitation; family benefits, including financial and education support; loans or loan guarantees for acquiring homes or farms and their upkeep and improvement; home remodeling for the disabled; nursing home care; alcohol and drug rehabilitation; counseling services; and burial and funeral expenses. Consult your nearest VA field office. Once you are admitted to any program, including active-duty VA loans and educational benefits, retain your VA file number for easy access to all future transactions.

Educational Assistance.   Any serving member of the armed forces or veteran having served in the forces since 31 January 1955 is eligible for educational assistance at the vocational, college, or university level in approved courses and institutions for up to thirty-six months. Three separate programs have been established over the period, and you may qualify for one, depending on your service entry and other factors.

1. The Vietnam Era GI Bill, administered by VA, supports those who entered service before 1 January 1977. Any benefits of the program yet unused may be converted to the current Montgomery GI Bill program (see below). Benefits must be used within ten years of release from active duty or from the beginning of such use, but no later than 1 January 2000.

2. The Veteran's Education Assistance program (VEAP) applies to those entering service between 1 January 1977–30 June 1985. It was a participatory program in which service personnel paid up to $2,700 to receive government matching funds for a maximum benefit of $8,100. Marines who entered active duty and paid into the program during the period are eligible for benefits, to be paid for a maximum of thirty-six months.

3. The Montgomery GI Bill sponsors active-duty and veteran personnel who began active duty after 30 June 1985 and accepted payroll deductions of $100 per month for the first twelve months of service. After completing the initial three years' active duty (or two active and four reserve service years), a serving member or veteran may receive at least $300 per year for a period up to thirty-six months. Various supplementary payments are also available. Eligibility ends ten years after release from active duty (or after the sixth active/reserve year of service). Personnel who graduated from a service academy or an ROTC scholarship program after 31 December 1976 are not eligible for the Montgomery GI Bill program. They may use the VEAP benefits, if applicable.

U.S. Employment Service.   Both the U.S. Employment Service and all state employment offices have counseling and placement facilities for veterans, to which you are entitled.

2128. Travel on Government Aircraft

Retired officers (but not family members) may travel, space available, in government aircraft within the continental limits of the United States. To arrange this, check with operations at the air station from which you wish to depart.

Retired officers and accompanying family members may travel, space available, on Mobility Command (AMC) overseas flights. To do so, report in person (with ID card and, of course, passport, visas as required, and immunization record) to the appropriate AMC "gateway" base. If your destination is the Pacific or the Far East, Travis AFB, California, is the place to report; for the Mediterranean or Latin America, it is Charleston AFB, South Carolina; for Europe, McGuire AFB, New Jersey, Dover AFB, Delaware, or Charleston AFB; and for Japan and Alaska, McChord AFB, Washington.

Space-available travelers are subject to being "bumped" by travelers on emergency orders at any point en route. Their baggage is limited to sixty-six pounds, and they must of course be physically present at the AMC terminal to be placed on the space-available waiting list (good for 30 days). Finally, anyone traveling in this category should have sufficient ready cash to proceed via commercial means if "bumped."

2129. Government Employment of Retired Officers

The Dual Compensation Act of 1964 repealed long-standing restrictions that hampered retired regular officers from holding government jobs. Today, with a few exceptions, retired officers, regular or reserve, may hold any civilian federal office.

Under the terms of Dual Compensation, regular officers retired for any cause other than combat disability received the full pay of the civilian job and (as of 1964, when enacted) the first $2,000 of their annual military retired pay, plus one-half of the balance of retired pay. Each time retired pay increases by reason of the cost of living, the $2,000 increment increased by the same percentage. As of 1999, it is $10,450. These fabled "double-dipper" penalties have been repealed by the 2000 defense budget, so that officers and warrant officers will no longer have to forfeit any portion of retired pay if they work for the federal government. However, no provision was made for back pay of the estimated 6,400 retired officers (1999), who fell under these former strictures.

Even with the present greatly simplified, more reasonable legislation on this subject, it remains complicated. Restrictions still in force limit officers participating in sales activities, employment as an agent of a foreign government, prosecution of claims against the government, participating in certain kinds of foreign commercial enterprises, or acting as an attorney against the United States without executive sanction. Certain specialist officers, such as those in procurement fields, are restricted from taking federal jobs for a certain period of time after retirement. In the event you have any doubts, consult DOD Directive 5500.7, Standards of Conduct, or the latest edition of *Handbook for Retired Marines*.

2130. Divorce

The decision to dissolve your marriage is an intensely personal one. Because of the structure of dependency benefits, however, an officer seeking separation or divorce needs to keep the commanding officer advised of administrative or social changes and needs to inform and provide documents to unit administration. Separation does not usually involve changes in dependency, but divorce does. In a divorce, identification cards must be recovered, your former spouse must be removed from the DEERS, and your remaining dependency obligations must be certified. The last means recertifying any children or other legal dependents and submitting a copy of the divorce decree and any accompanying support agreement to Headquarters Marine Corps. These may serve as references in case the government has to adjudicate elements of the decree. You should seek the most competent legal advice you can afford, so that an equitable arrangement can be determined as soon as possible. Adhere to your legal obligations so that the Corps need not intervene in your personal affairs and finances.

Garnishment of active duty and retired pay to meet the obligations of alimony and child support was authorized by Public Law 93-647 (1975). Garnishment was limited two years later under PL 95-30 to either 50 or 65 percent of the individual's aggregate disposable earnings received from the federal government, depending on whether the individual had remarried. A valid court order must be issued to garnish pay, naming the agency required to effect the garnishing and stipulating enforcement of child support or alimony obligations. Commanders are then required to forward such orders to the finance center for action.

In addition to support requirements, a divorced officer now faces possible division with a former spouse of military retired pay as property. The 1981 *McCarty* decision by the Supreme Court ruled that such pay was not subject to division as property, in effect safeguarding military pensions of those divorced before the date of the decision, 26 June 1981. But PL 97-252, effective 1 February 1983, contains a Former Spouse Protection Title that permits state courts to consider dividing military disposable retired pay as property between parties in a divorce regardless of the number of years the couple was married. Remarriage of the ex-spouse does not necessarily cause termination of the award. The title also extends health and commissary and exchange privileges to ex-spouses married during at least twenty years of active service.

The lesson of the above paragraphs should be clear: if ending a marriage, seek the best legal advice and consider the local laws and customary judgments most carefully before proceeding.

Foreign Divorces.   Medical care, quarters allowances, and other dependents' benefits have been denied in the cases of military personnel who have obtained foreign divorces, usually Mexican, and later attempted to marry some other person. You have the responsibility of preventing members of your command from the often tragic difficulties that can result from foreign divorce entanglements.

Three things come not back: the arrow that is flown, the spoken word—and lost opportunities.

—Omar Ibn, 581–644

22

Marine Corps Social Life

There was once an era when officers and their families lived, worked, and enjoyed social occasions within a rather insulated community of fellow service members. Most officers and families lived on board bases, and the nearby civilian communities offered less in the way of social attractions than did the bases. With the coming of the Second World War, the military services expanded and the separate military and civilian societies became more intertwined. In the postwar period, the larger peacetime military establishment and frequent expansions during the conflicts of the second half-century brought that old insular military society to a gentle close. Today, military officers live, commute, and mix freely with their civilian counterparts. The demands for recreation and social activities have far outstripped the capacity of the bases.

There still remain many enjoyable trappings of that old military society to enjoy and to share on occasion with your civilian friends. This chapter contains some useful information covering those traditional activities. A few have become extinct, for practical purposes, but are retained here for reference in the event that they could be revived in isolated instances or celebrated in a foreign country in which you serve.

As you become a Marine and join the corps of officers, you also must be prepared to share the time-honored and pleasant social traditions of your Corps. As you do so, remember one thing above all: the phrase, *"an officer and a gentleman [woman]"* is a current one in the Marine Corps. It means what it says.

2201.   Helpful References

This chapter is not intended to be an "Emily Post" for Marine officers but simply to deal with the military, and more especially the Marine, aspects of service social life. For more general reference, consult the latest editions of the following publications:

- *Service Etiquette* (U.S. Naval Institute). A sound general guide, indispensable in certain matters.
- *Social Usage and Protocol* (Foreign Liaison Section, Office of Naval Intelligence). This handbook, for many years withheld from general circulation by civil servants in ONI, is a comprehensive, useful *vade mecum* within its limits. Any officer going on attaché, Military Assistance Group (MAG), or naval mission duties should obtain a copy.
- *Social Usage in the Foreign Service* (Department of State). A useful compilation containing many excellent suggestions and much good advice.

SOCIAL OCCASIONS

2202.   The Marine Corps Birthday

As every Marine knows, the Corps was founded on 10 November 1775. From that day to this, 10 November has been the climax of the Marine Corps year, the top social occasion of the Corps.

The birthday of the Marine Corps is celebrated officially and socially by all Marines throughout the world. Not only do Marine units carry out the prescribed ceremony, but wherever one or more Marines are stationed—on board ship, at posts of other services, even in the field—10 November is celebrated.

How a Command Observes 10 November.   For a Marine command, the birthday includes prescribed or customary features, which are observed as circumstances permit. For Marines with other services, many of these items cannot be fulfilled exactly, but this list may serve as a guide:

- A troop formation (preferably a parade) for publication of the article from the *Marine Corps Manual*. The uniform should be dress blue A (which includes large medals). If blues cannot be worn, medals should be prescribed on the service uniform for this occasion. On shipboard, hold a special formation of the Marine detachment and get permission from the captain to pipe the birthday article over the public address system. If you are with some other service and only a few Marines are present, you may defer publishing the article until the evening social function.
- Holiday rations and, if the recreation fund can stand it, beer for the troops.
- Maximum liberty and minimum work consistent with the missions of the command.
- A birthday ball for officers and one for enlisted Marines. At each, a cake-cutting ceremony takes place.

At any schools or instruction scheduled for 10 November, you should emphasize the traditions and this history of the Corps.

The Birthday Ball. It is up to you to celebrate the annual birthday ball with pride, forethought, and loving care. Every Marine command must have one. If on detached service away from the Corps, the senior Marine officer present must arrange a suitable birthday ball, and it is up to every Marine to chip in to support it.

The birthday ball is formal, which means evening dress for officers possess-

Cutting the birthday cake is the high spot of the traditional birthday ball.

ing that uniform, or dress blue (with large medals) as a substitute. If you are not required to possess either evening dress or blues, wear service uniform.

The birthday ball is a command performance. Unless duty prevents, you attend. If resources permit, distinguished civilian guests and officers from other services should be invited, but not too many. Be sure that retired Marine officers and any Marine officers present from other countries are included.

The procedure for a birthday ball ceremony is described in Appendix VI. This procedure, of course, is a guide, and details may vary according to facilities, numbers of officers and guests, and local traditions. There is only one iron-clad rule for the birthday ball: *Make it a good one.*

2203. Mess Night

A *mess night* (sometimes called a "guest night" or a "dining-in night") is a formal dinner in mess by all members or by the officers of a particular post or unit.

Mess nights may be held on special anniversaries (such as that of a battle in which the unit has participated), to "dine-out" officers being detached, or to honor a distinguished guest or guests from another unit, service, or country.

In the U.S. Armed Forces, mess nights date back to the army's regimental messes of the pre–World War I days and to the days of the wine mess in the wardroom afloat, which ended abruptly in 1914 when Secretary Josephus Daniels imposed prohibition on the Navy. In this early era of a small Marine Corps with only a couple of hundred officers, the only permanent Marine officers' mess was that at 8th and Eye, and here in the Old Center House (torn down in 1908) the officers of Headquarters and the Barracks had their mess nights. Happily, the custom continues in today's successor Center House, as elsewhere.

Preparations.   The first step in preparing for a mess night is to designate the officer who will act as vice president. In some units, the vice president is traditionally the junior lieutenant present. However, it is good practice to rotate the post among all company officers on board so that all may gain experience. In any case, the function of the vice president, at least beforehand, is to undertake all preliminary arrangements—guest list (to be approved by the mess president), seating diagram (also to be approved), menu and catering, music, decorations, and so forth. The success of the evening depends on the vice president.

Subject to local or unit customs and to facilities that are available, here are specific arrangements which should be made for a mess night:

1. After approval of the guest list, invitations should be prepared and mailed or delivered at least two weeks in advance of the mess night. Each guest, regardless of organization or of sponsoring officer in the host unit, is a guest of the mess and should be so treated.
2. The table is set with complete dinner service—wine glasses, candles, and flowers. Unit or post silver and trophies should be used.
3. Unless the CO desires to preside, a field officer is detailed as president of the mess for the occasion; a company officer acts as vice president.

4. Uniform is evening or mess dress, or dress blues or whites. Civilians invited to a mess night should wear full dress with miniature medals if uniform is evening or mess dress; dinner jacket with miniatures, if blues or whites.
5. The National Color and the Marine Corps Color are placed behind the president's chair; guidons and drums may also be used as decorations.
6. The mess president sits at the head of the table, the vice president at the foot. Other guests and members take seat by rank (as in the wardroom on board ship), except that guests of honor are on the right and left of the president. A seating diagram should be posted in advance, and place cards and menu cards prepared. All preliminary arrangements are supervised by the vice president.
7. If available, a three- or four-piece military string orchestra should be detailed to provide dinner music. The orchestra should know the national anthems and regimental marches of guest officers. If suitable "live" music is not available, a good-quality PA system with taped or recorded selections will serve as a substitute. The musical program should be checked and timed by the vice president and should always include "Semper Fidelis" and the regimental march of each guest.

Procedure.   Officers assemble in an anteroom thirty minutes before dinner for cocktails and to greet guests. This should be the occasion for all officers to speak to guests and make them feel welcome. It is also the opportunity for each officer to pay respects informally to the senior officers present, COs especially. Dinner is announced in accordance with local custom. In some messes, "Semper Fidelis" is played; elsewhere, Officers' Call is sounded followed by a march (when drum and bugle corps is available, "Sea Soldiers" is a suitable march); still another variation is to play "The Roast Beef of Old England" (known and used in the "Old Navy" as "Officers' Mess Gear") on fife and drum. Whatever the signal, officers and guests proceed to their places. Each guest should be escorted by a member of the mess. A brief grace is said by the chaplain, if present, otherwise by the president. Officers then take seats. The ranking guest, seated at the mess president's right, is served first, then the president, and so on counterclockwise without further regard to seniority. Appropriate wines are served with each course. There should be no smoking during dinner, and no officer may leave the table until after the toasts, except by permission from the president. (If for any reason, official or otherwise, you arrive late, you should express your regrets to the mess president before taking your seat.)

After dessert, there is a short concluding grace, the table is cleared, and port decanters and glasses are placed on the table. The port passes clockwise until all glasses are charged. When the decanter (or both decanters, if two are used) has completed the circuit, the president raps for silence. If a foreign officer is present, the president rises, lifts a glass, and says, "Mr. Vice, His Majesty, King _____ of _____." The vice president then rises, glass in hand, waits until all have risen, and gives the toast. "Gentlemen, His Majesty, King _____ of _____." The orchestra plays the foreign national anthem, following which all say, "King _____ of

_____," drink, and resume seats. After about a minute, the president again raps for silence, the senior foreign officer rises, and says "Gentlemen, the President of the United States," and the orchestra plays the National Anthem. If no foreign guests are present, the first toast is to the President of the United States, and—in any case—the *concluding* toast is to the Marine Corps, during which, if music is available, "The Marines' Hymn" is played. The wording of this toast should be, "Mr. Vice, Corps and Country," and the custom has grown up (proposed long years ago by Colonel A. M. Fraser) that the vice president reply in words taken from a Revolutionary War recruiting poster of the Continental Marines—"Long live the United States, and success to the Marines!"* If the guest of honor is a Marine general officer, he or she may take this occasion to proceed to a few remarks. If the guest of honor is from another service, a toast to that service is in order. He or she may respond and speak. Toasts are not "bottoms up."

Before leaving the subject of toasts, note that toasts may be divided into four classes, and that they are given in the following order.

- *Toasts of Protocol:* Toasts to foreign governments or chiefs of state; toast to the President of the United States.
- *Official Toasts:* Toasts to other services, military organizations, government departments, agencies, or institutions.
- *Traditional Toast:* "Corps and Country."
- *Personal Toasts:* Toasts to individuals (distinguished guests, officer being dined out, and so on).

The traditional toast ends the formal part of the evening. Personal toasts and speeches may follow at a suitable interval afterward, as described below.

Following the toasts, coffee is served, the smoking lamp is lighted, and individual drinks or liqueurs may be ordered. At this point, or whenever the orchestra is released, the president may send for the leader and offer a drink. If speeches are planned (other than remarks associated with toasts), they are made now. In "dining out" an officer, the commanding officer makes brief, usually humorous remarks, whereupon the officer being honored replies in the same vein. In some messes, the orchestra remains and plays the regimental march of each guest, during which the individual stands. When speeches are over, the president announces, "Ladies and gentlemen, will you join me in the bar?" and the senior officers rise, following which the remaining members of the party adjourn individually to the bar and anteroom, where songs are generally sung and games played. All hands should remain until the ranking guest and the commanding officer leave, after which anyone may secure at discretion.

---

*In some messes and commands, the custom has grown up of emulating the Continental Marines by drinking toasts in rum punch rather than port. Here is the mix for "1775 Rum Punch": four parts dark rum; two parts lime juice; one part pure maple syrup. Add small amount of grenadine syrup to taste. Ice generously and stir well. The maple syrup was originally used during the Revolution because of the British blockade that cut off supplies of West Indies sugar cane.

Circumstances frequently do not permit a mess night with all formalities as to uniform, catering, and table service that are outlined herein, or all of them might not be desired. This should not deter an organization from making the effort. The idea is to do the best you can with what you have, and let the spirit of the occasion take care of the rest. Do not, in particular, let yourself be overcome or stultified by the apparent formality of mess nights; the object is the pleasure and comradeship of all hands. Reports that a few commands have actually rehearsed mess nights, if true, make the occasion ridiculous. A mess night is not a minuet.

As to timing, it is better not to schedule mess nights regularly. It is much preferable that officers begin asking when the next one will take place. Thus a mess night will be looked forward to with anticipation and never become a burden.*

2204. Military Weddings

As a Marine officer, you enjoy the privilege of having a military wedding. A military wedding is simply a formal wedding with traditional service embellishments. The characteristic features and ground rules of a military wedding are as follows.

Uniform. Marine members of the wedding party wear dress blue or white A with sword. Dress A uniforms call for medals, not ribbons. If the weather requires, wear boat cloak rather than overcoat. Even though wearing sword, and thus under arms, the bride and groom should not wear gloves, whereas the ushers should wear gloves throughout the ceremony.

Needless to say, all members of the wedding party wear the same uniform. If

---

*The costs of a mess night, like other "chip-in" Marine Corps functions, should be prorated by rank so that officers who make the most, pay the most. Here is the famous Schatzel formula for prorating by rank, which appears complicated but is actually quite simple:

Rank	Base Pay	Number Participating
Colonel	x	δ
Lieutenant Colonel	y	σ
Major	z	ν
Captain	α	ϕ
1st Lieutenant	β	Δ
2nd Lieutenant	λ	η

$$K = \text{total cost of the function}$$
$$E = x\delta + y\sigma + z\nu + \alpha\phi + \beta\Delta + \lambda\eta$$

$$\text{Colonel share} = \frac{Kx}{E} \qquad \text{Lieutenant Colonel share} = \frac{Ky}{E}$$

$$\text{Major share} = \frac{Kz}{E} \qquad \text{Captain share} = \frac{K\alpha}{E}$$

$$\text{1st Lieutenant share} = \frac{K\beta}{E} \qquad \text{2nd Lieutenant share} = \frac{K\lambda}{E}$$

officers from other services are included, they wear their nearest equivalent uniform. For an evening wedding, evening dress is worn.

Best Man and Ushers. Since your wedding is to be military, your best man and ushers should be regular or reserve officers. Inactive reserve officers may don uniform for the occasion. It is usual but not necessary for ushers to be the same rank as the bride or groom. The senior usher coordinates the military side of the ceremony and gives commands or signals for movements by the ushers and for the arch of swords.

The best man looks out for the groom. It is a nice compliment to your immediate commanding officer (if you are on those terms) to ask that he be your best man. The same pertains to the bride, if an officer, and the matron of honor. In any case, however, your CO and fellow officers should be invited to the wedding, and all will attend.

If the wedding takes place away from the bride's home, and her parents or near relatives cannot attend—as is sometimes the case in the service—it is appropriate for the commanding officer or other senior officer to give away the bride.

The Clergyman. You may choose either a chaplain or a civilian clergyman. A chaplain performs the ceremony in uniform or in vestments, according to the customs of the denomination. In some denominations (such as the Episcopal Church) ministers, whether chaplain or civilian, are permitted to wear military ribbons on their vestments and will do so if you request. The best man should see to this. If your wedding is an evening affair, it is appropriate for the clergyman to wear miniature medals on a civilian coat at the wedding reception.

Do not pay a chaplain for officiating at a military wedding. If you have a civilian clergyman, follow civilian custom regarding feeds. Again, this is something the best man should attend to. The same applies to fees for organist and music at the church.

Wedding under the Colors. If you wish, and if your denomination permits, the National Color and Marine Corps Color of your unit may be crossed above and in rear of the chaplain, or displayed during the ceremony in the chancel of the church. This is known as "A wedding under the Colors." It is an old tradition, signifying your spouse's acceptance into the Corps.

Handling the Colors for this ceremony is the responsibility of the senior usher, who, with designated ushers, receives the Colors (cased) from the adjutant, places them before the ceremony, and removes, cases, and returns them immediately afterward.

Wedding Present from the Unit. The officers of the bride's or groom's battalion, squadron, headquarters, or service school classmates (if at school when married) should present the couple with a piece of plate, such as a silver tray, water pitcher, or cocktail shaker, which is appropriately engraved. Some units have a standard type of wedding gift, which it is the duty of the adjutant to procure, engrave, and collect for. A typical inscription for such a piece of plate might read: From the Officers of the 1st Battalion, 5th Marines.

Social occasions can provide enrichment of the military professional's life.

If the wedding takes place at a school, it is up to the senior Marine officer in the class to see to this wedding present.

Arch of the Swords.   This is probably the best-known feature of a military wedding. It is carried out in this fashion:

After the ceremony, the senior usher forms the ushers in column of twos. and places them *immediately outside* the exit of the church, facing inboard. As the newly married couple passes through the portal, the senior usher commands: 1. Officers draw; 2. SWORDS. At the command of execution, ushers carry out *only* the first count of the movement and leave their swords raised, with tips touching, to form an arch under which the couple passes. After the newlyweds have passed, swords are returned on command by the senior usher.

Cutting the Wedding Cake.   The wedding cake is cut by the bride and groom together, using the sword. If a Marine Corps junior is being married, it is proper to use the father's sword. After the cake has been cut, the best man proposes a toast to the bride and groom, and, as the guests drink, the orchestra plays "Auld Lang Syne."

2205. Calls

The exchange of calls once received emphasis in military society far exceeding that on the "outside." Although at first glance a bit ritualistic, they did serve to break down barriers of seniority, widen one's circle of acquaintances, and disclose mutual interests that might otherwise have gone unnoticed. The Marine Corps far exceeds the size that it was in earlier times when tradition held that

Marines all knew one another. Calling has declined in the same manner that the old isolated military posts and their insular societies have expired. It is worth recording here, however, in the event that you arrive on an isolated station, which facilitates calling as a practice, or in the event that you serve in a foreign country still observing this practice.

2206. Kinds of Calls

Calls are of two kinds—official and personal. You will find the former covered in Sections 1820–1821. Official calls are rendered only between commanding officers, officers of state, and officers' messes. Personal calls are exchanged between officers and their families.

Although Marine Corps customs govern personal calls, some commanding officers have special preferences as to when and how calls are paid. Thus, before making any calls, check with the adjutant, and, if necessary, with the general's aide (or, if serving with the Navy, the flag lieutenant) in order to find out the local policies.

The procedures described below apply to small and medium-sized posts or organizations (individual ships and units no larger than a regiment). At large posts, at schools, and in Washington, the large officer population and the constant turnover have always prevented adherence to the protocol (but not the spirit) of formal calling.

Initial Calls.   Whether married or single, you pay a "visit of courtesy" on your commanding officer or reporting senior within forty-eight hours after you report. If your commanding officer or reporting senior is married, your spouse (if you are married) should accompany you. Unless your CO indicates otherwise, the uniform for this call is undress blue.

Some commanding officers will suggest a convenient time for this "visit of courtesy," even though it may not be strictly within the forty-eight–hour time limit. The important thing is that the call be made promptly and at a time when the CO and spouse will be in, the object being for you to meet them socially, and vice versa.

If you are single, after you have completed the foregoing call on the commanding officer, you should call in quarters on all field officers, and, if possible, on all married officers of the command. Unless local rules decree otherwise, wear civilian clothes for these calls.

If you are married and have your spouse with you, as soon as you are settled in quarters, on or off post, you may expect calls from other officers. Return each call within ten days. Wear civilian clothes for such return calls.

If you are married but not accompanied by your spouse, pay the same calls as a single person, provided your spouse is not expected to join you within a month. Once your spouse arrives and the family is settled, married calls will be paid as if you both had just arrived.

Calling Hours.   The hours for formal calling ("calling hours") are from 1700 to 1900 in the Marine Corps, Navy, Coast Guard, and virtually all foreign forces. In the Army and Air Force, however, you call between 1930 and 2100, after dinner.

Twenty minutes (or "one drink") is the accepted duration of a formal call.

"At Homes" and "Calling Parties."   On large posts, at schools, and in Washington, calling obligations are usually discharged through "At Homes" or "Calling Parties."

An "At Home" is a specified day and time (once a month or once a quarter) when a senior officer, such as a head of division at Marine Corps Headquarters or the director of a school, desires that callers present themselves at the officer's home. Refreshments are served, and, as on all formal calls, cards are "dropped." Attending an "At Home" is equivalent to a formal call made and returned between the host and those who leave cards. "At Homes" are rarely held by officers below general or flag rank, unless the host has an independent command.

A "Calling Party" is like an "At Home" but is given by the command as a whole rather than by an individual officer. In large commands, where general calling is not practicable, it is customary, once every six months or on the reporting of a new commanding general, to hold a "Calling Party" at the officers' mess. At a "Calling Party," the commanding general, other general officers, and their spouses form the receiving line; all other officers and their spouses attend and go through the line, although cards are not dropped. The mess provides refreshments. Attending a "Calling Party" is equivalent to required formal calls aid and returned—not only between the receiving officers and those who attend, but among all families at the party. Dress blue or white B is worn at calling parties.

"Calling Book."   In some commands, the CO or commanding general may have a "calling book." The "calling book" is kept in the CO's or commanding general's office (usually by the adjutant or aide). Officers who would otherwise be required to pay a personal "visit of courtesy" as outlined above, may meet this obligation by inscribing their names in the "calling book."

2207. Calling Cards

Correct selection and use of calling cards is of some social importance to an officer. For this reason, the following paragraphs cover a few essentials of card "etiquette."

Selecting Cards.   You can make few social mistakes as avoidable, as conspicuous, or as lasting as selecting the wrong kind of personal cards. The best way to avoid such bobbles is to have your cards engraved by a good stationer. In large cities, the better department stores usually have engraving services well qualified to advise you on the layout for a correct card.

Marine Corps Exchanges can order all types of calling cards and have brochures to illustrate the various types and styles of approved cards. Should you wish to purchase calling cards from commercial sources, any reputable engraver or stationer familiar with the correct use of letters and social forms, and the proper type and paper, can advise you competently. No matter with whom you trade, however, the general rules on cards are:

- Give your full name.
- Show full rank in the lower right corner. Avoid abbreviations: use "United States Marine Corps" or "United States Marines," *not* "USMC" or "U.S. Marine Corps." *Never* use "U.S. Marine Air Corps" or such incorrect terms.
- Be sure the card is engraved, not printed.
- Avoid fancy typefaces. Preferred types are shaded antique Roman, solid Roman, or Ideal Script.

Name and rank are engraved no larger than 9/64" for the capital letters, with lowercase letters of appropriate size in keeping with the size of the capital letters across the center, where the name is printed. Rank and service, in the lower right-hand corner of the card, are printed in letters 7/64" high.

The rank of general and field grade officers precedes the name, whereas the rank of company officers must be engraved one line above the service designation in the lower right-hand corner of the card. First and second lieutenants may use the rank designation of *Lieutenant.* Officers retired from the Marine Corps should have the word *Retired* engraved and centered beneath the service designation in the lower right-hand corner.

If married, you should also have a *joint family card,* as mentioned above, which lists your rank (but not the Corps), with a legend such as this: Lieutenant and Mrs. Fuller Barnett Henderson.

In addition to the general rules summarized here, much detailed information on card etiquette and customs is to be found in *Naval Ceremonies, Customs, and Traditions* by Vice Admiral William P. Mack, USN (Ret.) and Lieutenant Commander Royal W. Connell, USN (published by U.S. Naval Institute).

It is convenient, if you are married, to have what are known as "informals," or folded cards, inside which you or your spouse may pen short messages, invitations, or acknowledgments. The legend on the face of the "informal" is the same as that shown above for a joint family card.

After preparing your first batch of cards, most engravers will retain your plate. This makes it easy for you to reorder. It also permits you to modify the basic plate each time you are promoted. This is considerably less expensive than having a new plate engraved each time you wet down a commission.

Leaving Cards. Aside from obvious miscellaneous use (exchange between new acquaintances, enclosure with gifts, nameplates on doors, and so on), you should leave cards on the following occasions.

Formal calls. When you pay or return a formal call (discussed in Section 2206), always leave cards.

As an unmarried officer paying or returning a call, leave one card for your host, one for your host's wife, and not more than one extra for other adult ladies in the household—a ceiling, that is, of three cards.

If you are calling as a married couple, you leave cards on the basis just described. Your spouse may leave a card for each adult in the household visited.

Leavetaking.   When you are about to leave a post, you should leave a "P.P.C." card. P.P.C. stands for *pour prendre congé,* which is French for "to say goodbye." Write the initials P.P.C. on the face of your card, and affix it to the bulletin board of the station mess.

If, as a visitor, you have been accorded the privileges of a club, mess, or wardroom, ashore or afloat, always leave a P.P.C. card. Some clubs and messes have a section of bulletin board reserved for such cards. Other messes may have a mess "calling book," like the CO's calling book.

If you desire to leave P.P.C. cards for individual friends, you may mail them, have them delivered by a chauffeur, or drop them in person at the door.

"To Inquire."   When a fellow officer or a member of the household is seriously ill or hospitalized and unable to receive visitors, it is an appreciated courtesy to leave your card, inscribed "To inquire." This signifies that you have the invalid in mind and have asked after his or her health.

General Rules.

- Never leave more than three of any single card.
- When you call in person (which means in most cases), follow custom and turn down the top left-hand corner of your card(s).

CLUBS AND MESSES

2208.   Commissioned Officers' Messes

Every post or station has a commissioned officers' mess. The mess acts as a social focus for the officers and spouses of the post, it serves meals, and it sometimes provides accommodations for visiting officers.

The commissioned officers' mess is often referred to as "The Club" or "The Officers' Club." Like any club, the mess is a private association operated for the convenience of its members, who share its expenses. Although you are not automatically a member of any commissioned officers' mess just because of your rank and status, it is nonetheless habitual to extend privileges of a station mess to any visiting officer and family. At your home station, you are entitled to join the commissioned officers' mess upon payment of the required fees, if any, but you may be denied the privileges of the mess if you abuse them.

2209.   Officers Clubs and Unmarried quarters

Clubs and unmarried or bachelor officer quarters (BOQ) have three main functions: social recreation, meal service; and housing for bachelor, temporary bachelor, and visiting officer. Any officer assigned temporarily or permanently to a BOQ pays a fixed charge to take care of cleaning services, linen, and so forth. In certain BOQs with messing facilities, officers living therein pay for and take meals at given rates on a menu catered by the base officers' club. In a few cases (e.g., Camp Barrett at Quantico), the post central mess operates the officers' dining facility and serves (and charges for) the basic enlisted ration, which is habitually a good one. Where a BOQ does not have a messing capability, you take your meals at the officers' club (or possibly in an officers' section of a unit dining hall).

Closely related to the BOQ are its derivatives, MOQ and TOQ. An MOQ is a married officer(s)' quarters, usually an apartment building, and TOQ stands for transient officers' quarters.

2210. The Wardroom Mess

A wardroom mess is a commissioned officers' mess on board ship. The wardroom is the common room, recreational space, and dining room for the officers of a man-of-war. The wardroom mess is the organization through which the ship's officers cater their meals and meet most of their social and recreational needs while on board. Like any closed mess, the wardroom mess is a private association whose operation is paid for by members. Because wardroom messes fulfill essential functions of feeding and accommodation, they receive some government support. You will find notes about wardroom mess etiquette in Chapter 10. If you are going to sea duty, be sure to look up these rules—and observe them.

2211. Mess Etiquette

Before leaving the subject of clubs and messes, here are some general rules of conduct and etiquette that have always maintained the tone and correctness of Marine officers' messes.

Remember that the mess belongs to the members who support it. As a guest, defer to their ways and rules; as a member, assume responsibility for it and support it as your mess.

Attend mess meetings whenever they are held. You have no right to complain about the way a club is run if you are unwilling to attend meetings and voice your ideas at the proper time.

Dress conservatively and correctly at "the club." You can't go wrong, ordinarily, if you wear full uniform of the day or complete civilian clothes. Most messes publish and post their uniform rules. You, your guests, and your family members must abide by them if you expect to use the club.

Pay club bills promptly, sign chits legibly and accurately, and always be sure your checking account is in shape to meet any checks you write. The officers' mess is founded on the proven concept that a Marine officer's word or signature is his or her bond. Dishonorable disregard of your obligations as an officer will destroy your personal standing, weaken your mess, force irksome restrictions on other members, and bring swift retribution, which will mar your record.

Do not tip mess employees unless club rules expressly so authorize and encourage.

When you are a guest in a club or mess—unless the place is on a cash basis—do not attempt to stand drinks. If you are on temporary additional duty and thus become a member of the mess, however, you pay for your fair share. If, as a member, you see a strange officer alone in your mess, introduce yourself and extend hospitality; remember that a guest of any officer is a guest of the mess.

When you bring guests to the mess, be sure they are those you would entertain in your own home or introduce, as your friends, to the commanding general and spouse.

Whether in a private club or a service mess, remember that an officer of Marines is well mannered. If in doubt as to some nicety or ground rule, do the gracious thing. You will never go far wrong.

WASHINGTON DUTY

2212.   White House and Diplomatic Functions

The White House is a focus of social and official Washington. Some officers on duty in Washington may expect to be entertained at the White House, and a few are detailed to additional duty as Marine aides-de-camp at the Executive Mansion.

Because a White House invitation constitutes a presidential command, it takes precedence over any other social commitment, previous or not. If you receive a White House invitation, consult one of the aides to the commandant at Marine Corps Headquarters. The aide will tell you the uniform and give you whatever briefing may be in order.

Second only to White House functions in their requirement for fine attention to dress and etiquette are those conducted by the diplomatic corps.

Uniform is ordinarily worn for official parties at embassies or legations or those given by a military or naval attaché. The general rule is: undress blue or white for afternoon receptions and cocktail parties; evening dress for formal evening parties, black or white tie.

When at a foreign diplomatic party, be alert for and familiar with foreign badges and insignia of rank and with their national anthems. On occasions of this kind, your dignity, courtesy, and smartness set you apart not only as a Marine but as a representative of the United States.

2213.   Washington Calling Etiquette

Call on your reporting senior as if he or she were your commanding officer on a post, but don't wear uniform for this call as you might elsewhere. Because of the relatively large number of Marine officers in the Washington area, the commandant does not require calls. Field officers (and selected company officers) on duty in Washington may be invited to a reception or some other function at the Commandant's House, and attendance constitutes a call made and returned.

Subject to the foregoing ground rules, when in Washington you call on particular friends and acquaintances only, following the calling procedures that obtain elsewhere.

2214. Recreation in Washington Area

Navy and Marine Messes. The two Navy commissioned officers' messes are at Washington Navy Yard and at Naval Hospital, Bethesda, Maryland. Officers at MB, Eighth and Eye, have a closed mess for members only at Center House.

Other Services. The Army has two excellent (dues-charging) clubs: Fort Myer, Virginia, and Fort McNair (National War College), Washington. The Air Force has an outstanding club at Bolling AFB, Washington, and one at Andrews AFB, Camp Springs, Maryland. Marine officers, if they choose to frequent clubs and messes of other services, are eligible for membership in all of the above.

Private Clubs. The Washington area boasts two of the foremost military and naval clubs in the country: the Army and Navy Club (the "Town Club") and the Army and Navy Country Club (the "Country Club").

The Army and Navy Club, located on historic Farragut Square in Washington, is one of the senior private clubs in the United States and provides all amenities (including rooms for members and guests). The "Town Club" is a traditional meeting place for officers and their friends. The Army and Navy Country Club, in Arlington, Virginia, overlooking the city, is one of the coolest summer spots in the metropolitan area and a country club of first rank (with a first-rank golf course).

Both the Town and Country clubs allow newly commissioned officers to join, as nonresidents, with greatly reduced entrance fees well within your pocketbook. If you fail to take advantage of this privilege at the outset of your career, you must later buck waiting lists and pay relatively large initiation fees, which may make it impossible for you to be a member of these fine clubs. Membership on these terms is one of the best bargains open to a new officer; lose no time in taking advantage of it.

MARINE CORPS SOCIAL CUSTOMS

2215. Standing Social Customs

Certain social customs are observed throughout the Corps and deserve mention here.

Wetting Down Your Commission. Whenever you are promoted, you are obligated to hold a "wetting-down party." At this affair, your new commission (which is usually displayed at some conspicuous but safe vantage point) is said to be "wet down." When several officers are promoted together, you may join in a single wetting-down party.

Cigars.   If you are either newly promoted or a new parent, you distribute cigars or candy to all officers and staff NCOs of your unit.

Five Aces.   Any officer who rolls five aces when throwing dice for refreshments in a mess is obliged by tradition to buy a complete round of drinks for all the messmates present. In large messes, this custom is eased to the extent that you have to buy drinks only for your own party.

Entering a Mess Covered.   Unless you are on duty and under arms, if you enter a mess covered, you are liable to buy a round of drinks. Most messes adhere to and post the old rule: "He who enters covered here buys the house a round of cheer." In fact, some even have a bell and lanyard that may be rung by anyone present who spots an offender against this rule, thus signaling a free round.

Drawing Your Sword in a Mess.   The seagoing rule that any officer who unsheathes a sword in the wardroom must buy a round also applies on shore, if you are so unwary as to draw sword in any public room of an officers' mess. The custom goes back to the days of dueling, when this was one method of cooling off hotheads and restricting indiscreet sword-play.

Welcome on Board.   Whenever a new unit arrives at a post, or a transport brings in an appreciable number of Marines or Marine families, the local Marine commanding officer or representative, together with the post band, greets the newcomers.

Departure from a Post.   When a unit or draft leaves, the commanding officer, band, and friends see them off. If the move is routine, the band plays "Auld Lang Syne" as aircraft embarkation is completed, the transport casts off her last line, or the train gets under way. If the unit is on war or expeditionary service, "The Marines' Hymn" is the send-off. In either case, the departing unit should be played down to the airfield, dock, or loading platform by "Semper Fidelis."

Special Courtesy to COs and Senior Guests.   At any social functions—cocktail parties and receptions especially—you have certain special obligations to your commanding officer and spouse and to the guest of honor, if any. On your arrival (or on the CO's arrival, if later than yours), both you and your spouse should make it an immediate point to approach and speak to the CO and spouse. This is known as "making your number." Except when absolutely necessary, you should not depart before your CO and the guest of honor do so. If you must leave early, however, express your regret to your CO and ask permission. It is a mark of the worst military manners and social upbringing if either you or your spouse fails to observe these courtesies.

2216.   Social Do's and Don'ts

Common sense, tact, and ordinary courtesy are the fundamentals of social success in the Marine Corps. For fine points, you may wish to refer to the tested references listed in Section 2201 or to Emily Post, Judith Martin, or some other recognized social guide. The following pointers are supplementary, therefore, but worth your perusal.

When you are on a post, on board ship, in uniform ashore, or otherwise recognizable as a Marine officer, your conduct must be impeccable. "If you must raise hell," runs an old Marine proverb, "do it at least a mile away from the flagpole."

It was once written, "The ideal income is a thousand dollars a day—*and expenses*." Obviously you don't stand much chance of attaining this on service pay, although a few inexperienced or improvident officers try to live as if they had it. You cannot fool anybody as to how much you make, so live within your income.

"Good clothes open all doors"—be sure yours are correct both for style and occasion. And always check to see which uniform is prescribed, before you attend a social function.

"Whoever gossips to you will gossip of you"; "It is easier to be critical than correct"—avoid criticism about other officers, and never vent destructive criticism of your service, your unit, or your superiors.

Never serve bad liquor—"Use hospitality to one another without grudging."

Be punctual. It is never wrong to arrive exactly on time. For large cocktail parties, dances, receptions, and debuts, you may arrive *not later* than a half-hour after the announced time. For meals, be exactly on time. "Punctuality is the politeness of kings."

Don't load down social conversation with technical language or with labored application of Marine Corps terms to civilian matters. On the other hand, as a professional, learn the talk and nomenclature of the Corps. Use precise terms to convey precise meanings. Avoid undue shop talk and thus avoid the character whom Addison so well described:

> The military pedant always talks in a camp, and is storming towns, making lodgements and fighting battles from one end of the year to the other. Everything he speaks smells of gunpowder; if you take away his artillery from him, he has not a word to say for himself.

At a mess or at any official function, politics, religion, and sex are discussed (if at all) only with the greatest discretion. Whatever you do, never speak ill of your Corps or of any fellow officer in the presence of outsiders, civilians, or members of any other service. And remember always, insofar as public utterances are concerned, an American soldier has no politics and espouses no political party or cause.

Polite society is no place to play "the tough Marine." Courtesy and personal modesty are never more becoming than in an officer. Rudeness, abruptness, gory tales of blood and thunder, and coarse language usually show up the greenhorn or counterfeit, and certainly the ill-bred. "The bravest are the tenderest; the gentlest are the daring."

Remember that your spouse does not and cannot wear your rank. Be certain that he or she understands this quite clearly and does not exhibit a tendency to dominate the juniors or subordinates. This will only belittle your rank in the eyes of others. Insist, however, that your spouse receive due courtesy from all.

"Be prepared" is just as good a social motto for Marine officers as for Boy Scouts. Before you attend any social function, ascertain the dress, whether there will be a receiving line, who will receive, when the line closes, who of importance to the Marine Corps may attend. All these are the "EEIs"—essential elements of information—that help place you at ease and prepare you for any social eventuality.

Teach me to be obedient to the Rules of the Game.
Teach me to distinguish between sentiment and sentimentality,
  admiring the one and despising the other.
Teach me neither to proffer nor to receive cheap praise.
If I am called on to suffer, let me suffer in silence.
Teach me to win if I may; teach me to be a good loser.
Teach me neither to cry for the moon nor to cry over spilt milk.
                              —Lines framed in his cabin by King George V of England,
                                        while serving as a naval officer.

We are all members of the same great family. . . . On social occasions the formality of strictly military occasions should be relaxed, and a spirit of friendliness and good will should prevail.
                                                                    —John A. Lejeune

I

The Marines' Hymn

From the Halls of Montezuma
To the shores of Tripoli,
We fight our country's battles
In the air, on land, and sea.
First to fight for right and freedom,
And to keep our honor clean,
We are proud to claim the title
Of United States Marine.

Our flag's unfurl'd to every breeze
From dawn to setting sun;
We have fought in every clime and place
Where we could take a gun.
In the snow of far-off northern lands
And in sunny tropic scenes,
You will find us always on the job—
The United States Marines.

Here's health to you and to our Corps
Which we are proud to serve;
In many a strife we've fought for life
And never lost our nerve.
If the Army and the Navy
Ever look on Heaven's scenes,
They will find the streets are guarded
By United States Marines.

II

Commandants of the Marine Corps

Major Samuel Nicholas, 1775–81
Lieutenant Colonel William Ward Burrows, 1798–1804
Lieutenant Colonel Franklin Wharton, 1804–18
Lieutenant Colonel Anthony Gale, 1819–20
Brigadier General Archibald Henderson, 1820–59
Colonel John Harris, 1859–64
Brigadier General Jacob Zeilin, 1864–76
Colonel Charles G. McCawley, 1876–91
Major General Charles Heywood, 1891–1903
Major General George F. Elliott, 1903–10
Major General William P. Biddle, 1911–14
Major General George Barnett, 1914–20
Major General John A. Lejeune, 1920–29
Major General Wendell C. Neville, 1929–30
Major General Ben H. Fuller, 1930–34
Major General John H. Russell, Jr., 1934–36
Lieutenant General Thomas Holcomb, 1936–43
General Alexander A. Vandegrift, 1944–47
General Clifton B. Cates, 1948–51
General Lemuel C. Shepherd, Jr., 1952–55
General Randolph McC. Pate, 1956–59
General David M. Shoup, 1960–63
General Wallace M. Greene, Jr., 1964–67
General Leonard F. Chapman, Jr., 1968–71
General Robert E. Cushman, 1972–75
General Louis H. Wilson, Jr., 1975–79
General Robert H. Barrow, 1979–83
General Paul X. Kelley, 1983–87
General Alfred M. Gray, 1987–91
General Carl E. Mundy, Jr., 1991–95
General Charles C. Krulak, 1995–99
General James L. Jones, 1999–

III

Reading for Marines

All military laws and military theories which are in the nature of principles are the experience of past wars summed up by people in former days or in our times. We should seriously study these lessons paid for in blood, which are a heritage of past wars.

—Mao Tse-Tung, 1936

Marines and other artisans of war justly find perplexing the prospect of future war, for which they are charged to prepare. The answers to questions of who, when, where and to what aim will not grow less elusive in the future, of that we can be most sure. One method of preparing for the future, more and more espoused by Marines, lies in general reading in the only laboratory the soldier has, the study of the social sciences. The following suggests books and journals that will profit you as a Marine and as a professional soldier. Any such listing is bound to be arbitrary; many of the thousands of other writings on the military art will certainly prove enjoyable and beneficial as well. I have tried to suggest works of significant breadth and quality that remain available in bookstores, albeit difficult to locate in some instances. The reader will notice immediately a dearth of autobiography and biography, a field so obvious and rich as to defy selecting a few. In addition, you should read the excellent official histories of the Marine Corps and U.S. Army dealing with World War II, Korea, and Vietnam; the Second World War official histories of the United Kingdom, Canada, Australia, and New Zealand also make remarkably fine reading. Without further qualification, here are seventy books, grouped into seven categories, that cannot fail to improve your insight and skill as a professional.

GENERAL SURVEYS

M. Bartlett, *Assault from the Sea*
B. Brodie, *Strategy in the Missile Age* and *War and Politics*
M. van Crefeld, *Supplying War*
P. Fussell, *Wartime*
J. Hackett, *The Profession of Arms*
B. H. L. Hart, *Strategy*
M. Howard, *War in European History* and *Studies in War and Peace*
W. McElwee, *The Art of War*
A. Millett, *Semper Fidelis*
R. Preston and S. Wise, *Men in Arms*
C. Reynolds, *Command of the Sea*
T. Ropp, *War in the Modern World*
R. Weigley, *The American Way of War*

TECHNOLOGY

B. Brodie, *Sea Power in the Machine Age* and *Crossbow to H-Bomb*
W. McNeil, *The Pursuit of Power*

SOCIAL AND POLITICAL

M. Janowitz, *The Professional Soldier*
The Pentagon Papers ("Gravel" Edition)

CAMPAIGNS AND TACTICS

C. Barnett, *Desert Generals*
W. Belote and J. Belote, *Typhoon of Steel*
P. Calvocoressi and G. Wint, *Total War*
V. Chuikov, *Battle for Stalingrad*
T. Dupuy, *Genius for War*
J. English, *Perspectives on Infantry*
J. Ericson, *Road to Stalingrad*
B. Fall, *Street without Joy*
M. Ferro, *The Great War*
H. Guderian, *Panzer Leader*
J. Gunsburg, *Divided and Conquered*
J. Hackett, *Third World War*
B. H. L. Hart, *The Real War 1914–18*
W. Hughes, *Fleet Tactics*
S. Karnow, *Vietnam*

J. Keagan, *Face of Battle*
C. MacDonald, *Company Commander*
E. von Manstein, *Lost Victories*
S. Marshall, *Sinai Victory*
F. von Mellinthen, *Panzer Battles*
A. Moorehead, *Gallipoli*
S. Morison, *Two Ocean War*
E. O'Ballance, *No Victor, No Vanquished*
D. Rees, *Korea*
G. Rothenberg, *Art of Warfare in Age of Napoleon*
C. Ryan, *Bridge Too Far* and *Longest Day*
R. Weigley, *Eisenhower's Lieutenants*
H. Willmott, *Empires in the Balance*

CLASSICS

Caesar, *The Civil War*
K. von Clausewitz, *On War* (ed. Paret-Howard)
Josephus, *The Jewish War*
T. Lawrence, *The Seven Pillars of Wisdom*
Mao, *On Protracted War*
Tacitus, *Annals of Imperial Rome*
Thucydides, *Peloponnesian Wars*
Sun Tzu, *Art of War*
Xenophon, *The Persian Expedition*

MISCELLANEOUS

A. Collins, *Common Sense Training*
S. Marshall, *Men Against Fire*
S. Sarkesian, *Combat Effectiveness*

FICTION

P. Caputo, *Rumor of War*
R. Graves, *Goodbye to All That*
J. Hasek, *The Good Soldier Schweik*
E. Hemingway, *For Whom the Bell Tolls*
W. Mauldin, *Up Front*
E. Remarque, *All Quiet on the Western Front*
M. Shaara, *The Killer Angels*
J. Thomason, *Fix Bayonets*
J. Webb, *Fields of Fire*

Most of these books can be obtained through the Marine Corps Association Bookstore or the U.S. Naval Institute, with discounts offered to members. For cut-rate offers and sales, query the Military Book Club, Edward R. Hamilton Bookseller, Falls Village, CT 06031-5000, or The Scholar's Bookshelf, 110 Melrich Road, Cranbury, NJ 08512. For military history titles out of print, try The Military Bookman, 29 E. 93d Street, New York, NY 10128; or Antheil Booksellers, 2177A Isabelle Ct., North Bellmore, NY 11710. Perhaps the finest collection in the world is offered, at no mean price, by Francis Edwards, Ltd. of London.

PROFESSIONAL JOURNALS

Marine Corps Gazette
U.S. Naval Institute *Proceedings*
Journal of Military History
Military History Quarterly
Naval War College Review (free to active-duty officers)
Parameters (Army War College mails free to officers using billet title and address)
Military Review

More expensive, but useful, are the following:
Royal United Services Institute Journal
Armed Forces Journal International
Jane's Defense Weekly
International Defense Review

IV

Fellow Marines

The bonds of comradeship-in-arms that knit many of the corps of marines in today's world remain unusually strong. As a member of the world's largest (though not the oldest) of these military organizations, you should know of the other sea soldiers serving under foreign flags. Many of these—the older corps in Europe, the Latin American and East Asian corps of marines and naval infantry— enjoy long-term relations with the U.S. Marine Corps, and the respective commandants have exchanged messages and visits over the years.

This appendix has been expanded to include information, as known, on some of the other such corps, many of which had been regarded as "on the other side," depending on the varied courses of diplomacy.

THE ROYAL MARINES

I never knew an appeal to their courage or loyalty that they did not more than realize my expectations. If ever the hour of real danger should come to England, the Marines will be found the country's sheet-anchor.

—Lord St. Vincent

Britain's Royal Marines, elder brothers of the U.S. Marine Corps, were 111 years old in 1775 when our own Corps was founded. From inception, the infant American corps was modeled after its illustrious British prototype, and many of the traditions of our Corps today can be traced to the Royal Marines.

As a result, despite early fallings-out (as in 1775, at Bunker Hill, and in

1814, when Royal Marines burned Washington after the Bladensburg fight), the camaraderie between U.S. and British Marines is a tradition of both Corps, and knowledge of the Royal Marines is part of every U.S. Marine's fund of information.

The Royal Marines perform much the same duties as U.S. Marines, with certain variations. As is the case for one of our Fleet Marine Force commanding generals, the Commandant General, Royal Marines, serves as a "type commander" under the fleet commander of the Royal Navy. The fleet commander, under the present system (since 1993), delegates full command of the Royal Marines to the commandant general, who also has the right of direct access to the First Sea Lord, equivalent to the CNO of the U.S. Navy, on regimental matters of the Royal Marines.

The roles of the Royal Marines include the following: providing an amphibious commando brigade (with supporting army, navy, and air force personnel and units) capable of worldwide deployment, as well for traditional infantry tasks; detachments for navy ships and certain shore stations; special forces, such as the Special Boat Service (SBS); a special unit to protect nuclear weapons and sites; maritime counterterrorism; the Royal Marine Band; and other missions as the Navy Board may direct.

The uniforms of the Royal Marines are much like our own. Aboard ship and on certain shore duties, they wear blues. Their ranks, rank insignia, and field undress uniforms are those of the British Army, but the color of the service uniform is forest green. All Royal Marines wear a blue beret as one type of headgear, but members of commando units wear green berets, because green has always been the traditional commando color.

The official colors of the corps are scarlet, yellow, green, and blue. These colors appear on the Royal Marines necktie, which is worn with civilian clothing by all members of the corps.

Although Royal Marine Officers wear British Army rank badges, they are promoted and paid under the naval system. An officer can expect to be promoted to captain at about age 30 and would then receive the pay of a lieutenant commander in the Royal Navy or army major. Further promotion depends upon selection, with up to 60 percent of the captains reaching major at an average age of 37.5 years. A lieutenant colonel equates to a naval captain and a colonel to a captain of six years' seniority. As with the British Army, the grade of brigadier is an appointment position for a colonel, with two- and three-star grades the same as in other services.

The "Birth of the Corps Day," which corresponds to our 10 November, is 28 October of each year. The Royal Marines were organized in 1664.

The sovereign, or a member of the royal family, is captain-general of the corps. At present, this post is filled by the Duke of Edinburgh, husband of Queen Elizabeth.

The principal stations of the Royal Marines are the major barracks (Stonehouse) at Plymouth; Commando School, Bickleigh; Infantry Training

Center, Lympstone; Amphibious School, Poole; and a recruit depot and school of music at Deal.

Although U.S. and British marines have served side by side on many occasions, both Corps particularly cherish associations stemming from the Boxer Uprising and from the Korean War. In the Boxer Uprising, U.S. and Royal marines formed the backbone of the band of Western troops who defended the Legation Quarter in Peking throughout a long and bloody siege in 1900. In addition, in the International Brigade, which finally relieved both Peking and Tientsin, U.S. and British marines were formed side by side. Fifty years later, a Royal Marine commando was attached to the 1st Marine Division in Korea and served with the division throughout the Chosin Reservoir campaign. And it was at Suez, in 1956, that the Royal Marines conducted the first carrier-based helicopter assault landing ever executed in combat.

ROYAL NETHERLANDS MARINES (KORPS MARINIERS)

The *Korps Mariniers*—as the Dutch Marines are officially entitled—were founded on 10 December 1665 in the Dutch Wars, which caused the British to form the Royal Marines. One of the most important early operations of the Netherlands Marines was the amphibious raid up the Thames in 1666, one of the few occasions when foreign troops have landed in Great Britain since the Norman Conquest. Subsequently the *Korps Mariniers* performed normal sea duty and garrison duty throughout the Dutch empire. During World War II, when Holland was overrun by the Germans, several thousand Dutch Marines were trained at Camp Lejeune as the basis for reconstitution of the corps, and the relationship between our two corps has since been close. *Qua Patet Orbis* ("To the Ends of the World") is the Dutch Marines' motto; their uniforms, both service and dress, are similar to those of the Royal Marines and of the U.S. Marine Corps.

Today, the *Korps Mariniers* continues to serve as an integral part of the Royal Netherlands Navy. It provides detachments for ships and naval stations and takes responsibility for the physical, military, and ceremonial training of all Navy personnel. A battalion each is furnished to a British/Dutch landing force in the North Atlantic Treaty Organization (NATO) and the Allied Command Europe Mobile Land Force. From the latter battalion, two companies, known as *Qua Patet Orbis* units, can be formed for United Nations (UN) missions on twenty-four-hour and forty-eight-hour notice, respectively. Some four hundred Dutch marines guard installations in the Netherlands Antilles and Aruba. There is also a "special assistance unit" for counterterrorism tasks.

The headquarters of the corps is in Rotterdam, with principal barracks there and on the island of Texel. Amphibious training is conducted on Texel.

SPANISH MARINES (INFANTERIA DE LA MARINA ESPAÑOLA)

Dating from the *Tercios de la Armada Naval* of Spanish Armada days and earlier, Spain's *Infanteria de la Marina* can claim four centuries of service. Its men fought at Lepanto (1571) and with the Armada in 1588; defended Cartagena in 1741; took Sardinia in 1748; and served gallantly in the Peninsular War, Cuba, the Philippines, Guam, Morocco, Cochin China, the Spanish Civil War, and the Sahara (Ifni).

The missions of the Spanish Marines are to guard ships and stations and maintain trained expeditionary forces.

The *Infanteria de la Marina* today maintains *Tercios* (light infantry regiments) at El Ferrol and Cartagena bases and *Agrupaciones* (light infantry battalions) at Cádiz, Las Palmas, and Madrid. Each contains an expeditionary company in addition to guard companies. The *Tercio de la Armada* is a marine expeditionary brigade maintained at San Fernando (Cádiz) for duty with the fleet. It is colocated with the development and education center. The Major General Commandant has his office and staff in the Navy Headquarters, Madrid.

Spanish Marine officers' uniforms are those of the Navy, with distinguishing badges; enlisted Marines wear dress blue similar to those of the Royal Marines, and combat/utility uniforms resembling those of our own Corps. The emblem of the *Infanteria de la Marina* is an anchor (up-and-down) with crossed rifles, surmounted by the crown of Spain.

The Spanish Marines' motto is "Valiant on Land and Sea." Since 1701, the traditional colors of the Corps have been red and blue. As in the case of our own Corps, Horse Marines are both a tradition and a joke with the Spanish, dating from the fact that, during the nineteenth-century guerrilla operations in Cuba, "Navy Cavalry" mounted units were formed of Marines. The birthday is celebrated on 26 February for this, the oldest (1537) marine corps in the world.

ARGENTINE MARINE CORPS

The origin of the Argentine Marines goes back to 1807 when a naval battalion was organized to defend Buenos Aires against British attack. Subsequently, during Argentina's War of Independence, Marines served on board warships and conducted landing operations. In 1879, a Marine artillery battalion was formed, to man coast defenses at Argentina's seaports and naval bases. In 1947, following World War II, the corps was reorganized along modern amphibious lines, and a U.S. Marine adviser was provided. However, he did not accompany the battalion that spearheaded Argentina's seizure of the Falklands/Malvinas Islands by amphibious assault in 1982.

The major operating units of the Argentine Marine Corps include a cold-weather center garrisoned by a battalion in Patagonia, a riverine battalion on the River Plata delta, and another battalion at Rio Santiago naval base. The 2d Marine Force includes the Marine Brigade, an amphibious RLT, based at Puerto Belgrano.

The uniforms and ranks of the Corps are similar to those of our own. The annual birthday ceremonies are held on "Day of the Marine Corps," 19 November.

BRAZILIAN MARINE CORPS (CORPO DO FUSILEIROS NAVAIS)

The *"Fusileiros,"* as the Marines are known throughout Brazil, date their lineage back to the Portuguese Marines, which were founded in 1797. Units of this organization first came to Brazil in 1808, and 7 March, the date of their landing, is the birthday of the corps in Brazil—which was then an overseas dominion of Portugal and subsequently separated amicably from the mother country.

Brazilian Marines fought in their country's wars throughout the nineteenth century, including major riverine operations along the River Paraguay. The most recent expeditionary service of the *Fusileiros* was as part of the Inter-American Peace Force, which kept order in the Dominican Republic for fifteen months in 1965 and 1966, side by side with U.S. Marines during part of that time.

The Brazilian Marine Corps is divided into operating forces (which include a Fleet Marine Force and security forces and ships' detachments) and a supporting establishment, which functions in the same way as our own. The *Fusileiros'* headquarters and FMF are located at Rio de Janeiro.

COLOMBIAN MARINE CORPS

The first combat landing by Colombian Marines took place on 11 November 1811, less than a year after their organization during their country's War of Independence. Throughout the nineteenth century, the corps had its ups and downs, but it was permanently constituted as amphibious and expeditionary troops in 1937. Ever since 1948, during Colombia's prolonged struggle to win over banditry, the corps has been continually engaged in riverine, amphibious, and pacification duties. Like our own corps, the Colombian Marines carry out operations in both the Atlantic and the Pacific. The corps includes one tactical battalion. Virtually all its officers today are graduates of Basic or Amphibious Warfare Schools at Quantico, and many of its NCOs are also graduates of U.S. schools.

VENEZUELAN MARINE CORPS

The Venezuelan Marine Corps was formed on 22 July 1822—as in the case of most of the other South American Marines—during its country's War of Independence. During the nineteenth century, however, it became inactive, and it was not officially reconstituted until 11 December 1945.

The missions of the Venezuelan Marines include amphibious operations, counterguerrilla and pacification duties, and naval base security. The corps regularly conducts battalion-landing-team–level landing exercises, and over a third of its officers are graduates of U.S. Marine Corps Schools.

The Venezuelan Marine Corps is made up of four battalions, based at Puerto Cabello and Maiquetía, with headquarters at Caracas. All these units have been active in Venezuela's defense against guerrillas and bandits.

REPUBLIC OF KOREA MARINE CORPS (ROKMC)

The Korean Marine Corps, which has fought side by side with U.S. Marines in two wars—Korea and Vietnam—was founded on 15 April 1949 at Chinhae, destined to become the Quantico of Korea. Within less than two years, the 1st Korean Marine Regiment had become an integral part of the 1st U.S. Marine Division and played an outstanding part in the three years of hard fighting.

The primary mission of the ROKMC is to conduct amphibious landings as part of the national mobile striking force and to serve as a portion of the national force in readiness. In addition, like our Corps, it performs security duty for the naval shore establishment and is responsible for the development of amphibious warfare doctrine, tactics, techniques, and materiel.

In addition to maintaining a brigade in the mainline of resistance at Kimpo, the ROKMC has two main bases, Chinhae and Pohang. Marine garrisons or security units are found at Seoul, Paeng Yong Do, Cheju-Do, Pusan, Muk-Ho, Inchon, and Mokpo.

The uniforms of the ROKMC are similar to those of the U.S. Marine Corps. The official color of the Korean Marine Corps is scarlet. The creed of the corps, which serves as its motto, is as follows:

Loyal to the nation
Be ever victorious
Unite as a family
Honor is worth more than life
Love your fellow countrymen.

ROYAL THAI MARINE CORPS

The Royal Thai Marine Corps was formally organized on the U.S. Marine Corps model on 30 July 1955, but it also traces its modern existence to 1932, with historical antecedents to 1824. Its missions are amphibious operations, base defense, counterinsurgency and support of the Royal Thai Army. Naval ranks and titles are used throughout the corps. Combat operations include the 1941 conflict with France, border conflicts with Cambodia since 1961, insurgency actions throughout the 1970s, and action against a Vietnamese incursion in 1985.

Thai Marine operating forces consist of a combat division and a security regiment.

Sattahip, on the Gulf of Thailand, is the main base of the Thai Marines, but Chanthaburi, near the Cambodian frontier, is the secondary base. In addition to being headquarters for the corps, Bangkok is also the home station for a Marine garrison.

FRENCH MARINES (FUSILIERS MARINS)

In contrast to the Anglo-American evolution, French Marines started out as sailor-infantrymen, vice soldiers of the sea. This was the inspiration of Cardinal

Richelieu, as he founded the Sea Company in 1622 for landing party duties in the French Navy and raised a full regiment in 1627, the official year of origin. The *Regiment de Marine* became the *Fusiliers Marines* by an imperial decree of 5 June 1856, which confirmed their status as seagoing specialists. They have fought in all the modern conflicts of France, with particularly distinguished service in the world wars and in Indochina. Since 1963, the operating forces have formed a commando type battalion, the *Groupment de Fusiliers Marins Commando,* based at Lorient. Other marines serve in the school, also at Lorient, guard units, and ships' detachments.

These *Fusiliers* must be distinguished from other troops often reported as "French Marines." The latter are the former colonial infantry of the French Army that guarded and fought in the outposts of the French empire, most of which were administrated by the Navy Ministry. In the modern order of battle of the French Army, these *Troupes de Marine* units form motorized and parachute battalions of the 9th Marine Division. They are modern army units, not designed for service with the French Navy.

PORTUGESE MARINE CORPS (CORPO DE FUZILIEROS)

The Portugese Marines trace ancestry to a shipboard corps formed in 1585 to serve guns on board ship, defend the coast against pirate attacks, and serve in the royal guard.

The *Fuzilieros* have been integral to the Portugese Navy and use naval ranks and service uniforms. The corps' most intensive period of service came during the frustrating 1961–75 insurrectionist wars in the colonies of Guinea, Angola, and Mozambique, where some 13,000 men saw action.

Today, Portugese Marines guard ships and stations and provide a landing battalion for the navy, based in Lisbon.

RUSSIAN MARINES

The turbulent history of the Russian Marines began, as with many other modern trends, with Peter the Great. Soviet practitioners used the term "naval infantry" loosely for large detachments of sailors thrown into land battles, as well as specialized permanent troops. Peter, from the start, plainly titled his marines *Morskoi Soldaty,* or sea soldiers, and assigned them to sea regiments, beginning in November 1705. By 1715, experience gained in campaigns against Sweden caused him to more than double the force to five large battalions. Steady growth under Peter's successors came to an abrupt halt when Napoleon's invasion caused a permanent transfer of all the sea regiments to the Russian Army.

Not until the early 1960s did the Soviet Union reestablish the naval infantry. Each of the four Soviet Navy fleets received base security units and a landing battalion. A later expansion created a combined arms brigade in each fleet, complete with armored vehicles and heavy weapons. The Russian Republic continues to operate the naval infantry on a reduced scale commensurate with fleet operations.

ECUADORIAN MARINES

Founded officially on 12 November 1966, after a four-year trial period, the *Cuerpo de Infanteria de la Marina* of Ecuador guards the naval base of Guayaquil, provides an amphibious spearhead, and assists in internal security.

CUBAN MARINES

Even newer than the Ecuadorian corps is the elite Cuban naval infantry. First noticed in 1979 in a naval parade, the contingent has not exceeded one thousand men. It provides a motorized amphibious battalion for operating forces and has security and special operations elements as well.

CHINESE MARINE CORPS

Although no longer recognized diplomatically by the United States, the Taiwan Republic of China continues to field the second largest Marine Corps in the world. Founded on 16 September 1947 in the midst of the Chinese Civil War, the Taiwanese Marines expanded under U.S. assistance after 1951 and oriented themselves to the USMC organization of their advisers. After the tough Kinmen Island defense of 1958, the Taiwanese Marines settled into a taut peacetime training and readiness regimen that continues today.

With a Fleet Marine Force of two divisions, plus security units, the Taiwanese Marine commandant exercises command from Tsoying, with another major installation located at Fang-Shan. The colors are scarlet and gold.

Still somewhat obscure is the size and composition of the Marine Corps of the People's Republic of China. But with six-thousand marines assigned in peacetime and the modernization of the Chinese fleet, it is conceivable that it could rival the size and status of its island counterpart. Both Chinese corps can trace lineage to the earlier Chinese Marines of 1917, with antecedents dating to 1433.

V

Article 38, Marine Corps Manual, 1921

Every 10 November, the central part of the ceremony is the publication to all hands of Article 38, *Marine Corps Manual,* 1921, which was written especially for this purpose by John A. Lejeune, the thirteenth commandant. While this text and its introduction are found in the *Marine Corps Manual* today, it is reproduced here as a matter of convenience for those who do not have a *Manual* within easy reach.

On November 1st, 1921, John A. Lejeune, 13th Commandant of the Marine Corps, directed that a reminder of the honorable service of the Corps be published by every command, to all Marines throughout the globe, on the birthday of the Corps. Since that day, Marines have continued to distinguish themselves on many battlefields and foreign shores, in war and peace. On this birthday of the Corps, therefore, in compliance with the will of the 13th Commandant, Article 38, United States Marine Corps Manual, Edition of 1921, is republished as follows:

"(1) On November 10, 1775, a Corps of Marines was created by a resolution of the Continental Congress. Since that date many thousand men have borne the name Marine. In memory of them it is fitting that we who are Marines should commemorate the birthday of our Corps by calling to mind the glories of its long and illustrious history.

"(2) The record of our Corps is one which will bear comparison with that of the most famous military organizations in the world's history. During 90 of the 146 years of its existence the Marine Corps has been in action against the Nation's foes. From the Battle of Trenton to the Argonne, Marines have won foremost honors in war and in the long era of tranquility at home, generation after generation of Marines have grown gray in war in both hemispheres, and in every corner of the seven seas that our country and its citizens might enjoy peace and security.

"(3) In every battle and skirmish since the birth of our Corps, Marines have acquitted themselves with the greatest distinction, winning new honors on each occasion until the term 'Marine' has come to signify all that is highest in military efficiency and soldierly virtue.

"(4) This high name of distinction and soldierly repute we who are Marines today have received from those who preceded us in the Corps. With it we also received from them the eternal spirit which has animated our Corps from generation to generation and has been the distinguishing mark of the Marines in every age. So long as that spirit continues to flourish Marines will be found equal to every emergency in the future as they have been in the past, and the men of our Nation will regard us as worthy successors to the long line of illustrious men who have served as 'Soldiers of the Sea' since the founding of the Corps."

The inspiring message of our 13th Commandant has left its mark in the hearts and minds of all Marines. By deed and act from Guadalcanal to Iwo Jima, from Inchon to the Korean Armistice, from Lebanon to Taiwan, the Marines have continued to epitomize those qualities which are their legacy. The success which they have achieved in combat and the faith they have borne in peace will continue. The Commandant and our many friends have added their hearty praise and congratulations on this, our . . . birthday.

VI

Birthday Ball Ceremony

The following is an outline for conducting the Marine Corps birthday ball ceremony in a medium-sized command with drum and bugle corps (or at least a field music) and an orchestra available. Bear in mind that this is a guide and may be modified according to local resources and traditions.

- At H – 15 minutes, drum and bugle corps sounds *Officers' Call.*
- Adjutant (who acts as announcer) requests that officers and guests clear the floor for the ceremony. Floor Committee places line and stanchions (if used) to define ceremonial aisle and area.
- At H – 5, the drum and bugle unit (D&B), color guard, and honor guard form at exit, prepared to march on.*
- At H – 1, adjutant takes post on floor, adjacent to exit, and, at H-hour, when all hands are posted, commands, "Sound *Adjutant's Call.*"
- D&B sounds *Adjutant's Call,* then marches up the aisle to designated post, playing "Foreign Legion March," or "Sea Soldiers."
- (When D&B halts, historical pageant, if any, commences. At conclusion of pageant—or next event, if no pageant—orchestra plays "Semper Fidelis.")
- On first note of "Semper Fidelis," honor guard steps off.

---

*For an officers' birthday ball, honor guard consists of two officers of each grade; at small posts, where the ball is an all-hands party for the whole command, honor guard consists of two lieutenants, two staff NCOs, two sergeants, and two corporals. All honor guard members are covered and wear Mameluke or NCO Sword as appropriate.

- Honor guard, junior rank in lead, proceeds up the aisle two abreast, each pair at six-pace intervals. At six paces inside hall, senior person in leading pair commands, 1. Officers 2. HALT. Without further command, pair faces outboard, takes three paces, halts, and faces about. Six paces farther, the next junior pair repeats this evolution, etc. In each case the only spoken command is 1. Officers 2. HALT, the remaining movements being executed simultaneously in cadence without command. When the honor guard is posted, the orchestra stops playing.
- D&B sounds *Attention.*
- Senior Marine commander and honored guests (the official party) enter and march up aisle, face about, take post at head of aisle abreast of senior pair of honor guards, and receive honors (if a flag or general officer is present) from D&B.
- Orchestra commences "Stars and Stripes Forever." Color guard enters from exit and marches up aisle, halting abreast of next senior pair of honor guards. Music ceases when color guard halts.
- Adjutant, from original post at rear, proclaims, "Long live the United States, and success to the Marines!"
- D&B plays "To the Color." All covered officers come to hand salute. Colors then take designated post.
- Fanfare by D&B.
- Orchestra commences "The Marines' Hymn." Birthday cake is wheeled in from exit by four-person cake escort, followed by the adjutant. Cake is posted abreast of second senior pair of honor guards. Cake escort takes post in rear of cake.
- Adjutant steps front and center between cake and official party.
- Senior Marine commands, "Publish the Article."
- The adjutant then publishes Article 38, *Marine Corps Manual 1921,* and resumes post.
- Senior Marine steps forward to make remarks, followed by remarks, if any, by honored guest.
- At conclusion of remarks, adjutant steps forward and hands senior Marine an unsheathed Mameluke Sword (previously placed on cake table), with which senior Marine cuts cake while orchestra plays "Auld Lang Syne."
- Senior Marine then introduces and presents cake slice to youngest and oldest Marines present.*
- Cake escort then retires cake to a flank where it is received by waiters.
- D&B commences "Semper Fidelis." Senior Marine and official party retire from post and proceed to head table or box.
- Color guard marches off, followed by the honor guard in reverse sequence (senior pair leading). As the rear rank of honor guard comes abreast of next

*When senior to the senior Marine (for example, an ambassador, secretary of the Navy, etc.) the honored guest is asked to cut the cake by the senior Marine, who then introduces youngest and oldest Marines, who in turn receive slices from the honored guest.

pair, the senior of that pair commands 1. Forward. 2. MARCH, and the pair marches three paces inboard face right and left respectively, and step off without further command. The D&B marches off at six paces behind final pair of honor guards. On passing through exit, each D&B player mutes instrument so the music will seem to fade away in the distance.

- Floor Committee removes line and stanchions. D&B ceases playing, and ceremony is ended.

VII

Glossary

This glossary contains a compilation of terms currently peculiar to the Marine Corps. Certain terms might be recognized as belonging also to one of the other services; in such cases, however, the term has been incorporated here only by virtue of long inclusion as part of the Marines' distinctive vocabulary.

Airdale: Aviator.

All hands: All members of a command; everybody.

Ashore: (1) On the beach, as differentiated from on board ship; (2) any place off a Marine Corps or government reservation. **Go ashore:** go on liberty, or leave the reservation.

Asiatic (adj): Mildly deranged or eccentric as a result of too much foreign duty; (n) one who has "missed too many boats."

Aye, Aye, Sir: Required official acknowledgment of an order, meaning, "I have received, understand, and will carry out the order or instructions."

B & W (n): Solitary confinement on bread and water, now only authorized on board ship; sometimes spoken of as "cake and wine."

Barracks cap: Frame type, visored cap, so called because this type of headgear was traditionally prescribed for non-FMF organizations.

BCD (n): Bad-conduct discharge.

Binnacle list: List of men placed on light duty by the surgeon; in old days, it was posted on or near the binnacle.

Blue Book: *Combined Lineal List of Officers of the Marine Corps on Active*

Duty; also the *Register of Commissioned and Warrant Officers of the U.S. Navy and Marine Corps.*

Blues: Dress or undress blue uniform.

Boondockers: Field shoes or boots.

Boondocks (n): Woods, jungles, faraway places; semifacetiously defined as "that portion of the country which is fit only for the training of Marines."

Boot: A recruit.

Boot camp: Recruit depot.

Break out (v): (1) To unfurl; (2) to remove from storage; (3) to arouse.

Brig: Place of confinement aboard ship or ashore at a Marine Corps or naval station; the post prison. **Brig time:** confinement.

Brig rat: One who has served much brig time, a habitual offender.

Bulkhead: (1) (**n**) A wall; (2) (**v**) to complain against or asperse a superior while superficially pretending not to.

Cannon-cocker: Artilleryman.

CG: The Commanding General

Charger: Highly motivated, aggressive Marine (contraction of "hard-charger").

Chaser: Contraction of "prisoner-chaser," an escort for a prisoner or detail of prisoners.

Chew out (or on): Reprimand severely.

Chief messman: Permanently detailed assistant to the mess sergeant, in charge of all messmen and responsible for the police and good order of the mess hall.

Chit: Acknowledgment of indebtedness to a mess; a receipt or authorization; in general, a small piece of paper.

Chopper: Helicopter.

Chow: Food, rations.

Chow-down: To eat heartily.

Chow hound: One who appreciates food.

Class VI: Alcoholic beverages of any kind.

Clutch (n): A serious, sudden emergency.

Clutched-up: Nervous, panicky.

CMC: Commandant of the Marine Corps.

CO: The Commanding Officer.

Color sergeant: A distinguished noncommissioned officer given the privilege of carrying the National Color and of commanding the color guard.

Communicator: Officer or enlisted man assigned to or specializing in communication duties.

Corpsman: Enlisted man of the Navy Hospital Corps.

Cover (n): A Marine cap or hat; headgear.

Crummy: Untidy or unclean in person or uniform.

Crying towel: A towel said to be employed by those with many troubles or complaints to wipe away their tears; a crying towel is said to hang in every chaplain's office.

Cumshaw: (1) (n) Something free, gratis, obtained at no cost; (2) (v) to obtain something at no cost or with no accountability in the supply system.

Cut it: See "hack it."

D & D (adj.): Drunk and disorderly, an entry formerly made on the liberty list beside the name of any man returning from liberty in that condition.

DD (n): Dishonorable discharge.

Deck: (1) (n): The floor, the surface of the earth; (2) (v) to knock down with one blow.

DI (n): Recruit-depot drill instructor, ordinarily an experienced drillmaster.

Dinged (adj): Hit, as by a bullet; *to be* . . . : to be hit by enemy fire.

Doc: Navy hospital corpsman.

Doggie (n): Diminutive for "dog-face," an Army enlisted man.

Dope: (1) Information; (2) sighting and/or wind correction for a rifle under given conditions; *bad* . . . : misinformation.

Dungarees: Marine Corps utility clothing (obsolete).

Eight-ball (n): Worthless, troublesome individual; one who deservedly remains "behind the eight-ball."

Emblem: United States Marine Corps Emblem, or Corps badge, adopted in 1868, frequently referred to as the Globe-and-Anchor.

EPD (n): Extra police duties.

Extend: To lengthen a current enlistment by contracting to remain in the service one or more years after the enlistment would ordinarily expire.

Fall out (v): To assemble outside barracks, immediately prior to a formation.

Field boots: Heavy half-boots designed and issued for field service; boondockers.

Field Day: Day or portion of a day set aside for general cleanup or police of an organization or area.

Field hat: Broad-brimmed felt hat with four-dent crown, formerly worn on expeditionary service by the Marine Corps, but now worn only at rifle ranges and recruit depots; often erroneously called "campaign hat" (Army term for same type headgear).

First Soldier: First sergeant.

Flag allowance: Marines assigned to duty in an admiral's headquarters.

FMF (n): Fleet Marine Force.

Fore-and-aft cap: Garrison cap, also referred to as a "p-ss cutter."

Foul up: (1) (n): A mistake, botch, bungle, or confused situation; (2) (v) to confuse or bungle. **Fouled up:** badly confused.

Frock (v): To grant official permission for an officer who has been selected, but not yet made his number, to assume the style, title, uniform, and authority of the next higher grade.

Frost-call (n): A procedure within a command whereby all officers and other key personnel may be alerted by sequential telephone calls or other notification.

Furlough: Period of authorized leave for an enlisted man, not to be confused with a "48" or "72."

Galley: (1) Kitchen of a mess hall; (2) mobile field kitchen; (3) ship's kitchen.

Gear: Equipment. **Pack the gear:** measure up to Marine standards.

General mess: The enlisted men's mess.

Gizmo: Any miscellaneous, nondescript, unidentified thing or gadget.

Globe-and-Anchor: Marine Corps Emblem.

Greens: Marine Corps service uniform.

Grinder: Drill field.

Ground-pounder: See "grunt," below.

Grunt (n): Aviation term for a rifleman. See also, "ground-pounder," above.

Gung-ho: (1) (**n**) Aggressive esprit de corps; (2) (**adj**) hard-charging.

Gunner: Contraction of "Marine Gunner," the title for line warrant officers.

Gunny: Contraction for gunnery sergeant.

Gunship: Armed helicopter.

Hack (n): Arrest, officer's; *to be in or to be under . . . :* to be under arrest.

Hack it: To be competent or successful in a job or assignment, as, "Do you think Corporal Calkoff can hack it as a squad leader?"

Hands, all: All members of a command.

Happy Hour: Late afternoon period during which the price of drinks at an officers' or NCOs' mess is sharply reduced.

Hard-charger: Aggressive, dynamic, zealous, indefatigable officer or enlisted Marine; one who is professionally keen.

Hashmark (n): Service stripe worn on the uniform sleeve by enlisted men for completion of an honorable four-year enlistment in any of the U.S. Armed Services.

Head (n): Toilet facility; latrine.

Heel-and-toe watch: A condition during which watch-standers alternate tours, one individual relieving the other and vice versa for an indefinite period.

Hill, to go over the (v): To desert.

Hill, to run over the (v): To force an individual to desert or apply for a transfer or retirement, as, "Captain Hardnose certainly ran that brig rat over the hill."

Holiday routine: Condition during which routine drills, instruction, training, and work are knocked off (q.v.) throughout a command; routine followed on authorized holidays and Sundays.

I & I (n): Inspector-instructor, a regular officer assigned to supervise the training of a Reserve unit.

ID card: Armed Forces identification card, issued to every member of the U.S. Armed Forces.

IG (n): The Inspector General.

IG Inspection: An official inspection of a command or unit (usually annually) by the inspector general or representatives.

Iron Mike: Nickname bestowed on statue of World War I Marine in front of old Post Headquarters, Quantico (now the Marine Corps Association offices).

JO (n): Junior officer.

Joe: Coffee.

Joe-pot: Coffeepot, percolator.

Junk on the bunk: Periodic inspection of equipment or, more loosely, of clothing and equipment, displayed on the bunk.

Khakis: Summer service uniform (obsolete).

Knock off: To cease forthwith.

Ladder: (1) (n) Stairs or stairway; (2) (v) to adjust gunfire by a series of graduated spots in range.

Liberty: Authorized free time ashore or off station, not counted as leave.

Line company: Originally, a separate, numbered Marine company performing infantry duties (obsolete); now, the aviation term for ground units or organization.

Line duty: General duty in a ground organization of the Marine Corps.

Lock up (v): To confine in a brig (enlisted); to place under arrest in quarters (officer).

Locked up (adj): Confined or under arrest.

Main gate: Main entrance to a post, station, reservation, camp, or compound, at which a guard post is maintained.

Manual, the: *Marine Corps Manual.*

Mast: Navy equivalent of office hours (q.v.); upright spar supporting signal yard and antennas in a naval ship.

Messman: Nonrated enlisted man assigned to duty in the mess hall for a period of one month; on board ship, called "mess cook."

Mess sergeant: Noncommissioned officer in charge of an enlisted mess.

Mount-out (v): To load and embark for expeditionary service in amphibious shipping or transport aircraft.

NCO: Noncommissioned officer.

Nervous in the service: Jittery, fearful, apprehensive, especially when in forward areas.

Nonrated (adj): Not of noncommissioned or petty officer rank; . . . person, private, or seaman.

Number, to make: (1) To be promoted, when a vacancy occurs, to a higher grade for which previously selected; (2) (colloquial) to pay one's respects to a senior.

OD (n): Officer of the day.

Office hours: Periodic, usually daily, occasion when the commanding officer receives requests, investigates offenses, reenlists and discharges enlisted men, and awards commendations.

Officers' Country: (1) Officers' living spaces on board ship; (2) any portion of a post or station allocated for the exclusive use of officers.

Old man: The commanding officer.

Old salt: (1) Old-timer, experienced Marine; (2) sardonically, person who thinks he knows all the answers.

Out-of-bounds: An area or space restricted from use by normal traffic or prohibited to enlisted men, sometimes called "restricted area." Avoid "Off Limits," the equivalent Army/Air Force term.

Outside: Civilian life, sometimes colloquialized as, "Sergeant Boatspace is now on the *Outside*."

Overhead: Ceiling of a room (ashore) or compartment (on board ship).

Pass over (v): To omit an officer or staff NCO from a promotion list by promoting one junior to him in rank.

Passed over (adj): In the status of having failed of selection for next higher commissioned or staff NCO rank.

People: (1) Enlisted seamen or Marines; (2) one's subordinates, regardless of rank.

Pick up (v): To promote an officer who has previously been passed over (q.v.).

Picked-up (adj): In the status of having been selected for next higher rank after having been passed over one or more times.

Piece: (1) A Marine's rifle; (2) artillery piece.

Pipe up: Speak up.

Platoon sergeant: Senior noncommissioned officer in a platoon, executive to the platoon leader.

Pogey-bait: Candy, snacks.

Pogey-rope: Fourragère.

Police: (1) (v) To straighten or tidy up an individual, area, or structure; (2) (n) condition of neatness or cleanliness.

Police gang: Permanent working force assigned to the police sergeant.

Police shed: Structure or space assigned to the police sergeant for stowage of tools, gear, and supplies; the police sergeant's workshop.

Prisoner-chaser: See "chaser."

Property room: Storeroom for unit property, sometimes called "property shed."

PX (n): Marine Corps Exchange, a store maintained within the organization for sale of articles necessary for the health, comfort, and morale of the command.

Qualify: To attain the minimum qualifying score in weapons proficiency, to attain the rating of marksman.

Quarters: (1) Government housing at a post or shore station, for officers and NCOs with authorized dependents; (2) periodic, usually daily semimilitary muster of a ship's company (Navy).

Rack: Bed, bunk; sometimes referred to as "sack."

Rated man: Noncommissioned or petty officer.

Read off: (1) To reprimand severely; (2) to publish the findings and sentence of a court-martial.

Reading, take a (v): To sound out.

Record day: The day on which a Marine fires an individual weapon for record of qualification.

Recruiter: Marine assigned to recruiting duty.

Regulation (adj): (1) Strictly in accordance with regulations or adopted specifications; (2) issued from government sources (equivalent Army term, "GI").

RHIP: Colloquial abbreviation for the service phrase "Rank hath its privileges."

Rock-happy (adj): Eccentric or mildly deranged as the result of long overseas duty at a remote station, usually an island; akin to "Asiatic" (q.v.), but without cosmopolitan connotations.

Rocks and Shoals: Punitive articles of the Uniform Code of Military Justice.

Runner: Messenger, usually the field music.

Running Guard: Guard duty in which individuals have one tour on duty, one off, and then back on again with no intervening free period.

Rustbucket: Old, worn-out ship; Navy transport.

Sack: See "rack."

Saddle up (v): To put on packs and prepare to move out.

Salty: A seasoned Marine of any rank.

Scoop, the: Late news, information.

Scope out: To ascertain or verify a piece of information, as, "I'm not sure whether that's good or bad dope—you'd better scope it out."

Scuttlebutt: (1) Drinking fountain, or a container of drinking water; (2) unconfirmed rumor.

Seabag: Canvas duffel bag issued to each enlisted Marine for storage and transportation of uniforms and personal gear.

Seagoing: (1) (n) Sea duty; (2) (adj) pertaining to or assigned to sea duty; (3) (n) the uniform combination of blue trousers and khaki shirt.

Sea soldier: Marine.

Sea story: Yarn calculated to impress recruits or other gullible individuals.

Secure: (1) (v) To anchor firmly in place; (2) (v) to cease or terminate an activity or exercise; (3) (n) an outdated movement in the manual of arms.

782 Equipment: Individual combat equipment issued on memorandum receipt to Marine officers and enlisted men, so called because of the designation of the receipt-form employed.

Shanghai (v): To get rid of an individual by involuntary or surprise transfer.

Shift (v): To change uniforms, or from uniform into civilian clothing and vice versa.

Ship over (v): To reenlist.

Shook (adj): Dazed, groggy.

Shoot the breeze (v): To chat or conduct casual conversation.

Shooter: Marine whose avocation is marksmanship with the rifle or pistol; loosely, a Marine who has displayed special prowess with rifle or pistol, or who has served with distinction on a Marine Corps rifle or pistol team.

Short-fused: Very quick-tempered. Sometimes derivatively used in the nominative sense, as, "Gunnery Sergeant Piledriver sure has a short fuse."

Short-timer: One whose enlistment or current tour of duty is about to expire.

Shove off: To depart or leave, to get under way; an order to a boat to leave a landing or a ship's side.

Sick bay: Ship or unit aid station, dispensary, or infirmary.

Sick-bay commando: (1) Individual who spends undue time in hospital or at sick call; (2) malingerer.

Sick call: Daily period when routine ailments are treated at the sick bay.

Sight in (v): In general, to aim a weapon at a target; loosely used as synonym for "zero."

Skipper: Commanding Officer of a company, battery, squadron.

Skivvies: Underwear.

Slopchute: Post exchange restaurant or beer garden (equivalent of "Geedunk" on board ship).

Slop down (v): To drink in quantity and rapidly, beer especially.

Slop up (v): To eat in quantity and rapidly, without regard to table manners; to gourmandize.

Small chow: Hors d'oeuvres.

Smoking lamp is lighted (out): Smoking is (is not) permitted (originally, a lamp on board old-time ships used by men to light their pipes).

Snap in (v): (1) To conduct sighting and aiming exercises with an unloaded weapon; (2) to try out for, or break in for, a new job.

Snow (v): To fool, bewilder, mislead, or exaggerate.

Snow job: Misleading or grossly exaggerated report or sales talk.

Spit and polish (n): (1) Extreme individual or collective military neatness; (2) extreme devotion to the minutiae of traditional military procedures and ceremonies.

Spit-shine: (1) (v) To shine leather, employing spittle or tap water to remove excess grease and produce a high polish; (2) (n) an extremely high polish on a piece of leather.

Squadbay: Barrack room occupied by privates and junior NCOs.

Square away (v): To align, set in place, or correctly arrange an article, articles, or living space; when applied to individuals, to take in hand and direct.

Staff NCO: Noncommissioned officer above rank of sergeant.

Striker: (1) Apprentice or aspirant, attempting to learn a military specialty; (2) on board ship, the Marine entrusted with the ordnance maintenance of a single gun, sometimes designated "gun-striker."

Swabbie: Sailor.

Survey: (1) (n) Medical discharge; examination by authorized competent personnel to determine whether a piece of gear, equipment, stores, or supplies should be discarded or retained; (2) (v) to effect discharge or retirement of an individual for medical reasons; to dispose of an item of government property by reason of unserviceability; to obtain a second, third, or fourth helping of food.

Sympathy chit: Chit supposedly issued by those in authority, or by chaplains, authorizing an individual with many woes to obtain a prescribed amount of sympathy; expression used derisively to indicate lack of sympathy or concern over the plight of another.

Take off your pack: Relax.

Thirty-year Marine: Marine who intends to make the Corps a career.

Top: First sergeant. Avoid the Army term, "Top-kick."

Troop and stomp: Morning troop inspection, followed by close-order drill.

Two-block (v): (1) To hoist a flag or pennant to the peak, truck, or yardarm; (2) to tighten and center a field scarf.

Under way, to get: To depart, or to start out for an objective.

Utilities: Green or camouflaged field and work uniform.

Watch (n): Official tour of duty of prescribed length, such as guard or officer of the day.

Wet down (v): To serve drinks in honor of one's promotion.

Wetting-down (n): Party in honor of a promotion.

Whites: Marine Corps or Navy white uniforms; in the Marine Corps, worn only by officers.

Wing-wiper: Enlisted aviation Marine.

WMs (n): Women Marines (obsolete).

Word, the: Late news, usually well verified and reliable.

Work one's bolt: To resort to special measures, either by energy or guile, to attain a particular end.

Work over (v): To reprimand severely; (2) to place heavy fire on a target or area.

Working over (n): (1) Severe reprimand; (2) heavy attack by fire.

Zapped (adj): Killed in action. Occasionally used as a verb, as "Corporal Buttplate sure zapped that sniper."

Zero: (1) (v) To determine by trial and error the sightsetting required to obtain a hit with an individual weapon at a given range; synonymous with "zero in"; (2) (n) the sightsetting required to obtain a hit with a rifle at a given range.

TERMS AND USAGES TO BE AVOIDED

In recent years, as a side effect of unification, certain undesirable terms or expressions from outside the naval services have been picked up by a few individuals and used to the detriment of the authentic Marine Corps way of talking. Avoid especially the following unfortunate usages:

"Career" (as in :"career officer"): Say "Regular."

E-4 (and other similar ways of speaking of enlisted rank): Under no circumstances, refer to an enlisted person as "an E-3" or "an E-6," etc. This is as bad as calling him or her a "member." Give people their correct ranks.

EM: Just say "enlisted Marine." Even better, say, "Marine."

GI: Use "squared-away" or "regulation." *Never* speak of an enlisted Marine as "a GI."

Hitch: Use "enlistment." "Hitch" is an Army term dating from the horse cavalry.

Insignia (when you mean Emblem): Even though unified clothing procedures have designated the Marine Corps Emblem as "insignia, branch of service," this terminology should be absolutely shunned. The only acceptable word is "Emblem."

Medic: Army/Air Force term for a hospital corpsman or "aid man or woman" (also an Army/Air Force term). Always say "Corpsman."

O-Club: Speak of it as the "Officers' Club" or "Officers' Mess."

TDY: Army/Air Force term that now appears on many joint forms. Always use the Navy/Marine "TAD."

Trooper: Of Army airborne origin. Refer to an individual Marine as a Marine, never a "trooper." "Troops" as a plural is acceptable, but not "troopers." "People" is best.

ZI: Use "Conus," or just "the United States."

Index

The Naval Institute Press is the book-publishing arm of the U.S. Naval Institute, a private, nonprofit, membership society for sea service professionals and others who share an interest in naval and maritime affairs. Established in 1873 at the U.S. Naval Academy in Annapolis, Maryland, where its offices remain today, the Naval Institute has members worldwide.

Members of the Naval Institute support the education programs of the society and receive the influential monthly magazine *Proceedings* and discounts on fine nautical prints and on ship and aircraft photos. They also have access to the transcripts of the Institute's Oral History Program and get discounted admission to any of the Institute-sponsored seminars offered around the country. Discounts are also available to the colorful bimonthly magazine *Naval History*.

The Naval Institute's book-publishing program, begun in 1898 with basic guides to naval practices, has broadened its scope in recent years to include books of more general interest. Now the Naval Institute Press publishes about one hundred titles each year, ranging from how-to books on boating and navigation to battle histories, biographies, ship and aircraft guides, and novels. Institute members receive discounts of 20 to 50 percent on the Press's more than eight hundred books in print.

Full-time students are eligible for special half-price membership rates. Life memberships are also available.

For a free catalog describing Naval Institute Press books currently available, and for further information about joining the U.S. Naval Institute, please write to:

Membership Department
U.S. Naval Institute
291 Wood Road
Annapolis, MD 21402-5034
Telephone: (800) 233-8764
Fax: (410) 269-7940
Web address: www.usni.org